1994

# EDUCATING YOUNG CHILDREN
## Infancy to Grade Three

# EDUCATING YOUNG CHILDREN
## Infancy to Grade Three

SUZANNE LOWELL KROGH

Western Washington University

**McGraw-Hill, Inc.**

New York   St. Louis   San Francisco   Auckland   Bogotá
Caracas   Lisbon   London   Madrid   Mexico City   Milan   Montreal
New Delhi   San Juan   Singapore   Sydney   Tokyo   Toronto

This book was developed by Lane Akers, Inc.

This book was set in Stempel Schneidler by The Clarinda Company.
The editor was Lane Akers;
the production supervisor was Louise Karam.
The cover was designed by Carla Bauer.
The photo editor was Debra Hershkowitz.
Project supervision was done by The Total Book.
Arcata Graphics/Martinsburg was printer and binder.

*Cover photo credit:* Nancy Brown/The Image Bank

# EDUCATING YOUNG CHILDREN
## Infancy to Grade Three

Photo Credits appear on page 561, and on this page by reference.

This book is printed on acid-free paper.

1 2 3 4 5 6 7 8 9 0 AGM AGM 9 0 9 8 7 6 5 4 3

ISBN 0-07-035708-0

Library of Congress Cataloging-in-Publication Data
Krogh, Suzanne.
    Educating young children: infancy to grade three / Suzanne L. Krogh.
        p.        cm.
    Includes bibliographical references and index.
    ISBN 0-07-035708-0
    1. Early childhood education—United States.    2. Early childhood education–United States—Curricula.    3. Classroom management—United States.    I. Title.
LB1139.25.K76        1994
372.2—dc20                                                    93-1765

# About the Author

SUZANNE LOWELL KROGH is chair of Educational Curriculum and Instruction at Western Washington University in Bellingham, Washington. She received a bachelor's degree in history from Florida State University, a master's degree in early childhood education from the University of Maryland, and a doctorate in early childhood curriculum and instruction from the University of Oregon. Additionally, she holds a primary teaching certificate from the Washington Montessori Institute. Her interests in research and writing have focused on moral development and education as well as on curriculum integration. In addition to articles on these topics she has written the books, *Helping Children Choose* (with George Schuncke), *The Integrated Early Childhood Curriculum,* and *Literature Based Moral Education* (with Linda Lamme and Kathy Yachmetz). Most recently, Dr. Krogh has been studying the use of metaphor in the education of early childhood preservice teachers.

# Contents in Brief

# Contents

# Preface

*Educating Young Children: Infancy to Grade Three* is designed for students taking a first course in early childhood education whether in community colleges, four-year colleges, or universities. Normally the purpose of such a course is to provide prospective teachers of young children with a sufficiently broad and detailed exposure to the realities and the knowledge base of this field that they can answer such all-important questions as: Do I want to become a teacher? At what level do I want to teach and in what kind of situation? What kind of teacher do I want to become? To help students answer such questions, this text has the following characteristics.

## Foundations Focus

Understanding contemporary approaches, practices, and issues in early childhood education requires, I believe, some understanding of their origins. Consequently, history and theory play a prominent role in this text. In Part One, *Perspectives,* I provide students with an historical overview of early childhood education that includes the theoretical contributions of its major figures. Their link to contemporary approaches in early education is then examined in Chapter Two and their connection to specific teaching practices and curriculum activities is made explicit in Parts Three and Four.

In Part Two, *Providing Developmentally Appropriate Education,* child development is discussed both on its own merits and as a foundation for effective teaching. The four chapters in this section not only discuss the basics of physical, social, and cognitive development, but take a look at the increasingly diverse student population that characterizes today's schools. The effective early childhood teacher must be knowledgeable about both development and individual differences and be able to apply this knowledge daily in the classroom or center.

## Theory/Practice Connections

Throughout the book the focus is on applying what is known about theory and development to practical teaching and learning activities. This allows the reader to develop both a theoretical viewpoint and a concrete understanding of what it means to be a teacher of young children. For example, the Part Three chapters, which focus on classroom practices and processes, are full of practical guidelines regarding such matters as how children learn, how to build and maintain a supportive environment, how to guide children's behavior, and how to establish effective interactions with other adults. Likewise the curriculum chapters of Part Four all contain a unique section called "Making Connections," which ties the content of earlier, foundations chapters to the topics under discussion.

## Writing Style

The writing style employed in the text is deliberately informal and full of concrete examples. Experience has taught me that it is almost impossible to have too many concrete examples when trying to explain a viewpoint or illustrate a strategy. Consequently, I have used short scenarios at the beginning of most chapters to provide a source of illustrations for important content. The situations they describe are ones I have observed or experienced myself.

## Point of View

While the book contains information about a variety of educational philosophies, theories, and opinions, its own view is based on the *Early Childhood Teacher Education Guidelines* as laid out by the National Association of Education for Young Children. These guidelines have been approved by the National Council for the Accreditation of Teacher Education as well as the National Association of Early Childhood Teacher Educators. Their underlying theme is developmental appropriateness: providing children with educational experiences that mesh with their current level of development.

## Conversations

A unique feature of the book is the conversations that are found in each chapter. They introduce the reader to a variety of interesting and talented people who have something to say about early childhood education: classroom teachers, educational leaders, and consultants as well as noneducators with interesting opinions. Whatever their point of view or special interest, their opinions should provide the fuel for some interesting classroom discussions.

## Acknowledgments

With great appreciation I would like to acknowledge the many helpful reviewers whose insightful comments helped guide me through the long and arduous process of developing this text. Chief among these are Nancy Benham, Kent State University; Jacqueline Blackwell, Indiana University; Kathy Fite, Southwest Texas State University; Marsha Kaufman, Georgia State University; Sondra Langer, Leslie College; Helen Lewis, Indiana University at South Bend; Mary Ann Maggitti, Westchester State University; Joan Moyer, Arizona State University; and Lillian Oxtoby, Manhattan Community College.

Special thanks are also due to the sixteen colleagues who agreed to make their lives public by being interviewed and to the many unnamed teachers and children whose experiences have been called on to illustrate important points within each chapter. Finally, my editor, Lane Akers, deserves much gratitude for his insightful suggestions, encouragement, and devotion to seeing this project through to completion.

Suzanne Lowell Krogh

# Part One

# Perspectives

Today's young children need you. They need your commitment, your caring, your knowledge of their development, and your ability to apply that knowledge to their education. The world is more complex than it has ever been, and they need you to help them make sense of it.

Young children make up a large percentage of the total population, but they lack power and need you as their advocate. As individuals, they represent the complex diversity of a shrinking globe and a mobile society, and they need you to value them for their uniqueness. As future citizens, they depend on you to demonstrate what democracy means and to prepare them to contribute to society's health and longevity. Their perceptions of their own cognitive, social, emotional, and physical growth are limited, so they need you to understand their development. More, they need you to free them from the limitations that the stresses of their world continually present to them.

Working effectively with young children is a difficult and demanding challenge. As you will see in the next two chapters, teachers have met this challenge in a multitude of ways over the centuries. Today, there is still no single answer to the question of how best to meet the challenge, but the available answers are more satisfactory than ever before.

For more than a century, early education has been an area of important change. By now, there has been sufficient progress that we may safely say that the field you are entering has moved through its infancy and adolescence and is at the brink of maturity (Seefeldt and Barbour, 1990). There is a new feeling that the early childhood educator is a professional, a person who is equipped to provide knowledgeable guidance to children at one of the most critical periods of their lives.

Seefeldt, C., and Barbour, N. (1990). *Early childhood education: An introduction.* Columbus, OH: Merrill Publishing.

# 1

# Perspectives on History and Theory

OBJECTIVE

When you finish reading this chapter, you should be able to

- Identify significant leaders in early childhood education.
- Understand the major ideas and contributions to early childhood education of history's most important figures.

As you think about the chapter on your own, you should be able to

- Begin to formulate your own philosophy of early childhood education.
- Observe elements of historical influence in various early childhood settings.

When you look at a young child, what do you see? Surely your interest in pursuing a career in early childhood education means that you see beyond outward appearances: an open smile, an adorable outfit, a charmingly awkward pose. If you think of yourself as a teacher of this child, do you see a small being waiting eagerly for you to share the knowledge that you've gained over the years? Or do you see someone who will learn best if allowed to remain independent, with you as an occasional guide? Do you see this child as innately good, but in danger of losing that goodness within a hostile environment? Or do you see a child born neutral, ready to soak up the social environment as a sponge might?

All of these views, and many more, have been held by large groups of adults at different times in history. At times, the welfare of children and their educational needs have been of great concern; at other times, they seem to have been scarcely considered. For much of history, attitudes on children and education were simply taken for granted and change came slowly. Today, however, much research and thought are devoted to child development and early education. This doesn't mean that definitive answers have been found to questions about what children are and what they need to develop most adequately. It does mean that to be effective, we cannot simply take children's development for granted. The world is changing too fast, with more and more demands on children to perform at higher intellectual and physical levels. As teachers, we need to be aware of what these pressures do to children and to help them develop in the best ways possible.

One way to become more aware of our own attitudes and beliefs is to learn more about their roots. To do this, we must look back at key figures in history, for what we think today is part of an intellectual tradition that dates from antiquity.

## Some Ancient History

The centuries of prehistory are, of course, unknown to us, but we can safely assume that the education of young children during this period was directly related to survival issues and was nearly always the responsibility of the same-sex parent. Teaching techniques were probably quite simple and direct. We can relate to this method, for example, when we take a child out for her first walk in the woods. Since there may be poisonous plants and dangerous areas to avoid, we depend on simple instructions rather than hands-on discovery learning. Thus, in survival situations, we still retain a close kinship to our ancient ancestors.

Once beyond the survival level of instruction, however, we can begin thinking about what else children might need or want to learn and how we might best teach them. To look at the oldest recorded thoughts on early education, we turn first to the ideas of the Greek philosopher Plato and then move on to the Romans and the early Christians. At this point, you may wonder why we appear to ignore philosophies from other parts of the world. Our reason, quite simply, is that the cultures we discuss are those that still influence the way we view and teach children here in the United States.

## The Early Greeks

So, let us begin with Plato (427?–347 B.C.), who, in the fourth century B.C., could look at and respond to a fairly well-developed educational system and comment on the status of childhood itself. Although the Greek view of infants and young children varied from state to state, infanticide was a universal practice, particularly in regard to girls and infants with birth defects. At best, an unwanted infant might by "potted," that is, put in a pot or basket and left at a temple gate in hopes that someone who needed a servant might adopt it. As Lloyd deMause (1974) noted, "The further back in history one goes, the lower the level of child care, and the more likely children are to be killed, abandoned, beaten, terrorized, and sexually abused" (p. 1).

It is interesting to compare the treatment of young children as demonstrated in two city-states of that time: Sparta and Athens. In Sparta, education began at about age six and was probably available only to boys. Prior to that, boys might attend their fathers' club meetings and play informal games that involved stealing food off the table without getting caught. This was light-hearted training for the serious business of learning to wage war and keep down rebellions. The more serious education began at about the time we would send a boy off to elementary school, but in this case the sole purpose was to train warriors for the state. Boys were put into gangs, given scant provisions, and sent off to forage in any way they could; even murder was sanctioned. Girls were given training at home for domestic life, but they might also be provided with quasi-military training to prepare them to be wives and mothers of state warriors.

It was not to the Spartans that Plato wrote his philosophical views, however, but to the Athenians at a time when their government was in some disarray. In the context of describing the ideal state, Plato suggested a design for early childhood education. From birth to age six, learning should be informal, for "knowledge which is acquired under compulsion obtains no hold on the mind. So do not use compulsion, but let early education be a sort of amusement" (Gwynne-Thomas, 1981, p. 14). Good health and good social habits were to be inculcated by attentive parents who would provide plenty of close supervision; freedom was only to be earned over time.

For boys old enough to start school (at about age six), Plato argued that the racier stories about the gods should be cleaned up and presented in a more ideal fashion to impressionable young minds. His enthusiasm for musical training also came with reservations, and he suggested that music be chosen that would promote the right attitudes, particularly toward the state.

Children's rights are, historically speaking, a rather recent development. The further back in Western history one goes, the lower the level of child care, and the more likely children are to be killed, abandoned, terrorized, or sexually abused.

It should be pointed out that Plato's ideas about education were tied to an ideal republic that could only function successfully with a large slave class. In fact, the word *pedagogue* is almost identical to the Greek word for slave-teacher: an educated person, enslaved by victors of a battle, assigned as a child's tutor and companion.

Aristotle (384–322 B.C.), like his teacher and mentor Plato, believed that early education was important. He argued that children have varying talents and skills and that these should be enhanced. Thus, he may be the first writer to recognize the educational importance of individual differences (Osborn, 1980).

## The Early Romans

The inability of the Greek states to stop warring among themselves eventually led to their downfall, as Roman armies conquered them one by one. Once again, many educated Greeks found themselves in the role of teacher-slave, this time to the eager-to-learn Romans. Until their rise to power, Roman thought was considerably less sensitive, inventive, and curious than the

Greeks'. Roman education was restricted to the basic necessities of life: fighting, farming, swimming, and riding, for example. There was little to read except for the rules of the state gathered in "The Laws of the Twelve Tables," published in 450 B.C. Greek influence changed all that.

Perhaps the best known and most influential Greco-Roman thinker was Quintilian (A.D. 35–97). Born in Spain but educated in Rome, Quintilian felt that in order to produce young adults of good character, education must begin at the age of one. Responsible parents and tutors, as well as carefully chosen companions, were important because they set examples for impressionable youngsters. And examples were important in the development of character and speech patterns. According to Quintilian, what the child learned while young and still at home would have lifelong implications.

Quintilian recommended making lessons as interesting as possible. Encouragement should come from the use of praise and never from corporal punishment. Academics should be balanced with gymnastic training, Quintilian said, in order to promote health.

Rome's overexpansion eventually made it impossible for it to keep all its territories fortified and under control. As new groups of less educated outsiders began to conquer Roman territories, education began to decline until much of the learning of the past centuries was all but lost. Many centuries later it would be "found" again and recognized as the basis of some of the same issues we write about and discuss today. Regarding early childhood education in particular, we can look back to Plato for his argument for informal learning and freedom based on structured guidance. Today's controversies about appropriate literature and music for children were also considered by Plato. For the recognition of individual differences, we can look to Aristotle. And for role modeling and positive reinforcement through praise (vs. corporal punishment), there is Quintilian. That these positive ideals should have been lost from the mid-fifth to the eleventh century and beyond was definitely a setback in the education of young children.

## The Early Christians

By the middle of the fifth century A.D., the Roman empire had officially collapsed and new struggles for control took place. Most notable was the Christian church's rise to power. Earlier this had worked in favor of young children, since the newborn was deemed the owner of a soul and infanticide was considered murder and punishable. The Christian emperor Constantine made killing a child a crime in 318, and by the next century there were stipends provided to families that kept foundlings and orphans. In 313 Constantine decreed Christianity the official religion of the Roman empire, and Christian schools spread throughout much of Europe.

With the fall of the Roman empire, the influence of the Christian church began to be increasingly anti-intellectual. Fewer and fewer people were educated, and the newly emerging monasteries became the principal repositories of knowledge. Even there, however, intellectual freedom was highly constrained. For example, one monk who tried to translate all of Plato and Aristotle from the Greek to Latin was sentenced to die for his "crime." Over the next five centuries few children received an education: only those who planned to enter the monastery and those who belonged to wealthy families. As convents arose, girls were occasionally educated, particularly in what is now Germany.

The prevailing view of young children, what they were and what should be done with them, changed gradually from the Greek, Roman, and early Christian attitudes. As the concept of original sin took hold in religious thought, children came to be seen as inherently evil, thus condoning punishments that today we would define as child abuse. Further, the concept of childhood itself changed. As soon as children had outgrown the most helpless stages of infancy, they joined in the general adult life, both for work and play.

It was for later generations to term these centuries (from the fall of Rome to the rebirth of Greek and Roman ideas) the Middle or Dark Ages. The people who lived through this period knew little, if anything, about better times. But better times did come, and with them new interpretations of the ancient ideas that provide the foundation for today's views of early education.

The onset of the Renaissance (from the Latin meaning "rebirth") was very good news for young children. During the Middle Ages physical and sexual abuse had been widespread, even condoned by some of the great philosophers and religious thinkers. Although infanticide had been given up, it was still a difficult time for children, as some form of abandonment seemed the prime alternative to murder. The wet nurse, monastery, convent, and foster family were all acceptable avenues of abandonment, and infanticide still persisted, although it was more covert. For example, an unusually large number of babies were reported to have died while sleeping with their parents, who allegedly "laid over" the babies and smothered them. In addition, wet nurses could be paid to have an "accident." The beginning of the Renaissance produced an increasing number of child instruction manuals, demonstrating a new view of children that could only be an improvement on the previous centuries. These manuals and other writings show a new understanding of children's needs and identities as being separate from those of adults.

## The Roots of Today's Views on Early Childhood Education

Whereas the Middle Ages gave us no educational leaders in the field of early childhood education, later centuries did. Like ancient Greek and Roman philosophers, influential thinkers wrote about their ideas so that today we can look back and evaluate them. The Czech John Amos Comenius (Jan

Early Christian theology improved the treatment of children by holding that they, too, had souls. Thereafter, infanticide became punishable as murder. Later, as the concept of original sin took hold, children came to be viewed as inherently evil, thus condoning punishments that today would be defined as child abuse.

Amos Komensky) was the first to posit a complete system of education in the style of Plato. By the time he did, however, much Renaissance thinking had been altered by the period of religious Reformation.

## John Comenius

(Jan Amos Komensky in the original Czech)

John Amos Comenius (1592–1670) was a bishop in the persecuted Moravian church who spent most of his adult life in exile. Nevertheless, his educational ideas were widely received throughout Europe, his books were translated into more than a dozen languages, and he was invited by several European governments to reconstruct their educational systems. In succeeding centuries he was sometimes forgotten and that is surely now the case. Yet if any thinker was responsible for pulling education, including early childhood education, out of the Middle Ages, it was Comenius. Here are some of the things he said in his book *School of Infancy* (1633), which dealt with children to age six. Note how closely his ideas fit with our own.

Every one knows that whatever disposition the branches of an old tree possess, they must necessarily have been so formed from the first growth. . . . Man, therefore, in the very first formation of body and soul, should be molded so as to be such as he ought to be throughout his whole life. (p. 16)

. . . too much sitting still or slowly walking about on the part of a child is not a good sign. . . to be always running or doing something is a sure sign of a sound body and vigorous intellect. . . . (p. 46)

In this stage dialectics [reasoning] beyond the natural, or such as is obtained in practice, cannot be introduced. . . . (p. 46)

Although Comenius's views were in harmony with most of what we think about education today, his stand on corporal punishment reflected the tradition of centuries: "Why do you prefer the child's being detained in its natural foolishness, rather than to rescue it from its folly, by the aid of well-timed, holy, and salutary discipline?" (p. 59) His thinking in this instance was based on the religious justification that to spare the rod was to spoil the child.

In other areas, Comenius was truly ahead of his time. He even suggested that education should be universal and for both sexes. For Comenius, the best schooling in the early years could be found at home, with the mother as teacher.

Comenius was important in the development of educational methods and views, not just because his ideas provided an escape from medieval backwardness, but because their revolutionary nature affects us today. For example, the single most important issue in early education today is developmental appropriateness in children's learning. This concept comes directly from Comenius. He understood that younger children are best able to grasp knowledge that relates to their own lives and that learning must be concrete before it can be abstract.

Today for example, the study of history typically begins with the here and now and, as children grow older, adds on previous centuries. It was Comenius who first observed that young children need help in simply understanding yesterday and tomorrow and that they need to do this before trying to comprehend last year and beyond. Geography is another of the social studies influenced by Comenius. He realized that, just as children first understand time in terms of today, they first understand space in relation to what they can see around themselves. Thus, he argued that geography should begin with the study of familiar places. Science study also begins with what is nearest and dearest to young children: nature. Again, this idea originated with Comenius. His views on arithmetic appear in today's textbooks and lesson plans, too. He suggested that young children should begin by learning such basic concepts as a lot or a little. Although he said that small children could learn to count, he added that it would take several years for them to understand numbers. Research done in recent decades has proven him completely right. In this, as in so many other instances, Comenius was far ahead of his time. Perhaps that is one reason that, at a practical level, his educational ideas were not as widespread as his popularity might indicate. But it is his ideas that affected later educational thinkers, some of whom we will discuss in this chapter.

To help us organize subsequent history, we can create a family tree for early childhood education. Since Comenius's ideas were seminal, we will make him the root of the tree. As you read about each of the following people, you might like to refer to Figure 1.1 to see where he or she fits in the model. You will notice that as the tree grows it becomes more intricate. This reflects the increasing complexity of educational thought as the centuries pass.

## John Locke

An English philosopher of the following century is the next major member of our newly planted family tree. John Locke (1632–1704) was brought up in a Puritan family, but his adult thinking was more influenced by the scientific revolution than by Reformation Protestant thinking. At Oxford he studied, and later taught, Greek, rhetoric, and moral philosophy. In his mid-

FIGURE 1.1
**A Philosophical Family Tree**

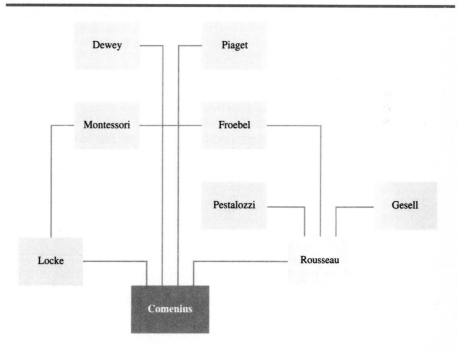

thirties, Locke's more practical and scientific nature eventually led him back to the university to study medicine. He never succeeded in getting his terminal degree and only practiced medicine a short while, but the balance between the scientific and the philosophical in Locke's thinking and education produced a like balance in his later writing on education. While working as the personal secretary to the earl of Shaftesbury and tutoring the earl's son, he began to formulate his views on education, which, along with his antiauthoritarian political ideas, were revolutionary for their time. The only major work on education published during Locke's lifetime was *Some Thoughts Concerning Education,* and this was not originally intended as a book for the public. A cousin and her husband asked Locke to write some letters giving advice on the upbringing of their son, and these were eventually published in book form. All Locke's philosophical and medical thinking, as well as his past experiences, went into these letters. So did his views on social class. His cousin's son was to be raised as a gentleman, and Locke differentiated the education of a future gentleman from that of a commoner's child. Thus, despite his increasing involvement in the politics of the Enlightenment, Locke did not propose the kind of universal education that Comenius did.

Nonetheless, Locke's ideas on early education represented new ways of looking at children and formed the basis for much of what we think and do today. His view of infants was that they are born with great potential for learning. Their minds, he said, might be viewed as white paper or an empty cabinet or a blank tablet. What they become as adults is then defined by their total education: "I think I may say that of all the men we meet with, nine parts of ten are what they are, good or evil, useful or not, by their education" (Cleverley and Phillips, 1986, p. 17).

Another idea that set Locke apart from the educational thinkers of his day was his belief that in educating children we need to be aware of individual differences.

> There is a difference of degree in men's understandings, apprehensions, and reasonings to so great a latitude . . . that there is a greater distance between some men and others in this respect, than between some men and some beasts. (Cleverley and Phillips, 1986, p. 18)

This concept was in contrast to the prevailing idea that there was a general mass of knowledge out there to be learned and everyone in a group or class should move along together in conquering it. For Locke, our minds might all begin as blank slates, but some slates are higher quality than others. In other words, Locke (1964) did not completely dismiss heredity and even said

> God has stamped certain characters upon men's minds, which, like their shapes, may perhaps be a little mended, but can hardly be totally altered and transformed into the contrary. (p. 43)

For young children, Locke wrote in favor of play and freedom, but he also supported disciplined living and even some deprivation for upper-class children, who were, in his view, overly pampered. While his ideas along this line were sometimes contradictory, Locke was consistent in arguing for a positive approach to both teaching and discipline:

> Beating then, and all other sorts of slavish and corporal punishments, are not the discipline fit to be used in the education of those who would have wise, good, and ingenuous men; and therefore very rarely to be applied, and that only on great occasions, and cases of extremity. (p. 35)

What Locke did advocate when discipline was necessary was stern, disapproving looks as well as shaming. To keep children from getting too spoiled, as well as to promote rugged health, he suggested cold foot baths, open air, loose fitting clothing and not much of it, a simple diet, and a hard bed. He may be the first educational philosopher to discuss toilet training, and on this subject he maintained his stern view, recommending regular visits with enforced sitting. For Locke, "A sound mind in a sound body is a short, but full description of a happy state in the world" (Weber, 1984, p. 24).

Much of Locke's thinking pervades early childhood education today, although the form it takes in practice may be much altered. As an example, consider his view that individuals are born like blank slates but that they may differ qualitatively. For Locke, this meant the permanent subjugation of some classes of people. Today, while there are those who still believe as he did, we generally argue that this attitude is potentially rascist, sexist, classist, or prejudiced in some other way. At the same time, it is possible to accommodate Locke's view of the blank slate in an updated, more democratic approach to teaching children from all walks of life.

When Locke said that the environment would create the child, he referred to its entire intellectual, social, and physical entity. Full learning experiences should involve input from all these aspects of the environment and include the child's use of all the senses. When you see a classroom with much opportunity for learning through acting on sensory materials, you may well be observing a classroom whose roots go back to Locke's seventeenth-century views. For the materials to be truly Lockean, however, they must have a learning goal connected to them. Locke believed that the environment should be controlled so that children learn what they should know. Some examples of what you might observe today would be math games using concrete materials, cardboard cut-out letters used in creating simple words, or perhaps wooden puzzles; all of these are sensory and all have specific learning goals.

Today's behaviorist psychology also owes some portion of its basic thinking to Locke. One of Locke's views was that children should be reinforced for their good behavior and intellectual successes. Little is accomplished, he argued, by approaching the child with a negative attitude or physical punishment. These should be saved for emergency cases. At the same time, Locke believed that too much reinforcement could have the wrong effect, making a child more demanding and spoiled, refusing to do schoolwork unless rewarded. Today's behaviorists have created classroom approaches to discipline that are much like those that Locke would have recommended. Reinforcements are positive, focus on negative behavior is avoided, and rewards are gradually withdrawn as behavior or performance improves. Since teacher behavior is usually more subtle to observe than learning materials, you may have to look longer and more carefully to see these influences from Locke. It may be nothing more than a carefully timed, "You worked hard at that, didn't you?" or the old standby, "I like the way Emily and Al are sitting," but these and other similar statements have a direct effect on children's attitudes and behaviors. Watch for them.

## Jean Jacques Rousseau

If you look now at our family tree, you will see that the next major figure is important enough to have a major branch of his own. Jean Jacques Rousseau (1712–1778), born in Switzerland not long after Locke died, combined philosophical and educational thought in his writings as Locke had done. Like Locke, he was an influential force for egalitarianism and democracy in his society, but the conclusions he reached were different enough from those of Locke to inspire a very different form of early education. Thus, on our family tree, Rousseau receives not only a major branch but one that grows in another direction.

In some ways it is difficult to believe that someone of Rousseau's background could affect both politics and education in the intense way that he did. His mother died while giving birth to him, and his father first spoiled and then deserted him. He was passed around among relatives and received little education, although by age ten he had read countless novels. Apprenticed to an engraver, Rousseau tired of the cruel treatment he received and ran away. He began the life of a wanderer, trying various occupations (clerk, secretary, music copyist, even priest) and usually failing. At age twenty-seven Rousseau was hired as a tutor to two young boys. He lasted just about a year, failing miserably at disciplining them in any way. But by now the wanderer was in France where he became involved in society and numerous love affairs, in particular with one woman from the lower class who became his lifelong companion (he eventually married her when in his sixties) and who bore him five children. All of these he abandoned to a foundling home.

How, then, did Rousseau manage to influence his own and future generations in two major fields: politics and child development? As one author (Wodehouse, 1924) has explained it, the enlightened gentlemen of the age of Locke were ready for new influences, something more of a "natural" condition and, "about 1760, a few books connected with this subject struck the general imagination with extraordinary force. They came from a somewhat lower cosmopolitan level, being the work of a rather disreputable Swiss from Geneva, living in France, who happened to have genius" (p. 101).

In his major work on education, *Emile* (1762), Rousseau seemed to idealize the details of his own life in the fictional biography of a "perfectly" brought up and educated boy. Was Rousseau abandoned as a child and did he abandon his own children? He could turn that into a positive experience for Emile, who would be given freedom to roam, play, and follow his spontaneous impulses. About this Rousseau wrote, "What is to be thought of that cruel education . . . that burdens a child with all sorts of restrictions and begins by making him miserable, in order to prepare him for some far-off happiness which he may never enjoy?" (Weber, p. 27)

The force of Rousseau's thought was much stronger than the details of his often sordid life. Let's take a look at some of his ideas on early childhood education because they eventually gave rise to many of the ideas we practice today.

Rousseau argued that early childhood education should come from all the senses, and that reading should not be pushed. In fact, he felt that it would be better for a child not to read at all until about age twelve. The teacher or tutor should not use direct instruction but should act as a guide. The teacher should be aware of the child's interests and let him follow those interests rather than prescribe a curriculum. Discipline should be primarily through the natural consequences of the child's actions. Much of the child's education should take place outdoors and emphasis should be placed on healthful development. One of Rousseau's views of the child set him apart from the traditional religious thinkers: Where they saw the infant as inherently evil, Rousseau saw him as basically good. "God makes all things good; man meddles with them and they become evil" (Weber, p. 27). Thus, the general approach in the education of the young child was to tuck him safely away from the world in a protected environment where the only influences were those of good.

We should note that Rousseau's ideal education was reserved for children of the middle and upper classes. Like Locke, he believed that little education was needed for the lower classes. In Rousseau's case, this could be justified by his idea of naturalism, in which the child is educated by his surroundings. The poor, he decided, could take care of what little education they needed right where they were. In *Emile,* Rousseau also revealed his attitude toward women.

> [Women are] specially made to please men, he said, to be useful to them, to make themselves loved and honored by them, to rear them when young, to care for them when grown up, to advise them, to console them, to render their lives agreeable and sweet to them,—these are the duties of women at all times, and should be taught to them from their childhood. . . . It is a law of nature that woman shall obey man. (Compayre, p. 84)

Locke and Rousseau proposed different views of early education based on different views of human learning. Locke saw children's minds as blank slates or empty buckets to be filled by the teachings of knowledgeable adults. Rousseau, however, saw children's minds as naturally programmed to unfold in their own way and at their own pace if given a secure environment by nurturing adults.

This was the "natural" woman who would be the helpmate of the free and unspoiled "natural" man.

Rousseau's ideas on education were complemented by his thoughts on politics. Much of what he wrote influenced antiroyalist thinkers and helped bring on the French Revolution, which he did not live to see. Occasionally, some progressive fathers of his century and the next actually tried Rousseau's ideas on their own little "Emiles," generally with disastrous results. He did not live to see this either, as his ideas on both politics and education had more effect after his death.

Today, you are as likely to see Rousseau's influences in the classroom as you are Locke's. Again, you can observe children interacting actively with materials that appeal to all their senses. But, in keeping with the concept of natural development, the materials will be more open-ended and their use determined by the children. Math materials might be sticks brought inside by the children. These could be played with in a free-form way, while the teacher would make informal comments to inspire learning. Books might or might not be available, and the teacher could well choose to tell a story rather than read it. Giving children materials for costumes and props so that they might invent little plays would take preference over providing structured reading. Time spent outdoors would focus on learning about nature in an informal way.

A basic difference between Locke and Rousseau affects what you see in the classroom today. Along with others of his time, Locke assumed that there is a discreet body of knowledge that people of the upper classes should learn and that the function of education is to make knowledge accessible and interesting. Rousseau, on the other hand, was more interested in process, or learning how to learn. You can observe this difference in outlook when you see children playing with materials that have right solutions (Locke's view) or when you see them playing with open-ended materials, creating their own learning (Rousseau's view). In most classrooms you will find some of each kind of learning, living testament to our inability to decide which is the better course to take. Many teachers argue that a combination of the two views provides the best learning, although many of them aren't aware that their argument is based on a conflict in ideology that has been around for more than two centuries.

Just as Locke's ideas were modified by succeeding generations, so were Rousseau's. Parents who took his ideas literally found themselves creating ill-mannered, self-centered, illiterate adolescents. Still, his ideas offered inspiration for more practical interpreters. In Rousseau's native Switzerland, a man of the next generation molded his ideas into a more useful form and succeeded in educating children in a more natural way than ever before.

## Johann Pestalozzi

Johann Heinrich Pestalozzi (1746–1827), like Rousseau, had an unhappy childhood. Born into a comfortably affluent family, his whole life changed at the age of five, when his father died. He was subsequently brought up by his mother and a family servant. Pestalozzi had a delicate constitution, and his apparently odd appearance and personality made him the object of other children's jokes. Even in his later years, commentators referred to his peculiar personality.

His motives in life were, from his early years, tied to the fate of the downtrodden. Like Locke and Rousseau before him, he was politically attuned to the need for some democratization in his country. Unlike them, he was sympathetic to the needs and deprivations of the poorer classes. As a young man he married and settled on a farm, having been inspired by his readings of Rousseau to seek the "natural" life. Soon he was providing a home for some twenty orphans and poor children. His poor business management ensured that he would eventually fail at the effort, but within a short time Pestalozzi published a successful novel, *Leonard and Gertrude*

Among the enduring contributions of Pestalozzi were his insistence on universal education for both the rich and the poor of both sexes and for early learning that moves from the concrete to the abstract through the use of manipulative materials.

(1781–1787), which made him famous and gave him some income. It contained his views on education, which were influenced by his earlier reading of Rousseau's *Emile*. In one important respect, however, he took issue with Rousseau. To Pestalozzi, unlimited freedom would not bring children to the desired educational level. In Pestalozzi's view, "Liberty is a good thing, obedience is equally so" (Gwynne-Thomas, 1981, p. 235).

In 1799, Napoleon invaded Switzerland and, after sacking the town of Stanz, left hundreds of children destitute. An orphanage was established with Pestalozzi in charge. There he was able to put into practice the domestic love, emotional stability, and sensory education he had been writing about. Although the French eventually returned and comandeered the orphanage for a military hospital, Pestalozzi's life career was begun. By 1805 he had established a school in the town of Yverdon, which, for twenty years, was an internationally known model of the latest in education.

In his school, Pestalozzi took Rousseau's basic ideas about natural education, freedom, sensory learning, and so on, and made them work. Rousseau had escaped his own life by writing about a fictional ideal; Pestalozzi chose not to deny his own experience but to use it to empathize with and help others. Although his writings were well known, it was his ability to put his ideas into practice that gave Pestalozzi his lasting fame.

Much of what Pestalozzi did and recommended still influences what we do with young children today. He believed then, as most of us do today, that poor children have as much right to education as their wealthier counterparts. In fact, it was Pestalozzi's intention to attempt a real elevation of their lives. Additionally, he matter of factly included girls in his educational plans, a radical departure from tradition. Although he believed in equal access to education for everyone, he also valued diversity, saying, "Idiosyncracies of the individual are the greatest blessings of nature and must be respected to the highest degree" (Weber, 1984, p. 29).

In the classroom, Pestalozzi geared experiences so that they went from the concrete to the abstract, a major innovation for his time. For the younger children there were "object lessons," what we might call manipulative materials, that gave children their first understanding of form, language, and number. The order, he said, would be to "steadily increase the range of their practical experience with things"; then the teacher would "do all that is possible to clear this experience from confusion and indefiniteness." Finally, when the concrete lesson was clear, the teacher would "supply them with words . . . going, indeed, a little farther in preparation for the future" (Pestalozzi, 1912, p. 93).

Today we would describe Pestalozzi's choice of natural, concrete materials as developmentally appropriate for young children. He also saw these materials as a way to interest young children in school. In his best-known book, *How Gertrude Teaches Her Children* (1801), Pestalozzi remarked at length on the wonderful freedom of preschool children and decried what traditionally happened to them once they attended school:

> [S]uddenly, after five years of blissful sensuous life, we banish all Nature from their eyes . . . we herd them together like sheep in an evil-smelling room; for hours, days, weeks, months, and years, we chain them unmercifully to the contemplation of miserable and monotonously unexciting alphabets, and condemn them to an existence which, in comparison with their former life, is repulsive in the extreme. . . . (Pestalozzi, p. 89)

In actual practice, Pestalozzi did not always live up to his own ideals. In extreme cases he might resort to corporal punishment, and sometimes his ideas about object lessons gave way to boring drills that he somehow convinced himself the children loved, despite the obvious agony visitors observed on their faces.

Today we can see both sides of Pestalozzi in action: the use of manipulative materials juxtaposed with drill materials that seem to get the job done faster and with fewer frustrations—at least for the adult. The latter approach, however, is not an example of Pestalozzi's thinking but of the normal adult's occasional impatience with children. Let us focus instead on his ideas that are still philosophically sound. Pestalozzi developed activities and materials that encouraged children to learn from the concrete to the abstract. If you observe first in a nursery school and then in a third grade you will, no doubt, see this developmental sequence in action. Four-year-olds, who gain an intuitive understanding of division when they share crackers equally among the group, can later transmit that understanding to pencil-and-paper problems, as long as they have something concrete to help them understand.

Another enduring contribution was Pestalozzi's insistence on universal education. He believed that both rich and poor, boys and girls deserved to learn. The increasing democratization of Western thought made such a concept more acceptable than it had been in previous generations. Today, we take for granted the right to free education, although the equalization of quality is often problematic. Still, if you are female and/or have grown up poor, you owe your education, in part, to the groundwork laid by Pestalozzi.

It was the observations of his school at Yverdon that made Pestalozzi famous throughout the world. For early childhood education, it was the visit of the German educator Friedrich Froebel to the school that was most important. His experience there transformed Froebel from a rural schoolmaster into a theorist and philosopher.

## Friedrich Froebel

Yet again, we have an example of an influential educator shaped by his own unhappy childhood. Friedrich Froebel's (1782–1852) mother died early in his life and Froebel later wrote, "This loss, a hard blow to me, influenced the whole environment and development of my being: I consider that my mother's death decided more or less the external circumstances of my whole life" (Shapiro, 1983, p. 19). At the age of fifteen he was apprenticed to a forester and began a lifelong attachment to nature. Perhaps it was this experience that contributed to his inability to stick with university studies and sent him off to work as a land surveyor, estate manager, forest department official, museum assistant, tutor, and, finally, rural school teacher.

Between 1808 and 1810, Froebel attended the training institute run by Pestalozzi at Yverdon. Although he came away accepting the basic principles of Pestalozzi's theories, Froebel felt that something critically important was missing: the "spiritual mechanism" that is the foundation of early learning. "Pestalozzi takes man existing only in his appearance on earth," he said, "but I take man in his eternal being, in his eternal existence" (Shapiro, 1983, p. 20). Froebel also rejected ideas, still popular with the followers of Rousseau, concerning education that was largely outdoors. Although he loved nature and wanted children to as well, he wanted to protect them from its more raw aspects.

Eventually, Froebel's concern for children's moral, spiritual, physical, and intellectual growth led him to focus on their needs just prior to entering school. He shared Pestalozzi's horror of what happened to five-year-olds whose uninhibited, happy lives were so radically changed by their entrance into school. What Froebel envisioned was a sort of halfway house between home and school, infancy and childhood, that would be attended by 4- to 6-year-olds. Because it would be a place where children were nurtured and protected from outside influences, much as plants might be in a garden, Froebel decided to call his school a *kinder* (child) *garten* (garden).

To make his kindergarten successful, Froebel knew that special teacher training would be necessary. He also decided that new concrete materials must be developed. They must be age appropriate for children's interests and have an underlying spiritual message. To meet the first need, Froebel began a training institute alongside his first school. For the second, he developed a series of play objects as well as singing games that seemed appropriate to the interests and education of young children and had a spiritual message as well.

The educational materials were divided into two groups: "gifts" and "occupations." The first two gifts were designed to be introduced in infancy by the mother, and Froebel fully expected babies to have a beginning understanding of what they were about. For example, the first gift was a yarn ball connected to a string, which was to be played with under the mother's supervision in such a way that the baby's senses and muscles would be stimulated. But Froebel also believed that the ball would "awaken spirit and individuality" while helping the infant intuit "unity" (from the shape of the ball) and "freedom" (from its swinging motion). Three more gifts introduced to children in kindergarten were small building blocks that would fit together in prescribed ways under the teacher's instructions.

It is important to note here that Froebel considered these directed exercises with their specific goals as a form of play. Compared to what most children in those days dealt with in their daily lives, it probably would have felt like very liberating play. Today, however, we would no doubt quibble that close-ended, prescribed, teacher-directed activities might be enjoyable but could not be described as play.

The occupations allowed children more freedom and included such things as weaving, bead-stringing, sewing, and stick-laying activities, as well as gardening. But even these held underlying spiritual messages that could be learned in such simple steps as the required and careful cleanup. This last step in every activity was considered "a final, concrete reminder to the child of God's plan for moral and social order" (Shapiro, 1983, p. 24). The essential harmony of the gifts and occupations had its counterpart in the songs and games that focused on social harmony. Break up a circle of children and you have an understanding of individuality; put it back together again and there is group unity. Teachers were to point out these symbolic acts to the children, and it was expected that the children would understand.

Froebel did not have the strong political inclinations of Locke, Rousseau, and Pestalozzi and, indeed, rejected political action as a way to achieve more rights for women, although it was a cause he championed. His definition of emancipation was that women would be permitted out of the home to teach. This may explain why his ideas for helping them included reform in child rearing and interaction with early education. One of his missions was to train women throughout the world in child rearing and teaching. Despite his rejection of politics, however, the Prussian government considered Froebel's ideas dangerous and ordered his schools closed in 1848. Despairing, he died four years later, not knowing that his educational ideas were about to take hold in the United States, bringing the still new country an early education system unlike anything it had ever seen before.

The same Prussian repression and political rebellions that closed Froebel's kindergartens also sent numerous educated citizens out of the country, many of them to the United States. Among these were a number of women trained in the Froebel system of early education, and it was they who were responsible for introducing the kindergarten to this country. The very first kindergarten was established in Wisconsin for German immigrant children, who were taught in German. Word of this new way of teaching eventually made its way to St. Louis, where the first public kindergartens were opened. Although those responsible for establishing the schools were native-born Americans, they coupled Froebel's ideas with those of the German philosopher Hegel. Just as today there are people who worry about foreign influences altering the "American way," so there were concerns held by parents and educators then that early education in the United States was being taken over by German ideals. Despite this setback, Froebel's ideas provided the major direction that kindergartens followed during the last half of the nineteenth century. However, in a country that was beginning to look toward scientific theories rather than metaphysics and religion as a way to understand children, his ideas were gradually replaced by those of more scientific thinkers. The most radical of these eventually gained sufficient strength to be called the Child Study Movement.

To a large degree, Froebel remains forgotten today except in his role as the developer of the kindergarten. His belief that young children can understand the spiritual symbolism behind the games they play has been discarded. The rigidly structured use of play materials has been abandoned in most quarters. The finely detailed, perfectly measured and produced learning materials have been replaced by mass produced toys. Some things remain, however: the concept that children of preprimary years learn best through some form of play, the feeling that group games help children feel a part of the whole, the idea that playing and working outdoors can lead to creativity and good health. Froebel's ideas of natural learning and play demonstrated his debt to Rousseau, while the goal-oriented activities and materials followed the lead of Locke. Thus, Froebel's place in the family tree branches from them both.

## John Dewey

One of those responsible for the demise of Froebel's kindergarten movement was John Dewey (1859–1952). Born, raised, and educated in Vermont, Dewey graduated from the University of Vermont at the age of twenty. He then spent three anxious months looking for a job and more or less fell into teaching when a cousin offered him a job at the high school where he was principal. Dewey taught Latin, algebra, and science, but his reading and thinking leaned toward philosophy. One of his former philosophy professors encouraged him to publish, and he had immediate success with three articles. This encouraged him to pursue a doctorate in philosophy from Johns Hopkins University. He moved quickly up the academic ladder, going from professorships at the universities of Minnesota and Michigan to one at the University of Chicago in 1894. It was at Chicago that Dewey first gained national notice and respect for the application of his philosophical ideas to the education of children.

As a young man, Dewey read the German philosopher Hegel and came to reject his ideas. This was important for his own later theories on early childhood education, because much of the symbolism in the activities, songs, and games of Froebel's kindergarten came from Hegel's philosophy. It was

Dewey believed that children learn by doing and that participation in democratic decision making, whether in or out of school, develops rational problem-solving abilities and social skills.

important, too, that Dewey came to the University of Chicago when he did because both it and other institutions nearby were in the midst of exploring new ideas in education. Even Froebel kindergartens in the area were interested in innovation and were considered far too radical by their more orthodox counterparts.

University laboratory schools were a recent innovation, and Dewey was instrumental in beginning one at Chicago. It included a kindergarten as well as the elementary grades. In putting his theories of early education into action, Dewey found himself caught between two popular but antagonistic philosophies: that of Froebel, which he considered outdated and rigid, and that of the more recent Child Study Movement, which he believed had gone overboard in attempting to be scientific. In the mid-1890s, the followers of Froebel were a force to be reckoned with, so, rather than striking out completely on his own, Dewey chose to reinterpret Froebel in his own image. As one example, he took Froebel's concept of unity (which we have seen expressed in children's circle games and in building blocks) and focused instead on unifying such concepts as learning and doing or child and society. Learning and doing can be united if we consider that young children are constantly active and are enthusiastic about learning, leading us to conclude that perhaps children can and should learn *by* doing. Child and society are also two dissimilar concepts that can be united. The individual child can learn to be a part of society if the school itself becomes a micro-society.

In addition to his different interpretation of unity, Dewey's view on play was unlike that of Froebel's. Children at the experimental university school used the Froebel blocks, but could play with them freely; there was no emphasis put on observing the unity of the whole and the individuality of the separate pieces. Play was free, there was more of it, and the rigidly timed lessons disappeared entirely. Dewey's ideas on play came from the American philosopher and psychologist George Herbert Mead, who believed that play was grounded in the child's social environment. From this idea, Dewey developed a whole new way of structuring the school, from the earliest years on. No longer did children play with pretend "symbolic" brooms and such. Now, they really took care of their own classrooms, structuring them as mini-societies. Further, Dewey believed that social development could best take place in classrooms with mixed ages. For him, the artificial divisions between grades were unnecessary and worked against children's social growth.

In the laboratory school, the subprimary classroom covered two years. To help the youngest children learn about society, teachers began with the already familiar home and the people in it. Bit by bit the outside world was then introduced. During the winter the children worked with Froebel building materials and arranged furniture and living spaces, while in the spring they could play outdoor games, study nature, and take walks in the city. All the while, they played and worked with far more independence than children did in a Froebel kindergarten. Fostering democracy in the classroom was a major goal for Dewey and one of his most lasting contributions to education.

In 1897 Dewey published a pamphlet that stated his pedagogic creed. Here are a few of his views. (In Chapter 5 you will find a "Conversation" about a school that carries on much of this Dewey philosophy.)

I believe that

- the only true education comes through the stimulation of the child's powers by the demands of the social situations in which he finds himself. Through these demands he is stimulated to act as a member of a unity, to emerge from his original narrowness of action and feeling, and to conceive of himself from the standpoint of the welfare of the group to which he belongs.
- the child's own instincts and powers furnish the material and give the starting-point for all education.
- the school is primarily a social institution.
- education, therefore, is a process of living and not a preparation for future living.
- the school must represent present life—life as real and vital to the child as that which he carries on in the home, in the neighborhood, or on the playground. (Dewey, 1964, pp. 427–430)

Dewey stayed at the University of Chicago ten years and then moved on to Columbia University in New York. His interests branched into other areas, but his influence on early education has been lasting, although sometimes misinterpreted or unpopular. Misinterpretation was probably inevitable as Dewey's philosophical views were simplified and watered down in their widespread application. He believed that learning by doing was important, not just for kindergarten children but for older students as well. He was a proponent of teaching children of all ages about democracy by helping them create democratic societies in their classrooms. These ideas in the wrong hands and directed by teachers who read little, if any, of his philosophy could lead to the kind of classroom anarchy that Rousseau's early followers experienced. And that was just what happened. By the late 1940s, Dewey-inspired education was coming under widespread attack. By the late 1950s, when the weak nature of American education seemed exemplified in the Soviets' jumpstart into the space race, Dewey's philosophy was blamed. The backlash led to a greater focus on academics and eventually a back-to-basics movement.

Of course, Dewey was never against academic learning. He believed, however, that children need to be actively involved in it and that academics should be meaningful to them. As the sterility of the back-to-basics approach became apparent, Dewey's ideas began to return. Today, as you see young children learn how to run "town meetings" in their classrooms, or observe a teacher who focuses on all aspects of children's growth, or learn to plan and teach a theme unit, you come in contact with education that has its roots in Dewey's thinking.

Because Dewey's philosophy did not agree with the didactic views of

Locke or the laissez-faire ideas of Rousseau, he is given his own branch in the family tree.

A bit younger than Dewey and on the other side of the Atlantic, Italy's first woman doctor was, at about the same time, developing an educational philosophy that might be placed somewhere between Froebel and Dewey. The thought of Maria Montessori held elements of both Rousseau and Locke, and thus she branches from both on our family tree.

## Maria Montessori

Maria Montessori (1870–1952) was born in a small town on the Adriatic Sea in the same year that Italy succeeded in unifying its various states into one nation. The spirit of optimism in the new country gave hope to women and the poor, both traditionally downtrodden. And while this hope was eventually squashed by those who clung to tradition, it was sufficient during Montessori's youth to give her the boost she needed.

When she was five the family moved to Rome. Her mother expected her to take an active interest in helping those less fortunate, so she knitted for the poor and befriended a hunchback girl in the neighborhood. As a young child in school she performed only adequately, but in time she grew interested in math and technical subjects. With the help of her mother, she overcame her father's objections and at age thirteen actually entered the kind of technical school few Italian girls of her time dared enter. For a time she considered going on to study engineering, but decided on medicine instead. This was totally unheard of for a woman, and when her father finally gave in, he insisted upon accompanying her to class each day. As might be imagined, there was much prejudice against her presence, but she matched her courage with enthusiasm and brilliance and eventually graduated with high marks.

As a new doctor, some of her research took Montessori to the University of Rome's psychiatric clinic. There, amid insane adults she saw large numbers of retarded children, placed there for lack of other choices. The inhumane treatment of these children touched her, and she began to read everything she could find on the education of the retarded. Eventually she decided that there must be some way to reach the children and found herself influenced, in some ways, by Rousseau. Although she disagreed with his idea of unstructured education in the wilds of nature, she liked his idea of developing the senses before abstract learning takes place. She also studied the work of Pestalozzi and Froebel and adapted them to her own use.

Since Montessori wanted to help retarded children, she also studied the writings of those who had been successful in that area. Soon, she was speaking at conferences about the need to educate retarded children, and she proposed a school along Froebel's lines. Before long she found herself appointed director of a teacher training institute that would be a pioneer in creating special education in Italy. Pulling her ideas from Froebel and others, Montessori experimented with teaching materials and activities, succeeding so well that her eight-year-old "defectives" eventually did as well as or better than normal children in state examinations for reading and writing.

For the next several years, Montessori moved back and forth between medicine and special education. During this time she developed a close relationship with one of her colleagues, gave birth to their son, and sent him off to the country to be raised by others. Only in his teens did she raise him herself, usually claiming that he was adopted or belonged to someone else (Kramer, 1976).

Meanwhile, Montessori was given the opportunity to test her educational ideas with children of normal intelligence when she was asked to start a daycare center in a new public housing project. Her success came quickly as she experimented with methods and materials and international fame followed. Some of the school's attributes were born of necessity, then remained because of their effectiveness with children. Aspects of the so-called Children's House (Casa dei Bambini) that were new in that time and place were insufficient materials to go around (to foster sharing), mixed ages (to promote positive interrelationships), freedom of movement and child-choice of materials (to enhance self-direction and democracy), structured activities for the youngest and newest (to provide a sense of stability and confidence), and real tools for real work (to demonstrate respect for the children's abilities and to help them adjust to the real world).

Just as Pestalozzi's and Froebel's teacher-training institutes had attracted enthusiastic students from afar, so did Montessori's. Several Americans learned Italian for the purpose of attending, and in the early years of this century Montessori schools began to bloom in this country. Soon, however, they were denounced by influential scholars and for a time almost disappeared. You have, no doubt, noticed that there are Montessori schools today, however, and this is due to their rebirth in the late 1950s when our society became newly concerned about academic learning for young children. The Montessori method, which encourages children to go as far as they can in their cognitive development, seemed for many an effective alternative for early childhood education.

Like Froebel, Maria Montessori did not live to see this resurgence of popularity in the United States. Her last years were largely spent in exile from Italy and its fascist dictator, Benito Mussolini. Her travels during the Second World War ensured the establishment of Montessori schools in India and the Netherlands. They also gave rise to her belief that if people, beginning in their early childhood, could have more learning and experience with democratic processes, they would be less likely to follow a Mussolini or a Hitler. It was a sentiment that no doubt would have been shared by John Dewey.

Montessori education has survived to this decade relatively intact. Although there are various approaches to training, some purists wanting to keep the schools as they were in Montessori's day while others arguing for updating them, a common element is found in all the schools. If possible, you should try to observe at least one Montessori classroom. There you will find a selection of materials designed to enhance learning through the senses, concrete math activities that help preschoolers intuit complex principles, and children moving independently and at will. It is likely that you will see little play in the free-form sense, and in this way, Montessori schools have a strong relationship to those of Froebel. Traditionally, Montessori schools have come under fire for their lack of creative experiences and free play. Responding to this criticism, many schools have added these elements to their programs, so you may find some differences if you observe in more than one place. In most Montessori schools there is some mixing of ages. The intent is to help the older children take responsibility for the younger while reinforcing their own learning, and for the younger children to learn to depend on and trust their older peers. Further, the mixing of ages is designed to foster the creation of a predemocratic society, or "society in embryo," as Montessori referred to it.

In recent years, the Montessori philosophy has been grasped by those who want to give children an early academic push. This is an unfortunate interpretation of her belief that children should be given the freedom to go

Montessori, like Froebel, believed in structured play for children. Her carefully crafted manipulative materials were designed to enhance learning through the senses. Play experiences based on these materials are still popular in early education classrooms today.

ahead in their learning if they so choose. Nevertheless, it fits with the growing trend for hurrying children along (Elkind, 1983). At approximately the same time that Montessori was beginning her children's house in Rome, a doctor and psychologist named Arnold Gesell was starting a much different trend in this country.

## Arnold Gesell

Arnold Gesell (1880–1961) received his M.D. from Yale after completing a Ph.D. in psychology at Clark University. For thirty years he carried on research at the Yale Clinic of Child Development, which had strong influences on childhood education, particularly for the early years. The roots of Gesell's thinking went back to Froebel, Pestalozzi, and Rousseau, so we will place him on that side of the family tree. Gesell's view of the child was related to that of a growing plant or tree or even an accreting coral. He believed that the seeds of adulthood are present from birth and what is most needed for proper growth is simply proper watering and fertilizing. Gesell's thinking put the most emphasis on the idea of the unfolding, predetermined plant, but it also left room for the influence of the (less important) environment.

The psychological term that Gesell gave to this automatic unfoldment was *maturation*. Related to it was the educational term *readiness*. Observational research in the Yale laboratory suggested to Gesell that there were ages and stages to all aspects of growth: physical, emotional, mental, and school skills. His research led him to establish norms for many behaviors within these areas. For example, he observed that children were biologically ready to read when they had attained a mental age of six and a half years. The school skill of reading, therefore, has the following developmental norms:

| | |
|---|---|
| 15 months | Pats identified picture in book. |
| 18 months | Points to an identified picture in book. |
| 2 years | Names three pictures in book. |
| 3 years | Identifies four printed geometric forms. |
| 4 years | Recognizes salient capital letters. |
| 5–6 years | Recognizes salient printed words. (Weber, 1984, p. 57) |

To Gesell's way of thinking, a child who does not reach these behaviors according to schedule is not a candidate for pushing. His hands-off attitude was reminiscent of Rousseau, as he argued the importance of waiting until the child demonstrates the appropriate readiness. Gesell's arguments were widely heard, and readiness became for many people in early education an important byword. Eventually he was taken to task by other psychological researchers, who noted that he had done his studies at the Yale Clinic of Child Development, where the children's parents were students and professors. In this privileged atmosphere norms were established that were posited for the population as a whole. Gesell's detractors saw this lack of broad-based research and regard for environmental influences as the fatal flaw of his life's work. Further, many have argued that the developmental schedules he established were too rigid and detailed to have universal application.

Nevertheless, Gesell's legacy lives on and work continues at the Gesell Institute in Connecticut. In the 1970s, Louise Ames and others published *The Gesell Institute's Child from One to Six,* along with such titles as *Your Four Year Old: Wild and Wonderful* and *Your Six Year Old: Defiant but Loving.* Each contained detailed descriptions of what one might expect at each naturally unfolding age. Although the idea of readiness is no longer as popular as it once was, there are still educators and school systems that make use of the Gesell philosophy. The transitional kindergarten is one manifestation of the philosophy in action. The argument for it is that although everyone in a graduating kindergarten class may be close to six years old, it is likely that some children lack the mental maturity that will make it comfortable for them to learn to read. Since reading is the core of first-grade instruction, it would be better, the argument goes, to put the unready children into a class of their own. There, they can make the transition to first-grade learning at their own speed.

Letting children learn at their own speed while developing, flowerlike, in an expected sequence, is a Gesell idea that dates back to Rousseau. And while it may be argued that this vision of children is a limiting one, the strength of the philosophy, in these days of pushing children too far too soon, is its reluctance to do so.

## Jean Piaget

There is one more major figure in early education to add to our family tree, although, as a scientist devoted to genetic epistemology, he preferred to leave the educational implications of his studies to other people. Jean Piaget (1896–1980), like Rousseau and Pestalozzi before him, was born in Switzerland. And, like theirs, his childhood was a difficult one, although perhaps not as radically so. In writing about it many years later, he explained that his mother, while "intelligent, energetic, and fundamentally a very kind person," also had a "rather neurotic temperament" that "made our family life somewhat troublesome" (Piaget, 1953, p. 237). To shut off this difficult part of his life, Piaget chose at a very early age to follow an interest in science, modeling himself after his father, "a man of painstaking and critical mind, who dislikes hastily improvised generalizations. . . . Among other things he taught me the value of systematic work, even in small matters" (p. 237).

Turning aside childish play for serious study, Piaget published his first scientific observation (of an albino sparrow) when he was ten. Later he apprenticed himself to a local natural history museum director and developed a lifelong interest in the study of mollusks. Although they were the

More than anyone, Piaget has been responsible for the "constructivist" view of learning, which holds that people actively create their own intellects through their self-chosen interactions with their environment. This view argues for play, experimentation and guided learning activities as opposed to direct instruction and lectures.

subject of his doctoral dissertation, they were not the focus of any further study until the last few years of his life. Instead, Piaget took a position in Paris analyzing responses to items on standardized intelligence tests. Soon, he noticed that similar wrong answers were given by children of similar ages, and this led to interviews with the children to satisfy his curiosity as to why this was so. From this initial experience grew a lifelong dedication to the study of the genesis or origins of human knowledge: genetic epistemology.

From Paris he returned to Geneva, Switzerland, where he did research at the Institut Jean Jacques Rousseau, observing and interviewing children in the "modified" Montessori school there, marrying one of his graduate students, then publishing observations of his own children in their early years. Most of his observations of and interviews with children were devoted to cognitive development, but he also published one major study of children's moral development as well. Although his studies were published in the 1920s and '30s, it was decades before they were translated into English and thus influential in the United States. In common with Montessori, Piaget discovered that eager American educators wanted to use his ideas as a means to push children beyond their developmental readiness.

While Piaget's ideas had elements in common with earlier philosophers and scientists, the way in which he fitted those elements into a new view was the work of a revolutionary genius. Piaget rejected the path of those who

## The Place of Males in Early Childhood Education: A Conversation with Larry Macmillan

*The presence of men in early childhood classrooms and centers has always been somewhat unusual. Today, newly defined problems may contribute to making them an even greater rarity. This interview provides insight into the thinking of one man who is sensitive both to children's needs and to current problems.*

Larry Macmillan has been associated with early childhood education since 1967, when he helped found a community preschool. Later he was a teacher/administrator in an early childhood center. Because he held authority in both these positions, Larry felt no discomfort being a male in a traditionally female career. But in 1974 Larry joined the teaching staff of a university day-care center, and for the first time he found that working with women could be problematic. He was the lone male in a staff that expanded to six teachers just as the women's movement was reaching its apex. While Larry was a supporter of the women's movement, he felt that the other staff members were so enthusiastic about it that they lost perspective on what was legitimately male. (He recalls an incident in which the other teachers refused his proposal that a target dot be painted on the insides of the toilets so that little boys could learn to aim properly; this was seen as divisive of the sexes.)

It didn't help when Larry's male relatives, successful in their more male-oriented careers, asked him when he was going to "get a real job." He felt ever more isolated and found the situation "demoralizing and undermining of self-concept." But Larry was committed to his career and to the children he served; he was not about to leave. To deal with his situation, he helped organize a support group made up of men with careers in the helping profes-

followed Rousseau in believing that children, like plants, simply needed good tending to grow to their genetically determined fullness. And he also chose not to take the path begun by Locke in which children, with their blank slate minds, simply waited to be written on by a nurturing environment. Both nature and nurture, he said, affect how humans develop, so that we need not

sions. Since there weren't other men in the local early childhood centers, he began to net-
work with others in his state. Larry hoped
these steps would help him "claim back some
of my inherent maleness." While the support
group no longer meets, he did find it helpful
for several years. In his more recent role as administrator of the center, he still keeps up
with his early childhood colleagues around
the state.

In the past several years, Larry has found himself affected by society's increasing suspicion
of men in child care positions. For the first
time he feels vulnerable to accusations of sexual abuse and is more careful in his interactions with children. He makes sure that his
male teachers are not placed alone in situations that expose them to suspicion, such as
the diaper-changing or nap rooms. Additionally, he helps them develop a high awareness
of the need to act in such a way that absolutely nothing could be interpreted as possible
abuse.

One approach to this that he now recommends for his entire staff is to avoid picking
up or hugging a child without asking permission first. Larry regrets the loss of spontaneity
this has engendered, but, he says, "What it
does is set up an interaction style that gives
children power. I think it's a key element to
the dispelling of concern, because parents can
see that their children are empowered and can
say no to physical contact."

Larry suggests some things for men to think
about before choosing early childhood as a career:

- Think about your motivation. You must be
  committed to the field. You need to be doing this for yourself and not for someone
  else.
- You have to build some sort of support system with other men. This will help you get
  through the times when others ask you
  when you're going to get a "real" job—and
  they will.

He also has advice for the women who work
with men in early childhood settings:

- It's important to realize that men may have
  different perspectives on children and education. Be ready to discuss their ideas with
  them; don't reject ideas simply because
  they're not what you're accustomed to.
- Don't automatically expect men to do the
  traditional "male" things in your center. If
  things are broken and need to be fixed, for
  example, don't always turn to a man.
  Just as you help both boys and girls play
  and work with all the materials, so you
  should model this behavior yourselves.

*To think about and discuss: What do you see as
the pros and cons of having men in the early childhood setting? Focus on such issues as benefits or
detriments to children, influence on society and history, and impact on the men who work with the
children.*

choose one path but must travel both. In Piaget's view, the child is born with
certain genetic traits and, as he develops, interacts with the environment to
construct his own intelligence. Piaget's view has been called interactionism or
constructivism, the latter being the more popular term at this time.

　　To Piaget, there are four factors that explain early development: maturation, direct physical experience, social transmission, and equilibration. It is *equilibration* that is fundamental to school learning and refers to the child's continual process of cognitive self-correction, whose goal is a better sense of equilibrium. There are two subcategories of equilibration: *assimilation* and *accommodation*. When children learn something new that they can just add on to their existing store of logic (cognitive structure), they are said to assimilate it. For example, a baby who can crawl and who has seen a ball but never one that is rolling, can put these two bits of knowledge together to crawl after a ball the first time she sees one roll by her. Piaget said that assimilation has a close identification with play, thus making play important to adequate cognitive development.

Accommodation, on the other hand, might be termed more serious learning. In this case, some part of the child's cognitive structure has to be modified to take in the new learning. Suppose our crawling child has never seen a ball and suddenly one rolls by. The spherical shape, the rolling movement, perhaps the color are all new, and the child must adapt her thinking to take all this in. Of course, she may still take off after it, but the learning is deeper. As you might guess, both assimilation and accommodation go on continually and in combination with each other.

Despite his reluctance to give much advice to educators, Piaget did have some general ideas as to what should happen in the classroom. From the constructivist view, if children create their own intellects, then they should be given the freedom to do so. This argues for play, experimentation, and guided learning activities as opposed to direct instruction and lectures. As one example, Piaget abhorred the behaviorists' view of mathematics as a drill subject and argued instead for a rich variety of experiences that would lead to deeper understanding. Such learning should begin with concrete activities and only slowly give way to abstract experiences:

> Mathematical training should be prepared, starting at nursery school, by a series of exercises related to logic and numbers, lengths and surfaces, etc., and this type of concrete activity must be developed and enriched constantly in a very systematic way during the entire elementary education, to change little by little at the beginnings of secondary education into physical and elementary mechanical experiments. (Piaget, 1972, p. 104)

Piaget (1972) argued that it is better to let children spend more time on a few problems, really working through them, than to cover a lot of territory: "It is in learning to master the truth by oneself at the risk of losing a lot of time and of going through all the roundabout ways that are inherent in real activity" (p. 104). This approach to learning is more closely related to the current Japanese methods than it is to American ones, and every report of mathematical achievement indicates that what the Japanese are doing is more successful than the American concern with vast coverage of material.

Early critics of Piaget faulted him for basing his worldview of children on studies done in his own home. Subsequent research by others, however, seemed to indicate that his creative genius made it possible for him to do successfully what others would frown upon. Today, early education is strongly influenced by Piaget, particularly when we put down the skillpacks and dittos in favor of less directive, hands-on learning. Meanwhile, research based on his ideas continues to go on so that it is perhaps too early to look back on his contributions as we have with our other historical figures. However, Piaget's place in the family tree is, and will be, a firmly established one.

## Other Contributors

Although the people we have just discussed are arguably some of the most important figures in the history of early education, there are many others who are worthy of our attention. Perhaps you have read about them, or soon will, in other contexts. Following is an annotated list of other names you should know.

### Socrates (470–399 B.C.)

Greek philosopher and Plato's teacher. Discussed the education of children under the age of six.

### Martin Luther (1483–1546)

German leader of the Protestant Reformation. Introduced the idea of music as a school study. Believed girls should be educated, too.

### Margarethe Schurz (1832–1876)

Founded the first American kindergarten in Watertown, Wisconsin, in 1855. Classes were conducted in German.

### Elizabeth Peabody (1804–1894)

Founded the first English-speaking American kindergarten in Boston in 1860.

### Susan Blow (1843–1916)

Opened the first public kindergarten in the United States in 1873 with the backing and sponsorship of *William T. Harris,* superintendent of schools, St. Louis.

### Margaret McMillan (1860–1931)

With the help of her sister *Rachel,* she founded the first nursery school dedicated to improving the health and general well-being of preschool children in England. The building was in the style of a lean-to and open to the elements. The curriculum included both cognitive and social focuses. (You will read more about the McMillan sisters in Chapter 5.)

### Patty Smith Hill (1868–1946)

A leader in the movement away from strict Froebelianism to more progressive education. She was influenced by Dewey as well as the psychologist *G. Stanley Hall,* both of whose philosophies were incompatible with much of Froebel's thought. At Teachers College, Columbia University, she cotaught a series of lectures with Susan Blow in which Hill's "common sense, practicality, and science" were pitted against Blow's "erudition, abstraction, and philosophy" (Shapiro, 1983, p. 167). From the point of view of most students and the administration, Hill came out the victor and Froebelianism took one more step toward a natural death.

### John B. Watson (1878–1958)

A psychologist who affected child rearing during the 1920s and '30s. A behaviorist, he recommended little affection between parent and child, suggesting instead that children be treated as adults and given handshakes rather than hugs.

### B. F. Skinner (1904–1990)

A behaviorist who believed that positive reinforcement is the impetus to increased learning. His thinking has influenced such school programs as assertive discipline, which makes extensive use of reinforcement. The use of extrinsic rewards for academic success is derived from behaviorist thought. (You will read more about Skinner in Chapter 2.)

### James L. Hymes, Jr.

On the original planning committee for Head Start, a past president of the National Association for the Education of Young Children, past vice president of the Association for Childhood Education International, and creator of the *Living History* series, in which he writes annual updates of events in early education.

### David Weikart

Founder of the Perry Preschool Project, which conducts research with disadvantaged children before and during the Head Start years. Follow-up studies have shown that the benefits of preschool are lasting, even into adulthood.

## Extending Your Learning

1. Choose one of the people listed in the last section and study his or her life and contributions to education. Share your findings with your class.
2. See if you can observe influences from centuries ago here in twentieth-century America. Make a list of characteristics associated with education inspired by Locke and another list for Rousseau. Observe at least two classrooms, noting materials, teacher's style, children's learning behaviors and movement patterns, and teacher–child interaction. Compare your findings with the rest of your class.
3. Is there one best way to approach early education? Discuss the historical philosophies and theories and their most positive contributions. Would it be possible to combine the best of each to create the perfect early education? Why or why not?

## References

Ames, L., Gillespie, C., Haines, J., and Ilg, F. (1979). *The Gesell Institute's child from one to six: evaluating the behavior of the preschool child.* New York: Harper & Row.

Boyd, W. (1914). *From Locke to Montessori.* London: Harrap.

Cleverley, J., and Phillips, D. (1986). *Visions of childhood.* New York: Teachers College Press.

Comenius, J.A. (1896, first published 1633). *School of infancy.* Boston: Heath.

Compayre, G. (1907). *Jean Jacques Rousseau and education from nature.* New York: Crowell.

deMause, L. (1974). *The history of childhood.* New York: Psychohistory Press.

Dewey, J. (1964). *John Dewey on education.* New York: Random House.

Elkind, D. (1983). *The hurried child.* Reading, MA: Addison-Wesley.

Gwynne-Thomas, E.H. (1981). *A concise history of education to 1900 A.D.* Washington, DC: University Press of America.

Kramer, R. (1976). *Maria Montessori.* Chicago: University of Chicago Press.

Locke, J. (1964). *John Locke on education.* New York: Teachers College Press.

Osborn, D.K. (1980). *Early childhood education in historical perspective.* Athens, GA: Education Associates.

Pestalozzi, J. (1912). *Pestalozzi's educational writings.* London: Arnold.

Piaget, J. (1953). Autobiographie, Jean Piaget. In *A history of psychology in autobiography,* vol. 4. Worcester, MA: Clark University Press.

———(1972). *The principles of genetic epistemology.* New York: Basic Books.

———(1972). *To understand is to invent.* New York: Viking Press.

Shapiro, M. (1983). *Child's garden.* University Park, PA: Penn State University Press.

Weber, E. (1984). *Ideas influencing early childhood education.* New York: Teachers College Press.

Wodeshouse, H. (1924). *A survey of the history of education.* New York: Longmans, Green.

# Perspectives on Today

# 2

When you finish reading this chapter, you should be able to

- Identify the three major theoretical views of early education.
- Understand some of the controversies surrounding the education of young children.
- Identify and define possible career directions in early childhood education.
- Know the positions taken by some professional organizations concerning early education and related teacher training.

As you think about the chapter on your own, you should be able to

- Begin to consider your own position on educational controversies.
- Have some direction about your own career in the early education field.

The history we read about in Chapter 1 has relevance for today's educators. Depending on their location on the family tree, most of the historical figures we profiled can be defined as belonging to one of three orientations that continue to influence our views of education. In this chapter, we first describe these orientations, then discuss contemporary issues and educational guidelines that have emerged from historical forces. Finally, we consider your own place in early childhood education: careers to choose and the steps within them.

## Three Orientations to Early Education

When a teacher sets out to educate, be it adults taking drivers' training, teenagers studying American history, or three-year-olds learning singing games, success is more assured if the teacher is aware of the intellectual and social maturity of the students. However, in the case of very young students, the teacher's awareness of development is most important because young children change so rapidly. Their stages of development and their learning capacity are more intertwined than at any other time in their lives.

For this reason, research in early childhood education is dominated by psychological as well as educational theorists. In Chapter 1 you met a number of historical figures who have been important to the field of early education. Some were more devoted to psychology and some more interested in education. For example, Froebel, Montessori, and Dewey, while aware of the importance of psychology and child development, were most concerned with education. Piaget, while realizing that his views had an important impact on education, focused almost entirely on cognitive and social/moral development.

In this section we look at three orientations to education: behaviorist, maturationist, and constructivist. While all three are based in psychology, only the second and third are grounded in theories of developmental stages.

### The Behaviorist Orientation

At the beginning of this century, the romantic ideas and ideals attached to Froebel's education were rejected partly because of Dewey's influence and partly because of a movement to make psychology and education more scientific. The scientific approach grew from the seventeenth-century influence of John Locke, who contributed one of the major branches to our family tree. You will recall that Locke regarded children's minds as blank slates, ready to be written upon by the environment. While he agreed that heredity plays some part in a child's makeup and capacity for learning, he believed that it was external forces that determined most of the child's progress. Furthermore, he rejected corporal punishment in favor of a positive approach to discipline.

By putting these two views together, you have the roots of modern-day behaviorism, the scientific approach to psychology and education that began its development early in this century. The person most associated with behaviorism, particularly in relation to classroom applications, has been B. F. Skinner. Skinner's two primary contributions to education were the teaching machines (now replaced by computers) that made programmed learning possible, and behavior modification, which has produced new approaches to motivation and discipline. The behaviorist orientation is built around mastery of the following concepts.

### Behavior

There are two types of behavior: reflexive, such as a knee jerk or eye blink, and operant, or voluntary. Operant behaviors, which are the focus of education, are controlled by their consequences, that is, by the pleasure (positive stimulus) or pain (negative stimulus) they produce. Behaviorists believe that proper stimulus management can produce desired social and cognitive behavior patterns in children.

### Positive Reinforcement

The frequency of desired behaviors can be increased by giving special food, toys, praise, hugs, or anything else the child sees as positive. For example, extra time on the playground is a positive reinforcer for most children and can be used as a motivator for academic work.

### Negative Reinforcement

Instead of adding a rewarding stimulus, as in positive reinforcement, something aversive is taken away. The traditional time-out corner is a common example. A child is behaving inappropriately and is therefore sent to the corner. As soon as the behavior changes, the child is permitted back, and the unpleasant time-out experience is thus removed. Negative reinforcement usually works best when it is followed by positive reinforcements that reward good behavior. If care is not taken, negative reinforcement can lead to punishment.

### Punishment

Skinner objected to punishment because of its undesirable side effects: anger, dislike of school, and the return of the undesired behavior. Researchers have found that punishment can change behavior, but it must be administered soon after the undesired behavior takes place.

### Nonreinforcement

In this case, the teacher simply ignores a behavior, either good or bad. A reason to ignore good behavior might be that it is time to wean the child from an expectation of continual rewards. In the case of bad behavior, nonreinforcement can often cause the child to stop the behavior because there's no reward in it.

### Behavior Modification

The child's behavior is modified, or changed, through the use of any of the methods just listed.

Teachers who subscribe to the behaviorist orientation must have very clear goals, and these must be stated behaviorally. For example, it is not enough to say that your class will understand addition. A specific goal must be established, such as attaining a score of 90 percent on a five-minute written quiz of addition problems with sums of 10 or below.

Learning is generally sequenced, moving from the simple to the more complex, from the concrete to the abstract. Usually, larger bodies of knowledge are broken down into more manageable pieces. The goals of learning

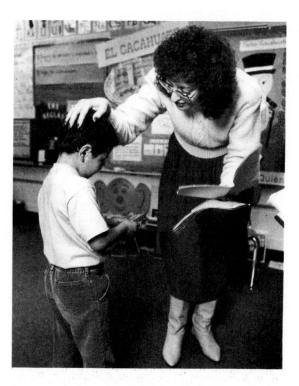

Behaviorists believe that human behavior is largely controlled by the positive and negative stimuli that organisms receive from their environment. In this picture a teacher is shaping behavior through the use of positive reinforcement.

are defined by the teacher, not the children, and the teacher controls the way in which reinforcements are used to help achieve success.

While a number of program models have been created based on the behaviorist orientation, and while most teachers occasionally use some aspects of behaviorist theory, even if only informally, it is in special education that behaviorist techniques are most pervasive. The clear-cut, straightforward approach, with learning broken down into small chunks, has had much appeal for those who work with learning-disabled children.

## The Maturationist Orientation

A plant matures according to a predetermined hereditary plan. It goes through completely predictable stages, from internal seed development to the attainment of its full height, weight, and shape. Although the plant's development can be affected somewhat if it receives too much or too little light and water, its stages of growth are still the same. According to maturationists, the same is true of children.

Historically, the views of maturationists can be traced back to Rousseau, who saw children as inherently good and needing only proper nurturing to achieve their full potential. Later, Arnold Gesell became the leader in carrying Rousseau's ideas into the twentieth century. His most influential theory, the one that has continued to have broad acceptance, was that much of a child's development takes place in invariant, predictable stages. Each stage is a major step forward, and, after it is reached, there is a period of consolidation before the next major step is taken. Other principles of the maturationist orientation include the following.

### Norms

Decades of observing children led Gesell to define what children are like and what they should be able to do at specific ages. These developmental expectations or norms were made for each six-month period of life.

### Readiness

Children should not be pushed into kindergarten or first grade just because they have reached a certain chronological age. First, they should be tested to see if they have reached prescribed intellectual and physical norms. If not, they should be held back until they are ready. Similarly, children should not be forced to read until they have reached their own internal maturational level of at least six years.

Children in a maturationist classroom are all at about the same stage of development. The teacher and the classroom environment nurture children but don't push them. Materials and activities are chosen because they are appropriate for the developmental stage of the children in the class. If children avoid them, this is a signal to the teacher that the level may be inappropriate, and not that some sort of reinforcement might make them more attractive. The teacher's role is "acceptance, gentle guidance, and facilitation of children's wants and interests," but "directing, correcting, or actively modifying behavior are questionable or undesirable" (Lay-Dopyera and Dopyera, 1990, p. 172).

## The Constructivist Orientation

This is the most recent theory of early education and, unlike the preceding views, does not stem from the teachings of a seventeenth- or eighteenth-century philosopher. Instead, it flows from the work of Jean Piaget, who studied children's thought processes by observing the children themselves. His hands-on, personal approach directly contradicted the American attitude that psychological research should focus on abstract laws of learning. Furthermore, Piaget wrote in a scholarly European style guaranteed to overwhelm the layperson and even most psychologists. It was at least four decades before his work found acceptance in this country. Now, however, Piaget's theories of development have the highest respect among psychologists.

Educational theory has also been altered profoundly by Piaget's thinking, which argues that children help construct their own intelligence through active exploration of their environment. Such a view is sure to produce a classroom that is quite different from a teacher-dominated situation where children are coaxed into learning what adults have decided is best for them.

Recall from Chapter 1 that Piaget believed children learn best by interacting with the world around them. They do this through accommodation (when something is quite new) and assimilation (when there is prior experience to build on). In Piaget's words, "The filtering or modification of the input is called *assimilation,* the modification of internal schemes to fit reality is called *accommodation*" (Piaget and Inhelder, 1969, p. 5). Remember, too, that these processes complement each other and occur simultaneously. In this theory, the child's biology is the important factor in the learning that comes right after birth. But, as time goes by, the child has more input from the environment and from social experiences, and these factors become more important than biology. By the time the child enters preschool, the environment and social experiences are primary influences in learning. The constructivist view is that children don't just passively absorb their environment; they actively operate on it.

As children learn, they progress through stages, but the constructivist view of these stages is a bit different from the maturationist. While the maturationist sees stage development as a predetermined, natural, flowerlike unfoldment, the constructivist argues that this is only part of the picture. When

According to maturationists, young children (like plants) develop according to a predetermined hereditary schedule that is modified according to the type and quantity of nutrients they receive from their environment.

children actively operate on the environment, their experiences influence their maturational processes. Thus, their learning is influenced both by environmental influences and by maturation.

Teaching in a constructivist classroom is more complex than in classrooms inspired by the first two orientations. One Piaget scholar has said, "To put Piagetian concepts into action requires, above all else, a thinking teacher. He or she looks beyond the child's verbalization and manipulation and tries to understand what they mean for the child. This way of looking at and thinking about children is far from easy. It adds, however, a new and satisfying dimension to teaching" (Millie Almy, quoted in Weber, 1984, p. 169).

The carefully sequenced, small bits of knowledge favored by behaviorists give children little opportunity to carry out the kind of exploratory learning constructivists feel is needed. The maturationists' use of developmental stages as a guide for planning is seen as necessary but not sufficient. In the constructivist view, the goals of learning are not so much a predetermined set of facts or a particular level of accomplishment, but opportunities for children to build on to their existing mental structures through active learning. Children

According to constructivists, children don't just passively absorb their environments; they actively operate on them and, in the process, have much to do with constructing their own intelligence.

are likely to be found experimenting, questioning, and planning. During the early years, and often beyond, hands-on materials are critical. Children may choose to learn alone for a bit and then join a group. They may choose to interact with a teacher for a while and later with their peers. Such self-regulated learning periods tend to be long and unstructured, rather than neat and orderly segments. In this way, experimentation and invention have an opportunity to develop.

## Summary

These three orientations to learning are quite different from each other. Although you occasionally will find schools that profess to be aligned with one or the other of them, it is more likely that you will see a mixture of two or even of all three in the same school. For example, you might visit a transitional kindergarten (maturationist) that teaches arithmetic through repeated drills (behaviorist) and has a long afternoon period when children experiment freely with many kinds of materials (constructivist).

In the next section we discuss some of the contemporary issues you will

face as an early childhood teacher. As you read about each issue, try responding to it according to each of the three orientations just presented.

## Current Issues

Numerous and complex issues face today's early childhood educator. All
of them reflect the society we now live in, and all will affect you in some
way as you enter the world of teaching. Among the issues are the following.

### Life in a Democratic Society

Participating in a democratic society is not always easy. The freedom to
make decisions about our laws, our leaders, and our own lives can be both
challenging and frightening. The possibilities for social and economic success
are no greater than the possibilities for failure. It takes both courage and
knowledge to live life to the fullest in a democracy, and both are ours most
fully if we begin to acquire them early on. Thus, as early childhood educators, we do children a great favor if we introduce them to democratic principles at the earliest possible moment.

This doesn't mean that we have to have elected classroom officers for
three-year-olds. However, we can provide decision-making opportunities in a
very concrete fashion throughout the day. We can increase the societal rights
for each child in our class while making everyone aware that there are responsibilities, too. It is possible to do this in an age-appropriate way for even
the very youngest children. In Chapter 9 there will be a complete discussion
of democracy in the classroom with ideas for you to try.

### Structured Versus Unstructured Learning

As you reflect on the three orientations to early education, you will want
to determine how structured your classroom will be. Typically, the behaviorist classroom is the most structured of the three.

Ordinarily, a structured environment includes carefully chosen materials,
each designed for specific purposes. Often, but not necessarily, the teacher
plays a rather directive role and may make more decisions than the children
do about what will happen during the day's highly scheduled events. In a
structured classroom the children know that if it's 10:00 A.M. Tuesday the
music teacher is on her way. They know, too, that there is a time to play
with blocks and a time for reading readiness activities, and one is usually not
permitted to interfere with the other.

In an unstructured environment, scheduling is more open and the children have more say in what they will do and when. The curriculum has a
basic plan, but it is also open to spontaneity. The teacher may choose to follow up on the children's interest in a beautiful flower brought in by one of

their classmates. The event might lead to a change in the day's plans or even to a full unit of study designed partly by the children themselves. In the unstructured classroom children are more independent and self-directed and often have more time to play.

Both types of environment have their pros and cons. The structured classroom offers children more security and stability but can also be more rigid and demanding. The unstructured classroom provides more freedom but can also lead to chaos and disorganization. On the surface, it would seem that the unstructured class would be more easily identified with the values of a democratic society, but this is not necessarily so. Montessori education, which is one of the most highly structured systems, is also dedicated to ensuring that children are introduced in a practical way to the concepts of democratic living.

At some point you will need to make your own decision about which approach is right for you. In Chapter 7 we'll discuss this issue more fully.

### How Much Play?

People who think and write about education have commented for centuries about the advantages of letting the youngest children learn through play. But different people in varying cultures and at different historical times have defined play according to their own—and often adult—perceptions. In some cultures, including our own, there is a pervading distrust of play despite decades of research which tells us that young children do most of their best learning through play. We keep wanting children to work at tasks that are more suitable for their older peers or even for adults. Although we remind ourselves that "play is the work of the child" and try it for a while, after a time the pressure to accomplish more in a shorter time leads us back to a work orientation.

We consider the issue of play in Chapter 7, where it is presented as the primary vehicle for early learning. Of course, children can't learn everything through play. As a teacher, one of your major decisions will be to determine when play is the most appropriate method for learning and when other, more structured approaches are desirable.

### School From What Age?

For centuries, this was really not an issue. Young children were educated, if at all, at home. Those philosophers and educators who wrote about teaching assumed that home was where the youngest belonged. However, for over a century now, nursery schools, child care centers, and kindergartens have become common and have gradually changed the status of early education. In 1965 just 10 percent of three- and four-year-olds in the United States attended school. Now, 39 percent attend (Walters, 1990). Some states have mandated public kindergartens so recently that you may not have attended one. Although many educational writers still believe that age five is too early to take a child away from home, some parents and educators feel that it is never too early to begin fostering a young child's development through school experience. Mixed into the argument is the need for more and better child care to meet the demands of families in which both parents work. For them, shortly after birth may be the time they want or need to send their child outside the home, and for most parents, having some educational experience built into the day-care situation is preferable to simple babysitting.

You may eventually choose to work in a center that houses the very youngest. If so, this is an issue of some importance for you. An advantage to teaching children early is that you can work with the families to plan the most advantageous educational activities for their children. Together, you can begin to foster children's growth in every area of development.

The other side of this issue is that children who begin school too early may feel bombarded and pressured by the constant attention given their progress. They may respond in negative ways if they are given insufficient time to play in their own way and to do things according to their own internal schedule. Well-intended early education may actually be a disservice to a child. As you read Chapters 3, 4, and 5, think about this issue in relation to the discussions on child development. Then decide for yourself what your own viewpoint is.

### Learning to Read

Among the issues embedded in the process of children's learning to read are the following: (1) how teachers should teach and children should learn (including the old debate about the role of phonics instruction); (2) whether parents should be involved or not, and if so, in what ways; and (3) whether children should learn to read in some systematic way or whether they should be submerged in a more informal, "natural" process. Pervading all these issues is another major one: *When* is the best time for children to start learning to read?

Over the centuries, traditional wisdom has held that the age of six or seven is, for most children, the critical period when learning to read comes most easily. Nevertheless, there have always been those who believed that age two is not too early to expose children to the printed word. They argue that the earlier we expose children to the idea of reading, the more easily they become accustomed to it and accept it as a natural part of their learning. Of course, an interest in reading doesn't usually come naturally to a two-year-old, since children of that age aren't quite sure just what kind of "toy" a book is. Thus, the parent or teacher must introduce the idea of reading in some direct way, perhaps using flash cards with large words printed on them.

The opposite point of view, that later is better, presents the argument that children will be more enthusiastic about reading if given the opportunity to discover it naturally as a meaningful part of their environment. This argument also includes the view that early gaps in reading performance tend to

The debate on when it is developmentally appropriate to begin formal education continues. Educationally oriented child care programs have shown that considerable learning can occur at very early ages, but many experts feel that too much attention to children's early learning produces harmful pressures.

disappear within a couple of years. In Chapter 11 the various issues concerning reading are presented with research findings to help you choose your own positions concerning this important school-related topic.

### Computers Versus Manipulative Materials

For centuries, observers have noted that young children seem to be most happy and successful in their learning when they are given concrete objects to manipulate. Even adults who distrust play as a method of learning are usually willing to grant young children at least some interaction with physical materials. Are computers a concrete material? Do they provide play, in the real sense of the word?

The arguments in favor of computers for young children are persuasive. These machines, which now pervade our society, will assume greater importance as technology develops even further. If young children learn to take computers for granted, they will have greater mastery and openness to new technology as they grow older. Further, age-appropriate software ensures that young children interact with computers in a playful and enjoyable way. We made similar arguments earlier in favor of when and how young children should be introduced to democracy.

Often, young children do take quite easily and happily to computer-based learning. For the primary grades there is even a very successful learning-to-read program sponsored by IBM. On the other hand, there are those who argue that using this kind of technology is similar to teaching children to read too early or putting them in school before they have had time to feel secure and comfortable at home. The question to be asked: Is it really necessary or desirable to push younger children into this learning mode that is a step away from truly concrete learning, when they can so easily and happily catch up later? Computer technology and software for young children are both in exciting developmental stages. As a new teacher, you may well be asked to make decisions regarding whether and how your children should interact with computers. In Chapter 8 you will find a "conversation" with an early childhood computer expert whose ideas may help you develop your own views and ideas.

### Cultural Pluralism

You undoubtedly have heard our nation called a melting pot and sometimes—when advocating ethnic diversity—a stewpot. This argument about what kind of national "pot" we should be is one that has existed in some form from the first decades of colonial settlement. As a teacher, you should be aware of the issues, particularly as they affect your interactions with children and their parents. You will need to consider these issues from several directions: How can you be most sensitive to each family's needs and desires regarding its ethnic identity? How can you best help all children feel good about their cultural heritage and also about their identity as U.S. citizens? In what ways can you be sure that children are accepting of each other's differences as well as similarities? When should you downplay children's commentary on differences and when should you seize the opportunity to educate regarding those differences?

Related to these questions is an underlying one concerning your own development: How do you deal with your own biases concerning children whose backgrounds are different from your own? Virtually everyone has prejudices of some sort. What you do about them may profoundly affect the well-being of many of the children you teach. Chapter 6 deals with the many sides of cultural pluralism, as well as with other differences among children.

### Government Intrusion

In the nineteenth century, when kindergartens first appeared, there were schools for rich children and schools for poor children, but they were all funded privately. Once they became a part of the public system, however, government control as well as funding became an issue. This is increasingly the case as more and more states provide access to free preschool education. Since the 1960s the federally funded Head Start program has been available, and by 1980 eight states provided some form of public preschool. By 1988, there was legislation in twenty-four states to fund prekindergarten programs (Walters, 1990).

As with other issues, there are pros and cons surrounding the growth of government-sponsored preschools and kindergartens. A century ago, wealthy philanthropists discovered that their devoted and impressive efforts to fund early education could not keep up with the waves of immigrants. Today, rising birthrates and increased immigration make private efforts even more inadequate at a time when the growing population of underprivileged children requires and deserves some sort of early educational intervention to offset its many disadvantages. Thus, it is imperative that government intervene in some measure to help promote the welfare of young children. The public recognizes this to the extent that politicians find it to their benefit to support new programs for ever-younger children.

Understandably, the agencies that contribute the funding want some say in what happens to their money, but the views of national and state agencies regarding how children should be taught and what the curriculum should include may not be the same as the local school's. In what way the money is apportioned is certain to create a battleground for power and control. We touch on this topic in Chapter 8. Although it won't be discussed in great depth, it is one that you need to be aware of and to keep informed about through the various news media.

## Teacher Preparation

As more states provide education for increasingly younger children and as more mothers enter the work force, thus expanding the need for child care, many more teachers are needed. Unfortunately, training for caregivers and teachers cannot keep up with demand. As a result, young children may be taught by unqualified people. In recent years, organizations concerned with the education and welfare of young children have felt impelled to create lists of expectations for caregivers and teachers. Additionally, some states have increased the legal requirements. New degrees and degree programs have emerged. Because of financial considerations, however, the debate regarding the amount of professional preparation needed by teachers and caregivers continues. Good child care and good education are expensive, and teacher salaries are often high on the list when budget cutbacks are attempted. Even dedicated teachers find it difficult to remain in what is sometimes a very low paying career.

## Guiding Principles for Early Childhood Programs

Today there are many ways to educate young children, and some of them have conflicting goals and philosophies. In part this is due to the issues just discussed, and in part it is due to the continuing conflict between the three historical views of childhood. In an effort to make sense of the large number of choices, several organizations have, in recent years, stated their positions concerning the welfare and education of young children. These positions are the result of consensus building on the part of various experts in the field of early education. Although these people may come from differing philosophical viewpoints, they have found that there is much that can be agreed upon by almost everyone. These position statements underlie the views of this textbook. In the next three chapters you will see how they relate to different aspects of children's development. Here, we provide an overview of those principles that today's experts feel constitute a good education for young children. Our source is the 1987 expanded edition of *Developmentally Appropriate Practice in Early Childhood Programs Serving Children from Birth through Age 8* published by the National Association for the Education of Young Children (NAEYC).

### Developmentally Appropriate Programs

This concept may be the single most important consideration for early childhood educators today. According to NAEYC, there are two sides to the issue: age appropriateness and individual appropriateness. For the first, it is important that teachers be aware of children's predictable stages of growth in all areas: physical, emotional, social, and cognitive. For the second, teachers need to know and appreciate each child's uniqueness and individuality and to provide activities and materials that are personally interesting and challenging. A major mode for doing this is play. According to NAEYC, "child-initiated, child-directed, teacher-supported play is an essential component of developmentally appropriate practice" (p. 3).

An illustration: In a suburban elementary school there were two kindergarten classes. One had a rigid program made up of daily work with dittoed phonics and math materials. Children were permitted to play only when their work was finished. For the slower children, this time never came, and they spent most days doing nothing but paper-and-pencil seatwork. Unfortunately, their slowness often had as much to do with their unreadiness to use a pencil skillfully as with their inability to understand the work. The second class had large periods of traditional kindergarten play: housekeeping and block corners, puzzles, paint, and so on. Because the principal demanded it, there was a certain measure of paper-and-pencil work in this class, too, but individual capabilities were taken into consideration. Toward the end of the year, the principal observed both classes and, being a rigid academician, gave the second teacher two choices: change to the first teacher's approach or leave. The second teacher responded that her method was closer to what she knew to be developmentally appropriate practice and that she couldn't, in good conscience, change. She transferred to another school. Her experience is one you may have. As you read this and other books about how children learn, think about the decision you would make.

### Curriculum that Integrates All Areas of Child Development

When we teach young children, we should not just focus on isolated areas of development (physical, social, cognitive, etc.) but realize that "any activity that stimulates one dimension of development and learning affects other dimensions as well" (p. 3). This is very different from the kinds of learning you have become accustomed to in high school and college and requires a very different way of planning your curriculum.

An illustration: Chris was an elementary physical education teacher intent on improving the fitness of a generally out-of-shape third-grade class. Each day he took the children outside for calisthenics and mile-long runs, and each day he charted the children's progress on his clipboard. At first the children groaned; then they became pleased with their increasing speed and ability to do the exercises; then they became intrigued by the clipboard. To humor them, Chris showed the children his markings, and a few of them begged to write down their improvement themselves. Soon, Chris realized that his record keeping was a major impetus in creating positive attitudes. He simplified the charts so that all the children could understand them, then trained the children to use them on their own. A final step was to place the charts on a sheltered wall where the children could record their progress without his supervision. At the end of the school year, every child in the class tested above the national average in every single skill. Additionally, their self-esteem was greatly improved, and they had learned valuable real-life math skills.

### Experiences that Are Concrete and Relevant to Real Life

It is totally inappropriate to teach very young children using abstractions and symbols. These should only be introduced and gradually increased throughout the primary grades. As NAEYC notes, "Learning takes place as young children touch, manipulate, and experiment with things and interact with people" (p. 4).

An illustration: A new but adventurous teacher wondered if introducing supposedly difficult math concepts at an early age would help children avoid fear of math later. Her idea was that, if they learned the concepts in a concrete way, the children would feel at home and comfortable with them. She rejected the "easier" operations of addition, subtraction, and multiplication in favor of starting with the "hardest": division. Choosing daily snacks as her material, the teacher broke up everything into small pieces, which the children learned to divide evenly among themselves. They also learned that left-overs went in a separate pile for the teacher. Soon they could say and understand such terms as *divide, division, divisor,* and *remainder,* and knew that the answer to a division problem was the amount each child had. Despite their solid understanding of the division process, the teacher didn't ask the children to write down their problems. After all, they were only four years old.

### Multicultural and Nonsexist Curricula

Children pick up cultural cues from the earliest years. It is entirely appropriate and desirable to focus on such issues at every educational level. To do so "enhances each child's self-concept and esteem . . . supports the integrity of the child's family . . . [and] enriches the lives of all participants" (p. 8).

An illustration: A first-grade teacher had a large number of children who came from non-English-speaking homes, and he was aware that some of the other children were beginning to make fun of their accents. He sought out the strong points of each child and determined that everyone should be an expert at something. It wasn't long before children were helping each other with tricks on the playground equipment, with difficult math problems and puzzles, and with standard English grammar and pronunciation. The teacher had believed he would need to couple this approach with lessons on cooperation and caring, but simply making each child feel expert at one thing developed the desired atmosphere.

### A Balance between Rest and Activity, Indoors and Outdoors

Children have a physical rhythm that is very different from that of adults. Teachers need to be aware of this and to alternate quiet and active periods in a flexible way, as the children need them. This is true all the way through the primary grades when, unfortunately, many teachers keep children inactive and indoors for the entire day. It is important to remember that "outdoor time is an integral part of the curriculum and requires planning; it is not simply a time for children to release pent-up energy" (p. 8).

An illustration: A kindergarten teacher complained to a colleague that her children were restless in the mornings no matter what she did to entertain them. "I practically stand on my head and all they do is fidget," she said. The colleague arranged to observe one morning and discovered what she had suspected: the teacher stood in front of the children, being as entertaining as possible and, yes, practically standing on her head. All the while the children fidgeted because they had to sit cross-legged on the floor and weren't allowed to move. The observer suggested involving the children actively in the morning activities, letting them role play most of what the teacher was saying. The teacher reported back the next day that the change was working so well that, when it really was necessary for the children to sit still, they were able to do so with almost no fidgeting at all.

As various minorities compose an ever larger portion of our school age population, it is imperative that teachers give minority children a chance to gain respect from the majority children by demonstrating mastery of their native culture.

### Opportunity to Communicate

Often, teachers seem to think only in terms of directly teaching children new information. This not only requires children to sit still for long periods of time, which is difficult, but deprives them of the opportunity to practice communicating themselves. It is important for teachers to understand the types of communication that characterize each stage of development, from the infant's crying and body movements to the primary child's lengthy conversations. To be educationally effective, communication should be two-way: "Children acquire communication skills through hearing and using language, and as adults listen and respond to what children say" (p. 10).

An illustration: One teacher of two-year-olds keeps a record of her conversations with each child. This is simply a chart on which each child's name is listed down the left side, with dates written across the top. Each time the teacher completes a one-on-one communication, she makes a check mark in the appropriate space, following up once or twice a day to be sure that no child is being neglected. Two pencils are kept handy, one of them red. A red check mark indicates that some special learning has taken place. At the end of the day the teacher checks the chart, looks for red marks, remembers the events (almost always successfully), and describes them on each child's individual record.

## Providing the Respect, Acceptance, Comfort, and Encouragement Children Deserve

When we respect children, we can help them learn from their mistakes, hear them out when they are frustrated and angry, and guide them to resolve their own conflicts. Teachers can help children's behavior become more mature only if they model desirable behavior. Consequently, teachers must avoid such actions as "screaming in anger . . . inflicting physical or emotional pain . . . insulting . . . threatening, or using frightening or humiliating punishment" (p. 11).

An illustration: If ever a teacher deserved to scream in frustration and anger it was Judy. Her second graders were the most difficult children she had ever encountered. But she recognized that, in many cases, the children's parents were drug addicts or alcoholics, which made simple survival a victory for the children. Her compassion led her to give an extra hug here and there. Before long, the children were responding with gratitude. Boys and girls alike came to her for hugs in the middle of their work, after completing their work, when they didn't feel like doing their work, or any time at all. When two children fought, Judy simply marched into the middle, threw an arm around each, and hugged hard. It worked almost every time.

## Good Parent–Teacher Communication

Everyone gains by good parent–teacher relationships. The children feel more confident and secure when they are aware of such interactions. Also, parents and teachers who share experiences have a better understanding of each child's needs and interests. Different points of view are recognized and dealt with. It is important to remember that "parents have both the right and the responsibility to share in decisions about their children's care and education" (p. 12).

An illustration: Three-year-old Timmy's behavior was taking a turn for the worse. Each morning he came in fighting mad, swinging his fists in all directions, even at the children who were older than he. This went on for several days, and his teacher decided it was time to contact Timmy's mother. She described the child's almost ritualistic approach to fighting stances, his lack of fear when taking on any child of any size, and her inability to communicate with him during these times. She wondered if Timmy might be watching a lot of television, especially shows with violence in them. Timmy's mother agreed that this was, indeed, the case, and the teacher asked if they might discuss a reduction in viewing time. But Timmy's mother said that she would just as soon "pull the plug." Over the next three weeks teacher and mother were in continual contact, and Timmy was aware of it. When he went home he reported his school behavior and vice versa. The change in behavior was dramatic. After only a few days Timmy stopped fighting and was always ready for a chat with his teacher. One day, after about two weeks, he hugged his mother and said, "You and Teacher love me a lot, don't you."

Now that you have read about historical trends in early education and the theoretical views, issues, and educational guidelines that have emerged from that history, it is time to consider your own place in history, to think about how you picture yourself in relation to young children.

The following section will focus on current expectations for people preparing for different jobs in early education. The overarching purpose of this section is to help you look at the different directions your career might take and the expectations, rewards, and difficulties associated with each. As you read this section, try to develop (if you haven't already) a very clear idea of what your future goals and accomplishments in early education could be.

## Careers in Early Childhood Education

An early childhood career provides a choice of age groups with which you can work. The early childhood years typically cover birth to age eight, and various programs divide these ages in different ways. Some schools segregate each age group, making it possible to focus on the changing needs of the child at each identifiable stage. Others place two or more age groups together so that the children can learn from each other. Before selecting a specific career, it would be a good idea for you to acquire as much experience as possible with each of these different age groups. It would also be helpful to try your hand at teaching both mixed-age groups and segregated-age groups. There are advantages and disadvantages to each approach, and, as you work with different ages, you will no doubt discover that you have favorites. There may even be some groups you are not comfortable working with at all. Try to identify your preferences and capabilities during your teacher training, as this is the time when it is easiest to experiment and take risks.

In addition to selecting particular age groups to work with, focus on specific roles within the educational establishment. In part this will be determined by the level of training you undergo, but there is still quite a bit of flexibility. You may decide to own your own school, and that could mean caring for a small group of children in your home or creating a larger enterprise with its own buildings and a large staff. Eventually you might not work with children at all, preferring instead to become director of a center or even to attend law school and specialize in education-related issues. As a teacher, you can work with privately run centers that are either nonprofit or profit-driven; teach in public preschools, kindergartens, or primary grades; or be employed in industry-associated care centers. Some public libraries hire people with early childhood training for their children's rooms, and there are hospitals that run nurseries or care centers for their patients or even the patients' visiting siblings. Wherever young children gather there is a career waiting for you. Here are some of the more traditional jobs in early education, along with expected preparation, responsibilities, and rewards.[1]

## Teacher Aide or Teacher Assistant

This job requires little or no training, and the pay, which is minimum wage or close to it, reflects this. An aide helps the teacher in whatever ways are needed, usually assisting children in activities that require adult help: preparing supplies, grading projects and papers, keeping the environment cleaned and straightened. Primary qualifications for an aide are to enjoy, respect, and relate well to young children. Often, people who begin working with children by being an aide discover that they enjoy the work and would like to take more responsibility. Naturally, this requires more education. There may be people in your class now who have followed this route.

## Associate Teacher or Assistant Teacher

An associate teacher has more credentials than a teacher aide, the most common being an associate of arts (AA) degree or a child development associate (CDA) certificate. The CDA program is offered by many community colleges and vocational-technical institutes that have early childhood programs, although it is also possible to be informally educated through in-service workshops. These programs require the student to demonstrate specific competencies in order to receive the certificate. The associate teacher, like the teacher aide, works under the direction of the regular teacher, usually in a center-based (as opposed to school-based) environment. The associate teacher supervises children as the teacher directs and may do some team teaching, particularly by reading stories or singing songs. Although this job generally pays more than the teacher aide position, the salary is still low.

## Teacher

In an early childhood center, a teacher will usually have an AA degree, possibly with the CDA certificate. Centers may also have teachers who hold a bachelor's degree, but the pay is generally lower than in the public schools,

---

[1]The sources for much of the information in this chapter are R. Bouverat, M. Reeves, and B. Skeen, "Resource Packet for Advising in the Preparation of Personnel for Early Childhood Education" (1988) and "NAEYC Position Statement on Nomenclature, Salaries, Benefits, and the Status of the Early Childhood Profession" (1984).

so this is less common. In public schools, kindergarten through the grades, entry-level teachers must have baccalaureate degrees, although some states are moving toward a required master's degree. As each state passes legislation to create publicly funded preschool education, decisions must be made concerning teacher training. In some cases, only the AA is required, thus lowering the personnel cost for the state; in others, a bachelor's degree is required.

In a school setting, the teacher is usually the highest-level person to come in contact with the children. In early childhood centers, the teacher may also answer to a head teacher. In either case, the teacher makes lesson plans based on the school's philosophy and goals, arranges and maintains the environment, keeps records of children's progress, and does the actual day-to-day instructing.

## Head Teacher

Typically found in an early childhood center rather than in a school, the head teacher coordinates the curriculum and classroom functioning with the other teachers and staff. The head teacher takes a leadership role in meetings and planning sessions and may do some training of aides. Depending on the center and the head teacher's experience and capabilities, his or her background might include an AA, a bachelor's degree, or even a master's degree. Head teachers can often, but not always, expect to earn as much as public school teachers.

In public schools there may also be a head teacher who is appointed by the principal or elected by other teachers, usually in the same grade. In this case, the head teacher is not expected to monitor the teaching or organization in other classrooms, but coordinates the curriculum, calls meetings for the group, and speaks for the group in communications with administrators. There may well be no extra remuneration for this task, but the teaching load might be reduced in some way. Most people reading this book will be training to be a teacher or head teacher.

## Program Director or Supervisor, Assistant Director, Educational Director, Curriculum Coordinator, or Resource Teacher

People in these positions have had experience, often in-depth, teaching young children. They have been successful at it and are willing to accept responsibility on a broader level. Their positions can be defined as a midway point between the administration and the teaching staff and generally provide pay that is above a teacher's but lower than an administrator's. These supervisors and coordinators are responsible for monitoring the programs of each teacher, coordinating curriculum, providing in-service programs, maintaining teaching materials, supervising testing, and spearheading program develop-

## *Starting Your Own School: A Conversation with Elise Webb*

*Most caregivers and teachers begin their careers by working for someone else, and most continue to do so. A few, however, dream of owning their own center or school. The subject of this interview is a woman who had such a dream and has succeeded beyond her greatest expectations.*

Elise Webb taught fifth and sixth grade until her first child was born. Then she chose to work part-time as the art teacher in a small private nursery school. Elise enjoyed the younger children, and, when the owner of the school moved away, she accepted the invitation to buy the business from her. As the school was only open half days, she visualized continuing in a part-time capacity. This would work well, she thought, with her obligations as wife and mother.

Learning that a half-day school meant full-time work was just one part of Elise's on-the-job training. "I had to become a major decision maker for the first time in my life. That was a major change in personality for me, but a necessary one." Furthermore, "I had never done anything financial and had to learn that side of the business from scratch." Then, too, there was purchasing, advertising, personnel decisions, public relations, painting, wallpapering, plumbing, and other upkeep. Finally, curriculum development took more time than Elise had ever imagined. Despite all this, both Elise and the school prospered.

Elise believes that starting small was important for success. Mistakes ("and there were many," she says) were relatively small ones, and she could learn as she went along. One step Elise took was to hire an accountant who was interested in nurturing and educating her. Among other things, he taught her how to do her own income taxes and to budget, and recommended that she incorporate.

One lesson learned the hard way was that hiring new teachers requires trust in one's intuition as well as reliance on résumés and recommendations. Elise believes that, once background checks and fingerprinting are taken care of, the rapport that develops during an interview can provide the most important information. She feels fortunate that almost every person she has hired shares her philosophy of education and is an enthusiastic and conscientious teacher.

From the beginning, Elise purchased high-quality materials for every aspect of the school. At the same time, she learned that making a purchase based on a quick perusal of the first interesting catalog can be foolhardy. She learned to comparison shop while keeping an eye out for quality. This approach makes it possible to splurge now and then on some special material.

As the school grew, Elise found that her style of decision making had to change. When there were only four or five teachers, almost everything could be decided by consensus. When the faculty grew to eight or ten, she found it necessary at times to make the tougher decisions herself, since consensus was more difficult to achieve. To her surprise, Elise found herself liking this kind of leadership. Her present style is to give teachers as much decision-making power as possible. When necessary, she steps in.

Although running her own small school took a lot of work, Elise found it rewarding. However, a problem arose that forced the school to be closed. Elise owned the school, but the property it was on was owned by a university that eventually decided to reclaim it. At first, the news was devastating, but before long Elise had joined with another educator to open a new school. In just a few years it grew to include nursery through elementary grades, and a day-care center has recently been added. The school is highly regarded for its commitment to quality child-centered education.

The second school came with its own set of lessons. At the outset, Elise found it beneficial to work closely with the local health department and other regulatory agencies. "Before we made any move at all we involved them," she says. "Because these agencies knew we cared so much, we never had any problems. Even now, as soon as we contemplate a change we call the various agencies right away and involve them." The relationship has been one of mutual trust rather than an us-against-them situation.

Elise has also learned that, as the school grows, good communication with parents becomes more difficult and more important. Teachers are available at the beginning and end of each day to talk informally, and the school publishes a parent handbook, school calendar, and frequent newsletters. Teachers post daily activities on the classroom doors.

One problem has been impossible for Elise to surmount. She has always wanted "to have my fingers in everything. But, it's counterproductive if you let yourself get pulled too thin. If you're outside with the children you can't be agonizing because you should be in the office doing paperwork, and vice versa. But, to be honest, I haven't worked this one out. And I probably never will." As Elise explains, "After all, the school is my baby. But the job would be impossible if we did not have an excellent faculty. I've learned that possibilities multiply when you have good teachers and trust their judgment."

*To think about and discuss: If you could start the center or school of your dreams, what would it be like? Talk your ideas over with the owner of a local school to determine the practicality of your dream. If you think you might like to follow through in the future, begin now to collect good suggestions.*

ment. People in these positions may have an AA, but can usually be expected to have at least a bachelor's degree and often some graduate work.

## Director or Principal

Whatever the school setting, these positions require the most responsibility and the most unpredictable working hours. They also provide the highest pay. A director or principal must be able to work well with faculty, staff, parents, and the community as needed. In addition to overseeing the staff, this person must also manage the school's budget, coordinating it with the school's academic and caregiving goals. A director or principal generally holds a bachelor's degree and, increasingly, a master's or specialist's degree. In some places, principals and directors even hold doctoral degrees. In this case, they are usually expected to contribute professional research or extra programs for the community. Directors and principals have almost always had several years of teaching experience.

As you study this book and have opportunities to work in classrooms, think about which settings you will feel most comfortable in. Then, choose an appropriate career direction and try setting goals for the next five years or so. Finally, be sure that you are acquiring the necessary training and credentials when you need them. While this advice might sound painfully obvious, many prospective teachers ignore such suggestions and eventually find themselves taking redundant courses, going back to school for requirements they overlooked, or changing careers because the credentials they need require too much time, effort, and money. It is well worth the effort to think through now what you will want to be doing over the next several years.

Some ideas for you to think about right now are contained in a position paper on teacher preparation. It was drafted by the Association of Teacher Educators (1990) (a professors' organization that your own instructor may belong to). The association, which deals with education at several levels, created a Commission on Early Childhood Teacher Education, which then worked closely with the National Association for the Education of Young Children to ensure that their views were coordinated and complementary. The commission concluded that early childhood teachers

- Must be knowledgeable about a variety of disciplines because the curriculum for young children is "an integrated whole and informed by children's interests."
- Need to understand the significance of play because it is a critical component of the classroom.
- Should understand developmental theories and be able to apply them in classrooms where there is concern for the child's whole being.

■ Must learn to value diverse kinds of families and learn to interact skillfully with parents, always valuing parents as educational partners.
■ Need to be able to work with and supervise other adults because they will usually function in teams.

As you embark on your program to become an educator of young children, try to keep these essential characteristics in mind. Be sure you choose courses and read books and articles that are devoted to them. The text you are reading now will deal with all five characteristics at an introductory level. Continue to pursue them in more depth.

In looking toward your future career, you will want to consider the different settings available to you. The next section describes the most common ones.

## Where Young Children Learn

### Nursery School

The concept of nurturing very young children lay behind the creation and naming of the nursery school. At the turn of this century, Margaret and Rachel McMillan noted with dismay the sad state of health in many of England's children. They created a school designed to give children plenty of fresh air, good food, and hygiene in addition to academics and socialization through play. Today, nursery schools do not usually need to focus on retrieving children's health, but they do maintain similar play-oriented curricula. In the United States a new twist has been added to some nursery schools. Many have become cooperatives, with parents sharing the responsibilities of running them, thus keeping costs down. Children who attend nursery schools are generally between the ages of two and five.

### Kindergarten

Typically, kindergarten is a one-year learning experience, immediately preceding first grade. The German name given to it by Friedrich Froebel has remained, but its character has changed in many ways. Froebel conceived of the kindergarten as a bridge between home and the primary grades, and for many decades it served this purpose in the United States. Now, many children attend nursery schools or child care centers. Consequently, kindergarten has become a different kind of transition experience, from the early childhood center instead of from the family. Curricula vary depending on the philosophy of the school. Traditionally, the focus was on play with an academic purpose, that being readiness for the first grade. Today, kindergartens have become much more academic. Many educators are concerned that the curriculum is simply watered down primary material, inappropriate to younger children.

## Transitional Kindergarten

Some children do not seem ready to enter the primary grades after one year of kindergarten. To ensure success in later years, the transitional program was created. This concept is a relatively recent one and remains controversial. Those who oppose the transitional kindergarten do not like the reasons that children are held back: they don't yet understand letter/sound relationships, follow directions well, work easily on paper-and-pencil tasks, raise their hands, or speak only in turn (Brewer, 1990). All these reasons indicate that children are expected to be ready to take on a first grade that is rigid, traditional, and intellectually deadening. On the other side of the argument, it is said that this extra year provides the extra help needed to avoid personal failure in the primary grades (Uphoff, 1990). Unless you work in a state that does not have transitional kindergartens (California has outlawed them), they will be one of the career choices available to you.

## Head Start

Head Start is a federally funded program for economically disadvantaged children. It primarily serves children over the age of three. Although it is now comprehensive in scope, it was begun in 1965 as a summer-only program focusing on health and social development. President Lyndon Johnson's War on Poverty promoted much creative thinking from the various governmental "warriors," and a number of social programs were begun almost simultaneously. Head Start was one of them and was seen as a way to close the gap between the lives of disadvantaged children and those of their wealthier peers during the summer before the start of school. Today, children may attend Head Start for two years, and programs have academic orientations along with health and socialization. Although there are variations in types of programs, an important component of all Head Start programs is their emphasis on parent involvement. By 1990, Head Start proponents were lobbying Congress for funds to reach all deserving children in the United States and to extend the program to infants and toddlers. The election of Bill Clinton as president in 1992 has increased expectations that these advances will come to pass. You will find Head Start centers in many locales in large cities and small towns alike. They may be attached to elementary schools or stand alone.

## Day Care or Child Care

The purpose of child care is to provide a secure and happy place for young children while their parents work. Typically it serves children from birth to school age, but it can also provide after-school care for older children. Types of child care centers vary widely and may be in homes (usually called family day care) as well as in other types of buildings. Educational components also vary widely and at times may not exist at all. In many countries child care is provided in some fashion for all working parents, but this has not been the case in the United States. Finding good care continues to be a nationwide problem for many families.

## Primary Grades

Traditionally, early childhood education has been thought of as encompassing birth to age eight. In some ways, ages six to eight are a transitional time between babyhood and middle childhood. The primary grades, grades one through three, are concerned with educating children during this transition. Because children develop so unevenly during these years, it is important that primary teachers have a good understanding of child development. Thus, you will observe that teachers in the first three grades often have training in early childhood as well as in elementary education.

## Extending Your Learning _____

1. From the career options discussed in this chapter, choose at least two that interest you. Interview someone who holds each position. Some questions you might ask:
   - What prompted you to choose this career?
   - What are your goals for the future? Will you continue with this indefinitely?
   - What are the most satisfying elements of your career? The most frustrating?
   - What are some ways I can prepare well for this kind of career?
   - What characteristics do you think that someone needs to do this?
2. Observe a classroom that makes good use of computers and one that doesn't. Be sure the children are about the same age in each. In which class are the children interacting more with each other? Are they interacting with each other differently? In which class are the children more independent and self-directed? Are the children learning different things? What are they learning that is the same? Which type of learning seems to provide more depth? Which more breadth? Give examples.
3. Observe a nursery school class and a primary grade class. List similarities

and differences in the teacher's style, children's interactions with each other, children's interactions with the teacher, kinds of materials, and the amount of freedom the children have.

## References

Association of Teacher Educators (1990). *Position paper of the ATE commission on early childhood education certification standards for teachers of children from birth through age eight.* Washington, DC: National Association for the Education of Young Children.

Bouverat, R., Reeves, M., and Skeen, B. (1988). *Resource packet for advising in the preparation of personnel for early childhood education.* Bellingham, WA: Western Washington University.

Bredecamp, S. (ed.) (1987). *Developmentally appropriate practice in early childhood programs serving children from birth through age 8.* Washington, DC: National Association for the Education of Young Children.

Brewer, J. (1990). Transitional programs: boon or bane? *Young Children* 45(6):15–18.

Lay-Dopyera, M., and Dopyera, J. (1990). *Becoming a teacher of young children.* New York: McGraw-Hill.

NAEYC position statement on nomenclature, salaries, benefits, and the status of the early childhood profession (1984). *Young Children* 40:52–54.

Piaget, J., and Inhelder, B. (1969). *The psychology of the child.* New York: Basic Books.

Uphoff, J. (1990). Extra-year programs: an argument for transitional programs during transitional times. *Young Children* 40(6):19–20.

Walters, L. (1990). Hi-ho, off to school wee ones go. *Christian Science Monitor,* 10 Sept., 14.

Weber, E. (1984). *Ideas influencing early childhood education.* New York: Teachers College Press.

# Part Two

# Providing Developmentally Appropriate Education

In their early years, children develop physically, socially, and intellectually faster than at any other time in their lives. Between infancy and elementary school they graduate from utter dependency on others to an ability to engage in complex sports, from communication by crying and laughing to adult-level speech, from ego-centered social interactions to play skills that can involve two dozen other children in their classroom. The quality of this development is dependent to a great extent on the quality of interaction children have with others in the environment. As a caregiver or teacher, much of the responsibility for quality interaction will rest with you.

Because understanding child development is so critical to a teacher's success, an entire chapter has been designated for each of the areas: physical/motor, social/affective, and cognitive. And, because children do not all develop on the same schedule or identically from culture to culture, there is another chapter devoted to diversity. Together, these chapters are designed to provide a philosophical foundation for everything you do when you interact with children in a center or classroom.

Each of the chapters provides an overview of the theories and philosophies connected to its subject. Then the theoretical and philosophical are made practical as we discuss how to apply them in the classroom.

Infants begin their lives learning through physical actions and experiences. Even into the primary grades, children retain their need to involve their bodies in learning, whether that learning is physical, social, or intellectual. Thus, we begin Part Two with a chapter on physical and motor development.

# 3

# Education for Physical and Motor Development

## OBJECTIVE

When you finish reading this chapter, you should be able to

- Identify stages of physical development.
- Identify stages of motor development.
- Relate developmental stages to approaches to education.
- Interact with young children in ways that promote their safety and health.

As you think about the chapter on your own, you should be able to

- Understand more about your own physical and motor development.
- Consider which teaching approaches might be right for you.

## DIFFERENT YET THE SAME

*It was spring and, as usual for this time of year, the kindergarten children were becoming more competitive physically, some of them trying to imitate the older children's team-oriented games. They had engaged in this kind of behavior before, but winning often seemed to equate with having the most fun or screaming the loudest. Losing, by whatever definition, might lead to tears or accusations of "No fair!" Now, some of the children were beginning to understand that winning might mean being the fastest or strongest or most tenacious, and that to win fairly meant to follow specific, unchanging rules. It was still difficult to lose, but tears could be fought back more easily. Physically, the children were changing, too, becoming stronger and more coordinated, and this made it easier for them to imitate the older children.*

*Their teacher, who had worked with kindergarteners for almost three years now, saw the same developmental pattern every year. Each spring she responded by altering their physical activities in subtle but important ways. During the fall and winter the children had played with balls of varying sizes, jumped rope, worked on gym equipment, held relay races, and so on. They continued to do so in the spring, but on occasion an element of competition was introduced. During this time, the teacher would observe the children carefully, making sure she wasn't pushing them too fast either socially or physically. This particular spring, she chose to begin by modifying the relay races.*

*This group of children seemed to love the races more than any other physical activity, and all year the teacher had been careful to structure them so that there were no winners or losers. Children were given a physical task (running, hopping, walking backwards, holding each other's ankles for a wheelbarrow walk), and each team finished at its own pace. Recently, some children had begun to care which team came in first. A few children appointed themselves informal monitors to be sure that participants stayed behind the line until it was their turn to start. The lines they stood in became a bit tidier, and taking a turn out of sequence was cause for outrage.*

*Observing these changes, the teacher knew that spring had, indeed, arrived. She gathered the class into a group and instituted a few basic rules: numbering off for taking turns, required contact with the wall at the far end of the race, and no "jumping the gun." Most of the children understood and accepted the new spirit of following rules.*

*At first, the teacher divided the teams as she always had, making sure that there was a mixture of abilities on each team. Within a short time, however, the children decided they wanted to divide into girl and boy teams. The differences between the sexes were immediately apparent. In the races where a ball had to be dribbled or thrown, the boys were almost always the victors. In the hopping, skipping, or galloping races, the girls proved superior. A brief class discussion concluded with an agreement that the teams should return to a combination of the sexes "because too many of us get our feelings hurt."*

*This was the first year in which the children had requested a team division along gender lines. Once the teacher had seen the difference in skills (she wondered why she hadn't noticed it before), she wasn't at all surprised to observe that during recess it was primarily boys who chose to kick the playground balls and begged to join in the older children's baseball games. Nor was she surprised to see the girls become obsessed with what appeared to be an ongoing game of hopscotch.*

This rather typical example of kindergarten life illustrates the complexity of physical growth and motor development that not only involve certain gender differences but are influenced by social and cognitive factors. For example, when children are no longer satisfied with a joyous free-for-all approach to sports and games, they are moving into a social stage in which interaction with their peers becomes highly important and following rules can become an obsession. Moreover, to understand and obey these rules takes a higher level of cognitive awareness. In short, physical, social, and cognitive development, while studied separately, are part of an inextricable whole. The younger the children you teach and care for, the more important it is to remember this. Infants learn about their intellectual, social, emotional, and physical worlds primarily through physical interaction. As children mature, these elements become more discreet, but throughout the years we cover in this text there is still considerable interaction. In Chapters 4 and 5 we will discuss the ways in which social and cognitive development occur. In this chapter, our focus is on physical development. Yet, it is important to remember that, much of the time, the three interact with each other.

For example, a baby may crawl after a moving ball, enjoying herself thoroughly for awhile. Soon, however, she begins to feel alone and seeks the familiar face of her mother. In her early infancy, this child would have assumed that, if she couldn't see her mother, then her mother was simply gone. This baby, however, having graduated to the next cognitive stage, responds to the sound of her mother who is, at that moment, behind her. She slaps the ball into her mother's lap in a pre-throwing fashion. If the baby and her mother continue with a game of handing the ball back and forth, then the baby is simultaneously learning both a physical skill and the social skill of cooperative play.

For another example of the interplay between types of development, we visit a third-grade class playing kickball at recess. Ordinarily, there are enough players to fill all the positions. Today, however, many of the children have other interests, and the kickball teams find themselves short of players. An argument ensues. It is caused by one boy who suggests that they play with just two bases. He has counted up and there are just enough people to make this work. "But," someone insists, "the rules say you gotta have three bases!"

"Well," the first boy counters, "if we all say it's okay to change the rule, can't we change it?"

"No!" respond some.

"Sure! Yes!" say others with equal vehemence.

In this situation, social and cognitive stage changes have invaded a predominantly physical/motor experience. Just as the kindergarten children in our earlier example were becoming interested in rules toward the end of the school year, first and second graders become even more intensely focused on them. Although all children don't always remember to obey the rules, they worry when they don't and they enthusiastically tattle when someone else doesn't. Toward the end of elementary school, they begin to understand that there are times when this is acceptable. The child who suggested changing the kickball game to have just two bases was moving into this more ad-

In the early years almost every kind of development is keyed to physical and motor development. Here children are not only practicing gross motor skills but are also learning about social cooperation.

vanced stage of understanding, unlike some of the children who opposed him. Sometimes squabbles on the playground are caused by this dissonance in social or cognitive awareness.

The alert teacher is aware of developmental changes in all three areas and responds appropriately to the children's dilemmas, problems, and questions. For example, the third-grade teacher above might first observe the children to see if they can work the situation out on their own. Chances are, they will. If the friction becomes too great, however, she might intervene and suggest that, yes, sometimes rules can be changed to suit the situation. This confirms the budding understanding of the more advanced children and provides the authority that the other children still need. To promote children's growth in all areas, it is important to deal with such social issues in order to make the physical experience go more smoothly. Once the issue of the bases has been solved, the children can more happily and easily concentrate on giving their full energy to the game.

The section that follows provides an overview of the physical and motor changes of infants and young children. As you read, try to relate the information to the third-grade kickball game, the baby with the ball, and the kindergarten relay races. When finished you should be able to tell why kickball was an appropriate game for third graders, why a crawling baby handles the ball the way she does, and why the boys and the girls differed in their relay race performances.

## Understanding Physical Growth and Motor Development

Physical growth and motor development are interdependent. The former refers to bodily changes over time and the latter to the increasingly competent use that is made of the body. Theorists generally define physical growth as a continuum, while motor development has been divided into discrete phases. For this discussion, each of the phases is presented and then followed by the physical growth that normally accompanies the phase. Although we will deal only with those that apply to young children, the entire set of phases includes *reflexive* (before birth to about six months), *rudimentary* (birth to about age two), *fundamental movement* (age two to six or seven), *sport skill* (age six or seven to about twelve), *growth and refinement* (age twelve to about eighteen), *peak performance* (age eighteen or younger, depending on the sport, to about thirty), and *regression* (middle and older adulthood). The last three phases will not be dealt with here. See Table 3.1 on page 83 for an outline of motor development and physical growth.

While everything is not yet known about the way children develop, the theoretical controversies are not strong ones. Our discussion reflects the widely accepted views of Gallahue (1982) and Gabbard (1992). Their own work draws on the results of research done by themselves and others.

## Reflexive Phase

Reflexes are involuntary movements made in reaction to a stimulus such as light or touch. It has been estimated that infants have about twenty-seven different reflexes. Most of these are present at birth and have been developing since two or three months after conception. Some reflexes will be useful throughout life: sneezing, blinking, yawning, and coughing, for example. Others disappear after about six months and reappear later as voluntary behaviors. Examples include the swimming reflex, in which an infant held at the water's surface immediately makes swimming motions, and the stepping reflex, in which the infant makes stepping motions when held upright in the air.

These early reflexes actually provide infants with a means of unintentional learning before they have reached the stage of active curiosity. Two primitive and critical reflexes that appear at this time are the rooting and sucking reflexes. Newborn infants turn toward the mother's or bottle's nipple when it touches their cheeks or lips; immediately following this, they begin to suck. These two reflexes are critical for the infant's survival. Another protective but not critical reflex is the Moro reflex. It is demonstrated when a falling or startled infant flings its arms and legs outward with its hands spread open; the child then moves its arms inward, fists clenched, eyes open, and cries out.

Although it is apparent that reflexive behavior gradually gives way to voluntary movements, the role that reflexive behavior plays in the development of voluntary movement is still not known. Reflexes probably have, at the least, an indirect connection since they build the infant's strength and muscularity as well as better postural control and balance. The connections between disappearing reflexes, such as swimming and stepping, and their later voluntary counterparts remains unclear. But some research seems to indicate that infants who are given practice in swimming and stepping during the period when these reflexes would ordinarily disappear are earlier swimmers and walkers than other infants.

By the time infants are about four months old, voluntary movements overtake reflexes. At this point, children can use the information learned from the reflexive phase in new ways through more intentional behaviors.

### Physical Development During the Reflexive Phase

While the brain of a newborn infant weighs approximately one-fourth of its adult counterpart, it soon doubles in volume, taking only six years to reach its full adult size. Before birth it begins as a long, hollow tube on the embryo's back. As the nervous system develops, the brain takes on its final shape, but it doesn't contain all its elements until after birth. For example, some of the brain's nerve cells and the white fatty sheath that protects them (called myelin) aren't formed until after birth.

The brain has two halves, called hemispheres, that are divided down the middle by a band of myelinated tissue known as the corpus callosum. Each hemisphere controls the motor behavior on the opposite side of the body. Further, each hemisphere specializes in its own type of thought processes. The left hemisphere is assigned language and logic, while the right controls music, art, emotions, and the understanding of spatial relationships. This hemispheric division of functions is known as brain lateralization and is present throughout life.

At birth, the infant's head accounts for almost one-fourth of its total height and is almost as wide as the shoulders and hips. In the following months and years other parts of the body, especially the legs, must grow more quickly than the head to achieve mature proportions. During the first year of life, as in the nine months preceding birth, growth is faster than at any other time of life. After a year, the typical infant has grown by 50 percent.

In the past twenty-five years, researchers have been learning much about the visual powers of newborns. In contrast to what was previously thought, we now know that the visual system is quite well developed at birth. The infant can focus on a nearby object or respond to a moving light. However, since the eyeball is still short, the infant is farsighted. Also, since the muscles attached to the lens are still weak, they can't make the quick adjustments that are necessary to focus well on moving objects. By the end of four months, however, the muscles have gained enough strength that the infant's eyes can adjust to moving objects as well as an adult's eyes can.

The infant's sense of hearing is strong and develops rapidly. Newborns have a primitive ability to discriminate between various pitches of different lengths. This important development is necessary for later language learning. Some researchers believe that by six months infants are almost as good as adults at sorting out sounds.

Infants have much to learn about their own bodies. For example, an awareness of their own separation from the rest of the world is a major learning. This awareness begins in the first month and steadily emerges as the infant grows and practices various movements. Although infancy is too soon to be looking for handedness (being right- or left-handed), up to 90 percent of newborns position their heads toward the right when they lie on their backs.

## Stereotypies

Any observer of babies notices a lot of kicking, waving, rocking, and bouncing. Anyone who has been pregnant is more than a little aware that these behaviors begin to occur before birth. Such behaviors do not take place automatically in response to a stimulus, so they cannot be classified as reflexive. Neither do they fit into our next major section on rudimentary behaviors because they lack any purpose or goal. Nevertheless, they are important to infants, taking up to 40 percent of their daily activity time. The movements, which are spontaneous, patterned, and repetitious, are called stereotypies. Forty-seven of them have been documented. They are most noticeable between six and ten months of age, at which point they begin to disappear.

Although the movements appear to have no purposes or goals, it is thought that they have developmental significance. It may be that they represent a stage in neurological maturation, preparing the infant for later similar actions.

## Rudimentary Phase

Rudimentary behaviors such as sitting and crawling are both basic and voluntary. Like the reflexive and stereotypic behaviors, they last until about age two, but, unlike them, they do not exist before birth. Rudimentary behaviors increase as the infant's nervous system matures, and their practice helps the infant establish postural and manual control as well as locomotion skills. The ability to engage in and control voluntary movements begins first with the head and neck, then moves downward to the legs. It also moves outward from the shoulders to the elbows and fingers. For example, infants can generally lift their heads and chests when they are two months old, sit up between six and eight months, and stand alone by about one year.

The rudimentary movement phase is sometimes divided into two stages. In the first, termed *reflex inhibition,* the child begins to reject reflexes in favor of voluntary movement. The movements are primitive, poorly integrated, and rudimentary, but they signify a step forward in development. The second stage is called *precontrol* and signifies greater control and precision. It appears around age one and lasts for about a year.

Rudimentary behaviors include movements that are basic for lifelong activity: moving the head and upper trunk, rolling over, sitting, crawling and creeping, standing, and walking. The child's demonstration of all of these behaviors progresses from primitive and immature to efficient and mature over different periods of time. For example, a four-month-old can sit fairly well if given support, can sit alone at about six months, and can move alone from a prone position to a sitting position at around eight months. Similarly, walking appears at about age one, with the first steps being uncoordinated side-to-side movements. Fully mature, straight-ahead steps become normal by the time the child is four or five.

### Physical Growth During the Rudimentary Movement Phase

The greatest activity of the rudimentary movement phase occurs in the middle of the infant's first year and continues until about age two. During this time, physical growth is rapid. Newborn body weight triples by the end of one year and quadruples by age two when boys weigh about 32 pounds

Basic activities like rolling over, sitting, and crawling belong to the rudimentary movement phase of development. This phase includes the beginning of voluntary control over body movements and lasts from about age 1 to 2.

and girls are a pound lighter. Handedness becomes more pronounced and body awareness improves to the point that babies can find a few body parts that are named by someone else. They are able to do this on themselves before they can do it on others.

## Fundamental Movement

Fundamental or basic movements are general activities such as running, jumping, throwing, and catching, which form the basis for advanced, often sports-related skills. At about age two, children begin their acquisition and by age seven are capable of efficient, coordinated, and controlled fundamental motor behaviors.

One such skill is running. While most children make an awkward try at running at about eighteen months, an elementary level develops between ages two and three and a mature running form and good speed are achieved at about age five. Jumping is another skill that appears in a primitive form at about eighteen months, when children often try jumping off a step or other high object. A real self-propelled leap is usually tried at about age two, but good height and distance are achieved at about age four or five. While both running and jumping are sports events that are engaged in and improved upon all the way through adulthood, the maturity these skills achieve in young children is basic and simple. It is also basic in the sense that such maturity is necessary for future sporting success.

What constitutes maturity in skills such as running and jumping is coordination and the skillful use of various body parts to achieve balance, height, distance, speed, and so on. During the early stages of running, children take short, flat-footed steps and lean rather far forward. Their arms move across the front of their body, and the swing is somewhat rigid. More mature runners lean just slightly forward, swing their arms at their sides, and use their legs more efficiently for fast forward movement. Jumping capabilities develop in a similar fashion. During the early stages children hardly crouch at all before jumping, and their arms remain fixed in one position. More mature jumpers learn to crouch more emphatically, use their arms in opposition to their body movement, and then, at the apex of the jump, stretch the trunk and one or both arms.

Hopping is a form of jumping that includes repetition of the same movement on one foot. The rhythm, strength, and balance that are required for this basic skill are more difficult than for any other form of jumping. A required preliminary skill is the capability of standing on one foot for a moment or two, and this becomes possible at about twenty-nine months. Children three and a half years old can hop between one and three steps; when they are five many can hop about ten steps, although some children really can't hop comfortably until they are about six. Girls tend to develop hopping skills more easily than boys.

Galloping, sliding, and skipping require a lot of balance, which probably explains why most children don't attempt these skills until around age four. Skipping is usually the last of the three to be mastered, and girls are usually more skilled than boys.

Boys, however, shine in throwing skills. While most children achieve a mature stage in overarm throwing, some, usually girls, never do gain a mature capability. Overarm throwing appears in its most primitive form at six or seven months, when babies can sit up on their own and try to propel an object to another place.

Catching capabilities tend to appear after throwing. The behavior begins at age two or three with trapping, in which body, arms, and legs are used. Catching is an activity that promotes a fear reaction in many children, causing them to turn their heads away from an oncoming ball, thus ensuring that they will drop it. With practice and increased confidence, most children lose this fear. In the fundamental phase, catching matures to the point of two-handed catches in easy situations. Catching a ball with one hand while moving isn't achieved until near the end of elementary school.

Kicking and striking are two fundamental skills needed in later sports. A simple placekick is the forerunner of dribbling or kicking a moving ball. Striking will be needed for tennis, softball, or baseball. Kicking skills begin to appear at about age two and, for most children, mature at age five or six. Children usually demonstrate a sidearm sort of striking at about three years and achieve an efficient form at four or five. Mastery isn't generally accomplished, however, until the end of elementary school.

Bouncing and rolling a ball are two favorite activities for young children. At age two, some children can bounce with two hands, at first just catching it on the rebound and later slapping it back down. At five or six children can dribble the ball as long as they stay in one place. Dribbling while moving takes some practice throughout the elementary years to achieve mastery. Children often try pushing a ball across the floor before they are one year old, although what it does, of course, is roll. Intentional rolling is attempted between ages two and four. By age six most children have mastered the skill.

The last fundamental skill under discussion is important in regard to children's ability to do most schoolwork. Manipulation has to do with the use of the hands and a mature, refined level may not be achieved until age eight, well after many schools expect such performance. Pincer movements can be made with the thumb and forefinger at about nine or ten months, and a frequent stereotypic activity is to flex the fingers repeatedly. At about eighteen months, children can hold a pencil or crayon and by nursery school age or first grade have been experimenting with assorted methods of holding on. Before age three, the most popular method is to wrap the thumb and all the fingers around the drawing implement in a power grip. The adult three-fingered method of holding on sometimes appears by age four, and reasonably mature skill has developed by age seven.

As with the large muscle skills, children gain coordination in writing and drawing from the inside part of the body outward. At first, they write or draw using the shoulder and arm, and then add the elbow. Wrist, fingers, and thumb are added last.

Accompanying manipulative development are stages in drawing that begin with random scribbling (ages one to two and a half). Children may watch the lines appearing on the paper, but it is mostly out of curiosity, not intention. They then advance to controlled scribbling (ages two and a half to three and a half), in which they look at the paper more often and seem to have some visual control over the marks. Scribbles are named later (ages three and a half to four), usually after a drawing is finished and the child realizes that the picture looks like something. Intentional attempts at representation (ages four to five) coincide with an improving ability to hold the drawing tool. As children gain real control of the implement, they move to a stage called pre-schematic drawing (ages five to seven). Baselines appear and, for the first time, figures with all their body parts stand on them. The final schematic stage (ages seven to nine) accompanies children's thoroughly comfortable grasp of the tool. The baseline grows thicker, representation is based on realism, and there is less experimentation.

### Physical Growth During the Fundamental Movement Phase

By age seven, children have increased their weight to seven times their birth weight. From the beginning of this phase and on through puberty they grow about 2 inches per year. Boys are slightly heavier and taller than girls and have more muscle and bone mass. Children's eyesight continues to improve during this phase, and adult levels of visual acuity (20/20 vision) are reached at about age five. Between ages five and seven, there is rapid improvement in the ability to focus on moving objects. Body awareness also improves, so that by age five or six most children can identify the major parts of their bodies and by age seven can name the smaller parts as well. (With some focused teaching they can do this earlier.)

Handedness is established by about age five, although changes may still be made until age ten. Since children begin school during this phase, the establishment of handedness is often of importance for teachers. Traditional views once held that clumsiness and learning disabilities accompany left-handedness, but these views have been discredited. Arguments about whether handedness is genetic or socially derived are long-standing and have not yet been resolved. Latest thinking and research argue on the side of genetic determination. Most important for teachers, left-handedness should not be seen as a warning sign that something is wrong with a child's development.

## Sport-Related Movement

During this phase, the fundamental movements that were established during the prior phase are refined and combined and applied to new situations. Depending on the theorist, the phase is divided into two or three stages that cover the elementary years and all of adolescence. Teachers can expect to see the beginnings of the first stage during the primary years as children start using the fundamental movements they have just attained by applying them to games. Hopping is essential for hopscotch; running is used in races and ballgames; kicking is applied to soccer and kickball; striking, catching, and throwing are essential for softball; better balance is needed for gymnastics and bicycle riding; and walking is taken for granted in just about every activity of life.

During this stage, children make roughly equal progress in both their gross and fine motor capabilities. The sport-related improvements have their counterpart in activities requiring the use of hands and fingers. Writing, drawing, painting, clay modeling, carpentry, and other handicrafts are all tackled with more confidence and capability. Children are able to stay within the

Table 3.1
MOTOR DEVELOPMENT AND PHYSICAL GROWTH

| AGE | MOTOR PHASE | BEHAVIORS | PHYSICAL GROWTH |
|-----|-------------|-----------|-----------------|
| Prenatal–6 months | Reflexive | Involuntary: blink, suck, cough, yawn | Brain still developing<br>Length increases 50% in first year<br>Limbs grow faster than head<br>Farsightedness normal<br>Differentiation of sound develops |
| Birth–1 year | | Stereotypies: kick, wave, rock, bounce | |
| Birth–2 years | Rudimentary | Voluntary basic: sit, crawl, creep, stand, walk | Birth weight quadruples<br>Handedness develops |
| 2–6 or 7 years | Fundamental movement | Run, jump, hop, skip, gallop, kick, throw, catch; pincer movements | Seven times birth weight<br>Gains 2 inches a year<br>20/20 vision<br>Handedness established |
| 6 or 7–12 years | Sport skills | Fundamental movements applied to games; handicrafts done with confidence | Gains 2 inches a year<br>Health stable<br>Baby teeth replaced<br>Heart, lungs increase in capacity and size<br>Center of gravity lowered |

lines on a written page. They may be enthusiastic about learning both to print and to write in cursive letters. During these years, boys and girls are very nearly equal in their motor development.

## Physical Development During the Sport-Related Movement Phase

Boys and girls are also nearly equal in their rate of physical development. Growth is slow and steady, averaging about 2 inches per year. Health is generally stable, although postural defects may emerge and should be attended to. All aspects of eyesight attain a high level of functioning. Baby teeth are replaced by permanent teeth. Energy levels are high, but children are generally able to sublimate their activity needs during school hours. Out of the classroom, they are able to engage in increasingly vigorous exercise as their strength grows and their heart and lungs increase in capacity and size. The children's center of gravity is lower, making balancing feats easier. In sum, this is a period of slow, steady growth, distributed fairly equally between boys and girls, in which many sports can be introduced with good results.

## FOSTERING PHYSICAL FITNESS AND MOTOR DEVELOPMENT

*As new parents in need of day care, Judy and Ron had an unusual advantage. Their urban apartment overlooked the backyard of a nearby child care center. While Judy stayed home from her teaching job in the final days of pregnancy, she spent much time watching the scene below, deciding if it would be a good place for her infant. After observing for some days, Judy decided that the center's major disadvantage was its yard, which was all concrete with a narrow dirt border for gardening and bushes. However, she liked the fact that on nice days even the youngest children were put outside in their infant seats.*

*Before deciding what to do, Judy and Ron visited another center several blocks away. The backyard was beautiful and the children seemed to be outdoors quite a lot. Back home, Judy and Ron were discussing their preference for the more attractive site when Ron looked out the window and noticed something he thought important. Caregivers were making full use of the unattractive concrete space by engaging children in ball skills, jump rope, and balance beam tricks. There seemed to be a balance of free play and informal instruction. Ron insisted that they return to the second center for another look.*

*The weather was chilly and overcast that day, and the children were all inside watching television. Answers to Ron's questions about use of the outdoors didn't please him. There were fewer balls and jump ropes and no balance beams at all. Further, play was entirely free with no instruction offered.*

*Realizing that such considerations weren't immediately important, Judy and Ron finally made their decision based on a further observation of the center next door. On another chilly, overcast day they noticed that all the children were outdoors playing, having donned an extra layer or two. Even the babies were out with blankets thrown over the infant seats. Despite their choice of an urban lifestyle, Judy and Ron were an outdoor, athletic couple. They felt that their child would thrive more outdoors and, when old enough, benefit from the skills instruction offered at the care center next door.*

*As soon as their daughter was born, she was registered there. For the next three years, Judy and Ron took their daughter next door, happy in their decision. On weekends they took hikes in the country, taking turns carrying the baby on their backs. As soon as she was in her first hard-soled shoes, their daughter began hiking, too. She especially loved climbing uphill and could do so for extended periods of time. Both parents were confident that the center's approach to outdoor play was at least partly responsible.*

Judy and Ron had a high awareness of their daughter's need for a healthy body and for developed motor functions and skills. They also realized that some intervention on the part of the adults who cared for her would be necessary to achieve these goals.

Judy and Ron had cause for concern. Several studies have been reported (Poest et al., 1989) in which children in day-care centers were found to have significantly less large muscle activity than children in nursery schools. This may show the difference in training received by caregivers, who typically have less information about children's physical needs than do trained teachers. Still, many parents and teachers, as well as caregivers, believe that providing children with free play opportunities is all the support that is needed to grow healthy bodies and develop motor skills. In one sense this is true. Free play opportunities are clearly preferable to sitting inside watching television while the play areas go unused. But playing freely, even with the best of equipment, does not guarantee skill development beyond the minimal level of performance. In one study of preschool children (Miller, reported in Poest et al., 1990), well-equipped play areas, with no instructional requirements, were used for social play rather than for motor experiences. The result was that the children scored significantly below normal in their motor development. This should not be surprising if we consider the way in which children develop skills. Learning to jump rope is an appropriate example. At first, children step all over the rope and have difficulty swinging it over their heads. A teacher, parent, or older friend can help by modeling or giving a careful hint or two.

Failure to achieve rudimentary, and then fundamental, motor skills can have long-term negative effects on children. These two levels of ability form the basis of sport-related skills, which are used through the school years and into adulthood. Very young children may not notice when others are unable to measure up physically, for they are too interested in their own progress. But, from the primary grades on, children who lack the basic skills have a difficult time keeping up and are subsequently not chosen to be on teams or included in group games. Such rejection can cause problems in friendships and self-esteem as well as feelings of frustration and failure. Children who have these negative experiences may well give up exercise entirely, and this can lead to ill health in later life (Poest et al., 1990).

Children's time in a center or school can and should contain plenty of movement experiences. These should take place both indoors and outdoors. They should be challenging, exciting, and focused on large motor development, as well as on aerobic capacity. Justifications for a major emphasis on motor activities are numerous.

1. Critical or sensitive learning periods are less likely to be missed.
2. Children's needs and desires for movement are fulfilled.
3. Rudimentary and fundamental motor patterns are developed and established. Infants develop motor capacities more quickly and, for older children, sport patterns are begun.

Children who lack basic motor skills run the risk of being rejected in games. Such rejection can lead to problems of self-esteem, frustration, and failure.

4. Exercise builds muscles, strengthens the heart, and enhances aerobic capacity.
5. Repeated practice helps develop attention span.
6. Movement games promote such social skills as cooperation.
7. For infants and younger children, much cognitive learning takes place through motor activities.
8. The drive to be a top-notch athlete may originate in early childhood, even in infancy.
9. Movement activities provide experiences in exploration, discovery, and creativity (Bowers, 1988; Flinchum, 1988; Gober and Franks, 1988; Grineski, 1988).

Despite these benefits, long known by educators, physicians, physical education specialists, and many parents, the current level of children's physical fitness and motor development is low and seemingly in an endless decline. As yet, there has not been sufficient research on young children to make definitive health-related claims for movement programs. But reports over the past ten years show the following:

1. Young children are exhibiting cardiovascular health problems that could well be remedied by aerobic exercise.
2. Most early childhood play periods, recesses, and sports don't promote cardiovascular fitness because they don't provide continuous movement.
3. Just 27.8 percent of preschool children in a major survey participated in a minimum level of physical activity.
4. Just 5 percent of elementary-aged children earn the Presidential Award for Physical Fitness, with 64 percent falling below the fiftieth percentile.
5. Many young children have not developed their perceptual-motor skills: visual awareness, auditory awareness, time awareness.
6. Obesity has been increasing continually since the 1960s, when 16 of every 100 children were found to be obese.
7. By the late 1980s, only one-third of all primary grade children were receiving daily physical education classes, while 37 percent took physical education one or two days a week.
8. Analysis of physical education classes may show that they are not providing sufficiently vigorous activity.
9. Schools are using recess as a substitute for physical education time, leading to little or no enhancement of children's fundamental skills (Grineski, 1988; Kraft, 1989; Poest et al., 1990).

While sufficient research is not yet available to argue just how much a movement program will help cure children's developmental and health-related ills, the following claims can still be made for good programs:

- Exploring and experimenting with movement helps children express pleasure in being players and movers.
- Participation in developmentally appropriate activities that are success oriented helps promote a good self-concept.
- Physical fitness is encouraged.
- Movement exploration, play on the equipment, and games help develop the imagination.
- Movement activities that include guided discovery and problem-solving components help develop cognitive processes.
- Learning new terms and discussing cooperative movement challenges can help children develop language abilities.
- Positive interpersonal interactions during movement experiences promote social development (adapted from Grineski, 1988).

## Essential Elements for Fostering Physical Development

Good motor development is essential not only for every child's physical well-being, but for emotional, social, and cognitive growth as well. Children feel good about themselves when they can do what others do; they can learn more easily the social skills that are attached to play when their motor capabilities are not in question; and the cognitive learning that takes place through motor activities happens more easily if motor development is good. There is overwhelming agreement between theorists, researchers, and observant educators that optimal motor development will not take place unless it is fostered by caring adults. It is critically important that teachers and caregivers plan carefully for good motor experiences. This is true even if a physical education teacher is assigned to the school. Too often, inadequate resources mean that this teacher cannot provide the daily program that young children need.

The early childhood curriculum should contain three essential elements to be effective (Gabbard, 1988). While these are generally covered in some way by a good physical education program, the regular caregiver or teacher can and should provide related activities as well.

## Movement Awareness

Eye-foot awareness is fostered by such activities as kicking, jumping, leaping, hopping, and walking. Eye-hand activities include rolling, bouncing, throwing, catching, and striking. When children become familiar with what their bodies are capable of doing, they are learning body awareness. When they can project themselves effectively in space, they are growing in spatial awareness. As they learn about moving up and down, in and out, left and right, or frontwards and backwards, they are increasing their directional awareness. Activities that include visual awareness help children's "ability to judge depth, distance, and distinguish an object from its surrounding background" (Gabbard, 1988, p. 67). Auditory awareness is increased as children learn to discriminate the sounds around them during activities and games. Tactile awareness grows as children manipulate the toys and other objects of the physical education experience.

## Fundamental Movement Skills

The foundational skills that make later sports success possible are divided into three categories: locomotor (moving through space) skills, such as running, jumping, and skipping; nonlocomotor skills, such as twisting, swinging, and swaying; and manipulative skills, such as throwing, kicking, and catching.

## Health-Related Physical Fitness

This essential element is supported not only by physical education associations but by the American Academy of Pediatrics. Children should have experiences that promote aerobic endurance (conditioning the heart and lungs through the increased efficiency of the body to take in oxygen), flexibility (the nonrigid use of muscles and joints through their full range of movement), and muscular strength and endurance (using the muscles to produce force with high effort and using them with less effort over long periods of time). A fourth component of fitness is body composition (the relative percentage of fat to body weight). Although body composition is influenced by hereditary factors and nutrition, experiences that promote aerobic endurance, flexibility, and muscular strength can have positive effects.

These are the essential elements for programs that cater to children of nursery school age or older. Working with infants and toddlers is similar in some respects. For example, as they increase their repertoire of movements, babies become more and more aware of what their bodies can and cannot do. Thus, caregivers need to provide plenty of opportunities for free and safe movement. At the same time, promoting locomotor, nonlocomotor, and manipulative skills for infants and toddlers is more a matter of encouragement and support than it is of education. The crawler, creeper, and beginning walker need to be placed in safe areas as they practice their skills. Gentle praise and expressions of joy in their accomplishments provide encouragement and sustain efforts. Providing infants and toddlers with opportunities to move safely and feeding them a well-balanced diet will do much toward promoting their physical fitness.

The teacher who wishes to foster good physical development can do so in a variety of ways. Observing children, establishing a supportive environment, using appropriate teaching techniques, and promoting creativity and playfulness are all important avenues to success. A word about each of these follows.

## Observing Children

As you will learn throughout this book, observation is an important part of teaching young children. There is much to learn by watching, and the information you gain can and should be put to use when designing curricula or helping individual children. This is particularly true in terms of physical and motor development because infants, toddlers, and young children are by nature so physically oriented. The ways they move and use their bodies can tell you much about their cognitive progress, their social attitudes, and their emotional state, as well as their physical and motor progress.

Take advantage of every opportunity to observe each individual child. Observation can be formal: make notes on what you see and keep a dated record for future reference. Much of the time, however, formal observation isn't possible because interaction with the class is necessary and desirable. Even at busy times, however, it is important to remember your observation role and to make mental notes that can be recorded and analyzed later on. Whether your observation is formal or informal, it needs to cover the range of developmental areas.

### Movement Skills

As you observe infants, you need to keep in mind that rudimentary movement skills are acquired according to each child's individual schedule. Nevertheless, general guidelines can be useful. For example, most infants can sit up by eight months. If you observe that a child of this age is still having trouble holding her head steady and shows no interest in trying to sit, it would be wise to mention this to the parents. They may have already conferred with their pediatrician, or they may be unaware that most other infants have achieved an ability to sit by this age.

Similar observations should be made of other rudimentary skills. First attempts at walking are generally made at about one year, although some children take longer. If many weeks pass and there is still no interest, or the child's attempts are hampered by obvious physical weaknesses, it may again be time to talk with the parents. Observation of first attempts at walking will reveal that

- arms are held high
- knees are bent in an exaggerated position
- hips are not rotated
- legs are kept wide apart for balance
- strides are short
- feet are flat turned out or in
- rhythm is choppy

As the child gains skill, you should observe that

- arms are swung at sides
- knees have a smooth action
- hips are rotated
- feet are close together
- strides are longer
- a heel-to-toe motion is maintained
- rhythm is smooth

As children learn to run, jump, hop, gallop, and so on, observe their development. Over time, progress should be made as described in the Fundamental Movement section on pages 76–79.

Additionally, observe differences between boys and girls. If you observe that some boys are having trouble skipping and galloping or that some girls are inept at throwing a ball, you may want to provide more play activities that include those movements.

Health-Related Fitness

Observe children as they run across the playground. Are there children who give up easily, who never seem to be able to run as long or as far as the others? Are there children (perhaps the same ones) who consistently lag far back and seem to have trouble moving easily? It may be that their aerobic and/or muscle endurance have not developed to capacity. You may wish to find opportunities to give them extra practice. This can sometimes be done simply by giving the entire class more focused running time, thus providing these children with the practice they need without making a public issue of it.

Muscle strength and flexibility can be observed in numerous settings. Watch children as they carry chairs across the room, build with blocks, move pieces of furniture in the housekeeping corner, and participate in various games. If there are children who seem to have less strength and flexibility than others, two approaches can be helpful. First, provide these children with instructions for moving or lifting most efficiently. For example, a chair seems less heavy and isn't so unwieldy when it is carried from the side than when it is lifted from the front, and children may not discover this on their own. Second, provide these children with plenty of opportunities to gain confidence in their abilities. When someone is needed to move a heavy box or help put the big blocks away, the children who need practice should be included as often as possible.

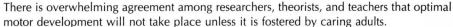

There is overwhelming agreement among researchers, theorists, and teachers that optimal motor development will not take place unless it is fostered by caring adults.

### Body Awareness

Body awareness contains elements of strength, flexibility, locomotor and nonlocomotor movement, and manipulation. It is a kind of spatial knowing and you will observe it primarily during movement activities rather than in everyday classroom life. You will want to observe if children coordinate parts of their bodies harmoniously; move in various directions with age-appropriate ease; sense whether their body movement is quick or sustained, accelerating or decelerating; and stop movement easily, either with the entire body or in part.

### Emotional State

Most observation is done visually, but touch can be an effective mode as well. Children's bodies become tense when they are upset, just as adults' do. Keeping in touch through occasional hugs or a hand on the shoulder should be more than an expression of affection or encouragement. Use this moment to observe the child's degree of relaxation or tension and follow through with caring questioning if appropriate.

### Social Attitudes

Social interactions may be intertwined with motor competencies. If you observe some children consistently standing at the sidelines watching others play, the reasons may be social (difficulty getting along with others) or physical (unable to keep up) or both (not chosen for the team because of delayed motor development). Sometimes children refuse to participate in a particular physical activity because they "don't like it" or "don't like the kids who are playing." Often this means that they lack confidence in the activity itself. Other times, they are enthusiastic about a particular activity and are highly capable in it, but their inability to get along with the other children makes the others reluctant to include them.

In all these situations, it is important to observe and perhaps ask questions until you have determined which elements of the problem are social and which physical. Once these are sorted out, appropriate solutions are more easily chosen.

### Cognitive Progress

In early infancy, cognitive progress is made almost entirely through motor activity. While this is less the case in later years, children continue to learn by using their bodies. "The movement experience enhances cognitive development because it adds another dimension (such as feeling/touching) to ideas, words, and symbols . . . movement and active play assist the child in memory processing and retrieval" (Flinchum, 1988, p. 63). Observe children as they build with blocks. As weeks go by, do they learn principles of balance and design? Watch them as they ride their trikes. Are they beginning to understand safety and the rules of the road? Keep an eye on everyone's manipulation of scissors, crayons, markers, and pencils. This is especially important in the primary years, when a child's grasp should be progressing to the adult form. Without ease in such manipulation, school progress may be hindered.

## A Supportive Environment

Try experiencing the environment, both indoors and out, as children do. Even child-sized furnishings are daunting to those who haven't yet grown into them. Bring your body level with furniture and playground equipment. Imagine what it is like to try to climb up on them. Once you have done this, see if there are adjustments you can make that will make life easier for the children. Or you may decide that greater challenges are appropriate just now and it is all right to leave things as they are. Or you may decide to make things more difficult. Other aspects of the environment deserve attention also.

### Equipment

When choosing what equipment will be used in movement activities, it is important to keep in mind children's developmental levels. Toddlers who can barely hold and toss a ball should probably not be given too many baseballs when they need to learn to catch a ball by trapping it with their entire upper body. Kindergarteners and first graders who are just learning to jump rope will be frustrated if there aren't enough ropes to practice their newly emerging skills. Careful observation of children's developing interests and capabilities will go a long way toward ensuring appropriate choices.

For most teachers, choice of stationary equipment is not an option. They must learn to use whatever the school or center provides. Choices can be made in how the equipment is used, however. If children are just about big, strong, and agile enough to use the jungle gym, it is the right time for some instruction. Never force children onto a piece of equipment; it is better to wait for them to choose it themselves. Just as important, there are few times when it is appropriate to help a child onto a piece of equipment. If you are suddenly called away or the child thinks the feat would be easy to do alone later, the activity becomes a dangerous one. If a piece of equipment is too overwhelming for the child to use alone, it would be better to steer him or her to something more manageable.

All transportable equipment should be kept in spaces that are easily accessible to the children. Blocks should be kept on low shelves, balls in boxes on the floor, trikes in an easily accessed single row, and so on. Rules for their use and enforcement of them will usually make management simple.

### Space

When you have movement activities, be sure there is enough room for children to move without hitting each other or the furniture. If space is cramped, set whatever rules are necessary for safety. It is also possible to have too much space. If the classroom features a large open space, children will quite naturally respond by running through it at all speeds and at all times. When this is the case, a good practice is to move a table or other piece of furniture into the open space to slow the movement through it.

As children become mature enough to understand rules about staying inside a particular area or they begin playing standard games, the concept of boundaries needs to be introduced. Take children in a follow-the-leader walk around the established boundaries. Show them landmarks along the way. Return to the starting point and have them visually define the boundaries from a distance. For the most part, children will then stay within the boundaries, although it is still essential for you to monitor them visually at all times.

### Time

In general, infants, toddlers, and very small children should be permitted to move whenever they feel the need or interest, since this is the primary way they learn. As children get older and sedentary learning becomes more important, teachers should still be sensitive to children's need to move. If the classroom has center time, some of the centers should incorporate movement. When possible, children should be allowed access to both indoors and outdoors when playtime or worktime is free.

Children in the primary grades should be given several movement breaks during the day, particularly if their learning time doesn't include movement experience. In addition to physical education and recess, a few minutes can be spent on calisthenics or stretching or dance or a run around the perimeter of the playground.

### Group Size

Another important decision concerns the number of children who will be included in movement activities. If the whole class needs a stretch, there is no question that everyone should be included. (Note: It is *never* appropriate to exclude children from such experiences as a type of punishment.) If instruction is to be given and/or equipment to be used, decisions about group size may need to be made. If movement experiences are included in center activities, it may be necessary for safety and interpersonal relations to limit the number of children who can participate at one time.

## Teaching Approaches

Depending on the time, place, and desired experience, you may choose a variety of approaches to providing movement activities. These can range from the very directive to the totally free.

A highly directive approach to teaching may be suitable when children are first learning a new skill or how to use a new piece of equipment. However, it is rarely appropriate to be very directive over a long period of time. Your intent should be to move into the background and let the children direct themselves as much as possible.

A first step in this direction is to pair children and let them teach and help each other. This arrangement is usually appropriate by kindergarten, but some older nursery school children may also try it. Children enjoy this arrangement when they work on such things as ball skills.

Small groups provide the opportunity for children to take turns teaching. They also provide a good vehicle for moving from direct teaching to problem solving. You might ask such questions as, "Can your group find a way to make the letter *A* using your bodies?" or, "Can you work together to act out the poem we just learned?" Involving children in problem solving is a teaching technique that leads to creativity and playfulness in children's movement experiences. Give enough direction when presenting the problem to provide focus. From there, the children are free to imagine and create. This approach can even be relied on when the movement experience is a brief transition be-

After initially modeling how to perform some motor activity, teachers often drift into the background to allow pairs or small groups of children to practice and teach each other.

tween work times or when the entire class is gathered in a circle on the floor: "Can you touch the line on the floor with just one finger and one foot?" "With one knee and your nose?"

Of course, playfulness may be most evident when children have no direction at all. Yet, during completely free times, children may choose not to use movement as a part of their play. While this isn't necessarily a concern, problem-solving movement experiences do provide both an opportunity to create and be playful and a natural way to develop motor skills.

## Considerations for Age Appropriateness

In our discussion of observation, the environment, and teaching approaches, some differences were noted between the needs and interests of the different age groups. We will now conclude this discussion with a closer look at these age groups. While careful observation of your particular children is the best way for you to determine what the most appropriate movement experiences are, it is helpful to have a general idea of the needs of each age group and some suggestions for meeting them. Those given here are adapted from Liselott Diem (1979) and Diane Lynch Fraser (1991).

### Infants

- Newborns are active but dependent on adults for assistance and stimulation.
  *Suggestion:* Several times a day, engage the infants in five to ten minutes of gentle movement experience.
- Newborns need freedom of movement.
  *Suggestion:* Avoid tight diapers and too much clothing. Provide a firm elastic mattress that absorbs movement and supports the body.
- Infants' body awareness is increased by being touched, held, and picked up.
  *Suggestion:* Let them feel your bare skin; cradle them slowly and quietly back and forth; avoid touching them with cold hands.
- Infants learn to move by adjusting themselves to the movement of the adults who hold them.
  *Suggestion:* Carry infants around whenever possible; change rhythm, tempo, and direction of your pace; repeat motions they appear to like; avoid sudden or violent changes that can promote fear.

### Toddlers

- Children run before they walk, falling from one step to the next. Awkwardness is inevitable at first.
  *Suggestion:* When you encourage a child to come to you, keep the distance

short and increase it very gradually; let the child learn to walk on different surfaces; allow the child to revert to crawling; don't push the walking idea.

■ Children need change in order to learn to differentiate between appropriate actions and use of muscles.
*Suggestion:* Give them hassocks and chairs to climb on; let them push chairs together for tunnels and bridges; let them roll around on the rug with a pillow; allow time for repetition and modification.

■ Learning to jump begins with jumping down from something.
*Suggestion:* Provide a mattress or mat as a soft landing spot and place a hassock within it for practice.

## Three- and Four-Year-Olds

■ Children tire easily after vigorous play.
*Suggestion:* Alternate active and quiet play.

■ Children are naturally curious and learn through all their senses.
*Suggestion:* Provide as many different materials as possible to use in movement experiences.

■ Children are developing the ability to symbolize their experiences.
*Suggestion:* Provide a variety of forms of expression, such as stories and music.

■ Children are naturally active and energetic.
*Suggestion:* Provide plenty of space for whole body movement.

## Five- and Six-Year-Olds

■ Children are learning to control their bodies.
*Suggestion:* Provide such muscle-control activities as run-and-stop or seeing how long they can stand on one leg.

■ Children are developing their powers of concentration.
*Suggestion:* Permit children to continue activities as long as their interest holds them.

■ Children begin to suggest taking turns.
*Suggestion:* Provide games and activities that allow this.

■ Children begin to form real friendships.
*Suggestion:* Permit them to choose their own partners at times.

## Seven- and Eight-Year-Olds

■ Children have highly developed large and small muscle control.
*Suggestion:* Provide experiences that are noncompetitive but support physical exploration and muscle control.

■ Children can work well collectively.
*Suggestion:* Let them work in pairs and threes, and later in larger groups.

## AIDS in the Early Childhood Setting: A Conversation with Terry Harville

*There are challenges in today's early childhood settings unlike those of any time in the past. One of the most worrisome to many teachers and caregivers is the presence of children who are HIV (human immunodeficiency virus) positive or who have progressed to the stage of suffering from AIDS (acquired immune deficiency syndrome). Because their condition can be contagious and because there are no laws requiring parental disclosure, nervousness is understandable. In this interview, a doctor who works with HIV and AIDS children shares helpful insights.*

One of about three dozen pediatric immunologists in the United States, Terry Harville works daily with children infected with HIV or who have AIDS. He cares deeply about them, concerned about the injustice of their suffering. He points out that they are almost all congenitally infected and thus are innocent victims. "These are children who deserve to live as normal a life as possible and to grow up normally," he says. Yet he sees that "the children's families are usually dysfunctional, with many mothers unmarried and infected by often absent fathers. In other words, the children are brought up in a socially poor environment. But to cut the child off is not the answer."

Part of the answer, according to Terry, is for teachers to overcome their own fear by being knowledgeable about what they observe and about what steps they can take to ensure their own and others' safety. Some things for teachers to know:

- A child is defined as having AIDS when the immune system has broken down sufficiently so that serious infections such as pneumonia or meningitis can be acquired easily.
- When children have AIDS they are frequently sick and thus absent from school.
- Since 1989 the drug AZT has been approved for infants and children. Children born since that time are less likely to have progressed from HIV to AIDS.
- Previous to the introduction of AZT, 90 percent of infected children would not be expected to live past their first birthday. At this point, it is not known how long the life

span can be extended, but many children are expected to live through elementary school and beyond.

- HIV and AIDS children never seem to be aggressive or angry. Encephalopathy (a disease of the brain) often accompanies the infection. Terry Harville and his colleagues hypothesize that the children's generally docile behavior can be attributed to this phenomenon.
- Infected children tend to experience physical and cognitive delays in development. Early diagnosis can point toward appropriate treatment that can help encourage proper development.

Because of advancements in treatment, because some children are not identified for several years, and because parents may not publicly admit their children's condition, teachers may be unaware of the presence of infected children in their classrooms. Even to the medical professionals a child might seem age appropriate in development until formal testing turns up such problems as functional illiteracy or deficiencies in long-term memory. Fortunately, many parents are forthcoming with the needed information, thus providing teachers with an opportunity to help. For some children, special education classes or physical therapy may provide needed assistance. A positive attitude toward children who are frequently ill and a willingness to help them catch up can go a long way to help. Terry offers some practical information and ideas for teachers:

- Transfer of the virus through saliva has not proven to be a problem, despite the theoretical risk.
- If an infected child is cut and bleeds, keep calm and apply pressure to the wound with a clean cloth. If you have an open wound, some other adult should treat the child.
- If you come in contact with the child's blood, wash the affected area with soap and water.
- If the child is hurt in a fight, or if there is biting, the accompanying saliva will help kill the virus. Even if the skin is punctured there is probably not sufficient blood transferred to transmit the virus.
- Caregivers who change infants' diapers should practice routine handwashing and disposal of diapers. There is no evidence that HIV is spread through excrement.
- Use common sense when attending any child who has been injured and is bleeding, since anyone potentially could be infected with HIV.
- HIV cannot be transmitted by hugging, kissing, touching, or drinking from the same glass.
- Animals and insects do not transmit HIV.

*To think about and discuss: Our knowledge of HIV and AIDS grows daily. Contact your local health agency for the latest information. Perhaps have this person address your class. Discuss ways in which teachers can be aware and safe while providing full care for and affection to HIV-infected children.*

■ Children are able to give more thought and judgment to decisions.
*Suggestion:* Take time to reflect back on and discuss problem-solving experiences.

## Keeping Well: Safety, Health, and Nutrition

Beyond the issues of physical fitness, there is the broader concern of how to keep children safe and healthy. The sections that follow focus on the caregiver's or teacher's responsibilities for the child.

### Safety

Infants and young children, eager to explore everything in their environment, have no way to know which elements in it are hazardous. Preschool, kindergarten and primary children, able to begin reasoning and making sound decisions, benefit from safety education.

*Poisons* should be kept out of reach for all children, most particularly younger ones. Cleaning compounds, used rags, and anything else that is unsafe need to be kept in closed cabinets that are accessible only to adults. Under no circumstances should materials that are in use be put aside, unsupervised, for even a few seconds. If an emergency arises or the telephone must be answered, the materials should be placed out of reach first.

Most parts of most plants are poisonous, making it imperative that very young children be closely supervised during outdoor play. When they are old enough to listen, talk, and obey, children can be told in a simple way that outdoor plant life does not go in the mouth. Nevertheless, as long as children are young enough to be tempted to taste experimentally, they should be closely supervised. Older children can learn of poisonous traits as part of their study of nature.

*Water* is a delightful substance for learning and play. It can also be hazardous. Infants and very young children, not yet in control of their bodies, can easily fall and drown in very shallow water. Anytime children are involved with water they should be closely supervised.

If the school's program involves interaction with a body of water, such as a creek, pond, or lake, adults must take responsibility for constant vigilance. For these experiences there should be extra adults present, with each one responsible for a few specific children or for a specific area. They should keep constant watch on those children in their care if the water is more than a few inches deep.

*Fires* are not common, but every center and school should have a plan for fire safety and every adult should be able to participate in the plan should the need arise. The plan should be written and posted in plain sight and be de signed with the assistance of the local fire department. Extinguishers should be available in such high-risk areas as the kitchen, and all adults should know how to use them.

As soon as children are old enough to walk they are able to participate in fire drills, although at first they should not be expected to stay in tidy lines. As children grow older they can be taught to stay in line, to walk with relative calm to a designated site away from the building, to drop and roll if they come in contact with fire, and even to use the fire extinguisher.

*Traffic safety* is a daily concern for children old enough to be mobile outdoors. A good guest speaker is the local "Officer Friendly" or other police officer. Rather than devoting this time to lecturing and questions, request that the officer take a few children at a time to the nearest crossing, preferably one with a light, to learn safe practices. Reinforce what the children learn by making simple traffic lights to use on the playground with tricycles and "pedestrians." Observe the children's role play and intervene as appropriate.

*Involving parents* leads to effective reinforcement of safety procedures, both at home and at school. Share with parents the plans that you have for safety education before you carry them out. If the parents' rules are slightly different than the school's, the children's confusion may create more danger than safety. If no rules are in effect at home, this is an opportunity to alert parents to the need for them.

## Physical Health

Healthy physical habits should be practiced by caregivers and teachers and taught to the children. For example, after changing a diaper, wash your hands with soap. As children learn to use the toilet they should also be taught to wash their hands. Children should always wash their hands before eating, and you can foster this process by setting an example and by explaining what they are doing and why. If facilities permit, it is a good idea for children to brush their teeth after eating. You can model and explain this behavior as well.

Every center and school should have a basic first-aid kit. To help children feel comfortable with it, demonstrate its contents to the entire group at a time when there are no problems demanding attention. A similar kit in the housekeeping corner and some instruction in how to use the contents will provide further comfortable familiarity.

## Nutrition

Children learn to choose and appreciate foods based primarily on what is placed in front of them. Thus, it is the responsibility of adults in their environment to introduce foods that are healthy and beneficial. Traditional emphasis on the four basic food groups (fruits and vegetables, dairy products,

FIGURE 3.1
**The Food Guide Pyramid is an outline of what to eat each day. It's not a rigid prescription, but a general guide that lets you choose a healthful diet that's right for you.**

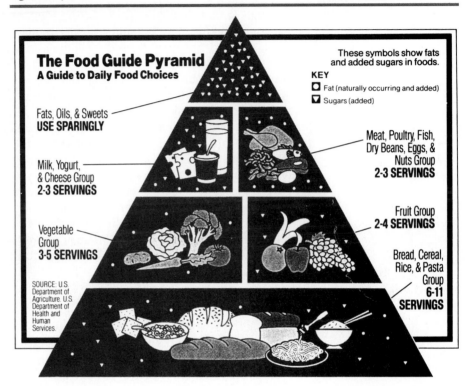

**The Food Guide Pyramid**
**A Guide to Daily Food Choices**

These symbols show fats and added sugars in foods.
**KEY**
☐ Fat (naturally occurring and added)
▼ Sugars (added)

Fats, Oils, & Sweets
**USE SPARINGLY**

Milk, Yogurt, & Cheese Group
**2-3 SERVINGS**

Meat, Poultry, Fish, Dry Beans, Eggs, & Nuts Group
**2-3 SERVINGS**

Vegetable Group
**3-5 SERVINGS**

Fruit Group
**2-4 SERVINGS**

Bread, Cereal, Rice, & Pasta Group
**6-11 SERVINGS**

SOURCE: U.S. Department of Agriculture. U.S. Department of Health and Human Services.

breads, and meat and its substitutes) has been replaced by the pyramid concept. The large base of the pyramid contains the foods that should be most emphasized; above this group are foods that should be eaten in lesser amounts.

For good nutrition education, food that is provided by the center or school should approximate the emphases of the pyramid. In other words, daily meals and cooking experiences should emphasize fruits, vegetables, and grains, while reserving sugar-oriented treats for special occasions.

Good nutrition should be accompanied by good eating habits. Children should learn to value the importance of food, eating it politely and while sitting down. Wandering around in the classroom with food may promote later habits of eating unhealthily on the run.

Encouraging children to try new foods is important but should not become a power play. Often, when children have time and energy of their own invested in meal production, they will taste foods that they wouldn't touch at home. Thus, group cooking efforts can be fun, informative, and adventure-some. It is important, however, to learn about any allergies before beginning cooking experiences. Try to choose a menu that everyone can eat so that no child feels left out. This may mean, for example, that you spend an entire year finding recipes that don't include wheat flour or milk, but the experience can be a creative and educational one for you as well as for the children.

## Extending Your Learning

1. Pair yourself up with an infant. Try to copy his or her movements for a period of ten minutes. How do you feel when finished? What did you learn about the importance of movement to an infant? In what ways do an infant's movements differ from your own?
2. Observe two toddlers of about the same age playing together. Compare the use of their bodies. In what ways is their large motor development the same? How is it different? Observe how they manipulate small objects and compare their dexterity. Compare their awareness of their bodies in space. Do they bump into objects? Move around or through them easily? How do they propel themselves through space?
3. Observe one boy and one girl at preschool during outside play. What similarities and differences do you see in their play preferences? In their use of large muscles? In their small muscle dexterity?
4. Play a team game with a group of primary grade children. Observe their regard for the use of rules. Observe ways in which social and emotional issues enter into the physical experience.
5. If you are working in a center or school, familiarize yourself with all safety rules, including plans for fires, earthquakes, tornadoes, or other problems associated with your area.

## References

Bowers, L. (1988). Children need playgrounds but playgrounds need help. *Journal of Physical Education, Recreation and Dance* 59(7):47–51.

Diem, Liselott (1979). *Child learn physical skills.* Washington, DC: American Alliance for Health, Physical Education and Recreation.

Flinchum, B. (1988). Early childhood physical education. The essential elements. *Journal of Physical Education, Recreation and Dance* 59(7):62–64.

Fraser, D. (1991). *Playdancing.* Pennington, NJ: Princeton Book Co.

Gabbard, C. (1988). Early childhood physical education. The essential elements. *Journal of Physical Education, Recreation and Dance* 59(7):65–69.

———— (1992). *Lifelong motor development.* Dubuque, IA: Brown.

Gallahue, D. (1982). *Understanding motor development in children.* New York: Wiley.

Gober, B., and Franks, B. (1988). The physical and fitness education of young children. *Journal of Physical Education, Recreation and Dance* 59(7):57–61.

Grineski, S. (1988). Teaching and learning in physical education for young children. *Journal of Physical Education, Recreation and Dance* 59(5):91–94.

Kraft, R. (1989). Children at play—Behavior of children at recess. *Journal of Physical Education, Recreation and Dance* 60(4):21–24.

Poest, C., Williams, J., Witt, D., and Atwood, M. (1989). Physical activity patterns of preschool children. *Early Childhood Research Quarterly* 4:367–376.

———(1990). Challenge me to move: large muscle development in young children. *Young Children* 4–10.

# 4

# Education for Social and Affective Development

When you finish reading this chapter, you should be able to

- Identify stages of social, moral, and affective development.
- Differentiate psychoanalytic, social learning, and constructivist theories of development.
- Differentiate children's everyday stress from more serious types.
- Relate developmental theories to approaches to education.

As you think about the chapter on your own, you should be able to

- Understand more about your own social and affective development.
- Consider which theories and teaching approaches might be right for you.

In Chapter 3 we saw the wide range of physical abilities that characterize the years of early childhood. In this chapter we will again observe remarkable changes in the first eight years of life, focusing now on the social and affective (emotional) aspects of development. Two separate rooms in a child care center illustrate some of the differences we can expect to see in children as they grow and develop.

## THE INFANT ROOM

*It is naptime and a dozen babies sleep quietly in the darkened room. Four caregivers sit together, talking quietly. On a counter nearby is a collection of bottles containing formula or juice sent from home. All is ready for the end of nap. The soft sound of a baby waking to put his pacifier back in his mouth is seconded by a noisier child who pulls herself up on the crib bars and makes attention-getting sounds. Each child is picked up by a caregiver, and the little group of four meets at the counter where the bottles are. The adults continue their quiet conversation in between talking to the babies and giving them their bottles. Side by side the group stays near the counter for about fifteen minutes while babies drink and caregivers talk. During this time the babies eye one another over their bottles, but when through drinking, they express little interest in each other. Instead, they watch the moving mouths of the people holding them, listen a bit to other babies waking up, and gaze around the room at whatever interests them for a moment. Now and then two adjacent babies look at each other, touch hands, and smile. But there is no sustained interest or real interaction.*

## THREES AND FOURS

*It is the end of naptime here, too, but the scene is somewhat different. The cribs have been replaced by low canvas cots. Again, there are a dozen children, but just two adults (who are now referred to as teachers rather than caregivers) and a mother of one of the children who works as a part-time aide. Two of the adults talk quietly in a corner, while a third lies on a cot near a child who had earlier needed comforting. It is to this third adult that the first waking child goes. She sucks her thumb and drags behind her a ratty security blanket brought from home. Removing her thumb, the child pounds on the back of the dozing teacher. "It's time," she says. "It's time to wake up. It's morning!" Although the teacher quiets the child immediately, her voice has awakened a light sleeper nearby. "It's morning?" he asks.*

*"Time for breakfast. Can I have some Sugar Pops?" He grins and the teacher grins back, acknowledging his little joke. She gives each a warm hug, then sends the two children to a far corner of the room to play quietly until other children start to wake up. They both drag their blankets along, then make little nests of them in the corner. They soon settle down to look at a book together, arguing about the plot line and the meaning of the pictures. This lasts but a few minutes, however, and soon each one is doing something different, though still side by side. Their dialogue goes like this:*

*She:*   *This baby* [a doll] *needs a bath. Do you want to wash it?*
*He:*   *If I'm quiet it's okay to play with the blocks.*
*She:*   *Okay, into the water you go.*
*He:*   *Quiet, quiet, don't fall down. Do you want to make something with me?*
*She:*   *What a nice clean baby!*

*The two children are clearly content playing next to each other and they do talk to each other, but communication is one way and about completely different topics. Neither seems concerned that the other does not answer questions.*

No more than three years separate the ages of the children in the two rooms, yet much has changed. In the infant room, the babies received most of their emotional support from the adults holding them. In the second room, the children were first drawn toward the adult. Apparently her hug was satisfying enough so that they could then take off together. The babies had little interest in each other beyond a brief touch, while the older children could sit down together and share a book, even if only for a short time.

Some aspects of social interaction had not changed greatly. All of the children spent much time focused on self. The babies looked outward but did little about it. The older children soon tired of their book and began to play independently. Their dialogue was really two overlapping monologues as they largely ignored each other.

Much of social/affective growth has to do with growing out of a focus on self and becoming more skillful at looking both outward and inward. The children in the second room are making good progress along these lines. Developmentally, they are right on schedule, as are the babies in the first room. Both caregivers and teachers knew just how to interact with the children. Part of this was common sense, but part was training, too. It wasn't just their own interest in continuing their conversation that led the two caregivers to stand side by side with the babies. They knew that it was to the benefit of the babies' social growth to be near each other even if they didn't interact much. In

Despite years of research and careful observation, scholars still do not agree about the ways in which social and affective development takes place.

the second room, the teacher knew that her charges were capable of playing harmoniously together without direct supervision; she also knew that a friendly hug would help promote the best results. To move beyond the common-sense level of interaction with children, it is important for you to have a good understanding of their social and affective development. You can then apply your knowledge in a way that best promotes their growth.

Understanding children's social and affective development is more complex than understanding their more easily observed physical and motor development. Historically, there have been several views of children's social and affective development, and the topic remains a controversial one. Despite years of research that have included philosophical considerations as well as observations of and interactions with multitudes of children, scholars still cannot agree among themselves about the way in which social and affective development takes place. In the following discussion we will make use of a variety of philosophical views. You may find that you agree with some more than others. Perhaps you'll be attracted consistently to one philosophical view; most teachers prefer to take what they consider the best of each and apply what works. The important point is that the decisions you make should be knowledgeable ones.

Before beginning a discussion of the different views, we'll do one more observation, this time of two boys in kindergarten. Then we'll take Charles and Pablo with us throughout our discussion of theory, philosophy, and practical applications.

*It was October when two new children, Charles and Pablo, showed up at Madeleine's kindergarten, within just a day or two of each other. By the time they arrived, the class was fairly well stabilized in terms of expectations, curriculum, children's behavior, and the general rhythm of classroom life. The intrusion was a bit unsettling for everyone, particularly the two new boys. They had to learn to fit into the various established norms. On top of all that, they needed to figure out how to make friends with the other children who had no need of them. (It's important to realize that their classmates had felt like Charles and Pablo not too many weeks earlier. Now, they were beginning to feel comfortably at home and therefore did not welcome the arrival of two strangers.)*

*Madeleine was well aware of the difficulties on both sides, and she spent time observing the new children's ability to fit in. After a week or so, she noted that all was going well, with one important exception. Charles was having much more difficulty than Pablo in making friends. Both boys wanted to play in the block corner more than anything else. Madeleine marveled at Pablo's skill in achieving a friendly reception. He was more adept at it, she thought, than many adults. Equally stunning was Charles's inability to choose the right attitudes and behaviors. Pablo's technique was to stand on the sidelines, quietly watching the children play. If someone dropped a block, he would pick it up, say simply, "Here," and hand it back. After a few days he began to offer tidbits of advice when there were building problems. Never did he ask to join the children, but, after the fourth day, Pablo was invited in.*

*Charles's approach was heavy-handed. On the first day he said in a loud voice, "Hey! Can I play with you?" It was more a statement than a question, and he followed it up by grabbing a few blocks and adding them to the current building project. "Hey! Not there," one of the boys said, and three children made faces of frustration and anger. Similar incidents followed over the succeeding days. Madeleine realized that the children were never going to accept Charles if she didn't intervene.*

*First, she helped Charles see that his tactics weren't working and asked him if he could think of any alternative behaviors. He couldn't. Madeleine suggested variations on Pablo's techniques and had Charles rehearse them, right down to the exact words he should say to the children in the block corner. She then went to the block corner and told the children what she had been doing with Charles. She asked that they respond appropriately to his new attempts at being a more skillful friend, but she did not say that they must accept his entry into their play.*

*Madeleine accompanied Charles to the block corner, listened as he politely asked if he might join in, heard the children's grudging acceptance, and stayed a few minutes to watch as Charles waited with forced patience for the others to give him something to do. She knew it would take some time for Charles to learn to interact with social skillfulness. She also knew that her continued efforts were an important element in her role as a kindergarten teacher.*

## Understanding Social and Affective Development

The section Fostering Social and Affective Development (see page 123) discusses in more depth the approach that Madeleine took with Charles. At this point, we will take a look at some views on development that can help explain how Charles and Pablo arrived at kindergarten with such vastly different personalities, views of themselves and others, and approaches to making friends.

### Development of Self and Personality

Forever, no doubt, parents have noticed that their newborn infants carry some incipient personality traits with them all the way to adulthood. The baby who objects to being left alone becomes the child who loves to gather lots of friends together for group games, then enters adulthood as the kind of person friends know they can count on and trust. The watchful infant who visually drinks in every movement and interaction between family members later worries excessively every time her parents fight and grows to adulthood overinterpreting casual remarks by her friends. Charles and Pablo, at age five, are already exhibiting traits they may have had since early infancy and will take with them in some form throughout their lives. Theorists and philosophers have speculated about the ways in which children like Charles and Pablo come to be the way they are. Three major schools of thought provide models of development that are quite useful for us as teachers.

#### The Psychoanalytic View

Erik Erikson (1963) presents the most time-honored and universally known view, one based on the work of Sigmund Freud. His "eight ages of man" provide a model of development that contains stages, or critical peri-

Erik Erikson proposed an eight stage model of personality development. Each stage involves a conflict between two forces (e.g., trust vs. mistrust), the resolution of which determines the rate and direction of "self" or personality development.

ods, in which we must all work out specific identity problems. In each of the stages there are two forces, one positive and one negative, that create a "crisis" to be solved. If, at each stage, we are at least somewhat successful in eliminating the negative and negotiating the positive, we will move on to the next of the eight stages with our egos strengthened. We take these successes and failures with us through our lives. An important element of Erikson's model is that it can be applied across all cultures; each of us relates to each of the stages and to the people we meet during those stages in ways that reflect our own cultures. Thus, success or failure may be defined somewhat differently depending on where we live. (Erikson's theory has a societal dimension related to each stage. If you study his ideas more thoroughly, you will no doubt find these interesting.) The first four stages relate directly to the early years, from infancy through elementary school.

**Stage 1: Basic Trust Versus Basic Mistrust (Age: birth to about twelve months).**    To be successful at Stage 1, an infant must have confidence that the major caregiver (usually the mother) is trustworthy. If the mother leaves, the infant must trust that she will come back; and, when hungry, the infant must trust that the mother will provide nourishment. The exact amount of food and demonstrated love isn't as important as the quality of the mother–infant interaction.

**Stage 2: Autonomy Versus Shame and Doubt (Age: about twelve months to three years).**   Children at this stage want to do things independently, most notably toilet activities, because their maturing musculature has made it possible to hold on or let go at will. Children's attempts at autonomy can be difficult for adults to deal with, giving rise to the ironically descriptive term the "terrible twos." For children to be successful in negotiating the Stage 2 crisis, there must be much reassurance from adults. Children need firmness, loving acceptance, and freedom of self-expression. Failure at this stage brings loss of self-esteem and self-control and may lead to a lifetime of self-doubt and shame.

**Stage 3: Initiative Versus Guilt (Age: about three to five years).**   Children at this stage bring much energy and initiative to their experiences. They like to plan and attack an activity just for the sake of the activity. This change in motives—from autonomy to pleasurable activity—makes children easier to live with, more loving and relaxed than they were in the previous stage. This attack-and-conquer attitude can have a negative side, however, in that the goals a child chooses for conquest may create a sense of guilt. This is particularly true if the child wants to take the place of the same-sex parent or to remove all the brothers and sisters who seem to be competing for the mother's attention.

**Stage 4: Industry Versus Inferiority (Age: about six to twelve years).** Sexually, this period is the lull before the storm of puberty, and this frees the child to focus more on being a worker and a producer than on being the conqueror of Stage 3. It's time for school, whether that means learning primitive farming or hunting skills or learning to read in the classroom. Children at this stage want to be industrious, and teachers can help them be successful by presenting new challenges at the right level. A child may feel discouraged, inadequate, or inferior and, in doing so, revert to behaviors from the previous stage. Adults working with children at Stage 4 must find the proper balance between learning activities that provide challenge and those that are too advanced and therefore discouraging.

Erikson's stage theory provides one useful framework for our observation of children's social and affective development. Charles and Pablo, for example, fit quite readily into Stage 3 as they attempt the conquest of making friends in the block corner. Charles is in danger of negotiating the crisis of this stage badly, but the conquest training his teacher gave him may help. Erikson's theory is not without controversy. Some may disagree with its grounding in Freudian theory. Others, as we will see in the next section, argue that the concept of stages is erroneous.

## The Social Learning View

Albert Bandura (1963, 1969) has researched the development of self and personality and arrived at quite different conclusions as to how they are formed. He and his followers have argued that trust, mistrust, autonomy, shame, doubt, and so on are slippery for the adult observer to define. Teachers and counselors might observe the same child's behavior and assign different psychological explanations to it depending on their own philosophy or educational background. Further, Bandura has argued that children don't all go through universally predictable stages; there is too much influence from such variables as family, biology, and culture. Rather, he says, children develop their personalities by modeling what is in their own environment. Since parents, brothers, and sisters typically constitute much of the child's environment, it shouldn't be any surprise that many personality traits seem similar across family members.

Bandura (1969) says that there are two ways that children acquire their values, attitudes, and social behavior. The first is through direct training by parents, teachers, and others in the child's environment. This, he says, is the least influential way that children learn. More important is "the child's active imitation of parental attitudes and behavior, most of which the parents have never directly attempted to teach" (186). This is indeed bad news for adults who subscribe to the old joke "Do as I say, not as I do." More seriously, it is an explanation for the frequent observation that abusive parents were themselves often abused by their own parents. Bandura's extensive observations of children showed that the more aggression they observed, the more aggressive they became.

Subscribers to the social learning view of development can find in it much that is practical for helping children develop. For example, Bandura (1969) and others have used the theory to eliminate even well-established fears in some children. In the 1960s, one of his studies showed that nursery school children who were fearful of dogs could overcome their fears by observing the behavior of a child who wasn't afraid. It took just eight brief sessions in which the modeling child, by interacting happily with a dog, changed the fearful children into confident ones who could pet and walk a dog, and even climb into a playpen with it. It is important to note that each of the sessions involved a small step away from fear, rather than a total immersion, sink-or-swim approach. Here is a case in which a specific fear was eliminated from children's personalities by intentional modeling. It may well be that some of the frightened children originally learned their fear by observing the fear of others, a case of learning through unintentional modeling.

In choosing role play as a means to help Charles, his teacher was applying the social learning view. As Charles practiced his part, the teacher also played a part, that of a child in the block corner accepting his overtures. Another approach might have been to have Charles quietly observe other children's interactions and to discuss them with her.

Bandura's view of development, like Erikson's, has its critics. It is based on the ideas of behaviorism, a philosophy that some find repugnant because it leads to the manipulation of children according to the dictates or whims of more powerful adults. There is a third view of development that contains elements of the first two, although it should not be considered a combination, or compromise, view.

### The Constructivist View

In Chapter 1 you became acquainted with Jean Piaget and the important terms and concepts he used to describe young children's development. Piaget's primary research interest was in cognitive development, but he also did some study of social/moral development. (He didn't deny the part played by emotions in children's lives, but he left that research to others.) Piaget's observations of children led him to theorize that cognitive and social/moral development are intertwined. Children's cognitive development can proceed without equal social/moral development. On the other hand, social/moral development is impossible without sufficient cognitive development. In other words, children can do morally good things, but for the moral development to be whole, they must also have the cognitive awareness to tell why they do the good things they do.

We can apply the constructivist view to Charles's and Pablo's experience in the block corner. Pablo had attended preschool for two years before entering kindergarten, and he had always been popular. He had learned quite early that the subtle approach was most successful for making new friends. He brought this learning with him to kindergarten and simply had to assimilate the new situation to it. Charles, on the other hand, was entering school for the first time. His previous social experiences were largely confined to his older brothers and sisters, who tended to bully him. Historically, his response was to attack new situations with forcefulness. This didn't work in the kindergarten situation, and Charles was forced to accommodate a whole new set of behaviors. Because this was so difficult for him, the teacher found it necessary to step in.

The constructivist theory has been used by Piaget's followers to explain children's expanding understanding of themselves. Remember that in constructivist theory, children progress through stages. Their progress is not influenced by inner sexual conflicts, as in Freud-based theories, but by their interaction with the environment. It is from this viewpoint that Hart and Damon (1985) have suggested four levels of development, two of which apply to the early years.

**Level 1.**   Children see themselves in very simple terms with no elaboration. Body features and material possessions are of most importance ("I am pretty and I have a doll."). If asked why this is important or interesting, the child is likely to answer, "Just because."

**Level 2.**   Children see themselves in somewhat more complex ways, uniting several characteristics at once, if only superficially. If asked why it is important that she is pretty, the child might answer, "Because I'm happy when Daddy says so." Children also begin to compare themselves with others at this stage, and their focus may be on their active qualities, for example, "I'm the fastest runner in my class." And why is this important? "Because I can win most of the races at recess."

As children get older, characteristics of the self become more synthesized and are eventually integrated into a personal or moral belief system. Much of self-development, no matter which theory is used to describe it, takes place as the child learns to interact with others. This social development also changes over time.

## Social and Moral Development

Once again, we can use any of the three theories as we attempt to describe how children grow in their understanding of appropriate social interaction. Erikson's eight stages of man can explain not only the development of the self but the ways in which people understand and interact with others. Bandura's social learning views are predicated on the child's social interactions and observations of others. Because of much recent research the constructivist approach has even more to say about social development and morality. In this section we will expand our understanding of development, primarily based on the constructivist theory.

### Friendship

Friendship was a major goal for both Charles and Pablo at the block corner. Their teacher knew this and when Charles was observed failing, she immediately planned ways to intervene. According to Damon (1977), "Friendship is the central social relation between peers during childhood. In fact, friendship is so basic that we often use it as a reference point from which to characterize all of our other social relations, peer or otherwise" (p. 137). William Corsaro (1985) points out, the "discovery of friendship is a major step in children's acquisition of social knowledge" (p. 121). Before this monumental discovery, children's social bonds are between themselves and their family members or caretakers. Although there may be brothers and sisters within the family, it's difficult for the youngest members to negotiate friendships and more likely that they will have to accept and adapt to the social milieu that already exists. Once there is an opportunity to interact with peers, Corsaro says, "children learn that they can regulate social bonds on the basis of criteria that emerge from their personal needs and social contextual demands" (p. 121).

Throughout life, people's personal needs and social contexts are continually changing. If we view the crisis in the block corner within the framework

In the primary grades, most children still can't put themselves in the shoes of their peers and understand their point of view in conflict situations.

of Erikson's eight stages, we see that success or failure in forming kindergarten friendships may well affect the success or failure at forming friendships when Charles and Pablo have graduated from blocks to baseball and on to their own marriages. Social learning theory might argue that Pablo's success will reinforce his perception of his subtle approach to making friends and that he will then continue to refine and adapt it, thus making many more friends over the years. Conversely, Charles's inability to make friends is likely to establish and reinforce an increasingly low self-concept. Constructivist theory, through the work of Robert Selman (1980), suggests that there are stages children pass through as they grow in their understanding of friendship.

**Stage 0.**   Close friendship as momentary physical interaction. Very young children are not yet aware of the psychological aspects related to choosing, treating, and keeping friends. For the very youngest, a friend may simply be someone who is close by and available. If jealousy arises at this stage, it has to do with a loss of toys or space rather than a loss of affection or attention. Similarly, conflict is resolved by simply going somewhere else to play with another toy or by using physical force. In either case, the child's attention is focused on the situation or materials (toys) at hand rather than on any psychological elements.

**Stage 1.**   Close friendship as one-way assistance. In the early elementary school years, children gain an awareness of the psychological element in friendships, the motives, thoughts, and feelings of both self and others. Children also understand that another's psychological experiences and needs may not be the same as their own. However, there is no understanding of reciprocity in relationships with others, that needs and interests may be complex, or "that friendship may be more than the accommodation of one person's behavior to the other's will" (Selman 1980, p. 138). Conflicts and their resolutions are seen as one-way; a problem that is felt by one child is caused by the actions of another. Mutual blame or complex causes are beyond the child's reasoning.

These two stages are observable in young children. A third stage emerges toward the end of elementary school. At this point children can begin to take the view of the other person, even an outside party who can understand the complexities for everyone concerned in a friendship negotiation.

## Sharing

When Piaget, and later Kohlberg, applied constructivist theory to moral development, they argued for justice as the foundation of all morality. They based their notion on ancient Greek philosophy. Sharing, or what Aristotle long ago called "distributive justice," has no doubt been a concern of friends and nations since the beginning of time. "For a young child," Damon (1977) says, "sharing is probably the largest part of friendship" (p. 71). Taking turns, using and trading each other's toys, are the physical realities of friendship, as we have just seen. Whether we speak of friends or of nations, fair distribution adds a moral element to the idea of social interaction.

A young child's sense of justice is quite different from an adult's. Damon (1977), like Selman, found in his research with young children that their reasoning and behavior proceeded from the physical and self-oriented to the more psychologically complex and other-oriented.

**Level 0-A.**   Children make choices because they want something, and they don't see a need to justify their decisions. "I should get it because I want it."

**Level 0-B.**   Children justify choices based on external, observable characteristics. "She gets it because she's big and pretty."

**Level 1-A.**   Children base choices on strict, inflexible equality. "Everybody gets the same, no matter what."

**Level 1-B.**   Children make choices based on merit and reciprocity. "The poor kids can have more if they work extra."

**Level 2-A.**   Children begin to realize that making choices can be more complex, and concern for people with special needs appears. "Everybody should get the same, but he gets a little more because he's poor and might starve."

**Level 2-B.**   This level appears toward the end of elementary school and, like Selman's friendship stages, requires children to understand reciprocity, multiple perspectives, and more subtle definitions of equality.

While children of the same age may reason and behave differently and move back and forth between levels, depending on the situation, some general ages can be assigned. Typically, preschoolers are observed at Levels 0-A and 0-B, kindergarteners at Level 1-A, and lower elementary children at Levels 1-A, 1-B, and 2-A.

Friendship and sharing are of primary importance in the social relationships between individuals from the very earliest years. At the societal level, establishing and obeying fair rules and laws is equally important.

## Rules

In the 1920s, Jean Piaget undertook a number of seminal studies of young children, then published several books describing them. His *Moral Judgment of the Child,* published in 1932, was the only book not focused on cognitive development. (In the next chapter you will learn more about his studies.) His study of moral judgment, together with his cognitive studies, led Piaget to formulate the concept of constructivism as a way of explaining the process by which children develop. The research we have just read about, done by Selman and Damon, was based largely on Piaget's studies done a half century ago in Switzerland.

How did Piaget get inside the minds of children to observe their developing morality? He played marbles with them! Although morality for young children can include such issues as sharing, authority, friendship, helpfulness, respect for property, truthfulness, keeping promises, caring, and obeying rules, Piaget chose to focus only on the last issue, viewing rules as the childhood precursor to laws in the larger society. He was less concerned with behavior than with children's unfolding sense of justice as demonstrated through their explanation and application of rules. He found that children moved from early heteronomy (willing submission to outside authority) to eventual autonomy with transitional stages along the way. Since true autonomy first appears during the middle school years, what teachers of young children can expect to see is heteronomy and the first of two transitional stages.

**Stage 1. Heteronomy.**   Children of preschool age are other-directed (heteronomous) and are inclined to obey authority even if they don't understand its basis. They assume that they know the rules, even if their understanding conflicts with what their peers also "know." And they only relate to rules as the rules affect their self-interests. If a rule conflicts with what a child believes or likes, it may simply be ignored or declared nonexistent. Children's relationship to authority figures lacks understanding at this stage. Big people should be obeyed and have the ability to punish simply because they are big.

**Stage 2. First transitional stage.** Authority figures are still important, but so is peer approval. Children develop a primitive understanding of rules, taking them very literally and ascribing them to a major authority figure: teacher, parent, or even God. Thus, disobeying rules or trying to change them can cause conflict with friends and much tattling. Stage 2 begins to develop during kindergarten and lasts throughout the primary years.

**Stage 3. Second transitional stage.** Because some eight-year-olds enter this stage, we include it here although it is often too much to expect of the typical third grader. Children learn to see the viewpoints of others and begin to understand that rules can be changed when advantageous. The views of their friends gradually become more important than those of authority figures, and real strides are made in understanding the concepts of fairness and justice.

Piaget's stages of heteronomous-to-autonomous development provide a useful framework for viewing social and moral development. The heteronomous child is controlled from the outside, by authority figures, and makes decisions based on expectations of and relationships with authority. Autonomy, on the other hand, indicates self-government. From our earliest years and on through life we all have experiences and thought processes that tend toward one direction or the other. When young children play with their peers they have opportunities to be autonomous. However, the decision-making segments of their lives generally occur under the auspices of authority figures who provide security, protection, and knowledge. Thus, younger children lead lives that tend more toward heteronomy. However, if development proceeds normally, they will move toward autonomy in the primary years as the opinions of friends become more important in their minds. It is the responsibility of adult caregivers and teachers to help children in the direction of autonomy while providing them with the security that gives them the confidence to become more independent.

In recent years there has been disagreement about Piaget's theory based on his reliance on the game of marbles. This traditionally has been a boy's game, which was certainly the case in 1920s' Switzerland. Piaget chose the game because its rules and traditions came from children rather than adults. He found that it provided an excellent source of children's reasoning—as long as the children were boys. Girls, he said, were less interested in the "splendid codification of rules" that led to greater understanding of law-based justice. Girls, in fact, generally chose not to play marbles but preferred such games as hopscotch, which requires little negotiation about rules. Further, if there was disagreement concerning rules, the girls wouldn't negotiate a settlement as the boys did, but preferred to withdraw from a game or close it down entirely. Piaget concluded that the boys' approach to their disagreements prepared them more successfully than did the girls' approach for adult understanding of law and justice. Thus, men were more likely to be moral philosophers, while women were often stuck at a lower and conventional level of moral thinking.

Since the 1970s some women researchers and moral philosophers, led by Carol Gilligan (1982), have challenged this view of female development. Gilligan pointed out that Piaget focused on boys' development, equated it with *human* development, then assigned girls to lower levels because their development was different. She took Erikson, Freud, and others to task for the same attitude. The concept of justice, Gilligan says, underlies male ideas of morality; the concept of caring is the basis for female morality. If little girls walk away from conflict during a game of hopscotch, they shouldn't be faulted for it, but observed for their developing ability to care for the feelings of others.

Staying within the framework of constructivism, Gilligan suggests that girls go through stages of moral development based on an ethic of caring. In response, Damon (1988) argues that, although cultural experience and expectations may direct girls toward caring and boys toward justice, it would be a good idea for us to help both sexes grow in each:

> It could help weaken the gender stereotypes that have limited the opportunities of girls and have contributed to the subordination of women. It should enhance the moral awareness of boys and girls alike. By removing gender-linked constraints on children's values we may provide children with their best chance to expand their moral horizons to the full limits of human potential. (pp. 102–103)

As children develop and grow in all areas of their lives—social, physical, intellectual—there is one affective element that influences them all and that can be both positive and negative. Once there was no name for it, but today we refer to it as stress.

## Stress

Stress is not new to our century or current lifestyle. From the birthing experience on, children have always had to deal with it. The children who were your ancestors may have felt stress while working long days in a factory or fighting in the Civil War or being kidnapped and dragged onto a slave ship. While these particular stressors may not face children today, there are others, equally horrendous, that may await them. On the other hand, stress can be part of a happy experience, and often the quality it has depends on the attitude of the child.

Kit and Elena were two six-year-old friends who attended a birthday party together. For Elena, it was a joyous occasion, and she entered into the games and other fun with enthusiasm. That there was some stress involved was demonstrated later at home when it took her almost two hours to calm down. For Kit, the experience was fraught with potential dangers. Would something be served that she was allergic to? Would she be hurt in the rowdier games? Would the other children want to play with her? Although everything turned out well, Kit went home and took a nap.

We have already seen how Charles and Pablo responded differently to their first week in kindergarten. No doubt, it was a stressful situation for both, but Pablo turned the stress to his advantage, while Charles was unable to do this. In succeeding weeks, Pablo's stressful feelings subsided while Charles's grew.

The stress, both good and bad, experienced by Kit, Elena, Charles, and Pablo is a natural part of life. Psychoanalytic theories such as Erikson's suggest that stress may be experienced during any stage of development if all doesn't go smoothly. Seefeldt (1984) maintains that "should some unbalance be present during a specific growth stage, or a lack of coordination between maturation, the environment and development occur, then stress would result" (p. 28). Social learning and other behavioral theories approach stress from an environmental point of view. Children receive stimuli from the environment and subsequently react with different degrees of stress. In part, their response is influenced by past experiences that were also determined by the environment. Constructivism argues that stress grows out of each child's understanding of a situation. This understanding, which each child constructs

Children's stress, according to constructivists, is greatly influenced by how they interpret situations. This understanding, which each child constructs through active manipulation of his or her environment, matures over time, clearing up some stressful thoughts and introducing others.

through active manipulation of his or her environment, matures over time, clearing up some stressful thoughts and introducing others.

The sources of childhood stress are various, some of them peculiar to our time and place, others more universal. Some of the more common sources of stress include the following.

**Prematurity.**   Too much stimulation from concerned caregivers, too little from rejecting parents, or unrealistic parental expectations may all cause stress in the premature infant.

**Learning Disabilities.**   Again, too much or too little stimulation, rejection or fear of it, and incorrect expectations can cause stress for the learning-disabled child.

**Gender.**   Boys seem to be more vulnerable than girls to stress and have higher rates of bed wetting, dyslexia, and school delinquency (Honig, 1986).

**Poverty.**   While young children often cannot compare lean times with comfortable ones, the stress felt within the adult family members can create a stressful situation for everyone.

**Hospitalization.**   Whether a parent or the child himself enters the hospital, the separation as well as the physical experience can cause great stress.

**Birth of Siblings.**   Sleep troubles, toileting problems, and behavioral disorders may appear when a new "competitor" enters the scene.

**Death of a Parent.**   Loss of a parent during childhood may cause emotional problems that last a lifetime.

**Divorce.**   Younger children especially may blame themselves, believing their bad behavior caused a parent to leave.

**School Learning.**   Teachers' own anxieties may be transferred to children. Previous unsuccessful experiences in school can lead to fear of new ones. Test anxiety can begin early when kindergarteners and even preschool children are subjected to standardized tests or entrance exams.

**Physical and Emotional Abuse.**   Any negative physical or emotional experience causes stress. The line separating normal experience from abuse is a fine one and may be different for different children.

**Sexual Abuse.**   Our greater awareness of this today provides us with the resources to cope with the problem.

**Neglect.**   This problem is a growing one, as more and more parents become drug dependent or unwilling to face the responsibilities of mature parenthood.

The stressors in this list can be the cause of great difficulty in children's development. There are ways teachers can help children, not only to cope with stress but to have positive affective and social experiences. In the next section we will discuss some of these methods.

## Fostering Social and Affective Development

Throughout this chapter differing views of development have been presented. Although theoretical in nature, each has been developed with a view to practicality so that clinicians and teachers can apply them in ways that are beneficial to children. Here, briefly, are some practical ideas based on each theory.

**The Psychoanalytic View.** Children need assistance in solving a major crisis at each stage of development. If you are working with two- or three-year-olds, their crisis is that of autonomy versus shame and doubt. They want to express their own opinions and make their own decisions (often negative), but they also need to know that you are there to provide consistency, security, and firmness. Try phrasing questions so that a yes or no answer isn't possible: "Do you want to help put away the trikes or put away the balls?" rather than, "It's time to clean up. Do you want to help with the trikes?"

**The Social Learning View.** Children model the behavior they see in the environment, so be sure that you model good behavior. Point out what you're doing very explicitly: "Oh! I spilled a little red paint on the table. I'll wipe it up with this sponge right away. Now, I'll rinse the sponge and put it back in its proper place. Then someone else can find it and use it."

**The Constructivist View.** Children need plenty of opportunities to learn on their own and make decisions in order to construct their own development. Your role is to create an encouraging environment and to provide growth opportunities. For example, children may be having trouble sharing during art projects. If the problem is extreme, you may decide to have sufficient numbers of scissors, crayons, and so forth available at all times so that conflict is avoided entirely. As the situation improves, you may remove some of the supplies so that children are forced to share and take turns.

It is possible and desirable to combine these views. For example, you can model sharing as you delete some of the supplies: "I see you need some scissors. I'll be happy to let you use mine. While you're using them, could I borrow your black crayon?" A number of classroom suggestions are offered in the next sections to help you foster children's social and affective development. Some are derived from a particular theory while others combine two or more theories. It is important for you to do more than take the ideas at face value. You should begin developing your own philosophical views of child development and evaluate classroom suggestions within that framework. If you fail to take this step, you may find it difficult later to pick and choose good teaching ideas and almost impossible to create solutions of your own.

## Fostering Social and Moral Development

In later chapters there will be ideas for promoting positive social behaviors as part of classroom management (Chapter 9) and ways to enhance social understandings through the social studies (Chapter 14). In this chapter we will consider steps that you can take to stimulate social development.

### The Social Classroom

Social development, by definition, indicates that children grow in their ability to relate to and cope within the larger society. This process begins with opportunities to interact with others. In many classrooms, teachers feel as though they must always be in charge, forever pouring knowledge into students' heads. Otherwise, they feel as though they aren't teaching. This type of classroom, however, gives children little opportunity to interact. Consequently, their social development may not progress in an optimal way.

Two suggestions may help you avoid this common teaching trap. First, listen to yourself. Are you overexplaining, offering too many instructions, repeating yourself? Are you giving children sufficient opportunities to ask questions, carry on discussions, share experiences and stories?

Second, create a physical environment and time schedule that allow children plenty of opportunities to interact with each other. Centers for learning and playing that permit free movement and choice encourage the most social growth.

### Friendship

As we have seen earlier, friendship is perceived differently by children as they grow older. You will undoubtedly have children at different levels of development in your classroom, even if everyone is close to the same age. Friendship skills are important from the earliest years. Even babies reject other babies who are surly or unresponsive and show preference for those who demonstrate more positive social behaviors.

For very young children, friends are those within playing distance. As they get older, someone who plays with them is considered a friend. Therefore, in the school setting, much of what children need is a set of tactics for entering groups so that they can join in the play. Almost all children develop approaches that are at least partly successful, but some have more trouble than others. We saw this situation with Charles at the kindergarten block corner. It is possible to list general principles for helping a child like Charles, and these can then be adapted to individual situations:

1. Observe the child closely to determine those skills that are lacking.
2. Choose one or two important skills on which to focus.
3. Talk to the child briefly, explaining the need to alter behaviors in order to enter play groups more successfully.
4. Recruit another child to play with the target child for a short time. After a few minutes, sit down and discuss how the new ideas helped.
5. Do follow-up observation and repeat the process several times.
6. Don't expect miracles, even when dealing with very young children. Remember, a lack in skills may have begun in infancy.

There are numerous questions you might ask when observing a child or group of children. Here is a selection drawn from the child friendship research of William Corsaro (1985):

■ Does the child regularly participate in a wide or narrow range of both peer and teacher-directed activities?
■ Does the child have difficulty in entering and being accepted into peer activities?
■ Does the child regularly participate in both large and small groups?
■ Is the child actively involved in peer culture?
■ Is the child frequently involved in disputes and disagreements?
■ Does the child actively participate in organized group or meeting times?

There will be times when you will be tempted to lecture the class on what it means to be a friend. Try to resist the impulse! As you know by now, your definition of friendship is sure to be at odds with theirs and they will be confused or tune you out. Instead, focus on the behaviors and skills that need shaping. As you tackle each skill, you will find friendships emerging.

## Perspective Taking

When we talk about stepping into another's shoes or walking in someone else's moccasins we refer to the need for understanding the perspective taken by a person other than ourselves. Very young children still have much to learn about their own perspective and can't be expected to understand others' viewpoints. When they first become aware of other viewpoints (usually in late nursery school or in kindergarten) they can only relate these to their own. By occasionally focusing on perspective taking, you can ensure that this important learning takes place.

When reading stories to the children, for example, try asking them how each of the characters feels about various events. By the primary grades you

Adults can use stories as the basis for "perspective taking" exercises in which children are asked how various characters involved in some dilemma or conflict might be thinking and feeling about their situation.

can discuss the feelings of the villains and talk about ways to improve their behavior.

When helping children to negotiate conflict, you can take steps to help them see others' viewpoints. The youngest children will impose their own feelings on a victim ("She *wanted* me to hit her") and can benefit from a reality check. Have the victim state how she feels both physically and emotionally, then have the perpetrator restate what the victim has just said. Children in late kindergarten or the primary grades can usually say on their own how the other child feels, but may regress to the earlier stage if it is in their best interest. One way to help a child see the viewpoint of someone he has just injured is to have them exchange shoes as a symbol of considering the situation from the other child's point of view. The gentle humor in this activity can help to relieve tension while giving the child a very concrete experience in being open to someone else's view.

### Sharing and Helping

Since the youngest children share and help only if it is in their self-interest, and primary children are learning to step into another's shoes, approaches to fostering sharing will differ depending on developmental stages. You can accomplish much by modeling behavior, but, particularly with younger children, you will need to accompany your behavior with simple and clear descriptions of what you are doing. Some explanation is necessary throughout the primary grades as well.

Try role playing, particularly at the beginning of the school year. Create a situation in which a child might need help, then ask her classmates to act out solutions. With the youngest children this will work best if you take a role, probably that of the child needing help.

Both helping and sharing can be promoted by carefully introducing new materials into the environment. You might teach a few children how to use the new materials, then appoint them "teachers" and let them demonstrate to others. Also, you can pair up an older or more experienced child with another who wants to try something that is new and a bit difficult. Finally, you can have limited numbers of some materials with well-understood rules for taking turns and sharing.

## Respect for Authority and Rules

In the earliest years, young children obey because authority figures have more power and they either don't consider questioning it or consider it in their self-interest to accept. By the primary years children are learning that rules and authority figures may both be flexible. In either case, children will respect and obey rules more readily if they have helped to create them. However, the youngest children should not be expected to obey more than two or three rules at a time.

Children of all ages need the security of knowing that teachers, aides, and other caregivers have authority. This does not mean that you must be authoritarian in your approach. You need to be loving, firm, and stable, while providing children with opportunities to make decisions on their own.

## Morality

A major way in which you can enhance children's moral development is to help them take responsibility for their behaviors, both good and bad. Taking responsibility for good behavior occurs when children share, help, or demonstrate friendship in a positive way. Normally, children enjoy the psychic benefits that come from such behavior and will often point it out to the world at large.

But children who realize they shouldn't have behaved in a certain way, or wish they hadn't done something, can often convince themselves that it never actually happened. Taking responsibility requires children to admit wrongdoing, take the consequences, and then do what is necessary to set things right. It is critically important for you as the teacher to follow through, monitoring their progress during all steps.

Damon (1988) suggests several basic understandings that should underlie our attempts to foster children's moral development:

- Just participating in normal social situations provides children with opportunities to learn about moral issues. They may need guidance, but they don't need special situations imposed from the outside.
- Moral awareness is shaped in part from emotional reactions to early experience: empathy that leads to moral compassion, shame and guilt that lead to obedience, love and attachment to parents that lead to respect for authority.
- Relations with parents and teachers introduce children to social standards and rules, leading to respect for the social order. When teachers and parents make firm demands, accompanied by clear explanations, positive growth is most likely to follow.
- Relations with peers help children learn procedures for dealing with others. Some of these procedures carry over into adult social capabilities such as compassion, fairness, and perspective taking.
- The environment children are in will determine, in part, some of their social attitudes. If girls are expected to be caring and boys expected to participate in activities that foster justice, this is the way they will develop. Teachers can create an atmosphere in which both sexes can learn caring and justice.
- Lecturing to children about moral values has little effect. Social interactions in the classroom need to be structured so that they naturally lead to the moral values that belong to a democratic society. (pp. 117–118, adapted)

## Stress

Stressful situations for children can vary from everyday interactions with friends to coping with criminal physical abuse. At the everyday level, your role will be to provide children with techniques and attitudes that will foster their best development. In the more threatening instances, you will need to do some observation and be aware of available professional help.

### Everyday Stress

Whether you are beginning a student teaching experience or starting the school year with a new class, the single most important thing you must do is get to know each of your children as well as possible. In this way you will be able to "read" them daily, knowing, often without being told, if someone is unusually stressed. Try these ideas to start:

- When children enter in the morning, greet each one with a special hug or place your hand just below the back of the child's neck. Does the child feel unusually tense? The cause may be disharmony at home or fear of something at school. In either case, you may need to take extra steps to be sure the child's day is a happy one. If unusual tenseness is followed by abnormal behavior, provide the child with opportunities to play alone quietly or with one or two easy-going friends.

■ Learn which children thrive best on variety and which need stability and predictability. If something new and exciting has been announced for the day, the children who prefer stability may begin the day in a bad mood or perhaps act out. If you know who these children are, you can be prepared for them before there are discipline problems. Greet them at the door as described above; then, if it seems wise, send them off to a quiet corner with a book. If you do this in a nonpunitive way, the children will come to understand what is happening and will appreciate your help.

■ Some children find the constant hubbub of large group interaction quite stressful. They may simply enjoy a quiet homelife, or may have late afternoons that include several more hours of raucous playing in a day-care center. Be sure there are quiet places for them to retreat, and give them the option of going there when they seem to be out of sorts, even if it means they miss something you consider important.

■ There are shy children who may be afraid of large group experiences. Let them stay close to you until they feel brave enough to move out. If that time doesn't come, encourage them to stay away from you for short periods of time. These can grow longer as you see progress or the children feel more comfortable.

■ At the beginning of the school year there are usually a few children who cry at the start of the day. If this continues more than a few days, suggest to the parents that the children be permitted to come late if this is at all feasible. Often, it is the pressure of getting dressed and rushing through breakfast to get to school on time that is stressful for both parent and child. A more relaxed attitude may well turn off the tears.

■ Separation anxiety is sometimes felt as much by the parent as by the child. It may be wise for the parent to stay at school for a short time each day. For the child, bringing a security blanket or favorite toy can help. Some children will cry no matter what techniques you and the parents work out. In that case, keep the child close to you unless he or she absolutely refuses. While you have a responsibility to make the school experience as positive as possible, at some point each child also must accept some responsibility for coping with this difficult situation. For some children this takes a longer time.

## Coping with Unexpected Events

From a very early age, some children are confronted with events in their lives that cause unusual stress: the separation or divorce of their parents, the death of a family member or pet, the absence of a parent who is in jail, the departure of an older sibling for college. These unexpected experiences re-

## The Home-Schooled Child: A Conversation with Janet and Ehren Nagel

*Despite the widespread popularity of home school-ing many people, including educators, have no ex-perience with home-schooled children. They worry that home schooling could have adverse effects and wonder if the children can keep up with others in their age group or learn to get along with peers. In this conversation we talk to a boy who has been educated at home since kindergarten and to the mother who teaches him.*

Ehren recalls his one year in nursery school fondly. "I liked everything except naptime," he says grinning. "Recess was best." His mother is not so positive. After one year, she removed Ehren because she was dissatisfied with the school environment, especially the influence of television on the children's social interactions. "The children would go home and watch the super-hero cartoons, which I thought were not appropriate for three- and four-year-olds. Ehren felt excluded because he wasn't allowed to watch the cartoons. I real-ized that I either had to let him watch and be a part of the group or I had no business asking him to try and fit in."

Janet explored several other alternatives, but couldn't find anything satisfactory. Then, her husband "said this outrageous thing. 'Don't send him to school!' It had never occurred to me not to send him to school, yet it seemed the only choice left." Soon, they were meet-ing other home-school families, and Janet started reading books that supported their choice.

In the following years, Ehren attended only one school: a parent cooperative in a remote area of Canada where they lived when he was eight. There were six children in his class and school met just three days a week. While Ehren was more advanced than the other chil-dren in math, he was the only one who could not read. Although the teacher was sympa-thetic and supportive, giving him more ad-vanced math and not pushing the reading, Ehren still found classroom learning constrain-ing and uninteresting. He could not get used to the idea that there was a specified time to do math and other times when it could not be done, or that he should be interested in a project about Indians because the teacher wanted him to be.

"From the age of five, Ehren had a desire to read," Janet says. "He had a friend who could read and wanted to be like him." Over a span of several years Janet and Ehren tried various approaches, but their brief attempts always ended in frustration, Ehren often in tears. "I kept telling him that children all grow differ-ently, and that one day reading would be easy for him. I always reminded him of all the things he was good at."

Despite his frustration, Ehren was able to take the long view. "In some ways I've always been slow," he observes. "Sort of like Einstein!"

Janet spent a lot of time during those years reading to Ehren, often biographies. "I read him things I liked," she laughs. Eventually, at age ten, Ehren sat down one day and started to read. He compares his rather sudden emergence into literacy to an earlier learning. "When I was three I wanted to tie my shoes. My mom showed me once and I could tie my shoes. I just wanted to read and I could." Meanwhile, Ehren continued to progress rapidly in math and science, even sitting in on a community college physics course where he was quickly accepted by the other students.

Ehren's social life has never been a problem, although it has often taken some extra effort. "It was always important to Ehren to have a friend," Janet says, "and sometimes that meant we'd have to drive him 45 minutes to get him to his friend's house." Janet says that, in general, home-schooled children are different in their social skills and that the difference is positive. She finds that they are more self-confident and more comfortable with people of all ages than are children who typically are exposed primarily to a single age group at school.

Ehren explains that there are different philosophies of home schooling. "There's organic home schooling where you just let the kid do what he wants. You do the subjects he's interested in. You say, 'The kids can teach themselves because they're smart.' Then there's home schooling where you say, 'You don't know anything and we're going to teach you.'" Janet interjects that, while some have coined the term *organic learning,* she feels that *student-led learning* is a better descriptor.

If the organic or student-led approach sounds much like Rousseau's view of education, it is and Janet (who holds advanced degrees in education) has found it best suited to her son's temperament and their home learning environment. "I'm more and more impressed with Ehren and with other home schoolers . . . just how much they accomplish without formal instruction. For most of human history people didn't go to school. This makes me go back to Rousseau and his idea that formal education should really start at about age twelve. This seems to be the natural pattern for unschooled children and I wish we could incorporate some of these insights about development into our institutionalized education."

Janet feels that because Ehren was a late reader, home schooling was a major advantage for him. In a typical school he would have been the subject of teacher concern, educational pressure, and peer condescension. She is sure that learning to read in school would have been as demoralizing for Ehren as she believes it is for large numbers of normal children like her son who are wrongly treated as problem readers. Instead, Ehren is now a supremely confident thirteen-year-old, who is as accomplished academically as his schooled peers and who has plenty of friends of all ages. But most important to her is that Ehren is curious, self-motivated, and his own best teacher.

*To think about and discuss: What kinds of children do you think would benefit most from home schooling? Why do you think some research shows that home-schooled children score above average in both academic achievement and social adjustment? What qualifications do you think the parents should have? What are your own strongest arguments for and against home schooling?*

quire some response from children. You may observe one or more of these coping mechanisms:

- *Denial.* A child acts as if a problem doesn't exist.
- *Regression.* A child acts a younger age.
- *Withdrawal.* A child becomes quiet, perhaps daydreams a lot.
- *Impulsive acting out.* A child acts impulsively or flamboyantly to conceal some problem.
- *Altruism.* A child attempts to forget the problem by helping others.
- *Humor.* A child jokes about a problem as a way to express pain.
- *Suppression.* A child may cry for a time, then play as if nothing were wrong, ignoring the problem temporarily.
- *Anticipation.* A child foresees and plans for the next stressful episode, which sometimes makes it easier to face.
- *Sublimation.* A child becomes absorbed in games, sports, hobbies. (Brenner 1984, pp. 5–6, adapted)

Depending on how these coping techniques are used, they may prove helpful or injurious. Brenner (1984) suggests three general ways you can help children as they deal with these difficult times in their lives:

*Remove at least one stressor.* If a child is dealing with an unusually difficult experience, look for other ways to make classroom life a bit easier. Jeffrey presented a difficult problem for his teacher after his grandfather, a labor union leader, was brutally murdered. The six-year-old managed to see some of the details on the evening news despite his parents' protectiveness, was aware that his parents were unusually upset, and was exposed to a daily round of reporters and law officials in the house. Not surprisingly, his work at school began to suffer, although he continued to play with his friends during recess. The teacher took Jeffrey aside, explained that she understood his difficulties, and suggested that he produce only what work seemed comfortable for him for a while. After a few weeks, the teacher noticed that Jeffrey was beginning to complete more of his work, and she began to encourage him to keep up with the rest of the class. Soon, Jeffrey was participating fully, although for the entire year he never was quite himself.

*Teach new coping strategies.* If a child is using only one or two techniques, such as those listed above, help him experiment with others. Ben's father was sentenced to a prison term. Like Jeffrey, Ben heard all about it on the nightly news. Both his mother and third-grade teacher noticed that his one coping technique seemed to be altruism. Ben helped everybody do everything from morning until night, and his behavior appeared obsessive. After a three-way conference, Ben, his mother, and his teacher worked toward helping him enjoy life more. He was encouraged to participate in games and sports, and it wasn't long before Ben's smile became more frequent. His altruistic behavior continued, though, a major bonus when his father left and Ben's help was both needed and appreciated at home.

*Transfer some coping strategies to other life situations.* A child may use a strategy that usually works well but in this case is less successful. It may be best to redirect the child in some way. Susan's parents were in the midst of an unpleasant divorce, and there was much yelling and crying at home. Like Ben, Susan chose altruism as a major coping technique. Her mother reinforced this helpful behavior by frequently expressing her appreciation. Unfortunately, Susan's kindergarten friends were not so pleased with her new behavior. She managed to offer help at all the wrong times, often interrupting others' games or giving advice when none was wanted. Susan's teacher knew little of her family problem but recognized the need to redirect her behavior. She suggested that Susan take care of all the animals and plants in the classroom for an entire week. The other children were a bit bemused by this change in the usual responsibilities, but accepted it without too much question. As it turned out, a second week was necessary, but at the end of the trial period Susan was beginning to participate in classroom activities with behavior that was more the norm. (Brenner, 1984, p. 7, adapted)

Be sure that there are quiet places where young children can retreat when they feel too much stress to participate in group activities.

Abusive Stress

Unfortunately, children today may feel stress that goes beyond the expected variety or even such tragedies as divorce and death. Your observation of a child may need to go beyond your normal checking up.
Symptoms of physical abuse:

- Exhibits bruises, welts, burns, broken bones, cuts.
- Wears hats, sweaters, or other clothing to cover evidence of abuse.
- Dresses inappropriately for the weather.
- Is aggressive or withdrawn.
- Seems unable to play or be spontaneous.
- Is stuck in an early stage of emotional development.
- Has a short attention span.
- Exhibits poor memory.
- Has inept social skills.
- Is overly solicitous of parents' needs.
- Is difficult to toilet train.
- Seeks affection indiscriminately from any adult.
- Avoids being touched.
- Responds negatively to praise.

Symptoms of emotional abuse:

- Comforts self through rocking.
- Is overly passive and compliant or aggressive and defiant.
- Exhibits speech disorders.
- Rarely smiles.
- Has inept social skills.
- Is detached from parents or overly solicitous of them.
- Shows inappropriately adultlike behavior.
- Is fussy, unresponsive, irritable.
- Is watchful, yet avoids eye contact.
- Seeks approval and attention and seems to want/need more.

Symptoms of neglect:

- Is underweight.
- Self and clothing are dirty.
- Is inappropriately dressed for the weather.
- Is constantly hungry and rummages for food.
- Tires easily.
- Shows untended medical problems, such as infected wounds.
- Is apathetic.
- Is hyperactive and exhibits uncontrolled, random behavior.

■ Has no friends.
■ Doesn't turn to parents for help; parents seem unconcerned.
■ Doesn't want to go home. (Brenner 1984, pp. 98, 101, 119, adapted)

If you observe two or more of these symptoms in a child, there may be cause for concern or even alarm. Your responsibility at this point is to get immediate help from trained professionals. Talk to your supervisor, director, or principal. Be sure there is follow-through. At the same time, do not automatically assume that the child's parents are guilty of abuse. Sometimes there really is a logical explanation for suspicious behavior and appearance.

Continue to observe and to listen and to be the child's advocate at all times and under any circumstances. These are the essentials in promoting affective development.

## Extending Your Learning

1. List the characteristics of your personality as you see them. Ask a trusted friend to respond to your perception of yourself. Revise by adding or subtracting characteristics.

   Next, interview your parents and others who knew you as an infant and/or a small child. What were your personality characteristics then? How do they relate to those you have now?
2. After completing the interviews in number 1, consider which of the three major theories of development given on pages 110–115 best describes your own development. Try writing an explanation of your development from the point of view of each of the three theories.
3. Various practical suggestions have been given in this chapter for promoting social and affective development. Using the theoretical views on development, label each suggestion as an example of the psychoanalytic, the social learning, or the constructivist view. Some suggestions may lend themselves to more than one theory.

## References

Bandura, A. (1963). *Social learning and personality development.* New York: Holt, Rinehart & Winston.
———— (1969). The role of modeling processes in personality development. In D. Gelfand (ed.), *Social learning in childhood,* pp. 185–195. Belmont, CA: Brooks/Cole.
Brenner, A. (1984). *Helping children cope with stress.* Lexington, MA: Lexington Books.
Corsaro, W. (1985). *Friendship and peer culture in the early years.* Norwood, NJ: Ablex Publishing.
Damon, W. (1977). *The social world of the child.* San Francisco: Jossey-Bass.
———— (1988). *The moral child.* New York: The Free Press.
Erikson, E. (1963, first published 1950). *Childhood and society.* New York: Norton.

Gilligan, C. (1982). *In a different voice.* Cambridge, MA: Harvard University Press.

Hart, D., and Damon, W. (1985). Contrasts between understanding self and understanding others. In R. Leahy (ed.), *The Development of the self,* pp. 151–178. Orlando, FL: Academic Press.

Honig, A. (1986). Stress and coping in children. In J. McCracken (ed.), *Reducing stress in young children's lives,* pp. 142–167.

Katz, P. (1983). Developmental foundations of gender and racial attitudes. In R. Leahy (ed.), *The child's construction of social inequality.* New York: Academic Press.

Krogh, S. (1990). *The integrated early childhood curriculum.* New York: McGraw-Hill.

Piaget, J. (1965, first published 1932). *The moral judgment of the child.* New York: The Free Press.

Seefeldt, C. (1984). Growth and development—a source of stress? In E. Humphrey (ed.), *Stress in childhood,* pp. 19–46. New York: AMS Press.

Selman, R. (1980). *The growth of interpersonal understanding.* New York: Academic Press.

# 5

# Education for Cognitive Development

Effective education for young children requires a broad focus sometimes referred to as education of the whole child. This whole-child focus includes attention to cognitive development. As in the preceding chapter, we will use examples from two real-life children to guide us in our discussion of theory and practical application.

## *DEIRDRE AND SAUNDRA: TOGETHER AND APART*

*Almost without exception, Montessori schools are academically oriented. When parents choose this kind of education, they often expect their children to engage in the three Rs at an early age. Although many Montessori children do just that, the philosophy does not advocate pressuring children in this direction. Instead, opportunities are made available for children to choose when they are ready. Frequently, an admiring younger child will trail after the older ones and, without trying very hard, pick up some advanced academic skill or knowledge. This was just what happened in the case of Deirdre and Saundra.*

*The girls were sisters. Deirdre was the older and had been in school two years before Saundra joined her in the same class. Saundra, who had just turned three, happily tagged after her sister during her first days in school. Five-year-old Deirdre took pleasure in showing her little sister the projects she was working on, especially the stories she was writing and illustrating and the books she liked to read. Since Deirdre was an early reader, she spent considerable time reading aloud to her younger sister.*

*Before long, Saundra felt at home and, while she still tagged after Deirdre, began to mix with children whose interests were different from her sister's. She was soon rejecting most literature-related activities in favor of math-oriented games. By the time she was four, Saundra thought it was great fun to join with the six-year-olds in memorizing addition flash cards. (Once, when she observed this, her sister groaned, held her nose, and disappeared across the room.) It became apparent, too, that Saundra's perception of spatial relationships was quite different from her sister's. One day the older children were learning how to map the classroom and Saundra, sensing that something interesting was happening, tagged along with her own pencil and paper. Before long she had produced a map of the classroom and, although it was drawn freehand rather than measured with a ruler, the spatial relationships were almost correct. Her results, in fact, were more accurate than the measured dimensions her older sister made. On the other hand, Saundra didn't read until she was seven.*

Stop for a moment and consider whether you identify with the intellectual inclinations of Deirdre or Saundra. Chances are, you won't have much trouble deciding since most of us are well aware of our intellectual inclinations. Some people are equally at home with either math or literature, but most of us lean toward one or the other.

Of course, people differ in other areas of learning. Saundra's ability to see spatial relationships was undoubtedly connected to her early ability in drawing. She wasn't yet four years old when she drew a profile of her mother's head, complete with ear and hoop earring. On the other hand, Deirdre loved to sing and dance and would make up new words to old melodies, then act them out as she sang.

As different as these two sisters were, they were both developing quite normally. While most children don't read as early as Deirdre or learn their addition tables as early as Saundra, an academic environment such as their Montessori school can make these achievements quite normal. If their lives have not been too harsh, young children are naturally eager to learn. They develop their intellects with no awareness that learning is often regarded by older children as *work*. Montessori herself described the youngest children as having "absorbent minds," and argued that teachers must therefore choose carefully what they place in the learning environment.

Montessori's vision of cognitive development was an extraordinarily open one for her time. By providing mildly retarded children with academic materials, she was able to show that their standardized test scores could exceed those of regular schoolchildren. She later duplicated that feat with disadvantaged children from a housing project.

But Montessori's vision of cognitive development is only one of several. Her detractors argue that, although very young children are capable of academic learning, there is no reason to give them this head start; with good teaching, they can reach the same levels of proficiency if they begin academic learning at a later point. Others agree that academic learning is appropriate but that it should be more directive and less open to children's free choice.

Even among those who agree that formal academic programs are inappropriate for young children, there is disagreement concerning what types of learning experiences are most appropriate. Some thinkers believe that young children should be left totally free to explore the world around them. Others argue that adult direction in the form of activities and materials are important to young children but should be geared to the children's interests. Each group's opinions of appropriate teaching practice are based on its vision of how children develop most naturally and advantageously.

As a future teacher embarking on your own cognitive journey, you no doubt would prefer that the researchers and thinkers give you definitive answers about how children's intellects grow and about the best ways to foster this growth. Such answers, however, may never be forthcoming. The best that can be done is to present you with different views of children's cognitive growth and their implications for teaching. You can then decide for yourself which ideas seem most appropriate for your own classroom. In the next three sections we will take a look at the different visions or models of cognitive development and show how to make these models practical. In the last section, Guidelines for Teaching, we will explore pedagogical principles that can stimulate cognitive growth irrespective of one's theoretical views.

## Three Views of Children's Cognitive Development

Across the centuries there have been many views of cognitive development. Three have been particularly influential in the history of American early childhood education. You have already been introduced to these views through the family tree of early childhood education on page 00. Here, we review these theories, then take the ideas a step further.

### The Child as Blank Slate

You were introduced to this view in Chapter 1 when you met the English philosopher John Locke. You will recall that his vision of the newborn's intellect was that of a blank slate waiting to be written upon by others.

In arguing that children learn best when they enjoy their education, Locke was responding specifically to the punitive, aversive approach to teaching so popular at the time. Although Locke believed that children needed variety in their subject matter and teaching approaches, he also felt that there was a prescribed body of knowledge to be learned and that directive, didactic methods when properly used could be very effective.

Locke (1964) felt that children's minds could deal with only one thing at a time and that it was important to make their education specific and sequential.

> Great care must be taken with children to begin with that which is plain and simple and to teach them as little as can be at once and settle that well in their heads before you proceed to the next or anything new in that science. (p. 178)

Most theorists would agree with Locke that children learn best when their subject matter is plain and simple. Presenting learning in a carefully programmed and sequential manner, however, is a hallmark of this view of cognitive development. Add to this the belief that the environment is continually writing on or shaping children's minds, and we have the seventeenth-century roots of twentieth-century behaviorism.

Perhaps the most influential contributor to an updated and more scientific application of Locke's ideas has been B. F. Skinner. In writing about his experiences in shaping behavior through manipulating the environment, Skin-

The "blank slate" view of learning emphasizes direct teacher led lessons where children supposedly absorb carefully structured lessons prepared for them by their teachers.

ner (1968) stated, "Comparable results have been obtained with pigeons, rats, dogs, monkeys, human children, and psychotic subjects" (p. 14). It was Skinner's belief that a broad variety of animals and humans develop according to the influences of their environments. No doubt he would have agreed with John B. Watson before him that he could be given

> a dozen healthy infants, well-formed, and my own special world to bring them up in, and I'll guarantee to take any one at random and train him to become any kind of specialist I might select—doctor, lawyer, artist, merchant-chief, and, yes beggarman and thief, regardless of his talents, penchants, tendencies, abilities, vocations, and the race of his ancestors. (quoted in Weber 1984, p. 77)

With Locke, Skinner preferred the idea of planned learning that follows a simple-to-complex sequence. Most important of all, he argued for carefully structured reinforcements during learning. He observed that teachers do reinforce children's efforts, but that too often their reinforcement is negative or aversive. Skinner argued instead for positive reinforcements and said that, for learning to be efficient, these must come almost immediately after the child engages in a learning activity. He observed, of course, that no single teacher can reinforce every child's learning within seconds of each effort. His solution was the invention of various teaching machines that, in many respects, pre-dated today's computer education.

Skinner proposed teaching machines that could be programmed sequentially for any subject area. However, he thought it especially useful for teaching mathematics, which he regarded as "one of the drill subjects." While his proposals focused on elementary and secondary education, computer programs have since been developed for even younger children. We will discuss this development in Chapter 7.

It is important to realize that the blank slate view of children's cognitive development places great reliance on the teacher, whether a parent, classroom teacher, or computer. Learning is controlled externally by the transmitting authority rather than by the learner. In Locke's time, this made great sense because of the generally accepted view that a static world produced a fixed body of knowledge that could be discovered and transmitted to the learner. For Skinner, the concept of externally directed learning also made sense, because he saw that much of a child's learning was made up of drills and the attainment of correct answers.

To behaviorists, learning involves modifying the child's behavior through carefully sequenced, simple-to-complex learning experiences that are reinforced positively until a targeted learning objective is reached. A good number of early childhood programs have been established that apply such views, many of which were begun during the early years of Head Start. This approach found much success with disadvantaged children. Lay-Dopyera and Dopyera (1990) provide a good summary of the attributes of behaviorist early education:

- There is a focus on very specific objectives.
- Subjects are broken into pieces and carefully sequenced before being transmitted to children.
- The teacher's role is to direct, correct, and reinforce desired behavior.
- The teacher shapes the learner by providing reinforcements.
- Children are moved as quickly as possible from working with real materials to abstract learning through language. (pp. 165–168, adapted)

Educators who subscribe to this view of cognitive development see themselves as directly responsible for the specific learning that children engage in. Detractors of this view consider such teaching to be manipulative and insensitive to children's feelings and attitudes about learning. It should be noted, however, that Skinner was quite concerned about children's feelings and attitudes. He rejected punishment because of "the negative emotions that are stirred up," and created his teaching machines so that learning would be emotionally positive as well as successful. Despite Skinner's concern, most behaviorists focus on behavior changes in the child, rather than on underlying feelings. To most behaviorists, underlying emotions can never be fully understood anyway.

## The Child as Unfolding Flower

The beginnings of this view were established by the writings of Jean Jacques Rousseau, whose ideas gave rise to the familiar argument about nature versus nurture. The nurture side of this educational battle is represented by Locke's vision of the child's mind as a blank slate that is filled (nurtured) by the environment. Rousseau's view of the child as naturally good, needing to be given freedom to develop as nature intended, assigns him to the nature side.

In this century, the primary standard bearer for the side of nature has been Arnold Gesell (1943), whom you also met in Chapter 1. Arguing for this position, he said:

> [Behaviorism] explains, of course, how totalitarian systems of education and government can mold their subjects to a pre-conceived model. But it does not sufficiently explain how this molding process also fails, and why an inexorable spirit of liberty defies it. [In the future] there will . . . be profounder spiritual insights, but even these must reckon with the laws and limitations of human nature, as embodied in infants and children. (pp. 358–359)

Anyone on the nature side of this argument views the child as developing in a biologically prescribed way. Gesell and his colleagues spent years observing infants and children in order to piece together a timetable of developmental changes and how they take place. These observations were presented to the public as indisputable facts, and texts for early childhood teachers were filled with charts, tables, and descriptions of "normal" development. You will recall, however, that Gesell established his norms based on observations of the rather privileged children attending the child study center at Yale University.

Today, there remain many followers of Gesell's theory, often referred to as *maturationism.* Their thinking about these "factual" stages, however, has been modified. While they still view children as maturing in predictable ways, most maturationists now view stage theory as "providing only a metaphor, a way to think about human growth, with the user involved in the determination of how far to accept analogies" (Weber, 1984, p. 171).

## The Child as Self-Builder

Although the first two views of the child are opposed in important ways, they are also similar in that cognitive development is viewed as passive. That is, children, as blank slates, simply receive the messages written upon them by their environment; or, as flowers, they receive environmental stimulation and then unfold in the way that nature has prescribed for them. In this third view, however, the child actively uses the input of the environment to construct his or her own intellect. This view has been known both as *interactionism* and, more recently, as *constructivism*.

Looking back once more at Chapter 1, we see that the roots of this view are in the work of Jean Piaget, whose theories emerged only in this century. Piaget did not reject the views of behaviorism or maturationism; instead, he argued that they didn't go far enough. He agreed that both the environment and biology affect the child's growth, but he also believed that the child's makeup includes the freedom to seek interaction with the environment and thereby to take an active part in constructing his or her own intellect. Piaget's theory, like Gesell's, is a stage theory, but is much less rigid and allows more latitude within each stage of development.

There are four major stages of growth in Piaget's theory, beginning at birth and extending through adolescence. As you read the following descriptions, keep in mind that a child's intelligence undergoes continuous change and that elements of more than one stage can be present at any time.

- *Sensorimotor period* (birth to eighteen months or two years): The physical senses and motor activities are the basis of the infant's cognitive development. Reflex actions, such as sucking and crying, begin in the stage, but, as the child matures, intentional behaviors and imitative behavior support learning.
- *Preoperational period* (two to seven or eight years): A major attribute of this stage is the child's ability to use one thing to symbolize another. A child may hold a block to his face to imitate his father shaving or pretend that a pile of pebbles will serve as birdseed. Preoperational children, while making increasing sense of their world, are limited in their understanding by what they can experience with their senses. They center their attention on just one thing at a time, making it difficult for them to make comparisons between objects or ideas or to understand that others may not view things as they do.
- *Concrete operational period* (seven or eight to eleven or twelve years): During this stage, children learn to decenter, making it possible to work with more than one variable at a time. They become more logical in their reasoning. Still, they need concrete objects to manipulate during much of their learning, and true abstract thinking is not yet possible.
- *Formal operational period* (eleven years to adulthood): The thinker at this stage can form abstract ideas, and think both logically and reflectively. While this stage begins at about age eleven, it can extend into adulthood. Perhaps you have had experiences in which it was difficult for you to grasp a new concept because it was too abstract. Possibly it made sense to you when something concrete was added to the explanation. When this happened, you were thinking at a concrete operational level; most likely you were later able to think about the idea more abstractly as a demonstration of formal operations.

Both the "unfolding flower" (maturationist) and the "self builder" (constructivist) view of learning emphasize child-directed activities. However, in the constructivist view of development children's active exploration of their environment is seen much more as a stimulus to development, whereas in the maturationist view, exploration merely enhances development.

While this summary of the Piagetian stages has been brief, it is important for you to grasp these theories. In subsequent sections of this chapter, and in future chapters as well, we will continue to refer to them when suggesting ways to make age-appropriate decisions for working with children. Piaget's research in cognitive development has been influential in recent decades in the curriculum of early childhood programs, the psychological approaches to dealing with young children, and the position statements taken by associations dedicated to the well-being of children.

## A Developmental-Interaction Approach

Many students, and teachers, too, would prefer not to align themselves with just one of these three views of cognitive development. After giving each its due, they would like to combine the best of each view into a new, unified whole. In recent years, an increasing number of early childhood thinkers have been attempting to do this in a theoretically sound way. The various stage theories you have read about here and in Chapter 1, with their qualitative shifts between each stage and their invariant sequences, are all respected. However, many scholars now see interaction happening on two different fronts. First, the child interacts with the environment; second, both the cognitive and affective phases of development interact with each other. The term *developmental-interaction* was given to this eclectic view in the early 1970s by Edna Shapiro and Barbara Biber. Weber (1984) has pointed out that "many theoretical and practical questions remain in attempting to integrate theories" (p. 185). In the coming years you probably will observe that much writing and thinking is heading in this direction.

## Aspects of Cognitive Development

In the previous sections we considered theories of cognition as they relate to wholistic development. To obtain a more complete understanding of how children's intellects develop, we must now look at specific aspects of cognitive development. Some of these pieces relate to children's language acquisition, others to mathematical understanding, and still others to the rest of the school curriculum.

### Language Learning

Depending on your view of the child (as blank slate, biologically programmed flower, or self-builder), you will see the impetus for language development differently. Can the child develop language solely as a result of environmental stimulus, or solely from genetic inheritance, or does the child construct his or her own knowledge? Although theorists differ in these views, we can make a number of observations that transcend theory and provide practical information for us as caregivers and teachers.

#### Spoken Language

Infants begin early on in their development to experiment with a variety of sounds. By the time they are ten or twelve weeks old they can be heard experimenting with varying levels of volume and pitch. In their first year of life, babies are already learning to listen to and imitate the people around them, signifying the beginning of their language education. By the end of the first year the first word is usually uttered, expanding to a vocabulary of twenty to fifty words by eighteen months. More than half of those words are nouns, but they provide the material for the infant's first combinations of words. By age four, children may have vocabularies that exceed 2,000 words. Such a rapid increase is made possible in part because of their increasing ability to use one thing to symbolize another, a feature of Piaget's preoperational period. By age five or six, children intuitively understand most of the basic rules of grammar, although it may take the rest of the elementary school years to formalize this knowledge and to learn the more complex structures. In fact, most people never master all of the rules of spoken or written language.

### Written Language

In the early years, drawing and writing are closely related. An infant who can hold a crayon enjoys making marks wherever they may land, a stage referred to as "uncontrolled scribbling." Most preschool children have moved to "controlled scribbling" in which they understand the relationship of crayon to paper and the concept that their markings actually have meaning. They eventually give these scribbles names, usually after the drawing is completed (Brittain, 1979). As soon as they begin to make representational drawings, children are also capable of forming letters, although they may have no idea what the letters mean. In the early stages of writing, children's letters may meander across the page just as their drawings do. However, by the end of kindergarten, more visual structure and appropriate directionality are often possible.

### Print Awareness

Before they can read, children must first learn the function of print and have a basic understanding of the form print takes (Mason, 1981). Adults reading stories to young children assume that the children look at the pictures and know that those other little marks are what tell the story. The children, though, may believe that it's possible to read the pictures and totally ignore the accompanying print. In two different studies, up to 20 percent of five-year-olds could not understand the purpose of print (Kontos, 1986).

## Mathematics Learning

Much of the research related to specific aspects of the development of mathematical thinking has been done by Piaget and his associates. Some of their discoveries follow.

### Conservation

The principle of conservation requires an understanding that a set of objects remains unchanged in its amount or quantity no matter how differently the individual parts may be arranged. A child who does not understand the idea of conservation may think, for example, that a long row of seven pennies has more money in it than a shorter row of ten pennies. Or that two equal amounts of clay, squashed into different shapes, become unequal in quantity. Children are not capable of understanding conservation until they reach the concrete operational stage, and they cannot easily understand mathematical concepts without it.

## *Still Learning from Children: A Conversation with Kathleen Holz*

*In 1914 a young woman, whose experience as an education student and teacher had convinced her that traditional education was in great need of reform, founded a small kindergarten in the Greenwich Village section of New York. Caroline Pratt's City and Country School eventually grew in both size and fame as John Dewey himself praised the school for its progressive education. Today Pratt's book,* I Learn from Children *is still published and the school is alive and well, serving neighborhood children from ages two to thirteen. This conversation is with its current principal.*

After her graduation from the well-regarded Bank Street College, Kathleen Holz was excited to be accepted as a teacher at the venerable City and Country School. For fifteen years she has worked with children between the ages of four and six, pausing only for a three-year teaching stint in Spain. Now, as principal of the school, Kathleen works side-by-side with teachers to ensure that the school's educational philosophy remains intact while adjustments are made for modern changes. Like Pratt and Dewey before them, the teachers remain committed to giving the children true experiential learning based on play. Now, however, issues of technology must also be considered. "Although it's a new age," Kathleen says, "children still need to learn from firsthand experiences. They want to know where bread comes from, why the men on the corner are digging up pipes, how the banks work. . . . But today we have TV to contend with." City and Country teachers deal with this pervasive intruder by disallowing TV play at school. "We try to get the children to act upon experiences that are real."

Kathleen admits that a TV orientation often competes with the teachers' commitment, particularly when children appear to be using materials such as blocks in a realistic way and the teachers suspect that what is in their minds is their latest favorite TV show.

A reality-based curriculum has always been the tradition of the school. In the early days, children could be taken on walks to the nearby warehouse district, through the meatpacking plant, over to the Hudson River to watch banana boats load and unload, to the blacksmith's, the cobbler's, and so on. Today, the neighborhood, Kathleen says, is "much more sanitized. It's not a busy port anymore and the stores and factories are wary to have us visit because of litigation." Still, the teachers continually work at finding places that show children the inner workings of the city that will provide inspiration for block building, story writing, and other experiences.

Reality-based literature about the here and now is an important part of the curriculum at

City and Country. In the storytimes that occur at least twice a day, "We don't read literature that's too scary or fantasy-like. We don't read fairy tales. We feel that they're not comforting and reassuring. At home it's easier to talk about concerns, but in a group it's a very difficult thing to handle. In groups, fairy tales only tend to excite or overstimulate in a way that's not positive."

Participation in real-world activities takes place right from the beginning. The three-year-olds, for example, are introduced to woodworking, complete with hammers, saws, and nails. The school's philosophy is to teach children the proper way to use materials, to set realistic limits, and then to let children experiment and learn by doing. In regard to woodworking, Kathleen explains that, "Once the proper way to use the hammer and nails is taught, there are no assigned projects until needed for group work such as building bridges for a city or mailboxes on a house." The same is true of other materials. "Clay, paper and crayons, paint and easel are always there. There's never a predetermined project to make."

Perhaps the best known learning material of the school is the huge collection of blocks. It was Caroline Pratt who invented the unit blocks observed in virtually every early childhood center today, and at City and Country they are used as the core learning material all the way through the second grade. In addition to the unit blocks there are cars, trucks, animals, and people, all of basic design and simple colors. Children supplement these with the cubic centimeter blocks which might represent food, dishes, plants, or whatever imagination decrees them to be. In the two-, three-, and four-year-old classrooms, there is no housekeeping corner, but dolls and their accessories are kept close to the blocks to be used as needed. Blocks are even the central material of the playgrounds where they are large and painted, and supplemented with crates and boards. With these basic materials, children create their own structures rather than play on manufactured equipment.

Caroline Pratt referred to her educational endeavor as an "experiment" and Kathleen, who still refers to it as such, explains why she has remained faithful to the school for so many years. "I approve of what we do here and I want to keep the experiment alive. There's much that's written now that corroborates what we have always done." For example, "The work of Piaget has borne out many of the ideas that Caroline Pratt had." Having an underlying philosophy is important to the continuation of the school, Kathleen maintains. "The teachers talk about what they do and they respect each other's ideas. There's a sense of continuity making each year build on itself. Also, children are discussed with respect and with an understanding of what is developmentally appropriate."

Like any private school, City and Country has periodic financial problems and the staff, including Kathleen, earn less than they would in a public school. Why does she stay? Kathleen explains simply, "This place gets into your system. I really believe in this kind of education."

*To think about and discuss: Does this school's philosophy that "play is the work of the child" coincide with your own philosophy of learning? Does it go too far? Not far enough?*

### Classification

Classification is an ability that begins in infancy. A baby who can differentiate her mother's voice from her father's has begun to classify. A child learning to talk may learn to say "man" and then apply the word to every person around. To an adult, this appears to be an erroneous label, but for the child it is beginning classification and the more complex reality will soon be understood. Young children can classify on just one level at a time, while concrete operational children can do so in more complex ways. For example, a preschooler might group a collection of plastic dinosaurs by color. The older child might do this first, then divide them according to size.

### Seriation

Seriation involves ordering objects according to some dimension of size or weight. Preoperational children have difficulty doing this, although they can usually identify the largest and the smallest items. Even early con-

Very young children can classify according to only one characteristic (size, shape, color, etc.) at a time, while slightly older children can classify according to two or more of these characteristics at the same time.

crete operational children must often rely on trial and error to order objects correctly.

### Number

Although many preschool children can count aloud or sing counting rhymes or even read some numbers, they may not necessarily understand the concept of number. Understanding number requires counting objects correctly without skipping over some or otherwise becoming confused. It includes aligning objects in a one-to-one correspondence or realizing that regrouping some objects does not change the total number of them. This aspect of development is achieved as children move into the concrete operational period.

## Other Types of Learning

While the following aspects of cognitive development may at times be related to language or mathematics, they are most often thought of as pertaining to other areas of learning, such as science, social studies, and art.

### Causality

Preoperational children lack the ability to understand cause and effect in a logical way. They may believe that objects in nature act in certain ways because they choose to. (The rain falls because it wants to make plants grow. The sun shines so the picnic won't be ruined.) There is much that is magical to the young child, and magic is frequently given as an explanation for cause-and-effect relationships. For concrete operational children, more logical explanations are usually plausible, particularly if they have concrete materials to work with. Ideas that are too confusing and abstract, however, may cause children in the primary grades to revert to more magical explanations.

### Transformation

Young children have trouble understanding transformations and may resort to fanciful explanations. Unless a child can actually see batter become a cake or a caterpillar become a butterfly, the transformation will make no sense. Throughout elementary school it is important that children have an opportunity to witness such changes firsthand and slowly enough so that they can begin to make sense of them.

### Space Concepts

There is a classic Piagetian task that describes the slow unfoldment of children's understanding of space. On a large board is placed a configuration of several papier-mâché mountains. Cards providing a view of the mountains from each of the four sides are also provided, along with a small doll that will be moved to each of the four sides in turn. A child is then seated on one side of the board and given the cards. As the doll is moved to each side of the board, facing the mountains, the child is asked to choose the card that shows what the doll is now seeing. Preoperational children have difficulty "seeing" the mountains from any position other than their own. It may be the middle of elementary school before some children are able to choose the appropriate card, realizing that the doll is seeing something different.

### Time Concepts

Although toddlers begin to develop a sense of time, particularly as it relates to their own daily schedules, children are about five years old before they begin to develop the adult sense of time. The sequence of learning for most children seems to be the concept of day, followed by week, month, and year, and finally short time periods such as minutes and hours. It is usually at about age eight when children can look at the future apart from their everyday lives (Bauer, 1979).

## Applying the Theoretical Views

The three views of children's cognitive development presented above are more than theoretical positions. They can be made quite practical if you use them as underlying philosophies for your classroom decisions. Here are a few examples to get you started.

### The Child as Blank Slate

Since teaching is usually directive, you should break intended learning into manageable segments. More complex ideas and abilities should build on simpler, more basic ones. For example, you might find that the "three-period lesson," which is employed in Montessori schools to teach new concepts, is useful.

Let's assume that you have a child of another culture in your class who is just beginning to learn English. You place in front of her three small objects that she can name in her own language but not in yours.

In the third period, the child must have internalized the names and be able to say them herself. You point to an object and say, "What is this?" If, at this point, the child is hesitant or uncertain, cut back to the second period. If she still has a problem, cut back to the first.

The child will know when she is doing well, because you can move on to having her identify other objects. It is important that you not disparage the child's attempts. Keep your voice and body language pleasant. Remember, positive reinforcement works much better than negative reinforcement.

## The Child as Flower

According to this view, it is important that you keep the child's readiness level in mind, never introducing a new concept or skill too early. If you err on one side or the other, it is better to wait too long than to introduce something too early. By following this advice, you will rarely need to rely on reinforcement to keep a child learning, since children who are developmentally ready to learn will usually be motivated as well. Readiness, in this view, is one of the most important considerations when planning for teaching.

If you subscribe to this view, you will want to test and observe your children's developmental levels. The Gesell Institute publishes an assortment of books that provide normative tables for you to use. For example, *The Gesell Institute's Child from One to Six* (Ames et al., 1979) suggests that at age twenty-four months the child enjoys the process of painting, but not the end result. Further, there is social enjoyment in painting on the same paper with another child. Since a two-year-old is likely to paint out of bounds "on table, easel, floor, own hands, other children" (p. 125), plenty of supervision would be in order. Such information tells you that it is unrealistic to expect representative pictures from this age child and that painting will be a popular but messy activity.

## The Child as Builder

According to the constructivist view, providing a stimulating environment and acting as a facilitator are two of your major roles as a teacher. To the greatest extent possible, learning will come from real experiences in the children's lives. Within that context, you can suggest questions that need to be answered and materials and opportunities to answer them at a developmentally appropriate level.

For example, daily snacktime offers a recurring opportunity to solve such problems as counting out the right number of crackers so that each person has enough but not too many. Voting on which of two songs to sing provides an opportunity to count the number in favor of each one and to decide which group is larger. Assigning one child to hand out two crayons to each person in the group gives real-life practice in division. An even number of crayons could be provided, or an odd number could be given, requiring the child to determine the remainder. As a facilitating teacher, you must be aware of the general developmental levels of your children and of their specific needs at the time.

## Developmental-Interaction View

This view is still in an early stage of development. Submitting it to a test of practicality, we might say that it is important first to have a general awareness of your children's stages. Then, since children learn by interacting with the environment, your job is to create the best possible learning environment.

Additionally, since cognitive and affective development occur together, you should keep both in mind when planning activities.

One area of the curriculum that offers rich opportunities for this view is environmental studies. A "litter walk" through a nearby park, for example, can sensitize the children to the esthetic consequences of people's careless treatment of their trash. Collecting the litter and bringing it back to the classroom allows for the scientific analysis of the trash in terms of its environmental consequences. For instance, the children, under your direction, can conduct experiments to determine when, or if, various materials decompose. The children's affective response to this cognitive information will depend on their developmental stage. If they are in the primary grades, they may well be inspired to begin a schoolwide program to combat litter in the park.

## Guidelines for Teaching

Chapters 10 through 16 provide an in-depth look at how to foster children's cognitive development in specific curriculum areas. In this section, we present some general principles for you to think about in your role as a facilitating teacher or caregiver. Where appropriate, we cite Deirdre and Saundra as examples.

### Act as a Role Model

Deirdre's and Saundra's teacher took her responsibility as role model quite seriously. Although most of the children were too young to be reading, in the adult sense of the word, time was set aside each day for everyone, including herself, to read silently. This teacher remembered her mother reading in bed each afternoon while she and her brother took their naps. Early on she mimicked her mother by nestling in bed with books, although she couldn't yet read. The teacher felt that this early attraction to books was partly responsible for her continued enjoyment of reading in adulthood. Thus, in her class, she would make a great show of settling down in a mood of contentment, answering children's questions about the plot and characters of whatever she was reading.

If you hope to pass on the excitement of learning, then you must show that you are enthusiastically involved in discovering new things. Young children learn very little from our moralistic lectures and much from the example we set. One quality that is especially important to foster in young children is *curiosity*. A healthy child is born with this trait and loses it only when the environment destroys it in some way. Children will know that it is all right to be curious when you demonstrate that it is appropriate. Some examples:

■ If you're not sure what a word means, look it up. Be sure to show any interested children how you use the dictionary, and communicate to them

One of the major goals of teachers is to encourage children's sense of curiosity. A healthy child is born with this trait and only loses it when the environment squashes it in some way.

that adults don't know what every word means and must continue learning new ones.

■ If you can't answer a child's question, don't be afraid to admit it. Instead, say that you don't know but would be interested in finding out. Then, the two of you (and any interested observers) should search out the answer together. It doesn't matter, of course, if the child can read or not.

■ If you have become interested in a new area of learning, share it with the class. The concept of lifelong learning may well be new to the children, and it is never too early to find out about it.

Another quality that children need to learn about is diligence in the face of learning experiences that may sometimes be difficult. While we want children to enjoy learning, it is also important that they know the rather different joy that comes from working through a complex or arduous task victoriously. Some suggestions:

■ If you have a silent reading time and the book you are reading is very long, the children will probably notice this and comment on it. You might say something like, "Yes, it's taking me a very long time to read this book, but it's a really wonderful book, so I don't mind it at all."

■ If you are working on the classroom environment in some way, let the children know how much effort you are putting into it. For example, if there is a new bulletin board going up you could tell them, "Last night I spent two hours working on the border, and I got very tired of it. But now that it's up, I'm glad I did it. It will be a pretty background for the good work you children will put up there."

As you model learning behavior, keep this consideration in mind: Children often don't know you're modeling unless you tell them that you are. While some children will notice you reading and deduce that it would also be fun for them, others may assume that it's something they can't do until they've broken the code. If you want to be sure that children get the picture, you may have to draw it clearly for them.

### Provide Developmentally Appropriate Practice

This is a phrase you will come across several times throughout this text, particularly in Chapter 7. It first gained wide usage in 1986 when the National Association for the Education of Young Children published a position statement on learning for young children. The prime instigator of their action was that, "[i]n recent years, a trend toward increased emphasis on formal instruction in academic skills has emerged in early childhood programs. This trend toward formal academic instruction for younger children is based on misconceptions about early learning. . . ." (p. 4). Some of their examples of developmentally appropriate learning activities for different ages groups are:

■ *Infants and toddlers.* These youngest children learn "through their senses . . . by physically moving around, and through social interaction" (p. 9). Infants who aren't yet mobile learn much when adults carry them around to observe the world, talk and sing with them, and provide objects for them to manipulate. Mobile infants and toddlers learn through their increasing grasp of language, and through toys and materials.
■ *Three-, four-, and five-year-olds.* Children change rapidly during these years, and NAEYC suggests approaches for each age that are slightly different. For three-year-olds, learning "should emphasize language, activity, and movement, with major emphasis on large muscle activity" (p. 9). Four-year-olds need more variety in their activities and can begin to enjoy such small motor activities as manipulating scissors and cooking. In teaching language to children, particularly five-year-olds, you should offer practice in a meaningful context rather than focus on isolated skills. For example, kindergarteners usually will find that tracing over the letters *c-a-t* is intensely boring and tiring. They more likely will be excited by finding a cat on their walk outside, then coming back and dictating stories about it. As they illustrate their experience, some children may attempt to write the

word *cat* on their drawings, or choose other words that interest them more.
- *Six-, seven-, and eight-year-olds.* Fatiguing, mechanical seatwork is developmentally inappropriate for most children in this age group. Instead, cognitive growth can best be fostered through hands-on activity and experimentation. Children at this age are newly interested in games and rules and can learn much by partaking in them.

## Ask What Is Worth Knowing

Many teachers neglect to ask themselves this all-important question: What should I teach that is most worth knowing? Instead, their choices are dictated by materials that are easily available, by the pressures put on them by parents and administrators, or by the commercially canned curriculum that is provided by the school. Somehow, the children are lost in the shuffle.

Saundra's teacher remembers the child's first day in school. Barely three years old, excited and scared, Saundra was ready to soak in any knowledge that was given to her. The teacher had met many three-year-olds before, but somehow Saundra seemed unique. It suddenly occurred to her that the responsibility of choosing what Saundra would learn was enormous; never again in her school life would this child be as open to learning.

Although the setting of this experience was a Montessori school, with its highly prescribed curriculum, the teacher was well aware of the need to ask herself: What is worth knowing? It wasn't long before she noted Saundra's precocious artistic talent, something that she might never have discovered if she had followed the narrowest approach to Montessori education, which includes little, if any, free art experience.

There are three stages at which you should ask yourself what children should know. The first occurs before you even begin teaching. As you study this text and take your other education courses, you should begin to formulate your own philosophy of education, including what knowledge you feel is most worthwhile. As you seek employment, you should again consider the question. When you visit schools where you might work, ask yourself if the available materials, curriculum philosophy, and administrative staff would be supportive of your goals. Ask questions that will help you arrive at your answer. The third stage occurs when you teach. This stage should never end. You should apply the question to individual children, as Saundra's teacher did with her, and you should ask it as you choose activities and materials for the entire class.

One group of early childhood writers summarized their view on this topic when they stated, quite eloquently, "When you choose what you will teach, we urge you to look at what is worth knowing, what we all need to know to help us become more human and to help our world survive. We believe that to attempt to achieve less gives children less than they need and less than they deserve" (Feeney et al., 1983).

### Relate Learning Activities to Real Life

One afternoon, just as the children were leaving for home, the first snow-flakes began to fall. Deirdre said, "I remember seeing snow once when I was little." A few feet away, Saundra held out her hand, stared at the white, puffy spot in the middle of her palm, and asked, "What's that?!" As soon as all the children had departed, their teacher began making plans for the next day. They lived in an area where snow was a major event, and the weather report predicted several inches for the coming night. The teacher realized that this new development would be of intense interest to the children all the next day and that it would be important for them to spend much of their learning time outdoors. She felt it worth her time, then, when she called every parent that night to request that they send their children to school the next day with appropriate clothing.

While some of what the teacher planned was designed to let the children freely enjoy the somewhat unfamiliar substance, there were other activities that led to cognitive learning. Further, her teaching methods were still in line with the Montessori philosophy of the school. This integration of learning objectives with children's real-life interests is an important goal. Whether you teach in a school with a prescribed curriculum, such as this teacher did, or have total freedom to choose what children learn, you should try to relate your lessons to real life.

Some of the children's interests and concerns will remain consistent over time, while others, such as the snow experience, may be brief. Part of your task is to decide how much time should be invested in projects and activities that are intensely interesting at the moment as opposed to other, more permanent topics. For example, Saundra's and Deirdre's teacher planned just one day of snow activities, being relatively sure that the weather would warm up soon afterward. But she made that one day an intensely snow-related one, in which the children were permitted to indulge their excitement for the entire time. Other topics could be less intensely covered but continue on for days or weeks.

What is important is to observe children as they play, talk to them about their lives whenever you can, and then make curricular decisions with this information in mind.

### Provide Well-Rounded Learning for Both Sexes

It has been noted that boys outperform girls in mathematics and the sciences, while girls perform better in reading and writing. This observation has validity throughout people's lives. Much research has been devoted to finding explanations for this phenomenon, and it may well be that a large portion of the responsibility rests with the early childhood teacher or caregiver.

The occasion for assigning this responsibility may be something as simple as free play. In the toddler room, materials are usually gender free, designed to provide plenty of manipulative experience and to promote motor skills and eye-hand coordination. Further, these toys usually can be used either indoors or outdoors without making special adjustments.

As children get older, toys become more gender specific. This happens at about age three. Selma Greenberg (1990), who researches early childhood curriculum, has hypothesized that it is at this point that negative changes in learning begin. She asks, "Does scientific illiteracy begin in the doll corner?" and answers in the affirmative. "Boys' toys," she says, "promote scientific and technological understanding" (p. 193). For example, cars and trucks provide opportunities to learn about motion and direction, blocks develop ideas about balance, and batteries and science kits teach about electricity and chemical properties. Since boys' toys take children outdoors much of the time, there are opportunities to explore and experiment with "space, motion, and direction on land, on sea, and in the air" (p. 193).

Girls' toys provide quite different experiences and skills. Playing with dolls and other small toys as well as cutting and pasting activities provides girls with an advantage in small muscle development. Since such activities are geared more toward the indoors, girls are generally around adults more than boys. These experiences—playing indoors with small toys and with adults present—provide girls with a distinct advantage when they first arrive in school. It is usually the boys who initially have trouble adjusting to the physical confinement of school and the paper-and-pencil orientation of much of schoolwork.

Yet, Greenberg (1990) argues, girls are also disadvantaged in that they come to school with less background to

> experiment, explore, and experience the physical forces of both nature and machines. Girls are denied the fun and delight of spatial and physical freedom. They have little opportunity to develop the "sense of" or "feel for" natural and mechanical actions, reactions, and interactions which make success possible in later science, mathematics, and technology experiences. (p. 194)

It is ironic that girls are most often viewed as having no learning deficits when they come to school, while boys are thought to be at risk. Thus, girls are less likely to receive the help they need to balance out their earlier lack of "boys' toys" experience. Greenberg argues that it is important that all children receive the full range of early learning experiences, but that it is especially crucial for girls. If they are guided toward more large-muscle, exploratory play in the early years, girls are more likely to be enthusiastic about science and technology in the formal school years.

## Provide Both Indoor and Outdoor Learning

In the early years of this century, two sisters in England, Rachel and Margaret McMillan, observed that many, even most, children were too unhealthy

When children are about three years old, their toys begin to be gender specific. Boys begin to play with trucks, balls, airplanes, etc., and girls with dolls. This is believed to contribute to the tendency of boys to outpace girls gradually in subjects like math and science, which involve the physical manipulation and exploration of objects.

to learn efficiently. Believing that more time spent in the fresh air would lead to healthier bodies, and thus increased learning, they founded the Open-Air Nursery School. Their concept of nurturing preschool-aged children was soon picked up abroad and nursery schools began to flourish.

While the general health of children is much improved today, it is still true that time spent outdoors contributes to children's health and, therefore, their capacity to learn. Unfortunately, many modern-day teachers have forgotten what the McMillan sisters demonstrated almost a century ago. Particularly in the primary grades, children are often deprived of time spent outdoors whether for play or for learning. The reasoning seems to be that there is so much to learn and so little classroom time to teach and test it, that outdoor time must be cut to a minimum. Yet one long-term study in France showed that letting children play outdoors for long periods of time actually raised academic scores (Bailey, 1976). In this ten-year study, children had just four hours of academics a day, while the rest of the day was turned over to games, gymnastics, swimming, and recreation. In the late afternoon there was art, music, and supervised study. With nearly one-third of their school day devoted to physical education in some form, the children actually did better on academic tests than their counterparts in traditional classrooms. The results were later replicated in studies conducted in Belgium and Japan. As you might suspect, the experimental children's health, fitness, discipline, and enthusiasm were also superior. While this study took place in the elementary grades and the McMillan sisters' school was for preschool children, the tie between the two situations should not be overlooked. Being outdoors really does improve children's capacity to learn.

Remember, too, the previous discussion of outdoor versus indoor learning. When children play outdoors, they learn concepts associated with the sciences, math, and technology; when they play indoors, they focus more on verbal skills. A balance is needed between the two.

## Remember Affect and Values

Many years ago, Jean Piaget concluded that cognitive growth could take place without a corresponding amount of moral development. However, he did not find the reverse to be true. He found that moral development could not take place easily unless there was corresponding cognitive development. In more recent years, proponents of the developmental-interaction approach have argued that cognitive and affective development are more closely related than even Piaget realized. There is an interdependence of such developmental processes as "acquiring and ordering information, judging, reasoning, problem solving, using systems of symbols . . ." and "the development of self-esteem and a sense of identity, internalization of impulse control, capacity for autonomous response, [and] relatedness to other people" (Weber, 1984, p. 186).

According to developmental-interactionists, this "integration of functioning" should be reflected in what we do with young children. They suggest that early childhood programs should "focus on process, on providing the experiences that make it possible for children to try out, shift backward as well as forward, to create where necessary the opportunities for . . . integration . . . in both the cognitive and emotional realms" (p. 187). Some suggestions for doing this include

- Interweaving work and play in the curriculum.
- Relating to children as individuals.
- Valuing individual differences in children.
- Permitting children to make decisions about their own learning.
- Creating more collective than competitive learning experiences.
- Making values education an integrated part of the curriculum.
- Realizing the need to rethink continually the learning experience.

Feelings, attitudes, and values are always a part of the cognitive experience, no matter how we may try to separate them. Deirdre and Saundra demonstrated this when they responded in quite different ways to the same experiences. Deirdre, for example, was uninterested in the math games that

Saundra loved. The low value she placed on them was no doubt due to the difficulties she had in understanding math concepts. In short, her negative attitude toward math had a cognitive basis. Additionally, Deirdre may have been somewhat jealous of her younger sister's mathematical abilities. Consequently, she may have convinced herself that she simply didn't like those games and then decided to choose activities that were more difficult for Saundra.

Each child you teach will bring a complex set of emotions and values that will influence his or her cognitive learning. As you recognize and support the individuality of the children and permit them to direct much of their own play and learning experiences, you will foster more integrated and complete development.

## Support Creativity

Just when educators from the United States began studying the "superior" education system in Japan, the Japanese became dissatisfied with their schools and began to look at American teaching methods. While the Japanese educators were pleased that their children's test scores were the highest in the world, they were concerned that there was so little creativity permitted in their schools. They felt that creativity must be cultivated if their country was to remain competitive in commerce. Americans have long recognized this need, but for us there has been another consideration as well. People who live in a democratic society must rely on individual initiative and creativity rather than government agencies to direct their lives.

Americans, however, have also worried that their education provides too little room for children to be creative. As one book on creativity advises parents, "Don't expect a lot of help from your local school system as you try to help your child improve his creative skills. Schools have to set up systems that make things easier—they do this by making all children adhere to easily managed daily routines and rules" (Belliston and Belliston, 1982, p. 2). Traditionally, the upper grades have caused the most concern in this regard, but in recent years academic pressures have threatened the existence of creativity as far down as the nursery school.

In the preschool years children are naturally creative as they try to make sense of the very large world around them. Once they reach the primary grades, however, they have learned enough that they no longer have the same compelling need to be inventive just to survive. The teacher's role in these two early stages is somewhat different. In the earliest years, we need to support children's natural creativity, protecting them from the academic pressures that so often are forced upon them. In the primary years, we need to support children's need to get things "right," while continuing to nurture their creative abilities.

Doris Shallcross (1981), a researcher in creativity learning, suggests several ways in which teachers can build a climate for creative behavior. She begins by pointing out some misconceptions regarding the development of creativity.

- Creativity does not mean there is chaos in the classroom.
- Students are not given total freedom to express themselves in any way they like.
- The teacher does not abdicate her role as the person in charge.

Instead, she says, teachers must always remember that they are responsible for the physical and psychological safety of their children and that children will be most creative if there is sufficient structure to make them feel secure. Shallcross (1981) offers the following suggestions for setting the stage for creative learning:

- Arrange the classroom so that there are different kinds of spaces for different kinds of activities and pursuits.
- Provide a safe place for each child to keep some personal belongings and tools to be used in creative projects.
- Provide a variety of stimuli to account for individual differences in creativity.
- Create an intellectual environment that challenges but doesn't overwhelm children. Their earliest experiences should have built-in success, with challenge being introduced gradually.
- Establish an atmosphere of trust by repeatedly proving your trustworthiness to children. Let them know you support their creative attempts, and don't ridicule them. (pp. 7–20, adapted)

In *How to Raise a More Creative Child* (Belliston and Belliston, 1982), the authors provide a number of suggestions that can be adapted easily to the early childhood setting. The following guidelines, for example, will help nurture creativity in either home or school.

- Support children's play. Be playful yourself.
- Don't try to force creativity on demand. Let it emerge naturally.
- A supply of "junk" enhances creativity. Keep a collection handy for inspirational use.
- Look at problems from a positive view and teach children to do the same. If you hear a child say, "This doesn't work!" use the opportunity to encourage such follow-up questions as, "How can I change it for the better?"
- If you don't know the answer to a child's question, research the solution together.
- Foster a questioning attitude, particularly by using an encouraging tone of voice.
- Ask children open-ended questions, rather than those that can be answered with a simple yes or no.

- Explore nature with the children. As the authors advise, "The more familiar your child can become with the world around him, the more data he'll have stored in his brain to use creatively."
- Learn to differentiate between creativity and naughtiness. Sometimes children may behave in certain ways because they are trying to learn or to solve a problem. They should be allowed to explore and make mistakes.
- Never ridicule. Look for the good. Praise freely but honestly. Be interested. (pp. 3–70, adapted)

These guidelines for teaching and the applications of theory that preceded them may seem overwhelming to you if you have not yet had any teaching experience. Yes, there is much to remember. It is wise, however, to develop your skills gradually. Take time to experiment with an idea or two, then reflect on your experiences before trying others. This step-by-step approach to learning about teaching will help ensure your success.

## Extending Your Learning

1. Make a list of academic experiences you can recall from your own schooling through the third grade. Be as specific as possible. Next, indicate whether each experience was primarily positive or negative. Finally, where possible, deduce the philosophy of learning (see pages 140–146) your teacher must have preferred for this experience to have taken place.

   Share the results in a small group. Try to conclude which modes of teaching were most positive for your group as early learners.
2. Form a group of three people, each of you taking the part of a teacher trained in one of the three major views of cognitive development. Debate your positions in terms of their scientific correctness and application to the classroom.
3. Observe two or three teachers present lessons or interact with a child or group of children. Try to determine which philosophy of cognitive development is best represented by their behavior.
4. Write a short essay describing and detailing ways in which your knowledge of child development can and should influence you as a teacher or caregiver.

## References

Ames, L., Gillespie, C., Haines, J., and Ilg, F. (1979). *The Gesell Institute's child from one to six: Evaluating the behavior of the preschool child.* New York: Harper & Row.

Bailey, D. (1976). The growing child and the need for physical activity. In J. Albinson and G. Andrew, *The child in sport and physical activity,* pp. 81–96. Baltimore: University Press.

Bauer, D. (1979). As children see it. In K. Yamamoto (ed.), *Children in time and space.* New York: Teachers College Press.

Brittain, L. (1979). *Creativity, art and the young child.* New York: Macmillan.

Belliston, L., and Belliston, M. (1982). *How to raise a more creative child.* Allen, TX: Argus Communications.

Feeney, S., Christensen, D., and Moravcik, E. (1983). *Who am I in the lives of children?* Columbus, OH: Merrill.

Greenberg, S. (1990). Does scientific illiteracy begin in the doll corner? In J. McKee and K. Paciorek, *Early childhood education 90/91.* Guilford, CN: Dushkin Publishing.

Kontos, S. (1986). Research in review. What preschool children know about reading and how they learn it. *Young Children* 42(1):58–66.

Lay-Dopyera, M., and Dopyera, J. (1990). *Becoming a teacher of young children.* New York: McGraw-Hill.

Locke, J. (1964, first published 1693). *Some thoughts concerning education,* ed. F. W. Garforth. Woodbury, NY: Barron's Educational Series.

Mason, M. (1981). From print to sound: Reading ability and order information. *Journal of Experimental Psychology: Human Perception and Performance* 7(3):580–591.

National Association for the Education of Young Children (1986). Position statement on developmentally appropriate practice in early childhood programs serving children from birth through age 8. *Young Children* 41(6):4–19.

Shallcross, D. (1981). *Teaching creative behavior.* Englewood Cliffs, NJ: Prentice-Hall.

Skinner, B. (1968). *The technology of teaching.* New York: Appleton-Century-Crofts.

Weber, E. (1984). *Ideas influencing early childhood education.* New York: Teachers College Press.

# Diversity Among Children

# 6

When you finish reading this chapter, you should be able to

- Identify and understand the characteristics of gifted children and children with special needs.
- Understand the challenges faced by children from minority groups.
- Recognize the similarities and differences in development for boys and girls.
- Begin creating an environment and curricula appropriate for diverse groups and types of children.
- Have an increased awareness of the complex role a teacher must play when dealing with diverse populations of children.

As you think about the chapter on your own, you should be able to

- Increase your awareness of your own feelings about various groups of people.
- Begin to deal with any negative attitudes you uncover and plan strategies for working through them.

# THE NEW REALITIES OF TEACHING

*The education committee of the state legislature was holding a public hearing on future directions for teacher education. Presentations were lively, important people shared ideas, and, despite disagreements, progress was made. One concern that everyone mentioned was the need to prepare teachers to deal with increasingly diverse populations. As one principal noted, "This year our soccer team had twelve languages represented!"*

*Then a kindergarten teacher spoke. "I know that some legislators think there should be fewer courses in teacher education," she said. "I would like to argue for more. Let me tell you what it's like to teach today."*

*"I have twenty-eight children. More than half come from single-parent homes or live with their grandparents or other relatives, and those relatives can change frequently. About twenty of the children qualify for the free lunch program. I have four who were crack babies, and their behavior is unpredictable. I never know when they'll start hitting or kicking or screaming, and I don't know what to do with them. How can I? The doctors don't even know. The children come from many cultural backgrounds and several nationalities. Four of them began the year speaking no English at all, and their parents don't speak much either. At the same time, I have four children who came to school with some knowledge of reading and will probably qualify for the gifted program next year. This is what today's teachers face. This is what they must be prepared for."*

*Until then, most of the discussion on dealing with diversity had been hypothetical and very general. The silence that followed the kindergarten teacher's remarks attested to the shock of today's reality that was suddenly felt by the participants.*

Not every kindergarten looks like this one, of course, but a growing number across the country do. It is the reality that you must be prepared for because there is a new "minority group" emerging: teachers who work in uncomplicated schools where almost everyone can learn with relative ease, where most of the parents still live together, where almost everyone is of the same race and socioeconomic status as the teacher, and where every child speaks English as a first language.

Perhaps you will find yourself a member of this minority group, but chances are good that you won't. The purpose of this chapter is to give you information about some of the diverse situations you may encounter and to help you think more deeply about your own feelings and capabilities for dealing with them. You are strongly encouraged to try the suggested activities at the end of the chapter, or to adapt them to your own situation. This should help you discover more about yourself as well as about the complexities of teaching today's children.

There are as many forms of diversity as there are human beings, and it is important that we as teachers treat children as the individuals that they are. At the same time, we can learn more about individual children's traits if we know something about the attributes of the groups they represent. In this chapter we will focus on four groups: gifted children, children with special needs, children from minority cultures, and children as members of their own gender. To begin, we will discuss the children who are most likely to be neglected at every stage of their education: those who seem to be always at the head of the class without ever trying very hard.

## The Gifted Child

When a teacher has a class like the one described above, it is tempting to assume that the children who appear to be gifted or talented can be left to fend for themselves. They can be depended on to keep up the class average on standardized tests, even without much attention being paid them. They are generally self-starters who don't need much instruction to begin new projects or learn to use new materials. They can be a delight to have in class because of their capabilities, and it is easy to take them for granted. But there are dangers in this attitude, as one young boy's parents and school principal found out.

*When Kenny was six, his family moved to the East Coast. For three years he had attended a preschool that encouraged gifted children to develop their interests and skills. In this nourishing environment, Kenny learned to read before he was five and enjoyed the challenges of adding, subtracting, multiplying, and dividing. He had an intense interest in what he called "sinetific spearments" and liked to draw pictures of the results.*

*When the family arrived in their new town in late August, Kenny's mother enrolled him in the small neighborhood elementary school. Kenny was a sociable child and had no difficulty making friends in his first-grade class. Nevertheless, it was only a short time before he began to complain of stomach pains in the morning and begged not to go to school. His mother then learned that he was not permitted to read* Hardy Boys *books, which his father had handed down to him and which he proudly took to school. Instead, he was forced to sit with the rest of the class drawing single letters in the air and on paper. The same was true with arithmetic. Rather than assigning Kenny something that would challenge him, the teacher insisted that he join the class in practicing writing single-digit numbers. When his mother questioned her, the teacher argued, quite rightly, that Kenny's handwriting was almost illegible and that she felt it important that he improve it before going on to other challenges. Shortly afterward, the principal sat in*

*on the class and observed the misery that was Kenny's day. After a confer-*
*ence with his parents, the principal moved Kenny to the second grade.*

*A promotion of this sort has always been controversial. Kenny's parents*
*feared that he might be a social misfit and that he would never succeed in*
*using his rather considerable athletic talents. But Kenny's delight in moving*
*to the new class soon put everyone's fears to rest. Since the second-grade*
*teacher had once been placed a grade ahead himself, he understood much of*
*what Kenny felt and needed. In a short time, Kenny had become a class*
*leader, both socially and academically. He could run faster than all the chil-*
*dren in his class, with the exception of one girl, and he soon declared he*
*was "in love" with her. The joy that was Kenny's that year carried him*
*through a third- and fourth-grade experience that was, once again, rigid*
*and uninspiring.*

Kenny's story is told here to demonstrate the importance of providing
gifted children with the school challenges that they crave and need. Without
a caring mother, alert principal, and knowledgeable teacher, Kenny might
well have turned off to school or developed a serious illness based on his
stomach discomfort. He might have ceased to produce quality academic
work, finally emerging from high school unable to enter a university despite
his giftedness. It is possible that he would have dropped out of high school
altogether. Scenarios like this are not unusual for gifted children, and society
loses much valuable talent as a result. As Merle Karnes et al. (1985) have
said,

> The result for the gifted child when home and school fail to foster pro-
> ductive habits and attitudes is underachievement, which not only de-
> prives the child of full development but robs the community of their
> most valuable resource, human talent. (p. 204)

James Gallagher adds,

> By the time the gifted underachiever has reached the middle elementary
> grades, his underachievement is a genuine life style, and major educa-
> tional readjustments or counseling over an extended period of time are
> often needed to change it. (quoted in Karnes, 1985, p. 204)

In 1991, Karnes and Johnson looked at more than twenty years of research on giftedness and summarized the current approach to providing appropriate education for gifted young children. The authors concluded that
there are few advocates for these children; that there has been no commitment to their early identification or the development of programs for them;
that teachers and parents alike are largely unaware of the importance of early
identification and special programming; that there is almost no teacher train-

ing for this group of children; that financial resources are needed for research, screening and assessment, and program development; and, finally, that special procedures for identifying handicapped and low-income gifted children are lacking and needed. It seems that, while other areas of special education have attracted attention and funding, gifted education, particularly for younger children, has been largely ignored.

Given the potential for positive individual growth and contribution to the community that the gifted child offers, and the potential for negative development that can come from ignoring this child, it should be apparent that caregivers and teachers need to put forth their best effort to provide this child with the best possible experience. Before discussing ways of doing this, it is important to define giftedness.

## Defining and Identifying Giftedness

What constitutes a gifted child? Is it simply being able to do better than others in school? A high IQ? In actuality, there are many facets to giftedness, and no single child demonstrates them all. A long-standing definition of giftedness covers six areas: intellectual ability, specific academic aptitude, creative or productive thinking, visual or performing arts talent, leadership ability or advanced social and emotional development, and psychomotor ability (Karnes and Johnson, 1991). Nevertheless, the focus in most educational settings is on intellectual giftedness. Kenny's early capacities for reading and arithmetic showed him to be intellectually gifted. At the same time, despite his early stomach discomfort, Kenny was emotionally mature and socially adept. He proved to be a natural leader. (At a parent conference his second-grade teacher described, with some amusement, the recent interest that about 25 percent of the class had taken in reading the encyclopedia. "Come on, guys," Kenny would say, "let's go find something to read in the encyclopedia!" and a group of friends would follow along with enthusiasm.)

Observers of gifted children point out that what these children are capable of doing is not what is so extraordinary; it is the age at which these capabilities appear. Characteristics that the alert teacher should look for include:

- A thirst for knowledge. Gifted children always want to know more and want to tell people everything they know.
- A need to feel a sense of progress as they learn.
- Single-minded devotion when learning a specific topic. Their concentration, even obsession, with a line of learning may make them hard to live with.
- An ability to make linkages between all kinds of things.
- Sensitivity to values that may make them precociously interested in fairness, honesty, truth, and justice. (Gallagher, 1986, p. 3, adapted)

Among the most characteristic behaviors of intellectually gifted learners are a deep sense of curiosity, intense focus on their current line of learning, the ability to make linkages between ideas, and a deep sense of morality and justice.

Other behaviors that might characterize some gifted children but that shouldn't be expected at all times include

- Spontaneously elaborating on new experiences.
- Making innovative or interesting patterns with blocks and art materials.
- Being unusually adept at doing new or difficult puzzles.
- Having a sense of humor in their conversation.
- Showing understanding of abstract concepts such as death, time, or fairness.
- Mastering a new concept, learning a foreign language, or singing a new song correctly faster than other children their age.
- Using an identifiable reasoning process when explaining why something occurs or how it can be used.
- Using advanced vocabulary and sophisticated words correctly and in context.
- Using their insatiable curiosity in their struggle to learn how things function.
- Constantly asking questions, enough to try the adult's patience.
- Having a heightened sensitivity to physical and emotional factors and to the people and circumstances around them.

- Having an extraordinary memory and attention span.
- Integrating adult themes into their dramatic play.
- As preschool children, showing the kind of understanding of game rules ordinarily found in elementary children. (Adapted from Hanninen, 1985, p. 194; Parke and Ness, 1988, p. 196; Wright, 1990, p. 272)

While encouragement of intellectual skills and talent is most critical for young children, it is also possible to identify and encourage leadership skills. Children who are gifted in this area typically show a social sensitivity well beyond that of their more egocentric peers. Some of the skills and situations that suggest leadership behavior in preschool children are

- High verbal abilities as measured on standardized tests.
- Ability to communicate ideas and feelings.
- Ability to give directions.
- Heightened sensitivity to the needs and concerns of other children.
- Being frequently sought out by other children for companionship, ideas, and help in making decisions.
- Easy interaction with their peers.
- Easy adaptation to new situations. (Hensel, 1991, p. 5–6)

Identifying gifted children can present a challenge (Gunderson et al., 1987). This may be especially true when dealing with a gifted child who has a learning disability (LD). A child in this category will have above-average intellectual potential accompanied by a basic psychological disorder that causes learning problems. Possible disorders might be seen in one or more of the following areas: oral expression, written expression, reading skills, listening or reading comprehension, or mathematics. When given IQ tests, gifted LD children often show depressed scores because of their disabilities, yet they may perform quite well on a verbal subtest. Their approach to learning is often reflective, slow, even plodding, which can be one cause of their poor test performance. Written compositions may be poor despite their insightful contributions to class discussions. Their usual disorganization affects their time management, study habits, and test-taking ability. It is easy for a teacher to mistake a gifted LD child's behavior for laziness or lack of motivation.

Since gifted LD children tend to expect a lot from themselves and to be upset when they can't perform as well as they had hoped, this lack of support from the teacher can further add to their frustration and self-criticism. Their frustration may cause them to give up on school entirely, to feel that they are failures, or to become socially isolated. Early identification can lead to future successes, but it takes some alertness on the part of the teacher. If you observe a child sending any of the mixed messages just described, it may be worthwhile for you to insist upon the kind of in-depth testing that could identify problems hiding an above-average talent for learning.

In summary, we can say that the earlier a gifted child is identified and provided for, the greater the chances are that this child will achieve his or her full potential in school (Delp, 1980). Arguing that identification should ideally occur before age six, Karnes et al. (1985) say that, "Motivation to learn, persistence at task, interpersonal skills, fundamental values, standards of quality, and self-concept are all strongly influenced by significant adults in the child's early years" (p. 204).

## Being a Teacher of the Gifted

Special training for working with gifted young children is quite rare. Enhancing some of your qualities, both personal and professional, and developing appropriate skills can certainly help. In one study (Whitlock and DuCette, 1989), "outstanding" teachers of gifted young children were compared with "average" ones and some important characteristics were identified. Outstanding teachers were:

- *Enthusiastic.* They were enthusiastic about their jobs, took pride in their children's accomplishments, were cheerful even in adversity, but were disturbed when a child was experiencing academic or behavioral problems.
- *Flexible.* These teachers adapted plans and lessons to follow up on children's interests, allowed children to develop their own style of work and to do assignments in their own way, and changed their approach to problem solving when situations demanded it.
- *Self-confident.* They had a positive but balanced view of their own capabilities, were willing to have their programs observed and evaluated, stated their views forcefully when opposed, and were willing to reinterpret policies or rules when it seemed to be in the best interests of the children.
- *Empathic.* They showed awareness of individual children's concerns and feelings as well as those of their parents, and they helped individual children with their personal problems.
- *Open.* The teachers involved children in decision making, were willing to be corrected by a child, and were concerned about treating children fairly.
- *Motivating.* They looked for creative ways to motivate their students. For instance, they would ask a series of questions to lead a child to alternative approaches to a problem, insist that children make their own choices about how to complete assignments or projects, and provide challenging (but realistic) activities.
- *Facilitating.* They were conscious of being facilitators rather than directive teachers. They did this by seeking out other people, information, or materials as resources; or they designed projects to follow up on children's emerging interests.

While such qualities as enthusiasm, self-confidence, and flexibility are desirable in any teacher, the ways in which they are expressed with gifted children may be just slightly different. For example, employing frequent changes in teaching approaches might be overwhelming for some children, or insisting that nongifted children design their own projects might be more than they can handle.

## Choosing and Developing Curricula

Unless you become a specialist in gifted education, there probably will be just a few children in your classroom who can be described as gifted. In many ways they will be similar to the other children and may not be gifted in all subjects or areas of development. This will offer many opportunities for them to be part of the larger group or to participate in cross-ability groupings. Normal interaction with many kinds of children is just as important to the development of gifted children as it is to other children. At the same time, it is important to provide some specialized experiences.

Theory, research, and practice all indicate that there are two underlying principles pertaining to the development of curriculum and teaching strategies for the gifted (Maker, 1986). The first is that the curriculum needs to be different qualitatively, not just extra work to fill up time. Many teachers, observing a gifted child finishing an assignment quickly, simply give him or her more of the same. While this may be an appropriate time filler, it can deaden a young child's interest in learning. The second principle is that the curriculum needs to build on the unique qualities of the gifted child. This means, for example, that some learning may be more abstract, complex, and comprehensive than it is for other children. Karnes et al. (1985, p. 205) suggest some ways to make the curriculum for gifted children a differentiated one:

- Encourage children to pursue a chosen interest in depth.
- Let learning be based on interest and needs rather than on the usual sequence of instruction.
- Let activities be more complex and abstract.
- Provide greater flexibility in the use of materials, time, and resources.
- Have high expectations for independence and persistence.
- Provide more opportunities for leadership.
- Encourage much creative and productive thinking.
- Put more emphasis on interpreting the behavior and feelings of self and others.

As you choose among these suggestions, keep in mind the age of the children. For example, abstract thinking may be seen in some gifted children in kindergarten and primary grades, but it will be quite rare in much younger children. Keep in mind, too, that a child may be gifted in some areas but may need more assistance in others. Finally, it is important to remember that, although gifted children usually work best when allowed to be independent, they should not be forgotten and ignored but given the attention they deserve.

In the next section you will read about a group of children which includes a variety of sub-groups. They will claim much more of your time and attention because of one characteristic: they all share the special needs they have that can prevent them from participating fully in their learning.

## The Young Child with Special Needs

Ever since Public Law 94-142, the Education for All Handicapped Children Act, was passed in 1975, more and more children with special needs have entered the mainstream of education. This act owes its heritage to the 1954 judicial decision known as *Brown v. Topeka Board of Education,* in which the Supreme Court declared that all children should have equal access to public education and that keeping one group separate did not provide equality. While intended to integrate schools along racial lines, this decision had far-reaching effects. It was finally argued that children with various handicaps—intellectual, social, physical, emotional—should also have equal access to what was called "the least restrictive environment." More and more, particularly in the case of younger children, the least restrictive environment has come to mean the regular classroom.

Coupled with this trend is another of equal importance to centers and schools: the growing number of children born with serious problems. Increased abuse of drugs and alcohol, a growth in the number of single-parent families, widespread poverty, and homelessness have all contributed to the increased numbers of children with special problems and needs. These two trends taken together can almost guarantee that you will face unusual teaching challenges in the years ahead.

The act of placing exceptional children with their normal peers is called *mainstreaming* because it takes children who would otherwise spend their developing years on the fringes of schooling right into the mainstream of normal learning activity. When PL 94-142 was first passed and it became apparent that mainstreaming was a coming reality, many people, ordinary citizens and education professionals alike, were fearful. They held "negative images of 'dumping,' 'sink or swim,' or of denying special needs of a handicapped child" (Safford and Rosen, 1981, p. 2). But more than a decade of mainstreaming and related research have shown that placing special needs children in regular classrooms has, instead, brought many benefits (Guralnick, 1990; Odom and McEvoy, 1990).

PL 94-142, passed in 1975, mandated that children with various types of handicaps be "mainstreamed" into regular classrooms for as much of the school day as possible. Participation in regular classroom life was felt to be "less restrictive" than segregation into special education classrooms.

For the child with special needs these benefits can include an opportunity to choose friends from all abilities, to develop skills more fully, to learn from nonhandicapped peers, to become self-reliant, and to be inspired by more advanced examples. At the same time, children from the regular classroom can learn to accept and be comfortable with those who are different, to understand that special needs children can also have talents, to be helpful and caring, and to know when and how to help (Hayden et al., undated, Morgan and York, 1981).

In 1986, the Federal Preschool Program and Early Intervention Program Act was passed. As Public Law 99-457, it has extended rights and services to special needs infants and preschool children. Day care, home-based care, parent and family training, medical services, and counseling are now all available.

Children may function inadequately because of genetic defects, emotional trauma, or chemical impurities absorbed from the mother before birth. Following are some of the causes for problems that you may observe in your work with children.

### Developmental Delays

For some children, cognitive, social, and physical development does not happen according to the expected schedule. While these children develop in the same sequence of stages as their normal peers, they do so at a slower rate and at a lower qualitative level. Their play can be less mature and more repetitive. Sometimes a developmental delay in one domain can affect performance in another. For example, a child may have the motor ability but not the cognitive ability to understand a task such as jumping rope or riding a tricycle. At other times, teacher emphasis on overcoming one weakness may lead to another. For example, children may become clumsy and weak, lack endurance, or be poorly coordinated if they are kept at their desks for long hours to compensate for cognitive slowness. Or they may not fully develop social skills when they are harshly punished, overprotected, neglected, or always given help—all fairly commonplace approaches to dealing with special needs children.

### Speech, Language, or Hearing Impairments

By age three a child's speech should be intelligible even to strangers, and by age eight articulation should be error-free. If a child doesn't fall within these guidelines, a speech disorder should be suspected.

Language disorders are of three types. The first is inner language, in which children have trouble figuring out their environment, which then causes them to use objects incorrectly during play or to not understand simple cause and effect. The second is receptive language, in which children have difficulty understanding spoken language at their developmental level. They may seem unwilling to obey requests or follow directions when, in fact, they can't relate spoken language to themselves or their experience. The third type of language disorder is expressive and is usually the most obvious. Children with this problem have a hard time communicating ideas or feelings, their sentence structure and vocabulary may be limited, or they may continually speak in very brief sentence segments.

A child who doesn't talk by age two or respond to loud sounds, or who watches other children for clues when the teacher gives directions, may well have a hearing problem. Hearing impairments are usually treatable medically if they involve the outer or middle ear. Impairment of the inner ear or auditory nerve is usually not treatable and is probably permanent. Sometimes a hearing aid may be of help (Patterson and Wright, 1990).

### Visual Impairments

Visual impairment may be partial or total. Because it is more easily noticed in infancy than other impairments, diagnosis has usually taken place before the child enters a center or school. If diagnosis has been accompanied by stimulating experiences, interactions with others, and opportunities for sensory exploration, the child may have developed well physically and socially. Often, however, this is not the case, and you may find that these other areas are underdeveloped.

### Attention-Deficit Disorder

Until quite recently, this disorder was labeled hyperactivity, but research has shown that, at times, an inactive distractibility is also a manifestation of the same problem. Classroom symptoms can include difficulty in sitting, calling out at inappropriate times, frequent interrupting, excessive talking, distraction, disorganization, lack of fine motor skills, and short attention span. Because they have difficulty controlling their behavior, ADD children also have a hard time making and keeping friends. Boys are six to nine times more likely to have ADD than girls, and the symptoms may not show up until school age, thus making the teacher an important part in identifying the problem (Buchoff, 1990). Many children with ADD are on medication, which reduces the symptoms but doesn't eliminate them entirely.

### Crack Cocaine Children

Children who have been exposed in the womb to crack cocaine are estimated to constitute 1 to 2 percent of all babies born nationwide. Research into the long-term effects is only beginning as the first wave of children makes its way through the elementary grades. For the first three months of their lives, these children are irritable, sleep with difficulty, and are hard to keep calm. Quite a few have birth defects, and they are more likely to die from sudden infant death syndrome (SIDS). From the very beginning they tend to withdraw from intimacy and stimulation, and this trait stays with them into the school years. Because they are difficult to deal with, they are likely to be passed around from adult to adult, thus depriving them of the continuity of affection they need in order to begin the hard task of forming attachments.

As they move into the preschool years, crack children "have a low tolerance for frustration . . . have difficulty structuring information, and . . . [are] easily overwhelmed by information coming in" (Rist, 1990, p. 5). Although these children are not brain damaged, they seem not to know what to do when placed in a free play situation. They may simply bat toys around aimlessly. Working with them in a highly structured, supportive environment with a low child/teacher ratio is important and should begin as early as possible. If identification and support are not given before kindergarten, the school years promise to be chaotic.

## Being a Teacher of Children with Special Needs

The handicapping conditions described in the previous sections vary widely, but they have one thing in common: the children who possess them need special attention in order to learn successfully. If the condition has been identified before the child comes to you, and you are within a school system, you can expect to be part of a team made up of an in-school specialist, one or both parents, and perhaps the child. Together you will design an individualized education program (IEP) that is tailored to meet the child's special needs. If the condition has been diagnosed and you are not part of a school system, help may be available from specialists within local agencies. Either way, you should not expect to shoulder the decision making without help from experts.

Since many disabilities are not diagnosed until children are in preschool, kindergarten, or even the primary grades, teachers have some responsibility for identification. This requires good observational skills and a thorough knowledge of child development. Once you suspect that a child has a problem, you should put in motion the testing process. If the child passes the tests but still exhibits unusual difficulties, you have a responsibility to continue searching for answers. It is important to keep in mind that large numbers of children are tested and the testing period is relatively short. You, on the other hand, are with the children all day over extended periods of time. Further, there are some handicapping conditions that may show up only intermittently and may not be evident during the testing time. If you suspect that testing has not shown the real picture, you should speak with the director, principal, or parents to arrange further observation and testing.

What children need most of all from you as their teacher is acceptance and a willingness to care for them at their individual level of development.

## Teaching Approaches for Children with Special Needs

Positive acceptance of special needs children involves more than attitude. Acceptance must be very explicitly modeled for the other children in the class. You can do this by being honest and open about disabilities, forthrightly answering questions the children may have. In these discussions, stress similarities that handicapped children have with others in the class. During any discussions and interactions be aware of the children's tone of voice and body language to ensure that they communicate acceptance.

You will need to adapt the classroom environment to accommodate special needs children. Hazards must be removed and materials placed in reachable settings. Independence is encouraged when a child with a disability can easily reach cubbies and coat hooks or a child in a wheelchair can negotiate the furniture placement or a blind child knows exactly where to sit at circle time. Where these arrangements are impossible, the rest of the children need to be trained to help as needed.

For many disabilities, it may be useful to encourage imitation. One way this can be done is to have duplicate materials and let two children work or play together. One of the children should be competent with the use of the materials so that the disabled child can imitate more easily. Imitations of verbal and motor responses can also be encouraged (Hanline, 1985).

In all cases, teaching children the way gifted and talented children are taught—by building on their strengths—can foster the greatest amount of success (Walters, 1990). All children, including special needs children, must be engaged in academically stimulating activities and discussions and must be expected to produce high-quality work and learn to their fullest capabilities.

A number of researchers (Buchoff, 1990; Morgan and York, 1981; Rist, 1990; Schneekloth, 1989; Weiner, 1990) have provided suggestions for dealing with specific disabilities. You will find that some of these ideas are useful with various handicapping conditions and with the class as a whole.

### Cognitive Disabilities

Interaction with younger children who are at the same developmental level is helpful for these children. So is teacher modeling. When you give directions, be sure they are brief and consistent and that you make eye contact with the child. Patiently provide repetition in many learning activities. Focus on successes, not failures, and give plenty of praise for participation and effort.

### Physical Disabilities

Avoid keeping the child in one place for more than twenty or thirty minutes. Be sure that the child can see what is necessary from any position he or she is placed. Allow extra space around the child for movement. Keep changes of clothing on hand.

### Speech or Language Disabilities

Avoid correcting mistakes; rather, restate the communication correctly. Allow the child plenty of time to talk. When you listen, show interest and make eye contact. Singing, fingerplays, poems, and chants should be provided daily.

### Hearing Disabilities

When you talk with the child, make eye contact, use the child's name, and speak clearly at a moderate speed. Avoid both mumbling and yelling. Be sure the child is seated for good visibility of every activity and teach the child to do this on her own.

Since many childhood disabilities are not diagnosed prior to entering school and since formal testing often fails to detect disabilities that occur only intermittently, it is often the classroom teacher, who lives with a child the entire school day, who first observes a child's special needs.

## Visual Disabilities

Take time when the child first arrives to orient him or her to the entire environment. Make sure the child knows where tables, desks, and the restroom are located. Move anything hazardous and work with the rest of the class to make sure that dropped articles are picked up before they can be tripped over. Help the child learn about real-life objects by providing objects to manipulate, such as locks and keys, parts that hinge or open and shut, and safe kitchen utensils. Help the child's physical development by designating an area that is safe enough to allow carefree movement. A large sandbox from which sharp-edged toys have been removed is ideal. Give the child plenty of activities that involve all the other senses and that include movement. When a large group activity is about to be changed, announce it clearly.

## Attention-Deficit Disorder

Keep the child away from distracting noises and active areas, such as near the doorway or the pencil sharpener. To promote organization, limit the number and type of materials that are available at any one time. Older children can make charts that list organizational activities to remember, such as cleaning up the desk before recess or stacking books to get ready for a library visit. Similarly, the daily schedule can be posted right on the child's desk. If a routine is to be disrupted, give the child plenty of advance notice and perhaps write down the information. When giving directions, do so clearly and make eye contact. Keep directions simple and give just one command at a time. Prepare the child for transitions to new activities by announcing them a few minutes ahead of time. Create a private signal that communicates, "You are not on task. It's time to get back to work." If this doesn't work and you must tell the child directly, look the child in the eye and say so quietly and privately. (ADD children's behavior will often get worse if you correct them publicly.) Realize that misbehavior comes from the disorder and not from willful disobedience. Ask the child to state what rule was broken. Be sure that any consequences are provided immediately; otherwise, they will not be effective.

### Crack Cocaine Children

Keep schedules and routines as stable as possible. If changes must be made, give advance warning. Try to keep the day's schedule smooth rather than fragmented and cut down on interruptions. Be flexible about the environment, removing materials if they are overstimulating and adding them when there is a need for enrichment. Make transition times orderly and help the child understand that there is a beginning, middle, and end to them. Keep the child away from distracting noises. The stability that is important for the ADD child is also important for the crack cocaine child. In as many ways as possible make the day less stressful and more predictable.

The children we have discussed in this section have disabilities that make them educationally at risk. There are other children who may also be at risk for reasons having to do with culture.

## The Young Child from a Minority Race or Culture

As an undergraduate, the author of this text majored in history and the social sciences, and also earned a certificate to teach high school. Armed with this totally inappropriate background, she took a job as a second-grade teacher in an international school in Japan. Here, in brief, is her story, complete with a lesson or two learned the hard way.

*Seven or eight nationalities were represented in my class, although Japanese and American children made up the majority. I soon noticed some cultural differences in the way different nationalities approached the concept of Go-*

*ing to School. The Americans sauntered in loudly, obviously having chosen their own, frequently mismatched, clothing; they might be nervous about beginning a new year with a new teacher, but they covered it up with bois- terous bravado. The Japanese children slipped in quietly, carrying briefcases and somehow looking as if they were in uniform even though the school had none; any nervousness they felt was covered by a façade of serious intent. The Chinese entered with sufficient seriousness to let me know they under- stood the importance of school, but with enough humor and flash to commu- nicate that they weren't particularly overwhelmed by the prospect. One In- dian child skulked in, looking a bit ashamed and hungry; another, looking better fed, observed the first child with some condescension and arrogance. He lost little time in announcing that she was inferior, both because of her family background and her gender. I soon learned that it would be impossi- ble to view children solely by their individual traits when much of their per- sonalities were formed by the cultures from which they came.*

*In the early 1960s there was little written about teaching in multicul- tural classrooms, and I made my way through trial and error. At some point I realized that the many groups could be unified only if we learned to sup- port each other and be happy in each other's successes. If a new child en- tered the class with little English or Japanese (the two languages of the school), linguistic "experts" were assigned the responsibility of working with the child whenever possible. The children took to the idea with enthusiasm. On occasion they even turned their recess time into a language lab complete with drill sessions and reports to me of progress made. I then carried this design into the rest of the curriculum, with the intent that every single child must have an opportunity to be an expert at something.*

*Despite the trial-and-error approach (or perhaps because of it), I learned some valuable lessons at the international school that I could take with me to later teaching experiences in the United States:*

1. It is as important to take a sociological view of children as it is to take a psychological one. The former provides the context for learning more about the child's culture and the latter about the child's individuality. Both are critical to fully understanding a child.
2. There are as many differences within single cultures as there are between them. This understanding is crucial if we are to observe children individually. This was true, for example, in the case of the two Indian children. They could more easily relate to children of foreign countries than they could to each other. It is essential for teachers not to lump together everyone from one nationality.

3. The multicultural classroom can become a mini-community if uni-fying activities and behaviors are fostered. A new classroom cul-ture is created that provides a safe haven for children who are just beginning to learn the complexities of living in a multicultural world.
4. Peer teaching is one powerful way to begin creating a classroom learning community. It requires that every child be recognized as having some expertise to teach others. Conversely, all children need to be aware that they can learn something from others, even from those they may think of as inferior in some way.

This experience from the early 1960s was considered quite unique for its time and would not have been easily replicated in the United States. Now, however, early childhood centers and classrooms are increasingly populated by children of different ethnic and cultural backgrounds. About 3.5 million schoolchildren come from homes where English is not the first language. At the same time, the majority of caregivers and teachers are still middle-class white females who often lack any knowledge of their children's backgrounds and have no idea what it is like to have to learn another language.

In this increasingly complex society, it is important that caregivers and teachers continue to learn about their children and their backgrounds. Here are some characteristics you might expect to find in your classroom that per-tain to three minority groups of long-standing in this country. It is important to emphasize that some children of these cultures might not exhibit these characteristics. It is just as dangerous to stereotype cultural behaviors and at-titudes as it is to ignore differences.

### Native Americans

There are so many variations on Indian culture that it is impossible to make generalizations about encounters with these children. However, some of the more frequently observed behaviors and attitudes are listed here, along with the misinterpretations or negative responses they often produce.

- Many Indian children are taught that it is rude to look directly at an au-thority when being spoken to. The teacher may find this behavior evasive and be tempted to say, "Look at me when I talk to you!"
- Speech patterns may be slower, conversation may include fewer "umm-hmm"s, and there are likely to be fewer interjections. This contrasts with the mainstream western psychological view that a person who interrupts is usually more intelligent.
- Group needs and cooperation take priority over individual goals, whereas the dominant school culture values competition.

- Physical punishment is rare, while in the larger society it is more frequently accepted. (Native American parents who use physical punishment have frequently spent their school years in off-reservation boarding schools where physical punishment was the norm.)
- Learning of new skills is done by observation and imitation, while today's mainstream education values curiosity and discovery learning.
- Extended families traditionally are the norm, with cousins and other relatives treated as brothers and sisters. Schools are more likely to treat children as individuals with no cultural connections. Teachers may be confused by the terminology used to describe relatives.
- Events on the reservation, designed to bring extended families together, often take precedence over children's attendance at school. Teachers often regard attendance at school (even in the earliest years) as of unquestioned importance.
- Property is not so rigidly assigned to individuals and possessions are shared with anyone who needs them. Whatever belongs to the group belongs to each individual within the group; Native American children may take or use others' possessions without asking. In the usual classroom, children are taught to share, but ownership is clearly defined and others' property must be left untouched until permission to use it is granted.
- Traditional Native American cultures view time as a continuum rather than as discrete units. Children may be sent to school when they are "ready," while teachers regard promptness and attention to designated clock time as important. (Sources: Little Soldier, 1985; Swinomish Tribal Community, 1991)

These differences will be most noticeable if the children live on a reservation or come from traditional families. Other children may adapt to the classroom as quickly as any Anglo child, but occasionally exhibit one of the listed behaviors.

### African Americans

Black children have a longer history than Indians of being assimilated into the majority culture and, consequently, differences are often not so noticeable. Still, their performance in school is, statistically speaking, not as highly rated on standardized tests as other groups'. Haynes and Comer (1990) offer some explanations for teachers to think about.

- *Poverty.* A black child is three times as likely as a white child to be poor. In fact, 52 percent of black children between the ages of three and five live in poverty, compared to 18 percent of like-age white children. Children who are poor live under stress, are concerned about being hungry, and may feel

## *(Mis)understanding the Minority Child: A Conversation with Bernie Thomas*

*Sociologists call them "taken-for-granted realities": the aspects of our culture that are so obvious to us that we don't think to question them. Educators who take their school culture for granted may fail to realize that a young minority culture child who has never been to school may regard the entire concept of schooling as a mystery. Such an unquestioning view of reality by school staff can have devastating consequences at a time when the number of minority children is rapidly increasing. If school culture isn't adapted so that minority children can fit into it, there is little chance that these children will ever experience academic success.*

Just as Bernie Thomas was scheduled to begin first grade at the Lummi tribal school, the school was closed down. Instead, he and about a hundred other children were bused ten miles to the nearest public elementary school.

More than three decades later Bernie remembers the first day with agonizing clarity. With no prior kindergarten experience to inform them, he and his friends boarded the school bus to ride many miles to a building they'd never seen for an experience they could only imagine. The driver let them out and the older, more knowledgeable children entered the building. That left Bernie and the other first graders outside, wondering where they were supposed to go. They soon noticed the playground equipment and enthusiastically headed for it. Before long, the vice principal discovered them and dragged them—some by their ears—into the classroom.

Almost immediately, Bernie felt inadequate. Children who had been to kindergarten knew their shapes, letters, and numbers. Some could even look at a circular object high on the wall and tell what time it was. When he realized that he was even expected to be able to write his name in those mysterious letters, Bernie felt so homesick he considered running away.

Within a few months, about 70 of the 100 Indian children had been moved to special education classes. Bernie knew many of the children and, even then, believed the school was misplacing them. He knew that the poorer boys stayed up all night fishing for their families and that by schooltime were too exhausted to stay alert for their lessons. Girls, who were silent in class, appeared incapable to the teachers, yet on the playground they talked freely and with understanding about their schoolwork.

Bernie was also aware that Indian children were regarded differently when it came to discipline. White girls chattered incessantly in class but weren't reprimanded; an Indian boy who talked out of turn might be paddled. White boys who acted out were largely ignored; Indian boys would be paddled or sent home.

Bernie was one of the fortunate thirty who remained in regular classrooms. By upper elementary school it was apparent that he was a superior student. As an adult, he began educating others and is now an independent consultant, sometimes to the very school system he first attended. Bernie looks back at his early school experience and avers that only one of the seventy children who were assigned to special education classes actually belonged there. Some have gone on to higher education, and most are successful in their jobs and their community. Their memories of their childhood school experience, however, are sometimes bitter and resentful.

Today there is a Head Start center on the reservation and the tribal school has been restored nearby. Bernie's daughter attends the Head Start program, and he marvels at the difference between her early knowledge and his. Still, he worries that if she ever transfers to the city school ten miles away, she will experience some of the cultural antagonism that he did.

Bernie suggests that teachers of Native Americans

- Be aware that children need to have their culture validated. As an example, if their tribe has complex intergenerational relationships, it should be understood that more relatives than parents may have interest in and influence on a child's progress.
- Visit the children's homes or reservation. Be a part of the community from time to time by being knowledgeable about holidays or special events.
- Avoid behaving in ways that are intimidating to the child's family. Explain the purposes of parent meetings; listen to their point of view; ask if instructions are clear.
- Find out the prior knowledge of the children as they enter school. Don't assume they know what other children know, and take time to find out what they do know that is unique.
- Include rhythm and dance experiences in the curriculum and teach some dances that are from the tribal culture.
- Realize that the children are developing biculturally and that there isn't one main American culture.
- Ask the parents and other relatives how they view their children. What do they see as the children's special talents and gifts? The talents that are valued may be different from those you take for granted.

*To think about and discuss: What are ways in which teachers validated (or didn't validate) your own culture when you were a child? What effect did this have on your learning and/or your feelings about yourself and others? Discuss steps you might take to ensure that you will not take for granted the reality of your students' educational experience.*

unsafe as a result of not belonging to the majority group. When basic
needs are unmet, such feelings as high self-esteem are luxuries.

- *Racial discrimination.* Despite the gains from affirmative action programs instituted in the 1960s, racial discrimination persists. For example, in urban
school systems where the black population is high, blacks tend to receive
an inferior education. The results of discrimination is evident in studies in
which young black children prefer to play with white dolls, viewing the
lighter racial characteristics as superior to their own.

- *Support groups.* The black nuclear and extended family and the black community are no longer as unified as they once were. Now, at least 40 percent of black children are brought up in fatherless homes and the number
of unwed black mothers is more than four times that of whites. These two
statistics imply a high level of poverty, since 75 percent of families headed
by a woman under age twenty-five are poor.

- *The role of schools.* Teachers may expect lower academic performance from
black children, and research has shown that low expectations result in low
performance. Academic standards should not be lowered for disadvantaged black children. They should be taught the mainstream ways of working, learning, and acting. Conversely, ". . . the mainstream child becomes
aware of and learns from non-mainstream ways of adapting, learning, and
coping" (p. 111).

As with Native American children, teachers must avoid stereotyping by
assuming that all black children share the above experiences. Refusing to assume that they will produce inferior work is one strong way to help these
children perform their best.

### Hispanics/Latinos/Chicanos

Children from Hispanic cultures represent many countries throughout the
world. While it is essential to avoid stereotyping, we can point to some common behaviors that you may observe.

- Even very young Hispanic boys may mimic their fathers by demonstrating
an independent, giver-of-orders mode of behaving. Hispanic girls, on the
other hand, may be submissive and subservient. Translated into classroom
behavior, the boys may appear aggressive and the girls passive.

- In Hispanic cultures courtesy toward authority figures is shown by lowering the eyes. We have discussed this trait in regard to Native American
children. The teacher should not regard this reaction as a sign of devious-
ness.

- Children from Hispanic cultures may be more demonstrative and noisy in
their greetings. Touching and embracing are more acceptable than in the
mainstream culture, and personal distance is much closer. Children may

Some demographers now predict that by the year 2020 approximately one half of the nation's school children will be from racial and ethnic minorities. Many will have a very limited proficiency in English and will come from home cultures that are different from that of their mainstream teachers.

respond more happily to their school situation if the teacher remembers this and provides them with extra hugs and pats.

- Reticence and indirectness are considered virtues. Even young Hispanic children may seem passive and too indirect to their teachers.
- Children who come from Spanish-speaking backgrounds are accustomed to hearing fewer tones in everyday speech. Mainstream English has more higher-range tones and to the very young ear this can actually be alarming. One teacher, who thought she was demonstrating enthusiasm, came across to her Hispanic children as angry because she "yelled" all day long. (Segal-Swan, 1980)

### Non-English-Speaking Children

Not many years ago, it seemed that if caregivers and teachers could learn some Spanish, they would be in a better position to help the non-English-speaking children in their care. Although about 73 percent of language-minority children are still Hispanic, today more than 150 languages are represented in schools around the country. Although learning multiple languages is beyond the scope of most teachers, learning the language of at least one minority group can still be useful. Teachers gain a better understanding of their children's linguistic struggles; they learn something about the ways in which "mistakes" can be used to increase knowledge; and they may even achieve the original intention for language learning by selecting the language that is used most by their children.

The look of the American child care center and classroom is changing. Not too many years ago, we somehow justified incorporating every new ethnic or racial group into the mainstream culture. Now, however, ethnic groups demand that their heritage not be denied. Consequently, multicultural education is proposed by most national education organizations, and it is appropriate even for the youngest children. The reason for this is that awareness of differences actually begins in infancy and awareness of political and emotional responses to differences begins in nursery school or kindergarten. Caregivers and teachers cannot ignore their children's awareness and interest.

## Development and the Minority Child

Those who work with young children sometimes hope that ignoring issues of race, ethnicity, and other differences in their classrooms will help the children stay unprejudiced. In actuality, children are aware of and affected by differences in a variety of ways.

### Racial Awareness

One important study (Katz, 1976) found that children begin forming an understanding of racial differences as babies and, by the end of elementary school have passed through the following eight (often overlapping) levels of perceptual and attitudinal development.

**Level 1.**   The child observes and has a basic awareness of racial cues such as differences in skin color or shape of eyes.

**Level 2.**   The child gains a rudimentary understanding that some races may be preferred over others. Typically, the mainstream race is preferred, but this may differ depending on the child's environment.

**Level 3.**   The child's perceptions of positive or negative attitudes are increasingly influenced by others, typically parents, caregivers, teachers, and other important people in the child's life.

**Level 4.**   The child learns that racial identification never changes.

**Level 5.**   The kindergarten child can identify, label, and recognize members of a physically distinct racial group.

**Level 6.**   For preschool-elementary children differences between groups become more important than those within groups.

**Level 7.**   Complex racial attitudes begin to develop based in part on what family, teachers, and peers have to say.

**Level 8.**   Attitude crystallization occurs about the end of elementary school.

These levels of development can have implications for those who work with children. For example, infants who are introduced to a new caregiver of an unaccustomed race may actually appear startled (Level 1). Or, if light skin coloring is viewed as preferable, darker nursery school children may try to wash off their own coloring (pre-Level 4). Ramsey (1987) found that as children learn to identify and label differences (Level 5), they tend to focus on skin color rather than on other features. She also found, however, that race was only one of many ways in which children regarded others as different, and that such identifications related to their Piagetian stage. In other words, preoperational children (who can focus only on one attribute at a time) would discuss another's race if someone brought it up, but otherwise would just discuss the other's hair length if there had just been a haircut, or the other's personality if there had just been a fight. By the primary grades, children would be more likely to coordinate all three elements into one observation (Piaget's concrete operational stage and Katz's Level 7).

### Awareness of Linguistic Differences

Children who learn to speak in bilingual or multilingual homes usually are aware when one parent more easily speaks one language and the other parent another. Sometimes children come from homes where the languages are often mixed. In either case, children seem to be able to sort out the linguistic codes and emerge from early childhood with a well-understood grammar in each of the separate languages (Huerta-Macias, 1983.)

Young children's awareness of what is happening when different languages are used is influenced by their developmental levels. For example, Ramsey (1987) tells of a kindergarten teacher who introduced the idea of people in foreign countries speaking different languages. The children were taught a few foreign words and sang songs in various languages. However, an understanding of geographic distance and cultural differences eluded them. One day (in demonstration of preoperational thought), two children were heard arguing about whether the children in a nearby town spoke a foreign language.

In contrast, one second-grade class studied Latin roots of both English and Spanish words and discussed how language changes, and the role early Roman soldiers played in carrying languages across much of the European continent. These children had achieved the stage of concrete operational thought and learned what they did by engaging in hands-on activities. Their teacher role-played with them; they made clay models of the stories she read to them; they visited a museum with Roman ruins; and they all could speak and read both English and Spanish (Krogh, 1991).

What remains most controversial about language learning in the United States is the degree to which speaking a language other than English weakens or strengthens the mainstream culture. Does bilingualism promote foreign cultures and thereby weaken the mainstream culture, or does it permit the mainstream culture to continue growing richer and stronger through contact with other cultures? In Chapter 1 we saw how German-speaking and German-influenced kindergartens in this country were once looked upon as a threat to Americanism. Learning the native language has always been the ultimate "fitting in" behavior, and fitting in means being comfortable with where you are. The controversy today swirls around the consequences of submerging non-English speakers into an English-only preschool (Schmidt, 1991). Some research seems to indicate that doing so may accelerate "children's loss of their primary language and threaten their ability to benefit from the parental guidance needed to keep them on track during their school years" (p. 11). Others disagree, and so the argument continues.

## Teaching for Cultural Understanding and Equity

There is much that you can do to help children understand and appreciate cultural and linguistic differences. As a start, you should

- Have a good understanding of and respect for other cultures. This is necessary so that you can adequately represent the cultures in the classroom.
- Avoid perceiving some cultures as inherently inferior. Children must be respected, not only for their individual integrity but for the culture that is their background.
- Learn to read the body language and emerging verbal capabilities of children from different cultures and linguistic backgrounds.
- Provide multicultural experiences even if you work in a one-culture setting.

## Choosing and Developing Curricula

Many articles and books are available that offer ideas for establishing a multicultural center or classroom (see, e.g., Derman-Sparks, 1989; Kendall, 1983; Ramsey, 1987). The focus of the center should be to help children understand that there are different ways of living and speaking and that these differences should be approached with respect rather than prejudice. Some helpful ideas include

- Avoid collecting and using stereotypic and inaccurate materials. For example, before introducing a new book to the children, check the story and its illustrations for stereotypes (such as darker people in subservient roles), for lifestyles (darker people in ghettos, lighter people in middle-class housing), for people in powerful positions (are the dominant ones always white?). This is especially true when choosing books that were written before the 1970s or even the 1980s.
- Visual materials should represent a broad cross section of cultures and ethnic groups. One group should not be overrepresented. Likewise, when choosing art supplies be sure that various skin tones are available and

Minority children should be given an opportunity to display their special cultural knowledge to mainstream children, as it gives them an opportunity to develop self esteem while simultaneously teaching about other cultures.

avoid communicating the concept that light, bright colors are good and dark colors bad.

■ Dramatic play, language, and music experiences should reflect a variety of cultures. For example, language and music experiences should include other languages, and dolls and puppets should represent different races.

■ Study all the holidays represented in your group. For kindergarten and older children, holidays that celebrate struggles over injustice are especially appropriate. Treat all holidays with equal respect; don't assume that those you yourself celebrate are "regular" and others are "exotic."

## The Child and Gender

In the earliest years of childhood, boys and girls play together with little regard for gender differences. However, as they mature, these differences, which may have causes that are both inherited and learned, become more noticeable. Vivian Paley (1984) observed domestic play in her own classroom over time and noted that

- At age three, everyone cooks and eats together, exchanges male and female costumes, and arbitrarily alters sexual identity.
- Around age four, boys become less comfortable playing in the doll corner. When taking on roles, they are happier as superheroes than as daddies or other domestic characters. While the girls may occasionally become super-heroines, they generally prefer to play mother or baby, and will continue to do so throughout kindergarten.
- At age five and six, children change the atmosphere of the doll corner forever. It is at this period that boys and girls try hardest to clarify the gender roles they will play in life. Only the less mature boys agree to play domestic characters in the doll corner, while the rest prefer noisy superhero roles. In turn, the girls create increasingly female domestic plots with more female characters.

It is not known how much of this gender difference in maturation is due to biology and how much to social learning. For example, the earlier maturation rate of girls is inborn, but the greater physical activity of boys may be both inborn and socialized (Lay-Dopyera and Dopyera, 1990). Boys are usually provided with toys and opportunities for action (building blocks, cars, and trucks), while girls are guided toward sedentary and quiet experiences with dolls and books. Yet, conscientious parents who provide their offspring with an array of toys and experiences often observe that their toddling boys reach for the trucks and the girls for the dolls. If young boys do play with dolls, they may use them as props in noisy adventures; if girls construct with blocks, it may be just enough to create a backdrop for domestic doll play. As Paley (1984) has noted, by age five or six children have clearly divided the genders in a traditional, stereotyped fashion.

While research and argument (both scientific and emotional) are still in progress (Gilligan, 1982), some important conclusions may yet be drawn. Young children need to sort out what is male and female about themselves and others and should be permitted to do so through exploratory role playing. They also need to grow up feeling that they are capable human beings who are free to fashion their own identity without stereotyped gender constraints. What caregivers and teachers say and do may have enormous impact on children's growth along these lines.

## Teaching for Gender Equity

"Sexism" has been defined as "any attitude, action, or institutional practice backed up by institutional power that subordinates people because of their sex" (Derman-Sparks, 1989, p. 3). People who work with young children may promote sexism, even if they are not aware of it. For example, as Lay-Dopyera and Dopyera (1990) point out, teachers may allow girls more freedom of choice when it comes to playing. Parents and teachers generally permit them to engage in the rough and tumble of "boy" play as well as encourage them toward the quieter "girl" play.

On the other hand, linguistic preference is generally given to boys because male pronouns are used in reference to all people and female pronouns to refer to the other, lesser sex. One researcher (Gelb, 1989) spent a year observing teachers of three- to five-year-olds talk to their children in this way. In science lessons, animals were almost always referred to as "he"; a mother dove, in fact, was described as sitting on "his" eggs. To see the effects of this misuse of language, Gelb then asked the children to tell stories about several animal or baby pictures in which the gender couldn't be determined. Close to 90 percent of the generic descriptions were defined in male terms. Gelb concluded that, by nursery school age, children of both sexes have already internalized the concept of females as invisible and that, "unwittingly, we are raising the next generation to accept the preconscious belief of their parents and teachers that maleness and humanness are equivalent" (p. 213).

As a teacher, there are numerous ways that you can promote gender equity in your classroom. Here are some suggestions:

- Avoid such comments to children as "Boys don't . . ." or "Girls never . . ."
- Listen carefully to your pronouns so that you can avoid the trap described in Gelb's research.
- When reading to children, modify stories that use male-only descriptors. Point out the strong acts of girls and the gentleness of boys. Help children appreciate the many sides of individuals.
- Choose browsing books that avoid stereotypical male–female roles.
- Be sure that classroom leadership roles are distributed fairly across both sexes.
- Post pictures that show a good balance of males and females in widely varying roles.
- Make "boy" and "girl" toys easily available to both sexes. Dolls may be placed in the block corner and blocks in the doll corner, or the two centers may be made into one large play center, even if temporarily.
- Create housekeeping corners that represent rooms other than the kitchen. Include in them materials for both sexes.
- Encourage and compliment girls in the traditional "boy" curriculum (math, science); encourage and compliment boys in the traditional "girl" curriculum (reading, writing, art).
- Avoid defining correct behavior as that typically valued by your own sex.

Sexism is defined as "any attitude, action, or institutional practice backed up by institutional power that subordinates people because of their sex." One subtle form of sexism is the unconscious tendency of many teachers to pose more questions to boys than to girls.

## An Observation of Self

We all have preferences and prejudices and sometimes we permit them to get in the way of our relationships with children. A few that this author has witnessed:

- The kindergarten teacher who regularly hugged the Haitian refugees and white children in her class, but couldn't bring herself to even touch the black children.
- The teacher in a private preschool who had far more than her share of the noisier boys because parents knew her to be the only teacher who would treat them with fairness.
- The teacher who left her "dream job" because it included responsibility for two handicapped children.
- The student teacher who looked with distaste upon several four-year-olds in her class who were just learning to speak English, concluding that they were incapable of "real learning" because of the "language barrier."

Young children feel the effects of such treatment, although they may have no understanding about its origins or meanings. They are quite likely to misinterpret a teacher's negative actions and attitudes since they are unable to step outside the situation and see it from an observer's viewpoint. They only know that something is wrong or believe that there is something wrong with them. The effects of such feelings can affect children for a lifetime. In the shorter run, they can inhibit children's success in school, both academically and socially.

Yet we all have preferences and prejudices of one sort or another. They may come from our life experiences, from the media, from our family, or from unthinking acceptance of our particular culture's stereotyped attitudes. For the sake of the children we teach, it is important to face our prejudices in a two-step process. First, we must find and define them. If they are deeply hidden within the culture we take for granted, this may be a rather difficult task. At other times, only brief reflection is needed to identify groups or types of people that we find difficult to accept. Second, we must deal with each prejudice in such a way that we avoid damaging children. Our ultimate goal should be to eliminate the prejudice entirely, but, in the short term, that may prove to be too difficult. A realistic alternative is to observe our behavior and then work on changing it.

As an example, in the cases mentioned above, the teacher who left her "dream job" probably did the handicapped children a service by doing so. The teacher who could hug only Haitians and whites observed other teachers around her, thought about what she was doing to the black children, and trained herself to hug them as well. She even kept a mental tally each day, counting the times she hugged each child to be sure it came out even. The teacher who was loaded down with noisy boys discussed the problem with the principal, who finally agreed with her that a facultywide discussion was in order. It became apparent, however, that for the other teachers (who were all women) the only proper behavior was quiet, submissive, and feminine. The next year, when there was a faculty opening, the principal hired a male teacher and the noisier boys were then distributed between the two teachers. And the student teacher? Her supervisors suggested that, unless she could be accepting of all children, she should consider another career. She left teaching.

For each of the difficult situations, a solution was found. In each case, the children were well served. In each case, the teacher or principal may have been unaware that prejudice existed until it was in full bloom. Yet those involved in each situation were willing to face a prejudice once it was identified.

Child care centers and schools today have more diverse populations than ever before. It is critical that those of us who interact with young children make certain that we do so in ways that are compassionate, fair, and accepting of all. In the next section, there are activities you can engage in that should help you take a better look at your own thinking.

## Extending Your Learning

1. From a group of children in a child care center or classroom choose two to observe: a child who is much like you and the child who is least like you. Criteria used for choosing the children can include any combination of physical, intellectual, or social characteristics.

   Observe both children for at least one hour, keeping notes about their activities, their interactions with others, and their capabilities as you perceive them.

   After you leave, think about the two children and your own response to them. As a final writing exercise, discuss which child you felt most attracted to and why.

   If everyone in your class does this assignment, you may want to discuss the implications of your findings as well as the steps you can take to make it possible to work more easily with children both like and unlike yourself.

2. Seek out teaching experiences with the diverse kinds of children discussed in this chapter. Try some of the suggested ideas for working with them. Discuss the results with their teachers, your instructors, and other experts. Expand your reading knowledge of the groups you find most interesting or difficult to work with.

3. "Adopt" a gifted child or a child with special needs. Tutor this child over a period of several weeks, and record the progress the child makes as well as the discoveries you make in teaching approaches.

## References

Buchoff, R. (1990). Attention deficit disorder: help for the classroom teacher. *Childhood Education* 66(2):86–90.

Delp, J. (1980). How to live successfully with the gifted. In S. Kaplan (ed.), *Educating the preschool/primary gifted and talented,* pp. 167–182. Los Angeles: National/State Leadership Training Institute on the Gifted and Talented.

Derman-Sparks, L., and the ABC Task Force (1989). *Anti-Bias curriculum: Tools for empowering children.* Washington, DC: National Association for the Education of Young Children.

Gallagher, J. (1986). The need for programs for young gifted children. *Topics in Early Childhood Special Education* 6(1):1–8.

Gelb, S. (1989). Language and the problem of male salience in early childhood classroom environments. *Early Childhood Research Quarterly* 4:205–215.

Gilligan, C. (1982). *In a different voice.* Cambridge, MA: Harvard University Press.

Gunderson, C., Maesch, C., and Rees, J. (1987). The gifted/learning disabled student. *Gifted Child Quarterly* 31(4):158–160.

Guralnick, M. (1990). Major accomplishments and future directions in early childhood mainstreaming. *Topics in Early Childhood Special Education* 10(2):1–17.

Hanline, M. (1985). Integrating disabled children. *Young Children* 40(2):45–48.

Hanninen, G. (1985). Effectiveness of a preschool program for the gifted and talented. *Journal for the Education of the Gifted* 7(3):192–203.

Hayden, A., Smith, R., vonHippel, C., and Baer, S. (undated). *Mainstreaming preschoolers: Children with learning disabilities.* Washington, DC: U.S. Government Printing Office.

Haynes, N., and Comer, J. (1990). Helping black children succeed: the significance of some social factors. In K. Lomotey (ed.), *Going to school: The African-American experience,* pp. 103–112. Albany: State University of New York Press.

Hensel, N. (1991). Social leadership skills in young children. *Roeper Review* 14(1):4–6.

Huerta-Macias, A. (1983). Child bilingualism: to switch or not to switch? In T. Escobedo (ed.), *Early childhood bilingual education: A Hispanic perspective,* pp. 18–30. New York: Teachers College Press.

Karnes, M., and Johnson, L. (1991). The preschool/primary gifted child. *Journal for the Education of the Gifted* 14(3):267–283.

Karnes, M., Shwedel, A., and Kemp, P. (1985). Preschool: programming for the young gifted child. *Roeper Review* 7(4):204–208.

Katz, P. (1976). The acquisition of racial attitudes in children. In P. Katz (ed.), *Towards the elimination of racism,* pp. 125–156. New York: Pergamon.

Kendall, F. (1983). *Diversity in the classroom: A multicultural approach to the education of young children.* New York: Teachers College Press.

———(1991). Studying the Romans and their language: Second graders create their own curriculum. *International Schools Journal.*

Lay-Dopyera, M., and Dopyera, J. (1990). *Becoming a teacher of young children.* New York: McGraw-Hill.

Little Soldier, L. (1985). To soar with the eagles. *Childhood Education* 61(3):185–191.

Mabry, M., and Rogers, P. (1991). Bias begins at home. *Newsweek,* 5 Aug., 33.

Maker, C. (1986). Suggested principles for gifted preschool curricula. *Topics in Early Childhood Special Education* 6(1):62–73.

Morgan, D., and York, M. (1981). Ideas for mainstreaming young children. *Young Children* 36(2):18–25.

Odom, S., and McEvoy, M. (1990). Mainstreaming at the preschool level: potential barriers and tasks for the field. *Topics in Early Childhood Special Education* 10(2):48–61.

Paley, V. (1984). *Boys and Girls: Superheroes in the Doll Corner.* Chicago: University of Chicago Press.

Parke, B., and Ness, P. (1988). Curricular decision-making for the education of young gifted children. *Gifted Child Quarterly* 32(1):196–198.

Patterson, I., and Wright, A. (1990). The speech, language or hearing-impaired child: At-risk academically. *Childhood Education* 67(2):91–96.

Ramsey, P. (1987). *Teaching and learning in a diverse world.* New York: Teachers College Press.

Rist, M. (1990). The shadow children: preparing for the arrival of crack babies in school. *Research Bulletin: Phi Delta Kappa* July, 1–6.

Safford, P., and Rosen, L. (1981). Mainstreaming: application of a philosophical perspective in an integrated kindergarten program. *Topics in Early Childhood Special Education* 1(1):1–5.

Schmidt, P. (1991). Report faults preschool English for language-minority children. *Education Week,* 1 May, 11.

Schneekloth, L. (1989). Play environments for visually impaired children. *Journal of Visual Impairment and Blindness* 83(4):196–201.

Segal-Swan, B. (1980). *Practical guide for the bilingual classroom: Spanish/English.* San Francisco: Alemany Press.

Swinomish Tribal Community (1991). *A gathering of wisdoms: tribal mental health: A cultural perspective.* Mount Vernon, WA: Veda Vangarde.

Walker, H. (1989). Towards anti-racist, multicultural practice with under fives. *Early Childhood Development and Care* 41:103–112.

Walters, L. (1990). Students take the fast track. *Christian Science Monitor,* 10 Dec., 12.

Weiner, R. (1990). What's working: Los Angeles preparing for "drug babies" with intervention models. *Education Monitor,* 9 Oct., 3.

Whitlock, M., and DuCette, J. (1989). Outstanding and average teachers of the gifted: a comparative study. *Gifted Child Quarterly* 33(1):15–21.

Wright, L. (1990). The social and nonsocial behaviors of precocious preschoolers during free play. *Roeper Review* 12(4):268–273.

# Part Three

# In the Classroom

The training you receive as an early childhood educator is quite different from what you would get if you were planning to teach high school. If your focus were older students, for example, your academic preparation would emphasize the attainment of content knowledge. Teaching methods probably would be presented in a course or two, and you would then be considered ready for an internship.

For the teaching of younger students, less course time is devoted to content, and more to learning how to teach. Those who plan to teach infants and very young children need comparatively little education in content but much more in teaching approaches, preparation of the environment, classroom management, and techniques for working with parents and other adults. Thus, you may find that Part Three is the most practical section of this text.

If this is your first experience with teaching, you may find that not every method works as well as you had hoped. Perhaps you feel uncomfortable trying out teaching and management methods that are foreign to your own childhood experiences. Or you may simply need more practice and should try again. You can benefit from discussing your experiences with the classroom teacher or your instructor to see what alterations would bring more success. If you do find success in your experiences, take time to analyze them; when you repeat an experience later, you'll be glad you did.

# 7

# Ways of Teaching and Learning

*Metaphor: A figure of speech in which a word or phrase usually applied to one thing is applied to another.*

Can you think of your teaching role as a metaphor? Perhaps you see yourself as an orchestra conductor: completely in charge of the situation, creating individual expression and overall harmony through the slightest movement of your baton. Or you may be like a camp counselor: informal, involving children in a variety of entertaining events, coordinating a wide array of ability levels in one big happy whole. Do you think of yourself as a mother hen? Perhaps you want to gather your brood about you, shielding them from the harsh world outside until you have helped them learn to fly a little. Even an inanimate metaphor is possible: You may think of yourself as the yeast in unrisen dough, bringing air and light to create a vastly expanded, more useful and appealing end product.

It would be good to take a moment here to actually choose a metaphor for yourself. It can be one of those just mentioned, or you can invent one of your own. Some other ideas you might choose:

■ Kindergarten Cop
■ Coach
■ Factory supervisor
■ Gardener
■ Pied piper
■ Best friend

The choice you make should have some relationship to the responses you have had to the first six chapters of this book. For example, in Chapter 4 you read of the psychoanalytic, social learning, and constructivist views of social development. If you were drawn toward the psychoanalytic view, then you might be attracted to the mother hen metaphor; if the social learning view, then perhaps the pied piper image; and if the constructivist view, then the coaching image may appeal to you. In Chapter 5, three views of cognitive development were themselves described as metaphors: the child as blank slate, as unfolding flower, or as self-builder. If the blank slate image attracts you, perhaps you see yourself as the chalk that writes on it. Or, choosing from the list above you could mix metaphors and become the orchestra conductor. If you see the child as an unfolding flower, you can, of course, choose to be a gardener. And, if the child is a self-builder, you can be the coach.

Choosing an appropriate metaphor has actually been used as a teaching technique by those who work with student teachers. There is a distinct advantage to such an approach. Suppose you have chosen "camp counselor" as the metaphor that guides your choice of teaching techniques. And suppose you are currently involved in a first-grade practicum and that you are having trouble with management and discipline. As you think about what is going wrong, you realize that your actions are not those of a camp counselor but of a factory supervisor. Every minute of the day is planned according to the dictates of the clock. Children must finish every bit of their work before they are allowed to use puzzles and games. Recess is exactly fifteen minutes, even if a game of kickball isn't quite over. Children work at their desks alone, each one dedicated to completing the packet of work you lay out each morning.

You must make a decision: Do you change your teaching so that your classroom feels more like camp? Or do you change your metaphor to reflect reality and do a better job of supervising your factory? Thinking through such a situation can help you understand better what kind of teaching and learning you value most. So, make a note somewhere of the metaphor you choose for yourself now. Then, when you have finished reading this chapter, see if it is the one you wish to keep.

In the sections that follow, various approaches to teaching and learning will be discussed, each with its strengths and weaknesses. At some time, you will no doubt use each one in some way, but one or two approaches should stand out as corresponding best to your own character and the image you have of yourself as a teacher.

The first approach to teaching and learning is the one that comes most naturally to children. Given a warm and supportive relationship with parents and other caregivers, infants of just a few weeks old begin to employ it entirely on their own.

## Learning Through Play

Perhaps the most difficult part of discussing children's play is defining exactly what it is. Some of its attributes are agreed upon by most theorists and researchers, but others are controversial. In addition, children may define the word differently than adults, and between children of different ages there are further disagreements.

### Attributes of Play That Are Broadly Accepted

#### Process over Product

The means rather than the end hold value. There are no extrinsic goals, although, within the play itself, children can decide to have goals. Perhaps two children are playing the piano, banging away happily, with no need to create anything other than as much noise as possible. Eventually, one of them suggests that it would be fun to create a song. They begin singing nonsense words accompanied by more raucous noise. When their mother walks by, they sing a variation of their "composition" for her, then go back to their original banging. It is important to note in this example that the decision to create a product was made by the players alone because it was a part of the play.

### Voluntarily Chosen

Play is not an obligatory activity. Two children may be involved in the same activity, side by side, yet one may be playing and another may not. For the first child, the activity was freely chosen; for the second, it was assigned by the teacher.

### Intrinsic Motivation

This attribute is related to the previous one. It explains why an activity is voluntarily chosen. Play experiences are chosen for their own sake and because they are inherently satisfying. They are not experiences that are chosen because of basic needs and drives, or because of social demands. A child fingerpainting with chocolate pudding may lick it playfully for the pleasure of the experience or, conversely, eat it hungrily in a nonplay mode.

### Nonliteral Use of Familiar Objects

When an object or toy is new to a child, exploration is necessary to learn how it is supposed to work. Once this knowledge is established, the child takes control of the object and uses it in unique but personally meaningful ways. Common examples include large cardboard boxes used as a house or car and a broom handle used as a baseball bat or horse. The former activity (initial exploration) is not play, but the latter (creative use) is.

## Attributes of Play That Are Controversial

### Pleasure

Although play obviously brings pleasure to children, this pleasure sometimes disappears in the midst of the play experience. For example, children may be afraid of jumping off the side of a pool, but the fact that they continue doing so suggests that overcoming fears and worries may be an integral part of play.

### Freedom from Imposed Rules

At times, this lack of outside control is critical to the play experience. At other times, however, the standard rules of a game are necessary for its enjoyment. For younger children who don't yet understand rules, freedom from them probably does make the difference between nonplay and play.

### Active Engagement

Again, there may be a difference between younger and older children. While younger children are almost always actively engaged in their play, older children may begin to daydream (mental play), an activity that some theorists suggest is their replacement for the dramatic play of younger children (Johnson et al., 1987).

## Child-Defined Play

Children in four kindergarten classrooms were interviewed by Nancy King (1986). When asked for their definitions of play, they focused on the context in which it occurs. To them, what qualified an activity as play was its voluntary nature. Anything the teacher assigned was viewed as work. Moreover, the less the teacher was involved in any activity, the more likely it seemed to be play.

King reports that the children's teachers were surprised at this definition because, to them, play was any activity that gave the children pleasure. However, the children stated that they could enjoy both play and work, but that play indicated a lack of adult involvement.

It is more than definitions of play, however, that have kept researchers,

The recognition that play, which has been referred to as the "serious business" of young children, is essential for their all around development, is a recent addition to the child-raising philosophies of Western culture.

theorists, and educators thinking about it. The meaning and purpose of play are also topics for consideration and debate.

## Theories of Play

Since definitions of play are difficult to agree upon, it should not be surprising that theories that explain the use of play in human life are often in conflict with each other. Toward the end of the last century and during the first two decades of this one, play theories were based on philosophical reflection and have come to be known as the classical theories. From the 1920s on, play theories have emerged from research, and we may refer to them as the modern theories.

### Classical Theories

There are four such philosophically derived theories and, as we will see, they are not totally focused on children's play.

#### Surplus Energy Theory

Every living being, according to this theory, generates a certain amount of energy to meet its survival needs. When the survival needs are met, there may be energy to spare. Play is the activity that is used to expend the extra energy. Since adults do more work, some of which may be devoted to taking care of children, children are left with more energy to expend and, therefore, play more. When teachers send children outside to "blow off steam," they subscribe to the surplus energy theory.

#### Recreation Theory

This theory takes the opposite point of view. Work is fatiguing and something is needed to restore the capability to engage in more of it. Sleep is one solution. The other is recreation through play. When teachers alternate intense work with play experiences they are using the recreation theory. Like soldiers pulled out of battle and sent for R&R, the children are being readied for further combat.

#### Recapitulation Theory

The concept of recapitulation has its roots in the nineteenth-century biological theory that the development of each human being follows the development of the entire human species from primitive to more modern forms ("ontogeny recapitulates phylogeny"). Adapted to the concept of play, recapitulation theory argues that young children engage in primitive activities and through playing these out, the primitive is dropped for the modern. Thus, young children climb trees like their primate ancestors; later they engage in gang play in imitation of tribal man or play out ancient hunting-with-a-club instincts in baseball games (Johnson et al., 1987).

### Practice Theory

Both animal and human behavior fit this theory. Infants are viewed as having only partially formed survival instincts that must be further developed through play. This play takes the form of practice for adulthood. For humans, this would explain the attraction that building materials, trucks, and war toys have for boys and that the housekeeping corner and dolls have for girls.

## Modern Theories

Within the modern research-based theories are two classical ones that deserve mention: psychoanalytic and cognitive.

### Psychoanalytic Theory

With its roots in the work of Freud, this theory argues that play provides a catharsis for children when they have had negative experiences. Through fantasy play they can take on the roles of those who have injured them and thus put themselves in control. As they play a role or a scene repetitively, children eventually play out the negative experience. Spanking one's dolls is a commonly cited example of a cathartic experience. Repeating a violent car crash or shootout may be helpful for today's TV-oriented children.

### Cognitive Theory

According to Piaget, there are three stages of play in which children engage, each one quite different from the others. Each corresponds to the cognitive stages you read about in Chapter 1: sensorimotor (birth–two), pre-operational (two–seven) and concrete operational (seven–eleven). Infants and toddlers play by practicing or repeating actions that are enjoyable to them. Preoperational children are capable of understanding symbolism, the concept that one thing can stand for another, and thus enjoy dramatic and fantasy play. Concrete operational children are learning about rules and social inter-actions that attract them to games with rules and teams.

Another component of Piaget's theory of cognitive development that applies to play is the mental structural change that takes place through the processes of accommodation and assimilation. Recall that accommodation in-volves taking something totally new into the intellectual structure; assimila-tion means fitting a new idea into previously held ideas. This is the element that relates to play. When children assimilate, they adapt something new to their own current organizational scheme. That is, they take an old idea and enhance it with new concepts by playing around with them. The two-year-old who learns how a doorknob is used almost immediately begins opening and shutting, first quietly and then with a bang. The behavior is repeated endlessly with different variations.

### Arousal-Seeking or Arousal Modulation Theory

Proposed in the 1950s and 60s by D. E. Berlyne and later popularized by M. Ellis, this theory suggests that humans continually seek an optimum level of stimulus for their central nervous systems. If children don't receive enough stimulation, they become bored and engage in play, a stimulus-raising activity. Or, they may change their play to be more complex and stimulating. Perhaps two children quietly watching television eventually become bored with their lack of physical activity and transfer the TV plot to their outdoor fantasy play. Soon they run out of plot and have no further ideas. They may then change the game to something new or go in search of other friends to increase the level of entertainment.

## Benefits of Play

Play is a natural way for children to learn, whatever theories and definitions are attached to it. Yet our culture has traditionally had a love–hate relationship with play that some attribute to the Puritan ancestry that undergirds so much of our society. In Puritan culture, work was revered above play and play was to be engaged in only after work—a lot of work—was done. Even today we justify the play of young children with philosophical statements such as, "Play is the work of the child." Without such a justification, we would have to invent some kind of work for babies to do. Despite its many benefits, as shown again and again by research, play continues to have a bad reputation, particularly in our very serious classrooms. Consider, then, the benefits of play to children.

### Play Can Enhance Cognitive Development

"Play, by virtue of its spontaneous, highly enjoyable qualities for children, acts as an energizer and organizer of cognitive learning" (Arnaud, 1971, p. 5). A three-year study of preschoolers (Saltz and Saltz, 1986) found that children who engaged in plenty of sociodramatic play and thematic fantasy play were approximately 10 IQ points higher than children who spent the same time engaged in other activities. The time spent was just fifteen minutes a day, three days a week over a seven-month period.

### Play Can Enhance Language Development

For children to develop language abilities, they must practice language. In language play children manipulate rhythm, sound, and form, often without much regard for the meaning or value of words. Few activities provide more opportunities to use language than sociodramatic play, and the results can be highly positive. This is particularly true when there is some teacher intervention and the children come from deprived backgrounds. In one short study, just eight training sessions on sociodramatic play increased children's ability to use longer and more complex sentences than children in a control group. In a longer study, daily sociodramatic training sessions were given for twenty-five weeks. The increase in sentence length and number of words used in free play was significantly higher for the experimental children than for the controls (Saltz and Saltz, 1986).

### Play Can Enhance Social Development and Skills

When children play with others, there are opportunities to share, take turns, negotiate, settle arguments, cooperate, learn the benefits of squelching negative character traits, and have and be friends. In social play children "learn a wide range of verbal and nonverbal communication skills for dealing with their peers' feelings and attitudes" (Spodek and Saracho, 1988, p. 17). Since children learn by active participation, denial of play may well inhibit the development of these skills.

### Play Can Enhance Emotional Stability and Affect

"The power of play in helping children master anxiety and normal developmental conflicts, as well as traumatic experience, has been exceedingly well documented in the psychodynamic and psychoanalytic literature . . ." (Arnaud, 1971, p. 5). The story is told of a preschool class (Brown et al., 1971) that witnessed a near fatal accident outside their playground. Both four- and five-year-olds responded in an age-related way to the incident. The fours became even more aggressive than usual and were permitted to express the aggression in their play, although they were carefully supervised. It took some time for them to get beyond this and to use group dramatic play as a coping tool. The fives turned immediately to group dramatic play, which helped them work through the incident. For both ages, the permission to play out the experience eventually led to dissipation of the stress.

### Play Can Enhance Children's Physical Development

"Large muscle activity through play is not a luxury. It is a necessity for young developing children" (Bowers, 1988, p. 48). In a time when electronic technology influences children to be ever more sedentary in their free time, the importance of active play should be increasingly highlighted. The skinfold thickness among primary grade children has increased significantly since the 1960s (Bowers, 1988) a sure sign that sedentary living and body fat percentage are correlated. Children need vigorous physical activity in which they can move and gain mastery over their bodies.

### Play Can Enhance Children's Creativity

For young children, creativity is developed in play situations that require the use of their imaginations. These situations come naturally to children as they enter toddlerhood, the period when symbolic play first becomes important. Imaginative play enhances creativity all through the elementary years, and time should be provided for it.

### Play Can Meet a Wide Variety of Children's Needs

In her book *Just Playing?* Janet Moyles (1989) helps answer the title's question by suggesting more than forty fundamental needs of young children that can be met by play. Here is an abbreviated version of her list. Through play, children:

- Have fresh air and exercise.
- Enjoy good health and healthy living.
- Enjoy a sense of physical and mental well-being.
- Have more opportunity to talk and develop language and communication.
- Write, draw, and generally make marks.
- Enjoy songs, music, sounds.
- Imitate others.
- Have occasions in which to be noisy.
- Are given an opportunity to love and be loved.
- Have interactions with other people of all ages and types.
- Use their imagination.
- Can have friends and be sociable.
- Learn to appreciate humor and be humorous.

Moyles then asks us to look back through the list and see how many of these needs we ourselves have. The answer: perhaps most, or even all. She then implies that some Golden Rule thinking is called for:

> Although they are not simply mini-adults, children are people with directly comparable feelings, emotions, social and intellectual needs to adults, albeit with a greater immaturity and naivety. Why, in this case, do we frequently expect children to do things we would hate to do ourselves and in which we can see no purpose? If we engage in some activity of importance to us, we would be more than a little enraged if someone constantly denied or put a stop to what we were doing! (p. 166)

## Developmental Levels and Related Issues

While children and adults have similar basic needs, the way these are answered by play experiences may be quite different. Both the motives behind play and the participants' understanding of the play experience change as children reach successively higher levels of development. One classical view divides play into four qualitatively different types of experience. Since this typology was first posited by M. B. Parten in 1932, it has been adopted, adapted, and argued over. Its longevity attests to its usefulness in studying the relationship between play and development. The four types of play in Parten's model are:

- *Solitary play.* The child plays alone and independently without reference to others. This is considered the most infantile form of play, a view that is seen as controversial by researchers who believe that solitary play can be a mature and happy experience.
- *Parallel play.* The child plays independently but alongside others. Two children may be doing similar things but not really play *with* each other. One child might say to the other, "I'm making a cake from this sand. Do you like it?" To which the other responds, "I got a new doll for Christmas." The first child is not in the least offended by the nonanswer.
- *Associative play.* The child plays with others in a similar activity but there is no negotiation, cooperation, or interest in subordinating the interests of self to the interests of the group. Several children playing house may want to be the mother or father. The teacher may need to intervene with the suggestion that all of them get to be mothers or fathers. Even though the group may end up with multiple parents and only one baby, this does not seem to concern children who are most concerned about their own needs.
- *Cooperative play.* The child plays with others in a complementary way. The negotiation, cooperation, and subordination that were absent in associative play become more the norm. The teacher is less likely to intervene in the houseplay problem. The children are more capable of working out a compromise in which, for example, they could agree to take turns playing parental roles.

## Development According to Age

While keeping in mind that children are individuals and that they develop according to their own schedules, it is still possible to make generalizations about the behaviors that caretakers and teachers can expect to observe.

### Infants

Play in this earliest period can be defined as *sensorimotor*. It relates to needs fulfillment and is expressed in oral activities, particularly those having to do with feeding. A common first play activity is to make rhythmic trills with the tongue against the mother's or bottle's nipple. Later, the infant experiments with sounds, breathing, and saliva control. Playfulness with the mother's breast or the bottle develops into playing with buttons, hair, or parts of the mother's face. Repetitive play with objects of this sort is practiced only by infants who have positive human relationships and is more frequent in active babies than in quiet ones (McFarland, 1971). Referring to Parten's typology, this period demonstrates solitary play.

### Toddlers

Toddlers enjoy experimenting with movements, and playing peek-a-boo or hide-and-seek. Filling and emptying, opening and closing are attractions. Toddlers may roam the house closing every door available, then opening them all again. Toward the end of this phase, *symbolic* or *imaginative* play begins as dolls and stuffed animals are used in a playful manner and sociodramatic play enters the scene. In sociodramatic play, children take on roles that are not their own, but they symbolize real people. At this age, this kind of play generally goes across both sexes, with boys willing to take on nurturing roles and girls acting out firefighters and other traditionally male roles (Pitcher and Schultz, 1983). Moving from solitary play to play with others, toddlers will most likely engage in parallel play.

One classic typology of play holds that play proceeds through four developmental stages that reflect the child's stage of cognitive and social development: solitary play, parallel play, associative play, and cooperative play. The children in this picture appear to be engaged in parallel play.

### Three-year-olds

Children are interested in the process of their play and have little use for goals or objectives of any sort. They may enthusiastically clean a housekeeping corner that has just had a thorough cleaning. Three-year-olds cannot yet separate fact from fiction, so they become the characters they play rather than simply pretending to be them. Collecting or gathering is an interest that may motivate them to place all the puzzles or books or dolls into a wagon and drag it about. Sometimes in their sociodramatic play at school they will take on the part of the mother in an effort to feel better about having left her (Brown, 1971). By age three, girls are likely to have less physical contact in their rougher play. There is much teasing and silly wordplay. Three-year-olds are still happy playing alone, frequently engage in parallel play, but also begin associative play.

### Four-year-olds

Enthusiastic, raucous, and sometimes wild are all typical descriptors of four-year-old play. While boys are more physical, aggressive impulses characterize both sexes. Male and female roles become clearer and take on exaggerated and stereotypical form. Girls like to dress in extensive jewelry, high heels, and scarves. Boys look for full cowboy regalia or superhero capes. These roles are now understood as divorced from reality. Rough play is highly favored by the boys, while girls prefer teasing and play that is sometimes physical but less rough. Both sexes enjoy bathroom humor and vocabulary. Associative play is most commonly found at this age.

### Five-year-olds

"Rough-and-tumble play, silliness, and teasing reach their zenith among boys, and descend to their lowest level among girls, in same-sex contacts at age 5" (Pitcher and Schultz, 1983, p. 60). The understandings that came about at age four also achieve greater heights. Sociodramatic play includes both real-life and fantasy roles, and children have no trouble differentiating between role playing and reality. Play is used effectively to deal with outside experiences that have upset or otherwise influenced the children's lives. For example, some children are already attracted to games with rules (hopscotch, kickball) that become increasingly important during the elementary grades.

### Six- to eight-year-olds

Games with rules are new attractions and the rules are taken very seriously. They may not always be followed, but they are always an issue. Pretend play continues to be interesting to children and, particularly toward the end of this period, is sometimes carried out through staged plays. The themes tend toward the bloody, with "ambush and attack, killing and death. They are peopled by ghosts, statues that come to life, grisly folk heroes . . . vampires, and people who turn out to be very different from what they purport to be . . . and remember, they are . . . developed by *normal* children" (Arnaud, 1971, p. 11). In the roles they play, boys show a concern for their physical strength and girls for their physical attractiveness.

## Guidelines for Teachers

Before the 1960s, when the psychoanalytic theory of play was dominant, the general opinion was that teachers should not intervene in children's play. Since children were working out their inner conflicts, they should be left alone to do it in their own way. Since that time, two developments have changed this view. First, cognitively oriented theories became more widespread and accepted. Second, Sara Smilansky (Johnson et al., 1987), an Israeli researcher with a cognitive orientation, experimented successfully with the concept of play training. Her research demonstrated that there was value in adult intervention in the play experience.

Smilansky's observations that low-income immigrant children were less involved in sociodramatic play than middle-class Israeli children led her to believe that some sort of intervention might be used to increase the duration and quality of play in the disadvantaged group. In her subsequent research, two approaches were used: outside intervention in which teachers made suggestions, from the sidelines, for improved play; and play participation, in which teachers actually played and modeled effective behaviors.

Decisions about the degree of intervention were left to the judgment of the teacher, based on her own observations (Smilansky, 1968). If the child wasn't playing at all (Level 1), the teacher would suggest a play theme, a role for the child, and the activities that would go with the role. At the same time, the teacher would try to get input from the child to avoid taking over the child's play. For example, she might ask the child to choose a toy or two from an available selection. Then the teacher would use the choice to help in selecting a theme. If the child engaged in dramatic play but persisted in solitary behavior (Level 2), the teacher would leave him in that theme and role but would encourage other children to join in, perhaps suggesting complementary roles for them. When children participated in sociodramatic play (Level 3), the teacher would intervene only if she observed that some element was missing.

Smilansky reports that, at first, the children were amazed when teachers joined them in their play, but after a very few days they began to take the interventions for granted. Children who received more attention were not viewed with jealousy by the others. As play became more competent and the teachers began to pull out, there was no request that they return. "The impression we gained was that the children accepted the adult participation as a temporary measure only, and when they had mastered the art of playing among themselves, they felt no particular need to be dependent upon the adults" (p. 50). While the immigrant children did not achieve the play competence of the native children, Smilansky points out that improvement did take place rather suddenly. However, interventions that took place over a period of days could not be expected to wipe out the deficits of several years.

Smilansky's study was influential in other parts of the world where studies were constructed to verify her findings and to expand what was known about the benefits of play training. Studies in the United States, England, and Canada, using variations of the two teaching approaches, produced very positive results. One such study reported: "Play training not only brought about gains in creativity, verbal IQ, perspective taking, language development, and conservation attainment, it also led to improvement in social skills such as cooperation and impulse control" (Johnson et al., 1982, p. 23).

As Smilansky's study and the follow-up research have shown, teacher intervention can be useful whether it involves intense help for deprived children or occasional suggestions for those who are largely successful in their play. In reflecting on these studies, a panel of researchers in early childhood play (Curry, 1971) suggested that teachers should

- Regard themselves as facilitators, stage setters, and listeners.
- Realize that high-quality play doesn't just happen and that their intervention may be essential.
- Use play sounds and gestures to get the play going ("Hey! I think I'll try out *this* car. Vroom, vroom . . .").
- Introduce new cognitive elements into the play using a familiar context so that children can easily understand ("This car is red and that one's blue. What color is the car you're playing with?").
- Avoid interpreting play too deeply if they don't know the child and the family well.
- Arrange the school setting to meet the needs of children from various cultures (e.g., the housekeeping corner might contain representative articles from the homes of different cultures).
- Supply nonstructured toys for the higher socioeconomic child (e.g., unpainted wood toys or blocks of varying shapes).
- Supply more structured toys in a sufficient number for the lower socioeconomic child (e.g., blocks that are brightly colored, which have obvious relationships to each other, but which still leave room for some creativity might be useful).
- Avoid supplying too many toys for either group, as this may stultify their creativity in adapting ordinary objects to play purposes.

## Four Approaches to Involvement with Play

An observational study of teachers in British preschools yielded four approaches to teacher involvement that work with young children. Johnson et al. (1987) elaborate on these findings with some useful suggestions.

### Parallel Playing

In parallel play, the teacher sits next to the child engaging in a similar activity. While the adult may make comments about what is going on, there is no attempt to enter into a discussion.

Benefits of parallel play can be: the adult's presence lets the child know that the play is worthwhile; the child may feel comforted by the adult's presence; the child may play longer with the adult there; and the child may try different ways of playing with the materials after watching the adult.

### Co-playing

In this case, the teacher plays with the children but lets them stay in control. The teacher may say something to extend the play, but is still careful not to take over.

The benefits of letting the children know that their play is worthwhile and encouraging the children to play longer are the same in co-playing as they are in parallel play. In addition, co-playing provides an opportunity to build rapport with the children and to extend play activities.

### Play Tutoring or Training

This approach was discussed at length in regard to Smilansky's studies. It relates most directly to sociodramatic play. Teachers can observe children to determine if the elements of this kind of play are present. If they are not, then outside intervention or participation in the play can be chosen. According to Smilansky, there are five elements that should be present in fully developed sociodramatic play: role-play and verbal declarations of the role; make-believe transformations in which objects, actions, and words substitute for real ones; social interaction, requiring at least two children in the play; verbal communication; and persistence, meaning sustained play episodes (Johnson et al., 1987).

## Intervention in Toddlers' Play

The fully developed sociodramatic play that is the goal for preschool children and beyond is too advanced for toddlers unless adult intervention is provided. An approach called infant and toddler-centered activity (McCune, 1986) can be effective for caregivers. Play sessions are held with one child, or

Although many experts believe that play is the primary means by which children learn, there are many occasions for teachers to engage in direct instruction as, for example, demonstrating essential skills such as how to hold a pencil or to write letters and words.

possibly two children, each week. The room or small area should be child-proofed to make it possible for the child to engage in any activity without prohibitions. A few toys should be present to provide focus for the session, but the child should take the lead in deciding what to do. The caregiver sits on the floor near the child, playing by invitation only. The session generally lasts between fifteen and thirty minutes according to the child's interest and the time available.

Benefits of this approach include those mentioned above in parallel playing. There is also time to observe the child in a way that other activities do not permit.

Many children today spend much of their time in front of the television set, ignored by busy or absent parents. More than ever teachers are noticing that children come to school with underdeveloped play skills. The research done by Smilansky and others has informed us that teachers can help to rectify this situation. It is not necessary and it is not sufficient to simply watch from the sidelines as children play. The benefits of play are so extensive that even a little intervention can make a big difference in what children are able to do and learn.

Today, play is regarded by many early childhood specialists as the most important means by which children learn. As we have seen, it offers many advantages. At the same time, there are other modes of teaching and learning that can be effective and are important to consider. As children grow older and move from the nursery to the kindergarten and primary grades, these other methods are more often observed than is play. This may or may not be positive, as we shall see.

## Learning Through Direct Instruction

Of all the other choices of teaching methods, direct instruction is perhaps most removed from play. Whereas play is child-centered, direct instruction is teacher-centered. Play at its best is flexible in design, with little teacher intrusion; direct instruction at its best is planned to the last detail and keeps the teacher at its center.

Traditional direct instruction simply involves a knowledgeable person (the teacher) imparting knowledge to a less informed person (the student). The direct instruction we read about today, however, is more complicated. It is a well-planned, very structured methodology in which the teacher presents material in small steps, asks the students to answer questions that have right and wrong answers, calls on the students in an ordered fashion, and gives immediate feedback for the answers (Sprinthall and Sprinthall, 1990).

Today's direct teaching is based on principles that have developed after several decades of research. These include:

- *Daily review.* If the current topic has been addressed before, children are provided an opportunity to clarify any confusion as the teacher reminds them of their earlier learning.
- *Presentation of new material.* First, the teacher tells what the lesson's objectives are. Then the new material is presented in small, easily managed steps. This is done at a brisk pace to keep the students' attention. The teacher checks continually for student understanding.
- *Guided practice.* The students are given an opportunity to use their new skills under teacher supervision. In a sense they teach the teacher, answering questions by demonstrating what they have learned.
- *Provision of correctives and feedback.* Correct answers are to be acknowledged clearly so that students understand when they are right. Incorrect answers are identified immediately for the student and corrections made.
- *Independent practice.* Students work on their own to reinforce what they have learned. Worksheets are a common form of independent practice for young children.
- *Weekly and monthly reviews.* These reviews provide students time for

more practice, thus encouraging higher achievement. (Sadker and Sadker, 1991, pp. 90–91)

These principles are translated into specific sequential steps for practical use. One approach, described by Arends (1988, p. 367), relates closely to the principles. He lists five steps the teacher should take:

1. Provide objectives and explain why the lesson is important. Get students ready to learn.
2. Demonstrate the new skill or present step-by-step information.
3. Provide and structure initial practice.
4. Check for student understanding and provide feedback.
5. Provide extended practice and help students transfer new knowledge to different or more complex situations.

While some proponents of direct instruction argue that this approach is applicable to students of all ages and in all subjects, there are some aspects that are not easily incorporated in an early childhood setting. Young children are seldom ready to listen to a teacher state the objectives of an upcoming lesson. Getting the children ready for the lesson will be more successful if the teacher uses an interesting introduction, perhaps incorporating new or related material that is attention getting. Extended practice may also not be of much interest to young children. While keeping their attention through the main presentation can be exhilarating for both teacher and students, follow-up worksheets and drill may actually work against progress. The initial excitement and interest are too often replaced by a feeling of drudgery. For very young or immature children, a brief follow-up may be all that is possible.

A four-step lesson sequence that is used in Montessori schools with children who are three-years-old and up may be more appropriate in the early years. It is used when new information, such as the names of new or unfamiliar objects, needs to be taught efficiently and directly. In this format the teacher

1. Prepares the children in any way that draws their interest. (Simply holding up an unfamiliar object is usually sufficient.)
2. Lays out the objects (usually no more than two or three) and, pointing to each in turn says, "This is a_____."
3. Calls on individual children to identify the objects. "Show me the _____."
4. Asks individual children to name the objects. "What is this?"

This sequence of steps can be adapted to instruction for skill attainment. In Step 2 the teacher says, "This is how to_____." This is followed by Step 4 in which the children demonstrate the skill.

Guidelines for Teachers

There are a number of guidelines that, if followed, can make a direct instruction lesson most successful even for young children.

- Keep groups of children small when possible.
- When demonstrating a skill, be sure you have first mastered it yourself. Rehearsal may be important.
- Be sure that any practice you assign is meaningful and not too long.
- Provide feedback as close as possible to children's answers or practice.
- Be specific in your feedback. Tell a child exactly what is right or wrong; avoid being too general.
- Emphasize praise in your feedback.
- If you must say something negative about a child's performance, be sure to follow up with the correct information.

While the position of this book is that direct instruction is inappropriate for much, or even most, of young children's learning, there are times when it is quite useful. When children want or need to learn a skill such as tying shoes, buttoning a coat, or using the bathroom correctly, direct instruction is the most efficient approach. At other times you may wish to use direct instruction to show how to use a new classroom material that takes special handling or to play safely on playground equipment. For the most part, however, experiences that approximate children's natural play activities seem to be most beneficial.

---

Learning Through Teacher Facilitation and Guidance

While play is the ultimate in child-directed learning and direct instruction is completely in the hands of the teacher, there are many methods of teaching and learning that fall somewhere in between. The role the teacher plays is one of facilitation and guidance. *Facilitation* indicates making learning easier; *guidance* refers to leading, pointing the way, or being a model.

The role of the child when the teacher facilitates and guides is a flexible one. The general goal for the child is to be a self-starting, self-directing, motivated, lifelong learner. To get to that point, however, much growth in cognitive, social, and emotional independence is needed. Each child develops at his or her own level and pace, and these may well be quite different in each of the areas of learning. For example, a kindergarten child may have learned to read in a supportive home environment and come to school ready to curl up in a corner with a book or to write short stories independently. This same child might well be afraid of soiling her hands with fingerpaint or mud. Self-direction and motivation are not part of her attitude toward these learnings. Instead, she will learn by following teacher direction, or by modeling the teacher's behavior, or by working with other, more confident children.

Whether we speak of the teacher's role or the child's, facilitation and guidance require flexibility. The following types of teaching and learning can be mixed, matched, or used independently. While the skilled teacher observes children closely and chooses methods to fit specific situations, children are themselves often aware of the ways in which they learn best. As one first grader said to his teacher (with just a shade of indignation), "Don't make Peter and me read in that group. It doesn't work on us. We want to read alone."

## Peer Teaching

Both in and out of school, children teach each other naturally, informally, and without prompting from parents or teachers. Brothers and sisters, cousins and friends help each other learn the culture ("Do what he says . . . he beats kids up"), adjust to new situations ("If you're gonna be in our club, you have to learn this song"), adapt to polite society ("Don't chew with your mouth open; it's gross"), accomplish athletic goals ("No, you catch the ball like *this*"), and attain academic success ("No, no, you're counting that all wrong . . . here, I'll show you"). Left to their own devices, children teaching each other are very direct and often negative, as these quite typical quotes demonstrate. With some guidance and facilitation from the teacher, however, peer teaching can have a positive effect in the classroom.

One major benefit is to the peer teacher. Learning is reinforced when children teach others what they have just learned. They are forced to clarify the information in their own minds, organize it in some way, and teach it clearly if their "students" are to be successful.

The benefits to those being taught by their peers include a shared sense of competence and self-direction, an opportunity to work on their own without teacher intervention. In addition, peer teaching may mean that children can learn something faster than by waiting for the teacher to take time with them.

The teacher's role has several facets. It is important to choose partners who are compatible; to assign a peer teacher who knows the information well enough to teach it, and, when possible, someone whose knowledge is new enough to be enhanced by this sort of practice; to give enough direction that learning will actually take place, but not so much as to be intrusive; and, finally, to know when to back off and leave the children alone.

Peer teaching can be as immediate and informal as having one child help another learn to tie his shoes. It can be as institutionalized as inviting somewhat older children into the class every day after lunch to listen to your be-

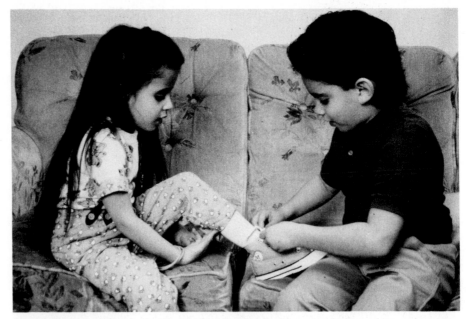

Peer teaching occurs constantly out of school, so when one child teaches another in a classroom environment, it is nothing new. The advantages of peer teaching include the ability of one child to understand the learning difficulties of another, to communicate in the language of childhood, and the tendency of the peer teacher to reinforce his or her own learning through the act of teaching.

ginning readers or to read stories themselves. In all its various forms, it promotes self-confidence and pride in both the peer teachers and their learners. And it provides the classroom teacher with some effective teaching help.

## Group Discussions

Like peer teaching, group discussions happen naturally in children's lives. Similarly, this approach to teaching can be facilitated and guided in the classroom. Children as young as three are often capable of group discussion if it is done appropriately.

When children work and play together, problems, confusions, and concerns may arise. Sitting down together to discuss the issues and come to conclusions is not too difficult when an adult facilitates. The teacher can help the children state the problem, assist them in taking turns talking, help them explore their feelings and attitudes, summarize all points, and lead the children to the most beneficial conclusion.

From about age four, a daily time can be set aside for whole group discussions. If this is too difficult for a class, separating into two or three groups with an adult in each one may be preferable. Topics for discussion might include:

- The upcoming activities for the day. The teacher and children plan together for the times that have not yet been decided. In the primary grades this may seem impossible within the often pressurized schedule, but it is an important goal. Planning of this sort gives children a sense of power and control over their lives and a feeling of investment in their own learning.
- Analysis of the day's events so far and readjustments, as necessary, for the rest of the day. This discussion occurs about halfway through the morning (for a half-day program) or just after lunch (for a full-day program). Children are permitted to bring up any topic they wish, whether it is interpersonal or academic or simply what they are feeling. The teacher facilitates by providing a sense of direction to the discussion and leading toward closure.
- Wrapping up the day's experiences and discussing what will happen the coming day. Children feel secure when they go home with a sense of closure and know what to expect the following day.
- Sharing or "show-and-tell." This kind of group experience can be deadly if not treated with skill. All children want to share whatever object or story they have brought from home; no children have a need to listen to others do the same. Yet sharing provides an opportunity for children to be the star for a few minutes and to learn to do so with skill. Turning individual sharing events into group discussions can help the entire class feel a part of the act. A minute-glass can be placed in full view of the speaker and, when it has emptied, time is called for questions and answers. The length of this time can also be limited by the minute-glass. Additional help for these sessions can be had by dividing the class into two or three groups, each led by an adult. It may also be desirable to assign children to particular days for sharing.

Whenever a discussion takes place, it is beneficial to include within it some ritual. This is determined by the teacher and helps provide structure for the situation. For example, in sharing sessions the teacher might always say after each contribution, "Thank you. If anyone has a question, please raise your hand." At the end of the questions and answers an appropriate conclusion might be, "Thank you all for your questions and answers. If it is your turn to share next, raise your hand." As the class grows more skilled in carrying on the discussions, the teacher can begin to pull back, turning over some leadership to the children. In kindergarten and primary classes it should become possible to leave the group entirely.

To do this, begin by asking one child to take your part. For the first day or week stay next to the child who is in charge, providing prompts as necessary. These usually aren't required often if you have been consistent in keeping the rituals. Children will know them so well that the discussion leader will easily adopt them, and the rest of the class will respond appropriately. When the children seem confident, withdraw from the group entirely and busy yourself with a task nearby. If any children begin to disturb the procedure, simply sit near them for a short time. If there is too much confusion or commotion, take charge again until the children are ready to try once more. This may take a few more days, weeks, or even months. If a particular class seems to have special difficulty, try breaking up in smaller groups and keeping the child-directed period to a very few minutes.

## Role Play

As we saw in the section Learning Through Play, children take on dramatic roles in their everyday play. There are times when this natural desire to play roles can be used to good instructional effect.

Suppose the class is about to take a field trip to a place that many or all of them have never visited. Thinking about this kind of unknown can be frightening for some children. For all the children, the more they know about the upcoming experience, the more they will learn once they are there. While informing the children about what to expect is helpful, acting out the events and behaviors before the trip promotes confidence, appropriate behavior, and fuller learning. Some portions of the role play can be more teacher-directed, particularly if there are safety considerations or disciplinary behaviors that need to be addressed. Other segments can be more open to children's interpretation if the field trip will include time for free play or creative experiences.

Role play in the classroom can be used for academic learning as well. Acting out the characters in a story is a way to dramatize what has been read; asking the children to imagine different endings to the story and act them out sends their thinking in new directions. As children become old enough to study historical events, playing the roles of real characters from the past makes them more real and easier to understand. Geography offers another opportunity for role play as the class acts out the decisions people make to move from one region to another. Math learning is enhanced when children play the role of various objects being regrouped. In some way, almost any academic learning can be adapted to role play. The main benefit of such an approach is that it makes use of the most meaningful real material of all: the child's own body.

## Learning Alone and Together

In the preschool years, learning to be together harmoniously is a major accomplishment. By the primary grades, most children have a definite preference for cooperative ventures. Still, at all ages, children prefer at times to play and work alone. It is important for caregivers and teachers to be aware of changing preferences and to honor them when possible. There are advantages to each type of learning.

## Learning Alone

Even infants should learn to be alone at times. Self-sufficiency and independence can be fostered if some alone periods are arranged from the very earliest weeks of life. It is critical, however, that caregivers be sensitive to the amount of time a child who can't yet verbalize his or her feelings is left alone. The periods should be short and discomfort avoided so that solitude is viewed as a positive experience.

In a center or school, where children are surrounded by a crowd of other human beings for the entire day, almost all of them will relish some time alone. Time and space need to be provided so that they can get away as needed.

In many, probably most, of this country's schools children from the primary grades and up learn chiefly on their own. Desks are placed in rows, individual work is given, and sharing information is considered cheating. This approach to learning can present problems: If new or complex assignments are made, working alone may lead to more confusion than learning; it is hard to stay motivated for long periods of solitary time; unless a desk is placed in total isolation, there is a natural desire to interact with nearby students, and this may well be expressed in competitiveness or misbehavior. On the other hand, working alone may be effective for doing simple tasks; for getting into a good book; for learning something that no one else has an interest in; or when children haven't been working well together and need some time alone before starting over.

The teacher's role in promoting effective solitary learning is twofold. First, it is important to be sensitive to children's needs or desires to be alone at times. In addition to the reasons just discussed, children may want to work out an academic problem alone or to cure a bad mood with some solitude. The second part of the teacher's role is to choose this type of learning when it is appropriate but to avoid overdoing it. Placing children in silent rows of desks for long periods of time may lead to feelings of isolation and boredom rather than to independence.

## Learning Together

Children can learn together from infancy, but in the earliest years the experience is not a cooperative one because the necessary social and cognitive skills have not yet been developed. Thus, caregivers of infants and toddlers can expect children to learn from each other by observation, but much more than that should not be expected. Preschoolers, on the other hand, are capable of rudimentary cooperation. These cooperative skills increase steadily until, in the primary grades, cooperative learning can emerge as an important and powerful tool for academic, social, and emotional success.

## Teaching an Ungraded Class: A Conversation with Linda Bennie

*In the United States, most kindergarten and primary classes are organized around traditional grade levels. Ungraded classes are rare and generally experimental. In Canada, the entire province of British Columbia has moved to an ungraded/continuous progress model for kindergarten and primary curricula, and other grades are due to follow. In most of British Columbia's seventy-six school districts, curriculum resource people, called "primary helping teachers," were assigned to ease the transition. This interview is with one of those helping teachers.*

Linda Bennie is one of three primary helping teachers in Surrey, British Columbia. For three years, her focus in supporting Surrey's 600-plus primary teachers has been the implementation of the province's ungraded primary program. The new model is similar to some found in the United States, but with a slightly different twist. In the United States ungraded classrooms have multiple ages, but in British Columbia this may or may not be the case. Instead, each school is permitted to create some classes of a single age, others of two ages, and still others of three or even four ages. Schools have experimented with different combinations.

As Linda explains, an ungraded class in British Columbia is "a state of mind" in which teacher and child work together to promote the greatest learning for the child. That learning "is not lockstep, is not evaluated by standardized tests, is not established according to artificial timetables, and is not tied in to promotion from one grade to the next." A motto of the program is that "all children are moving forward, but not all children are moving together."

The curricula for this new project have been developed from the philosophy of developmental appropriateness. As Linda puts it, "Chil-

dren come to us at different developmental levels. Just because they're chronologically five doesn't mean they're five physically, emotionally, or intellectually. We can't really expect all children to perform in the same ways when, realistically, they come to us at different points along a continuum. Also, we have to take into account what we know about the way kids learn. Intellectually, physically, and socially, individuals take big leaps or hit plateaus at different times. So you just can't expect everybody to be at the same place at the same time."

Linda emphasizes that British Columbia's new program is not simply concerned with academics, but is focused on the development of the whole child. As such, it has five developmental goals: physical, emotional/social, social responsibility, artistic and aesthetic, and intellectual.

It is believed that, within this new program, "there will be very, very little retention. It is expected that the vast majority of children will go on to the intermediate program." Evaluations include more than intellectual progress. "We look at other areas as well," Linda says, "for example, if the child is physically immature, tired, and not able to stay at school all day, or emotionally not ready to stay around so many children. We need to be more flexible in the ways we evaluate. It can't just be intellectual development." British Columbia's teachers are working toward keeping track of children's progress through various means, including observation, conferencing, portfolios, and student self-evaluation. The focus is on formative, as opposed to summative, assessment.

For the most part, the curriculum is now integrated by using umbrella themes. Gone are the earlier "scope-and-sequence expectations," which were much more rigid. In their place are "widely held expectations" that provide teachers with reference points by which they can identify children who may need extra help. Additionally, in specific subject areas such as mathematics, areas of emphasis are suggested for teachers under the broad headings of early primary or late primary.

After the first full year of implementation, Linda and another primary helping teacher did in-depth interviews with a number of kindergarten and primary teachers who had chosen to organize children into dual-year and multi-year classes. They found that a major advantage for teachers in these age groupings is that they get to work with the same children for more than one year. When children come back from summer vacation, for instance, the teachers know immediately where to begin their instruction. Further, the returning children know the classroom rules and routines.

Since teachers are now expected to use observation and anecdotal records in an ongoing assessment of their children, they find this easier when they have known the children for a longer period of time. Other pluses to the new system are the advantage of sharing ideas and information across the ages and the increased confidence that children gain in asking each other for help.

Linda's interviews brought out two problems with these types of age groupings. First, some long-time kindergarten teachers found that, with older children in the same class, it is difficult to spend much time engaging in such favorite activities as fingerplay or early childhood action games. The older children quickly become bored and potentially disruptive. Second, having widely mixed ages in physical education classes produced a variety of problems ranging from safety concerns to curriculum and space problems. Some schools are dealing with this by separating the ages during physical activities.

Based on extensive observation and interviews with teachers, Linda is enthusiastic about the new program. While dual-age or multiage grouping provides the most advantages, Linda believes that ungraded teaching can be done with any kind of class. "The main thing is that you focus on each class as a group of individuals," Linda advises, "not as a group of 'grade two's' or 'grade one's.' The task of a teacher in an ungraded primary class is to assess where each child is and to facilitate movement along the developmental continuum."

*To think about and discuss: A few pros and cons to teaching in an ungraded classroom are listed here. Create your own list of concerns and positive feelings about the concept. What do you think would be the concerns from the student's perspective? The teacher's perspective? The parents' perspective?*

Cooperative learning can bring a number of benefits if skillfully used by the teacher. Interdependence is fostered when a group of children can achieve success only as a unit rather than through their individual contributions. Negotiations, controversies, disagreements, and consideration of alternatives are all a part of collaboration. Children have an opportunity to teach and learn from each other as well as to respect each other's capabilities and talents. Finally, cooperative learning provides children with practice in getting along with others in the larger society, an important lifelong skill.

Since cooperative learning is an emerging capability in the preschool and kindergarten years, teachers should observe their children to determine their degree of readiness. Play activities that require cooperation offer many clues. In the block area, for example, children must engage in collaboration to make complex structures. If the teacher observes that their interactions are skillful and effective, the children are probably ready to transfer these skills to other situations.

These situations can grow informally out of the children's own expressed interests as well as from the teacher's plans. In one kindergarten, the children became fascinated by the many play possibilities offered by a single refrigerator box brought in by a student teacher. Soon, the student teacher was scouring the backs of stores for discarded appliance boxes. The result was a "box city," which took up more than half the kindergarten space. In between the arrival of the first box and the final establishment of the city, much cooperative learning took place.

When two additional boxes were brought in to join the first one, the student teacher held a whole-group meeting to determine what would be done with them. A brainstorming session led to a very long and creative list of things that could be made and done with the boxes. The student teacher suggested that much of the list consisted of buildings that could be found in their community and that they might want to make a whole city of boxes. The children were immediately enthusiastic. The first five buildings were identified (a fire station, a grocery store, a house, etc.), the student teacher was "commissioned" to scrounge for more boxes, and the children decided to work in groups. In consultation with his directing teacher, the student teacher decided that the group members would be determined by the adults rather than by the children. In this way, particular skills such as leadership and ingenuity could be spread across all groups.

In the following weeks, the children learned to plan, to share materials, to take turns at tasks, to help each other, and to be flexible when the plans didn't turn out as hoped. A small degree of competitiveness developed as each group tried to make its building more beautiful than the others. But, as more boxes were added to the collection and the city grew larger, classwide interdependence began to build. The boxes were taking over the space and something had to be done. Eventually, many of the class activity centers were housed within the boxes, but only after much discussion and negotiation between the children, the teacher, and the student teacher.

As children reach the primary grades, their social skills gradually reach the stage that co-operative learning activities are possible. Research has shown that cooperative learning not only results in strong cognitive gains, but that it does much to enhance positive social skills and attitudes.

Cooperative activities such as this, which grow out of children's interests, are appropriate in the primary grades as well. Unfortunately, academic pressures often make such ventures almost impossible. Yet it would be quite possible to take the kindergarten box city and include appropriate primary learning activities within it. Beginning mathematical skills could be applied to measuring spaces, boxes, and their relationships to each other. Signs, instructions, rules, and so on could be written and read. Officials of the city could be elected and a government established. Stores could sell their wares, with children learning to pay and give change in correct amounts.

More often, cooperative activities in the primary grades grow from the established curriculum. Any established projects can be done cooperatively. The role of the teacher is to set up groups so that skills are shared fairly equally, to teach collaboration skills as they are needed, to make sure that learning materials are sufficient, and to be available when help is needed. The teacher should avoid imposing his or her authority unless an emergency makes it necessary. It is more helpful when teaching collaboration to turn problems back to the group for resolution. Usually, it is the teacher's prerogative to assign tasks to the appropriate children. For example, if a group were putting together a report, a highly skilled reader might be assigned to work through an encyclopedia, while a beginning reader and writer could make a simple table of contents for the report.

The teacher's role as a facilitator and guide is at its best in cooperative learning. This is true also in the case of learning/interest/activity centers.

## Activity Centers

Centers will be discussed at greater length in Chapter 8. Here, we focus briefly on their contribution to the teaching and learning process.

Typically, a center is an area that has its own theme (blocks, housekeeping, math). It usually remains in some form throughout the school year, although short-term centers may reflect a particular classwide learning project. Time spent at centers may range from a few minutes to the entire day. Perhaps the whole class uses centers in one particular time block, or else children choose them individually, interspersed with other activities.

The teacher's role includes careful, sometimes extensive, preparation. The materials selected for the centers must be age-appropriate, keeping in mind that the interests and capabilities of the children may vary widely. Further, the teacher must choose between materials that are totally open-ended and those that are more directive. Goals must be determined, from free exploration to specific learnings.

Finally, decisions must be made about scheduling. Three basic models are common, although one has clear advantages over the others. One scheduling model is to have a specific "center time" in which children are allowed to explore each area freely for a set period. The teacher then signals the children that it is time to rotate to another center. While this method has the advantage of ensuring that every child gets to every center, it does not allow children to become engrossed in a single activity and explore it to the fullest. This may be even more frustrating than the opposite disadvantage, which is that some children in a group may lose interest in a center and become bored or disruptive. A second model is to have centers open for children when they finish other, more prescribed work. In this model, centers are viewed as a reward for completing tasks. While some children may be motivated to work harder to get to the (perhaps more interesting) centers, they may also simply work faster . . . and more sloppily. Other children may never get to the centers at all if they work too slowly or have trouble with their assignments. The third model makes use of blocks of time in which children can move freely according to their interests. If the teacher observes that some children spend all their time at one or two centers, this can be discussed and worked on. If a center's materials are being misused, they can be removed temporarily. If a center is being avoided, the teacher can highlight it, perhaps annointing it "the center of the day." The third model provides the most flexibility for both students and teachers. It also doesn't create the frustrations of being attached to a center for an assigned period of time, and it ensures that all children have an opportunity to use the centers.

Once preparations are complete, the teacher must determine the best way to introduce the center or its newest materials. Some activities are best served if they are explained or demonstrated first, while others should simply be placed in the center for children to discover.

During the time in which children use the centers, the teacher's role is to observe and to intercede only when it is necessary for discipline or when some learning can be enhanced. Observations should inform the teacher of adjustments that might make the centers more effective. They should also tell the teacher much about individual children's current learning levels and capabilities, about their social development, and about their emotional strengths and needs.

Centers offer children several advantages. There are opportunities for choosing between materials, between centers, and between other students to interact with. Whether the materials promote totally free exploration or have some guidance incorporated in them, children must interact without constant teacher direction. In all these things, independence and self-governance are promoted. Most centers are designed to promote creativity as well. As children make choices and decisions, as they explore and construct, new directions are taken and old restrictions are left behind. Finally, centers, at their best, provide opportunities to learn through play-oriented activities.

Learning through teacher facilitation and guidance is child-centered, rather than teacher-centered. Children's interests are considered as plans are made, and the children themselves direct much of their own learning.

## Developmentally Appropriate Practice

In 1987 the National Association for the Education of Young Children (NAEYC) published a landmark position statement, *Developmentally Appropriate Practice in Early Childhood Programs Serving Children from Birth through Age 8* (Bredecamp, 1987). The impetus for this publication was the "trend toward increased emphasis on formal instruction in academic skills [that] has emerged in early childhood programs." NAEYC argued that this trend "is based on misconceptions about early learning" and that research in recent years has affirmed "that children learn most effectively through a concrete, play-oriented approach to early childhood education" (p. 1). The position statement is extensive, covering both child development and curriculum issues. The contributors to it were hundreds of early childhood specialists, although the statement's primary writing was done by a special commission. In the following section, the primary points having to do with teaching and learning are listed. They provide important guidance for anyone who aspires to work with young children. As in the report itself, the points are separated into age groups and into appropriate and inappropriate practices.

## Infants

It is *appropriate practice* when adults

- have many face-to-face interactions with infants.
- talk with and sing and read to infants extensively.
- hold and carry infants to provide a wide variety of experiences.
- give gentle, supportive responses. They respect infants' beginning efforts at communication with imitations of sounds.
- observe and encourage infants at play, sometimes offering additional ideas.
- praise infants for their efforts and accomplishments.
- engage in infant games (peek-a-boo, five little piggies) with children who are interested.

It is *inappropriate practice* when adults

- leave infants in cribs, playpens, or seats without adult attention for long periods of time.
- use harsh voices, shout, or use baby talk.
- ignore infants' responses.
- interrupt infants' playtime, snatching toys away from them, or imposing their own ideas of play on the infants.
- criticize infants for their clumsy efforts at new skills.
- view play as a time filler rather than as a learning experience.

## Toddlers

It is *appropriate practice* when adults

- have plenty of one-on-one conversations with children.
- simplify their language for clarity, but also help children learn new words and appropriate sentence structure.
- support children learning new skills by providing help when it's necessary and allowing children to do what they are capable of.
- provide children with limited options and respect their preferences.
- permit children to roam around or to sit and parallel play with toys and objects.
- praise children for their accomplishments.
- realize that such routine tasks as eating, toileting, and dressing are important learning activities for toddlers and treat them as such.
- play reciprocally, modeling imaginative play behaviors.
- support extended periods of play so that play can become more complex and mature.
- respect toddlers' solitary and parallel play.
- read, sing, tell, and act out stories frequently.

- expect toddlers to explore and manipulate art materials and do not expect finished products.
- provide exploratory outdoor activity, particularly making use of sand and water play.

It is *inappropriate practice* when adults

- dominate the talk with toddlers.
- use baby talk or language that is too complex.
- impatiently take over tasks that toddlers are learning slowly.
- don't intervene when children are highly frustrated.
- don't give children choices but expect everyone to do the same thing.
- criticize toddlers for what they cannot do or for their clumsy struggles for mastery.
- do not play with toddlers because it seems silly or boring.
- try to make toddlers play together rather than supporting their solitary and parallel play.
- force a large group to watch an activity without opportunity for participation.

## Three-Year-Olds

It is *appropriate practice* when adults

- support children's play by helping when needed, but permit them to do what they can on their own.
- provide opportunities for three-year-olds to demonstrate and practice their developing self-help skills, although toileting accidents, spilled food, and other problems require extra patience.
- recognize that children this age may exhaust themselves, especially when trying to keep up with the older children. Plenty of naps or restful periods are provided.
- provide opportunities to play at all levels from solitary to parallel to play with one or two others.
- permit children to enter and leave the group during stories, songs, and other group activities.
- provide plenty of time and space for exercising large muscle skills.
- provide plenty of uninterrupted time for persisting at and practicing self-chosen tasks and newly developing skills.
- provide plenty of materials for practicing fine motor skills. Process is valued over product.
- provide plenty of materials for exploration and learning about the environment.
- support developing language by patiently listening, answering questions, and speaking clearly.

It is *inappropriate practice* when adults

- are impatient and do tasks for children that they could do alone.
- expect children to be independent and on their own for long periods of time.
- expect children to participate in whole group activities and don't permit them to leave.
- require children to do activities together or to share toys.
- restrict large motor activity to short outdoor recesses.
- become impatient when children want to repeat tasks many times.
- insist children repeat tasks they're not interested in.
- expect such fine motor skills as cutting, coloring within the lines, or following a teacher's modeled drawing.
- avoid the use of some materials because they are too messy or take too much time to clean up.
- limit language or music activities because the children may be too silly or loud.

## Four- and Five-Year-Olds

It is *appropriate practice* when adults

- provide experiences for learning in all developmental areas: physical, social, emotional, intellectual.
- respect individual differences in ability and interests.
- design appropriate activities for differing abilities, development, and learning styles.
- permit children to select many of their own activities.
- expect children to be physically and mentally active.
- permit children to work individually or in small groups most of the time.
- provide concrete learning activities with materials that are relevant to children's own lives.
- facilitate learning by moving among children asking questions, offering suggestions, adding more complex materials and ideas.
- provide opportunities for self-directed problem solving and experimentation.
- provide many opportunities to see how reading and writing are useful before giving instruction in letter names or word identification.
- provide daily opportunities for children to use large muscles and express themselves freely and loudly.
- provide daily opportunities for developing small muscle skills.
- provide daily experiences with art and music.
- use developmental assessment of children's progress and achievement to plan the curriculum, identify special needs children, and evaluate the program.

It is *inappropriate practice* when adults

- focus classroom experiences on intellectual development to the neglect of other areas.
- evaluate children only with standardized tests, expecting all children to perform the same tasks at the same level.
- measure children's worth by how well they do on standardized tests.
- use highly structured, teacher-directed lessons almost exclusively.
- expect children to sit down and do paper-and-pencil tasks, or sit passively, for long periods of time.
- use large-group, teacher-directed instruction much of the time.
- dominate the curriculum with workbooks, ditto sheets, flashcards, and other similar abstract materials.
- emphasize rote memorization and drill.
- require children to work individually at desks or tables most of the time.
- fragment cognitive learning into content areas such as math, science, or social studies with times set aside to concentrate on each.
- limit opportunities for large muscle activity.
- provide art and music only if there is extra time.

## Primary Grades

It is *appropriate practice* when adults

- design curriculum for all areas of development.
- design curriculum that helps children learn how to learn, to establish a foundation for lifelong learning.
- design curriculum and instruction that develop self-esteem and positive feelings toward learning.
- permit children to move at their own pace in acquiring academic skills.
- expect and accept different levels of ability, development, and learning styles.
- integrate the curriculum so that learning of traditional subject areas takes place primarily through projects, learning centers, and playful activities that reflect children's interests.
- encourage children to evaluate their own work and help them figure out how to improve it.
- view errors as a natural and necessary part of learning.
- provide learning materials and activities that are concrete, real, and relevant to children's lives.
- work together with children to select and develop projects.
- plan frequent outings and visits from resource people.
- change activity centers frequently so there are new things to do.
- make use of peer tutoring and learning from others through conversation.

- provide multicultural and nonsexist activities and materials.
- provide outdoor activity daily.

It is *inappropriate practice* when adults

- focus the curriculum on the intellectual and neglect other areas of development.
- measure children's worth by how well they do on such things as standardized tests.
- evaluate children against the group norm and expect everyone to meet the same academic level.
- divide the curriculum into separate subjects taught in isolation.
- provide art, music, and physical education only once a week and only through teaching by specialists.
- use instructional strategies that revolve around teacher-directed reading groups for most of every morning, whole group lectures, and whole group discussions.
- regard projects, learning centers, play, and outdoor time as embellishments and frills.
- use most of their planning time to correct worksheets and other seatwork rather than for planning enriching activities.
- expect children to work silently and alone on worksheets and other seatwork during most work times.
- limit materials primarily to books, workbooks, and pencils.
- try to motivate children to learn through external rewards and punishments.
- test children regularly on every subject and teach to the test.

The NAEYC position statement owes a historical debt to the writings of John Dewey and to the open education movement of the 1960s and '70s. It also relies on the findings of educational research from more recent decades. The position statement will be referred to again within the next two chapters, and its views on integrating the curriculum provide the basis for the chapters in Part 4.

## Extending Your Learning

1. Observe two preschools or kindergartens for at least two hours each. Record the length of time spent on play, directed learning, and varieties of facilitated learning. Compare the two classes with each other in relation to noise levels, degree of child–child interaction, and, to the extent possible, the amount of learning that took place. Try to picture yourself in each setting. Which would you choose? Why?
2. Observe children playing and practice some of the intervention techniques

described by Sara Smilansky and others. Make note of when you feel you intervene too extensively or not enough. Go back and try again.

3. If you are currently working in an early childhood setting, make a checklist from the NAEYC position statement for your age group. Share it with your directing teacher and discuss implementing it in your experience there.

## References

Arends, R. (1988). *Learning to Teach.* New York: McGraw-Hill.

Arnaud, S. (1971). Polish for play's tarnished reputation. In N. Curry and S. Arnaud (eds.), *Play: The child strives toward self-realization,* pp. 5–12. Washington, DC: NAEYC.

Bowers, L. (1988). Children need playgrounds—but playgrounds need help. *Journal of Physical Education, Recreation and Dance.* 59(7):47–51.

Bredecamp, S. (ed.) (1987). *Developmentally appropriate practice in early childhood programs serving children from birth through age 8.* Washington, DC: NAEYC.

Brown, N. (1971). Three-year-olds' play. In *Play: The child strives toward self-realization,* pp. 26–38.

Brown, N., Curry, N., and Tittnich, T. (1971). How groups of children deal with common stress through play. In *Play: The child strives toward self-realization,* pp. 26–38.

Curry, N. (1971). Consideration of current basic issues on play. In *Play: The child strives toward self-realization,* pp. 51–61.

Johnson, J., Christie, J., and Yawkey, T. (1987). *Play and early childhood development.* Glenview, IL: Scott, Foresman.

King, N. (1986). Play and the culture of childhood. In G. Fein and M. Rivkin (eds.), *The young child at play,* pp. 29–42. Washington, DC: NAEYC.

McFarland (1971). The first year of life. In *Play: The child strives toward self-realization,* pp. 7–8.

Moyles, J. (1989). *Just Playing? The role and status of play in early childhood education.* Philadelphia: Open University Press.

Pitcher, E., and Schultz, L. (1983). *Boys and girls at play: The development of sex roles.* New York: Praeger.

Sadker, M., and Sadker, D. (1991). *Teachers, schools, and society.* New York: McGraw-Hill.

Saltz, R., and Saltz, E. (1986). Pretend play training and its outcomes. In *The young child at play,* pp. 155–174.

Smilansky, S. (1968). *The effects of sociodramatic play on disadvantaged preschool children.* New York: Wiley.

Spodek, B., and Saracho, O. (1988). The challenge of educational play. In D. Bergen (ed.), *Play as a medium for learning and development,* pp. 9–22. Portsmouth, NH: Heinemann.

Sprinthall, N., and Sprinthall, R. (1990). *Educational psychology.* New York: McGraw-Hill.

# The Physical Environment

8

OBJECTIVE

When you finish reading this chapter, you should be able to

- Design an indoor environment that takes into account the ages and developmental levels of the children who will use it.
- Design on outdoor environment based on the same developmental differences.
- Make adjustments in already designed environments to make them more appropriate for the children who will use them.

As you think about this chapter on your own, your should be able to

- Coordinate your ideas for environmental design with your developing preference in learning philosophies and theory.

The usual rectangular shape of a classroom or playground may seem straightforward and simple, but the challenges of planning and using these spaces effectively are many and varied. Some examples from real-life early childhood settings illustrate the kinds of problems teachers can expect to face as well as some possibilities for dealing with them.

■ *One kindergarten teacher tried every discipline technique she knew to keep children from running the length of the room, frequently bumping into and injuring others. She finally realized that the wonderful open space in the center, just right for whole group discussions and movement activities, was also an open invitation for wild, abandoned play at inappropriate times. One obvious solution was to move furniture into the area, but dragging it back and forth for different activities didn't appeal to her. She decided to start small and simply placed her own rocking chair right in the middle of the empty space. That was all it took! The space no longer looked like a freeway and was no longer treated as one.*

■ *In a crowded urban area a small, private preschool–primary school was established in a large, old house. While the rooms were large and airy, there was no space for the children to play except on the roof. This did not seem to bother the preschoolers, but by first or second grade, the children obviously needed space to run. Fortunately, there was a park nearby and the primary grade teachers soon began making twice weekly outings. At first, these were seen as a way to provide running and playing space, but the teachers soon realized that the park was a potential learning laboratory as well. Before long, science studies took place primarily in this new learning space.*

■ *Another urban preschool–primary school had exactly the opposite problem. While it was located in the heart of the city, the building and grounds were rented from a family who had lived there for three generations. The house was huge and the grounds were extensive and forested. Although there was a large, grassy playground area, it contained no playground equipment. Often, children would tire of the few available toys and quietly find ways to disobey the strict rule to stay out of the forest. One afternoon, the teachers were discussing ways to expand the school's small garden. It occurred to one teacher that, if they put a new garden area adjacent to the forest, it might act as a barrier and the children would be less likely to escape. The plan was tried, with every child in the school having an opportunity to help create the new garden. This gave everyone an interest in seeing that the garden stayed healthy and cared for. The result was that no one walked over or beyond the garden, not because it was a barrier, but for fear of damaging the emerging plants.*

■ *A new teacher of four-year-olds was faced with an unusually confining space. The classroom was so tiny that there was just enough room for a few tables, some round and some rectangular, and a few storage shelves along the side. After several weeks of trying to cope, she asked two other teachers to help her plan more efficient use of the space. Eventually, one table was laid on its side against the wall and an old bedspread was draped over it. Inside were placed a few pillows of varying sizes. The children were delighted and changed the identity of this newly created space every few days, or even several times within a day. Sometimes it was designated a quiet library, at other times a cage in the zoo, a place to play house, or a jet on its way to faraway places. Because the table now took a little less space, it was possible to create a small movement area in one corner.*

As these examples show, the physical environment is central to the teaching/learning experience and to the way children feel about their centers and schools. Environmental issues include the size of the space, the way the space is divided for varying activities, the appropriateness and sufficiency of furniture and materials, environmental safety, the appropriateness of the environment to the ages of the children it serves, and the attention given to coordinating the indoor and outdoor settings. All these issues will be considered in this chapter.

The first consideration in planning the environment is the character and needs of the children within it.

## Children and Their Environment

Much of what children need in their environment is related to their age and stage of development. The physical, emotional, social, and intellectual needs of an infant are far different from those of a seven-year-old. In its position statement, *Developmentally Appropriate Practice in Early Childhood Programs* (Bredecamp, 1987), the National Association for the Education of Young Children addresses the environmental needs of varying ages as well as their implications. As each age group is considered, the NAEYC position will be the basis for discussion.

### Infants and Toddlers in the Center's Environment

NAEYC points out that accidents are a major cause of infant death. Thus, the environment must be completely safe while still designed to foster curiosity and mobility: "All the indoor and outdoor areas, the equipment, toys, and furniture in a good program are designed to ensure children's safety, while promoting their urge to explore" (p. 29).

Infants and toddlers need plenty of room to learn how to use their bodies. For infants, the space should be arranged so there is room to roll over, play alone quietly, and to learn to crawl. For toddlers, there must be room to run as well as walk. Well supervised times should be provided for exploration on the floor. Infant and toddler rooms need washable carpeting that is kept sanitized.

Infants learn most and are happiest if they move about the environment. The caregiver's role is to carry, rock, swing, and take infants on carrying "tours" of the entire center, giving them an opportunity to see the variety that is in their environment.

Toddlers need play spaces, both indoors and out, that are separated from those of older children. Because their social skills are in the earliest stages, they should be permitted to move between areas with groups of children and more private spaces with room for no more than two children.

Variety in the center's furnishings supports development. Soft elements, such as pillows and padded walls, counterbalance hard elements, such as rocking chairs and mirrors. All furnishings should be monitored for total safety. Adults should look for loose nuts and bolts, fraying strings and wires,

In designing spaces for infants and toddlers safety is of paramount importance. There should be sufficient space to permit safe movement, toys should not be small enough to swallow, and furnishings and equipment should be padded whenever possible.

and broken materials. This should be done continually so that there are no unpleasant surprises for the children or their caregivers.

For the sake of both cleanliness and the children's contentment, there should be separate areas for sleeping, feeding, diapering, and play. At the same time, it is desirable to have occasional low sounds enter the sleeping area so that infants learn adaptability. Likewise, infants on carrying tours should stop by a diapering event to get a different perspective on how it works and to have a chance to be sociable.

Attention should be given to the decor of the surroundings since even infants respond positively to rooms that are cheerful as opposed to dingy and dark. Since contrasts in color and design are interesting to infants and toddlers, bright colors in distinctive patterns should be used in the decor. For infants particularly, design should be simple so their immature eyes can focus more easily. Pictures and other decorations should be placed at two levels: near the floor for crawling infants and toddlers, and at adult eye level for the times when they are carried.

Atmospheric conditions are an important consideration, particularly for infants. For good health it is important to provide fresh air and maintain the right temperature and humidity. Infants and toddlers need time both indoors and outdoors. Excursions to the outdoors are often neglected, however, especially when the weather requires children to be bundled up. However, the health benefits are such that it is well worth the time and effort to take them outside.

The same principles of safety, color, and design that help determine the center's environment are also important in terms of toys and other materials. For infants, toys should all be too large to swallow but small enough to be grasped and manipulated. Mobiles should be placed within view, but should no longer be used once an infant can reach for and grasp them. Responsive toys are far preferable to those that infants just watch—a rubber duck that squeaks when squeezed is far better than a wind-up duck that just waddles on by.

Outdoors, there should be play equipment for the toddlers that includes opportunities to climb, go around, in, and out of, and other apparatus that require adult supervision, such as swings, jungle gyms, and low slides.

As babies become mobile they acquire interest in increased physical challenges. The center should have a number of low, padded climbing structures and steps available for exploration. Toys should be kept on low, open shelves rather than in jumbled and confusing boxes or on high shelves where only adults can reach them.

Even babies are interested in books, but these should be designed for their interests and capabilities. The books should be of heavy cardboard with rounded edges rather than of easily torn paper pages. Pictures should be brightly colored and of simple, rather than complex, design. For older toddlers, books with paper pages are appropriate, but caregivers should not expect them to remain unsoiled.

For toddlers and for infants who are mobile, the physical environment should respond to three aspects of development, each of which contains a polarity: (1) the need for independence versus the need for dependence, (2) the growth of motor ability versus undeveloped motor competence, and (3) a sense of being in control versus the sense of being controlled (Bergen et al., 1988). Thus, the recommendation to provide room for exploration while making sure that the surroundings are safe, the suggestion of softly padded but adventuresome climbing materials, and the suggestion for responsive over observational toys are all appropriate for infants and toddlers.

## Preschool and Kindergarten Children in the Center or School Environment

Young children, especially preschoolers, and kindergartners, need plenty of space and time to exercise large muscles and expand their physical skills. Riding tricycles, throwing and catching balls, running, jumping, balancing, galloping, hopping, and skipping are all important skills that require space, both indoors and out.

Fine motor skills develop during these years as well. Puzzles, pegboards, beads for stringing, scissors, woodworking and construction sets, and art materials are all appropriate, but not for all children or at all ages. The youngest children should not be expected to use scissors, and even some five-year-olds may need to rip and tear rather than cut. Woodworking sets are most appropriate for kindergarten children, as are the more complex puzzles. The youngest children should not be expected to provide, or care about, finished products. It is the process that is important, and, indeed, for the development of fine motor skills, this should be the focus for all ages.

For preschool children especially, it is important that materials and time for exploration of the environment be provided. This is a time in life when natural curiosity is high, and a well-prepared environment can foster its continued development. Blocks of many sizes and shapes; dramatic play props that change with children's interests; sand and water tables or boxes with plenty of scooping, measuring, and pouring utensils; toys and tools with various gadgets for manipulation—all these provide good opportunities for engaging in exploratory activities.

For children in the preschool-kindergarten years, the environment should include a wide variety of activities that encourage them to learn through active exploration and interaction with others. Young children are not yet ready for disciplined, long-term sitting or for standing in perfect lines to march down the hall. Further, there is no point in creating an environment that attempts to foster such behaviors, for these are not the ways in which young children grow best.

## Computers and Young Children: A Conversation with Karen Klein

*When computers were first proposed for young children's learning, most early childhood educators reacted with great concern. In due time, software was created, research began, and the controversy became more thoughtful and balanced. In this conversation we talk with an early childhood expert who has come to believe in early computer experiences and has her own education computer consulting company, Kkids, Inc. in Bellingham, Washington.*

Karen Klein began her teaching career in California with first graders and, after four-years experience and a master's degree, started teaching kindergarten. Although her experience began in the 1960s, much of what we now regard as new attitudes toward developmental appropriateness was an integral part of her teaching philosophy: whole language, discovery learning, problem solving for higher level thinking skills, thematic instruction, and interdisciplinary curriculum units. A favorite part of Karen's job was developing curriculum based on these philosophies. Eventually she began to team teach with a kindergarten teacher who shared her views on children's learning.

In the mid 1970s, they had what Karen calls "a Cinderella experience." At a reading conference they met the president of a publishing company and, somehow, found themselves describing for him the curriculum and materials that they had developed. Before long, the two had turned over to the company just about everything they had ever created for their class room, leading to publication of a complete kindergarten curriculum entitled "CROSSTIES: A Discovery Approach to Learning." Marketing tours, speaking engagements, and new product development followed.

In 1979, Karen moved to Portland, Oregon where she spent seven years as early childhood coordinator for the city's schools and as a curriculum consultant to area Headstart centers. During that time she was appointed director of a K-1 computer lab program in fourteen elementary schools, a new direction for Karen and one that required intensive training. "It was in that capacity that I began my immersion in the technological world and to begin speaking publicly about children and computers."

Much of what Karen had to say about the subject reflected the concerns of the time. She remembers one particular speech from the early 1980s. "I still have a copy of that speech. It was all about the cautions, worries, and dangers of sitting little children in front of a computer: moving away from concrete, hands-on experiences; robbing kids of valuable time just as if they were in front of a TV; isolating kids from social interaction; decreased language development; and focus on a learning medium that would put girls at a disadvantage."

While most early childhood educators shared Karen's views, research results began to show that "the findings were dramatically different from what we feared. There's definitely a role for young children and computers. For example, language development actually increases. Of course, the setting must be correct. If children are allowed to talk and interact in the classroom, they'll talk to each other at the computer and their social development increases."

Key to this development, Karen says, is the quality of the software. "If it's software that's developmentally appropriate, that promotes problem solving, reasoning, and thinking . . . rather than skills and drills . . . kids get into it. Just as there's a block corner where they

have to figure out how to build a structure without things falling off, there are similar opportunities on the computer. And computers also model dramatic play. Kids make objects on the computer move around and they talk to them, just as they do in the doll corner."

Karen also points out that children may have an easier time manipulating objects on a computer than with the usual classroom manipulative materials. In her current work as an independent consultant, she has observed this phenomenon firsthand. Not long ago, for example, she was introducing young children to a new computer game for which there were related concrete materials. Deciding to introduce the "real-life" construction activity first, she found that some of the children had trouble making the pieces work together but, later, had no trouble with the computer version. Conversely, other children preferred working with the concrete materials first. Karen points out that with computers, as with any material, it is important to take into account the needs of individual children.

*To think about and discuss: Do you have reservations about using computers with young children or do you believe they are developmentally appropriate? Discuss your views with others who disagree. Read some current research and consider your position. How does your own level of expertise with computers affect your attitude toward teaching with them?*

## Primary Children in the School Environment

Although children in the primary grades have outgrown their infant dependence on the physical environment as the primary source of learning, it is still of great importance. Children of this age still learn most effectively through the manipulation of concrete, hands-on materials mixed with a judicious use of somewhat more abstract materials. Further, they still learn best when they can interact with each other or, at times, choose to be alone. Small group work is attractive to most, and they are well ready for learning projects requiring cooperative decision making.

Needs and interests such as these argue against the traditional classroom environment in which desks are lined up in rows facing the largest chalkboard and an ever-in-charge teacher. Instead, there should be centers that include opportunities for reading and writing, math games, science experiments, and other learning experiences. Tables or desks can be placed so children can work in clusters. There should also be facilities for children to withdraw from the group and be alone. These might be out-of-the-way desks, a small, cozy reading corner, or even a large refrigerator box with a desk or chair inside.

The materials in the activity centers should be changed frequently so that children have new things to explore, although old familiar materials should also be brought back and updated for expansion on earlier learning. A center might contain a variety of materials within one curricular area, such as a reading center with many kinds of books. Or it might be stocked with variations on one topic of study, such as different games and activities for learning subtraction tables. Children could choose any of the materials and the teacher would be assured that, at the reading center children were learning something about reading and at the math center they were getting practice with subtraction.

Other materials for the primary grades that are "concrete, real, and relevant to children's lives" (Bredecamp, 1987, p. 69) are blocks, cards, games, woodworking tools, arts and crafts materials, including paint and clay, and scientific equipment. Such materials run counter to the more traditional programmed textbooks, workbooks, and pencils. For the greatest success in learning, primary children should be able to choose from these varied centers for much of the day with correspondingly less time spent on worksheets and other seatwork. Again, this is opposed to the traditional model of requiring children to complete their prescribed seatwork before permitting them to make use of interesting activity centers and materials.

## Children with Special Needs

Chapter 6 presented a number of suggestions for working with special needs children, many of them related to the environment. If you are working with such children, you may find those suggestions a place to start. In addition, you should confer with available specialists and the children's parents to learn what environmental adjustments might benefit these children. In general, extra sensitivity is critical to their well-being. Visually impaired children, for example, need to know where things are and to spend their time in nonhazardous surroundings. Children with emotional problems need consistency in their environment and little or no clutter. If there are several children with such problems, it may be worthwhile to simplify the entire environment. If there is just one child, he or she can be trained to focus on a limited number of activity areas, and then these can be simplified. Children with problems in physical development need materials and equipment that give them a sense of accomplishment and control. Those who are delayed mentally also need materials that lead them to a feeling of mastery.

The various challenges faced by special needs children are unique to their own situations. It is up to the teacher to be sensitive to those needs and to turn to experts who can better define those needs and provide skills, materials, and ideas for coping with them.

## A Nonsexist, Nonracist Environment for All Children

In ways both subtle and obvious, adults send messages to infants and young children that teach them society's expectations about their gender and their race. In recent years, we have become aware that such messages can have a negative effect on development and that these messages are often sent to children in the way we create the classroom environment.

As you prepare the environment for your children, step back and look for evidence that both sexes are welcome in all areas, both indoors and outdoors. A place to start is the housekeeping corner. Are there plenty of clothes for both boys and girls? Do dolls and their clothes represent both genders?

Most frequently it is the boys who gravitate toward the block corner and the girls who head for the housekeeping corner. Cross-migration can be encouraged by placing the centers next to each other and intermingling some of the materials. Thus, girls find themselves enjoying the creation of a special bed made from blocks in which to place a favorite doll. And boys discover the need to dress in the right clothing to play in the block structure they have just built.

The library area needs careful attention. Check books, particularly the older ones, for people in sex-stereotyped roles. Are the girls always submissive, helpless, and in need of rescuing? Are the boys rewarded only for their strength and bravery and never for their caring behavior? Are children of different races pictured? If so, is one race (probably white) always in the dominant or more successful role? It is not necessary to throw out every book that presents these stereotypes, but it is important to be sure of a proper balance.

The pictures on the walls should be checked in much the same way the library is. Boys and girls need approximately equal representation and they should not appear only in sex-stereotyped roles. If pictures hung or posted in the block area show nothing but energetic young boys and those in the housekeeping area present only girls caring for dolls or keeping house, children will readily get the message that this is their expected behavior. Likewise, it is important that different races are portrayed. Children need to see their own races represented so that they will feel valued and not invisible. They also learn from seeing other races portrayed with which they are not familiar. This can help prepare them to meet such people in a way that leads to understanding rather than to confusion or negativity.

## The Uses of Space

The way space is used, both indoors and outdoors, can affect how children learn, how content they feel, and how they interact with each other. A room that is too cramped may lead to irritability and fighting; a room that is too open can cause feelings of insecurity or a sense of being lost. An outdoor area in which all activities cross each other could be unsafe or encourage dissension. Outdoor equipment that is designed only for the older children can be overwhelming and even unsafe for the younger ones. Conversely, a well-designed environment can go far to promote emotional well-being, prosocial behavior, and intellectual growth. Underlying all decisions about environmental design should be the needs of the children who are served.

### Indoor Space

Deciding how to divide the available space is more than moving furniture around. There needs to be a conceptual base for making decisions. For example, one way to divide space is into open and closed areas. David Day (1983), who has written extensively on this topic, argues against thinking that bigger is necessarily better. While he believes that open space provides room for young children to move freely and, perhaps, have more opportunity to make choices, he also believes that even very young children need privacy now and then. Further, sound travels more readily in open areas, thus making the creation of quiet spaces more difficult. Thus, as you prepare the environment, you need to be sure that there are places where one or two children can be alone as well as sufficient space for large and small groups to gather. Activity areas should be laid out so that they are not in competition with one another, and the type of space provided should not contradict the activity placed in it. As an example, the nap area or library center (usually closed spaces) should not be placed next to the music and movement area (necessarily open space). Further, such areas as the library center are generally more inviting if they are cozily closed off than if they blend into the more open spaces. Centers that are located in buildings with many small spaces (perhaps a renovated house) can separate such areas by placing them in different rooms. Single-room classes can divide spaces with book and toy shelves or with inexpensive screens.

Once the areas are established, observe children using them. Day (1983) suggests asking such questions as: Are the children using each area? Are they using each as it was intended to be used? Can children move easily from area to area? Does the arrangement encourage and support combining materials from adjacent areas? Is such use appropriate or disruptive? Does the physical setting support and allow for the full range of child behavior?

Figure 8.1 shows one way to arrange a classroom when the concept of open and closed space is used. It is most appropriate for a preschool or kindergarten class. The same concept would be possible to adapt for older or younger children.

Another way to conceptualize indoor space is on a continuum from quiet to active. This can be intersected with a second continuum from wet to dry (Bergen et al., 1988). In this model, the room would be divided into four main sections, each with its appropriate level of noise and wetness. Figure 8.2 shows how this works. Figure 8.3 shows how this concept might be

Many experts believe that children respond best to small areas reserved for specialized activities: reading, music, block play, napping, etc., and that by allowing children to choose their own activities within these "centers" it is possible to develop self-direction and independent decision making.

FIGURE 8.1

**An Environment Using Open and Closed Space**

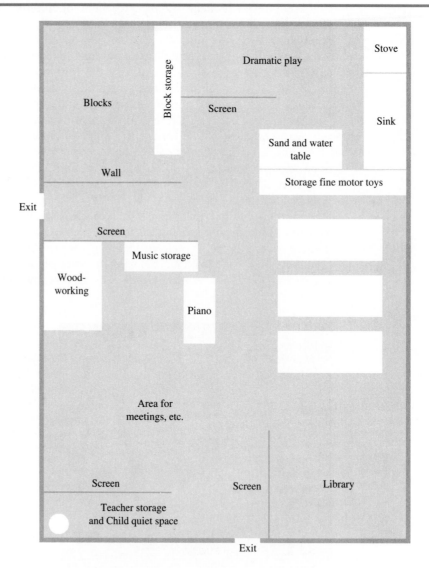

put into practice. As in Figure 8.1, adaptations could be made for other ages.

In conceptualizing your indoor space, it is important to consider your curriculum goals and teaching philosophy. One way to do this is to reconsider the metaphors of Chapter 7. If you see yourself as mother hen, you will

FIGURE 8.2 (Adapted from Bergen et al., 1988)

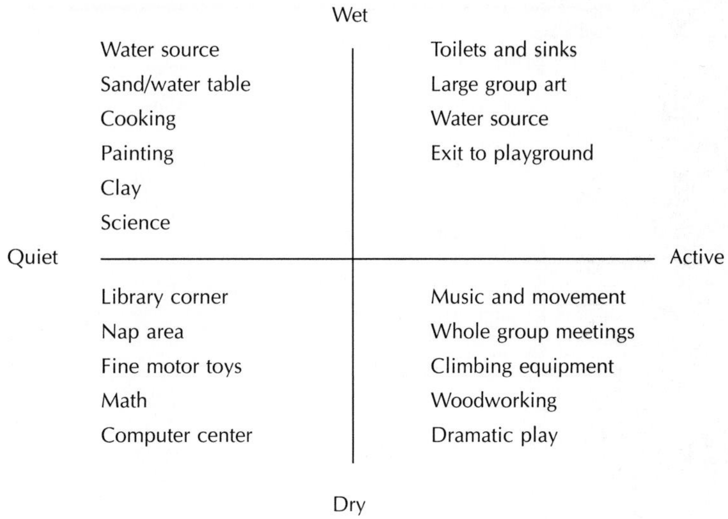

Wet

|  |  |
|---|---|
| Water source | Toilets and sinks |
| Sand/water table | Large group art |
| Cooking | Water source |
| Painting | Exit to playground |
| Clay |  |
| Science |  |

Quiet ————————————————|———————————————— Active

|  |  |
|---|---|
| Library corner | Music and movement |
| Nap area | Whole group meetings |
| Fine motor toys | Climbing equipment |
| Math | Woodworking |
| Computer center | Dramatic play |

Dry

need plenty of "nests" for small group activities and a good open space where you can easily gather the total group together. If you are the coach, you will need similar small group areas to which you can travel easily to support whatever is taking place. The feeling of the room might be somewhat more open and active than the mother hen's, although at first it would look quite similar.

Another approach to spatial decision making is to reconsider the philosophies presented in Chapter 1. For example, if you like Locke's concept of the child as a slate to be written upon (a metaphor itself), then you need a spatial arrangement in which you are in control. This places you at the head of a classroom with rows of desks in front of you. In a class of younger children, you might place a comfortable rocker in the center of the room where you can observe everything that goes on while children come to you for instructions.

Once you are well aware of your preferred philosophy or metaphor, some focused questioning is in order. One elementary teacher (Shenkle, 1988) reports that she began asking such questions about the "classroom geography" after she realized that her own room's physical environment contradicted her goals. A value for her was lively whole group discussion, while her classroom design was that of children seated in rows. "I suddenly realized that my students were talking to each other's backs," she reported. *"What kind of communication is this,* I asked myself" (p. 62). That first question led to many years of questioning:

FIGURE 8.3

**An Environment Based on Quiet-Active and Wet-Dry Continuums**

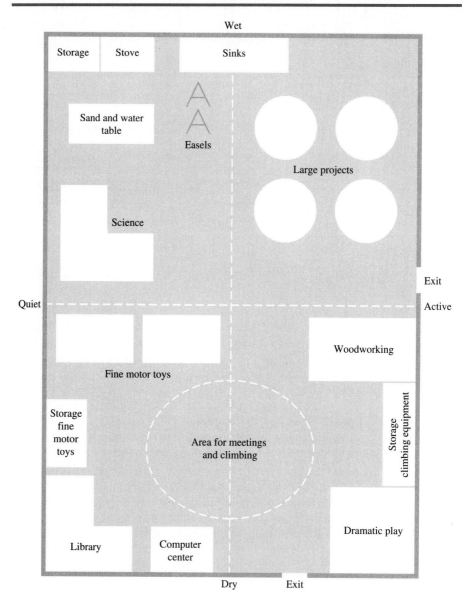

Over the years, I came to see more and more that in defining my classroom's geography and climate, I was also defining my values, my teaching style, and my goals for the students. And even though I usually didn't make any radical changes, just thinking about the how and why of my room arrangement stimulated other questions. (p. 62)

Some of the questions Shenkle (1988) asked herself were these:

- What do the students and I need to do here?
- What work will we be doing as a whole group?
- What work will we be doing in small groups?
- How will the movement of students around the room affect the work areas?

Other questions that might be asked by teachers and caregivers who work with younger children and infants are:

- Which activities will be more physical and which less so?
- How much time will be devoted to naps and will children all sleep at the same time or in staggered shifts?
- Which activities require sufficient space for extra adult supervision?
- Which activities will be messier than others?
- And other questions unique to your situation.

### Furnishing the Indoor Environment

A major part of conceptualizing the use of space is to plan the positioning and use of furniture and learning materials. The decisions you make should reflect your philosophy of teaching and learning so that the environment sends consistent messages to the children about the ways in which they are expected to learn. The author once asked her early childhood students to interview the kindergarten through third-grade children in their practicum about the meaning of the physical environment. Two of the questions, and some of the children's answers, were:

Q: Why do you sit in rows?
A: "So the teacher can see us better and we'll be good."
   "So we'll be quiet."
   "So the teacher can stand in back and we won't know if she sees us do something bad."
Q: Why is the teacher's desk so big?
A: "Because she's the boss."
   "She has to keep all that stuff. We're not allowed to touch it."
   "She's big and we're little. You have to be big to get a big desk."

The answers to both questions clearly have to do with who is in control, with who owns the classroom. Most of the children's answers seemed to fall in this category. Few of them focused on the possibility of convenience brought about by rowed seating or of the teacher simply having more possession to store in that big desk. Perhaps some of the teachers in these classrooms saw themselves as running a child-centered program, and perhaps their curriculum was just exactly that. The arrangement of the furniture, however, sent a different message.

As you determine what furniture to use and how it will be arranged, think about what it means to be a child in your classroom or center. It helps to lower yourself, physically, to view the room from the child's vantage. You may then see how enormous the teacher's desk actually appears to a primary grade child or how confusing a forest the furniture seems to a toddler.

While most teachers and caregivers must accept much of the furniture as it comes to them, they should make as many choices about the furnishings as possible. Chairs and tables need to be more than "child size." They need to be supplied in a variety of sizes so that children of different heights are comfortable. For toddlers just learning to sit above floor level, small stools or benches offer an easy introduction. Stools and chairs that can be stacked out of the way are helpful, particularly in smaller rooms. Different types of tables provide flexibility for various activities. For example, pairs of rectangular and trapezoidal tables can be pulled apart for small group use and joined together for large art projects and cooking. In addition, there should be smaller tables where children can sit in pairs or alone. Even into the primary grades, tables provide more flexibility for teaching and learning than do desks.

Other important furnishings relate directly to the curriculum.

- *Art:* Both tables and easels are useful surfaces. Drying racks for finished pictures should be close enough that children can, on their own, remove the paintings and place them to dry.
- *Music:* To prevent frustration, instruments and supplies that are off-limits during free choice times should be placed out of sight. Those that children may use should be hung on a pegboard or rack or else placed on shelves in their own labeled areas. An old cassette player that children can learn to use on their own is preferable to a brand new one that they can't touch. Multiple headsets plugged into one long electrical plug strip make it possible for several children to listen at one time without disturbing the rest of the class.
- *Housekeeping or dramatic play:* Shelves, sink, refrigerator, doll beds, table, and chairs are the basic furniture. To these should be added dress-up clothes that change occasionally to match current themes of interest or recent field trips. Dolls should be of both sexes and from different races.
- *Blocks:* There should be sufficient space allowed for construction so that every block can be used if desired. Storage space should be such that

blocks can be stored neatly according to their sizes. Picture labels remind children of which sizes go where.

- *Woodworking:* One area inside and one outside provides the best coverage. If the room is small and the noise of hammers unacceptable, the inside area can contain very thin wood and glue while the outside can be reserved for hammers and nails. Wood should be kept in a scrapbox and the tools carefully hung on a pegboard.
- *Water and sand tables:* These too should be both inside and out. Outside sandboxes should have covers for keeping sand clean. Inside tables need plastic sheeting under them to rescue the sand that goes overboard.
- *Library:* At least one rocking chair, plus another comfortable chair or two, and a few large pillows make the area inviting. The bookshelves can be used as dividers to wall out outside noise and activity.
- *Math, science, social studies areas:* Materials will change according to interests, themes of study, and developing capabilities. Materials currently not in use should be stored out of sight. Those in use should have sufficient storage space, preferably on open shelves within reach of the children, and labels to indicate where they belong. For nonreaders, the labels can be pictures, but even some three-year-olds can "read" written labels.
- *Large motor area:* Unless you have plenty of supervision available, it is usually best to have just one or two pieces of apparatus in use at a time. Other choices should be stored out of sight.

Each of these areas will be quite different depending on the ages of the children you teach and care for. Some of the areas may even be absent if they are inappropriate for the age. Nevertheless, primary teachers are urged not to eliminate the early childhood interest areas until children have really outgrown them. Blocks, for example, can be used for complex building projects during social studies experiences. A balance beam along an out-of-the-way wall provides a lighthearted transportation route as well as practice in a physical skill.

## Activity Centers

For those who work with children from about age three and up, it makes good sense to place furniture and materials into subject-oriented activity centers. As children work and play in such centers, they can learn firsthand what art, music, and other curricular subjects actually are. If a center crosses curriculum lines, it will probably follow some theme that provides a learning focus. Also, a center is more likely to foster child-centered learning than is a traditional classroom in which children sit in rows focusing their attention on the authority figure behind the big desk. When children are permitted to direct their own learning, they have more opportunities to discover what their real interests are and to follow up on that discovery. Self-direction also leads to

The shift from child-centered, preschool classrooms with free movement between activity centers to highly structured, teacher-centered primary grade classrooms is a difficult transition for many young children.

independent decision making, learning from one's own mistakes, and social interaction skills.

Children who gain these skills in a preschool and kindergarten setting sometimes have difficulty adjusting to a primary classroom in which there is a more traditional environment. At times, teachers in the primary grades fault these children for their "bad" behavior and blame the schools they have come from. Close examination of one such situation, however, demonstrates other forces at work.

*The teachers in the lower school were barely on speaking terms. Each year, the first- and second-grade teachers became more appalled at the impudence of the children who came to them from the kindergarten. The most badly behaved seemed to be those who had also attended the preschool. The preschool and kindergarten teachers felt defensive, certain that they were providing a developmentally appropriate education for the children. However, they couldn't explain why the children's behavior disintegrated once they entered first grade.*

*The principal finally insisted that the two groups of teachers get together to discuss the issue and to see what might be done. The feelings of hostility were so great, however, that one or two teachers refused. The principal agreed to intervene. She spent almost two days observing the preschool and kindergarten classes. She saw children as young as three years choosing their own activities for as long as two hours. She observed these same children deciding when they wanted to be alone and when they wanted to work or play with others. It was the same on the playground, with the older children more inclined to play in complex group situations. In all, there were three classes and in each one there were times when the entire group gathered together for singing, dancing, or discussion. At such times, children willingly took turns talking and listening to each other, rarely interrupting but also being quite assertive about having everyone's full attention when it was their own turn to talk.*

*The principal then observed the first and second grades. The atmosphere was quite different. Children sat in rows, listening to the teacher or working alone on their own. The second-grade children seemed reasonably well adjusted, but the first graders were clearly having trouble. They continually talked out of turn, forgetting that the teacher was always in charge and that they could never talk unless given permission. Twice, while the principal was there, a child forgot to ask permission to go to the restroom, simply wandering out the door. Each time the teacher upbraided the offending child and rolled her eyes at the principal. On the second day another child wet her pants and was sent to the office, in disgrace, for a change of clothing. On several occasions over the two days, children left their seats to sharpen their pencils and were severely reprimanded by the teacher.*

*Once the observations were concluded, the principal talked first with the first- and second-grade teachers, asking for their views on the problems. To the principal, their opinion seemed to be summarized in the complaint that "these children think they can go to the bathroom or sharpen a pencil whenever they feel like it. They have no respect for authority." The principal then asked if they had ever observed the preschool and kindergarten classes. They never had. She asked if they knew what the philosophy of the other teachers was. They didn't.*

*By this point, the principal realized that there were two critical issues to be settled: (1) a wide disparity in teaching and learning philosophies and (2) a lack of communication or smooth transitions between the two levels. The hostility between the teachers didn't concern her nearly as much as the disservice that was being done the children. The first graders seemed miserable and the second graders, while adjusted, not much happier.*

*The principal explained to the primary teachers that the children came to them after one or two or even three years of learning how to be indepen-*

*dent in a classroom that valued self-direction and decision making. She pointed out that the children, even at age three, were capable of knowing if they needed to go to the bathroom or if a pencil needed sharpening. She suggested that the abrupt change to an authoritarian environment was causing dissonance and great consternation for the children. She further suggested that it was absolutely necessary for the two groups of teachers to meet to discuss what their values truly were. Unless they could reach some sort of agreement, children were going to be damaged.*

*At last the teachers agreed to begin discussions. Changes were not made quickly or easily, as each "side" believed that its approach to teaching and learning was the right one. Over the next two years, though, the furniture in the primary classes began to be moved about sometimes for small group discussions. A few learning centers appeared. Children were permitted to use the restroom without asking, but they did pick up a wooden pass on their way out the door. In one class, pencils could be sharpened at any time, while in the other it had to be done at specific break times. Permission from the teacher, however, was not necessary.*

*For her turn, the kindergarten teacher began to rehearse the children in the late spring for first grade. The children practiced sitting in one place quietly, and they tried formal group discussions for short periods. They took two or three visits to the first grade, where buddies showed them around the room, and they met the teacher, who turned out to be not so terrifying after all.*

While there were quite a few elements that created dissonance for the children moving from the preschool to the primary classrooms, the majority of them came from environmental disparities. The younger children became accustomed to learning centers and a policy of free movement. Within that environment they became, of necessity, self-directed learners and independent decision makers. As such, they gained confidence in themselves and respect for others. The environment of the primary grades spoke to the children quite differently. Its rigid rows of desks and policy of no free movement without teacher permission said to the children that they were no longer capable of making their own decisions, that the teacher was the sole person responsible for running the classroom affairs and, therefore, the only one deserving of respect. The children were, quite literally, put in their place.

The lack of communication between the teachers in the two divisions exacerbated the problem since the children were left to sort out, totally on their own, the disparities between the two environments. While good continuity between environments is the most desirable situation, it is possible for them to be different and hospitable to children at the same time. What is required is close communication between the teachers and a shared understanding of each other's philosophy of education.

## The Outdoor Environment

From infancy on, children need opportunities to be outdoors, and this need is not terminated once they enter the doors of formal schooling. The air is different outside; the sounds are different and they carry differently; and, for children old enough to be mobile, the body moves differently outdoors. The space available is usually greater than that inside, providing children with more opportunity to engage in large-motor play. Further, the outdoor play equipment is usually designed to foster more large-motor play than the indoor apparatus.

In a review of play-research literature, Johnson, Christie, & Yawkey (1987) listed some differences between being indoors and outdoors. Preschool boys prefer playing outdoors, while girls are more inclined to remain inside. Related to this finding is another that girls engage in more make-believe play indoors while boys are more likely to do so outdoors. There are also differences between socioeconomic classes. Lower-class preschool children were involved in more dramatic play and for longer periods of time outdoors than were middle-class children. Because of these differences, it is important to provide children sufficient time both outdoors and inside. Gender and class differences are then taken into account naturally, and all children have access to their preferred playing and learning areas.

David Day (1983) has argued that the outdoors, in some respects, should be considered an extension of the indoor program. Despite the fact that the environment is different in many ways, he believes that, in both settings, children should be able to be "excited and calm, intense and casual, cooperative and protective, gregarious and reserved, attentive and preoccupied." Day points out that the outdoors can be used just as effectively as an indoor science center for serious and sustained inquiry; that creative play can be pursued in either place; that children can learn to negotiate good social relationships outdoors just as well as inside. "In short, outdoor areas can support the same developmental and curricular goals as the classroom if the staff believes that they have this purpose" (p. 239).

In a study by Michael Henniger (1985) indoor and outdoor play behaviors of nursery school children were compared. The researcher concluded that, "with the right equipment and careful teacher planning and encouragement, any desired play type could be stimulated in the outdoor environment . . ." (p. 153). He observed that social play was well stimulated outdoors and that cooperative play (the highest level of social play) was about equal in either setting. Being outdoors was especially beneficial for the boys of all ages and for older children of both sexes. As Henniger noted, these children may feel inhibited by the limitations of space, the softer floor covering, and the necessarily low noise levels of the indoor setting. Outdoors, they engage in the more active dramatic play roles that they prefer. Some ways to bring the indoors out could include:

- Placing painting easels outside when weather permits.
- Assigning each child, or teams of two or three, to a few square feet of ground for exploration of its contents. This can be adapted to any age from toddlerhood on.
- Creating a marching band using homemade instruments or those already in the classroom collection.
- Placing chairs and benches under a favorite tree for a book corner.
- Providing children with buckets of water and large brushes with which to "paint" the exterior walls and walkways.
- Collecting and using natural materials such as pebbles, rocks, and sticks for classification activities or for learning arithmetic processes.

Unlimited numbers of similar ideas are possible. For many teachers, coming up with extended lists may require an extra effort in creativity. Traditional teaching and our own classroom learning experiences have been focused primarily on the indoor environment, making such thinking a particularly mind-stretching activity. Children, however, do not see such divisions between indoor and outdoor learning unless adults socialize them in that direction.

While much of the indoors can be brought outside in some form, the outdoor setting also provides unique activities and materials. In recent years several studies have explored the ways in which children use playgrounds and traditional and more modern playground equipment.

Some of the most comprehensive work done in this field has been by Joe Frost, who has studied children at play on various styles of playgrounds, some of them designed by himself. In one study (Campbell and Frost, 1985), second graders at one school were observed playing in two types of play environments. One was a "traditional" playground that included seesaws, a merry-go-round, swings, slide, and trapeze bars as well as a dirt playground area. The other was a "creative" playground with three kinds of commercial climbers, a slide with enclosed platform, tire swings on swivels, movable seesaw, boat, and a platform structure that came with materials such as planks and crates for constructing purposes. In a corner shack were stored riding, dramatic play, and game equipment.

Observations showed that the amount of cooperative play was about equal across both groups and at about the level generally expected of seven-year-olds. There was more dramatic play and construction play on the creative playground as might be expected, given the inclusion of appropriate materials. What was surprising was the marked increase in solitary play on the creative playground. The design of the playground and its greater variety of choices made it easier for children to play independently. Frost believes this is a plus and cites other researchers who, like himself, believe that solitary play should not necessarily be viewed as a lower-order form of play.

In a related study (Frost and Campbell, 1985) at the same school, the second graders favored movable equipment or features. For example, on the traditional playground, the swings, merry-go-round, and seesaw were preferred over the fixed climbing apparatus. Likewise, on the creative playground, the play house with its movable props and other movable materials, such as the boat, were most popular. In general, action-oriented equipment and equipment designed for dramatic play were the most popular. Games equipment (various kinds of balls, etc.) was less popular. Frost points out that this observation conflicts with Piaget's observations that the preference for dramatic play reaches its peak between ages three and six, then fades out about age seven in favor of games with rules. One possible explanation, Frost says, is that playgrounds traditionally have come equipped with static play equipment (and frequently not much of it) so that teachers prematurely push children into playing games with rules to give them something to do.

The ultimate in playgrounds with movable parts for construction and dramatic play is the "adventure playground" pioneered in Denmark in the 1940s and quickly adopted all over Europe (Pedersen, 1985). These playgrounds are situated wherever there is a vacant lot, often one that is temporarily waiting for a building to be constructed. Much material is provided,

Numerous studies have shown that children prefer play equipment that is flexible and complex rather than fixed, simple, and oriented to a single use.

from hammers and nails to shovels and boards. Additionally, there may be live pets, a bonfire site, and/or gardens. The playgrounds are government sponsored and there are always adults in charge. Adventure playgrounds are few and far between in the United States, the argument often being that they are intrinsically unsafe and inherently noninsurable. Yet, the statistics demonstrate that adventure playgrounds actually have a higher safety record than traditional playgrounds, probably in part because of constant adult supervision.

Children below the age of six or seven are probably not capable of the intense kind of construction that is the hallmark of adventure playgrounds. Nevertheless, even very young children can combine pieces of equipment to make their own play structures. As Spodek et al. (1991) point out,

> Sawhorses, ladders, cleated boards, large hollow blocks, large wooden packing crates, and other such pieces of equipment can be combined and recombined to provide a variety of play structures. . . . The fact that children can continually modify and elaborate the structures they build means that these structures are continually being renewed, providing novelty and a sense of adventure and challenge that permanent structures cannot offer. Since they are created by the children themselves, such structures are even more attractive. (p. 199)

Thus, we see that the spirit of adventure playgrounds is possible in early childhood settings, even if major constructive projects are not undertaken until the elementary years. An important point in favor of adventure playgrounds, or the derivative form suggested by Spodek et al. (1991), is that in study after study children preferred play equipment that was more complex over that which was simple or oriented toward a single use. This has even been the case when preschoolers have been observed (Steele and Nauman, 1985).

While most studies of children's interaction with the outdoor environment have focused on the kindergarten age and older, Steele and Nauman (1985) researched infants and toddlers between the ages of ten and thirty-five months. They constructed two types of sandbox (one 6 by 8 feet and one contained in a tire); two kinds of slides (one traditional and one with an attached tunnel); two kinds of cubes (one more open and one almost totally closed); and two "neutral logs," which were cardboard boxes painted green and taped shut (one vertical and one horizontal).

The findings of this study can be helpful to those who want to make the most of their infant outdoor play area. The larger sandbox was popular with all ages, even when children were playing alone. The tire sandbox was used only by children who were close to two years or older. The more open cube was enjoyed by all children, but the closed cube was avoided by the younger ones. The fact that it was somewhat dark inside seemed to put them off while, at the same time, providing an interesting challenge for the older children. The older children also preferred the slide-tunnel combination and the horizontal log. No children of any age chose to play with the vertical log.

The researchers added to these conclusions the observation that the older toddlers were especially attracted to the slide with tunnel, which could be used by several children at a time and in a variety of ways. In other words, just as preschoolers and school-age children are attracted to the more complex equipment, so are toddlers. Apparently, it is only the youngest infants who are best served by very simple outdoor equipment.

### Dealing with Reality

While studies of children in the outdoors lead to conclusions such as the desirability of complex over simple play structures and for equipment varied enough to support both solitary and social play, in reality teachers must often adapt to a very fixed and different sort of situation. You may have a play area that is large but has little or no equipment. You could have plenty of apparatus, but the components may be so close together that there is no clear, safe pathway through the area. You could even be confined to a rooftop or to a particularly small backyard. By following some basic principles and guidelines, however, you can make adaptations that will improve the situation. The following suggestions, which can be adapted to your own teaching site, can help get you started.

There should be both open and closed spaces.

- *Ideal:* Playhouses, clustered low bushes, or low walls alternate with open fields for running and games.
- *Adjusting for reality:* Large appliance boxes can serve as hideaways, or portable folding screens can create temporary walls. Either can be placed against an inner building corner for a cozier effect. To create more open space, confine any added equipment and materials to one section of the play area, leaving a comparative feeling of openness and freedom in the remaining space.

In warm weather, wet as well as dry areas should be available.

- *Ideal:* The building contains well-placed outdoor spigots for flexible use for gardening, water tables, shallow pools, and art cleanup.
- *Adjusting for reality:* Water play and activities are important enough to make some adjustments. Keep a water table filled with water and covered when not in use so that it need not be changed too often. The same can be done with a shallow wading pool. Watering cans and buckets of water carried outdoors in the morning supply the rest.

Permanent equipment should be sized to the children and should be free of defects and sharp edges.

- *Ideal:* A playground area should be sectioned off for each age group in the center or school. The apparatus should be designed for each group.
- *Adjusting for reality:* It may be necessary to schedule playground times for different ages. Firm rules should be established about who may or may not play on which equipment and on height limits for climbing. A buddy system can be developed in which older children help watch out for the younger. Whatever the situation, adults should constantly monitor the equipment for any unsafe protrusions, broken parts, etc.

Apparatus should be sufficiently complex for creative play.

- *Ideal:* In each age-group section of the playground there is at least one piece of permanent equipment that is designed for age-appropriate complex play.
- *Adjusting for reality:* It is possible to expand the interest level of simple apparatus by supplying boxes of various sizes as well as items that will inspire dramatic play, such as steering wheels, tires or inner tubes, large blocks, and a box of durable dolls or stuffed animals.

There should be places for quiet and solitude.

- *Ideal:* Shade trees away from the main flow of play are supplemented by small benches facing away from everyone.
- *Adjusting for reality:* A portable screen can be set up to one side with a few sturdy chairs behind it. A chalk line might be drawn even farther out as a sort of "moat" over which noisily playing children do not cross.

There should be equipment that fosters social interaction and group play.

- *Ideal:* The pieces of complex apparatus contain linked platforms on which children can gather socially as well as wide slides which can be used by several children at a time.
- *Adjusting for reality:* Close to any piece of play equipment, place low benches facing each other. Children may be permitted to drag one or two of these around for construction purposes, while one or two others must remain for social interaction.

## Safety

An underlying and basic environmental issue is safety. This is true both indoors and out. A very careful survey must be made, at the children's height, to be sure that there is nothing sharp, electrical, or toxic within reach. If you will be carrying infants and toddlers, then it is equally important to check for these hazards at the adult level. This careful checking should be thoroughly done before a school or center opens for the first time, and it should continue informally every day thereafter. Of course, safety concerns will change somewhat depending on the age of the children. For example, toddlers do not have the physical dexterity to handle saws and hammers, but kindergarten children find them an exciting challenge. For toddlers, then, these tools need to be kept completely out of reach, while kindergartners need careful instruction in their safe use.

As children mature enough to help care for their environment, they should be permitted to share in its actual upkeep. The housekeeping area is a good instigator of sociodramatic play in which children imitate the roles of adults, but it does not provide the immediacy and reality of actually caring for the school environment. Another housekeeping area, a real one, is necessary for this purpose. It will be a much smaller corner and will contain real versions of some of the contents of the dramatic play area. Safety considerations are a must when supplying this corner. With some careful planning, however, you can establish safe procedures while encouraging children to participate in the care of the room. Such encouragement demonstrates your respect for the children's capabilities. The children will feel this and respond positively to it.

- Real brooms and mops should be supplied since the toy versions are generally ineffective. Handles can be cut to the children's size for manipulative ease and safety. Cleaning rags can be half size. There should be a disposal bag and children should be trained to deposit used rags in it.
- Metal polish can be made by melting Lava soap with a little water over a low flame. When the soap has softened somewhat, mix it with the water and press into a small container. A furniture caster cup is about the right size. A damp cloth can be rubbed over the soap and then used to polish almost any metal, including silver.
- A good wood polish substitute is hand lotion. A small amount can be placed on a dry cloth and rubbed well into the wood. It is harmless to the wood and can actually work up a good shine.
- A little lemon juice or vinegar mixed in water makes a good liquid spray for cleaning glass.

When you consider safety before introducing any activity or material, then the majority of your attention can be devoted to the intellectual, social, physical, and emotional needs of the children. This is as it should be.

Checklists of safety considerations can be useful as you begin your work with young children. The two that are given below are divided between indoor and outdoor safety. The first list is, in part, adapted from suggestions by the Public Action Coalition on Toys (Spodek et al., 1991).

## Maintaining Indoor Safety

1. *Electrical outlets and cords.* Are all open outlets plugged? Can children pull over an appliance by grasping a cord? Are in-reach appliances available only to sufficiently mature and trained children?
2. *Plants.* Are these out of reach to children who may put pieces of them in their mouths?
3. *Fire extinguisher.* Is there one readily available? Does every adult know how to use it?
4. *First-aid kit.* Is there one readily available? Is every adult familiar with its contents and their correct application?
5. *Furniture.* Are dangerously sharp corners covered by some sort of padding? Are there splinters and other imperfections that need smoothing out? Are some pieces of furniture easily pulled over by crawlers and toddlers? Are the slats on the baby beds far enough apart for a child's head to fit through or get stuck in?
6. *Toys and other materials.* Are there sharp edges, exposed nails, sharp wires, or pins? Are there detachable or easily broken parts that can be swallowed? Are there parts that can pinch? Are projectile toys (rockets, airplanes) capable of inflicting eye injuries? Are all cords on crib toys shorter than 12 inches to avoid strangulation? Will the toy be safe when used in its surroundings?
7. *Toileting facilities.* Are sufficiently high step stools supplied for toilets or sinks? Is the hot water turned down to a safe temperature? Are cleaning supplies kept completely out of reach? Are the facilities cleaned at least once a day?
8. *Diapering facilities.* Are there straps for confining babies while diapers are being changed? Are pads cleaned immediately after any leakage? Is the cleaning solution kept out of reach?
9. *General use.* During the day, is the floor kept safe for mobile infants and toddlers? Are toys and other materials regularly picked up and accidents immediately cleaned up?

## Maintaining Outdoor Safety

The following checklist is suggested by Frost and Wortham (1988). While you may have little control over some items, you should think about ways to adapt your situation for those that are missing.

1. A fence (minimum 4 feet high) protects children from potentially hazardous areas (e.g., streets, water).
2. Eight to 12 inches of noncompacted sand, gravel, shredded wood, or equivalent materials is in place under and around all climbing and moving equipment.

3. Resilient surface is properly maintained (e.g., in place, noncompacted, free of debris).
4. The equipment is sized to the age group served, with climbing heights limited to the reaching height of children standing erect.
5. There are no openings that can entrap a child's head (approximately 4 to 8 inches).
6. Swing seats are constructed of lightweight material with no protruding elements.
7. Moving parts are free of defects (no pinch, shearing, or crush points; bearings are not excessively worn).
8. Equipment is free of sharp edges, protruding elements, broken parts, and toxic substances.
9. Fixed equipment is structurally sound—no bending, warping, breaking, or sinking.
10. Large equipment is secured to the ground, and concrete footings are recessed in the ground.
11. All safety equipment (e.g., guard rails, padded areas, protective covers) is in good repair.
12. The area is free of electrical hazards (e.g., unfenced air conditioners and switch boxes).
13. The area is free of debris (e.g., sanitary hazards, broken glass, and rocks).

The list of safety concerns is practically endless; consequently, maintaining safety necessarily takes effort and time. However, for infants and young children just learning to adapt to the adult world, this issue is of critical importance to their well-being and even, in extreme cases, to their survival.

## The Children's Role

While adults have the ultimate responsibility for planning and preparing the environment, children should also have some input. Their suggestions, however, may be radically different from our expectations. Three examples illustrate how children of different ages and in different settings restructured a portion of their environments.

■ *One school had a fenced play area that was planted heavily with trees. At one end was a complex piece of play equipment interspersed with other smaller apparatus. The four- and five-year-olds chose to ignore the commercial elements of the playground entirely. Instead, they moved to the trees and spent days collecting every stick they could find and heaping them in one pile. Eventually, some of the children began classifying the sticks according to size, and there emerged three or four piles. During this time much* discussion took place as to what should be done with the sticks and it was finally decided that a fort should be built, although some of the four-year-olds seemed uncertain as to just what a fort was. Soon, a shaky and irregular structure began to emerge. Each day a part of it had to be rebuilt before additions could be made and much negotiation took place regarding ways to make the structure sturdier. Before it was anywhere near completed, dramatic play began with soldiers, mothers, babies, and other inhabitants bringing the fort to life. Meanwhile, the expensive adult-designed apparatus went unused.

■ One kindergarten teacher was a self-described "neat freak" who coped with the normal classroom mess by making sure that at the end of each day absolutely everything was perfectly cleaned up and put away. One day the children asked her to leave standing the complex block structure that they were building with blocks. They argued that it wasn't finished yet, that there was much left to do, and that they hadn't yet had an opportunity to engage in the play for which the structure was designed. The teacher took a deep breath and gave her permission because she was, she said, "a flexible neat freak." The structure was left up for more than two weeks and eventually took up almost a quarter of the classroom. Not long afterward, the teacher went to a late afternoon meeting in another school and, passing a kindergarten classroom, peeked in. To her surprise, there was a very complex block structure not unlike her own children's. While this structure wasn't much larger, the room was smaller and therefore more than half the space was covered. Seeing the teacher still working inside, she stopped to chat. The second teacher explained her patience with the situation by saying, "Well, of course it's a mess, but it's their mess. I also consider it their classroom, not mine. In a few days or so, if they don't notice that it's getting inconvenient to move around, I'll help them notice it. Then we'll discuss what we ought to do instead."

■ There were only fifteen second graders, eight boys and seven girls. The teacher tried several variations in the seating arrangement, usually regrouping for different projects as the year went along. It wasn't until March that it occurred to her to give the children an opportunity to invent a seating arrangement of their own. It began with a large group discussion in which a unanimous decision was made to split into two groups: boys and girls. The teacher left each of the groups to decide what they wanted to do as long as it didn't infringe on the space rights of the other group. She first observed the girls trying to deal with the problem of popularity and cliques. They agreed that everyone should feel happy with the outcome but had trouble deciding who should sit next to whom. Finally, someone came up with the idea of a circle, and this met total approval. Minimal furniture movement

If children were allowed to choose their own furnishings, what do you suppose their rooms would look like? In one such experiment, they chose not to have any tables or traditional chairs, preferring instead to lie or sit on the floor while engaging in their favorite activities.

*took place, and the girls settled down to making the space clean and attractive. Meanwhile, the boys decided they wanted to face each other with a space in between to place their backpacks. Two of the boys tried hard to go along with the majority, but their own problem was one of negative social interaction. Each, for his own separate reasons, found it necessary to get away from others rather frequently. The teacher had spent the year helping them learn how to do this gracefully rather than angrily. Thus, this new face-to-face arrangement was causing them problems. With minimal discussion, however, each of the problem boys chose to place his desk at one end of the two rows, at a 90-degree angle facing inward. This made it possible to simply slide his desk back and away from the group when anger struck. Despite the fact that the two new seating arrangements made the room much more crowded, the children loved it because they had thought of it themselves. They spent many weeks navigating some very narrow spaces in order to make it work.*

In each of these examples, the children assumed their environmental leadership roles with little or no hesitation. On the playground, no adult requirements were ever given, and the children simply chose to play among the trees rather than on the equipment. In the kindergarten classroom, the children knew that their teacher loved neatness, but their relationship with her was close enough that they could request a change. Once they had power, they kept it as long as they could. In the second-grade classroom, the children were accustomed to directing much of their own learning, so being allowed to move furniture around was easily received. In all three situations, an underlying premise was that the children had some ownership of their environment. When children know this, or at least sense it, they have the confidence to engage in environmental development.

Johnson et al. (1987) describe a research project in which all the equipment and furniture was removed from a preschool classroom and placed in the hall. The children were told that they could bring in whatever they needed and place things where they wanted. After several weeks, everything was back in the room except the tables and chairs and a piano. They preferred to play and work on the floor, and created a large empty space in the center of the room that served a variety of activities.

This experience and the three just described demonstrate the unique ways that children think about their environments. They make each one fit their current interests and needs. Too often, adults second-guess the results of such designs before they happen. While it would not be prudent to permit children to design their environments at all times, the experience does provide them with opportunities to learn from their own decisions. And it provides teachers with a better understanding of their children's needs and interests.

## Extending Your Learning

1. Observe one or two children on a playground for at least thirty minutes. Write down everything they do, making special note of ways in which they adapt to the environment. When you are finished, review your notes and make recommendations regarding ways the environment might be better adapted to the children. Always keep safety factors in mind.
2. Observe an early childhood classroom in which computers are integrated into the environment. Note the value the teacher and children place on this technology, its relationship to more traditional materials, and its popularity with each sex. Afterward, interview the teacher and a few children about what you have observed.
3. Choose an age group of children, either the one you are teaching now or the one you would most like to work with, and design your ideal classroom or center for them. Include the outdoor environment as well. Attach a written justification for the overall plan based on your own philosophy or metaphor of teaching and learning.

## References

Bergen, D., Smith, K., and O'Neill, S. (1988). Designing play environments for infants and toddlers. In D. Bergen, (ed.) *Play as a medium for learning and development*, pp. 187–208. Portsmouth, NH: Heinemann.

Bredecamp, S. (ed.) (1987). *Developmental appropriate practice in nearly childhood programs serving children from birth through age 8.* Washington, DC: NAEYC.

Campbell, S., and Frost, J. (1985). The effects of playground type on the cognitive and social play behaviors of grade two children. In J. Frost (ed.), *When children play,* pp. 81–88. Wheaton, MD: ACEI.

Day, D. (1983). *Early childhood education: A human ecological approach.* Glenview, IL: Scott, Foresman.

Frost, J., and Campbell, S. (1985). Equipment choices of primary-age children on conventional and creative playgrounds. In *When children play,* pp. 89–92.

Frost, J., and Wortham, S. (1988). The evolution of American playgrounds. *Young Children* 43(5):19–28.

Johnson, J., Christie, J., and Yawkey, T. (1987). *Play and early childhood development.* Glenview, IL: Scott, Foresman.

Henniger, M. (1985). Preschool children's play behaviors in an indoor and outdoor environment. In *When children play,* pp. 145–150.

Pedersen, J. (1985). The adventure playgrounds of Denmark. In *When children play,* pp. 201–208.

Shenkle, A. (1988). Shaping the classroom landscape. *Learning,* Sept., 61–64.

Spodek, B., Saracho, O., and Davis, M. (1991). *Foundations of early childhood education.* Englewood Cliffs, NJ: Prentice Hall.

Steele, C., and Nauman, M. (1985). Infants' play on outdoor play equipment. In *When children play,* pp. 121–128.

# 9

# Guiding Children's Behavior

## OBJECTIVE

When you finish reading this chapter, you should be able to

- Identify and define models and approaches to discipline.
- Relate models and systems of behavior management to specific psychological theories.
- Understand developmental differences in behavior that can be expected from young children.

As you think about the chapter on your own, you should be able to

- Observe the behavior management techniques of professional teachers and understand their intent.
- Begin formulating your personal philosophy of discipline.
- Begin experimenting knowledgeably with a variety of techniques.

A supervisor of student teachers once observed, laughing, "They really change their tune after they've been on the firing line a few days, don't they? Every semester my student teachers begin by writing idealistic entries in their journals about how they're going to be the 'children's friend.' Then they get in the classroom and practically forget the children in their own effort to survive."

While many student teachers do go through this unfortunate transition, there are others who do not. Some work hard at trying the management methods they learn in their classes. A few seem naturally blessed with the ability to bring out the best behavior in children. Maureen was one such student. After several successful practicum experiences, she looked forward to increased independence and responsibilities in her final internship. As you read what happened on the first day she was permitted to take over the class on her own, think about the decisions Maureen made and the specific behaviors she used to make a very complex teaching situation work smoothly.

*Maureen was barely 5 feet tall and wore her blonde hair in bouncy, young-ish curls. When she walked down the hall she was frequently mistaken for one of the sixth graders. Her supervising teacher worried that Maureen wouldn't be respected by her first-grade children, so she gave Maureen responsibilities rather slowly. It finally became apparent to the teacher, however, that Maureen was an exceptionally capable manager, and they began to make plans for her to take over the class for an afternoon.*

*The teacher's preferred style was direct instruction and whole-group activities. Maureen wanted to institute activity centers, and the teacher gave her permission. The teacher felt comfortable with Maureen's proposal because two parent volunteers who could help her would be present. They agreed, however, that the children would respond best to Maureen if the teacher were absent.*

*On the morning of the appointed day, Maureen was given time during the opening announcements to explain the afternoon's plans. As she moved to the teacher's chair, two children in the back began giggling to each other. Maureen said nothing but stared directly at them. They soon became quiet and she announced, "When it is my turn to talk it is everyone else's turn to listen. When it's your turn to talk, I'll listen quietly to you." No one interrupted again as Maureen briefly told the children what they would be doing and what behaviors and rules were expected of them. Some of the rules were new because, although they weren't necessary for the usual whole-group instruction, they were important for centers. These rules she wrote on the chalkboard and everyone practiced reading them aloud.*

*After lunch the children filed in quietly and the teacher disappeared. By now, the two parent volunteers had arrived and stood in the back gossiping about this "child teacher" who was, more than likely, "going to fall flat on her pretty little face." Their giggling to each other was not unlike that of the two children earlier in the day. Maureen overheard a bit of their discussion but chose to ignore it for the moment. It was important to get the children started first.*

*During the lunch hour, Maureen had moved all the furniture into carefully prepared learning centers. Each one had clear, simple instructions written on a large card placed in the middle of the center. For the moment, the children sat on the floor as they joined Maureen in reviewing the rules:*

1. Children may go to another center when they want.
2. Children must clean up their work before they leave a center.
3. Children may talk quietly at the centers.
4. Finished work goes in the teacher's basket.
5. Each center can have as many children as there are chairs.

*Of the five rules, only number 4 was familiar to the children. The usual whole-group instruction did not allow them to select their activities, to talk whenever they wanted, or to decide if there was room for them at their chosen center.*

*As soon as the rules were reviewed, Maureen let the children know that she would assign them to their first center, but, after that, they were on their own to choose where they wanted to be."Quietly walk to your center when I call your name," she announced, and the children did so. As soon as they were at their centers reading the directions, Maureen walked over to the two parents. In a self-assured voice she told them which centers she wanted them to work at and exactly what she wanted them to do there. The parents became serious and obedient and seemed to try their best to do what was expected of them.*

*Maureen spent her time roaming through the centers, helping children when necessary, answering questions, and asking some of her own related to the work at hand. When it was time to clean up, Maureen rang a small bell. It was the first time the children had ever heard it, and they stopped, startled. "Thank you," Maureen said quietly. "That's just what you should do when you hear the bell. Stay just where you are and listen carefully for your instructions." She described the few steps required for putting the room back the way it had been in the morning. As the children and the parents pitched in to get everything back in order, Maureen continued to roam the room, helping where necessary. When the regular teacher returned, the children were back in their usual seats and Maureen was reading them a story.*

*Although it was her first afternoon in charge of the class and also the children's first experience with so much freedom, there was not one problem with discipline in the entire two-and-a-half-hour center time.*

As you read about Maureen's experience, some of her management techniques might have been apparent to you. Others might have been less easy to see. The following discussion highlights a number of techniques that Maureen and others have found successful.

### Preparation of the Environment

Every center was carefully planned and everything was in place. Although the children were given freedom between and within the activities, nothing about the materials was left to chance. There was plenty of every supply that would be needed, thus eliminating any fighting over materials or confusion about what was expected.

Another control of behavior was the inclusion of the most appropriate number of chairs at each center. This number ranged from two to eight, depending on the activity. While one or two children occasionally seemed bored or impatient, their mood never lasted long because new places were constantly opening. Limiting the chairs worked well for Maureen in another sense. The activities in the centers were new to her as well as to the children, since she had never been given the opportunity to try them out before. Of course, some turned out to be more successful than others, and the children quickly tired of the less interesting ones. The chair rule, however, kept them from crowding the more popular centers and allowed Maureen to observe which centers needed improving or replacing.

### Clear Rules and Directions

When children know what is expected of them, they are more likely to behave correctly. They are usually relieved to have clear rules and expectations to follow. The instructions at the centers provided enough guidelines to eliminate confusion, but not so many as to be overwhelming.

Maureen determined what rules were needed by visualizing the way she wanted the afternoon to go. She would have preferred to have fewer rules and decided later that number 4 could probably have been eliminated or just mentioned in the initial instructions. During the activity time, three or four children did try to squeeze into a center where there weren't enough chairs. The first time, Maureen said in a voice that carried but wasn't terribly loud, "Please read rule number 5 and tell me if you should be here." After that, the children at a center would simply remind the extra child of the rule and there was no problem.

Teachers who develop and help children practice a few, sensible rules and routines during the first three weeks of the school year have fewer discipline problems and less confusion in their classrooms than teachers who do not.

### Rules and Directions Presented with Adverbs

It is not enough to tell children *what* is expected of them. It is just as necessary to tell them *how*. When Maureen said, "Quietly walk to your center," she properly placed the adverb *quietly* at the beginning of the instruction. Even experienced teachers sometimes wait too long to tell their students how something should be done; consequently, they find themselves shouting qualifying instructions over a noisy, rambunctious class.

### Attention-Getting Signals

Although Maureen had planned to tell the children about the bell in advance, she forgot. As she found out (to her relief), the introduction of a new signal works well, with or without an accompanying explanation. It is important to use signals, such as the bell, only as long as they are effective. As soon as a signal seems to become part of the background noise for the children, it is time to switch to something else. Flicking a light switch, playing a sound on a musical instrument, or clapping your hands are all potentially effective but must be monitored for the time when they lose their originality and become candidates for ignored background noise.

### Knowing When to Intervene

Maureen observed two similar behaviors and responded to them in very different ways. When the children giggled, she immediately did something to thwart the behavior. She knew that it was the kind of behavior that could easily get out of hand and lead to a larger control problem. This ability to nip inappropriate behavior in the bud is one of the most difficult skills for student teachers to attain. Too frequently, they either fail to catch the initial instance of the behavior or wait until it has spread before taking action. Maureen was unusually adept at sensing when trouble was brewing, and this was one reason for her success.

Maureen also knew that behavior doesn't always have to be dealt with immediately. When the parents began giggling in the background, she sensed that it was about her and that the commentary was probably negative. She also knew that, as adults, they wouldn't let their behavior get totally out of hand. A similar decision might be made if two mature and usually well-behaved children engaged in such behavior. In this case, the teacher might choose to let them have a momentary respite from their usual excellent behavior, knowing that it probably wouldn't last more than a short time.

### Body Language and Voice Control

When Maureen stopped the two children from giggling, she did it simply by staring at them. This is the famous (or infamous) "teacher look" and Maureen had mastered it early in her program. The "look" doesn't necessarily work for everyone, and some teachers may prefer not to use it. The point, however, is that Maureen was making careful use of body language to convey a message. Young children instinctively "read" what the teacher's body is saying, so it is important for teachers to decide what messages they want to send and then be sure their bodies "say" this.

For example, a teacher who smiles continually, even when angry, sends confusing messages to children who may "hear" the smile and not the words. Likewise, a very tall teacher who tends to hover over the children may make them feel either threatened or overprotected. In the first example, the teacher might wonder why the children don't respond to her reprimands and, in the second example, why they aren't learning independence.

Skillful use of the voice is absolutely essential for teachers. Most of the time, a quiet voice works best. This is even true when children become loud and out of control. In such a situation, a whisper might actually work best since most children will usually stop and try to hear what is being said. Generally speaking, when teachers save their loudest voice for emergency situations, children will respond by quickly paying attention. Continual shouting for children's attention generally results in their tuning the teacher out. Maureen never found it necessary to speak in a loud voice and never spoke until she had the children's attention. This worked especially well when she rang the bell for attention. In the startled silence that followed, Maureen was able to speak to the entire class with a very quiet voice, to which the children gave their total attention.

### Roaming

The children in Maureen's class, to some extent, were on their own. Yet, because Maureen spent most of her time walking between centers and communicating with them, there was always the feeling that the teacher was there. This affected the children's behavior in two ways. First, for those children who might be inclined to use materials inappropriately or to disobey the rules of the center, the sight of the approaching teacher would redirect their inappropriate behavior almost before it began. Second, it gave the children the security of knowing the teacher was there if they needed her. Both these elements of control are important to children who are just being introduced to learning in activity centers. The unfamiliar freedom can lead to inappropriate behavior and to feelings of insecurity so that, at first, the presence of the teacher is important. Once the children are accustomed to such learning, the teacher can even leave the room for awhile and, ordinarily, nothing changes.

### Balanced Freedom and Structure

Maureen was well aware that the freedom she was about to give the children would be unfamiliar to them and would need to be limited at first in order to avoid anarchy. Consequently, she chose to provide some structure by assigning the children to their first centers. In this way, they began their independent decision making confident of their ability to get started. Since the afternoon went well, Maureen could probably start the next session by letting the children decide on their own where to go first. Even then, some structure would be important to avoid chaos. Maureen would probably need to call on children one or two at a time to decide where they wanted to go. Another technique would be to have the centers set up before the start of school and, as children came in individually, they could go to available centers.

Part of the art of teaching with activity centers is knowing how much freedom to give children. This, in turn, will depend on the newness of the situation, the experience and ages of the children, their individual personalities, and the character of the class as a whole. Each year, month, and day will be different, and teachers must learn to be sensitive to the changes.

### An Interesting Curriculum

Sometimes activity centers will follow a theme. (Ideas will be discussed in coming chapters.) In Maureen's case, the activities were related to a variety of subjects being studied in the class at that time. In either case, what is being studied must be of interest to the children if their behavior is to be easily controlled. While some of Maureen's centers were more interesting than others, almost all of them provided something new and intriguing for the children. Experienced teachers find that, when the curriculum is interesting, behavior problems often have little or no opportunity to develop. The children are too involved with the learning at hand. When classwide behavior problems do develop, it is important to analyze the curriculum as one of the foremost possible culprits. A good curriculum may be the single most important element in fostering good behavior in young learners.

### Self-Confidence

This trait may well have been Maureen's most important possession in making everything run smoothly. Whether in a practicum or in her internship, she never doubted that she was the teacher and that this fact carried certain responsibilities and expectations. Everything about her body language, actions, and verbal communications conveyed this understanding to children and adults alike. Despite her small size and youthful appearance, she was even able to handle a couple of unruly adults.

Maureen's self-confidence became an important factor toward the end of the afternoon session. She had not planned to read a story to the children. Instead, she had hoped to create something of a grand finale by showing an interesting film. As desks and tables were being moved back to their original positions, she rolled the film projector into place. However, after the lights were turned down and the shades drawn, it became obvious that the projector wasn't going to work properly. With twenty minutes left in the day, Maureen quietly gathered the children around her on the floor at the front of the room. She managed to avoid any appearance of being dismayed. She raised the shades but kept the lights off for a quieter feeling and then reached for a book. Part of a teacher's self-confidence is knowing how to fill an unexpected gap, and Maureen was well prepared with several books, songs, and movement activities. While a quiet story didn't provide the grand finale Maureen had hoped for, it did ensure that the children's behavior would be exemplary when the teacher returned.

Maureen was not an experienced teacher, but she was learning to be a successful one. Her willingness to risk the experience of activity centers when her supervising teacher didn't use them was a good indicator of her self-confidence. So was her willingness to have her university supervisor (this author) observe the entire adventure. In our postteaching conference, it became apparent that not even Maureen was aware of all the things that she had done right. She learned on the spot that roaming the centers kept inappropriate behavior in check and that forgetting to explain the bell signal did not spell disaster. It was a surprise to her when I complimented her on immediately using the silence after the bell signal to speak to the children quietly. She didn't know, until we discussed it, that she might have had only a few seconds of silence to claim the airwaves as her own, and she explained that she had spoken in a quiet voice only because she was tired. Moreover, Maureen was still a bit disappointed that she hadn't been able to impress her teacher and university supervisor with the "grand finale" film she had planned. I suggested that her teacher was probably more impressed by the quiet demeanor of the class that came from the winding-down character of the story reading. While the film might have been a good activity academically, the story was the better choice in terms of student behavior.

Maureen's experience was with a first-grade class, and her expectations were appropriate for the six-year-olds in her charge. Although most of the management techniques just described could easily be adapted to children of other ages, to do so means being aware of children's behavioral characteristics at different stages of their development. The following section briefly reviews the relationship between developmental levels and classroom management techniques.

## Age-Related Behavior

Verna Hildebrand (1990) has suggested that it is important to understand how young children feel and think because, only then, can we understand what is appropriate behavior and what needs correcting. It is important, she says, to realize that age-related behavior may often be appropriate even if it doesn't meet an adult standard of goodness: "The positive or 'good' behavior of children is sometimes overlooked by parents and teachers because you may get so obsessed with correcting or eliminating their 'bad' or negative behavior" (p. 274).

In its position paper on developmentally appropriate practice, the National Association for the Education of Young Children (Bredekamp, 1987) makes a similar point.

> Understanding behavior that is not unusual for young children, such as messiness, interest in body parts and genital differences, crying and resistance, aggression, and later infraction of rules and truth, is the basis for appropriate guidance of young children. Developmentally appropriate guidance demonstrates respect for children. It helps them understand and grow, and is directed toward helping children develop self-control and the ability to make better decisions in the future. (p. 12)

You have already read, in Chapter 4, about age-related social and emotional development. Some of this information will reappear in the following discussion as it relates specifically to the issue of discipline within the center or classroom.

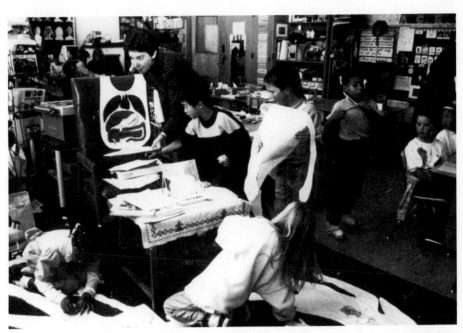

Effective teachers use a variety of strategies to control the classroom behavior of their children: roaming around the class; using body language and a calm, firm voice; using signals (bells, claps, turning lights off); and, most important, providing an interesting curriculum.

### Infants (Birth–Eight Months)

There is no such thing as a badly behaved infant. In the early months, babies begin to make sense of the world around them, and this includes learning to communicate effectively. They express both discomfort and pleasure unambiguously. Even in these early months, their emotions can include pleasure, anger, anxiety, fear, sadness, joy, excitement, disappointment, and exuberance. Adults should not expect them to hide any of these emotions or be able to change them with ease.

Future behavior can be influenced by the interactions that take place between adults and infants. If infants' needs are met, they will be their happiest. If they are not hungry, overly tired, wet or dirty, they will feel more secure and trusting of the adults around them. Their view of the world, as they learn to make sense of it, will be essentially positive, and they will have the confidence, as they get older, to act in positive ways. Small amounts of attention throughout the day should be sufficient for most infants in the child care center, and it is important to leave no child unattended for long periods of time. It is almost impossible to "spoil" infants in the center with too much attention.

### Older Infants (Eight–Eighteen Months)

As infants become mobile, their ability to express preferences and emotions grows. For the first time, they may express emotions and desires that are in conflict with those of their caregivers. When this happens, discipline emerges as an issue. Older babies begin to attain a strong sense of self and to assert themselves in various ways. They may express negative feelings, sometimes strongly. They also show anxiety when they are separated from their parents, and their feelings toward them are intense.

### Toddlers and Two-Year-Olds

The understanding of self as an individual increases dramatically. This is often expressed in one word: "No!" Adults who can phrase questions that have no yes or no answers will have the greatest success with this age. These young children want to explore everything and see themselves as powerful and creative, action-oriented people. They often display aggressive feelings and behaviors, but may also develop fear of the dark or of monsters. Mood shifts are frequent and "no" may not be heard for awhile during a happy period, then suddenly emerge when adults are least expecting it. Adults can help children through this ungraceful time if they are nonjudgmental, supportive, and present when needed.

### Three-Year-Olds

Some of the behaviors just described for two-year-olds often do not appear until close to the third birthday. But, eventually, three-year-olds become more cooperative than toddlers and want to please adults. Adults, however, should be prepared for occasional reversion to toddler behavior complete with thumb sucking, crying, hitting, and baby talk. If adults understand that this behavior is usually caused by fatigue, fear, shyness, or discomfort in a new situation, it should give them enough compassion to see the situation through. At these times, it is better to give affection, support, and comfort than to ridicule children for acting like babies.

### Four- and Five-Year-Olds

Exuberance might be the trait most commonly associated with behavior at this age. Children are loud, active, and sometimes aggressive. While there is much to be enjoyed about this time, self-control makes children more acceptable in the larger society. Teachers can facilitate this in a positive way by modeling and encouraging appropriate behavior, by redirecting children to other activities, and by setting clear limits on behavior. Conversely, teachers who spend their time punishing behavior, demeaning children when they misbehave, or making them sit and be quiet are less successful in helping children adapt.

### Six-, Seven-, and Eight-Year Olds

Children are fascinated with rules, although they may find it more interesting to watch someone else follow them than doing so themselves. They become ever more interested in impressing and getting the approval of their peers, often at the expense of the adults around them. Children may become overstimulated and act silly or overly excited and get carried away with chasing, screaming, or wrestling. Teachers can best deal with these behaviors if they observe them in the developmental stage and take advance measures. Redirecting children to calmer activities is more effective and more just than punishment.

While there are many explanations for children's behaviors, the simplest and most obvious is frequently that of normal human development. As you work with children of different ages, try to analyze your feelings about their behavior. If you feel comfortable and frequently charmed with a particular age group, you may have found your professional niche. On the other hand, if you find yourself constantly irritated by an entire classroom of children, you might do well to seek another age group with different behavioral patterns. While choosing the right group to work with is one basic consideration in achieving a happy and supporting atmosphere for children, your own personality and the management strategies that tend to fit your personality may be just as important.

## The Teacher's Role in Guiding Behavior

### Teacher Personality

Like it or not, teachers are behavioral models for their students. Consequently, much of your classroom atmosphere will be merely a reflection of your own personality. If you have a dramatic play area, you can expect to see yourself—mannerisms, tone of voice, exact language, and all—played out on occasion. If you are loud of voice and personality, your class will probably pick up on this. Conversely, your class is more likely to be a quiet and calm one if that is your nature. In short, your relationship with students can be helped or hindered by characteristics of your personality. This, in turn, will affect the kind of behavior children engage in. Dinkmeyer et al. (1980) list five teacher attitudes that may hamper their relationships with students and possibly encourage negative behavior.

- "I must control." When teachers believe they have to control children, they are asking for either overdependency or rebellion. Such teachers may demand that children ask permission before they move or speak or they may encourage tattling (referred to as "snoopervision"). Dinkmeyer suggests instead logical choices and freedom within limits.

- "I am superior." Teachers who feel this way are overly impressed by their own knowledge, experience, and responsibilities. They forget that children should be regarded as equal in human worth and dignity. No matter how young children are, Dinkmeyer argues, they can be treated as human beings and (with the exception of dangerous situations) be trusted to learn from experience.

- "I am entitled." This attitude arises from the concept that, because someone is a teacher, respect should come automatically. "Because I'm the teacher and I said so" might be a typical pronouncement. Dinkmeyer believes that there should be mutual respect between children and their teacher. Dominating, controlling, or overprotecting children fosters distrust; firmness mixed with kindness is more likely to foster trust and mutual respect.

- "I don't count." Teachers sometimes go too far when they give children greater rights. They need to retain their own rights and believe in their own value and abilities. In short, they should avoid becoming doormats. This happens, for example, when children repeatedly ask for the same instructions over and over and the teacher continues to respond, inconvenient though it may be. Teachers who turn the class over to their children risk creating an atmosphere of anarchy. Even very young children sense when their teacher "doesn't count." It makes them feel insecure, and they may respond with out-of-control behavior. Mutual respect can only emerge if teachers stand up for their own rights while respecting those of the children.

- "I must be perfect." People who are perfectionists often expect perfection of those around them. As teachers, they may resent the mistakes their students make, and young children make them often. Further, children need to be permitted to make mistakes because they learn so much from them. A teacher's fear of failure, Dinkmeyer says, may rub off on the children, and they begin to believe that what they do is never good enough. They may become overly dependent on outside opinion about their creations and activities, afraid to try anything new, and derogatory toward others as a way to make themselves feel better. As teachers we need to have the courage to be imperfect, to realize that mistakes help everyone to learn, and to let children know this.

## Modeling

Since young children intuitively understand our personality traits and since they tend to pattern their behavior after our own, we can turn this phenomenon into a positive force for the development of appropriate classroom behavior. The philosophical basis for choosing this approach to influencing behavior comes from the work of Albert Bandura, a contemporary psychologist. Bandura and his colleagues (1963) showed how negative the influence of teacher modeling can be on children. In this study, children ages three to six watched adults punch, kick, and yell at a big inflated doll. Later, these children and others who had not seen the adult behavior got to play with the doll. Those who had witnessed the adult violence were twice as likely to treat the doll violently as the children who had not seen the negative behavior. They even imitated the exact words of the adults. One psychology text, reporting on this study, speculates that, "had the adults danced with Bobo rather than punching it, the children, too, would have behaved in this gentler fashion" (Sprinthall and Sprinthall, 1990).

While young children often unconsciously mimic adult behavior, we cannot assume that they will pick up on the good behavior we want them to model. To help focus their attention on desired behavior, it is sometimes necessary to verbalize what we are doing as a means of reinforcing learning or making it more explicit. For example, you might walk carefully through a portion of the room saying, "I'm walking carefully around Tim's and Heather's blocks because I don't want to knock them down."

Another approach is to demonstrate appropriate behavior and then follow up by practicing it consistently. For example, you might gather the entire class around you to show everyone how to use a large new juice pitcher. You show that it must be held carefully, with two hands, if a small child is pouring from it. Despite the fact that you could easily pour with one hand while holding the glass with the other, you must remember to pour the two-handed way ever afterward or children may try to copy your more "adult" method. The results, of course, could be disastrous.

Modeling should always accompany any "lecture" you give the children. If you want them to differentiate between indoor and outdoor voices, then you must not only tell them about it, but be sure to speak more quietly indoors. If children are permitted to sit on chairs but not on tables, then you must do likewise, despite the greater comfort of sitting at an adult height.

Consistency is an important part of modeling. Children need the security of knowing that the behavior they are imitating is approved and that the rules won't suddenly and inexplicably be changed. Therefore, it is important for you to be careful in planning what behaviors to model and also to follow through by continuing to practice them.

## Withitness

This is a term coined by Jacob Kounin (1970) after observing teachers who were and were not alert to what was going on around them. Maureen, whose experience opened this chapter, demonstrated withitness when she stopped the giggling of two children before the behavior spread and when she observed the giggling of the two adults and chose not to stop it. In both cases, she was "withit" enough to realize that undesired behavior was developing and was then able to make a knowledgeable decision about what to do next. Withit teachers often sense that something is about to happen even before the children begin to act. Teachers lacking in withitness are more likely to let inappropriate behavior develop and spread before doing anything about it.

Withit teachers seem to be aware of all simultaneous happenings in their classroom even when they are not directly in charge of all activity. While this capability emerges with time and experience, there are some management techniques, such as the following ones, that can help teachers develop this quality.

- When children are lined up to go somewhere, appoint one child as line leader and be sure that child knows exactly where to go and what behaviors are appropriate. Then stay at the end of the line. You should not expect young children to walk in perfect order, but careful observation should tell you if someone is about to misbehave.
- Explore every part of your classroom carefully and find at least one place from which you can see everything. When working with infants and very young children this is absolutely essential for safety. When you teach older children and have established good rapport and behavioral expectations, it

One of the keys to a well managed classroom is finding an advantageous spot from which to monitor all classroom activity. To be a "withit" teacher means being aware of everything that is going on in your classroom and being able to anticipate events even before they happen.

may be all right to have a private place or two that are for the children's unsupervised use. For all other teaching circumstances, if you cannot find a satisfactory viewing place, you should move furnishings until you have created one. Then, when you are in a situation that requires you to stay in one place while the children move freely, this place is available to you for supervision.

■ When you talk to or work with a single child or a small group, do not let yourself forget the rest of the class. If your interaction with the target group extends more than one or two minutes, you should start eyeballing the rest of the classroom. You should do this almost continually while still treating the single child or small group with intense interest.

■ Never turn your back for more than a very few moments on the largest part of the class. If you are working with a single child or small group, do not sit down near them facing the wall. If you want to sit at a table with several children and you see that the only available chair is one facing the wall, ask a child who is facing the room to move to it. Then you take the chair that is better for surveillance purposes. Children will almost never ask you why you want to make the trade. If they do, simply explain that you need to see the whole class in case someone needs help.

## Thorough Preparation

Many discipline problems can be eliminated before they even happen if the environment and the day's schedule of events are carefully planned in advance.

### Planning Ahead

One way a beginning teacher can make the class run smoothly is by planning every detail of the day and even rehearsing some events and the accompanying dialogue. Careful planning includes arranging the furniture most effectively, selecting and eliminating materials, figuring out how children will move and work most easily among all the furniture and materials, and having contingency activities ready in case something goes amiss, as when Maureen's projector failed.

### Routines

Young children feel most secure when they know what happens when. Children with temporary or long-term emotional problems are especially aided when classroom routines are completely predictable. Once the routines are well established, they can occasionally be broken for a special event or for the enjoyment of the group, but the routines should still be considered the norm.

## Transitions

The periods between events and activities are often more important than the activities themselves when it comes to maintaining appropriate behavior and an atmosphere of calm. Some transitions should be part of careful planning as, for example, when a teacher plans a whole group dance experience to be followed by story time. The dance activity allows relatively noisy, unstructured behavior, while the story time requires a planned transition to quiet, more passive behavior. Other transitions, such as moving from snack time to outside play or the cleanup behavior that follows art activities, should be built into daily routines. Finally, some transitions must be handled on the spot, as might occur when the children have suggested a new activity and the teacher is flexible in permitting it.

When you plan a transition, it is important to think not only about what will be done but how it will be done. If it is necessary for children to line up, for example, you need to use a method that will ensure that they line up in an orderly way. Calling individual names or identifying small groups, such as those who are wearing specific colors, will more likely produce a state of calm than simply telling everyone to line up at once. Since a major goal of all behavior should be to help children become self-directing and responsible, good transitions should lead toward this goal.

## Fairness To Children

Bernard Spodek (1985) suggests the following guidelines for managing children's behavior. These guidelines focus on establishing and communicating to children fair expectations for their behavior.

- Behaviors expected of children should be known to them. Sometimes children's actions may appear to be misbehavior but are actually the result of ignorance. Instructions need to be given repeatedly and in different contexts before children understand them. This is particularly true for younger children.
- Children need to know why particular rules exist. Children should know the reasons for the rules they follow, even if they don't completely understand the rules. When such explanations are given, children are more likely to want to follow the rules.
- Children should have opportunities to observe and practice proper behavior. Demonstrations of proper behavior by the teacher and follow-up practice with feedback from the teacher make it easier for children to follow through on their own.
- Expected behavior ought to be possible for children. Developmental appropriateness applies to behavior just as it does to academic learning. Children should not be thought of as miniature adults whose misbehavior indicates that they are defective in some way.

- Children cannot be expected to behave properly at all times. Adults aren't expected to behave perfectly all the time, and children shouldn't be either. Children deserve even more patience in this regard than adults do.

## Fostering a Democratic Atmosphere

Psychiatrist Rudolf Dreikurs (Dreikurs et al., 1982) spent many years observing human behavior and focusing, most specifically, on child misbehavior. His work with children in and out of classrooms convinced him that the most effective way to promote good school behavior is for teachers and administrators to create a democratic atmosphere. Underlying this atmosphere must be a thoroughly democratic sense of social equality because, "The basic cause of conflict in the classroom is social inequality among individuals and groups. If the social relationship among people is unstable, it inevitably leads to conflict and disharmony" (p. 69). He hastened to add that teachers must understand the difference between democracy with its social equality and anarchy, which comes from permissiveness. Freedom and order must be carefully balanced in a successful democracy. Dreikurs made some valuable observations about schools, teachers, and children as they relate to a democratic atmosphere:

- On equality: "To most adults it seems preposterous to consider a child as an equal. . . . The mere assumption that children should be treated as their equal is an absurd idea to them." But, he insisted, "Lack of qualities or abilities should never deprive a person of respect and of equal voice" (pp. 69–70).
- On mutual respect: In the classroom there should be "respect for the dignity of others and respect for oneself. . . . Mutual respect is based upon acceptance of the equality of human beings, independent of individual differences, knowledge, information, abilities, and position" (p. 70). For Dreikurs, it is as important for teachers to respect children as it is for children to respect the teacher and each other.
- On shared responsibility: "Children are more than willing to accept guidance from adults if ideas are not imposed on them and if they feel that their opinions and suggestions are taken seriously. This does not necessarily mean that the teacher is obligated to do what they suggest. . . . The curriculum should, however, be flexible enough to give students and teachers a chance to follow the inclination and interest of each class" (p. 70).
- On teachers' versus children's rights: Teachers who claim they treat their children with respect and have a democratic atmosphere "are often not aware of how they violate this principle the moment their prestige is at stake." Children may be expected to obey rules that teachers do not feel obligated to follow, especially in private. "They believe that the children

will not notice if they eat behind the door of their coat closet or in a cor-
ridor. Children are very much aware of what the teacher is doing. They
often discuss this practice by the teachers among themselves" (p. 75).

■ On the characteristics of a democratic classroom: "In a democratic classroom the pupils and the teacher are united in planning, organizing, implementing, and participating in their common activities. The teacher . . . has
the duty and the responsibility to give direction, to help each child to increase his ability to take part effectively in group settings, and to be able to
make and carry out group decisions" (p. 76). Dreikurs added that a combination of firmness and kindness is critical to the teacher's attitude toward
the class. *"Firmness* implies self-respect; *kindness* implies respect for others. .
. . We can resolve our conflicts without either fighting or yielding, by both
respecting others and respecting ourselves" (p. 76).

In the many ideas he proposed for "maintaining sanity in the classroom,"
Dreikurs did not simply suggest that teachers find a midway position between autocratic control and permissiveness. While he argued that the former
leads children to rebellion and the latter promotes anarchy, his point wasn't
for teachers to try to avoid either extreme or to adopt a little of each. Instead,
he believed that teachers needed to reach children from within themselves.
Democracy, he believed, offered the best means to creating in children the
self-worth and respect for others that would make the classroom run
smoothly. (The full implications of this view are discussed in the upcoming
section, Systematic Training for Effective Teaching.)

To see how Dreikurs' ideas apply to children in the early years, we can
look back to some of the developmental stages described in Chapter 4. Selman's (1980) theory of friendship development provides a perspective on
children's abilities to engage in mutual respect. At Stage 0, the stage most
widely observed in the preschool years, children do not yet relate to the psychological aspects of choosing, treating, and keeping friends. If there are disagreements, they have more to do with disputes about the use of toys or
space than they do about the loss of affection or attention. At Stage 1, which
appears in the early elementary years, the psychological element in friendships enters children's awareness. Children most often view disputes from
their own point of view, however, and mutual blame or responsibility are
usually too complex to consider. Keeping in mind the limitations of these
two stages, teachers can help promote mutual respect in the preschool years
by focusing on the care and use of toys and other materials. In the primary
grades, children can be asked to take the first steps toward putting themselves
in others' shoes, but discussions should be kept simple and clearly focused.

Piaget's (1965) theory about the development of children's understanding
of rules provides another way of applying Dreikurs' ideas to the early years.
In the preschool years, children are most often at Stage 1, in which they behave heteronomously. For them, authority figures rule imperiously and at
whim. Authorities are to be obeyed just because they are bigger, older, and

have more power. Authorities may make rules and punish just because they feel like it. At Stage 2, most typical of the primary grades, children begin to understand the reasons for rules and usually interpret them very rigidly and literally. Although rules now have reasons, they are still created by authority figures who must know why they are important.

In the preschool classroom, it is usually best to deal with the Stage 1 view of rules by simply having as few rules as possible. Two or three rules are all most very young children can handle, and these should be associated with the most important issues of safety. In kindergarten, an extra rule or two may be added, and children can often help create them. By the end of kindergarten and into the primary grades, children should be involved as much as possible with the creation of rules. As teacher and children discuss the need for smooth functioning of the classroom, and decide together what rules could be established to ensure success, the mutual respect and democratic atmosphere championed by Dreikurs can emerge.

The concept of a democratic atmosphere in the school was transported to the early childhood classroom by Maria Montessori (1969). Like Dreikurs, she believed that mutual respect, equality, and shared responsibility should be the hallmarks of a classroom run with fairness. She, too, believed that autocratic teachers encourage rebellion and that permissiveness leads to anarchy. At the same time, she observed in children developmental stages similar to those of Piaget and Selman, leading her to the conclusion that full-blown democracy wasn't possible in the preschool years but that it could be instituted in many respects in the primary grades. In either place, however, a democratic *atmosphere* should be possible. In her own words:

- On teachers requiring absolute obedience: Teachers who require children to do just as they say, attribute to themselves almost biblical power in which "God made man in his own image. . . . Naturally, the adult does not realise that he is putting himself in God's place. . . . Within the child is the work of a creator much more exalted than the teacher, the mother or the father, yet in spite of this he is at their mercy" (p. 255).
- On dealing with the willfulness of very young children: "Conscious will is a power which develops with use and activity. We must aim at cultivating the will, not at breaking it" (p. 254).
- On what happens when young children are provided with an opportunity to "create" a democratic society in their classroom: "It is interesting to see how, little by little, [the children] become aware of forming a community which behaves as such. They come to feel part of a group to which their activity contributes. And not only do they begin to take an interest in this, but they work on it profoundly . . ." (p. 237).
- On the difference between the classroom societies formed by preschoolers and by primary school children: Montessori observed that a true society could only be created by children in the primary years, while that in the preschool years might be called a "society in embryo." In the earlier stage,

social cohesion emerges intuitively and almost unconsciously. "This unity born among the children, which is produced by a spontaneous need, directed by an unconscious power, and vitalised by a social spirit, is a phenomenon needing a name, and I call it *'cohesion in the social unit.' "* The older children look at their society differently, she says. "Children then want to know the customs and laws which men have adopted to guide their conduct: they seek to have someone in control who will govern the community." Both these stages—cohesion and organization—are important for children growing up to live in a democratic society because "the two things interpenetrate. Society does not depend enitrely on organisation, but also on cohesion, and of these two the second is basic and serves as foundation for the first" (pp. 239,241).

Montessori devoted much of her life to developing methods and materials for the schools that bore her name. Her interest in promoting the development of a sound society for children of every age led her to create methods and materials that may sound very familiar to you. Many of them have been incorporated into other models of teaching and many seem to be the result of common sense. Looked at closely, however, you can see how they can be used to promote democratic behavior in children and thus help create a democratic society within your classroom.

- A close-knit classroom community promotes the mutual trust that is necessary for democracy to develop. One way to help achieve this is to mix ages within your classroom, because in a multiage classroom children can learn to take care of and to trust each other. (See the interview with Linda Bennie in Chapter 7 to see how well this can work.) If this isn't possible, occasionally invite children from other classes or your children's brothers and sisters.
- Responsibility for and caring about others are related characteristics. One way to foster these is to limit the available materials, thus forcing children to learn to share and be unselfish. When confronted with a situation in which there aren't enough scissors and crayons to go around, and when given proper guidance in dealing with the situation, such learning can take place. But proper guidance, including discussion and role play, is essential so the children can actually see how the system works.
- Taking care of the environment is an adult responsibility in most schools. However, when young children are entrusted with various housekeeping tasks and are shown how to perform those tasks, their sense of environmental responsibility and competence tends to grow. Whether indoors or out, this means trusting children with real tools for cleaning, gardening, and so forth. To make this work well, it is important to demonstrate how each tool works and to give each child an opportunity to practice using it. If small versions of a particular tool aren't available, long handles can be cut off the lightest weight adult models. Young children take their respon-

One way to help children realize the necessity for sharing is to limit the available materials. However, the situation should be accompanied by guidance from the teacher.

sibilities quite seriously when given such trust, and teachers who are accustomed to cleaning up after their children will probably be surprised at how little work remains for them to do.

■ A truly democratic society (or democratic "society in embryo") can emerge only if the participants create it on their own, with little or no influence from an autocratic authority figure. One way to do this is to let the children choose when to be social and when to work or play alone. You can achieve this in part by offering both individual and group activities. Then, for as much of the day as possible, children should be permitted free choice of both kinds of activities. If you observe that a particular child never interacts with other children, it is appropriate to guide him toward occasional interaction or to find out if there is a deeper problem that should be handled. In general, however, if you try to force group cohesion, you will only encourage the continuation of an authority–follower relationship.

■ Management of inappropriate behavior without resorting to punishments or other authoritarian responses was always a goal for Montessori. This was true even in situations that threatened to disrupt the entire class. In such situations, Montessori suggested that the teacher survey the class, looking for the best behaved children, then speak quietly to each one individually, redirecting their activities as necessary. Since these better behaved children are the ones most likely to benefit from redirection, that portion of the class should soon begin to settle down. The teacher should then continue on with the rest of the class, saving the most troublesome children for last. This method is the reverse of that found in most classrooms, in which the most badly behaved children are targeted first.

Redirection was recommended by Montessori for frequent use in disciplinary situations, both large and small. She believed that if children could find materials and activities that successfully engaged them, then they wouldn't have a need to misbehave. At that point, they would become more self-directing in both their learning and their behavior.

- Self-discipline is vital to any democratic society, and children can be encouraged in this direction when teachers help them learn to choose what they want to do and where they want to be. A child who complains that "there's nothing to do" needs help in decision making. Pointing out that the room is full of things to do may be counterproductive, since the overwhelming quantity of materials may well be the child's problem. Instead, the teacher might offer to help the child choose and then suggest no more than just two ideas. If necessary, this can be followed with a comment such as, "You don't want either of those choices? Then *you* choose something." If the child still can't decide, the teacher returns to the first choices, or lists one of them and adds another new one. The key is to stay with the child until he or she has actually begun some activity. If there isn't sufficient time for this, the teacher should take the child along while attending to other tasks, occasionally asking if the child is ready to try choosing again.
- Living in a democracy requires the courage to take risks now and then and the self-confidence to make independent decisions. Montessori believed that the proper mix of classroom materials could help develop these traits. In her view, children who are in need of reassurance or more self-discipline can be guided in this direction through experiences with structured materials and activities. Other, more adventurous children should have the opportunity to direct their own learning and take risks with more creative and open-ended activities. Some children will always need more structure, but they should not be denied experiences with the risk-taking activities. Conversely, some children will usually be self-directive and creative but will occasionally need the comfort of more structure.
- Finally, it is important to realize that freedom, democracy, and independence should be allowed to emerge gradually. If offered at the start of children's experience in school, they will soon slide into the chaos of anarchy. Children first need the security of knowing the limits on their behavior and what the school expects of them. When beginning a school

year or creating a group of younger children, the teacher will need to be more of an authority figure than will later be the case. At the same time, the teacher should constantly be looking for ways to step out of the authority role, and here Montessori again suggests special preparation of the environment. If shelves and containers are kept relatively empty at first, there is less stimulus to confuse the children and promote inappropriate behavior. With fewer materials to choose from, the teacher can select some for demonstration, more easily guide children in their decision making, and maintain a calm atmosphere. One place to begin demonstration of materials is with the real housekeeping tools suggested above. If the children become busy taking care of their environment, they gain both self-direction and a sense of caring. As the teacher observes this happening, more materials can be introduced and more self-direction can be encouraged. This should happen gradually, until freedom, democracy, and independence have emerged as natural attributes of the classroom environment.

## Systems and Models of Behavior Management

A good number of package approaches to guiding behavior have emerged over the past decades. They have been created in response to the continuing need of teachers to find more and better ways to deal with this omnipresent issue in their classrooms. These various models of behavior management are often known by the names of the people who created them. Some of the better known models are briefly described here. Later, we will take a closer look at two very different systems.

### Rudolf Dreikurs

Dreikurs' (Dreikurs et al., 1982) background as an Adlerian psychiatrist led him to develop a model of discipline focused on the causes of children's misbehavior. He identified four short-term goals of misbehavior: the desire for attention, the desire to display power, the desire for revenge, and the desire to just give up, expressed in a display of inadequacy. Central to this model was the idea of providing children with the logical consequences of their behavior as opposed to letting them achieve any of the four goals mentioned above. In this view, children should be helped to understand that their goals are inappropriate and that they will not be achieved through misbehavior. Furthermore, they should understand why a particular consequence was chosen for them. As we have seen, Dreikurs was also dedicated to making classrooms more democratic and believed that teachers should deal with misbehaviors in such a way as to promote democracy.

### Applying the Model

In Dreikurs' model, the teacher's role is to identify the goal of a child's behavior and then deliver logical consequences. If, for example, a child in your class makes loud noises during circle time or catches your attention and then pretends to run away from the playground or yells "Look at me" just before using a snack plate as an airplane, he is probably seeking attention. Unless the child is putting himself or others in danger, the most logical consequence to such attention-seeking behavior is to ignore him totally or to simply remove him from the area.

## Haim Ginott

Good communication between teacher and child is the hallmark of Ginott's (1972) approach. The best known element in Ginott's view of communication is that adults should attack the problem behavior and not the child. The message teachers should convey is that, "I like you, but this behavior is unacceptable." The teacher is viewed as someone who is there to help children solve problems, who will communicate well with children, support their efforts toward self-esteem, and have the patience to realize that good self-discipline develops over time.

### Applying the Model

Perhaps there are two children who cannot seem to get along with each other. If one chooses a special toy the other immediately wants it and uses physical force to get it away. You may remove the offending child from the area and calmly but firmly say, "In this classroom, hitting and snatching toys away from other children is not permitted." This comment is designed to focus attention on the behavior and not to belittle the child. You would then listen to the child's side of the story and, perhaps, learn that she feels offended because every time she wants to use this particular toy, the other child races to get there first. By listening to the child's view, you find that the situation is deeper than it first seemed and the child feels as though her point of view is respected.

## William Glasser

A psychiatrist, Glasser (1985) created his model of behavior management based on an approach he called *reality therapy*. In school settings, the goal of this model is to develop responsible classroom behavior. To achieve this goal, children need to become aware of why things sometimes don't work for them in school. However, this encouragement of self-awareness must be accompanied by fostering self-esteem. Glasser suggests that teachers help children avoid failure by finding academic and other tasks that have a good chance of success. He also suggests that, once children are aware of the causes of their inappropriate behavior, they should commit themselves to corrective action. The teacher's role is then to assist the children in making sure the commitment is fulfilled. For older children, a written plan for changed behavior may be useful.

### Applying the Model

The best known classroom technique in Glasser's model is the class meeting, in which children discuss their feelings about how school is going and about their relationships with each other. While this takes time out of the day, it does bring to the surface some concerns and events that might otherwise remain hidden. Children as young as three can usually participate in such meetings, as long as there are older children serving as models. Otherwise, it may be best to wait until children are on the older side of four, or even five, before beginning such meetings. A time that works well to have the meeting is right after a playground period or after lunch. Children can then look back on the day and share their feelings about how things are going and discuss ways to make the coming hours work well. You need to emphasize the idea that feelings can be positive as well as negative and that everyone feels better when praise is given. Children will then be encouraged to thank each other for such things as assistance in getting on a high swing, for being picked up after a fall, or for help with an especially hard math problem.

Two other models of behavior management will be discussed in more detail. Because they are more fully developed than the approaches just described, they are often referred to as management systems rather than models. As you work with children in different settings, the chances are good that you will encounter elements of one or the other system in practice. Because they are so different, it is unlikely that you will see the two of them mixed to any great extent. The first approach, labelled *assertive discipline,* views children from a behavioristic standpoint, while the second one, known as *systematic training for effective teaching* (STET), comes more from a psychoanalytic perspective. As you read about the characteristics of each, and about their strengths and weaknesses, you should consider where your own preferences lie. If you feel strongly opposed to one or the other, you may find this useful to know when determining where you want to be employed.

## Assertive Discipline

Assertive discipline is modeled after assertiveness training. This approach to behavior management is the work of the educator Lee Canter (Canter and Canter, 1976), and grew out of his observation that the management methods in operation during the early 1970s were inadequate for increasingly difficult classrooms. He also argued that models such as those we have just discussed had been misinterpreted by teachers, and this led to fallacies in their thinking, which, in turn, led to chaotic classrooms. An additional problem Canter observed was that many teachers had accepted the "Myth of the Good Teacher," in which an effective teacher is viewed as one who can always control the class without outside help from the principal or parents. Canter believed that it was time for teachers to "take charge" and, essentially, stop being pushed around by disobedient children. It was also time that they insisted upon cooperation from parents and their school principal. Only then would they be able to meet their own very real needs to have the room quiet and calm enough to accomplish the teaching that they were hired to do.

The model Canter created was very specific in its suggestions and step-by-step instructions. For example, the teacher should clearly convey to the children what rules he or she has deemed necessary for the smooth functioning of the class. This list is then backed up with a specific sequence of consequences to use when the rules are broken. Generally, the sequence provides for increasingly serious consequences each time a rule is intentionally broken. For example, following the first instance of intentional misbehavior, the child's name is written on the board; the second time, a check is placed beside it and there is a consequence such as a missed recess; the third time, the child is sent to the office and the parent is called, and so on. (The sequence can be adapted to the needs of a specific school or age group.)

The sequence includes such in-class consequences as time-out, or isolation, in which the child sits in a corner for ten to twenty minutes; time-out in another classroom, where the child takes his work along; removal of a privilege such as free time, recess, physical education, or a field trip; or detention after school, considered particularly effective if a child hasn't finished her work.

In addition to consequences for breaking rules, there are rewards for doing well. One approach is to place an empty jar in full view of the class, with the suggestion that good behavior will, over time, result in more and more marbles being placed in the jar. When the jar is full of marbles there will be a special trip or treat, such as lunch at the nearest fast-food restaurant or an in-school party.

Canter's recommendation that teachers take charge, be assertive, and demand their rights to teach, clearly found an audience. In the early 1980s, assertive discipline became quite popular in the western United States and soon spread throughout the country (Duke and Meckel, 1984). Teachers learned the system through workshops or at conferences. Experience seemed to show that the system is most effective when adopted by an entire school. Such schools generally declare themselves assertive discipline schools, and every teacher hired must agree to buy into the system. For this reason, it is important for you to consider carefully the extent to which you would feel comfortable using assertive discipline in your own classroom.

A strength of assertive discipline is that children know exactly where they stand and exactly what will happen to them if they disobey the rules. Such

Common to several models of behavior management is the idea of helping children understand the consequences of their behavior. In each model, however, it is important to detach the specific instance of misbehavior from the child's general feelings of self-esteem: that is, to make him or her understand that even good people sometimes do bad things.

consistency can provide a feeling of security. For teachers who are timid about standing up for their rights or who need the structure of a system to give them the courage to talk to parents or to expect support from the principal, assertive discipline provides some help. Many teachers seem to fit into one or all of these categories and find much to praise in the system.

Others have found that there are problems. Canter himself has seen his ideas misused in much the same way he observed previous methods being misunderstood. For example, in the 1970s he suggested writing children's names and the follow-up check marks on the chalkboard. Problems arose when teachers used the technique in overly punitive ways, or claimed that children were upset by seeing their names written in public, or the same few children constantly had their names written. Canter has since recommended using a clipboard or notebook. Other problems are inherent in the system itself. When the teacher becomes overtly assertive and adopts a take-charge mode of behavior, it is clear to the children that the teacher is the authority figure. In some cases, this may be important for getting the attention of a difficult class. If it is kept up, however, there will continue to be a teacher versus children atmosphere in which any growth in classroom democracy will be nearly impossible. Furthermore, while this atmosphere may reduce teacher stress, it may unintentionally increase child stress. Canter claims that children are relieved when clear limits are set for them, but with a teacher versus chil-

## The Role of Race in Discipline: A Conversation with Simon Johnson

*Our conversation in this chapter is with a long-time principal, professor of education, and consultant to schools who has had an abundance of experience with management and discipline issues. It is his view that race is a component of discipline that cannot be disregarded. In our conversation he shares some ways that teachers of young children can face racial issues with success.*

Simon Johnson is the director of a university office assigned to recruit and support minorities as education majors. He is committed to diversifying the teaching profession and enlarging understanding between the races in school settings. Most of Simon's work in education has been in the south. As schools began to integrate in the 1960s, his experience, expertise, and educational background made him a valuable resource, particularly to white teachers who didn't understand the behavioral patterns of black children. Eventually, he put his philosophy and discipline suggestions into a book for teachers, which is now in its second edition.*

In recent years his expertise has grown to include the Hispanic cultures that have moved into much of the south. Regarding school behavior and attitudes, he says, "Sometimes the only difference between children is the color of their skin, if they are all growing up in the same neighborhood. If the families are above the poverty line that makes a difference. Then, the children are usually pushed to be successful in education. They're taught how to succeed in life."

*\*Better Discipline: A Practical Approach,* Springfield, IL: Charles C. Thomas, 1990.

It is the less fortunate children who seem to behave in racially distinctive ways according to Simon, and he feels this is particularly the case with disadvantaged African-American students. When these children enter nursery school or kindergarten for the first time, their behaviors may well be the same as those of the white children. Soon, however, peer pressure mounts not to "act white" by succeeding in school. Then these disadvantaged black children may begin to behave inappropriately by fighting, talking back to the teacher, and acting out in other ways. Their nonverbal behavior may include a refusal to look the teacher in the eyes or, conversely, to stare hard and defiantly. To the teacher these children are difficult discipline problems. According to Simon, however, "the children are mostly trying to show their friends that they are with them. They would rather have friends than good grades or a good relationship with the teacher." For younger children, who need a close relationship with the teacher, making this behavioral decision can be traumatic. "They cry a lot," Simon explains, "because of the conflict within themselves as to what they should and shouldn't do."

When any child performs poorly in school, excuses tend to be made, and Simon sees racial differences in these. "It doesn't matter if they are in kindergarten or the university, the same racial patterns apply, he says. "If a white kid isn't successful he'll say, 'I could have done it but I had something more important to do;' or maybe, 'Mommy didn't help me.' Minorities, particularly blacks, will say, 'the teacher doesn't like me' or 'she doesn't look at me the same as the other kids.' While Hispanic children's excuses are close to those of blacks, they will often offer no excuse at all. 'I just didn't do it' is all they will say." Such differences are largely based on differing family cultural values and Simon believes that teachers have a responsibility to learn about these differences in order to improve their work with children.

Additionally, he draws on his experience and observations to provide some concrete suggestions for promoting better discipline:

- Avoid sending children to the principal. It is better to talk out problems with the child yourself.

- Don't push children into a corner by threatening them. Black children especially will feel obligated to take the challenge and threaten right back.
- Either in words or attitude avoid the message of "Shut up and sit down." A black child especially will respond with, "Make me."
- Don't take children's negative responses personally. Remember that much of what is said is done for its effect on peers.
- Be sure to praise the children who need it, even if it is for something minor.
- Arrange it so that everyone in your class can have some success.
- Model polite behavior such as saying "please" and "thank you." This is a powerful change agent for behavior.
- Remember that children who live in deprived neighborhoods have to fight for survival. It should not be surprising if they bring their coping techniques to school. Discuss with them other ways to settle arguments. Such possibilities may be news to many children.
- Attend conferences where you can talk with others about your problems. You may find that others have more of them than you do.
- Keep good records of your interactions with children of other races. If you are accused of prejudice, be ready to explain what actions you have taken and why.

*To think about and discuss: Have you been mystified by the behavior of children of different races? Discuss these experiences with teachers and education students of those races. As you ask for explanations, keep your thinking receptive and nonjudgmental.*

dren situation, someone must be the winner and someone the loser. It is clear to the children that they must be the losers and, as such, must behave in specified ways to avoid punishment. The feeling that most children derive from such a situation is quite different from that which comes from helping to make rules and consequences themselves, based on the agreed upon needs of the classroom.

When the teacher is so clearly the authority figure, children have little or no opportunity to learn conflict resolution skills. Canter argues that children do learn self-discipline. However, when responsibility is only for oneself, the teacher must be relied upon for resolving interpersonal problems. In addition, if assertive discipline is used in a kindergarten class, there may well be a number of children who are not yet capable, in the Piagetian sense, of following rules.

While assertive discipline remains controversial, it also remains popular in much of the United States. When observing in schools, look for it in action and judge its results against what you have learned about developmentally appropriate practices.

## Systematic Training for Effective Teaching

Developed by Don Dinkmeyer, Gary McKay, and Don Dinkmeyer, Jr. (1980), STET is a very different response to the difficult school management problems that seemed to emerge in the 1970s. They began by developing a course for effective parenting and then adapted it for teachers. All three are educational and counseling psychologists who subscribe to the ideas of Rudolf Dreikurs. Dinkmeyer and his colleagues begin their program by introducing Dreikurs' four goals of misbehavior, then proceed to help teachers master their application. Examples, charts, and illustrations abound in their handbooks. Further, they deal more fully than did Dreikurs with those teacher characteristics that may hamper relationships with students. They provide numerous examples and charts that help teachers understand themselves in their relationships with children.

The authors suggest that an essential attitude that teachers should have toward children is that of encouragement, which they define as "helping students believe in themselves and in their abilities" (p. 69). This encouragement should accept children as they are and should help them "develop the courage to be imperfect." Teachers must avoid making negative comments about their students, should identify their talents, and avoid such discouraging factors as negative expectations, unreasonably high standards, competition, overambition and double standards. "Be an asset finder, not a fault finder" they conclude.

Another crucial element in the STET system is good listening skills with techniques borrowed from the psychologist Thomas Gordon. They use his approaches to reflective listening and his "I-messages." In reflective listening, the teacher processes the child's feelings and states them back to the child so that he can clarify his feelings and move the discussion forward ("You feel angry because Jimmy hit you"). I-messages are designed to convey the teacher's feelings about a situation to the child without the more usual accusatory "you" attached ("When I see you children fighting I become impatient because I need to spend the time teaching you").

The STET approach to working with children is designed to increase children's power in directing their own lives. An encouraging climate and respect for students as individuals are considered crucial for increasing democracy in the classroom. Rather than promote the image of teacher as authority figure in a take-charge role, the authors suggest quite the opposite:

> When we commit ourselves to the principles of a democratic classroom, we show our belief in the importance of offering choices. . . . Students begin to feel trusted when we allow them a voice in classroom policies, even in learning procedures. Similarly, students are more likely to benefit from disciplinary measures they helped tailor for themselves. . . . Offering choices, getting students involved in their educations, helps reduce the occasions for misbehavior. (p. 132)

### Punishment versus Logical Consequences

A major difference between the STET approach and assertive discipline is the view on punishment. In assertive discipline, punishment is built into the sequence of steps that follow disobedience: sitting in isolation, trips to the principal's office, or the loss of recess, for example. The STET authors suggest that logical consequences that relate directly to the misbehavior make more sense to children and do not create the negative feelings that punishment does.

Canter would argue that, when children disobey rules and are aware of the consequences, they actually make a choice. He suggests that teachers say such things as, "Since you have disobeyed this rule three times, you have chosen to sit in the corner." Dinkmeyer would counter by saying that the child's motives for disobedience may be much deeper than simply obeying or not obeying rules.

The strengths of STET include its emphasis on respect for children, its insistence on getting to the bottom of children's problems rather than treating the external situation, its preference for democratic processes, and its avoidance of punishment. The arguments that STET might have against it are that it requires much more observation of children than does assertive discipline, that teachers lacking sufficient training might misidentify children's problems, and that much time may be required to do this kind of management effectively.

STET and assertive discipline differ widely in the ways they view teachers and children and the roles they each play. As a teacher, it will be your re-

**Table 9.1**

CONSEQUENCES OF BEHAVIOR

| PUNISHMENT | LOGICAL CONSEQUENCES |
|---|---|
| 1. Expresses the power of personal authority. | Acknowledge mutual rights. |
| 2. Is arbitrary or barely related to the situation. | Are directly related to the misbehavior. |
| 3. Implies moral judgment and equates deed and doer. | Imply no moral judgment and separate deed from doer. |
| 4. Is concerned with past misbehavior. | Are concerned with present and future behavior. |
| 5. Threatens. Treats the offender with disrespect. | Are invoked in a friendly manner after feelings have calmed. Imply good will. |
| 6. Demands obedience. | Permit choice. |

SOURCE: Dinkmeyer, McKay, and Dinkmeyer, 1980, pp. 139–140.

sponsibility to choose carefully between available behavior management systems or to create your own approach based on your understanding of child development and educational theory. A final consideration is the age of the children you work with. Infants and toddlers are not advanced enough to understand management systems. However, teachers of preschoolers may find bits and pieces of the approaches useful, while teachers in kindergarten and above will need to consider the options most carefully.

## Extending Your Learning

1. Choose two schools or centers with different approaches to behavior management. Spend at least two hours in each observing teacher–child interactions. Write down instances in which you saw a behavior problem effectively dealt with. After you have left, analyze why the method worked. Then consider the long-term effects on the child and on the classroom atmosphere and the probable long-term success of the method.
2. Review this chapter and choose the ideas that you would most like to try at this time. If you are in a placement or have access to a classroom, discuss the ideas with the teacher or director and, with permission, try them out. Ask the teacher or director to help you analyze how well the ideas worked.
3. Discuss in class the pros and cons of each of the approaches to behavior management described in this chapter. Add arguments of your own to those already presented. Discuss with each other which approaches are most likely the ones you will adopt and why.

## References

Bandura, A., Ross, D., and Ross, S. A. (1963). Imitation of film-mediated aggressive models. *Journal of Abnormal and Social Psychology* 66:3–11.

Bredekamp, S. (ed.) (1987). *Developmentally appropriate practice in early childhood programs serving children from birth through age 8.* Washington, DC: NAEYC.

Canter, L., and Canter, M. (1976). *Assertive discipline.* Santa Monica, CA: Lee Canter and Associates.

Dinkmeyer, D., McKay, G., and Dinkmeyer, D., Jr. (1980). *Systematic training for effective teaching.* Circle Pines, MN: American Guidance Service.

Dreikurs, R., Grunwald, B., and Pepper, F. (1982, first published 1971). *Maintaining sanity in the classroom.* New York: Harper & Row.

Duke, D., and Meckel, A. (1984). *Teacher's guide to classroom management.* New York: Random House.

Ginott, H. (1972). *Teacher and child.* New York: Macmillan.

Glasser, W. (1985). *Control theory in the classroom.* New York: Perennial Library.

Hildebrand, V. (1990). *Guiding young children's behavior.* New York: Macmillan.

Kounin, J. (1970). *Discipline and group management in classrooms.* New York: Holt, Rinehart and Winston.

Montessori, M. (1969, first published 1949). *The absorbent mind.* Madras, India: Kalakshetra.

Piaget, J. (1965, first published 1932). *The moral judgment of the child.* New York: The Free Press.

Selman, R. (1980). *The growth of interpersonal understanding.* New York: Academic Press.

Spodek, B. (1985). *Teaching in the early years.* Englewood Cliffs, NJ: Prentice Hall.

Sprinthall, N., and Sprinthall, R. (1990). *Educational psychology: A developmental approach.* New York: McGraw-Hill.

# 10

# Working with Other Adults: Parents and Aides

## OBJECTIVE

When you finish reading this chapter, you should be able to

- Place today's parent involvement and use of aides in historical and cultural context.
- Understand your role as a teacher relating to parents.
- Understand your role as a teacher relating to aides.

As you think about the chapter on your own, you should be able to

- Consider some solutions to today's problems related to good school–parent involvement.
- Plan ways in which you can work best with other adults as a part of your responsibilities.

While the care and education of infants and young children is the major responsibility of the early childhood professional, much time is also devoted to interacting with other adults: the children's parents and classroom teaching assistants or aides. It is important to remember that parents are the children's first teachers, both chronologically and in order of importance. Consequently, your relationship with parents can go a long way toward making your teaching efforts successful. The same is true of aides, who contribute time, effort, and talent toward making your teaching a success. Further, they look to you for expertise and guidance, thus making personnel management a part of your job. While the larger segment of this chapter is devoted to the topic of parents, relating well with aides should remain a priority as well.

## Working with Parents

As an early childhood educator, you will be deeply involved in relating your children's needs, interests, and development to their home experiences. Since your children will never be closer to their parents than they are now, the more closely you are able to work with parents, the more successful your educational efforts with their children are likely to be.

The children entrusted to your care come from increasingly diverse backgrounds and experiences. In a kindergarten class today you might well find that most of the mothers work full- or part-time; half of the children are from single-parent homes; one or more children may be homeless; one or more may have been born addicted to drugs or are HIV positive; several live below the poverty line; one or more occasionally come to school with suspicious-looking bruises; two or three begin the year having learned to read at home; one or two have traveled extensively, even to other countries. Rarely have schools and centers been asked to deal with such complexity in children's backgrounds all within one site. A look back at the history of parent education and parents' involvement in their children's education should provide a better perspective on the situation today.

### A History of Parent Education and Involvement

It has always been the responsibility of parents to provide nourishment, comfort, safety, and education about the world to their offspring. However, the way parents go about fulfilling these responsibilities has changed over time and across cultures. In the past century, a proliferation of child care manuals and magazines has been added to the traditional passing down, from one generation to another, of the best methods of child rearing. Likewise, the role of the school in relation to parents has changed, depending on societal needs and historical events. In the last half of the nineteenth century, four historical and cultural developments in the United States influenced parent–child interaction: the end of the Civil War, industrialization, urbanization, and vastly increased immigration.

## The Nineteenth Century

Up until this time, small, rural, self-contained communities assumed the responsibility for enculturating and educating their children. Both family and church aided the school in this process. In the Northeast, for example, the Puritan tradition brought from Renaissance England held both school and family responsible for educating children to the point that they could read the scriptures on their own. In the Southwest, however, the Spanish Catholic tradition left scripture reading to the priests and, consequently, the education of children was according to the interests of the family. In the Southeast, wealthier children were sometimes sent back across the ocean for their education, while slave children usually received no education at all. For them, learning to read was usually forbidden entirely.

The end of the Civil War and of slavery meant that black children could now be educated. Missionaries from Northern churches quickly descended on the South, devoting their money and time to building churches and schools. Yet the rural economics and politics of the time ensured that black children, no matter what their education, nearly always ended up as poor sharecroppers or in menial labor jobs. Outside the South, ever increasing immigration and industrialization brought the growth of cities and the demise of many small rural schools. Poor immigrants pouring into the cities crowded facilities beyond capacity. As parents went off to find work, children were left to fend for themselves in uncomfortable and unhealthy conditions. Consequently, early childhood education became viewed by some philanthropists as a way to rescue these children and to teach their parents the culture of the new world they had so recently entered. Early education centers were established and funded by these philanthropists, with part of the budget reserved for parent education. The centers were often established in settlement houses, institutions that provided social services, recreation, and education to the urban poor.

After the Civil War, as more and more men sought factory day jobs away from the home, women began to assume a wider variety of roles within the home. As they became a more powerful force within the home, a new era of greater equality arose, encouraging the formation of women's clubs. Many of these had a strong interest in parent education (Berger, 1991). As you read in Chapter 1, the influence of Friedrich Froebel on early education during this time was extensive. Froebel viewed mothers as critical to the education of infants and young children and his book *Mother Play and Nursery Songs* was translated into English and widely read. During the 1870s, books and articles for teachers and parents, based on Froebel's ideas, increased greatly in number. "Pestalozzi and Froebel's belief that parents are integral components of education influenced the educational roles of parents. A climate for change, the possibility of perfectibility of man, and reverence for motherhood prevailed. Thus, the time was ripe for the parent education movement to begin" (Berger, 1991, p. 53).

By the 1880s, women's influence in child development issues was high, and organizations founded by women became instrumental in promoting parent education and involvement: the Child Study Association of America (CSAA), the American Association of University Women (AAUW), the National Congress of Mothers (which eventually became the PTA), and the National Association of Colored Women (ACW). The high impact of these associations has been lasting and, from the beginning, included such parent activities as child study groups, lectures, conferences, consulting services, libraries, magazines and other publications, and leadership training.

In addition, new magazines were founded, such as *Good Housekeeping, Ladies' Home Journal,* and *Woman's Home Companion.* These often contained articles on child rearing. While the advice given to parents in earlier centuries would have focused on breaking the will of the young, devil-inspired child, there was now an underlying assumption that children were born good and that proper motherly guidance would ensure continued goodness. "Mothers were idolized as the epitome of purity and goodness, and children were thought to model after the mother in their character development. . . . Character was best formed through provision of a good home with love and affection between mother and child. . . ." (Berger, 1991, p. 57).

### 1900 to the 1950s

By 1909 the federal government was visibly in the business of parent education when it held the first White House Conference on Child Welfare. The Children's Bureau, which is now part of the Department of Health, Education, and Welfare, was established in 1912 as an outgrowth of the conference. By 1914 it was publishing "the most widely distributed pamphlet of all times": *Infant Care: Your Child from One to Six* (Nedler and McAfee, 1979, p. 7). Subsequently, the pamphlet has undergone several revisions that reflect changing child-rearing philosophies. In fact, the first edition reflected the move away from the prevailing focus on providing children a warm, loving home environment and toward a new focus on routine and strict discipline.

While each age seems to have room for conflicting philosophies of child rearing, the general trend from the late 1880s to about 1910 was to emphasize love and acceptance. Then, from 1910 until the 1930s, a new trend linked to behavioral psychology began promoting obedience rather than acceptance and physical warmth between parent and child. The new focus on routine and discipline during this latter period meant that infants were no longer fed on demand but according to a rigid schedule, and they were to be totally weaned by their first birthday. Yet other philosophies vied for parents' attention, from the child-centered views of John Dewey and Arnold Gesell to the sexuality theories of Sigmund Freud. Whatever the philosophy, however, the emphasis on the importance of the early years caught parents' attention. The 1920s were destined to become the heyday of parent education.

Parent organizations seemed to spring up everywhere, and they might or might not be associated with a school. Their membership became more middle class and educated than had been the case when classes for poor parents were first established in settlement houses. This increased involvement of the middle class led to the establishment of the first parent cooperative nursery schools during the 1920s, generally under the sponsorship of a university or college, and most notably in California. By 1929 there were 500 cooperatives in the United States (Nedler and McAfee, 1979). PTA membership grew from 60,000 in 1915 to 875,000 in 1925 and to almost 1.5 million in 1930 (Berger, 1991).

While parent education continued through the 1930s, the stock market crash of 1929 and the resulting Great Depression served to renew interest in providing help to the poor. There was even a federal program that hired unemployed teachers to organize and direct nursery schools. The intention was to attach these nursery schools to local public schools when the financial crisis was over, but this was a largely unfulfilled plan. The philosophical disagreement between the behaviorists, who regimented and disciplined, and the child-centered philosophers, who opted for natural development, continued. The latter group, however, had gradually become more popular, helped along by a book for new parents. By 1946, when Benjamin Spock first published *The Common Sense Book of Baby and Child Care,* his somewhat permissive and vaguely Freudian point of view ensured that the book would be a best seller. Looking back a decade later he said:

> When I was writing the first edition, between 1943 and 1946, the attitude of a majority of people toward infant feeding, toilet training, and general child management was still fairly strict and inflexible. However, the need for greater understanding of children and for flexibility in their care had been made clear by educators, psychoanalysts, and pediatricians, and I was trying to encourage this. (Spock, 1957, p. 1)

Spock went on to say that, by the mid-1950s, parents were more likely to err on the side of permissiveness than strictness.

The event that most influenced the direction of parent education and involvement during the 1940s was World War II. Suddenly, millions of women worked while men served in the military. Nursery schools and day-care centers became a home away from home to more and more young children. The view of these schools and centers seemed to be that parents were important for physical care and emotional support, but that the nursery school should see that the child was appropriately educated. The prevailing view seemed to be that parent involvement should largely be confined to open houses and parent–teacher conferences (Nedler and McAfee, 1979). This view continued at least throughout the next decade, and even today remnants of this separatist attitude create a barrier to good parent–school interaction.

## 1960–1990

The political and emotional turmoil that characterized the 1960s preoccupation with civil rights and Vietnam once again produced new views of parenting, including the notion that fathers were important. While Dr. Spock continued to be influential, the psychologist Haim Ginott (see Chapter 9) added another view to parent–child interactions. According to Ginott (1965), parents should talk openly with their children about their own feelings and encourage their children to do likewise. Parents should work hard to encourage their children's self-esteem. This should be done by discussing the appropriateness or inappropriateness of a particular behavior or situation while remaining supportive of the child himself. While educated, middle-class parents read both Spock and Ginott, less fortunate parents had become increasingly left out of the mainstream of parent education and involvement.

Under Lyndon Johnson's presidency, this situation was tackled with more enthusiasm than had been seen since the 1880s. This time, it was the government, rather than private philanthropy, that led the newly named War on Poverty. The war included an early education division entitled Head Start, which began with an eight-week summer session in 1965. Federal money was provided for administration by local agencies, and within a few months the program was expanded with additional infusions of funds. More children could now be reached and they were kept for an entire year. The goal was to stop the cycle of poverty by reaching children in the earliest years. From the very beginning, a parent involvement component was included, and from then until today, "encouraging and facilitating parent involvement is a mandated responsibility of every Head Start staff member" (Mallory and Goldsmith, 1990, p. 37). Parents were provided with parent education classes, job training, literacy programs, and opportunities to volunteer in the classroom. While Head Start has undergone much development and change since the mid-1960s, and funding has always been less than generous, the parent component has remained.

One study (Leik and Chalkley, 1990) found that even greater parent involvement than is required by Head Start can bring increased benefits. In the study, a "regular" group of parents, whose four-year-olds attended a center, were permitted to participate in Head Start as much as they wished, while an "enriched" group participated in special activities. For the enriched group, there were support groups for the mothers, computer games that encouraged interaction between mother and child, and special parent–child group activities and games. At the end of the year, children in the enriched group had an increased sense of their own competence and social acceptance, while parents in both groups had a higher view of their children. In this study, there was an additional control group made up of children and parents on the Head Start waiting list. No improvement was found for them, in any area, at the end of the year. The researchers concluded, "At this point, there is good reason to believe that involving parents in Head Start as co-participants with their children, rather than simply as home-based teachers, fosters the type of family environment that helps the children most in the long run" (p. 38).

Another parent-focused program sponsored by Head Start has been the program known as Home Start. Begun in 1972 to bring education, health, and social services to children and their parents at home, this program and similar ones have mushroomed until by 1990 they totaled more than 4,500 throughout the United States (Powell, 1990). However, an important difference exists between the Home Start program of today and that of earlier years. Originally, there was a deficit-reduction orientation in many of the programs, which meant that the parents were assumed to need the help of the home visitor and the home visitor was expected to change both the parents and the children for the better. Now, a more collaborative relationship is encouraged, and the competence of the parent is to be respected. At the same time, a new problem has arisen as funding has stayed low: home visitors have caseloads that are far too large, and their supervisors are too overburdened to provide the support and supervision needed to maintain an effective program (Powell, 1990).

A smaller Head Start–related program that has existed since 1967 is the Parent-Child Centers for infants and toddlers. In recent years, policy makers and early childhood services leaders have called for the expansion of these programs (Pizzo, 1990). Happily, the Human Services Reauthorization Act of 1990 not only reauthorized the Head Start program, but provided for the expansion of the Parent-Child Centers. This amendment seems to be based on positive and sound reasoning. The accompanying report of the Committee on Education and Labor states:

> It is the Committee's belief that the Parent-Child Center amendment is warranted for several reasons including the fact that one out of every five children in the U.S. lives in poverty. Growing numbers of children are born with signs of drug or alcohol addiction, gang warfare is rising, school dropouts and teenage pregnancies are increasing every year. It is imperative that we provide appropriate prevention strategies earlier rather than attempting to deal with them later when they are larger and more serious. (Quoted in Pizzo, 1990, p. 31)

The implications in this statement for the inclusion of parents in Head Start programs are many. Many of these parents may still be in their teens and may be drug or alcohol addicts, school dropouts, and so on. Recognizing these problems, Head Start has always integrated parents into every program.

Writing about the strengths of Head Start's parent component, Nancy Mallory and Nancy Goldsmith (1990) argue that "Head Start makes a difference in families' lives. Parents who enroll their children in Head Start acquire parenting skills and learn how to interact in increasingly positive ways with their children. Head Start encourages parents' aspirations for their families" (p. 38). As an example, they describe a couple who enrolled one of their three children in Head Start. At the time, the wife was pregnant with a fourth child and the husband had trouble retaining a job because he didn't like working for others. The Head Start program made them feel needed and important by showing them how to become leaders and to take control of their lives. Now, just a few years later, they own and manage their own business. In their words: "We feel Head Start played a major role in changing our lives by changing our attitudes about ourselves. . . . Head Start bestowed on us an attitude toward life that will benefit not only us but our children as well" (p. 38).

The 1980s brought ever-growing family pressures: in more than half of the two-parent families, both parents worked; few companies were willing to provide flexible work schedules and job sharing; the extended family had almost ceased to exist; problems with drugs, child and spouse abuse, violence,

As Head Start has gradually evolved since its beginning in 1965, researchers have found the effectiveness of a program generally increases as the amount of parent involvement in the program increases.

and AIDS infiltrated all socioeconomic classes; and, while one child out of five lived in poverty, for black children the ratio was almost one in two and for Hispanics, one in three (Berger, 1991). At the same time, middle- and upper-middle-class parents tried to provide an ever-increasing amount of enriched education for their children, including (but certainly not limited to) sports, dance, and music experiences. While having two incomes was often responsible for making such enrichment possible, time became the insufficient resource. One mother wrote despairingly,

> We decorate refrigerators with schedules, compose and photocopy holiday letters to our friends telling them, in eerie detail, exactly how successful (and did we mention busy?) our children are. Instead of being embarrassed by this obsession to have every waking moment of their lives filled with a skill acquisition, we brag about it. The litmus test of parenting is being on the run. . . . The term "late bloomer" has been extinguished from our lexicon. (Hummel, 1992, p. 8)

For all classes of parents, stress has become a strong presence and a major topic of study and discussion in parenting classes offered by schools, hospitals, and social agencies (Berger, 1991). The stresses of living in these times have also contributed to the continuing lack of parent involvement in their children's centers and schools. While the Head Start experience has demonstrated that parent involvement is beneficial to both children and parents, the more common practice remains much like that of the World War II years when open houses and parent–teacher conferences were the primary points of contact. Even with so few expectations, teachers find that many parents do not appear. For the 1990s, one of the primary challenges for teachers of young children is to involve overly busy, overly stressed parents in the education of their children in a meaningful way.

The remainder of this discussion will focus on parent education and involvement in today's environment. As we have seen, this includes a variety of unique and difficult challenges that require understanding and cooperation between parents and teachers. A first step toward achieving this goal is for teachers to be aware of the rights parents have concerning their children and their children's education.

## Parents' Rights

The rights that parents hold fall into three categories: rights provided by law, rights determined by group consensus, and rights based on philosophical argument. While the last two categories are most subject to change and are the least binding, all three categories are subject to removal at various times. In other words, parents must often fight for their rights, although sometimes they are not even aware of what those rights are. One task you can and should take on as a teacher is to be sure parents know their rights.

### Legal Rights

The right to education is not established in the United States Constitution. Instead, rights and provisions for education are determined by each state. Nevertheless, some related issues have been decided by federal court decisions. In the 1920s, Supreme Court cases established the right of parents to teach their own children and to choose parochial over public schools. While every state has a compulsory attendance law, generally requiring that children start school at age five or six, most states also permit parents to teach their children at home.

Another right parents have held since the 1974 Family Educational Rights and Privacy Act was passed, is to have access to their children's records. Health files, grades, school records, and any other documents kept at school are legally available to the parent. Parents also have a right to demand privacy concerning their child's directory information. At their request, the school may not share with anyone such data as name, address, telephone number, and birth information.

Other rights are related to families' religious preferences. Parents who are Jehovah's Witnesses may request that their children not participate in holiday festivities or in the pledge to the flag. Parents who are Christian Scientists may request that their children be exempt from innoculations or medically oriented health lessons. Each state's laws concerning religious rights are different, although the right to abstain from pledging to the flag was established by a 1947 Supreme Court decision. In general, parents who have requests related to their religious beliefs have taken the time to ascertain their rights and will discuss them with you. Your role is threefold: (1) to cooperate in accordance with your state laws, (2) to respect the parents' views even if they disagree with your own, and (3) to take whatever steps are necessary to make the situation comfortable for the children. This may include arranging special activities for them or advising parents of days when they may prefer to keep their children at home.

One right that has remained problematic is that of corporal punishment. As of 1989, thirty-three states still permitted it. While parents might request that corporal punishment not be used, schools do not necessarily abide by their requests. Nevertheless, schools do not have the right to use corporal punishment harshly or excessively and may be criminally liable if they do.

### Rights Decided by Consensus

While any state, or even a school district, can establish parental rights, there are five parental rights that emerged from the first White House Conference on Families, held in 1979 and 1980. Forty-eight of the fifty states held meetings over the course of a year in which such needs as quality day care were discussed. The parental rights that were agreed upon were related specifically to the day-care issue and include the following:

■ The right to observe and talk with faculty before selecting a facility.
■ The right to access to the facility to observe their children.
■ The right to a regular exchange of information on their children and meetings with personnel.
■ The right to be informed about standards of quality that the child care faculty has pledged to meet.
■ The right to review formal evaluations of the program. (Hildebrand, 1990)

While these rights were designated as appropriate to day-care situations, they could well be adapted to other early childhood centers and classrooms. Whether parents are paying through private tuition or indirectly through taxation, their desire to know as much as possible about the site they entrust their children to should be honored.

### Rights Determined by Philosophical Views

The position paper *Developmentally Appropriate Practice in Early Childhood Programs,* published by the National Association for the Education of Young Children (NAEYC), includes a number of expectations that caregivers and teachers should meet when dealing with parents. These are based on NAEYC's philosophy that children deserve developmentally appropriate care and education and that this philosophy must be shared with their parents.

■ Parents should be respected as the child's primary source of affection and care.
■ Parents should have the opportunity to talk daily with staff about their child's progress.
■ The parent–teacher relationship should be considered a partnership with mutual understanding as a goal.
■ Teachers should listen to parents' concerns and goals for their children.
■ Teachers should be respectful of cultural and family differences.
■ Parents and other family members should be welcome in the classroom at appropriate times and assist with decision making when appropriate. (Bredecamp, 1987)

A somewhat different focus on parental rights has been suggested by Alice Honig (quoted in Spodek et al., 1991). In a "Parents' Bill of Rights" she states that parents have the right to

■ Knowledge about child development.
■ Observation skills for more effective parenting.

- Alternative strategies for problem solving and discipline.
- Knowledge about how to use a home for learning experiences with children.
- Language tools and story-reading skills.
- Awareness of being the most important early teachers of their own children.

Honig's "Parents' Bill of Rights" is more of a societal ideal than a reality, since few people innately possess such skills and knowledge. Consequently, some kind of parent education seems to be in order. While much parent education traditionally has been provided by churches, government agencies, hospitals, mental health clinics, colleges, and senior family members, teachers and caregivers may also find themselves answering questions and providing information.

## Parent Education

> Parent education aims to help parents become better informed about child rearing and about family life as it affects child rearing. . . . Society expects parents to perform many roles in relation to their children, and it is these parenting roles on which parent education focuses. Although no one can tell parents exactly what they should do to raise the kind of children they want, parents are eager for information to make parenting easier and more fulfilling. (Nedler and McAfee, 1979, p. 58)

Parent education sponsored by the center or school may be a major part of your life as a teacher or it may play a very minor role. At the very least, you will find that parents want to communicate with you informally about the problems and joys of raising a child. Often, they will seek suggestions from you about their current child-rearing problems. Good classroom observation and interaction, as well as a clear understanding of child development and behavior management techniques, will make it possible for you to share effective ideas. If you regard this communication as a reciprocal arrangement rather than a situation in which you do all the talking and the parent does all the listening, a climate of mutual respect will be established. Such a climate will make parents feel comfortable enough to establish ongoing communication patterns. Without it, they may feel intimidated or defensive. They may even be condescending if you're not a parent yourself.

While such informal day-to-day parent education is an integral part of any teaching job, other, more formal approaches are also common, such as the commercial parenting programs that centers, schools, and libraries sometimes sponsor.

Commercial Programs

One of the first commercial parenting programs to be developed was the one created by Haim Ginott based on his 1965 book *Between Parent and Child*. In Chapter 9, we discussed his philosophy of good communication as the basis of good relationships and behavior. For a time, particularly in the 1960s and '70s, parent study groups focused on his ideas.

Another popular program has been parent effectiveness training (PET) developed by Thomas Gordon. It, too, is based on the concept of good communication and was referred to in Chapter 9. Gordon created the "I-message" in which the parent shares feelings about an uncomfortable situation, rather than commanding the child to reform. Active listening, in which children are encouraged to find solutions to their own problems, is also a part of Gordon's system of communication. The goal for communication about problems or for conflict resolution is to create win-win situations in which everyone is the victor and no one has to lose.

Systematic training for effective parenting (STEP) (Dinkmeyer and McKay, 1976) is the predecessor to systematic training for effective teaching, which was described in Chapter 9. A major goal of this program is to move parents away from feeling as though they must be authoritarian to be successful and to show them ways to create a more democratic atmosphere in the home. Conducting democratic family meetings is one skill parents are taught. In addition, they learn to develop their skills in listening, resolving conflicts, and exploring alternative solutions to problems. Use of encouragement and logical consequences for behavior are also taught as ways to improve behavior.

Commercial programs such as these are most likely to be used if a teacher or administrator, parent or group of parents, has heard of them or taken a course and would like to share the experience with others. More often, a parent education program is built on the specific needs and interests at a particular center or school.

## HOW ONE PROGRAM EVOLVED

*Andrea Lohman is an early childhood educator who has devoted much of her career to working with young children in preschools sponsored by the Lutheran Church. Two underlying philosophies have supported her work: commitment to developmentally appropriate practices (DAP), as outlined by NAEYC, and dedication to the Christian principles of each sponsoring church. It was Andrea's feeling that the children's parents were not as aware as they could be of the practical classroom applications of the dual philosophy. Further, she felt that the schools could do more to show parents how the DAP and Christian educational foundations could be adapted to the home. She decided to take responsibility for creating a parent education program to fill this need.*

*The program Andrea developed consisted of six two-hour sessions, held in the evenings, for both mothers and fathers. Much of the time was spent sitting in the children's small chairs, sometimes engaging in the same activities that the children found enjoyable. While Andrea occasionally lectured, she favored interactive experiences and was always ready to be interrupted with questions or discussion.*

*The first session was devoted to a discussion of children's faith development. Here, the dual philosophies merged as Andrea shared some Piaget-based concepts of children's growing understanding of spiritual issues and then explored ways in which developmentally appropriate practices would apply. Succeeding sessions focused on the ways young children learn, the importance of play, physical growth, health and self-esteem, and friendship. While all the sessions contained references to the NAEYC philosophy, the religious principles were always an integral part as well.*

*At the end of each session, Andrea asked the parents for brief written feedback and she kept her own journal. Her hope was to learn from the experience, perhaps make adjustments, and share the program with other church-related schools. From their comments, Andrea learned that the parents not only learned more about their children but about themselves. They appreciated the opportunity to let their hair down and do some of the things their children did. "Adults need to be kids" one of them said, and another wrote, "Play helps grown adults, too." Andrea was interested to learn that the most popular session seemed to be the one on self-esteem. Indeed, she wrote in her journal that it had the highest participant involvement and interaction, possibly because it was a topic some parents had been reading about at home, thus providing a basis for sharing with each other.*

*What Andrea found most difficult was when the parents sometimes sought more specific information than she was able to give. As a nonparent, there were times when her knowledge was more theoretical than it was practical, even though she was accustomed to children in the school setting. She felt a bit humbled, she wrote in her journal, when she realized how much "parents struggle with the 'real' stuff, like 'Can my children jump on the sofa?' or, 'What do we do when our four-year-old twins pretend their three-year-old sister is a whale?' "*

*In planning for future parenting programs, Andrea believes that the one thing she would change would be to involve the parents more in deciding what should be covered. Her original intention was to share with them the dual philosophy of the church preschools, but she concluded that there are other issues of parental concern that will, no doubt, arise if parents are given the opportunity to provide input.*

Andrea's experience in developing a parenting program illustrates just one of many approaches that are possible, based on the needs of a specific situation, in this case a church-based preschool curriculum. Her experience also shows the current broad acceptance of developmentally appropriate practices and the need to provide parents with hands-on experiences.

Your own involvement with parent education may not be as extensive and formalized as Andrea's. However, you may occasionally see a particular need, as she did, and create a program related to that need. It may be more likely that your role will be to direct interested parents toward community programs. Certainly, the role modeling you do with children will be noted by the parents. Thus, the developmentally appropriate ways in which you teach children may well be educating their parents also.

## Parent Involvement

Just as parent education can take many forms and range from minimal informal contacts to intensive commercial programs, so, too, does parent involvement in the center or school have a broad range of possibilities. One principal (Galen, 1991) has described the parent involvement in her elementary school along a continuum. That is, while many parents participated in some way, some were involved more heavily than others. The occasion for sharing this information was to report on the school's success in moving beyond the traditional open house/parent conference level of interaction. Some selections from the list demonstrate the wide variety of ways in which parents can involve themselves in their children's education.

HIGH parents, trained by teacher, assist in writing conferences, learning centers, computer use.
Parents read to children.
Parents make presentations or present hands-on activities.
Parents participate on committees that set school policy.
PTA parents work on implementation of special activities.
Parents make instructional materials as directed by teacher.
Parents assist in school library, checking out and shelving books.
Parents participate as room mothers or room fathers.
Parents attend classroom plays and presentations.
Parents attend parent/teacher conferences.
Parents are asked to join PTA.
LOW parents are encouraged to read school's handbook for parents.
(adapted from Galen, 1991, p. 19)

Research has shown that parents' involvement in their children's classrooms has a positive effect on student achievement. Teachers can enlist parents to assist with such activities as reading, language games, fingerpainting, field trips, or plant and animal care.

Other ideas for parent involvement suggested by Spodek et al. (1991) include assisting small groups of children with language games, music, art, or short math and science activities; being available to talk with and listen to the children as they work; supervising cooking, pet care, fingerpainting, and other special activities; taking one or two children on short trips in the neighborhood; and helping with arrival and dismissal times. For parents who can come to school but who don't feel comfortable working directly with the children, other activities may be more appropriate: recording attendance, assembling samples of children's work for booklets or displays, arranging details for field trips, gathering information for various teacher reports, preparing materials for class activities, and locating resources and materials in the community. Parents who can't come to school during class time can also participate by laundering or mending clothes from the dramatic play area, collecting scrap materials for craft projects, painting or fixing broken toys, serving on telephone committees, making instructional materials, arranging field trips, or working on a parent newsletter.

There is a growing body of research which shows that student achievement is positively related to parents' participation in their children's educations (Galen, 1991). This fact alone argues for working hard and creatively to involve parents. Nedler and McAfee (1979) and Spodek et al. (1991) suggest that a serious commitment to parental involvement means planning such activities before the children even reach the center or school. Making parents feel welcome and necessary begins early by

- Sending information packets about the program and its expectations for parents and children. Included should be pamphlets that describe the curriculum and program goals, ways parents can help their children make an easy adjustment to school, and a special note to the child that might include a picture of the center or school.
- Inviting the parents and children to visit the center or school. Advance information should include the place to check in, parking arrangements, and any rules of courtesy. Ideally, a special room or corner in the main office should be designated for visitors to sit, talk, and perhaps have a cup of coffee. Staff or volunteers need to be available and to welcome people openly. Parents should be permitted to take time to observe in a classroom or two and then to discuss their experience with the teachers.
- Holding an orientation meeting at which parents can learn about the program. Parents can be given a schedule of activities, the school's policy on behavior, and information on parental responsibilities. It is important to provide time for parents to talk together informally.
- Arranging for a smooth and comfortable registration. Staggering registration appointments and schedules may eliminate confusion. Materials answering predictable parent questions can be sent ahead of time. Low chairs, tables, some interesting toys for the children and an opportunity to visit the classrooms can make the experience more pleasant, especially for the children. Special resource people such as the nurse, speech therapist, or even the cook should be available to answer questions.
- On the first day of school, parents should be encouraged to come with their children. This may be as important for the parents as it is for the children, because they too may find the separation traumatic.

Nedler and McAfee (1979) argue that taking these early steps has positive results for both child and parent:

> The child and parent have been prepared gradually, are familiar with the school setting, and are much less likely to be apprehensive or anxious about the new experience. Parents who have received clear messages of welcome are more likely to be comfortable and excited about the new roles they might assume. (p. 53)

In addition to taking these first steps to make parents feel welcome, the center or school must consider some ongoing attitudinal relationships with parents. Nedler and McAfee list nine ways to facilitate good teacher–parent relationships that will help lead to active parent involvement. They are described here with the addition of some experiences, both positive and negative, that demonstrate the importance of their points.

1. *Teachers need to be aware of differences in parents, and this information must be reflected in the programs that are developed.* Getting to know each parent individually is critical to make this work. One three-year-old's parents owned a pet shop, and they occasionally brought animals to share with the class. Another parent volunteer was allergic to most animals with fur. The teacher made sure that the days such animals came, the allergic parent had a job to do in the main office.

2. *Teachers should "forget the idealized, romanticized picture of the American family and learn to accept parents as they are."* They need to realize that most parents really are concerned about their children, to acknowledge that child rearing can be incredibly difficult, and to be openly supportive of the different ways parents can reach their goals. A second-grade teacher had eight nationalities represented in his classroom. He soon realized that his parent/ teacher conferences were not going as well as they could because he didn't understand the cultural bases of many of the parents' comments. It took him just a few evenings to read a bit about each of the nationalities and to learn enough to ask knowledgeable questions about the parents' views.

3. *Teachers need to respect the fact that it is the parents who are the real experts when it comes to knowing their own children.* They need to listen to what the parents have to say, share what they see in the classroom, and then work as partners for the children's best interests. One kindergarten teacher was concerned about the out-of-control behavior of one boy. She called in a school psychologist to observe and together they worked out a reward system to correct the child's misbehavior. The program had already been started, and wasn't working terribly well, when the teacher had her first conference with the boy's mother. She then learned that the mother had coped with similar problems of her own at kindergarten age and, based on that experience, was doing quite different things to try and help the child. Wishing she had spoken with the mother first, the teacher adjusted her thinking and her approach to the boy's problems.

4. *Parents should be given genuine opportunities to participate in making school decisions.* Teachers need to realize that there will be times when they disagree with the parents' ideas but that knowing the parents' mindsets can be valuable when it comes to implementing school programs. One Montessori school was a parent cooperative and, one year, a couple of the fathers decided that the teachers should be more accountable for the progress of their pupils. They put forth the idea that charts should be made showing how many children in each class had "mastered" each of the pieces of Montessori equipment. Teachers with the highest score would get the biggest raises. The teachers were horrified at this total misinterpretation of Montessori's views of individualized, self-paced learning. Banding to-

gether, they realized that they hadn't been doing a sufficient job of parent education. The result was a monthly newsletter containing articles about Montessori's philosophies, and guest-teacher visits at the parent meetings in which the teachers answered questions about what was happening in the classrooms. The fathers eventually agreed to retreat from their plan until they received more information on the Montessori philosophy. While they later tried to reintroduce the plan, other parents had become sufficiently knowledgeable that it was voted down.

5. *Parents need to be involved in planning and selecting activities, resource people, long-term goals, and so on.* Teachers who want to maintain total control over their classrooms, with little parent input, can expect a high parent dropout rate. In the previous section you read about one school's success in increasing parent involvement along a continuum. A major step in the school's plan for expansion was to create a planning committee of both teachers and parents. Remarking on the essential need to have a group of this sort the principal said, "Representation of parents on the planning committee is the *only* insurance of parental support" (Galen, 1991, p. 20).

6. *Since we all need feedback and reinforcement in order to retain our interest in an activity or project, teachers should remember to praise the efforts and successes of both parents and children.* A preschool teacher spoke at an open house about the need to limit children's television watching. Her concern, she told the parents, was that she was seeing far too many incidents of superhero-related violence. After a brief discussion, the parents agreed to cooperate and the teacher soon noticed a difference in the children's behavior. Although she saw many of the parents before and after school, it didn't occur to her to mention the change in the children or to thank the parents for their cooperation. Little by little, she began to see the undesired behavior return. Speaking to individual parents, she realized that their efforts should have been more openly appreciated. While the teacher was able to reestablish the TV policy, the parents' original friendliness toward her never quite returned.

7. *Teachers need to realize that parents are busy people and have many other important commitments.* Some parents may be too busy to be involved at all. In their planning, teachers should be practical and not expect parents to do more than is reasonable. One kindergarten teacher discovered that all the parents of her new class, both mothers and fathers, worked full-time jobs. Realizing that there would probably be a good number of tired families to deal with that year, she decided to scale back her usual hopes and expectations for parent participation. Realizing, too, that the parents probably didn't have as much opportunity to interact with their children as they would like, she redesigned the open house, holiday programs, and parent/teacher conferences so that they were all interactive and included the children. For example, instead of having the children produce skits and perform music for the Christmas program, she arranged activity centers for

parent–child participation and topped the evening off with parent–child carol singing. The following year there were several mothers who weren't working, but the previous year had been so positive that the teacher repeated many of its experiences, including the Christmas party.

8. *Teachers will be more effective if they learn about and accept the different cultures, value systems, attitudes, and traditions of the community in which they work.* The parents in one multicultural community took the initiative in ensuring that the elementary school teachers learned about their cultures and especially about their family values. Each year, each teacher was invited to the homes of most of the children in the class, usually for an informal dinner. Most of the parents didn't choose to lecture the teachers about what was important to them, but they did seek, by modeling and informal conversation, to enlighten the teachers. While the results were uneven (quite a few parents responded negatively to the idea and some teachers enjoyed the parent initiative more than others), most teachers appreciated the better communication and greater knowledge.

9. *It is important for teachers not to get complacent when their parent involvement program is going well.* Each year, new children and parents will require new efforts to accommodate new needs. The kindergarten teacher described in number 7 was aware of the need to make adjustments when she discovered a class full of working parents. While she kept many of the successful elements the following year, she found that other elements needed to be different. Two of the mothers and one father who worked nights were eager to participate in their children's education. They jumped at the chance to plan extensive and elaborate field trips and the teacher, who really preferred trips that involved walking around the school neighborhood, had yet another adjustment to make. She did it in good humor, appreciating the richness of experience the children were getting that year.

As we have seen, parent involvement takes many forms and requires many qualities of the teacher: understanding, compassion, respect, self-confidence, alertness to needs, flexibility, and a sense of humor, to name a few. What underlies success in getting parents involved is good communication.

## Parent–School Communication

Communication can be one way or two way. One-way communication might include newsletters, handbooks, announcements, or yearbooks. Two-way communication includes casual contact before and after school, classroom visits, parent education groups, PTA meetings, school programs, parent/teacher conferences, and home visits. The last two are examples of formal communications that you should know how to participate in as you begin your first experiences in teaching.

## Dialoging with Parents: A Conversation with Tom Logan

*For the beginning teacher, communication with parents can be daunting, particularly if the teacher is younger than the parents and/or has no parenting experience. In this conversation we talk with Tom Logan who has been on both sides of such communication: as a teacher and administrator and as the parent of a young child. From his perspective, good communication boils down to two basic necessities: effective dialoging and mutual respect.*

Tom Logan has been involved with Head Start, off and on, since the late 1970s when he directed a Head Start center that was a part of the Florida system of centers for migrant laborers and their children. Today he is administrator of the fourteen Florida centers belonging to the East Coast Migrant Head Start Project. The centers are open during each year's growing season, from October until June. As the migrants move farther north for the spring and summer seasons, other centers open for them.

Tom points out that the migrant Head Starts may have commonalities with the traditional model of Head Start, but that there are also differences. "In the migrant centers, 80 percent of the families are Hispanic and are intact, even extended families. Additionally, they are all working families who are required to have migrated at least once within the past twelve months. And, although traditional Head Start centers serve preschoolers, primarily four-year-olds, we serve infants through preschool age. We're open twelve hours a day as a care center for the children while their parents work in the fields." The migrant program is just different enough that it has its own funding and office in the Washington, D.C. Head Start headquarters.

While the migrant centers serve an important child care function, they also provide education. Tom explains that their educational program is committed to developmentally appropriate practices and follows the guidelines of the National Association for the Education of Young Children (NAEYC). While the centers' educational practices are grounded in developmental theory, they also take into account the cultures of the families and involve the parents in their children's education.

"Next to education," Tom says, "parent involvement is the most important component of the centers' functioning." He reminds us that, "from Head Start's beginnings in the 1960s, parents have been an integral part of the model. In the case of the migrant centers, we deal with working parents and often they don't speak much English or have an awareness of the edu-ca-tional and social service opportunities available to them. An important part of what we do is educate them about these opportunities."

One of the fourteen Florida centers is less a care facility than a parent-child center. Staff make home visits and parents come in for prenatal care, to learn parenting skills and developmentally appropriate practices for child rearing, and to gain career development skills. While the national Head Start model includes a sprinkling of parent-child centers across the country, the Florida migrant center is different in that it also includes an infant-toddler care center to serve the working parents.

Whether in the parent-child center or at any of the others, there is a commitment on the part of Tom and his staff to view parent education as a two-way street. The families might be Mexicans who speak Spanish, Guatemalan Indians who speak a Mayan dialect, Haitians who speak Creole, or Americans, both black and white, who speak English. Just as their languages differ, so do their views on child rearing and the Head Start staff are trained to respect others' views. "There's a true dialog," Tom says and the result is that "what occurs in the classroom is a mix of theoretically based developmentally appropriate practice and the local cultures."

One aspect of child care that requires careful dialog is that of discipline. The centers are committed to nonpunitive discipline while many parents look to punishment as a means of control. Often they doubt that the centers can discipline effectively without it. "Lecturing the parents won't work on its own," Tom

says. "So, we urge parents to volunteer and observe. When they see how we interact with the children they realize that our nonpunitive approach doesn't result in chaos and disrespectful children. We have to remember that parents and staff share the same goal: children who are well behaved and successful. At first we may disagree as to how to get to that goal, but once the parents come in they see how our approach works."

Along with good dialog between center and parent there must also be mutual respect, according to Tom. "We don't see ourselves as working with families with deficits. Instead, our dialog has the purpose of making parents more confident that they're providing good care for their children. We do this by respecting the families and their cultures. We don't propagandize and impose standards on anybody. Those deep, emotionally held views of child rearing can't be approached from such a shallow perspective. People won't respond to your ideas about change in child rearing practices unless they feel they're respected. And they always know if you respect them or not. If they believe you don't, they won't take your ideas seriously." Important too, Tom says, is to really listen to what the parents have to say because they just may be able to educate the educators. "They may well have important things to say that can lead you to change your own practices."

*To think about and discuss: If you had to interact with parents from a culture whose child rearing practices were quite different from your own, how would you deal with the need to respect those differences? What would be the dialoging skills essential to successful communication?*

To get the maximum benefit out of a parent-teacher conference, the teacher needs to plan it carefully, to have examples of the child's work at hand, to listen to what the parents have to say about their child, and to begin and end the conference on a positive note.

### Parent/Teacher Conferences

While much of your communication with parents will be informal—brief chats before and after school, telephone conversations, or quick notes home—there will be times when the more formal conference is necessary. The purpose is usually to discuss children's progress with their parents, but it might also be to deal with a major problem that hasn't been solved by more informal means. In either case, the situation is a delicate one and, if good communication is to result, deserves preparation and thoughtfulness before, during, and after the conference.

Before the conference, it is important to gather up the child's files and work products and determine how they will be used in the discussion. Any notes you have kept on the child's progress should be reviewed. Most important, decide what the primary goals of the conference will be and consider the most effective ways of achieving them. It is sometimes difficult to schedule conferences since so many parents work or have other obligations. Some creativity may be in order, such as meeting very early, before class begins, or during a time when an aide can take over the class. You should allow at least twenty minutes for the conference, with an extra ten-minute buffer if possible.

Begin the conference with a positive attitude, no matter how difficult the situation may seem to be. Even if the parents are coming to discuss a major problem, be sure to begin and end the meeting with a positive comment about the child. Expect to listen as well as talk. By asking the right questions you can learn enough about a child to reach a better understanding of academic or behavioral situations that need improvement. If you are open, receptive, and accepting, parents are more likely to share insights into their child's behavior at home and their successes and failures in dealing with the child.

During the conference, be sure to make good use of the materials you have gathered. Concrete evidence of what you are saying will mean much more than vague commentary. Be sure to point out ways in which the child has been improving, even if the general trend has been negative. Avoid comparing this child with others in the class, focusing instead on the child's own progress. Don't argue about the child with the parents. If they don't understand what you are trying to communicate, it may be better to wait until another time when you have more concrete evidence to share with them. Be sure that your communication is as clear as it can be. One reason parents may not understand is that teachers use too much educational jargon or have a different view of the child than the parents do.

After the conference, be sure you follow through on any decisions that were made. Telephone or send notes home concerning the child's progress, if that was an issue. Finally, make a brief summary of the meeting to keep in the child's file. If important decisions were made about specific problems, it might be a good idea to send a copy to the parents, requesting feedback if they are in disagreement with any points.

### Home Visits

Home visits have enough potential that Head Start and many nursery schools require teachers to make them at least once a year. Some school districts delay the opening of kindergarten by a week or more so that teachers can use the time for home visits. While still a formal style of communication, home visits can be less threatening than parent/teacher conferences. The home atmosphere itself is less formal than the school, and parents may feel greater self-confidence when communicating in their own territory.

If there is time for only one home visit in a school year, probably the best choice is at the very beginning. Parents have an opportunity to observe the teacher interact with their children in the children's accustomed settings; the teacher has an opportunity to observe the children interact naturally with their parents and to see their home surroundings; and the children can meet their new teacher in the safety of their own homes. Because the parents and children are usually looking forward to the new year, they are likely to anticipate the visit with more excitement than nervousness. With some advance thought and planning, the teacher can build on this positive affect to ensure that the visit is not a disappointment.

When making your first contact with the parents, make sure they know that the visit is a commonplace one that all parents participate in. Also, inform them of the purpose of the visit. If it is just to get acquainted, say so. As a matter of courtesy, as well as practicality, give them plenty of advance notice to allow for schedule adjustments. You can and should take time to verify or send a written reminder of the appointment time.

Take something with you to give each child and ask the child to bring it to school on the first day. A pencil or a few crayons would be suitable. You might also take some paper and ask the child to draw a picture that will be made into a class collage on the first day. Children feel additional security when they can make such a connection between home and school. Something tangible for the parents may make them feel more comfortable also. A brochure they haven't yet seen, a newsletter (even a sample from the previous year), a schedule of events, and a list of helpful "junk" contributions are possibilities.

Be a good listener, not just a transmitter of information. Parents may feel comfortable enough in the home environment to open up more than at any other time during the school year. Learn as much as you can about their child and the parent–child relationship, but do it without prying.

Don't overstay your welcome. Decide in advance what the maximum time will be (probably forty-five minutes) and stick to it, even if you are enjoying yourself. As pleasant as the visit may be, there is still some tension involved for everyone, and the family may be as relieved to see you go as they were happy to have you arrive.

## Diversity in Families

Throughout this book references are made to dealing with children from diverse backgrounds. Consideration must also be given to their families. As a teacher or caregiver, you will find that the structure of the children's families may often be quite different from your own. Probably a minority of them will fit the once traditional family image of father/mother/two children. There will be single mothers and an occasional single father or custodial grandparent. Some parents may still be in their teens and struggling to take their place in an adult world they're not ready for. Others may be mothers who had their first child after spending twenty years in a career. There may be foster parents or adoptive parents. Some may be undergoing the trauma of divorce, while others are dealing with remarriage and trying to blend two previously broken families. Some parents may be physically handicapped or have other children who are. It may be that some of your families are recent immigrants or migrant families who won't stay an entire school year. Whatever their situation, and however different from you they are, all these families deserve

Whenever meeting with parents of minority children, teachers should remember that it is the business of the school and its teachers to respect and accommodate student diversity rather than look upon cultural differences as deficits to be overcome.

your profound respect. It is tempting, at times, to feel sorry for people who are struggling with their nontraditional or different situation. But pitying can lead to patronizing behavior. Compassion may well be in order, but this should be coupled with the realization that the family is coping, learning, and resourceful. Admiration for what the family has been able to do and an attitude of building on those strengths will be more productive than pity, prejudice, or condescension.

Doreen Croft (1979), who has spent many years working with diverse families and children, suggests some generalizations that will make the school experience more positive for everyone. She points out that the "different" child and family are not deficient, and being clear about this will improve the way you deal with them. Within a single ethnic group you can expect to find wide variations in attitudes, values, and personalities. If you assume that all representatives of a group view the world in the same way you will lose valuable communication. Further, the socioeconomic status of a family may influence their relationships with others more than their ethnic background. For example, the values held by an upper-class black family will be closer to those of an upper-class white family than to those of lower-class blacks. Children who come from low-income homes often learn responsibility at a very early age, while children from high-income homes may have no responsibilities but greater academic advantages.

Croft points out that the home teaching strategies of different groups may be quite different than those to which you are accustomed. For example, while your upbringing may have favored competition over cooperation, families from other cultures may prefer their interactions the other way around. Communication and behavior styles may vary between different cultures, thus making it necessary for parents and children to make adjustments to the school's patterns. In fact, research has shown that the lack of continuity between home and school may be one reason for a child's social or academic failure at school, and a knowledge of this may help parents and teacher seek solutions. Despite the many obstacles that cultural diversity may place in the way of parent involvement, these families often have a very high interest in their children's education. For them, education may represent an escape from poverty or a way into the cultural mainstream, or away from the prejudice against handicaps. As their children's caregiver or teacher, you represent and symbolize much of the hope they need to feel.

Croft (1979) offers some practical suggestions that will help you face the challenge of working with families having special needs. She points out that "there are no easy rules to follow. However, the teacher who is willing to expend some extra effort . . . will find the task a rewarding one" (p. 43).

- Be patient with parents and children from different cultures who may not want to deal with problems in the same way as most others.
- Be supportive and encourage parents to express their feelings.
- Use plenty of praise to reinforce their efforts on any project.
- Realize that it takes time to build confidence in teacher and school.
- Don't push your knowledge and education on parents.
- Avoid relating to poor and different families out of a sense of pity. Provide respect, compassion, and guidance instead.
- Make rules and expectations clear and be sure they are understood.
- Admit your lack of knowledge of their culture or nationality and seek information from the parents.
- Support children's different native languages while helping them to learn standard English.
- Speak in complete sentences to all children and, in particular, to adult family members who are just learning English.
- Adapt all parent programs to serve the special needs of all families.
- Don't be misled by standardized test scores, which can be culturally biased. Instead, judge children's educability using your own teaching experience.
- Have family activities that encourage social interaction among all groups in the center or school. Recognize that minority groups also have misconceptions and prejudices about each other, and use these occasions to clear up misunderstandings and create bridges. (Adapted from Croft, 1979, pp. 42–44)

Whether parents come from other cultures or from your own, your interactions with them require consideration, planning, and skill. While working successfully with children is a teacher's highest priority, dealing well with their parents can enhance that success.

## Working with Teacher Aides

Providing out-of-home care of infants has always required enough adults to provide safety and comfort. In most instances these adults have included a primary caregiver who is supported by one or more aides or assistants. In modern times, the first organized effort to make use of teacher aides was in the mid-1950s in Michigan (Gattmann and Henricks, 1973). The postwar baby boom was just beginning to increase school enrollment, and aides were seen as a way of providing necessary adult supervision within existing budgets. Since the motives were largely financial, rather than educational, there was much resistance from Michigan teachers. Later in the 1960s, with the infusion of federal money into early education, the ability to hire aides took on new meaning. By then it was believed that teachers could do a more effective job of teaching if they had assistance with routine classroom duties. A contemporary survey showed that as much as 30 to 40 percent of a teacher's day was spent in nonteaching duties, leading to the conclusion that the service of an aide would offer substantial relief. Some political writers of the time argued that aide jobs could be given to unemployed men and women, many of them minorities. Thus, the modern concept of the teacher aide really began as a part of President Johnson's War on Poverty.

Today's teacher aides come from all walks of life and degrees of experience and training. An aide might be someone who is just out of high school and deciding on a career, a mother who wants part-time employment while her children are at school, an immigrant with a teaching degree that doesn't transfer, or a member of a senior citizens volunteer group. What the aide does in the classroom is determined, to some extent, by his or her background.

Most teachers are grateful to have aides available. It provides them with more time and energy to devote to the education of their children. Whereas the availability of aides may not increase the amount of time given to interactive teaching, it does provide more opportunity to plan and implement different and more creative instructional techniques, to guide and counsel children, and to observe the children and their progress. This increase in observation time in turn may lead to more individualized instruction. More specifically, the aide can help teachers with the following:

■ *Management tasks,* such as preparing teaching materials; creating bulletin boards; filing papers in children's folders; taking attendance; checking and replenishing supplies; collecting lunch or milk money; checking on the temperature, fresh air, and lighting; preparing snacks and setting up for lunch; and arranging field trips.

■ *Supervisory tasks,* such as assisting children with their outdoor clothing or changing wet or dirty clothes; helping the teacher in an emergency when a child is hurt or ill; assisting with playground, hall, and bus duty; helping to organize and supervise recess and outdoor game time; helping to care for children in large group or assembly programs; taking children to and from various places within the school such as the cafeteria, library, or nurse's office; acting as a chaperone on field trips; and helping children learn to play together.

■ *Instructional tasks,* such as supervising a group sharing time; reading a story to a small group; listening to children read; playing rhyming games, finger games, and guessing games; singing favorite songs; taking charge of a group working on a special project; helping children learn how to use new materials or tools; supervising computer use; helping children catch up when they have been absent; showing children how to clear, organize, and put away materials; and helping children locate information.

Which of these activities are assigned to the aide depends on the aide's education, experience, and maturity. As the teacher, it will be your responsibility to determine what is the best use of your individual aide's talents and capabilities. It will also be important to realize that with each new aide these decisions must be made over again. A newly hired person may have little or nothing in common with a previous aide.

## Orientation and Training

Just as the teacher must adjust to each aide, so must each aide adjust to the teacher. The smoothness with which this takes place is primarily the responsibility of the teacher, although the aide should participate in as positive a way as possible. Some sort of orientation and training will be necessary, even for the most experienced aides.

For a beginning teacher, training and working with an aide may be somewhat uncomfortable, particularly if the aide has many years of experience or has worked elsewhere as a regular teacher. Further, working with an aide is a form of personnel management, for which teachers are given little or no training. Nevertheless, it is possible, even without such training, to approach a relationship with an aide in ways that can ensure success.

Introducing a new aide to the people and places connected with your center or school is a good way to make him or her feel at home from the beginning. Show the aide how things work, whom to see for various emergencies, and which parts of the playground require extra supervision. Be clear about what is and isn't permitted on the site: rules for personal use of the telephone, length and flexibility of time for breaks, customs regarding personal use of the refrigerator, and so on. It is embarrassing for people to learn after the fact that they have broken rules they didn't know existed.

At the beginning, let the aide know the hourly and daily schedule and what times are most flexible. Tell him what rules you have for cleanup and completion of work. Let him know what behaviors to expect of the children at different times. Are they permitted to look at books during nap? Does everyone have to come to a whole-group activity or may they finish an individual project?

Communicating your philosophy of teaching and behavior management is important so that the aide understands why some things are done and not others. For example, if you have decided to promote democracy in your classroom and your inexperienced aide has only the authoritarian classes of her childhood as a point of reference, then much of what you do may seem chaotic to her. Or, if you use activity centers and the aide has only experienced rows of desks, she may think the children can't be learning anything. It isn't necessary to explain everything the first day, but giving an overview is a good idea. This can be followed up with explanations of specific events as they happen. After helping two children work out a disagreement on their own, you can explain to the aide that this is one way you encourage their independence. (She may well have been wondering why you didn't "take charge" and show them "who's boss".) Or, when she admires the clay replica of an ancient Indian village the children have produced, you can discuss the difference between this activity and what children learn from filling in blanks on a worksheet.

Take time to introduce the aide to the children and do it in such a way that they consider him a teacher, too. If the children have been in school long enough to be acculturated to the classroom, suggest that they share the rules and routines with the aide. It may not have occurred to many of them that an adult doesn't automatically know everything. Not only will this suggestion provide them with this social learning, but it will be a way to increase their self-confidence as they realize they actually know more about their school life than does this new adult.

Whether the aide is experienced or totally new to the occupation, start her off doing routine sorts of tasks. This will help her get oriented to the setting and to your expectations. It will also give you an opportunity to observe her work habits and her ways of interacting with the children. With time you can add more responsibilities, including instructional tasks, if the aide is ready for them.

Most of all, be sure to provide positive feedback as the aide learns your routines and expectations, interacts successfully with the children, and performs clerical work quickly and efficiently. Being an aide is never very rewarding financially, and an appreciative word from the teacher can go a long way toward making the job more attractive to come to each morning.

## Extending Your Learning

1. In a small group, list three or four of the strongest reasons to have a parent involvement program. Then discuss the possible reasons that these programs are rare, or fail when they are tried. Discuss some possible ways that teachers can help reverse the situation.
2. Discuss the ways in which parenting is different now than it was when you were young. If there are students of two generations in your class, compare them as well. Then discuss ways in which teacher behaviors and approaches to parents must be different today than they were previously.
3. If you are in a field placement, ask to be included in a parent–teacher conference. Before it begins, ask the teacher about goals for the conference and what approaches to interaction he or she expects to use.
4. If you are in a field placement, you probably already feel like an aide in some respects. Keep a journal for several days in which you reflect on your feelings, your relationships with the teacher and the children, and the ways in which you learned the routines, rules, and teaching expectations. At the end of several days, write a final entry in which you summarize what you have learned that you want to remember when you are in charge of your own aide.
5. If you are in a field placement, ask the director or teacher if you may change roles for a period of time. Ask for permission to work with your supervisor as if he or she were your aide. At the end, request feedback on your performance.

## References

Berger, E. (1991). *Parents as partners in education.* New York: Merrill.

Bredecamp, S. (ed.) (1987). *Developmentally appropriate practice in early childhood programs serving children from birth through age 8.* Washington, DC: NAEYC.

Croft, D. (1979). *Parents and teachers: A resource book for home, school, and community relations.* Belmont, CA: Wadsworth.

Dinkmeyer, D., and McKay, G. (1989). *Systematic training for effective parenting.* Circle Pines, MN: American Guidance Service.

Galen, H. (1991). Increasing parental involvement in elementary school: The nitty-gritty of one successful program. *Young Children* 46(2):18–22.

Gattmann, W., and Henricks, W. (1973). *The other teacher: Aides to learning.* Belmont, CA: Wadsworth.

Ginott, H. (1965). *Between parent and child.* New York: Macmillan.

Hildebrand, V. (1990). *Guiding young children.* New York: Macmillan.

Hummel, L. (1992). Vacation almost killed me. *Newsweek,* 27 July, 8.

Leik, R., and Chalkley, M. (1990). Parent involvement: What is it that works? *Children Today* 19(3):34–37.

Mallory, N., and Goldsmith, N. (1990). Head Start works! Two Head Start veterans share their views. *Young Children* 45(6):36–39.

Nedler, S., and McAfee, O. (1979). *Working with parents.* Belmont, CA: Wadsworth.

Pizzo, P. (1990). Family-centered Head Start for infants and toddlers: A renewed direction for Project Head Start. *Young Children* 45(6):30–35.

Powell, D. (1990). Home visiting in the early years: Policy and program design decisions. *Young Children* 45(6):65–73.

Spock, B. (1957). *Baby and child care.* New York: Pocket Books.

Spodek, B., Saracho, O., and Davis, M. (1991). *Foundations of early childhood education.* Englewood Cliffs, NJ: Prentice Hall.

# Curriculum for Young Children

# Part Four

In the introduction to Part Three, the argument was made that methodology is more critical to the successful teaching of young children than is content knowledge. This does not mean, however, that content is unimportant. Choosing interesting and important knowledge to impart is a vital element of the teacher's role. So is knowing how to put pieces of the curriculum together into a coherent whole.

Much of the content learning in an early childhood classroom is not divided according to subject matter. Quite often, children do not know that what they are learning is language or math, social studies or science, art or music or movement. Instead, they may go home talking about dinosaurs or spring flowers or fairy tales. This is because much of the early curriculum is integrated in some way, often according to themes of study. Yet, while the children may not consciously divide the curriculum into subject areas, the teacher must be able to do so and make sure that each one is present in some way.

The chapters in this final section are based on this dual focus of curriculum development. An overview is presented in Chapter 11 with extensive descriptions of planning and assessing integrated curricula. In subsequent chapters, each area of the curriculum is discussed individually, then integrated in some way with other areas.

Because it is important not to forget the developmental foundations of planning and teaching, there are sections in each chapter designed to help you make connections. After all, a good understanding of child development is useful only if you know how to apply it.

In the final chapter you will be asked to help write the sections devoted to making connections between development and curriculum. When you can do this, you will be well on your way to teaching success.

# 11

# The Curriculum: Planning, Creating, Evaluating

## OBJECTIVE

When you finish reading this chapter, you should be able to

■ Differentiate curricula based on their theoretical bases.
■ Identify the sources of curriculum and discuss the worth of each in educating young children.
■ Understand the importance of the NAEYC guidelines for appropriate curriculum content and discuss their practical application.
■ Define, explain, and evaluate scope-and-sequence curriculum, subject-based curriculum, and integrated curriculum.
■ Discuss and evaluate methods of assessment.

As you think about this chapter on your own, you should be able to

■ Begin designing theme-based curricula.
■ Integrate assessment techniques into the curricula you develop.

*Curriculum is an organized framework that delineates the content children are to learn, the processes through which children achieve the identified curricular goals, what teachers do to help children achieve these goals, and the context in which teaching and learning occur.* (NAEYC and NAECS SDE, 1991)

This definition of curriculum is a broad one and much of it has been the focus of earlier chapters. The "processes through which children achieve the identified curricular goals" were discussed in Chapter 7. "What teachers do to help children achieve these goals" was also a focus of Chapter 7. The "context in which teaching and learning occur" was a topic in Chapters 3 through 6, as well as in Chapter 8. However, the first part of the definition, "the content children are to learn," has yet to be examined and will be the focus of the remaining chapters of this text. It is this portion of the definition that refers to the "what" of teaching, while the others refer to the "how" and the "when."

In the United States, there is no national curriculum to tell a teacher what should be taught, although many school districts rely on some sort of scope-and-sequence approach to content coverage. Nonpublic schools, particularly nursery schools and child care centers, must decide for themselves what is important content for their young learners. In early childhood, more than in any other age group, the "what" of the curriculum is the responsibility of the teacher, either working alone or in cooperation with others in the school.

As a curriculum developer, the teacher needs to decide on a philosophy of education that takes into consideration the ways children learn best at different ages, what kind of environment is most preferred, and what methods of teaching are most appropriate. Philosophies that do not attend to these considerations will not produce informed content decisions. While a variety of philosophies and combinations of philosophies are available for teachers to choose from, for the purposes of this discussion, we will organize them into two contrasting points of view. By doing this, we can focus our discussion more easily on the ways in which philosophical choices affect content decision making.

## Choosing a Philosophy

The first philosophy of early learning comes from the behaviorist tradition of B. F. Skinner. It gained its greatest prominence in the 1960s when some Head Start centers experimented with it and when several large-scale curriculum programs were developed and implemented across the country. The preschools, kindergartens, and primary classes that adopted a behaviorist approach created programs with an academic focus. That is, in these schools it was assumed that children were there to learn important information from a predetermined body of knowledge. Further, in these schools children are believed to learn best when they

- sit still and pay attention to the teacher.
- do assigned (often pencil-and-paper) work.
- make minor choices about such things as color of paper to use (but not about which project to do).
- obey and follow directions well.
- reserve their own initiatives for free play and recess.
- confine discovery learning to finding the right answer from among several choices.
- stay quiet unless a teacher-led, formal discussion is held.
- conform to the learning rate of the whole class as determined by the teacher.
- follow the teacher's plans good-naturedly.
- confine problem solving to packaged problems from a purchased curriculum.
- memorize facts and wait to be told by the teacher if answers are right or not.
- work with a teacher who is almost always right, who approves of them when they are right, and disapproves when they are wrong.
- passively await adult evaluation and praise, with no self-evaluation expected. (Greenberg, 1990, p. 74)

In academically oriented programs, children's progress is assessed by an assortment of tests, thus making mastery an important issue. When children master, often by way of rote learning, such information as letters, shapes, and numbers, they are provided positive reinforcement such as stars, smiley faces, and other colorful stickers. Instruction is generally teacher-centered and direct, and the schedule is followed closely. The content emphasis is on reading and math or the subskills that lead to them, and on social-cultural knowledge such as the calendar, colors, and classroom courtesies. Often the curriculum structure and materials are purchased as a package. The teacher in these classrooms is most definitely in charge, at least from the children's point of view. However, given a packaged curriculum, the teacher may not share this feeling.

The content of the curriculum in this first philosophy is focused mainly on the child's intellectual development. The second philosophy argues that the content children learn should be far broader and more child-centered. Its basis combines the thinking of both maturationists and constructivists. While there are differences between the views of various theoreticians, philosophers, and educators who espouse a child-centered curriculum, there are more commonalities than disagreements. Names you have read about in this book that can be associated with the second philosophy are Jean Piaget, Erik

The behaviorist philosophy leads to teacher-centered classrooms where teachers spend considerable time teaching a preset curriculum using direct teaching methods. In contrast, the constructivist philosophy leads to child-centered classrooms where children have much freedom to move around and choose which activities they will pursue.

Erikson, John Dewey, and Arnold Gesell, as well as David Weikart, one of the early founders of Head Start who has spearheaded the establishment and continuing success of High/Scope, in Ypsilanti, Michigan.

This second philosophy has been integral to traditional early childhood education in the United States for much of this century. It originally developed alongside the child study and psychoanalytic psychology movements, absorbing some of each and adding compatible elements from other views over the years. Children in schools that subscribe to this second philosophy are assumed to be active learners who learn best when they

- move at will.
- become involved in projects—planning, collaborating, and discussing them with friends and adults—thereby becoming purposeful and creative.
- choose among "live" activities, as opposed to worksheets that merely represent what is live.
- initiate activities, discover, dismantle, and reassemble in a richly prepared indoor/outdoor environment.
- construct understandings at their own rate of intellectual development.
- solve problems and grapple with challenges that come up naturally, as opposed to those that are created out of context and presented to the children in bite-sized portions.

- work both with adults who mingle and with informal interest groups, skill groups, and social groups.
- evaluate their own work and behavior with both peers and adults.
- feel intrinsically rewarded by the satisfaction of a job well done, as opposed to feeling extrinsically rewarded by stickers.
- experience spontaneous encounters with learning as their minds meet interesting, puzzling, or intriguing things that capture their attention. (Greenberg, 1990, pp. 70–71)

Embedded within this list are possibilities for all types of learning experiences: intellectual, physical, social, and emotional. In other words, the content of education in this philosophy is viewed in terms of the whole child. While variations of this philosophy have been emerging for decades, its most common label today is developmentally appropriate practice (DAP). You have read about DAP in earlier chapters, particularly in association with position statements from the National Association for the Education of Young Children (NAEYC). While the behaviorist philosophy has its place, and some successes have been reported in its approach to academic learning, it is the position of this text that the broader, more child-centered view of DAP is more appropriate for young children. Consequently, this second philosophy will underlie the discussion in these final chapters.

## The NAEYC/NAECS SDE View of Early Childhood Curriculum

In 1990 a consortium of early childhood organizations, under the sponsorship of the NAEYC and the National Association of Early Childhood Specialists in State Departments of Education (NAECS SDE) "reluctantly" developed a set of guidelines for curriculum content and assessment. The groups explained their reluctance by saying that "early childhood professional organizations are so opposed to the specter of one best curriculum, that in the past, we have avoided the task of defining appropriate curriculum" (NAEYC and NAECS SDE, 1991, p. 22). The decision was made to go ahead, however, at a time when national reports and critiques of education were calling for sweeping educational change. It was believed necessary, for the welfare of young children, that early childhood organizations should make their positions known.

The *Guidelines for Appropriate Curriculum Content and Assessment in Programs Serving Children Ages 3 Through 8* grew from the consensus of the early childhood organizations that the widespread use of scope-and-sequence curricula has failed both schools and children. Scope, in education, refers to the breadth or range of learning, while sequence refers to the order in which learnings take place. In this approach to education, important learning is predetermined by adults, and children are then introduced to it according to the breadth that is deemed appropriate and in the order that appears to be logical. In practice, this approach leads to rote memorization and drill and practice of isolated academic skills, frequently utilizing worksheets and other pencil-and-paper activities. The behaviorist philosophy underlies most scope-and-sequence approaches to curriculum.

The concern of virtually every early childhood organization has been that such an approach to curriculum and learning "does not reflect current knowledge of human learning and fails to produce students who possess the kind of higher-order thinking and problem-solving abilities that will be needed in the 21st century" (p. 23). For example, while learning according to the behaviorist philosophy may improve basic skills in the three Rs, such success is not accompanied by improvements in reading comprehension, writing fluency, or math problem-solving ability. "In addition, it is evident that our schools are failing to produce future generations with even a working knowledge of the natural, physical, and social sciences, much less the kinds of minds that will create new knowledge in these areas" (p. 23). Early childhood organizations believe that, to rectify this situation, there must be a curriculum that includes "meaningful, relevant learning experiences . . . and a broad range of relevant content, integrated across traditional subject matter divisions" (p. 23).

Another concern expressed by the early childhood organizations is the response of schools to children's early failure. Instead of curriculum analysis and improvement, a "blame the victim" point of view pervades many schools, leading to other solutions: children are tested for kindergarten entry and placement; entry ages are raised; children are retained in preschool, kindergarten, or first grade (up to 30 percent in some districts); and transitional classes between kindergarten and first grade are added. Such "solutions," the organizations argue, are so widespread that it is apparent that children are currently considered defective and, as a result, curricula are not meeting their developmental levels.

In response to these inappropriate solutions, NAEYC and NAECS SDE suggest that curriculum development should instead be based on more appropriate sources of the curriculum: child development, individuality of children, content of the subject areas, cultural values, parents' desires, and the knowledge that children need to function well in society.

As the guidelines were developed, an effort was made to avoid "the three most common fallacies that mark curriculum debate": (1) emphasizing the process (strategies) of learning to the exclusion of content; (2) emphasizing content to the detriment of process, and (3) arguing that there is one, best, universal curriculum for all children. Since the organizations take the position that there is no one best curriculum and that content should be chosen by knowledgeable teachers, they agreed not to advocate any one model curriculum. Instead, they would suggest guidelines, a framework for decision making.

Guidelines for Curriculum Content

There are twenty guidelines designed to give teachers the standards and principles they need to make knowledgeable judgments about the curriculum. They were chosen with the view that they would be appropriate for all children ages three through eight. (The decision not to include younger children was based on the current position that a planned curriculum is not appropriate for infants and toddlers.) While programs for children with special needs can be designed according to these guidelines, curriculum developers may find that, by using these suggestions it is possible to include many special needs children in the regular program.

While twenty guidelines may seem to constitute a large list of points to keep in mind while creating a curriculum, each one is important to children's welfare. The list that follows includes explanations for each guideline:

1. *The curriculum has an articulated description of its theoretical base that is consistent with prevailing professional opinion and research on how children learn.* While you have just been presented with two opposing philosophies, it is the second philosophy of developmentally appropriate practices that is currently considered the most appropriate by early childhood organizations. Nevertheless, the behaviorist approach has been integral to curriculum development in many states over several decades. As you prepare to develop curricular ideas, you should find it helpful to refer to the attributes of each philosophy. As you make your plans, check back to see that your philosophical view is consistent. If it is not, be sure that you can justify the variations.

2. *Curriculum content is designed to achieve long-range goals for children in all domains—social, emotional, cognitive, and physical—and to prepare children to function as fully contributing members of a democratic society.* Whatever the age of your children, be sure that your curriculum is designed to meet the needs of the whole child. In the preschool years, the social, emotional, and physical aspects of development are often emphasized to the exclusion of cognition. In the primary years, the opposite is often true. In addition, the curriculum should reflect the fact that, in this country, children must be prepared from the earliest years to live in a democratic society. Such democratic ideals as community involvement, freedom of choice, equality, fairness, and justice should be reflected in the curriculum. This means providing for choice among learning activities and allowing children of all abilities and both sexes to participate to their fullest.

3. *Curriculum addresses the development of knowledge and understanding, processes and skills, dispositions and attitudes.* Children need to be exposed to content, learn about it, and, finally, attain a real understanding of it. In addition, children should learn skills in such a way that they will want to apply them. Positive feelings about learning will emerge if the curriculum is interesting and relevant. For example, rather than drilling arithmetic facts

and skills with no application to real life or any explanation of their usefulness, introduce children to these concepts by charting outdoor science explorations, by making change in the classroom "store," or by adding up the class milk money before sending it to the office. Children are more likely to see the need for learning arithmetic in the second approach than they are in the first.

4. *Curriculum addresses a broad range of content that is relevant, engaging, and meaningful to children.* For all of us, it is easier to learn, understand, and remember what is relevant and meaningful to our lives. This is most true for young children, who have not yet acquired our adult capabilities for making connections or abstracting meaning from small bits of information. The closer you can make the curriculum relate to your children's interests the easier it will be for them to learn. This argues for the second approach to arithmetic in number 3 and against the first. It also suggests that children will learn their letters and word attack skills more easily in a context that is immediate and meaningful than through workbook drills or tracing exercises.

5. *Curriculum goals are realistic and attainable for most children in the designated age range for which they were designed.* Achievement of this principle may be one that requires some extra effort on the part of the beginning teacher. First, it is necessary to know what learnings are appropriate for the age range of the children in the class. Efficiency in teaching and learning is greater when curriculum takes this into account. Examples of inefficient teaching and learning that are often required include the introduction of place value in first or second grade and clock reading in kindergarten and first grade. Many hours of frustration are devoted to these learning goals before children are ready for them when they could be achieved with much less effort at a later time.

   Second, it is important to create a curriculum that is flexible enough to permit children to work simultaneously at different levels using different activities and learning styles. This does not mean that the curriculum has no unity to it. An arithmetic center, for example, might focus on addition while providing a variety of games at different levels from which children are permitted to choose.

6. *Curriculum content reflects and is generated by the needs and interests of individual children within the group. Curriculum incorporates a wide variety of learning experiences, materials and equipment, and instructional strategies, to accommodate a broad range of children's individual differences in prior experience, maturation rates, styles of learning, needs, and interests.* This guideline is an expansion of point 5 and indicates that the teacher must make decisions about which of the children's interests to follow up on and which to ignore or save for another time. Young children have many interests and some are universal enough that they can become part of the whole group's curriculum. At other times, a child who is an independent learner can go off on his or her own to explore a particular interest. One role of the successful

teacher is to learn to differentiate between curriculum interests that are appropriate for the whole class and those that are best left for individual pursuits or that would best be ignored for the time being.

7. *Curriculum respects and supports individual, cultural, and linguistic diversity. Curriculum supports and encourages positive relationships with children's families.* As you plan the curriculum, it is important to take into account the needs of children who speak little English. This means balancing games and activities that require lots of verbal interchange with others that require less. Written instructions in an activity center can be accompanied by simple pictures that demonstrate what is to be done. The multicultural nature of the United States should be taken into account by providing knowledge of minority cultures present in the classroom along with knowledge of the dominant culture.

8. *Curriculum builds upon what children already know and are able to do (activating prior knowledge) to consolidate their learning and to foster their acquisition of new concepts and skills.* This guideline refers directly to the current rejection of scope-and-sequence learning. It is important to realize that there is no single body of knowledge that must be known by all children at each specific age. Thus, the curriculum should be designed so that each child connects new learning with what he or she already knows. This argues for curricular choices within activity centers and for open shelving as opposed to large numbers of whole-class, teacher-directed lessons.

9. *The curriculum provides conceptual frameworks for children so that their mental constructions based on prior knowledge and experience become more complex over time.* When children are presented with numbers, letters, shapes, colors, and other specific learnings, confusion and disinterest often ensue unless the concepts can be placed in some sort of context. Frameworks such as themes, units, or projects can be designed to offer specific learnings (e.g., numbers) within a larger context (e.g., to take necessary measurements), thus making them more meaningful to children.

10. *Curriculum allows for focus on a particular topic or content, while allowing for integration across traditional subject-matter divisions by planning around themes and/or learning experiences that provide opportunities for rich conceptual development.* Young children do not understand learning that is separated into adult-defined subject areas. When curriculum is integrated across subjects, it is designed to build on the natural way children learn (see Chapter 5). Integrating the curriculum also helps children make connections between their educational program and the home. When children read and write about the nature walk they took in the woods or make a map of where they went, connections are made and learning comes naturally.

11. *The curriculum content has intellectual integrity; content meets the recognized standards of the relevant subject-matter disciplines.* While subject areas are most effectively taught in an integrated manner, you still have a responsibility to respect the academic integrity of each discipline. This is true no matter how young the children are. You need to be particularly careful in regard

The NAEYC curriculum guidelines encourage children's active participation in activities that are meaningful in terms of their prior learning and their current developmental level. The constructivist philosophy is central to these guidelines.

to scientific knowledge where children's books sometimes create confusion by presenting a mixture of scientific accuracy and magical views. It is your responsibility as the teacher to help the children sort out one from the other. Finally, the literature, art, and music you share with children should all be selected for their high quality.

12. *The content of the curriculum is worth knowing: curriculum respects children's intelligence and does not waste their time.* Children and their teachers should not have to waste time with curriculum that has been well learned previously or that is too far advanced and could be learned more easily at a later time. There should be a good match between what matters to the children and what they spend their time learning. By focusing on what is meaningful to them, children learn to function capably and adapt to the world around them.

13. *Curriculum engages children actively, not passively, in the learning process. Children have opportunities to make meaningful choices.* Children need active, concrete learning experiences, particularly when dealing with new concepts or information. For instance, no mathematical exercise or concept should be worked out with pencil and paper (an abstract activity) until children have had an opportunity to work with hands-on materials and are comfortable with them. At both the concrete and more abstract levels of learning, choices in the curriculum keep children actively interested and

engaged. In the case of mathematical exercises, a variety of materials devoted to each concept can keep children fascinated for extended periods of time.

14. *Curriculum values children's constructive errors and does not prematurely limit exploration and experimentation for the sake of ensuring "right" answers.* While today's researchers, theorists, and education leaders advocate children's actively constructing their own knowledge, the demand for accountability often makes constructivist learning no more than a slogan. Quickly achieved high test scores often become more important than constructed learning with its exploration, experimentation, and acceptance of mistakes. It is possible, however, to plan the curriculum so that there are a few activities that "teach to the test," while most activities are designed for constructed knowledge. One activity that can be quite successful is to role play test taking. Test sheets or booklets can be made up that look similar to the real ones; seating arrangements can be altered to match what will happen on test day; regulation pencils can be used; and the clock or a timer can be incorporated into the activity. If you approach this role play as an interesting game, yet one of importance, the children will almost always take it in that spirit and approach the actual test day with self-confidence. This activity takes little time, leaving the rest of the schedule open for more meaningful learning.

15. *Curriculum emphasizes the development of children's thinking, reasoning, decision-making, and problem-solving abilities.* The development of all these attributes is related to constructivist education as well as to democratic decision making. When children can truly work out problems in their curriculum rather than focus on right and wrong answers, they begin to mature and become self-reliant. Searching for a word in the dictionary requires more problem-solving skills than memorizing it from a teacher-made word list, and creating a self-designed paper flower demands more decision making than cutting one out from a pattern book.

16. *Curriculum emphasizes the value of social interaction to learning in all domains and provides opportunities to learn from peers.* Much traditional learning has emphasized competition over cooperation, and individual effort at the expense of teamwork. Yet experience, observation, and research have demonstrated that children's intellectual learning is enhanced by social interaction. The one way for children to learn to cooperate in their work and play is to give them plenty of practice. Curriculum activities should be planned so that there are plenty of opportunities for children to interact with each other. Some activities can be designed so that they require teamwork, while others might allow children to choose whether to participate with others or do things on their own.

17. *Curriculum is supportive of children's physiological needs for activity, sensory stimulation, fresh air, rest, hygiene, and nourishment/elimination.* Remember that children's bodily needs can be quite different from an adult's. Sitting for long periods of time is difficult, and requiring children to learn in this

fashion is unnatural, inhumane, and counterproductive. If children are sitting cross-legged on the floor, the difficulty is especially great. If you spend much time in front of the class, you may not realize how long the children have been sitting, because you yourself are getting plenty of activity during the presentation. Thus, you should plan a balance of active and inactive curricula.

Fresh air and exercise are critical to children's health and important to their learning. Children who have indoor work to finish should never be deprived of their active time outdoors, despite the popularity of this punishment. Frequently, this punishment is used for children who do not concentrate, pay attention, or complete an assignment, but their nonperformance often stems from a need for fresh air and exercise. Denying them the outdoor experience makes it even harder for them to concentrate. In such cases, giving these children extra time outdoors in exchange for greater classroom effort may prove helpful. Under no circumstances should children ever be deprived of food or required to wait to use the toilet.

18. *Curriculum protects children's psychological safety; that is, children feel happy, relaxed, and comfortable rather than disengaged, frightened, worried, or stressed.* To promote the psychological safety that enhances learning, teachers should develop curriculum that is challenging but within children's developmental levels. When the content is over their heads, or introduced too soon, it may promote confusion or even fear. These feelings, in turn, may lead to mental disengagement from learning or to even greater stress. When the curriculum makes children feel psychologically safe, more learning takes place.

19. *The curriculum strengthens children's sense of competence and enjoyment of learning by providing experiences for children to succeed from their point of view.* This guideline asks teachers to move beyond creating curriculum that is simply fun for the children. While it is important that children love what they do at school, it is also important that they actually learn something. Rather than looking at curriculum as entertainment, you should create learning experiences that provide children with positive feelings based on their increased competence, progress in learning, and the realization that they have accomplished something important.

20. *The curriculum is flexible so teachers can adapt to individual children or groups.* While good planning is necessary for a successful curriculum, room should also be left for change when it proves to be important or desirable. For the beginning teacher, this may prove difficult at times because so much effort goes into planning that it seems a shame to leave out an activity, or too much work to add more materials or activities. It may help, when planning curriculum, to keep some activities in reserve to fill unexpected gaps or to substitute for less successful activities. It is also good to keep in mind the real purposes and goals of curriculum design. As one student teacher said when his intricately planned curriculum met

with little enthusiasm but he found himself forging ahead with it anyway, "I was so wrapped up with what I wanted to accomplish that I completely forgot the children!"

The basis of all curriculum design is children and their right to grow in all the domains: intellectual, emotional, social, and physical. As you think about these guidelines and apply them to your own curriculum planning and implementation, keep in mind that they will make the task more enjoyable and, ultimately, more rewarding.

## Planning the Curriculum

As you first begin planning curriculum, you may find that the process seems quite involved. However, once your school experience begins, you will find few experienced teachers who go to the trouble of writing out goals, objectives, needed materials, and so on, as you will be instructed to do in this section. Even so, most of these teachers first learned to plan by working through all the steps. With experience, many of them found that they could operate effectively through memory and some careful advance thinking. It is possible, though, to take such steps as goals and objectives so much for granted that it is easy to lose sight of them. Even experienced teachers should occasionally refresh themselves with the more elaborate written plans you are about to learn.

### Planning Curriculum Goals and Objectives

Curriculum *goals* are similar to goals in other walks of life. They are simply the ultimate aim of whatever you are doing. In the case of curriculum, however, the definition is characterized by nonspecificity: curriculum goals represent the overall purposes of a unit, project, or entire program. For example, if you have just purchased new classroom materials, your overall goal might be for every child to try them out before the end of the week.

Curriculum *objectives* are more specific and more precise. They can be identified as actual behaviors that will be accomplished by a portion of the curriculum. In the case of the new classroom materials, one objective might be that each child will learn to use the hammer and nails safely.

When planning a curriculum, it is important that goals and objectives relate to all domains of children's learning: intellectual, social, emotional, and physical. In Table 11.1, you can see how this might work in three different curricular plans.

Table 11.1 presents three quite different examples of the kinds of curriculum goals and objectives you might find yourself planning. If you read

**Table 11.1**
EXAMPLES OF GOALS AND OBJECTIVES

---

**Goal:** Every child will experiment with new classroom materials by the end of the week.
  *Objective:* Each child will design and create at least one product of choice at the woodworking table.
  *Objective:* Each child will participate in two or more small group games.
  *Objective:* Each child will have an opportunity to work with a favorite new material at least twice.
  *Objective:* Each child will learn and demonstrate the ability to use the hammer and nails safely.

**Goal:** Children will appreciate literature through use of the library corner.
  *Objective:* Each child will identify at least two books at his or her level and read them.
  *Objective:* Children will understand and obey the rule that all books must be returned to the shelves when finished.
  *Objective:* Each child will demonstrate an enjoyment of literature by being able to choose at least one favorite book.
  *Objective:* Children will balance more active experiences with relaxation by spending at least a few minutes each day in the library corner.

**Goal:** Children will be exposed to classical music and composers throughout the year.
  *Objective:* Each child will learn about the life of at least one composer.
  *Objective:* In small cooperative groups, children will choreograph dances to ballet music.
  *Objective:* Children will demonstrate self-reliance by composing brief individual songs.
  *Objective:* Children will participate daily in free movement to classical music.

---

through them carefully, you should note a similarity between them: in each case, the first objective relates to intellectual growth; the second, to social growth; the third, to emotional growth; and the fourth, to physical growth. Still, it is difficult, even when dealing with precise objectives to avoid some overlap. In real life, the four learning domains cannot always be completely separated. For example, the third objective in the classical music curriculum is intended to demonstrate learning in the emotional domain, but it advances cognitive learning as well. Can you find others that might overlap?

In Table 11.1 the sample goals and objectives are curriculum-oriented (new materials, literature, classical music). This is not the only way to assign them. It is also possible to develop them in terms of the learning domains. Some examples of goals in each domain might be

- Intellectual goals:
    Children will learn by solving problems.
    Children will appreciate poetry.
    Children will enjoy and welcome intellectual challenges.
- Social goals:
    Children will learn to work in small groups.
    Children will learn to respect each other's property.
    Children will assume responsibility for care of the classroom.

- Emotional goals:
  Children will learn to work independently with confidence.
  Children will be able to persist when work is difficult.
  Children will appreciate and trust their peers and teacher.
- Physical goals:
  Children will have desirable health habits.
  Children will increase in both fine- and gross-motor control.
  Children will have a balance of active and restful experiences.

As you plan children's activities within each unit or project or portion of the day, you will, of course, need to go beyond goals and objectives and into the specifics of what will happen and the materials you will use.

## Planning Activities

Activities work best when planned for a large block of time in which children can choose from among materials and experiences. When the amount of time is generous, there is plenty of opportunity for children to make choices, try new materials and experiences, work with friends, or be alone with an interesting project. Some of the materials and activities, such as centers or water tables, will remain available for long periods of time, perhaps for an entire school year. Other materials may be brought from the children's homes or other outside sources, and are only on short-term loan. Still others will be part of a current unit of study, project, or theme. While all materials and activities should relate to the goals and objectives, it is the specific unit, project, or theme that generally requires written planning.

As an example, consider a unit or theme in which children learn about transportation. Table 11.2 outlines one way to approach planning for the unit's opening. While many of the activities for the unit will be in activity centers, this introductory experience is whole-group and teacher-directed. The teacher here has chosen these particular materials because the northern climate and sporting interests of her children's families will ensure that the children know something about skiing. Their knowledge will differ, however, according to their experience with either downhill or cross-country skiing, two related but slightly different sports that require somewhat different equipment. In this description of the activity, note that the teacher has built in an informal pretest that will help determine the direction the activity takes.

### Making the Format Your Own

The format for planning an activity given in Table 11.2 can be altered to meet your own needs and preferences. For example, you may be a teacher

Although most experienced teachers probably don't go to the trouble of writing out every step of their unit and lesson plans, it is recommended that beginning teachers do so in order to keep their lessons focused on larger curriculum goals and to insure that needed materials and time are available.

who likes to remember materials with a check-off list. Thus, rather than limit yourself to a two-line Materials section, you might prefer to list each item. Or, you might prefer to include more explicit instructions to yourself in the Procedure section. For example, in Step 1, you might want to remind yourself to place each of the four skis in front of several children in the circle so that everyone has an opportunity to handle something as you talk. Once you gain experience and know what you need to write down and what you can count on yourself to remember, you can refine the system to suit your own needs.

Note that the Evaluation section includes a follow-up activity. In early childhood education, this is frequently one of the most effective ways of evaluating children's learning after a structured or whole-group activity. The informality of the activity center offers you an opportunity to chat with children individually and see how much they have learned, what their enthusiasm level is, and where their learning might head next.

Note also that the steps listed in the Evaluation section are directly related to the goals and purposes. This relationship is essential to successful planning and can be forgotten if the planning isn't carefully done.

**Table 11.2**

WHAT ARE SKIS FOR?

**Goals:**
1. Children will be introduced to the unit "Transportation" and look forward to it with enthusiasm.
2. Children will learn about premodern concepts and modes of transportation.

**Objectives:**
1. Children will identify similarities and differences between downhill and cross-country skis.
2. Children will identify the purposes of each type of ski.

**Materials:**
   One pair cross-country skis with poles and boots
   One pair downhill skis with poles and boots

**Procedure:**
1. In whole-group circle, teacher lays materials on floor. Teacher asks children to identify and describe as they are able.
   Teacher asks children to share experiences using materials.
2. Teacher asks individual children to explore materials and respond to questions about similar and different attributes of downhill and cross-country skis, then boots, then poles.
3. Teacher asks whole group to consider reasons for similar and different physical attributes. As hypotheses are presented, teacher or individual child demonstrates with materials. Teacher encourages further hypotheses.
4. As children begin to understand the different functions of the two types of equipment, the teacher leads the discussion toward an emphasis on ancient skiing as a mode of transportation.
5. Teacher uses students' discovery to tell them about the new unit of study. Children are also informed that the ski materials will be available in an activity center for independent exploration.

**Evaluation:**
1. Teacher observes children at each step for enthusiasm and adjusts activities accordingly.
2. Children respond to teacher's questions and demonstrate understanding of attributes and purposes of the materials.
3. Teacher observation of the follow-up activity center will include further questioning for understanding as well as for encouragement of further exploration.

## Planning the Daily Schedule

Goals and objectives should underlie the entire day, even if they are flexible or do not take the formal written form shown in Figure 11.2. On-the-spot objectives may be created informally whenever you need them. For example, when you see a child spilling milk again, you may think, "Tommy spills from that pitcher every day and has begun to think of himself as clumsy. Today I'll give him the blue pitcher and fill it just halfway. He can then be successful, feel better about himself, and have an easier time learning to pour the right way." Likewise, goals may be planned for a week, a day, or even a part of the day when the need arises. Perhaps the morning has been a contentious one, with children seeming to pick fights for no reason. You determine that many of them are tired after a long weekend and decide that, for the rest of the day, the goal will be to have positive social interaction among all the children. You then redesign your planned schedule to make that happen. One approach would be to provide a longer, more relaxing afternoon snacktime, during which you will converse quietly with the children rather than use the time to prepare activities, as you usually do. Your objective might be for the children to talk quietly and pleasantly with each other.

While some goals and objectives are written and others are simply noted mentally, it is important that you do have them. They give structure and meaning to the day and guidance to your planning, both short- and long-term.

While each day will be different in some respects, taking into account children's changing needs, interests, and abilities, there should still be structure and stability to the schedule. Children feel more confident and secure when they know what comes next and can count on a basic rhythm in their daily routine. At different times of the year you may find it advantageous to make a major change or two, but this should be discussed and planned for with the children. For example, at the beginning of the year, you may want to begin the day with a structured activity followed by a free-choice activity time. Later in the year, the children may feel more comfortable and energized by coming into a classroom that is already prepared for its free-choice time. The descriptions of the following components of the day should be considered as guidelines, keeping in mind that flexibility is always necessary.

### Arrival Time

The activities associated with arrival time should remain fairly stable so that children feel comfortable and secure when beginning their day. If changes are made during the year, be sure children are prepared for them. Arrival time provides an opportunity for the children to settle into the rhythm of the day and for you to have a one-on-one interaction with each child. This is often a good time for children to choose freely from among quieter, table toys and games. In the primary grades, the school may have expectations, such as roll call and lunch money collection, or ceremonies, such as the salute to the flag. Much of this time can be wasted if children spend much of it waiting around for each of the daily requirements to be over with. Thus, quiet games are also a good place to start the day in the primary grades. Furthermore, primary children can be trained to collect the lunch money, check their own names on the roll, and interrupt their games quietly when the schoolwide pledge begins.

### Activity Time

While this portion of the day will look quite different depending on the age of the children, the time of year, and the current curricular interests, there are some similarities. For all groups at all times, this is a period of open movement when children can work individually or in small groups, choosing their own activities. Your role is to circulate among the children, observing, encouraging, interacting, and helping them plan, make decisions, and formulate questions to answer. Since the children will be moving freely, planning for activity time includes providing enough activities so that there are always extras to choose from. Sometimes most of the activities will pertain to a unit or theme and will have been carefully planned with written-out goals and objectives. At other times, the materials will have been chosen from among those readily available. These should be selected to provide a balance between challenging and basic, active and quiet.

The beginning and ending of activity time should both be planned. Simply turning children loose at the beginning is an invitation to chaos. Children will need instructions before they start, even if it is just a quiet reminder as to how activity time should begin. Children who are learning to read will often enjoy the challenge of printed instructions at activity centers. Cleanup time is made easier if there is a rule that children put materials away as soon as they have finished using them. Then, when the activity time is over, the cleanup will take far less time and there will be fewer instances in which children try to figure out who messed up what. Even toddlers can help with cleanup, particularly if adults work beside them, explaining what is happening and how it is being done. From about four years, children are generally able to establish a set routine that is followed each day. A final bit of planning for activity time is to be sure that enough time is allowed for adequate cleanup. (See Chapter 9 for further suggestions for transitions.)

Whether your children are with you half-day or all day, a well-planned activity time is essential for intellectual, social, emotional, and physical development. If the children are present for the full day, a second activity time should take place in the afternoon after nap or rest. For preprimary children, this may be an outdoor play time, a walk around the neighborhood, or exploration of materials that weren't used in the morning. For primary children, the afternoon activity is another work period, but intensive intellectual work may be too much. This is especially true if the weather is very hot or if it is a major holiday period.

## Outdoor Activity Time

The regular activity time can also be the best time for outdoor experiences. To make this work, there must be enough adults available to supervise at all times. During activity time, the outdoors can be used by children who need a bit of fresh air, a respite from studying, or a chance to move their bodies. It can also be a secondary site for the indoor activities. Some children simply enjoy being outdoors more than inside and are happy to take work out with them. In addition, many materials can be moved outdoors when the weather is good and you have enough assistance.

In most centers and schools, however, there is an outdoor period when the entire class has an opportunity to play. This frequently is scheduled right after the morning activity time, after lunch, after nap, or just before it is time to go home. No matter how busy your schedule is or how many expectations are placed upon you, you should include plenty of outdoor time. A change of scenery, an opportunity to use different muscles, to stretch a bit, and to be in the fresh air are all important to young children. With good equipment, there are also opportunities to learn important physical skills. Children who seem unable to concentrate on their indoor work, or who are tired or unhappy, are often helped by being outdoors, thus making the indoor atmosphere more positive after the outdoor activity period. Because its attributes are all so positive, outdoor time should not be planned as a reward for good indoor behavior, but as an important and integral part of the day.

### Lunchtime and Snacks

Depending on the age of the children and on the length of the day, you may have one, two, or perhaps no snacks each day. For toddlers, the snack works best if an aide can prepare it, out of their view, and have them enter the snack area with the food immediately available. If this is impossible, it should be prepared as completely as possible, in advance. By the time chil-

Teachers should be sure to account for transition time in their planning. Well-planned transitions from one activity to another can be the difference between an orderly classroom and a chaotic one.

dren are three, they are usually able to pour from a small pitcher and clean up after themselves. This makes it possible to incorporate a snack center into the activity time. You will need to plan this carefully with the children, making sure there are clear instructions about how many crackers or pieces of fruit each child is permitted to take, how many children may eat at one time, and what the cleanup process is. The first few days you try this, there may be one or two children who take too much, and there will always be occasional spills. The benefit of the snack center is the independent behavior and social interactions it fosters.

Lunchtime is at its best when children can eat together in small groups, serving themselves family style. Helpful adults can teach them the most efficient ways to serve from a large dish to their own smaller ones, the best ways to use their utensils, and simple first steps in good manners. Sometimes, lunchtime in public schools is a grim period when discipline is maintained by permitting no child to talk or a chaotic period in which the noise and mess build. One elementary school turned around the behavior in its lunchroom by renaming it a restaurant. The food personnel and the principal shifted the long rows of tables into smaller clusters and then covered them with tablecloths (old sheets dyed in pleasing colors) and jars of fresh flowers. Attractive menus were posted and mellow music was piped in. While the children knew in advance that changes were coming to the lunchroom, they were given no new and stern rules of behavior. The changed atmosphere, however, altered the children's behavior immediately and the improvement was permanent. If lunchtime in your school is unpleasant, you might consider some changes of this sort.

### Ending the Day

Whether children are with you half-day or all day, enough time should be permitted that there is a feeling of closure and some understanding of what to expect the following day. A whole-group gathering to discuss the day's events can help children recap their learning, evaluate activities, and determine how they can be improved upon. This meeting also provides an opportunity for children to help plan upcoming events and activities. While much of the planning is your responsibility, children should be a part of it, too. The closing discussion is a good time to look both backward and forward, making plans that fit the flow of events and children's development. This discussion can be carried forward to the following morning if needed, and another planning session held before activity time begins.

Whatever the day has been like, it is important to end it with a positive feeling. Children should go home feeling comfortable about returning the next day, and they should come back the following morning feeling positive and prepared for what is to come. They will feel happiest if they have had some part in making the plans.

## Moving Toward Curriculum Integration:
### A Conversation with Pam Lee

*Experienced teachers as well as teachers in training are often dubious about integrating subject matter into themes and coordinated units. Tradition and logic both argue against such an approach. Further, the creativity and labor involved in making the change can be overwhelming if the change isn't made with care. Here, one teacher explains the transition she and her colleagues made and the results it brought.*

Four teachers make up the kindergarten team in Pam Lee's school. Through joint planning and task sharing they shape a yearlong curriculum that is made up of a series of thematic units. Yet, not too many years ago they taught quite differently, obediently following county directives to teach reading from the prescribed basals and following the chapters in the mandated math book. "I hated it," Pam says now. "It was boring to the children and boring to me, too."

Back then the kindergarten teachers occasionally would interject a brief unit that was of more interest than the usual basics. It was a unit on butterflies that gave them the impetus for long-term major change in curriculum. Children and teachers alike loved the unit. Pam remembers saying, "Look how interested they are! Look at how much they're learning!" At first, the teachers viewed the butterfly unit as science learning, but they soon noticed that the children, on their own, were reading complex scientific terms. Their interest in the subject matter impelled the children toward advanced reading performance while they con-

tinued to struggle with the basal-mandated vocabulary of "easier" words.

The teachers decided to try creating larger units that would incorporate various areas of the curriculum. Each one would take major responsibility for developing a unit, with the other teachers adding ideas. At first, they were careful to work the units around the mandated county competencies. For example, they would write theme-related stories for the children that would include words from the prescribed lists. More recently, the teachers have experimented with ignoring the lists. Pam is one who feels comfortable with the decision. "The children are learning words that are even more difficult than those on the lists" she says. "As their teacher I observe the children and, as I do, I begin to know what they've learned. I don't have to give them progress tests. The letters and sounds are all coming and I don't even have to teach them. They emerge on their own as the children write and work with each other. The children like books so much now that they choose them during free *play* time. It was never like that before."

While Pam manages to put most or all of the curricular areas in one thematic unit, she doesn't necessarily confine them to the unit alone. This is particularly true in reading, where children may choose nonrelated books to look at and read. It is also true in math where, in order to cover some skills, she may find it important to include nonthematic activities.

One concern of teachers who consider curriculum integration is the issue of standardized test scores. Pam has found that none of the children's scores have gone down and that some have gone up. There has been an additional bonus: As the kindergarten teachers began incorporating most of their curriculum into themes, they found that the required continual progress tests were impeding their ability to do the integration well. They negotiated a new system with the principal in which testing is now done only at the beginning and end of the year.

Another concern for those who are dubious about integrated learning is the effect it has on special needs children. There is fear that, without special attention and drill, they will somehow fall further behind. Pam has found that the opposite is true. As an example, she talks about Matt, a child with a learning disability. He is unable to read at any level, frustrated when he tries to learn letters and sounds. Yet during a recent unit on dinosaurs he learned most of their names and life habits. Matt is currently learning the functions of the human heart as part of another unit. Pam is excited about Matt's enthusiasm toward learning. She argues that, if she were using the basals, Matt would still be unable to learn his reading skills because he is not ready for them. In addition, his frustration would turn him off to learning and lower his self-esteem. In this integrated approach to learning, children are provided with opportunities to learn at their own rate according to their own level of development. As further argument that this is so, Pam points out that two of the boys in her current class make frequent trips to the library to check out third-grade level books.

As Pam considers the excitement of her children and their academic growth, and her own increasing enthusiasm for teaching, she concludes simply, "I *know* this is the right way to teach."

*To think about and discuss: This kind of teaching has its critics, particularly among those who believe it is important to focus on the acquisition of important skills. Another argument against it is that too much time is required for preparation and too much time is spent learning unimportant topics and ignoring the basics. Try arguing both sides of the issue, then come to your own best conclusion. If possible, observe teachers who subscribe to both views before you make a final choice.*

## Creating the Curriculum

When learning is meaningful to children, they accept it more enthusiastically, are better able to make connections to other learnings, and retain it longer. Several approaches can be used to enhance meaningfulness, one of which is to involve the children in creating their curriculum. Group planning at the beginning and end of the day is an important step in this direction. Participation in this activity provides children with the intellectual stimulation of considering what learning is important for them, with experiences in negotiation and positive social interaction, with enhanced self-esteem as they realize their views are respected and utilized, and with the opportunity to practice decision-making skills.

Meaningfulness is also enhanced when the teacher is flexible enough to permit spontaneity in the curriculum. A good curriculum and an atmosphere of receptivity should stimulate children's curiosity about the world. Curiosity, in turn, leads to questions of some importance as well as momentary whimsies, either of which may need exploration to answer satisfactorily. The flexible teacher stands ready to alter or enhance the curriculum to take into account children's changing interests.

A third way of providing meaningfulness is to create a curriculum organized around themes of current interest rather than around traditional classroom subjects. Historically, themes of interest have been an acceptable approach in the preschool years but only intermittently accepted in the primary grades, where accountability requirements, rather than children's actual needs, often drive the curriculum. In recent years, however, as the connection between meaningfulness and learning has become more widely accepted, the use of interdisciplinary themes, projects, or research problems has become more widespread in kindergartens and primary classrooms. It has been suggested that, "[i]n classrooms where skills and subject matter are interwoven, children experience a curriculum that is not fragmented skill-work, occurring within units of experience based on a common idea. Units of study are not contrived but rather flow naturally from children's interests" (Fountas and Hannigan, 1989, p. 136). Two other writers suggest that "[t]his argument for alternatives to the disciplines as the structures of curriculum emerged in the 1920's and has reappeared every ten to fifteen years since . . . a concept which keeps emerging with such regularity is one of such usefulness that it simply will not be ignored. Humans seek integration; specialization, though secure, doesn't feel as good. We want to grasp things on a higher and higher order of interrelationship. We need connectedness" (Harter and Gehrke, 1989, p. 14).

This integrated approach to curriculum creation has demonstrated success in promoting thinking, experimenting, leadership, self-initiation, higher test scores, academic retention of skills and knowledge, and enthusiasm for academics (Glover, 1990; Jersild et al., 1939; Sontgerath, 1989). Although more research is needed about the ways children think and make connections in their learning, teachers who have used integration as the organizing framework for their curriculum find it an exciting approach. Pam Lee, who has taught both integrated and nonintegrated curriculum in kindergarten, is an ardent supporter of integration using umbrella themes that include the subject disciplines. (A conversation with her may be found on pages 366–367.) Other teachers, particularly of the youngest children, integrate subsets of interest (rather than subject disciplines) into one large theme. Both approaches are represented in the following examples of curriculum integration.

## Creating a Curriculum for Older Toddlers or Young Preschoolers

Very young children are just beginning to learn about colors, and some preschool programs choose to study them in depth. You might, for example, decide to focus on one color each week in a unit that covers as many weeks as there are colors to study. Unless interest remains unusually high, you would probably limit the unit to the three primary colors and, possibly, one or two secondary colors such as purple (a favorite of young children). Planning for this unit will require that you first consider your overall goals and then plan for each week, always keeping the larger goals in mind.

### Step 1: Choose the Broad Goals

Some examples of whole-unit goals that take into account different developmental domains are

1. Children will understand differences between the three primary colors. (cognitive)
2. Children will appreciate the beauty of differing colors. (emotional)
3. Children will begin to learn about working together. (social)
4. Children will participate in and enjoy movement experiences. (physical, emotional)

### Step 2: Divide the Unit into Logical Segments and Plan Each One

In this case, you will divide the unit according to each color, one week to a color. Other times, the unit may not be large enough that such division is desirable or necessary. Or, you may divide into time segments that are less tidy than doing one topic per week. For our purposes, we will focus on a segment devoted to the color yellow.

### Step 3: Make a List of Activities and Create a Curriculum Web

Some of the activities that might work well in a study of yellow would be

1. Write a note home to parents requesting donations of materials and reinforcement of learning. Before sending the note, read it to the children and have them "decorate" it using a yellow marker.

2. Make butter.
3. Tie yellow ribbons on each child's wrist each day.
4. Find yellow in picture books.
5. Teacher wears something yellow each day and children identify it.
6. Make instant vanilla pudding with yellow food coloring added.
7. Have a bouquet of different colored flowers, some of them yellow. Each child chooses one yellow flower to put in an individual pot.
8. Plant marigold, zinnia, or other easy-to-grow seeds with yellow flowers. Place the empty packages on sticks and plant them at the end of each row as identifying markers.
9. When children wear yellow, ask other children to identify it.
10. Using any appropriate music, children dance freely trying to keep yellow balloons aloft, or trailing yellow streamers.

As you plan your unit, creating a curriculum web will give you a visual idea of what the coming weeks will be like. In the center of the web you will place the theme title. Each major area of study within this theme will have its own radial line, in this case, one that belongs to the color yellow. From each line will radiate smaller lines in which you write the activities you have chosen. Those that are similar in focus, such as cooking or clothing-related activities, will be clustered. By doing this, you can see if there is a focus that has too many activities or is underrepresented. In Figure 11.1, we see that the color yellow has its strongest focus on clothing-related activities, while only

FIGURE 11.1
**Curriculum Web—Theme of Interest**

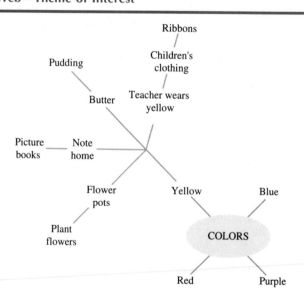

one activity uses movement. The plans for the other colors should take this imbalance into account.

## Creating a Curriculum for Primary Children

While curriculum planning for younger children generally avoids focusing on the subject disciplines, the opposite is true in the primary grades, and often in kindergarten. While the older children still learn most naturally according to themes of interest, the academic demands of these years ensure that subject disciplines will be an important part of planning. In that regard, the integrity of each discipline should be respected. Part of this respect is identifying and explaining the disciplines to the children. Failure to do so may lead to confusion for the children or to an embarrassing teaching experience, such as that of one second-grade teacher. It was close to Thanksgiving and the children were studying the Pilgrims and Indians of the New England region. Everywhere throughout the room there was evidence of their study, even including whole villages made from clay. One morning the principal dropped in, bringing with her the district superintendent. The superintendent said to a group of children, "I see you do lots of social studies in here." The children

Activities of natural interest to children such as the one shown here can be used to teach a variety of concepts from across the curriculum: how to measure (math), where rocks and dirt come from (science), what sort of language and customs the people in China (their destination) have (social studies) and how to share the digging and recording process (cooperation).

looked puzzled and turned to the teacher for help. "Social studies?" they asked. "What's that?" After that, the teacher identified the disciplines to the children, who found them quite interesting and spent the rest of the year enjoyably sorting them out on their own each time a new theme was introduced.

Another example of curriculum integration involved a third-grade teacher who wanted to take advantage of the fact that her school was situated in a neighborhood in which school, homes, church, and shopping were all within close walking distance. She knew that the children had studied the community in the first grade since it was a focus of their state-mandated social studies text. She believed, however, that further study of the topic could focus on new sites and issues and make use of the third graders' more mature capabilities. The enthusiasm with which the children tackled this "old" topic demonstrated to the teacher that she hadn't been wrong. Her role, then, was to make the children's study sufficiently challenging while reinforcing their earlier learnings.

While this was primarily a social studies project, the teacher integrated other areas of the curriculum where it was advantageous. Some of the activities she chose were

1. Interviews with employees, owners, ministers, and priests about their job responsibilities and reasons for choosing their careers. Small teams were assigned to do each interview, and their findings were placed in a class book.

FIGURE 11.2
**Curriculum Web—Subject Disciplines**

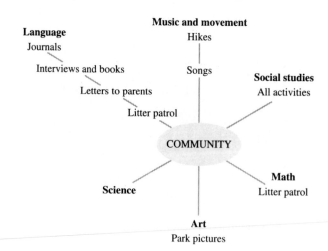

2. Writing personal letters to the children's parents, then tracing each step of the letters' delivery through the postal system. The children then created a wall diagram showing the entire process and also wrote an accompanying explanation.
3. Devoting another wall to a gradually evolving community map. The first entries were based on their walks to various places. Later, an easy-to-read realtor's map was used to fill in the places that hadn't been visited.
4. Hikes to determine the outer reaches of their mapping territory. It was decided that whatever street was fifteen minutes from their school in each direction would be the "frontier."
5. Spur-of-the-moment song compositions to make the hikes seem shorter.
6. A litter patrol activity that grew from children's concerns about an otherwise attractive "pocket" park. They weighed the sacks of litter and estimated the cubic feet, then wrote a letter to the editor of the local weekly newspaper asking fellow citizens to cooperate in keeping the area clean.
7. A trip to the park after the litter was cleaned up. Children drew crayon pictures of their favorite scenes.
8. Individual journals in which children wrote about their own responses to each of the activities.

When the teacher made the curriculum web, she divided activities among the subject disciplines. Figure 11.2 shows what these eight activities looked like when webbed.

Just a brief look at this web makes it apparent that this unit is totally lacking in science activities, and that math and art are underrepresented. You will also note that it is possible for some activities to appear in more than one discipline (litter patrol) and for others to fit only within social studies (the wall map). These observations can alert you to under- and overrepresentation in the academic curriculum. It may not be necessary or important to include science in the community unit for instance, but seeing that empty space on the web can remind you that science should be a focus at another time.

Another way to determine if there is under- or overrepresentation is to check whether each of the developmental areas or domains has been attended to. For this, another type of web can be created. It also contains the disciplines, but has an additional focus on human development.

This second web illustrates that all developmental domains have been considered in some way. This type of web is less common than the first one but deserves consideration if you take seriously your mission to educate the whole child.

As you plan a curriculum, whether it is for an hour, a day, or a year, you will need to consider how to evaluate the success of what you have created, then use your evaluation to plan for the future. The final section of this chapter is devoted to this important topic.

FIGURE 11.3
**Curriculum Web—Developmental Domains**

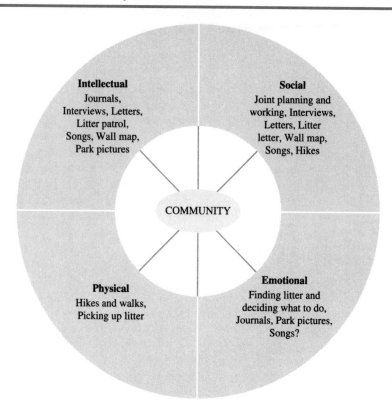

## Evaluation

Evaluation and assessment are words that are used interchangeably in education. In dictionary terms, they indicate the determination of something's value. In education, we evaluate or assess the value of our curriculum, the materials we use, the children's performance, and our own teaching effectiveness. Evaluation should be integral to early education because it helps teachers plan curriculum and instruction, determine what to communicate to parents, identify children who need special assistance, and assess whether the program is meeting its goals (NAEYC and NAECSSDE, 1991).

Evaluation of some sort should be ongoing in any center or classroom. The effective teacher continually evaluates the various aspects of the program. Much evaluation is done informally, as when it is noted that the Lego blocks aren't being used because they are stored out of the way, or that some books chosen for the current theme unit are popular and others aren't, or that a large minority of the children are having difficulties with the eighth and ninth problems on an assigned math project. Likewise, teachers continually and informally evaluate the progress of individual children, perhaps noting that Tony can now settle down with a book since he discovered sea mammals, or that Jorge no longer picks on Violet now that there are extra tricycles, or that Paige has begun to pay more attention during circle time. Such informal observations, while indispensable to smooth classroom operation, need to be supplemented with more formally gathered information that comes from a variety of sources.

## Evaluation Techniques

More formal evaluation is done through a variety of techniques. Traditionally, some form of testing is the first thing that comes to mind when the words "formal evaluation" are mentioned. However, in early childhood education, formal assessment can take a number of forms, while testing, in any form, is viewed with skepticism and concern.

### Observation

While you will observe your children on an ongoing informal basis, to do so in a more formal way requires skill and practice. First, your techniques should be so unobtrusive that your children will become accustomed to them and act naturally while you are using them. If your classroom is one that promotes independent learning, you should have observation opportunities throughout the day. One approach is to carry a clipboard or hard-backed notebook with you and devote single sheets of paper to individual children. These can then be filed in portfolios kept for each of them. At first, some children may question you about the clipboard or the fact that you are quietly watching without interacting. One way to answer their questions is to tell them you are interested in the materials they are using and in what they like to do. For the first day or two you might even read a few of your comments to them. Soon, however, they should come to accept your behavior and lose interest in it.

Successful observation requires that the observer suspend judgment until there has been time to reflect on what was seen. This usually takes some trial-and-error practice. For example, you may wish to spend time observing a child who is having trouble being accepted by others during group play. First, you must completely avoid letting this child or any others know that you have singled him out. Thus, your observation must appear to take in the entire group, which, to some extent, it will. Second, you should record only what you see and wait until later to make judgments. Such phrases as "seems to be," "looks happy today," or "he just couldn't wait to . . ." are judgmental. Instead, be more specific and just describe behaviors that you see: "He stands

2 feet from the occupied tricycle and pats the rider on the head four or five times," or "He grabs the largest block from Andy and, when Andy cries out, smiles and walks away." When you have time to reflect back on what you observed, you may be able to verify your initial impression about why the child behaved the way he did or how he was feeling at the time. Then again, it may take a string of similar observations for you to see a pattern and make an informed judgment. It is sometimes helpful to write your evaluations in a pencil or ink color that is different from the observation. That way, you can write both at the bottom of the page and in the margins and easily differentiate observations and analysis.

### Checklists and Rating Scales

If you create these yourself, the preparation time will be longer than grabbing a clipboard and noting your observations. However, they do provide focus, structure, and convenience in analysis. Some checklists can even be used by children on their own if the items to be checked off are either pictured or easily read. You might choose this method when a number of tasks need to be completed or when everyone should have at least one turn with new materials.

While checklists require a simple yes or no response, a rating scale asks for a finer judgment. This can be useful when you want to observe the interactions of individual children with various materials and types of learning. One way to rate the child would be according to *always, sometimes,* or *never.* Another might be on a scale of 1 to 3 in which 1 signifies that the child has completely mastered a skill or is beyond being interested in an activity, 2 signifies that the activity is just the right level for the child, and 3 indicates that the child is not yet ready to be interested and should be reintroduced to the activity sometime in the future.

Checklists and rating scales can be carried around on your clipboard and notations made when there are small bits of time. At other times, they will be provided to you by your school district and you will be required to make formal use of them.

### Self-Evaluation (Children)

When children evaluate their progress, they are taking responsibility for their own learning. The checklists described above can be thought of as one form of self-evaluation. You can also interview children informally about what they have been learning. Some appropriate questions might be, "What is one important thing you learned today?" "What was difficult for you yesterday that is easy today?" "Did you learn something this morning because you tried especially hard and didn't give up?" "Is there something you're learning about now that seems too hard for you?" "What are some things you know, now that you're five, that you didn't know when you were four?"

### Self-Evaluation (Teacher)

This topic is handled in depth in Chapter 7. It is discussed here briefly as a reminder that evaluation of what happens in the classroom should always include a careful look at what we ourselves are doing. If children show little interest in or success with the curriculum, it may be that the curriculum needs improvement, not the children. If they refuse to pay attention during a teacher presentation, it may be that the presentation is, in actuality, a long and boring lecture. Conversely, if there is sudden interest or understanding where before there were problems, it just may be that you are doing something especially right.

### Portfolios of Children's Work

In recent years, portfolios have moved from being unwieldy, haphazard collections of children's work to carefully put together evidence of progress. This change has come about largely because much instruction in language and reading has become holistic and less amenable to standardized testing. The result has been the need to find an ongoing method of evaluation that makes use of many kinds of materials. Well-kept portfolios should include checklists, rating scales, children's self-evaluations, examples of work in all areas of the curriculum, and anecdotal information.

An expandable folder for each child is probably the best version of a portfolio. These should be kept easily available to children as well as to you. Occasionally, it would be well to sit down with individual children and go over their materials, helping them see where they have progressed and discussing where more effort may be needed. Portfolios also provide highly effective evidence to use during parent conferences.

### Report Cards

Moving from the richness of a portfolio to the shorthand communication of the report card is difficult for many teachers. At the early childhood level, many schools do not require report cards or, if they do, the reports are in narrative rather than grade form. If you are required to send home report cards, make good use of children's portfolios in making your evaluations. If the report card is nothing more than grades or a checklist, be sure to take time to add a narrative that will have more meaning for both parents and children. When possible, supplement the card with a parent conference and a discussion with each child, using the portfolio to assist you.

### Standardized Tests

Standardized tests are tests that have been tried out on many children for the purpose of establishing performance expectations that differ by age and grade. They are administered with specific directions, predetermined time frames, and carefully monitored conditions. They may be norm-referenced, which means that there is a median or average score for each age and grade and individual scores are measured against this norm. Or the tests might be criterion-referenced, in which case the test maker (who is sometimes the teacher) decides that certain behaviors (criteria) are evidence that the curriculum goals and objectives have been met. The test maker then creates questions to see if the children can perform these behaviors. A weekly spelling quiz and arithmetic test, designed by the teacher, are examples.

In early childhood education, criterion-referenced tests are generally considered less effective ways of evaluating children's progress than are the less formal methods such as observation, self-evaluation, and so on. Norm-referenced tests send even stronger danger signals to early childhood specialists. Historically, they have been used in inappropriate ways, such as for identifying which children will be admitted to or rejected by a program, for tracking children according to ability, for placing children in special education classes, or for failing them in a subject or grade. While norm-referenced tests might be well used as one piece of evidence in a decision-making process, they should not be relied on as the sole source of information. Young children have not yet developed test-taking skills or an appreciation of the importance the tests may have to their lives. A child in a bad mood may score poorly on a test that might be easy another day. Or, a child who is afraid of the examiner, the room, or the test itself may just refuse to perform.

NAEYC (Bredecamp, 1987), in a statement of concern about such tests, has said,

> Accurate testing can only be achieved with reliable, valid instruments and such instruments developed for use with young children are extremely rare. In the absence of valid instruments, testing is not valuable. Therefore, assessment of young children should rely heavily on the results of observations of their development and descriptive data. (pp. 13–14)

Teachers of young children will do well to rely on evaluation techniques other than tests unless there is a strong reason for using them. One such use would be to identify services helpful to a child with special needs. Another might be to conduct research aimed at improving some aspect of young children's education.

## Extending Your Learning

1. Observe an activity in a child care center or classroom, then create a lesson plan for it according to the format in Table 11.2. Share the plan with the

teacher and discuss whether you have correctly analyzed the plan's components.

2. Choose one age level and plan a one-day curriculum. Use a real classroom if it is available to you. Check your curriculum against the NAEYC/NAECS SDE guidelines. Can you justify any components that do not meet the guidelines? Do you agree with all the guidelines, or do any seem unrealistic to you? Why?

3. Observe a single child for twenty to thirty minutes, using a clipboard or notebook. In a pen of a second color, analyze what you have seen. Then analyze your observation capabilities. Where did you succeed? What needs improvement?

## References

Fountas, I., and Hannigan, I. (1989). Making sense of whole language—a pursuit of informed teaching. *Childhood Education* 65(3):133–137.

Glover, M. (1990). A bag of hair: American first graders experience Japan. *Childhood Education* 66(3):155–159.

Greenberg, P. (1990). Why not academic preschool? (Part 1). *Young Children* 45(2):70–80.

Harter, P., and Gehrke, N. (1989). Integrative curriculum: A kaleidoscope. *Educational Horizons* 68(1):12–17.

Jersild, A., Thorndike, R., Coldman, B., and Loftus, J. (1939). An evaluation of aspects of the activity program in the New York city public elementary schools. *Journal of Experimental Education* 8:166–207.

National Association for the Education of Young Children and National Association of Early Childhood Specialists in State Departments of Education (1991). Guidelines for appropriate curriculum content and assessment in programs serving children ages 3 through 8. *Young Children* 46(3):21–38.

Sontgerath, M. (1989). What goes 'round, comes 'round. *Momentum* 20(1):40–44.

# 12

# Language and Literacy

When you finish reading this chapter, you should be able to

- Plan language and literacy experiences in relation to children's physical, social/moral, and cognitive development.
- Plan language and literacy activities taking into account the needs of individual children.
- Begin to choose language and literacy activities based on your own philosophy of how children develop.

As you think about this chapter on your own, you should be able to

- Consider ways in which language and literacy learning might be integrated throughout the day.

A major part of being human is the variety of ways in which we communicate: by speaking or signing, by writing to and for others, and by reading what others have written. Skilled communication underlies most successful human interaction, while failed communication can lead to unpleasant misunderstandings, rifts within families, botched business dealings, even war. No wonder that parents, schools, communities, and nations place great importance on children's language learning. Historically, parents have seen to their children's learning of spoken language, while schools have been responsible for the teaching of reading and writing. In recent years, however, the lines between school and home have become blurred. On the positive side, educational research has shown that there is much to learn from home-style language and reading instruction. Less happily, more and more children are arriving at school with inadequate communication skills. As research continues and knowledge expands, philosophies of language teaching and learning come in conflict with each other. The result can be very different-looking educational settings.

To demonstrate what is happening in the schools, two recent language-learning episodes will be described. They took place on opposite sides of the United States and represent very different ways of thinking about how young children learn language.

---

## EPISODE ONE: RAISING THE TEST SCORES

*Eastside Elementary School is one of two schools located in a small and rather poor Southern town. The principal is dedicated to proving that "his" children can perform as well as those who live in the wealthier areas nearby. To further that ambition, he spends much time studying the scores the children achieve on their standardized tests. His approach to learning is what he likes to call "good old-fashioned," meaning that an observer in the school would find children and teachers, at all grade levels, facing each other in formal rows and engaged in drill, practice, and direct instruction. This highly regimented approach to teaching and learning seems to pay off since, on standardized tests, the children at Eastside regularly outscore the children on the other side of town.*

*All Eastside's teachers, with the exception of an occasional kindergarten teacher, have embraced the "good old-fashioned" approach to teaching and proudly share the children's test scores with parents and visitors. Not long ago, the principal analyzed the kindergarten scores and noted that the most rigidly traditional teacher seemed to produce children with the highest language scores. The differences in the scores were not statistically significant; that is, they were so small that a researcher would probably attribute them to chance. But the principal argued that the differences were testimony to the superiority of the most traditional teacher and immediately ordered the other two kindergarten teachers to emulate her teaching methods. One teacher agreed to the change; the other asked for and received a transfer.*

*The next year all three kindergarten classes focused on reading readiness skills. They followed the guidelines of the county-adopted basal readers with close attention to detail. Rarely was a prescribed activity omitted, and suggested sequences were followed carefully. The teaching methodology was a combination of direct instruction and follow-up seatwork. For example, if the children were studying the letter M, the teacher might lead them in naming all the objects they could think of that started with that sound. These would be listed on the board and the M's underlined. The teacher would then show the children a series of attractive pictures and ask them to find objects within the pictures that began with the M sound. Related seatwork would consist of worksheets containing a number of pictures, some of them possessing names beginning with M. The children would be instructed to color the M pictures and leave the others blank. Since the follow-up tests in the basal reading series and the questions in the standardized tests both emphasized such finite skills as these, the children were well trained to perform at a high level on such tests. At the end of the year, all three classes performed almost identically. A researcher, however, might argue that the performances were almost identical before the cross-class consistency was required.*

This traditional approach to teaching, with its highly directed instruction complemented with independent practice, has been common in the United States for decades and, in one form or another, since our earliest schools. The second episode describes a type of classroom that is newly popular, although, it, too, has been seen in various forms since earliest times.

## EPISODE TWO: WHOLE LANGUAGE, WHOLE CHILD

*Shady Grove School is located in a working-class neighborhood in the Pacific Northwest. While the building shares with Eastside the same standard school architecture of the 1970s, the teaching and learning atmosphere is quite different. The principal of Shady Grove is fascinated by the latest developments in reading and language instruction and has encouraged her teachers to experiment with them, even at the risk of short-term failure. In this newest approach, there is less emphasis on skill attainment and drills and more on integrating language experiences into the entire curriculum.*

*Assessment is more likely to be done through analysis of portfolio collections of children's work than through standardized tests. To see how this works in practice, consider the following description of a single hour in one third-grade class.*

*The third graders have been studying generational histories within their own families. They have interviewed older relatives and are now bringing to class interesting artifacts that have historic meaning to their families. The session begins when the teacher briefly explains the day's project, then models for the children what she expects them to do. First, a student teacher from the local university shares a sample of lace that has been in her family for over a hundred years. As she does, the teacher takes brief notes on a large index card. Next, the teacher shares the notes with the children and explains that she has just modeled what the children will be doing in pairs. She explains that the person who has taken the notes will then share with the class what he or she has learned from the owner of the artifact. The teacher proceeds to model this final behavior.*

*The children seem to understand immediately what it is they are to do. They are permitted to pair up with anyone they like, and this is done quickly. The results, however, are not uniform. Quite a few children model the teacher and student teacher almost perfectly, asking pointed and appropriate questions, skillfully sharing artifacts, and taking concise and focused notes. Other children are distracted by the novelty of the artifacts and forget to take notes. When they do, the process seems difficult for them, although they have had the experience before. The teacher reminds them that note taking does not require perfect spelling or penmanship and that it is all right to draw a picture if a word is too hard to spell.*

*The children respond to the announcement with renewed confidence, and no one hangs on the teacher asking for help in getting things right. One child, concerned that her toy carousel horse might not be described adequately, dictates the notes to her partner. "Write that it's blue and green and red," she commands, then, "Now write down that it was my grandma's." There is one deaf child in the class and a full-time interpreter explains as necessary both to him and to his partner. Two children are mainstreamed from a special education class and halfway through the hour a specialist enters to work with them. She helps them to focus on the note taking and to write down a few words that will help them make their presentation. The room hums with activity as children work in their pairs, and the teacher and student teacher float among them, giving help where it seems needed, briefly checking in on pairs who are doing fine on their own.*

*With ten minutes to spare before lunch, the first three pairs share their partners' artifacts with the class. They are almost uniformly successful in following the model established by the teacher and student teacher forty-five minutes before. In just one case, a child has trouble reading her notes. The teacher chooses not to intervene and the child's partner provides sufficient and uncritical help so that the presentation proceeds satisfactorily. After each presentation, the entire class applauds. When the teacher promises that there will be time later in the afternoon for more presentations, the children reluctantly agree to leave for lunch.*

These two episodes differ greatly in their view and treatment of young children. In the Eastside classrooms, the teacher is clearly the authority figure (although only the children may think so, given the overshadowing presence of the principal). At Shady Grove, the teacher is a leader but allows the children to participate in decision making. The children are often permitted to choose who they will work with, their performances are permitted to vary, and everyone is expected to be supportive of each other's presentations. While teachers in both schools are fond of their children, the relationships are somewhat different. At Eastside, the children stay quietly in their seats unless given permission to talk or leave. At Shady Grove, children must obtain permission to leave the room, but they are otherwise free to move about and talk as they wish unless someone (not necessarily the teacher) has the floor.

The underlying assumption of how children learn is quite different in these two settings. At Eastside, learning is viewed as something that happens from the outside in; teachers are the knowledge givers and children the recipients. Good teaching happens when the children prove themselves on classroom quizzes and standardized tests. At Shady Grove, learning is viewed as something that happens from the inside out. Teachers facilitate learning in such a way that children engage in self-directed and self-chosen activities. Good teaching happens when the children remain enthusiastic about language and literacy, choosing, on their own, to learn more.

The view of the way children learn to read is quite different in the two settings as well. Eastside follows the traditional philosophy that reading readiness skills, such as letter recognition and letter sounds, should be learned first and that reading will then follow with greater ease. Kindergarten and the early weeks of first grade are designated the reading readiness time, and true reading becomes appropriate after that. Conversely, the teachers at Shady Grove believe that literacy emerges over a long period of time, possibly even from birth. Fluent reading is a major step in the process, but it shouldn't be separated out in such a way that there is first a series of readiness skills and then reading itself. Rather, many interrelated experiences lead to literacy and are different for each child.

These two ways of viewing children's learning of language and reading both have their roots in the history and theory that you read about in Chapters 1 and 2. Perhaps in reading about the two different programs, you have already been reminded of some of the people and theories that have been discussed.

Traditional approaches to reading (seen here) use an outside-in view of reading, that is, children being taught a set of "readiness" skills, prior to actual reading. A newer approach entitled "whole language" sees reading as an inside-out process with children learning to read according to their own schedules as a result of pursuing literacy activities that are innately interesting to them.

## Making Connections: Perspectives on History and Theory

While we can probably never know how and when humans began to use words in their oral communication, the written record is somewhat more clear. From cave pictures that represented events in people's lives communication progressed to two basic systems of writing. The first, called logographic, makes use of shorthand pictures, each one of which represents a word. Chinese characters are today's most widespread example of logographic communication, although the Sumerians of ancient Mesopotamia are thought to be the originators of the idea (Adams, 1990). Although a literate Chinese needs to learn between 4,000 and 5,000 characters, the Chinese have stood by their difficult and complex system. In the Middle East, however, alterations were made when writers started using symbols that represented syllables in words that couldn't be pictured. Later, symbols were used to represent initial consonants, and these were passed from language to language. Eventually, some of these symbols reached the Greeks, who, it is believed, misunderstood some of those they found unpronounceable, confusing them for vowels. In this way, the alphabetic system was created, an invention as important to social history as to language development. No matter what the language, its alphabet has fewer than fifty symbols to learn, thus making reading available to almost anyone at any level of society. Conversely, learning thousands of characters is an activity reserved for those who have the leisure time to invest—that is, the elite.

In English we use an alphabet system, one that is far from perfect. As you think about teaching young children to read and write, consider the problems our language presents as expressed in this poem fragment:

> I take it you already know
> Of tough and bough and cough and dough?
> Others may stumble but not you,
> On hiccough, thorough, laugh and through.

(For the entire poem, see Adams, 1990, p. 20.)

While other languages may provide fewer alphabetic stumbling blocks than English, all of them contain irregularities or exceptions. Further, an alphabet system of any type is inherently more abstract than early picture writing. Thus, moving children beyond their early inclinations to communicate by pictures and into an alphabetic system takes some sort of teaching. *How* children can best be taught is the argument of centuries.

## Early Views of Teaching

Comenius (Jan Komensky) believed that learning should be enjoyable to children, that they need concrete objects to make new ideas meaningful, and that the first language of school should be their native language. While Comenius was responding to his contemporaries' preference for teaching in Latin, today's research is beginning to show that children can read a second language most easily if they learn in their own language first. His view that learning should be enjoyable and concrete led educators in very different directions from the dominant practices of his day.

John Locke, who agreed that children should enjoy learning and that teachers should make use of concrete objects, viewed children's minds as blank slates to be written on by adults. Thus, learning to read comes from external sources such as adult teachers who impart their knowledge in some form of direct teaching and who provide rewards for successful learning. In this century, Locke's philosophical heirs are usually considered to be the behaviorists who propose providing rewards for good effort and who break learning into a chain of manageable pieces. Each piece is linked to the next until the fullest possible understanding is eventually reached. Skillful teaching includes knowing when the learner has been pushed too far along the chain, and perhaps cutting back to the nearest manageable piece. Learning to read and write from this philosophical viewpoint suggests working from parts to whole, or from learning letters and sounds to the actual act of reading and writing. Drill and practice are viewed as necessary to mastering the pieces so that, eventually, reading and writing will be skillful and fluent. Episode One on page 381 presents a modern-day example of this philosophy of teaching. Teaching goals are clear, disciplined practice is provided, and at the end the children have achieved the levels of competency that their teachers set for them.

Jean Jacques Rousseau also agreed with Comenius that children should enjoy learning and that concrete materials were important. This led him in quite a different direction, however, as he argued that children shouldn't be pushed to learn. In his view, reading and writing will happen when the children are ready and interested. A few of his contemporaries experimented with this sort of education for their children, eventually bemoaning the fact of the children's continued illiteracy, as well as their undisciplined behavior. Rousseau's philosophical heirs in this century are those who continue arguing against pushing children, although their views aren't usually as extreme as his.

## The Twentieth Century

One notable attempt at a Rousseau-like atmosphere was Summerhill school, founded in England in the middle of this century by A. S. Neill. In this school, children were never pushed to read. Neill observed that, as soon as a real need or interest arose, a child would learn to read quickly and with little frustration. Neill was even willing to wait until the high school years for this to occur.

Arnold Gesell and his maturationist philosophy provided a slightly different twist on the Rousseau tradition. To the maturationist, children are ready to read when they have achieved the level of a "normal" six-year-old (more specifically, a 6.2-year-old). Since children achieve this level at different times, the teacher must observe individual progress closely so that a child isn't pushed too far too soon. Prior to the time when reading can be introduced successfully, reading readiness activities are appropriate. Here, the Rousseau-like philosophy may be replaced by Locke-like goal-oriented activities in which information is presented in pieces. Phonics games, for example, might help children approach readiness.

Because developments across the centuries can take so many turns, the legacy of Rousseau can lead to different models of reading. In the broadest terms, a Rousseau-inspired reading curriculum would look more like Episode Two on page 382, with its emphasis on letting children choose the friends they work with, on employing flexible grouping and timing, and on promoting reading and writing as a natural activity that fits into whatever else is happening. In the maturationist interpretation, however, while the pace of learning has a Rousseau-like naturalness, the teaching methodology may be more reminiscent of Locke's goal orientation. Another difference, and a critical one, is the view of reading itself. To the maturationist, there is a prereading period in which special "reading readiness" activities prepare the child for the real reading ahead. Inherent in the earlier Rousseau philosophy, and exemplified in the Summerhill model, is the view that reading development is all of a piece, that early experiences with language are as much a part of learning to read as the eventual act itself. Thus, when the child is ready to read it may appear to happen suddenly and spontaneously, when, in actuality, the child's whole life experience has been leading to the glorious moment.

The development of reading and writing instruction in this country has not, by any means, followed the Locke–Rousseau dichotomy exclusively. A variety of other factors have also influenced the picture. In colonial times, for example, Bible study was the most important reason for learning to read. During this period a two-step teaching methodology prevailed that was a simplified version of that in Episode One: teach the phonetic and alphabetic codes and then have students read (Adams, 1990). Until the middle of the nineteenth century, when more varied reading materials became available, this approach to reading remained fairly constant. As a way to get around the boredom of the repetitive practice required of their teaching system, educational leaders began recommending that children learn meaningful words first and the phonetic-alphabetic rules later. It took patience to convince teachers and parents that this new approach would work, but the method finally gained acceptance in the second quarter of this century, coming to be called the "look-say" approach. While the teaching of phonics was not dispensed

From colonial times to the middle of the nineteenth century learning to read followed a two-step, skill-based methodology that involved teaching the phonetic and alphabetic codes and then giving children drill and practice in applying these skills.

with entirely, it was provided only gradually; children spent most of their time trying to memorize unfamiliar words to add to their vocabularies.

Although the look-say method was not the only one used in the United States during this time, it was common enough that a critical 1955 book called *Why Johnny Can't Read* rang a bell with just about everyone, even becoming a best seller. In this critique of reading instruction, Rudolph Flesch decried the look-say system, arguing that the only children who could read well were those who were able to intuit the alphabetic and phonic systems. He maintained that, in a democratic society, every child should be able to read well and that meant providing heavier instruction in phonics.

Much research followed the publication of Flesch's book and, to a great extent, his argument was borne out: children who had early instruction in phonics became better readers. Yet teaching methods focused on phonics can become just as rigid and inadequate as those focused on looking and saying. Eventually, two camps emerged, each adamantly opposed to the other, thus making it difficult to combine the best of each in a rational way.

In the 1940s, the idea of a "language experience" approach emerged, but it didn't begin taking hold until the 1960s. As its name implies, the approach seeks to tie reading and writing to real-life experiences. Children were provided with many experiences in and out of the classroom: field trips; group activities in science, social studies, and math; discussions and storytelling; drama, music, and art. Each experience was recorded on charts and lists, magazines and newsletters, and in child-generated books that became classroom reading material. However, language experience tended to become routinized over time, losing some of its early excitement and popularity (Goodman, 1989).

## Literacy Learning for Today

Meanwhile, a similar but expanded approach was stirring interest. In New Zealand, the writing, research, and teaching of Sylvia Aston Warner, Marie Clay, and Don Holdaway led to literature-based reading programs in which children were immersed in trade books and magazines rather than in formal, school-oriented readers. Additionally, teachers would produce oversized "Big Books" of children's favorite stories and give them repeated readings. Since New Zealand's education system was influenced by John Dewey, it is not surprising that this new approach gained favor in this country as well. Dewey believed the curriculum should be integrated rather than taught in isolated segments; that children should be involved in their own learning, grappling with real problems; and that reading, writing, and oral expression are tools for expressing what has been learned in these real experiences. Likewise, Piaget's view of self-constructed knowledge provided additional support for an approach in which children are more self-selecting in what they read, tell, or write about.

In the United States, however, official support of the move away from basal readers and programmed instruction was lacking. In its place, teacher-support groups were created, the first and best known being Teachers Applying Whole Language (TAWL). This term—"whole language"—emerged in the 1970s from various sources. As Yetta Goodman (1989), one of the early and continuing leaders in the movement, explains it,

> The early users of the term were not consciously naming a new belief system or movement. We were talking about some new ideas about language, about teachers and learners, and what these meant in terms of implementation, and we needed new language to express our new meanings. (p. 115)

Ken Goodman (1992), Yetta's husband and another major leader in the movement, adds that it was the Canadians who popularized the term: "They needed a term to differentiate their developing educational philosophy, programs, and practice from the skill-drill, text-test model they saw in U.S. schools" (p. 195).

While some critics of whole language argue that it is nothing more than an updated language experience methodology, whole language proponents answer that, while it shares the same basic tenets, it is in actuality much more. For example, whole language relies less on the teacher as producer of charts, lists, and so forth, and hands over much of the writing activity to the children. This approach is based on emerging research that shows that children learn to write by writing and that imperfect spelling is a useful stage in their development. Whereas language experience tended to give writing duties to the teacher until children were able to write with some skill, whole language proponents believe that invented spellings are both permissible and useful learning tools. They further argue that their approach was needed since the early language experience approach was losing momentum (Y. Goodman, 1989).

Defining whole language has always been problematic. Joanne Yatvin (1991), active in establishing a schoolwide whole language program, says that "whole language is the belief that language learning depends on the learner's motivation and self-confidence, and the integration of real language use into learning activities" (p. 2). Dorothy Watson (1989), one of the principal founders of TAWL, suggests that whole language is difficult to define because teachers come to it by way of their individual paths and because definitions change as new ideas are explored. Her own best definition is a rather lengthy explanation:

> Whole language is a point of view that language is inherently integrative, not disintegrative. It follows that language is learned and should be taught with all its systems intact. That is, all the systems of language—semantics, syntax, and graphophonemics (call it phonics if you must)—

are maintained and supported by pragmatics (language in natural use) and must not be torn apart if language is to be learned naturally. (p. 133)

She adds that children's culture must also be a consideration in deciding how they will best learn language, because language develops within a culture. Yatvin and Watson both list principles that support whole language. The following list combines their thinking.

- *Children should have real purposes for reading, writing, speaking, and listening as well as choice in what they do. Choice is the beginning of ownership in both reading and writing.* Whole language teachers invite children to read, write, and participate in activities through carefully orchestrated sets of choices. To do this, it is necessary to know about their children and how they learn, and about language and subject matter.
- *Students can take ownership and responsibility for their own learning.* The teacher's role is to facilitate an environment in which learners are provided with experiences that challenge them at the optimum level. Thus, children are empowered by choosing many of the books they read and the topics they write about, and by learning to correct their own spelling and grammatical errors and to revise and rewrite.
- *Since language is a living, changing communication tool, it can never be perfected or completely mastered.* Whole language philosophy argues against the concept of mastery or a static must-be-right model of literacy.
- *Language users can learn as much about communication from getting language wrong (producing a nonstandard form) as they can from getting it right.* Whole language promotes risk taking rather than an obsession with perfection. Inevitably, mistakes, miscues, misinterpretations, and misconceptions will arise. The personal logic of the child is valued as the method for effecting corrections.
- *Stopping students while they are producing an oral or written message in order to make surface-level corrections may hinder their linguistic and cognitive progress.* Whole language includes attention to standard forms, but this is not done during the period when meaning is being constructed.
- *The language arts are integrated in a whole language program just as they are in life outside the classroom.* When children write, read, listen, and speak in response to meaningful situations, they learn the necessary standard forms in a natural way.
- *All content areas are grist for the literacy mill. Classroom activities should integrate reading, writing, speaking, and listening across the curriculum.* Children listen, speak, write, and read about all areas of the curriculum and about things that are important in their lives. Teachers use the content areas to promote oral and written language and, conversely, use the language arts to support the content areas.
- *The classroom itself is a strategy that promotes learning.* One tenet of whole language is to facilitate learning by creating a learning community in which

children feel comfortable and excited about absorbing, discovering, producing, and communicating knowledge. One way to make this happen is to foster informal groupings that permit children to work in pairs, in small groups, or on their own.

■ *Children's language and thought have their roots both in the home and in the community. Good instruction builds on the knowledge and strategies they have been developing from birth.* Parents are invited to become part of the whole language process. The teacher's role is to work with—not without and not for—parents.

■ *Whole language teachers believe that the principal purpose of evaluation is to inform learners.* It is believed that knowledge of children's school learning should spread outward from the learner to the family and eventually to the community and legislature. When the sequence works the other way around, and children and teachers must endeavor to meet the testing expectations of people and organizations far removed from them, then the children and the teachers become the pawns rather than the principal actors in the learning process.

■ *Whole language teachers are cautious about what they accept as evidence of students' abilities and learning.* They are aware that standardized tests yield a narrow view of what children are able to do. And, while they are also aware that the public places its greatest trust in these test scores, they persist in evaluating progress through children's self-evaluation; through observation; and through keeping portfolios of written work, pictures, anecdotes, tapes, and notes from conferences.

The teachers at Shady Grove School base their teaching on these principles, although, in the best tradition of whole language, they put their own interpretation on the principles in order to meet their specific needs. For example, while whole language enthusiasts generally shun standardized tests of any sort, the Shady Grove teachers make use of placement tests to help them divide the children in various groupings for different projects. In addition to letting the children choose their partners, groups are sometimes made up of children with similar skills and reading attainment or, at other times, with children whose differences complement each other.

Although their principal supports their experimentations with the whole language approach, the teachers at Shady Grove are well aware that there is considerable skepticism on the part of other teachers around town. This skepticism has spread throughout the United States as whole language has become increasingly popular. For educators accustomed to traditional approaches to the language arts, there is some fear that, given the growing enthusiasm for whole language, many teachers may go overboard in their efforts to make learning enjoyable. Whole language enthusiasts, it is feared, may not provide the skills training and direct instruction that are needed by many or most children to read capably. Although the principles of whole language provide for such teaching, many adherents either philosophically reject anything resembling drill and practice or believe they are not "supposed" to be using such techniques. In actuality, the primary objection to direct instruction, according to whole language educators, is that it usually means "direct focus on 'skills' which can be easily and immediately tested with an 'objective test' for 'mastery'" (K. Goodman, 1992, p. 197).

By the early 1990s, some thinkers began exploring ways that whole language and systematic direct instruction might be combined. To do so successfully could mean avoiding the too common backlash against new ideas and simultaneously meeting the philosophical needs of educators from different views. As one writer who argues for compromise has said (Spiegel, 1992),

> [W]e must avoid either/or positions that reject out of hand the possibility of blending and blind us to the value of different perspectives. Advocacy of systematic direct instruction does not mean that indirect instruction is considered of no value. On the other hand, advocacy of whole language does not mean that children are left alone in a state of benign neglect. . . . If bridges are to be built, we need to think in terms of a continuum rather than a dichotomy. (p. 38)

While many teachers are still just learning to implement whole language, others are already firmly entrenched in it, and still others remain true to traditional teaching. At this time, a combination of methods appropriate to specific classes and children seems a likely and sensible direction. To demonstrate some ways in which the traditional and whole language approaches can be blended, one more school will be described.

## EPISODE THREE: MAKING CHOICES

*At Tanglewood School, as at Shady Grove, the principal is supportive of teacher experimentation. While some of the teachers have remained resolutely traditional in their approach to teaching reading, others, particularly the first-grade teachers, are working to incorporate whole language ideas into the curriculum. However, even the first-grade teachers have resisted diving in head first, believing that traditional reading groups also have much to offer.*

*For example, they prefer to ability group the children for formal reading sessions each day. As one teacher argues, "If I have a child who comes in here reading* Charlotte's Web, *why would I expect that child to participate in reading with children who aren't quite sure what a word is?" What happens in the reading groups, however, may call to mind some whole language thinking. The first-grade teachers dislike their district's basal series. Thus, they are more likely to seek out interesting stories and books, prefera-*

*bly in multiple copies. Predictable books are treasured for their ability to give children the feeling they are reading before they actually can. In fact, repeated experiences with these books lead some children to actual reading.*

*While much work goes on in small groups, pairs, and individually, there are also times when an entire class comes together. When this happens, the chosen activity is one that is appropriate and enjoyable for children at any level. For example, the teacher might place a collection of small cardboard letters in an envelope and give one envelope to each child. The letters are spilled out and children are invited to try spelling two-letter words, then three-letter words, and so on. Since the collections are identical, children who are unsure of themselves can watch the others and learn from them. In addition, the teacher might walk among the children asking such questions as, "What do you think that says?" or "How does your word compare with Mike's?" Children aren't usually told their words are wrong, but, if they are ready, they are encouraged to rethink what they're doing. Another way in which a whole group activity might be individualized is to give the class the same activity with differentiated guidelines. For example, in a creative writing session, children who need extra help are given the beginning words of a sentence, which they can then complete on their own, while other children are provided with a blank piece of paper accompanied by extensive discussion concerning the assignment.*

*For the teachers at Tanglewood, combining the traditional and whole language approaches makes them feel comfortable and secure while allowing them to explore newer options. As researchers begin mixing the traditional and whole language methods, some are concluding that the combined approach may be the most effective in meeting the needs of most children.*

As you observe and work in classrooms, talk with teachers about their views on language development and teaching. Try out some of their ideas with children and begin to develop the philosophy that works best for you.

## Making Connections: Perspectives on Development

The distinctive language capabilities of humans remain somewhat of a mystery in terms of *how* language is learned. Theories and research provide us guidelines, but thus far no definitive answers have been reached.

### Theories of Language Acquisition

The *behaviorists,* whose roots lie in John Locke's blank-slate theory of learning, argue that adults provide the language model and children learn by listening to and imitating them. Positive reinforcement from those same adults encourages children to continue their development. While this theory must be considered incomplete (Morrow, 1993), it does have practical value. Young children frequently ape the words, phrases, poems, and songs they hear around them, although they often lack the cognition and vocabulary to reproduce everything accurately. When that occurs, they simply substitute a similar-sounding word or phrase that has meaning to them. One Midwestern child, trying to sing "God Bless America," apparently could not conceive of an "ocean white with foam" and substituted "to the ocean's telephone." A Japanese two-year-old sang every verse of "My Darling Clementine" although she didn't understand a word of English. Her amused parents, who had taught it to her, noted that she occasionally lapsed into a Japanese word when she forgot the English sound. Two years later, when the child was enrolled in an English language nursery school, it became apparent that her imitation was turning to some minimal understanding. Between the ages of two and four, the child had continued to sing the song everywhere she went, largely because of the positive attention she received both publicly and privately.

Negative reinforcement, or no reinforcement at all, can also affect children's language development. A child who is continually told to be quiet or to "shut up" is likely to do just that, particularly if the words are said in a

Behaviorists, whose roots lie in John Locke's blank-slate theory of learning, argue that adults provide the language model and incentives for children to learn by imitation.

negative tone of voice. Unfortunately, much language learning takes place through practice, and this child loses out on important development opportunities. The same is true for children whose parents rarely speak to them. Such environmental deprivation in the early years can have lifelong negative implications.

*Maturationists* view language learning in the tradition of Rousseau: children are preprogrammed for innate development. As children observe their social environments, they begin to understand how language works. They begin to intuit naturally the necessary rules and conventions of their native language and begin to communicate intelligibly. While children need to hear language in order to understand it, adult instruction is not essential because cognitive maturation will lead naturally to language functioning. Children will naturally experiment with and test the linguistic rules that govern the language around them. As they generate more complex language, children unconsciously create a more complex rule system. The linguist Noam Chomsky (1965) has been a leader in developing a maturationist model for today. He theorized that infants are born with an innate "language acquisition device" that is part of their human brain structure. This genetic inheritance makes it possible to learn language upon contact with other language-speaking social beings.

To *constructivists,* language is both genetically determined and environmentally influenced. In the biological sense, humans have the ability to communicate through language. Young children make use of this ability as they respond to the sounds in their environment. Two theoretical researchers in this field, Jean Piaget and Lev Vygotsky, have greatly influenced today's views of how children learn language.

According to Piaget, children's first words—or their approximations—are egocentric, centered on their own interests and actions. In the early years, their communication relates to those things they have experienced through the senses. Further, young children believe that those who communicate with them perceive and understand things in the same way that they do. When Peter was three, his grandparents mailed him an Indian headdress. Within a few days they telephoned and asked him if he had received it. Instead of answering directly, he laid the phone down, ran to his room and put on the headdress, ran back to the phone and, lifting it, asked, "Doesn't it look good on me?" As children move from preoperations to concrete operations, they begin to realize that others have perspectives that are different from their own. Linguistically, they begin using this knowledge to construct speech that takes into account the views of others. If Peter had received the headdress two or three years later, he would understand that his distant grandparents couldn't see it on him and that it was his responsibility to inform them of how good it looked on him.

An early contemporary of Piaget was the Russian Lev Vygotsky (1962). His unfortunate early death meant that his contributions to the psychology of learning were limited. However, his influence on theoretical views of language learning has continued to this day. According to Vygotsky, infants begin to develop speech without understanding that its purpose is to communicate. Instead, they develop a kind of inner speech that only gradually becomes connected to external communication. It is the adults in their environment who encourage the transition from speech as a private toy to speech as a social tool. The first step in this transition process begins when children being to understand something of what adults say to them even if they are unable to communicate themselves. With repeated interactions, children begin to pick up adult meanings and use them, making the adult role less necessary.

## Linguistic Systems and Children's Language Development

In Chapter 5 you were introduced to language learning in relationship to general cognitive development. It would be useful to review the section Language Learning on pages 146 to 147. The more formal discussion here expands on this information.

By the end of kindergarten, most children have learned the basics of their native language. Doing so means they have mastered five systems of language.

- *Phonology* is the system of language sounds. In English there are forty-four phonemes, or individual sounds. Infants begin by approximating the sounds they hear, perhaps dragging a "blankie" in one hand, carrying a "baba" of "mik" in the other. With practice and maturity, children learn the sounds that make up words, rules for combining sounds, proper articulation, and intonation patterns.
- *Morphology* deals with the internal structure and formation of words. For example, young children begin to learn that adding an *s* makes a word plural. Soon they generalize this rule even in incorrect ways referring to men as "mans" or to a flock of sheep as "sheeps." Morphology also includes changes made to words to indicate different tenses and, again, children overgeneralize at first. "I goed" or "I sleeped" make good sense structurally, but not culturally. By the end of kindergarten, children have figured out most of the basic exceptions to the rules.
- *Syntax* is the grammar of language, the system for placing words in phrases and turning phrases into sentences. Sentences take varying forms such as questions, comments, and exclamations, and children must learn the differences between these. A beginning effort at this complex skill occurs when a baby uses a single word with varying intonations to indicate different sentences. An eighteen-month-old boy toddled into the kitchen all smiles and said to his mother, "Daddy!" to indicate that his father had just arrived home. Before long he was back, pointing his finger toward his father's study and crying, "Daddy," which this time meant he had wandered

in while his father was trying to read an important letter and had been curtly dismissed. His mother carried him back to the study, explained to her husband their child's sadness, then handed the child to him. When his father gave him a warm hug, the child broke into a smile, looked at his mother, and laughed, "Daddy," which no doubt meant, "Daddy and I are happy together after all." Two-word sentences also appear at about this age, and from there progress continues until, by the end of elementary school, most complex sentences are attainable.

■ *Semantics* is the system children must learn for giving meaning to words. In the beginning, words that are repeated over and over take on meaning for the infant, as long as the objects they represent are present at the same time. The toddler whose "Daddy" communication represented sentences was also very aware of the meanings attached to what he said. As preschoolers mature in their linguistic understanding, they can give more complex meanings to words, but are still tied to their egocentric view of the world. When a kindergarten teacher asked her class to define the word "family," one child said, "It's my mom, my cat, my dog, and me." Another answered, "Me, my daddy, my mommy, Gramma, and Billy." If the children had been a year or two older, they would most likely have given a dictionary definition rather than their egocentric ones.

■ *Pragmatics* refers to the application of language to specific and cultural situations. The social interactions of a neighborhood, region, school, church, and so on help determine the accepted rules of communication. Children intuit many of the rules and are taught others by parents, school, and older siblings. Cultural changes can cause discomfort for children if they move or begin to attend school with children and teachers of different backgrounds. One teacher moved to a Southern state after a lifetime in the North. In the first hour of the first day of class she found herself saying heatedly to three different children, "Don't you 'ma'am' me!" when they answered "Yes, ma'am" to her questions. When the third child burst into tears it finally occurred to the teacher that, in her own nervousness at being new, she hadn't picked up on the polite culture of her young children and had caused them much discomfort. In the same town nearby was a private school that had recently become integrated after years as a whites-only school. Black children as young as four quickly learned to speak standard English in the classroom while, on the playground, their speech patterns changed depending on the color and culture of the children they played with.

Phonology, morphology, syntax, semantics, and pragmatics are all elements of linguistics that young children need to learn to communicate successfully. Given a supportive environment and normal maturation, success is generally ensured. Since not all children have these advantages, it is good for the teacher to be aware of each element, its role in language development, and its importance to communication.

## Making Connections: Diversity Among Children

If all children arrived in their classrooms with equal access to language skills, teaching would undoubtedly be easier but certainly not as interesting. One of the challenges facing today's teacher of young children is the fact that children arrive speaking different dialects and, with increasing frequency, different languages. Some come from families in which they are read and talked to daily; others may never have seen a book and rarely communicate with family members. Still other children may have language delays for varying reasons of health or mental capacity. The teacher's responsibility and challenge is to try to meet the needs of them all.

### Children with Dialect Differences

If you teach in an area of more than one culture or race, you may find that some of the children in your class speak a dialect that is different than what you usually hear. It is important to realize that a dialect is not simply deficient standard English, but a way of speaking that has its own consistent vocabulary, morphology, and syntax, all of which the dialect-speaking child must learn just as other children learn standard English. The Northern teacher who had to accept being called ma'am was almost as startled to hear one child ask another, just before recess, "Are you fixin' to go out?" To which the other responded, "Uh huh. I'm either gonna jump rope with Peggy Jane or play tag with the boys, one. . . ." One what? the teacher wondered. And fixin'?! The elements of the local dialect that were new for this teacher included vocabulary ("fixing" rather than planning or preparing), morphology ("fixin' " with its lack of a final *g,* though this is common to many cultures), and syntax (". . . or play tag with the boys, one . . ."). In this case, the dialect was a regional one. Other dialects are the property of social classes or ethnic groups. Although the Northern teacher's Southern career got off to a rocky start, by the second or third day she came to understand that her own dialect was not necessarily superior, even though it was the one most commonly heard on national television news.

Teachers must walk a tightrope between valuing children's home dialects and introducing them to standard English. There is no reason children can't learn to be "bilingual," as the black children in the private school demonstrated. But first they must recognize that there are different ways to talk. As they learn to read stories in standard English and as they continue to hear them, some children will automatically pick up on the differences. Additional learning can be fostered by reading stories that are written in dialect and discussing the differences with the class. Inviting a guest speaker with an unfamiliar dialect, then discussing his or her speech, further heightens awareness. (Be sure, however, that the speaker knows what will happen and agrees to it.)

## Children Whose Native Language Is not English

The United States is experiencing an immigration wave in which a high percentage of the incoming children speak languages, such as Japanese or Vietnamese, that have little or no relation to English. Further, these may not be languages that any of us traditionally learn to speak in school. These two facts alone make comfortable assimilation difficult. Add to them a situation in which a large urban area might have more than two dozen languages represented in its school population and the situation becomes a challenge for everyone.

It is commonly assumed that, through play, younger children easily absorb the dominant language of their peers. This, however, is not necessarily the case (Logan, 1990). If there are others who speak their native language, the children may choose to play only with them, reserving their contact with English for the formal, teacher-directed experiences. Further, they come from a variety of backgrounds, just as the native speakers do, and may have a learning deficit in their native language that impairs their ability to pick up a second language. For children who can find no one in the center or school who can understand them, the situation may well be frightening.

The teacher's role must be a sensitive and supportive one. Underlying all teaching techniques and interventions should be a respect for each child's own language and culture. Today's terminology for identifying children new to English is the unfortunate limited English proficiency (or LEP), which carries with it an attitude of deficit rather than one of expansion on what is already known. You can help new children in a variety of ways:

- Arrange with the principal or director to meet with new children and their parents before they join the classroom. This provides an opportunity to make the child feel comfortable and to inform the teacher of the extent that linguistic intervention might be necessary.
- Prepare the class for the new child once the meeting is held. Role play in which the children are placed in a foreign situation where no one understands them can be helpful. A follow-up discussion of ways to make the new child feel welcome is useful, particularly if moderation is stressed. (Sometimes a class goes overboard in their enthusiasm, making the new child feel overwhelmed and subsequently confused about how to behave.)
- The child's parents, or others from the same culture, can be invited to share artifacts, games, dances, and stories from the culture. The class can be taught some basics of the language. If the new child is permitted to be the language teacher, self-esteem and respect are fostered.
- Use flexible grouping to place LEP children with native speakers to work on projects. Provide guidance to the group in assigning nonnative speakers to jobs that require a degree of English that is challenging but still manageable.
- Avoid placing LEP children in isolated groups or excluding them from ac-

tivities where they won't understand. Much language learning takes place through observation and listening. At the same time, if there is more than one child who speaks the same language, be sure that there are informal times when they can relax and communicate with each other if they so choose.

Finally, it is good to keep in mind what Gonzales-Mena (1976, quoted in Morrow, 1993) has said concerning the help teachers can give nonfluent children:

- Children are eager to learn English when there is an openness and an acceptance of them, their culture, and their native language.
- Language should be taught as part of the total, integrated curriculum, not as an isolated subject area.
- Because children learn through their senses and through physical activity, they will learn language best when they can examine and explore real objects and act out new expressions. Pictures can help, but action provides a stronger imprint.

## Children with Developmental Differences

Children do not all develop in their language capabilities at the same rate, although most do fall into a generally similar pattern. Outside that general range, almost every class will have a few children whose language capabilities are delayed or advanced. Each one of these children deserves your best efforts and an opportunity to excel to the greatest extent possible.

### Giftedness in Language Development

Frequently, children who talk more easily than others and read fluently with little instruction are ignored in favor of attention to children experiencing more difficulties. In actuality, many of these gifted children learn best if provided considerable independence. There is a difference, however, in leaving a child alone because you are too busy to pay attention to him or her and leaving the child alone because it is part of a well thought out plan of encouragement.

Children who have a talent for early reading also enjoy being read to. Further, they can read to very small groups of their friends or to younger children. One kindergarten teacher trained his early readers to read stories to the class just as he did: holding each new page up so that everyone could see the pictures, permitting children to ask questions and make comments, and leading a brief discussion at the end. At least three other children, inspired by and perhaps envious of their friends' leadership opportunities, began making heroic efforts at learning to read so that they, too, could read to the class. In varying degrees, all three were successful.

Children who can read early, and others who are on the verge, are frequently capable of very interesting composition, although their handwriting may not yet be competent. These children can be introduced to the computer keyboard or to small, cutout cardboard letters. While dictation is always a good approach, the computer or cardboard letters provide the independence a creative child may sometimes prefer.

In the primary grades, gifted readers and writers may become interested in pursuing a research topic in great depth. The teacher who facilitates this kind of learning goes a long way toward fostering the greatest learning for these children. Due to time constraints, in-depth research must sometimes be done at the expense of other activities. It is up to you as the teacher to decide if another activity is sufficiently important that the research enthusiast must participate. If this is not the case, then you should inform the child of the choice to be made, let the child decide which to do, and then respect the child's decision. (While respecting the decision may seem obvious, all too frequently teachers present the options and then convey by their facial expressions or body language that they really would prefer that the child join the larger group. It is important to give options only if you are willing to live gracefully with the child's choice.)

### Developmental Delays in Language

Identification of children's special needs can make your work easier. Sometimes, however, it is not yet known that a child has a problem or a specific problem may not have been identified yet. In one preschool class, for example, a three-year-old seemed to speak in total nonsense syllables, although her intonations were those of a person communicating in complete sentences. Just as her parents were making appointments to have her tested, the child became comprehensible, continuing to talk with the same intonations but, finally, making sense. In the same class, a four-year-old boy had a similar problem, although some of his words could be understood. For almost a year, his parents had taken him to various doctors and even a university medical school to try to identify the problem. No one seemed to have an answer. Meanwhile, the child began observing a couple of five-year-olds who were composing words and stories with the cardboard cutout letters suggested above. He expressed an interest in joining them, and the teacher helped him sound out the letters so that he could make the "real words like those big kids" that he hoped to emulate. In about three weeks the teacher called the child's mother in to observe an amazing development. As the child learned to read the words back, he began to hear what they should sound like and to pronounce them correctly. The mother and the teacher joined forces to teach the child, in an informal and nonthreatening way, to read. He joined in enthusiastically, and was soon talking normally.

These two experiences demonstrate the high probability that early child-

hood teachers will frequently be closely involved in the early stages of identifying and possibly remediating children's special needs. Some of the special
needs that are related to language and literacy are

- *Visual impairments.* Legally blind children will probably not be mainstreamed into your class, but some children with low vision may be.
Learning materials with large print are available for them. These children
also need plenty of tactile and auditory experiences.
- *Hearing impairments.* The way children hear language will affect their speech
and reading capabilities. It may also affect their behavior. If a child consistently pays no attention to you, be sure there is no hearing problem as you
look for corrective solutions.
- *Cognitive delays.* Children with mental retardation may need the services of
a specialist while spending some hours mainstreamed into your classroom.
Be sure that, when these children are in your classroom, both you and the
other children treat them with respect and include them in all activities.
Even if they can read just a few words in a story, they should be given this
opportunity. And, if they cannot express themselves as well as the others,
they should still be given the chance to contribute orally. Plan to work
with the specialist and with the children's parents to determine the optimum level of challenge.

For all children with language delays, contact with language in all its
forms should be introduced throughout the day. Even though they may not
respond with the skill of other children, it is important that these children engage in plenty of conversation, hear good literature read, and learn to read
and write to their highest ability.

## Oral Language, Written Language, and Reading

Language, by definition, is a *system* of sounds that are used to communicate orally or in written form. While infants are not born knowing any of the
systematic elements of communication, they begin to learn them almost immediately as their parents and other caregivers respond in differing ways to
their cries, gurgles, and coos. Later, young children learn the additional systems of reading and writing (literacy). At each step of the way, from infancy
onward, the quality of children's oral and literacy production is influenced by
the quality of interaction with significant others.

The traditional approach to teaching language and literacy separates out
oral, writing, and reading experiences in order to focus on each more adequately. Conversely, the whole language approach views language learning as
an integrated activity in which oral language, writing, and reading interact

with and complement each other. No matter which approach you take, it is important to consider each element of language when assessing each child's learning needs.

## Oral Language

Quality oral language experiences foster competent language development, while a lack of them will almost certainly impede progress. For example, as the infant repeats, "ma, ma, ma, ma," she observes that her mother smiles; she also sees that "pa, pa, pa, pa" brings a smile to her father. The predictability of the response provides the infant with a first cue that there are rules in language. If those same parents don't respond to the ma's and pa's, the infant may lose interest in making the sounds and an opportunity for learning has been lost. Continued lack of quality interactions may lead to delay in oral language development. This, in turn, may cause delays in learning to read and write. Reading and writing are also systematic activities, and the more the young child has experience with oral language as a system, the easier it will be to acquire other new skills. Further, richness in oral expression translates into more creative writing and more comprehension in reading than does sparse oral experience.

### Infants

In their first months, infants communicate by crying when they are in distress, by smiling and vocalizing to initiate social contact, and by babbling and laughing. They listen to conversations and engage in their own private monologues. From about eight to eighteen months, babbled "sentences" become longer while a few words can be pronounced clearly. Vocal signals other than crying can be used when assistance is needed. The National Association for the Education of Young Children (Bredecamp, 1987) recommends a number of appropriate practices for caregivers based on observation and research. They suggest that caregivers

- engage in many one-to-one, face-to-face interactions with infants, speaking in a pleasant, soothing voice.
- hold and carry infants frequently, talking to them before, during, and after moving them around.
- talk while engaging in routines such as diaper changing, feeding, and changing clothes. They should explain what will happen, what is happening, and what will happen next.
- respond to and imitate the sounds infants make. These should be respected as the beginnings of communication.
- respond quickly, soothingly, and tenderly to signs of distress.
- talk, sing, and read to infants frequently. (pp. 34–35)

## Toddlers

Toddlers and two-year-olds continually build their vocabulary, perhaps reaching a total of 200 words, which they begin to combine with each other for increasingly skillful communication. Toward the end of this period compound sentences that include nouns, verbs, adjectives, and adverbs begin to appear. Toddlers and two's can explain the use of many household items, recount the events of the day, and begin to play pretend games, using fantasy in their accompanying language. NAEYC suggests that caregivers

- continue frequent one-to-one, face-to-face conversations.
- let toddlers initiate language, and continue the communication, waiting patiently for the sometimes slow and awkward responses.
- label and name objects, describe events, and reflect feelings such that children have opportunities to learn new vocabulary.
- sing, do fingerplays, act out simple stories, and tell stories on a flannel-board or magnetic board, letting the children manipulate the figures.

## Preschoolers

Preschool children continue their rapid language development. The younger children, especially, do not care for much group participation, prefer to talk rather than listen, and often ask questions they already know the answers to. While this trait is at times annoying to adults, particularly when the word *why* appears so repetitiously, understanding caregivers and teachers recognize that children do this to start a conversation or to practice answering questions themselves. Preschool children are enthusiastic about learning new vocabulary and place importance on getting the names of things right. One well-meaning father, not wanting to confuse his child with too many technical words said to his child, "Look up there at that noisy airplane!" and the four-year-old responded with great disdain, "Don't you know that's a helitopter?" Throughout the preschool years, children's communication becomes more adept as they learn to make longer and more complex sentences. NAEYC suggests that caregivers and teachers

- speak clearly and frequently to individual children and listen to their responses. When they make errors in grammar, repeat the sentence correctly so that they can hear what it should be like. There is little benefit to spending much time with direct corrections unless they are requested.
- respond quickly, appropriately, and patiently to children's efforts at conversations. Provide plenty of opportunity for informal talk between peers and between adults and children.
- recite poems, finger plays, and nursery rhymes; facilitate play of circle and movement games.

It is estimated that, by age two, many children have a vocabulary of 200 words or more that they can combine into various sentence structures, including compound sentences.

## Primary Grades

Primary children, having acquired most of their adult grammar and a vocabulary adequate for most communication, have also been exposed to several years of television. This gives them vocabulary far beyond that of previous generations. However, their understanding of what they are saying may be quite different from that of adults. Primary children learn much through verbal interaction, including interaction with each other. To their recently achieved sentence structure and vocabulary they are ready to add negotiation, cooperation, and other social skills. NAEYC suggests that teachers

- occasionally ask children what they mean by certain adult words they are using. This allows comprehension to be checked. At other times, a definition can be worked informally into the conversation. If this is done non-judgmentally, children are interested and happy to know what words really mean.
- provide opportunities for learning in small heterogeneous groups in which student planning and decisions are necessary.
- provide time for informal conversation both in the classroom and on the playground.
- read books to the children that contain a modest amount of new vocabulary, which is both read in context and discussed for meaning. One approach is to preview the upcoming chapter, pulling out words that proba-

bly won't be understood and presenting these to the children before the read-aloud session. The words can then be highlighted or emphasized during the actual reading.

## Writing

While a number of researchers have tried to observe and describe some sort of stage development in early childhood writing, no one has succeeded completely (Morrow, 1993). Some of the steps that parents, caregivers, and teachers observe on the way to competent writing include drawing pictures to tell a story or communicate, scribbling in a format that looks like cursive writing, and may move from left to right; imitating letter forms, stringing actual letters together randomly, placing letters together to make words, using invented spelling, and, finally, producing words that resemble adult writing.

Drawing on broadbased research with young children, Lesley Morrow (1992, pp. 234–236) suggests that the following elements pertain to early writing acquisition:

- "Children's early literacy experiences are embedded in the familiar situations and real-life experiences of family and community." Many families don't realize how much writing is a part of their lives and that the young children in the family observe and copy such activities as writing each other notes, making grocery lists, and sending holiday greetings. It appears that young children learn much about writing in this fashion, even across cultures and classes.
- "As a process, early writing development is characterized by children's moving from playfully making marks on paper, through communicating messages on paper, to making texts as artifacts." At first, children don't care about the product of their mark making, losing interest in it once they are tired of writing. Once they learn that the symbols have meaning, interest in the product grows.
- "Children learn the uses of written language before they learn the forms." Observers of scribbling children have noted that the children seem to know what their writing is for before they know what the conventional forms are.
- "Children's writing develops through constant invention and reinvention of the forms of written language." When preschool children learn to write it is through experimentation, not through direct teaching. As they observe, model, and interact with others more literate than they, children develop increasingly recognizable symbolic representation.
- "Children need to work independently on the functions and form of writing that they have experienced through interactions with literate others." When children are given time to invent, experiment, rehearse, and explore writing on their own, competent writing emerges.

Morrow points out that, while we have seen much new theory building and research about emergent literacy in recent years, it is the thinking about emergent *writing* that has made the biggest break with tradition. Until recently, children were given crayons, markers, and paper to develop their motor coordination in preparation for writing, but it is now seen that children as young as two are learning about literacy as they begin making marks on paper. Based on what we are beginning to know about emergent literacy, Morrow suggests the following objectives for language instruction in home, care center, preschool and kindergarten, through first and second grade:

- Children should have enjoyable experiences with many kinds of print on a regular basis.
- Children will regularly observe adults writing, both for work and for leisure, and should have opportunities and materials for doing so themselves.
- While others can suggest topics to write about, children should be permitted to make the final decision based on what is most meaningful to them.
- Children's efforts at writing should be responded to as meaningful communication even when they are scribbles, random letters, or invented spelling.
- Children should be encouraged to use writing for a wide range of purposes: lists, cards, letters, songs, stories, expository pieces, books.
- Children should have varying types of writing read to them, which may eventually serve as models for their own writing.
- Writing should be integrated throughout the curriculum.
- Teachers will point out sound–symbol correspondences as the spoken word is transformed into written form.
- Children should be shown how to write letters in manuscript and how to use common punctuation symbols such as periods, commas, and quotation marks.

When children become aware of the functions of print, and begin to make some standard letters and to invent spellings, a number of activities and teaching approaches become possible. A *writing center* can be established and filled with tools appropriate to the children's age and development. Colored markers make a popular first writing tool. Paper of different sizes, some of it folded to make greeting cards, can be introduced and changed as children's interests change. *Word banks* can be kept for each child in his or her private envelope. Each envelope contains index cards with one favorite or important word written on each. Often these are names of relatives, pets, and good friends that the child can refer to during writing sessions. *Journal writing* permits children to reflect on the day and on their private feelings. It helps if the teacher models this activity the first few days, writing and reading the entry aloud. The teacher's journal can be kept in a public place where children can examine it for format or ideas.

Choosing some writing to *publish* involves more formality and perfection than writing in journals or jotting notes or keeping lists. When a story or expository piece is deemed interesting or important enough for publication, it goes through a series of systematic steps to completion. This is as true in the classroom as in professional life. Calkins (1986) suggests five steps: prewriting (brainstorming to generate ideas), drafting (the first attempt at writing), conferencing (reflecting on the draft and discussing it with a peer or teacher to determine possible changes), revising (making the changes for a second draft), and editing (making minor changes in punctuation, spelling, grammar, etc.). Publication outlets are only limited by one's imagination: mini-books for the class collection or school library, newsletters home, reports and other papers posted on walls for visitors to read, or gift stories to accompany handmade greeting cards.

## Reading

Recent theory views learning to read as a process that begins at birth and lasts throughout life. Young children emerge into literacy through informal life experiences and continue developing on a continuum of increasing competence (Freeman and Hatch, 1989; Strickland and Cullinan, 1990). This theory contrasts with the traditional view that reading readiness activities must precede the formal act of reading, which normally begins at about age six. Before that time, say the traditionalists, experiences with reading materials cannot be classified as reading itself. At this point, continued research has not demonstrated that there are convenient stages in reading development that we can use to categorize children's progress. In the last two decades or more, three general strands of development seem to have been identified in a variety of research efforts (Morrow, 1993). The first is that of *functions,* in which children take a first step toward reading by learning how print functions. This step often occurs as children begin to identify popular fast-food restaurant logos, road signs, labels on cereal boxes, and other meaningful signs. The second strand is *forms,* in which children learn the shapes of letters and words as well as the sounds that go with them. *Conventions* is the third strand in which children learn the rules of literacy, such as movement from left to right, spaces between words, and so on.

Don Holdaway (1986), one of New Zealand's leading reading researchers, suggests that there are four processes that help children learn to read. The first is *observation* of other people reading (i.e., modeling); the second, *collaboration* with someone who encourages the child; the third, *practice,* in which the child tries out some of the new learning; and the fourth, *performance,* when the child reads for others, sharing new skills and enjoying the approval this generates. Since these processes begin early in life, those who are involved with children should be aware of the need to encourage their development from the earliest years.

The concept of *scaffolding* was introduced by Jerome Bruner in the 1970s, and refers to the ways in which adults elaborate and expand on children's language attempts, thus facilitating their growth to a higher level (Boyle and Peregoy, 1990). Reading stories to young children is an example of scaffolding in that it introduces them to language and story patterns that will be useful later when they begin reading and writing on their own. Reading aloud to children is one of the most useful ways of introducing them to the act of reading, and one of the most effective tools seems to be predictable books. These are books that have repeated phrases, obvious cues in the text, or pictures that help children make sense of the story (Conlon, 1992). Reading the same book again and again may not appeal to the adult reader, but this technique seems to encourage reading as children become more and more familiar with the text. Adult readers should also permit children to ask questions, discuss the plot, join in on familiar words and phrases, and share related personal experiences.

A reading-rich environment that includes the presence of print in many forms is an important part of reading development. There should be labels, lists, signs, charts, posters, restaurant menus, notepads, stamps and envelopes, and greeting cards in addition to a good collection of picture books, poetry, informational books, and Big Books (Freeman and Hatch, 1989). Language experience activities in which children dictate words and stories help them see firsthand how stories are written and read.

As children begin to get the idea of reading, opportunities will present themselves to facilitate skill building in specific areas. These skill-building opportunities are usually generated by children on a need-to-know basis and they generally occur in the context of a meaningful experience. While the method of teaching the needed skill may be direct instruction, skill building today is unlike that of earlier years when instruction was given out of context. In other words, skills that were once taught in isolation for their own sake are now taught as part of an attempt at meaningful, real-life communication.

One example of an important skill area is the alphabetic principle. Traditionally, the alphabet has been taught for its own sake, usually before reading instruction begins. Often, each letter is given its own week and activities are designed to highlight it. Research in recent years, however, has shown that such in-depth teaching is not necessary (Reutzel, 1992). Once children begin to understand the alphabetic principle by learning a few letters, they generalize to others without further training. As children learn to read, more of the alphabet is revealed to them naturally. Observant teachers will note which letters are unfamiliar or difficult for specific children, and learning experiences can then be provided. Alphabet activities can include an alphabet center stocked with magnetic letters, puzzles, sandpaper letters, games, chalkboards, tracing papers, and stencils for informal exploration. Alphabet books, songs, chants, and poetry provide natural means toward learning alphabetic order.

Although this chapter has separated oral language, writing, and reading from each other for discussion purposes, it is important to remember that they are really part of an inseparable whole that is directly experienced by children. Further, since language and literacy are the basic tools we use to explore all areas of human knowledge, their use and mastery extend across the entire curriculum.

## Language and Literacy Across the Curriculum

As infants learn to communicate their interests, needs, desires, and feelings, they do so in every aspect of their lives. Language is not just learned for its own sake but because it is an integral part of the child's entire world. Unfortunately, language learning is often compartmentalized and decontextualized in school settings. Rather than embracing natural language learning opportunities that may arise as part of any school activity, too often reading and writing are reduced to narrow exercises devoid of any meaning. Caregivers and teachers who foster language and literacy throughout the day and in many natural situations can do much to stimulate language development.

The following ideas and activities are suggested ways in which language and literacy can be an integral part of the entire curriculum. To incorporate them, and others you add on your own, is as much an attitude as it is conscious planning.

### Ideas and Activities for Math

- Create "story problems" from everyday activities. These can be conversations carried on about naturally occurring events: deciding how many napkins are needed for a snack table, counting children in line, counting the number present, and figuring out how many are absent. The problems can also be more hypothetical as the children grow older and are aware of mathematical processes. "What would happen if . . . ?" questions can be created for almost any occasion.
- Create story problems in conjunction with short stories you write for the children to read independently or in pairs. These can be integrated right into the body of the story or added at the end.
- When children learn new math processes they can write about them in their journals or in letters to take home to their parents. As they describe what they have learned, they reinforce the math learning while expanding their writing and critical thinking skills.
- Cut up paperback versions of favorite stories and place the pictures of the plots' sequence of events on cards. Number the cards on the back and/or write the ordinal numbers. Children tell the stories to each other and place the cards in order. They check their accuracy by turning the cards over and reading the numbers. Children can also recreate the story, placing the cards

## Writing Stories for Children: A Conversation with Jane Hilleary

*As you read aloud to children you may find yourself thinking.* I could write a story like this! *More frequently, you may find yourself unable to find just the right book to relate to current projects in social studies, science, and so on, and will want to try writing something appropriate for classroom use. In this conversation, we talk with a woman who has spent many years writing such informal stories and now has begun professional publishing. You may find her experiences and suggestions helpful.*

As a single mother raising seven children, Jane Hilleary had little time or inclination to pursue career interests. She held a series of part-time jobs and expended the rest of her energy on caring for her family. "Being alone with the children, trying to find activities that we could all do together, was the first step in my becoming interested in writing. The one thing the whole family enjoyed doing together was reading aloud."

Jane explains that this family activity led her to an interest in "fiddling around with" writing herself. Feeling the need for guidance, she enrolled in a correspondence course. While she now believes the course was far too expensive, it did give her the encouragement and discipline she needed to complete a story and submit it to outside criticism. In the succeeding years, Jane continued to "fiddle around" with her writing, bring up her children and, eventually, return to full-time work as a secretary.

In 1988, Jane achieved her first professional success with the publication of *Fletcher and the Great Big Dog* (Houghton Mifflin). First pub-

lished in hardback, the book is now available in paperback as well. It has even won an award sponsored by a New Jersey elementary school: The Smallwood Drive School's Children's Choice Award. In 1991, *Fletcher and the Great Big Dog* beat out several well-known books written by far more famous authors and Jane was presented with an inscribed trophy.

Jane considers the possible reasons for her book's appeal. "Editors and critics have liked the book's strong and predictable plot, repetitive language, and the fact that it deals with real concerns. One critic cited its use of prepositions such as into, across, and between as adding to its appeal to young children.

While she looks forward to her imminent retirement as a time to devote to more writing, Jane has already begun trying to publish a sequel to *Fletcher*. Despite three attempts, however, she has been unsuccessful in satisfying the high expectations of the editors. "I think I've been trying too hard. My plots are contrived. I need to just go with the flow as I did with the first book, which seemed to almost write itself . . . a good example of right-brain activity. I didn't allow my left-brain editor to kick in until I started the rewrite process."

Jane suggests trying to write the first draft of any story in the freest way possible. "I think you stifle the writing if you try to make it perfect the first time you put it down. It isn't going to be perfect, and you aren't as creative when you try for perfection."

Like all writers, Jane sometimes has trouble facing a blank piece of paper or an empty computer screen. One favorite approach is to do what she calls "warm-ups". For example, she might think back to the time when she was in kindergarten or first grade. Next she lists events that were momentous to her at that time. She chooses one and starts writing, letting the thought flow freely. "With no expectations, this allows you to experience the flow of thought without the censorship of your left brain. And if you've chosen the age level you intend to write for, it puts you in that frame of mind."

In general, Jane says, "There is no substitute for practice. She advises setting aside a certain amount of time several days a week to "just write, write, write, write, write!"

Jane says she loves computers and that when she gets serious about real publication she uses one. But, for first drafts and warm-ups she likes the connection to her writing that pen and a pad of paper give her. She also likes to change her writing site. She might be propped up in bed one evening or, another time, in a lounge chair in her backyard. "The change of scenery helps to keep you from stagnating," she says.

If you are really serious about getting good feedback from your efforts, Jane says, you should have your friends and colleagues try your stories out on their children. Getting together with others who are writing children's stories can also be helpful. Reading your efforts to each other often provides new insights and suggestions for improvement.

Finally, if you do decide to try writing, be sure, Jane says, that your stories' endings are happy and satisfying. The ending that leaves the reader hanging or unsettled is for older, more sophisticated people. In *Fletcher*, the great big dog first scares Fletcher (a young boy) who tries to escape him. But the dog follows after and Fletcher, trying even harder to escape, eventually becomes lost. Together they retrace their steps and, together, they find their way home again, friends forever. It is an ending that leaves young children feeling contented and secure.

*To discuss: Try writing a group story with others in your class. Keep in mind the elements of success suggested by Jane Hilleary. Then, read your story to different groups of young children and note their responses. Was the writing experience as interesting or as difficult as you thought it would be?*

out of their original order. If desired, they can then turn the cards over and renumber them in their new order.

## Ideas and Activities for Social Studies (and Social Experiences)

- When children are having difficulty interacting successfully with others, provide them with direct instruction in oral communication skills. Help them with brief phrases that are likely to win them more friends. "Gimme the trike!" for example, can be replaced by "Will you let me use the trike when you're finished?"
- As children enter in the morning, hand them index cards on which are map outlines of a country or state (these can be drawn freehand with a marker). There should be duplicates of each small map so that children will end up with partners. Children first find their country or state on the class map or globe and then find their partner; or they first find their partners and search together for their country or state. The children remain partners for the rest of the morning or the day. (Children as young as four can do this if the drawings and maps are very clear. Older children can write the names in the outlines.)
- Place "coffee table books" of interesting places in a center for informal perusal. Help advanced readers read the captions under pictures they find interesting. Or write a few brief sentences yourself about some of the most interesting pictures and place the paper in the appropriate page for children to discover and read. Children who are not yet ready to read enjoy hearing stories about interesting places. Generally, these should be factual rather than fanciful so that children can first sort out the reality of unfamiliar places.

## Ideas and Activities for Science

- Any science experiment that involves equipment can benefit from labeling. Make a label with the name of each piece of equipment and tape it on. If the item is to be put away, make a matching label in its proper place. Even children who aren't quite ready to read can match labels and put equipment away properly.
- After any observational experience, such as a nature walk in the woods or a session outdoors looking at insects, have children dictate everything they recall observing. Write their ideas on a chart. Stretch the experience by putting aside time to reobserve very soon afterward. Take the experience chart with you and try to add more observations.
- Primary children can keep journals or write "lab reports" of their experiments in science. These can be free-form or can have a more formal format, using printed questions with spaces for answers. Some suggestions:

1. List the steps you took in the experiment.
2. What is one important thing you learned?
3. Draw a picture of the most interesting part of the experiment.

## Ideas and Activities for the Creative Arts

- Whenever children learn a new letter, part of speech, punctuation mark, or word, have them act it out in some way. Letters, for example, can be made with the whole body or parts of it; they can dance on the wind; they can be frozen in space and then melted to the floor.
- Favorite stories can and should be acted out whenever possible. This can be done formally, in play form, with children playing parts, or it can be done informally as you read the story to the children. With a minimum of rules (e.g., no noise as you move), children can become active participants in the reading or telling of a story.
- Use music experiences to play with various kinds of sounds. Let children substitute words and nonsense syllables for the original ones. Make up whole new verses or try singing the verse from one song to the tune of another.
- If you are singing or humming while holding an infant, repeat the same words to the same tunes rather than being inventive. The child will eventually grasp the patterns of sound and learn to expect them.
- Whenever possible, let children tell you about the pictures they are drawing, but don't force the issue. Sometimes children enjoy dictating stories about what they have done, but at other times they prefer to let the picture tell its own story. Respect their artistry and ask permission first.

## Extending Your Learning

1. Review the two episodes that opened this chapter. Which one more nearly describes the experiences you had in your first years of school? In what ways are your memories positive or negative? Compare your experiences and memories with other students in your class.
2. Interview two or three children about television shows they enjoy. As they use program-related words that you believe the children may not actually understand, ask for their definitions. Informally discuss the dictionary definitions with them while making note of their own first interpretations.
3. Model enthusiasm for reading by keeping a book with you to read at odd moments. If you are working with children, share a bit about your book with them, telling them what you like about it and a little about the characters. If they are interested, read a short section to the children, paraphrasing where necessary to help their understanding.
4. Model enthusiasm for writing by keeping a journal of what happens in

your center or school. Choose events that can be shared with the children, then do share.

## References

Adams, M. (1990). *Beginning to read: Thinking and learning about print.* Cambridge, MA: MIT Press.

Boyle, O., and Peregoy, S. (1990). Literacy scaffolds: Strategies for first- and second-language readers and writers. *The Reading Teacher* 44(3):194–200.

Bredecamp, S. (1987). *Developmentally appropriate practice in early childhood programs serving children from birth through age 8.* Washington, DC: NAEYC.

Calkins, L. (1986). *The art of teaching writing.* Exeter, NH: Heinemann.

Chall, J. (1983). *Stages of reading development.* New York: McGraw-Hill.

Chomsky, N. (1965). *Aspects of a theory of syntax.* Cambridge, MA: MIT Press.

Conlon, A. (1992). Giving Mrs. Jones a hand: Making group storytime more pleasurable and meaningful for young children. *Young Children* 47(3):14–18.

Flesch, Rudolph (1955). *Why Johnny can't read.*

Freeman, E., and Hatch, J. A. (1989). Emergent literacy: Reconceptualizing kindergarten practice. *Childhood Education* 66(1):21–24.

Goodman, K. (1992). I didn't found whole language. *The Reading Teacher* 46(3):188–199.

Goodman, Y. (1989). Roots of the whole-language movement. *The Elementary School Journal* 90(2):113–127.

Hatch, J. A. (1992). Improving language instruction in the primary grades: Strategies for teacher-controlled change. *Young Children* 47(3):54–59.

Holdaway, D. (1986). The structure of natural learning as a basis for literacy instruction. In M. Sampson (ed.), *The pursuit of literacy: Early reading and writing,* pp. 56–72. Dubuque: Kendall/Hunt.

Logan, T. (1990). Controlling involvement: A naturalistic study of peer interaction in a bilingual, bicultural preschool. Univ. of FL. Unpublished dissertation.

Morrow, L. (1993). *Literacy development in the early years.* Boston: Allyn and Bacon.

Neuman, S., and Roskos, K. (1990). Play, print, and purpose: Enriching play environments for literacy development. *The Reading Teacher* 44(3):214–221.

Reutzel, R. (1992). Breaking the letter-a-week tradition. *Childhood Education* 20–23.

Spiegel, D. (1992). Blending whole language and systematic direct instruction. *The Reading Teacher* 46(1):38–44.

Strickland, D., and Cullinan, B. (1990). Afterword. In M. Adams, *Beginning to read: Thinking and learning about print,* pp. 424–434. Cambridge, MA: MIT Press.

Vygotsky, L. (1962). *Thought and language.* New York: J Wiley.

Watson, D. (1989). Defining and describing whole language. *The Elementary School Journal* 90(2):129–141.

Yatvin, J. (1991). *Developing a whole language program for a whole school.* Midlothian, VA: Virginia State Reading Association.

# 13

# Mathematics

## OBJECTIVE

When you finish reading this chapter, you should be able to

▪ Plan mathematics activities in relation to children's physical, social, and cognitive development.
▪ Plan mathematics activities taking into account the needs of individual children.
▪ Plan mathematics activities using a variety of teaching methods.
▪ Incorporate mathematics into all areas of the curriculum.

As you think about this chapter on your own, you should be able to

▪ Have an increased awareness of natural mathematics experiences in daily life that are available for children's learning.

The field of mathematics includes an array of subfields, skills, and systems, many of which are appropriate for study, in some form, by young children. Among the more commonly taught topics are classification, seriation, counting, numeration, measurement, geometry, graphing, and arithmetic (addition, subtraction, multiplication, and division). Even without instruction, very young children intuit mathematical principles. When Matt was two, the lunch he liked best was a small cup of soup surrounded by a small sandwich cut into four triangles. This usually proved too much for him, however, and he regularly left one of the sandwich pieces, which his mother then ate. One day, feeling quite hungry, his mother ate "her" section of the sandwich before Matt walked in the kitchen, then spread the other three pieces out to fill the plate. (She, like you, had read about Piaget's experiments showing that young children believe that there are more objects when the objects fill a larger space.) As Matt sat down, however, he looked concerned, then faintly outraged. "Where's de udder one?!" he demanded. Whether it was his understanding of number or of spatial relationships or both that prompted Matt's reaction, it was clear to his mother that his mathematical ability had outdone her attempt to circumvent it.

A controversial study by Karen Wynn (Associated Press, 1992) indicates that infants as young as five months may have some understanding of arithmetic. Using 4-inch-tall Mickey Mouse dolls, Wynn would place one or two of them on a shelf. Then, with a screen to block the infant's view, she would put in another doll or take one out, creating a visual addition or subtraction problem. The screen was then removed and the infant could see that there was now one more or one less doll. Although the screen was used, the infant could watch each step as it happened. Following this first part of the experiment, Wynn would add a third doll when the infant didn't know it. Thus, when the screen was removed, the infant would see a "wrong answer." Wynn then timed the number of seconds that infants looked at "right" and "wrong" answers and discovered that they looked longer at the wrong answers. Wynn's conclusion was that the longer time spent looking at the unexpected or "wrong" numbers of dolls indicated that the infants had a basic, intuitive understanding of addition and subtraction. Detractors argue that Wynn's results may just show that the infants stared longer at the wrong answers because they "violated an expectation," and the behavior may not really demonstrate that they understood a change in quantity. Nevertheless, this study may inspire other researchers to evaluate the mathematical thinking of infants and younger children, perhaps leading to Wynn's conclusion that the ability to grasp the basics of arithmetic may be inborn, just as language is.

Whether mathematical concepts begin to be learned in the first months of life, or whether awareness starts with the missing piece of a sandwich, there are many ways in which the real world can bring informal math learning to young children. Children need to play with mathematical concepts just as they do with language, although this view has not been widely held in this country. Nevertheless, it may be that a lack of informal and playful mathematical experiences is one cause for the poor performance of American children on international mathematics tests.

In recent years, cross-national mathematics tests have demonstrated that children in the United States fall further behind the children in many other countries the longer they stay in school. Yet, when they first enter preschool or kindergarten, American children arrive with the same possibilities for growth as do children in other countries. Further, these disturbing results happen despite the dedicated efforts of countless teachers to provide their children with sufficient mathematical learning. In this chapter we will explore some of the ways in which young children can be turned on to mathematics and tuned in to real understanding. We begin with a description of one teacher-researcher's experience with first graders. What she learned from them may provide some clues as to what may be going wrong in American schools and what might be done to turn them around.

## THREE WAYS OF LOOKING AT ARITHMETIC: ONE TEACHER'S EXPERIENCE

*Suzanne Colvin (1987) was an early childhood teacher of considerable experience as well as a graduate student interested in the ways young children learn mathematical concepts. For her primary doctoral research, she decided to explore the ways that first graders learn to add and subtract. Suzanne wondered why most of the children were able to memorize the required addition and subtraction facts but didn't seem to have a clear understanding of what they were doing. Story problems were difficult for almost everyone. The school principal and the three first-grade teachers shared Suzanne's concern and agreed on a cooperative plan that they hoped might lead to some answers.*

*Suzanne's plan was to teach math to all three of the classes, focusing specifically on the introduction of addition and subtraction, for a period of seven weeks. To be sure that all three classes started out on an equal footing, she administered readiness tests to every child. Since the classes had already been divided according to age, sex, and entrance test scores, Suzanne wasn't surprised to learn that the three classes were just about equal in their readiness to begin addition and subtraction. A few children were eliminated from the study. Those who already knew how to add and subtract, or weren't ready to learn, were given specialized activities by their own teachers while Suzanne worked with the other children. Suzanne then planned three completely different teaching approaches for the three classes. To find out how successful each one was, she gave tests to all the children before her instruction started. After seven weeks, she gave everyone the same tests again to see what improvement had been made. Then, to check on the permanence of the learning, she came back once again, after four more weeks, and gave the children similar tests.*

*The three teaching approaches represented different philosophies of how children learn mathematics. The first approach Suzanne called "traditional." The children in the traditional class were taught according to the instructions in the commercial textbook that had been adopted by the school system. The text was organized along the lines of the traditional American approach to teaching addition and subtraction. First, the children are given facts, or number sentences, to learn. Then, to help them learn the facts and apply them to real situations, story problems are presented that make use of the just-learned facts. This first approach was the one the school had been using for some years, probably because it conveniently coincided with the approach taken by the text publisher.*

*The second approach reversed this process. First, the children were presented with story problems, which they discussed, drew, or role played. The stories were those that related to the children's own lives or were interesting to them in some way. Once they had, as a group, figured out the answers, Suzanne showed them how to represent the problems and their answers using written symbols. Because she immediately followed up the story discussions with information about symbols, Suzanne called this approach "immediate."*

*The third approach was more like the second than the first. The children in this class were also presented with story problems before symbols. In this case, however, the children didn't learn about symbols until the sixth week. Instead, they spent five weeks discussing and acting out many mathematical story problems in a totally informal way. Because the symbols weren't presented to the children until the last two weeks of the project, Suzanne called this approach "delayed."*

*As she began teaching the children, one of the first differences Suzanne noticed between the groups was their attitude toward story problems. While the immediate and delayed classes seemed to enjoy the stories and spent considerable time discussing different ways to solve them, the traditional class seemed to have no interest in them at all. For them, getting right answers to the addition and subtraction problems was all important and the stories merely a distraction, barriers to quick attainment of the facts. It was not surprising when, in the posttest, this group was the only one of the three that made no progress in solving story problems. The children in all three groups had performed inadequately in the pretest, generally guessing at possible answers rather than trying to figure them out. After seven weeks, the immediate and delayed groups tackled the stories with confidence and interest; the traditional group continued with guesswork.*

*The tests also required the children to work with story problems and number sentences together. For example, Suzanne might say, "I have two blocks and you have three. That's five altogether. Can you write a number sentence that shows what we just did?" Or, conversely, she might show them the number sentence and ask them to make up a story to go with it. After seven weeks, the immediate group did best in writing number stories to go with the sentences, but after four weeks of extra practice, the delayed group did just as well. The traditional group never did catch up. When it came to inventing stories to go with the number sentences, the delayed group did best after seven weeks and the immediate group caught up with them after another four weeks. Again, the traditional group did poorly.*

*Since the traditional group spent so much time practicing addition and subtraction facts, Suzanne thought that this might be where they would outperform the other two groups. However, after seven weeks the immediate group outperformed the others, while after another four weeks everyone was about the same.*

*Other testing showed that the immediate and delayed groups understood arithmetic symbols better than the traditional group, even though the traditional children spent more time studying them. And subtraction was harder for everyone than addition was.*

*For Suzanne, the conclusions to be drawn for teaching were obvious. Although all three approaches eventually helped children answer addition and subtraction problems with equal correctness, the traditional approach was far less effective in helping children understand what was going on or apply those memorized numbers in meaningful ways. Continual, daily exposure to story problems appeared to Suzanne to be the most beneficial approach to take with young children. She also began to wonder if it was really appropriate to introduce children to subtraction quite so soon.*

The questions raised by Suzanne and the questions and answers that grew out of her experience with the three classes are some of those that have been discussed and debated by mathematics educators in recent years. It took many centuries of theorizing and practicing to come to this debate.

## Making Connections: Perspectives on History and Theory

Throughout history, mathematical concepts and systems have been developed in response to real-life problems. For example, the zero, which was invented by the Babylonians around 700 B.C., by the Mayans about 400 A.D., and by the Hindus about 800 A.D., was first used to fill a column of numbers in which there were none desired. For example, an 8 and a 3 next to each other is 83; but if you want the number to read 803 and you put something between the 8 and 3 (other than empty space), it is more likely to be read accurately. Another example of early applied mathematics is demonstrated in the Egyptian development of simple arithmetic and geometry so that boundary markers in the fields could be reset after the annual spring flooding of the Nile (Baroody, 1987). When it comes to counting, tallying, or thinking about numerical quantity in general, the human physiological fact of ten fingers and ten toes has led in all mathematical cultures to some sort of decimal system.

History's early focus on applied mathematics is a viewpoint we would do well to remember today. A few hundred years ago a university student was considered educated if he could use his fingers to do simple operations of

Many mathematics researchers believe that the best way to teach the meaning of mathematical symbols is to first introduce students to meaningful story problems and then to show them how to substitute symbols for important characters or items within the problem.

arithmetic (Baroody, 1987); now we expect the same of an elementary school child. The amount of mathematical knowledge expected of children today has become so extensive and complex that it is easy to forget that solving real-life problems is the ultimate goal of mathematical learning. The first graders in Suzanne Colvin's classes demonstrated the effectiveness of tying instruction to meaningful situations.

You will recall that more than 300 years ago, Comenius pointed out that young children might be taught to count but that it takes longer for them to understand what the numbers mean. Today, classroom research such as Suzanne Colvin's demonstrates that young children need to be given meaningful situations first and then numbers that represent various components and relationships within the situations.

The influences of John Locke and Jean Jacques Rousseau are felt today as well. Locke shared a popular view of the time that the world was a fixed, mechanical system with a body of knowledge for all to learn. When he applied this view to education, Locke described the teaching and learning process as writing this world of knowledge on the blank-slate mind of the child. In this century, Locke's view continues to be a popular one. It is especially popular in mathematics, where it can be more easily argued that, at least at the early levels, there is a body of knowledge for children to learn.

B. F. Skinner, who applied this view to a philosophy of behaviorism, referred to mathematics as "one of the drill subjects." While Locke recommended entertaining games to teach arithmetic facts, Skinner developed teaching machines and accompanying drills, precursors to today's computerized math drills. One critic of this approach to mathematics learning has said that, while it may be useful for memorizing numbers such as those in a telephone listing, it has

> failed to provide a powerful explanation of more complex forms of learning and thinking, such as memorizing meaningful information or problem solving. This approach has, in particular, been unable to provide a sound description of the complexities involved in school learning, like the meaningful learning of the basic combinations or solving word problems. (Baroody, 1987, p. 13)

Rousseau's views of how children learn were quite different, reflecting his preference for natural learning in a supportive environment. During the late eighteenth century as today, this view argues for real-life, informal mathematics learning. While this approach is more closely aligned to current thinking about the way children learn than is the Locke/Skinner approach, it can have the undesired effect of giving children so little guidance that they learn almost nothing at all.

The view that seems most suitable for young children at this point in our history is that inspired by cognitive theorists, primary among them Jean Piaget. Three types of knowledge were identified by Piaget (Kamii and Joseph, 1989), all of which are needed for understanding mathematics. The first is physical, or empirical, knowledge, which means being able to relate to the physical world. For example, before a child can count marbles by dropping them into a jar, she needs to know how to hold a marble and how it will fall downward when dropped.

The second type of knowledge is logico-mathematical, and concerns relationships as created by the child. Perhaps a young child holds a large red marble in one hand and a small blue marble in the other. If she simply feels their weight and sees their colors, her knowledge is physical (or empirical). But if she notes the differences and similarities between the two, she has mentally created relationships.

The third type of knowledge is social knowledge, which is arbitrary and designed by people. For example, naming numbers *one, two,* and *three* is social knowledge because, in another society, the numbers might be *ichi, ni, san* or *uno, dos, tres.* (Keep in mind, however, that the real understanding of what these numbers mean belongs to logico-mathematical knowledge.)

Constance Kamii (Kamii and DeClark, 1985), a Piagetian researcher, has spent many years studying the mathematical learning of young children. After analyzing teaching techniques, the views of math educators, and American math textbooks, she has concluded that our educational system often confuses these three kinds of knowledge. Educators tend to provide children with plenty of manipulatives, assuming that they will internalize mathematical understanding simply from this physical experience. Or educators ignore the manipulatives and focus instead on pencil-and-paper activities aimed at teaching the names of numbers and various mathematical terms, assuming that this social knowledge will be internalized as real math learning. Something is missing from both approaches, says Kamii:

> Traditionally, mathematics educators have not made the distinction among the three kinds of knowledge and believe that arithmetic must be internalized from objects (as if it were physical knowledge) and people (as if it were social knowledge). They overlook the most important part of arithmetic, which is logico-mathematical knowledge. (p. 13)

In the Piagetian tradition, Kamii argues that "children should reinvent arithmetic." Only by constructing their own knowledge can children really understand mathematical concepts. When they permit children to learn in this fashion, adults may find that they are introducing some concepts too early while putting others off too long. Kamii's research has led her to conclude, as Suzanne Colvin did, that first graders find subtraction too difficult. Kamii argues for saving it until later, when it can be learned quickly and easily. She also points to studies in which place value is mastered by about 50 percent of fourth graders and 23 percent of a group of second graders. Yet place value and regrouping are regularly expected of second graders!

As an example of what children can do earlier than expected, Kamii

(1985) points to their discovery (or reinvention) of negative numbers, a concept that doesn't even appear in elementary math textbooks. Based on her experiences with young children, Kamii argues that it is important to let children think for themselves and invent their own mathematical systems. With Piaget, she believes that children will understand much more, developing a better cognitive foundation as well as self-confidence:

> Children who are confident will learn more in the long run than those who have been taught in ways that make them distrust their own thinking. . . . Children who are excited about explaining their own ideas will go much farther in the long run than those who can only follow somebody else's rules and respond to unfamiliar problems by saying, "I don't know how to do it because I haven't learned it in school yet." (p. 14)

## NCTM Standards and NAEYC Position

In recent years, the National Council of Teachers of Mathematics (NCTM) has given much consideration to the international failure of American children in mathematics, and has devised a set of standards that echo, in many ways, the Piagetian perspective of Kamii. The *Curriculum and Evaluation Standards for School Mathematics* (1989) prepared by the NCTM addresses the education of children from kindergarten up. Some of the more important standards are:

- *Children will be actively involved in doing mathematics.* NCTM sees young children constructing their own learning by interacting with materials, other children, and their teachers. Discussion and writing help make new ideas clear. Language is at first informal, the children's own, and gradually takes on the vocabulary of more formal mathematics.
- *The curriculum will emphasize a broad range of content.* Children's learning should not be confined to arithmetic, but should include other fields of mathematics such as geometry, measurement, statistics, probability, and algebra. Study in all these fields presents a more realistic view of the world in which they live and provides a foundation for more advanced study in each area. All these content areas should appear frequently and throughout the entire curriculum.
- *The curriculum will emphasize mathematics concepts.* Emphasis on concepts rather than on skills leads to deeper understanding. Learning activities should build on the intuitive, informal knowledge that children bring to the classroom.
- *Problem solving and problem-solving approaches to instruction will permeate the curriculum.* When children have plenty of problem-solving experiences, particularly concerning situations from their own worlds, mathematics becomes more meaningful to them. They should be given opportunities to solve

problems in different ways, create problems related to data they have collected, and make generalizations from basic information. Problem-solving experiences should lead to more self-confidence for children.

■ *The curriculum will emphasize a broad approach to computation.* Children will be permitted to use their own strategies when computing, not just those offered by adults. They should have opportunities to make informal judgments about their answers, leading to their own constructed understanding of what is reasonable. Calculators should be permitted as tools of exploration. It may be that children will compute by using thinking strategies, estimation, and calculators before they are presented with pencils and paper. (Adapted from Trafton and Bloom, 1990)

The National Association for the Education of Young Children, in its position statement regarding *Developmentally Appropriate Practices* (Bredecamp, 1987), arrives at views of teaching mathematics to young children that reflect those of Constance Kamii and the NCTM. Their position regarding infants, toddlers, and preschoolers is that mathematics should be part of the day's natural activities: counting children in the class or crackers for snacks, for example. For the primary grades they are more specific, identifying what is appropriate and inappropriate practice. Table 13.1 summarizes their guidelines.

The NCTM Standards, the NAEYC position statement, and studies with young children carried out by such researchers as Constance Kamii and Suzanne Colvin bring us to today's best analysis of how children learn mathe-

**Table 13.1**
**APPROPRIATE MATHEMATICS IN THE PRIMARY GRADES (THE NAEYC POSITION)**

| APPROPRIATE PRACTICE | INAPPROPRIATE PRACTICE |
| --- | --- |
| *Learning is through exploration, discovery, and solving meaningful problems. | *Learning is by textbook, workbooks, practice sheets, and board work. |
| *Math activities are integrated with other subjects such as science and social studies. | *Math is taught as a separate subject at a scheduled time each day. |
| *Math skills are acquired through play, projects, and daily living. | *Timed tests on number facts are given and graded daily. |
| *The teacher's edition of the text is used as a guide to structure learning situations and stimulate ideas for projects. | *Teachers move sequentially through the lessons as outlined in the teacher's edition of the text. |
| *Many manipulatives are used including board, card, and paper-and-pencil games. | *Only children who finish their math seatwork are permitted to use the few available manipulatives and games. |
| *Noncompetitive, impromptu oral "math stumper" and number games are played for practice. | *Competition between children is used to motivate children to learn math facts. |

matics. The conclusion these researchers and theorists have reached are based not only on their work with children, but on their understanding of child development. A brief review of each area of development and its relationship to mathematical learning should demonstrate the importance of such understanding for you as a teacher.

## Making Connections: Perspectives on Development

In this chapter as in the previous one, the connections in this section are made with Chapters 3, 4, and 5, which dealt with the various aspects of early development. We begin with cognitive development.

### Cognitive Development and Mathematics

In Piaget's theory of development, children in the sensorimotor and preoperational periods are intellectually tied to empirical evidence. Before they are seven or eight years old, they make sense of their world by their response to the physical environment around them. And, since they generally center their attention on one thing at a time, comparisons between objects or ideas are difficult for them. Even when they have entered elementary school, children need concrete objects to help them make connections and decenter their attention. Therefore, even though we warned against depending solely on the manipulation of objects as a means to mathematical understanding, those objects remain an important part of children's move toward logico-mathematical understanding. Several areas of learning are affected by these developmental phenomena.

As an example, children have trouble conserving objects or number until their thinking approaches the concrete operational stage. Before that time, they focus their attention on a single, interesting attribute such as the shininess of some pennies over others, the beautiful red shade belonging to the wooden geometric shapes they work with, or the amount of space the pennies or shapes take up. Piaget referred to such abstraction of physical properties as empirical, or simple, abstraction. Preoperational children cannot take the next step of reflective abstraction, which requires making a mental relationship between or among the objects. This mental, reflective step is necessary for learning number concepts. The lack of it explains why preoperational children cannot understand that, by spreading out a row of ten pennies to fill a bigger space, the amount remains the same. Without the capability of reflective abstraction children cannot operate on numbers unless they are related to physical objects right in front of them. Since children throughout the primary grades are moving into, but not necessarily safely harbored in, concrete operations, mathematics teaching should take this into account.

Current research in mathematics education emphasizes the use of exploration, discovery, and manipulative materials to help solve meaningful problems.

Placing objects in a series according to size is difficult for children who focus on one thing at a time. You can ask preoperational children to choose the smallest and largest objects in a series. If they do this first, they can then place some of the remaining objects in order, but don't expect perfection until concrete operations have been reached. Seriation activities and materials provide an interesting challenge to children at the mature end of the preoperational stage, then suddenly become boring once they have achieved a mathematical understanding of seriation. At that point, you might try giving the children several sets of seriation materials to coordinate into complex patterns.

Preoperational children also have difficulty with the order of numbers. You have, no doubt, heard a small child rote count, "One, two, three, seven, six, ten." If the child is given a group of objects and can count them fairly well, it may appear that he also understands ordering and counting fairly well. But if you interview the child carefully, you may find that he believes that the numbers he recites are actually names for the objects and might just as well be Sam, Joe, and Stephanie. Thus, even with the assistance of manipulative materials, the child has not yet learned the mathematical meaning of the numbers but can only focus on their socially determined names. This does not mean you should avoid giving preoperational children objects to count, but it does mean that you cannot force the mathematical understanding on them. The children will construct their learning on their own schedule.

The same is true of classification. Since young children focus on one attribute at a time, it will be awhile before they can classify objects in more complex ways. Geometric wooden shapes, for example, are popular classification materials which preoperational children enjoy grouping by a single attribute, such as color or size or shape. While teachers can encourage them to think of making more complex relationships, understanding of such groupings as small green circles or large blue triangles is gained as the children construct their own meaning.

Clock time is usually a topic in early elementary mathematics texts, yet most children have just recently acquired the adult concept of what time is about. Many children are about nine years old before they can solve time problems on a logical, rather than trial-and-error, basis. Throughout the primary grades, some children believe that when they move quickly the clock does the same. Much time may be spent in frustrating workbook exercises that have little real meaning to the children. Here is another case in which children may memorize the socially defined numbers but not have a good understanding of their meaning. During the primary years it is best to use the clock in informal ways that relate to the life of the classroom. Children might make their own paper plate clocks with hands made from tagboard and fastened with a brass paper fastener. They can then compare times to the classroom clock, set them ahead for upcoming events, or just explore informally.

## Social and Affective Development and Mathematics

Mathematics is one curricular area where social learning theory can be applied to good effect. According to this theory, children learn behaviors and attitudes (both positive and negative) as they are modeled by adults. Since many children learn to dislike or fear mathematics at a fairly young age, it may be that teachers need to change their own attitudes toward this subject and convey more enthusiasm to the children. Just as you set an example of enthusiasm for literature, you can find ways to show your own interest in mathematical experiences. Let children see you use a yardstick to measure a new bulletin board and talk about it aloud. Pace off game areas on the playground, counting your steps so that children can hear you. Have children help you count the milk money (and act as if you enjoy it). When you introduce new mathematics topics or discuss problems, do it with confidence and enthusiasm, just as you do for an interesting new story. Make mathematical exploration an exciting adventure for children by being excited yourself.

Social interaction with the teacher is also important to constructivist theory, but the focus is somewhat different than in the social learning theory. In constructivist theory, people are not considered the source of feedback for the development of logico-mathematical knowledge; the child's internal thought processes account for this. Instead, the teacher's role is to cast doubt in children's minds about the adequacy of what they are thinking, or to help them consider, on their own, alternative ways of coming to desired answers. The teacher should remember that, for young children, the exact answer is rarely as important as the thinking process that produces a reasonable answer. In the constructivist view, the teacher needs to interact with the children, but development takes place when there is less direct teaching and more encouragement.

According to constructivist theory, social interaction with peers is also important to mathematical development. Conversely, social competence is aided by cognitive development, thus making peer interaction doubly effective. Egocentric young children feel no need to make sense when they talk to others. As they have social interactions, however, they begin to realize how necessary it is to engage in coherent communication, to avoid contradicting oneself, to reason logically, to make true statements, and to use words that will be understood by others. "The desire to 'make sense' and to exchange points of view with other people undergirds the child's growing ability to think logically" (Kamii and DeClark, 1985, p. 26).

Further, having the opportunity to engage in peer dialogue has been shown to be effective in improving children's mathematical understanding. In one experiment (Kamii and DeClark, 1985), groups of three children were given juice and different shaped drinking glasses, then assigned the task of dividing the juice into equal quantities. With one child serving as pourer, all three of them debated the equality of amount between a glass that was short and wide and one that was tall and narrow. A replica of the first glass was offhandedly given to the children to use "if needed" after they had started their attempt at equality. This experiment is a version of a Piagetian conservation task, which tests children's ability to determine equality of liquid between differently shaped containers. In this study there was, in addition to several groups of three, an equal number of children who served as a control group and did not have the juice-pouring experience just described. When given a posttest, the children who had the juice-pouring experience had made significantly greater progress in being able to conserve liquid than did the children in the control group. There was carryover progress as well: the children who had the juice-pouring experience also improved significantly in other types of conservation tasks. This and other studies appear to demonstrate the benefits that come from providing children with opportunities to discuss and debate mathematical problems rather than assigning quiet, independent seatwork.

## Physical Development and Mathematics

Infants and toddlers attain most of their cognitive learning through physically active experiences. While quite a bit has been learned about very early language acquisition, mathematical studies such as the infant "counting" experiment described at the beginning of this chapter are only beginning. Nevertheless, it may be assumed that, to begin learning mathematical concepts, some activity is essential.

While physical development is not as closely tied to cognitive development as children get older, it still is of importance. For example, children become able to grasp a pencil at about eighteen months, but may continue experimenting with various grips until first grade. Since the adult three-fingered method of gripping isn't established for all children until about age seven, demanding that younger children engage in pencil-and-paper math activities is inappropriate for physical as well as cognitive and social reasons. Since boys are more likely to develop their small motor functions later than girls, they are at a special disadvantage when pencil-and-paper learning begins early. Yet it is entirely possible that you will see classes of four-year-olds seated at tables, or even desks, struggling over math worksheets. Children this young not only have trouble grasping the pencil effectively, but also need to move more often and more extensively than is possible when engaged in worksheet learning. While one answer to the problem might be to give the children frequent recesses, this solution does not address the inappropriateness of doing such activities in the first place.

In addition to making mathematics learning a natural part of the day, it is also possible to create activities that permit children to be physically active. Some of the teaching suggestions at the end of this chapter are designed with this goal in mind.

## Making Connections: Diversity Among Children

When you approach the teaching of mathematics in an informal way, taking advantage of natural experiences, you have gone one important step toward providing each child with individually appropriate learning. Giving children the opportunity to reinvent mathematics on their own at their own pace is a second important step. A third step is to observe children with care. When you do this, you may find that an occasional child rejects the manipulatives, having somehow intuited that it's more mature to work answers out mentally. This same child is likely to be one who will become deeply involved in complex projects, perhaps losing sense of time or refusing to join the rest of the class in other activities until satisfied that his or her work is done. Interests for this child may also be ahead of the rest of the class.

If your curriculum and attitude toward teaching are both flexible, you will be able to let this child learn at his or her own pace, just as you will be able to provide appropriate learning activities for the children who can't seem to keep up with the others. In a classroom where children develop at their own pace, it is possible that the other children will not be aware of the few who are having difficulties. Once you are aware of their developmental level, you can provide materials and activities that meet their needs.

Of special interest in mathematics is the long-standing difference in performance between boys and girls. There is still some debate as to whether boys are genetically more capable of some mathematical understandings, such as spatial relationships, than are girls. Whether or not this proves to be the case, one continual problem for the girls has been that they are not *expected* to do well and teachers often make excuses for them, permitting them to escape permanently to the library corner. One approach that Piaget (1975) usually found to be successful was to delay the use of numerical symbols until there had been considerable experience with stories and manipulatives—the same approach as that taken in Suzanne Colvin's third class. Using this

Although there is some debate as to whether boys' competitive edge over girls' in mathematics has any genetic basis, it has been repeatedly shown that teachers contribute to the poor mathematical performance of girls by projecting a lower set of mathematical expectations for them.

approach, Piaget found that most of the reluctant girls eventually came to enjoy mathematics.

---

## Mathematics Concepts

Children begin their mathematical learning as infants. Babies in their cribs observe the space between the bars and, making an intuitive measurement, grab them accurately enough to pull themselves up. Playing with balls, they come to understand the shape of a sphere and what happens to it when it is pushed. As they shove a clothespin in a plastic bottle, or a geometric solid into the similarly shaped hole of a plastic ball, they intuit information about measurement. In early classification experiences they learn to differentiate clothing from food or toys. And, if Karen Wynn's (Associated Press, 1992) infant experiments are right, infants even intuit addition and subtraction concepts.

Through their daily experiences, toddlers, preschoolers, and primary children also learn mathematics concepts in a natural way. When two-year-old Matt demanded, "Where's de udder one?" he demonstrated intuitive counting and understanding of spatial relationships. When children share cookies or other snacks, they engage in division, even to the point of puzzling over what to do with the remainder when the sharing comes out uneven. If they decide to solve the problem by breaking up the cookies, they gain experience in fractional division. Real-life experiences such as these are essentially "story problems" in which some understanding of number is used to solve a problem situation.

Because daily life presents so many opportunities to learn mathematics in a natural way, and because such learning provides young children with the most meaningful and easily remembered mathematical understanding, teachers need to consider such possibilities as they create their curriculum. Mathematical learning for young children is much more than the traditional counting and arithmetic skills; it includes a variety of mathematical concepts.

## Classification

Classification is the placing of objects or ideas into groups that are alike in some way. Teachers classify all day long as they put tired children down for naps and read stories to those who are awake, send the boys to one bathroom and the girls to another, give children a turn on the trikes who didn't have one yesterday and send everyone else to play on other equipment, select books for the library corner based on a particular theme and put the rest on an out-of-the-way shelf, spoon the applesauce into small cups and pour juice into larger ones, and send home the children whose parents have arrived and keep the others in the classroom. This list could almost be endless, yet, for the adult, such classification is so much a part of ordinary life that little or no conscious effort is involved.

For young children, classification cannot be taken for granted. Rather, they must develop their understanding of grouping according to like attributes. Their first attempts have little logic to them. A child might pull a red block from a group, *then* decide to put all the red blocks together . . . at least until he notices the stripe down the side of one block and then begins seeking other blocks with stripes. Sometimes, the child groups objects together for reasons that are not apparent to the adult observer, perhaps offering explanations of the decision that seem nonsensical. As children grow in their understanding of classification, they are able to group objects according to a single property, such as color, shape, or size. Still later, two or more properties can be coordinated, and ideas as well as objects can consciously be grouped.

Teachers can provide numerous opportunities for children to learn classification skills. What is important is that the materials and activities relate to the developmental levels of the children.

*Preschool* children are still learning who they belong to and what belongs to them; what things are theirs and what things belong to others; where some objects belong and how they are used. Thus, belonging is an appropriate concept for learning to classify objects and to understand their relationships (Read and Patterson, 1980). Informal conversations can include such teacher comments as "This is a book; it belongs inside," "This is Janey's stuffed dog; it belongs to her," and "The mop and the broom belong in the housekeeping corner."

Preschool children also benefit from experiences that focus on likenesses and differences. Interesting objects should always be available to sort. Variety should be provided based on children's changing interests or themes of study. If you have children who still explore objects by putting them in their mouths, be sure that the objects you choose are large enough to be safe and give extra attention to cleanliness. One popular source of objects is the natural environment surrounding the school or in a nearby park. Sticks, small rocks, and leaves can be brought into the classroom to be separated from each other. Then each of these groups can be regrouped according to the children's own definitions of sameness and difference. Big sticks might be separated from small ones and yellow leaves from green ones. Other ideas for sorting materials include:

- squares of various types of fabric, all the same size
- buttons of different sizes and colors
- pairs of shoes to be matched or separated by color
- postcards with pictures that have some obvious similarities
- holiday greeting cards that have some obvious similarities
- *large* nuts, bolts, and screws
- seashells

*Kindergarten* children and some four-year-olds need time for informal sorting experiences, but are also ready for teacher questions and larger challenges. For example, a child sorting buttons might be asked, "Are all the gold buttons alike? Can you find a way to separate them again?" Try to let the children discover that some of the buttons have two holes and some have four rather than simply telling them to put one group in one pile and the second group in another.

*Primary* children continue to need experiences in classification. Commercial attribute blocks (plastic geometric pieces in varying sizes, thicknesses, and colors) provide numerous ways of grouping. In addition to physical attributes, numbers of objects within a set can be used to classify. A large jump rope can be placed around a group of children and the rest of the class challenged to create sets of equal size. Or children can work in pairs to challenge each other to create equal sets from boxes of materials such as buttons and small blocks.

## Ordering (Seriation)

Sequencing objects from first to last is known as ordering or seriation. Going from first to last may involve increased height, darkening shades of a single color, increased width, and so on. In your daily life you probably arrange bills in your wallet in order of their value and arrange drinking glasses in the cupboard according to size, activities that provide order to your life but little intellectual challenge. For young children, understanding seriation takes until the first, second, or even third grade to accomplish. Counting numbers can be considered as seriation, but only when the child has a true understanding of what the numbers mean. Before that, counting is simply a rote activity.

*Preschool* children begin learning to order objects by doing simple comparisons. The teacher can observe children putting dolls away and ask which one is largest and which is smallest. Then, moving to other children putting blocks away, the teacher might ask which is heaviest and lightest or which is longest and shortest. There are also commercial materials made specifically for classification. One Montessori material, which is also manufactured in varying forms by different companies, is a long wooden block with a row of varying sized holes in its top. Into this fit cylinders (with knobs for handling) of increasing size. Preschool children engage in such fitting activities most easily if they fill the smallest and the largest holes first. From there, they typically find the proper holes by trial and error. The same is true if they try to order the cylinders correctly outside the wooden block. Although preschoolers can eventually get the cylinders in the right order, their trial-and-error method indicates that their sense of seriation is still in the beginning stage and does not yet include the ability to use logic rather than physical observation to achieve their goal.

*Kindergarten* children continue to enjoy seriation activities and some will begin to do so in a more logical way than trial and error. Many of the materials that are used for classification can be used for seriation as well. Shells or buttons, for example, can usually be ordered according to size and, with some teacher preparation, a few can be ordered according to color variations. Abstract concepts that do not involve matching objects can be introduced, although children may not fully understand them. Examples include *before* and *after; yesterday, today,* and *tomorrow;* and the smaller ordinal numbers *first, second, third . . . tenth.*

*Primary* children can increase their ability to use ordinal numbers, particularly if teachers build practice into the normal flow of the day. When materials are passed out, they might simply be counted (cardinal numbers) one day, but identified according to their order (ordinal numbers) the next. Similarly, as children stand in line they can count off in cardinal numbers one time and ordinal numbers another. The primary child's understanding of seriation is such that he or she can arrange eight or more objects in ascending or descending order without resorting to trial and error. The child also understands that, in a line of people arranged according to height, the second person is taller than the first, and the third is taller than both the second and the first (Read and Patterson, 1980).

## Counting

When adults or older children count, it is generally for the purpose of identifying how many objects or ideas are in a group or groups. For each number named there is a single object or idea to match it. Counting with such one-to-one correspondence is known as rational counting. For very young children, consistent matching of object or idea to number name is not yet possible. While they may be able to count, whether it is just a few numbers or many, this skill is a memorized one known as rote counting. A child who counts by rote does not automatically associate objects or ideas with the numbers.

*Preschool* children should have counting experiences, although they will be confined to rote learning. Songs, chants, and rhymes with numbers in them such as "Ten Little Indians," "Five Little Monkeys," "When I Was the Age of One," and "This Old Man" teach children the number names and give them beginning experiences in matching numbers to objects. In the everyday life of the classroom, there are numerous opportunities for counting: the number of children present, the number of children at a table, the number of crackers for each child and the total number for each table, the number of dolls in a baby carriage or blocks in a pile. Preschool children will not usually engage in such counting activities on their own, so the teacher must be alert to opportunities and exploit them.

Some *kindergarten* children, particularly toward the end of the year, may be on the brink of rational counting. Consequently, plenty of counting experiences are in order. As they learn to read numbers, it is a good idea to plan activities that match the numbers to objects. This may be done with either commercial or homemade materials. For example, using two sets of large, unlined index cards, you can write or glue large numbers on one set and then have children match them with the second set which pictures groups of objects. Laminate all the cards for longer life. The groups on the picture cards can be of two types: (1) groups in which all the members are the same object, size, and color and (2) groups in which members have less relationship to each other. The second type might picture several children of varying appearance or a cluster of different toys or even objects that have no relationship to each other at all. This second type of grouping forces the children to start classifying groups based solely on their numbers rather than on physical attributes.

*Primary* children feel comfortable counting. Consequently, when they begin learning to add and subtract they tend to use counting techniques. Teachers need to remember, however, that a concrete operational child still needs concrete objects to understand counting or any other skill. Keeping this in mind, teachers should provide primary children with plenty of informal counting experiences related to objects and events in the school day. Oral games can be played that help the children realize that each succeeding number represents one more than the preceding number. For example, you might count to 25 with a group of children, stopping now and then to say something like, "We just got to 12. What number came before it? Is 12 more or less than 11? What number comes after 12? Is it more or less than 12?"

## Addition and Subtraction

As Suzanne Colvin (1987) learned in her study of first graders, children find addition easier to understand than subtraction. In Suzanne's classes, both processes were introduced at the same time after pretests had shown that both processes would be new to all the children. Both were introduced with the same amount of care, using the same methodology, and an equal amount of time was spent studying each. Perhaps one reason that addition is easier is that it more closely resembles the positive direction in which children normally count. While addition and subtraction are formally introduced in the primary grades, informal preparation using everyday events can begin well before then.

*Preschool* and *kindergarten* children can be given opportunities to join sets and count the objects in the newly created set. However, there should be no pressure to memorize the problems or answers (Maffei and Buckley, 1980). The same materials that are used for classification—commercially purchased items or objects picked up on nature walks—can be adapted for making and joining sets. Or children may be ready to start with just one set and count on

Rational counting, that is, matching numbers to physical objects usually begins toward the end of kindergarten and continues into the primary years with greater and greater efficiency.

from there to tell how many more they need to reach a specific number. One game (Maffei and Buckley, 1980, p. 147) suggests giving children a few fish crackers, which they then place on a blue sheet of paper (ocean). You will have chosen a total number, 5, for example, that will be the same for all the children. The number of fish you first give to each child can be fewer than or equal to this total. Ask each child to tell you how many more fish will be needed to make five, then give the child that many even if the answer is wrong. Brief questioning can focus on how the child came to ask for that number. The child then should count the total and discover, with little assistance from you, any need to recount. Once five fish are in each child's ocean, suggest various movements and ask questions that promote further thinking: "One fish swims on the top of the ocean while the others swim at the bottom. How many are swimming at the bottom? Send a fish to the top to keep the first one company. Now how many are at the top? All the fish except one swim to the bottom and a monster fish [the child] comes along and gobbles it up. Now how many are left?" Continue in this vein until all the fish are eaten.

Since *primary* children have more difficulty with subtraction, some theorists and researchers argue that it should not be introduced in the first grade. Instead, children should first feel comfortable with addition, taking time to understand it rather than being pushed into memorizing tables of sums (Kamii and DeClark, 1985). Primary children should be permitted to use manipulative materials in ways that are meaningful to them rather than being pushed into pencil-and-paper exercises or teacher-directed, manipulative activities.

One phase that young children go through is called "counting all." They are first given six objects to count and then five objects to add on. Their approach is to start their count all over again with the very first object and count all the way through to the eleventh object. While many educators try to "cure" children of this time-intensive practice, others argue that this is just one example of the way children develop their logico-mathematical understanding, and they should be allowed to outgrow the practice on their own. Defending this second view, Constance Kamii (Kamii and DeClark, 1985) argues,

> If children are left alone to add numbers on their own, they *will* figure out a way that is appropriate for them. If they do not figure out a way, this means that addition is too hard for them and ought not to be imposed on them. If they count-all, most first graders will sooner or later give this up, just as toddlers give up crawling when they become able to walk. (p. 69)

For many primary teachers, the challenge is to make sure that their children are given time and opportunity to really understand addition and subtraction as opposed to meeting an imposed set of deadlines for memorization of facts or place value procedures. One way to achieve this goal, even in the most rigidly prescribed situations, is to avoid numerous practice sheets and multitudes of problems. The Japanese approach with young children, which has earned them the world's highest math scores, is to focus on one or two problems during a single learning session. Children are encouraged to think of as many ways as possible to solve a problem and to share those ways with each other and with the teacher. Such intensive problem solving and social interaction have proven far superior to the usual American practice of assigning large numbers of algorithmic practice problems in which children try hard to reach teacher-approved answers.

Children in the primary grades are interested in, and should be permitted, much interaction with their peers. Thus, they should be given more group games and fewer independent worksheets. Games played with dice or cards can be invented or purchased. (Good sources of ideas are three books by Constance Kamii and her teacher-associates: *Group Games in Early Education, Young Children Reinvent Arithmetic,* and *Young Children Still Reinvent Arithmetic.*) Various tossing games using available classroom materials provide experience in addition. For example, you might use a wastebasket and playground ball and count one or two points for every basket. Or an infant's ring-toss game can be adapted for a similar score-keeping game.

## Measuring

Measurement deals with the extent, dimensions, or capacity of things. Most measurements in the adult world take place according to standardized units such as feet and yards, centimeters and meters, and pints and quarts. Before children can participate in and understand standardized measurements, they must be able to conserve in the Piagetian sense. If nonconserving children are shown two strips of paper of equal length, they may easily use their observational ability to state that the strips are, indeed, equal—but only if they are laid side by side. If one of the strips is moved laterally, they may then argue that it has become longer than the other one. Similarly, if presented with a short, wide pitcher of water they will believe its quantity increases when poured into a tall, narrow pitcher. Children who cannot mentally conserve size or amount from one position to the next are not ready to use standard measurements, which are based on logic.

*Preschool* and *kindergarten* children, however, can engage in nonstandard measurement activities. Further, it is appropriate to have yardsticks, plastic quart jugs, measuring cups, and measuring spoons present in the classroom where they can be used in many ways and identified by their proper names. Some informal measurement activities might include:

- Using the entire length of a yardstick or broom handle to measure a wall, to compare lengths of different sections of the room, or to decide on the size of a garden.
- Using a measuring (or other) cup to see how many times it must be filled with water or sand to completely fill a quart, liter, or gallon jug.
- Using balance scales to compare the weights of rocks and sticks, buttons and magnets, or anything else of a small size. Determining how many of one item equal the weight of another provides additional practice in counting.
- Using long strips of paper to measure children's height. Write the name of the child on each one and lay it out next to the others on a line. Taking just a few at a time, they can be ordered according to height. Toward the end of kindergarten, a large class project can be to seriate the entire class using these strips.

*Primary* children are ready for more formal measurement, using standard rulers, weights, and containers. These should be introduced in simplified form, and such materials are readily available as part of classroom equipment. At the same time, nonstandard measuring activities should not be totally abandoned and can be relied on for approximations and for times when the informal approach may provide a better feel for and understanding of an object.

## Geometry

Geometry is the study of shapes, both flat and three dimensional, and their relationships in space. Geometry enters infants' lives from birth as they attempt to make sense of the shapes in their environment: crib bars, stuffed animals, mother's breast and face, the door to the bedroom. Geometric shapes become some of the first intentional scribbles made in young children's drawings, and they delight in their awareness of the shapes around them.

Such natural interest deserves encouragement and informal teaching intervention. In the 1950s, two Dutch educators developed a theory of stage development in geometric understanding. The van Hiele theory has gained acceptance in the United States in recent years, and applies to children from the early years through high school. An important tenet of the theory is that children do not grow through the stages automatically but, with teacher assistance, will do so competently (Teppo, 1991). What children are exposed to in the early years sets the stage for learning in geometry throughout their entire school experience. Through the primary grades, children are at the earliest, visual, stage in which they explore their environment to learn to identify the shapes within it. Activities such as describing, modeling, drawing, and classifying help them develop a spatial sense.

*Preschool* and *kindergarten* children can learn much from playing with blocks (Jensen and O'Neil, 1982). They can

- compare and seriate shapes. Start with single shapes and have children compare two pieces according to size. Later, more pieces can be added until several items of one shape can be seriated.
- classify and name shapes. Provide two shapes at first then, after much practice, add a third and fourth. Make large loops of yarn on the floor or provide boxes to place the blocks in. A good game to play for naming is Pass the Block. Children sit in a circle and, as music plays, they pass blocks in one direction. When the music stops, each child names the shape he or she holds.
- trace and feel shapes. Children trace around a block with pencil, then color it in if desired. With a little practice, they can superimpose different shapes on one paper, coloring in some of the sections. Blocks can also be used as items in a "mystery bag." Two or three familiar shapes are placed in a bag and children take turns reaching in, feeling a block, and identifying its shape.

Plane figures can be explored through active interaction. Colored tape is laid on the floor in geometric shapes large enough for children to walk on. Ask the children to jump, walk, crawl, and so on across specific shapes. They might count the number of children who can fit in one triangle or the number of steps it takes to walk the perimeter of a square.

*Kindergarten* and *primary* children continue to learn best from working with manipulatives and may find the illustrations in math textbooks confusing. Some materials that are appropriate are tiles, pattern blocks, attribute blocks, geoblocks, geometric solids, colored cubes, and tangrams. Computer games in which geometric shapes appear from different angles help children overcome their misunderstandings of book illustrations, which may show a shape from only one or two viewpoints. Some appropriate activities are

- building structures with various types of blocks to enhance spatial visualization.
- folding and cutting activities such as origami or snowflake making.
- exploring the indoor and outdoor environments to identify shapes and angles made by people and nature.
- reading maps.
- making graphs.
- playing Tic-Tac-Toe, Battleship, and other games that use grid systems.

All day long there are opportunities for children to increase their awareness of mathematics in the world around them. Mathematical phenomena may not always be as obvious as those of language, however. Thus, the teacher must take extra care to include mathematical learning whenever natural learning situations arise. Often this means recognizing opportunities to incorporate mathematics into other areas of the curriculum. The final section of this chapter provides suggestions for doing this.

## Focus for Mathematics: Curriculum Integration

Whether your usual curriculum is integrated or separated according to subject disciplines, it is possible to incorporate mathematics learning in many ways. The ideas that follow should be considered springboards to others of your own. Try adapting them to different classroom situations and curricular topics. The activities are divided according to subject disciplines and, within each section, from the simplest to the most difficult. Of course, you should consider the needs of individual children when determining the appropriateness of each activity.

As a beginning organizer, a curriculum web as shown in Figure 13.1 can be drawn.

## Math Activities for Curriculum Integration

### Language

**1. Shelving Books.** Two-year-olds are especially fond of making everything straight, and just as fond of making everything a mess. Three-year-olds love to dust and scrub, and sometimes like to make everything straight. Let preschoolers help you keep the library corner clean and straight and they will gain the added benefit of self-confidence, knowing you respect them enough to tackle an adult project.

Turn the activity into a math experience by putting all the *tall* or *large* or *big* books on one shelf and all the *short* or *small* or *little* books on another.

FIGURE 13.1
**A Planning Web for Mathematics Activities**

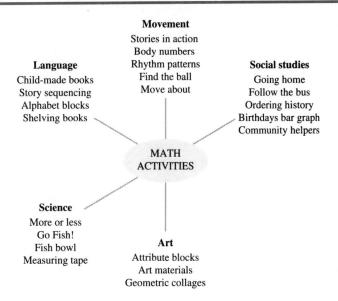

**Movement**
Stories in action
Body numbers
Rhythm patterns
Find the ball
Move about

**Language**
Child-made books
Story sequencing
Alphabet blocks
Shelving books

**Social studies**
Going home
Follow the bus
Ordering history
Birthdays bar graph
Community helpers

MATH
ACTIVITIES

**Science**
More or less
Go Fish!
Fish bowl
Measuring tape

**Art**
Attribute blocks
Art materials
Geometric collages

(Choose which vocabulary they will learn. If they know some of the words, introduce the others.) First, scrub, rinse, and dry each shelf. Then dust each book carefully and individually, repeatedly using the vocabulary of comparison.

**2. Alphabet Blocks.** This will work best outdoors or in an open space. Draw a line that children can stand behind. Each child takes a turn throwing an alphabet block over the line. The letter that turns up on top of the block is matched to other blocks that have turned up similarly before it. If it is the first time the letter has appeared, a new set is started. You should identify the letters' names, but children should not be required to memorize them.

While this is essentially a language activity, it requires classification, a math-related skill. Counting can be added to the activity at the end of the game as the children count how many blocks there are of each letter.

**3. Story Sequencing.** Commercial flannel board figures are available for well-known stories. They can also be handmade. Typically, there is one figure for each of the main characters and perhaps some props that move the plot along. If the collection does not include props, they will need to be made for this activity.

As you read or tell the story, characters are placed (by you or children) in an appropriate arrangement for each stage of the story. Vocabulary should focus on what happened *first, second, third,* and so on. Later, children can do the

## Mathematics as Elephant: A Conversation with Kathy Richardson

*Children in the United States continue to perform behind their counterparts in other countries on mathematics tests. Yet, there are many dedicated teachers who expend much effort in trying to provide the best learning for their children. In this conversation we talk with a mathematics consultant who specializes in the early years. She thinks she may have some answers to this very American dilemma.*

Kathy Richardson was teaching second grade in a California school when she attended a math workshop that changed her life. It was given by a first grade teacher who was struggling, as was Kathy, with ways to counteract the 1970s focus on behaviorism and the rigid curriculum that had grown from it. Kathy had been looking for someone who could help her meet the needs of individual children and Mary Baratta Lorton, the workshop leader, proved to be the support she needed.

Baratta Lorton's approach to teaching was closer to a philosophy of constructivism than to the prevailing behaviorism and Kathy felt both comfortable and excited by such an approach. Enthusiastically she volunteered to try some of the ideas in her own classroom. Eventually, Baratta Lorton published her ideas as the book *Math Their Way* (Addison-Wesley, 1976) and presented workshops throughout the country. After Baratta Lorton's death in 1978, Kathy continued to work with the philosophy and ideas she had learned from and shared with her. This resulted in a book, *Developing Number Concepts Using Unifix Cubes* (Addison-Wesley, 1984) and related video

tapes.* Today, Kathy is an independent consultant who works with school districts as they plan long-term change in their mathematics curricula and practices. She also works with teachers from around the country who present the workshops** she has developed based on her book and videotapes.

Kathy believes that there are two areas that cause problems for teachers as they try to improve mathematics instruction for young children. First, they often believe their responsibility is to have children work with the abstract symbols they will have on standardized tests rather than to help them understand concepts. "This approach assumes that mathe-

---

*Look at Children's Thinking* (videotapes). Norman, OK: Educational Enrichment, (1990).

**Developing Math Concepts* (workshops). Norman, OK: Educational Enrichment.

matical symbols have meaning to kids. In my workshops I try to show teachers how such an assumption leads to rote learning."

The second difficulty for teachers is that "they get lost in preparing and planning activities. The teachers look for activities that may be fun for the kids but they don't always know if they are dealing with important mathematical ideas." The frequent result is that "they have children play games that are too easy for them."

Kathy points out that the notion of what is developmentally appropriate in math remains controversial. For example, "there's the controversy about when to teach place value. The mistake is in thinking we can define ahead of time when it's right to present a particular idea. When we try to do that, we put limits on children; we oversimplify or we ask them to do something they can't understand and can learn only by rote. Instead, we need to look at the individual child in light of what we know about development. When individual differences are taken into account and appropriate learning experiences provided for them, then children can verify their thinking for themselves. They won't rely on checking with the teacher to see if they've gotten things right. When that happens, the teacher will know that the experience was developmentally appropriate."

Kathy believes it is possible to take individual needs into account even in a crowded classroom. "I suggest giving children what I call *expandable tasks*. You may be teaching number sense, for example. You then provide carefully selected multilevel activities that focus on this concept and let children choose the tasks that are within their range of understanding." Kathy's years of experience teaching children from preschool through second grade have convinced her that children are instinctively able to make appropriate choices at their own levels of capability. Yet, she says that "it is difficult for teachers to really trust that kids will choose what's right for them." Helping teachers provide activities that meet a range of needs within the classroom is a major focus of her workshops.

Kathy sees a new problem on the horizon as more emphasis is placed on curriculum integration and theme learning. In this approach, math tends to be trivialized, be made incidental, or even get lost entirely. While she agrees that it should be part of thematic learning, "math is also a discipline and that means there should be time to focus on it." She recommends a regular math period from the time children are about five years old.

Kathy explains the problem with today's shift from rigid subject matter to integrated theme learning by using the Blind Man and the Elephant analogy. "We used to teach mathematics as though it were the elephant in pieces. 'Here's the tail. This is what the trunk looks like.' Then we realized that teaching elephant pieces wasn't working. So we said, 'See? Here's the whole elephant.' We began to look at the elephant as though it were a big, gray blob and we stopped analyzing the pieces. But we need to look at the pieces in light of the whole." Kathy says that we need to place math in the context of umbrella themes while still remembering its importance as a discipline.

*To think about and discuss: Choose a math concept that is appropriate for young children. Discuss ways in which it can be taught to children of different levels of understanding. List ways that fit into interdisciplinary themes and ways that focus on math as a single discipline.*

Mathematics concepts can be integrated into almost any kind of lesson. In this picture, the teacher could easily teach sequencing concepts within the framework of the story she is reading by asking the children what happened first, second, third, and so forth.

activity independently. As you pass by and observe, use the ordinal numbers informally with the children.

**4. Child-made Books.** When children write their own stories and make books from them, they can count the pages, being sure to count the backs, too, if they have been written or drawn on. Children can then count the number of words per page, or the number of total words. Discussion can focus on whose book is *biggest, smallest, longest,* or *shortest.* Children will have to debate the merits of counting pages versus number of words to determine size.

## Science

**5. More or Less.** Throughout the year, children enjoy collecting items from nature: sticks, pebbles, shells, dirt samples, and more. These items can be counted and compared in different ways. Large rocks can be counted and their numbers compared with small pebbles, yellow shells with pink ones, large sticks with small ones. If children are just beginning to count, make smaller subsets of larger collections. If they are beginning to read numbers, place a card or tag with the counted total next to each set. When the counting is completed, discuss which set has the most and which the fewest.

This is a good time to emphasize the difference between *much* and *many, less* and *fewer.* (*Much* and *less* refer to mass quantities. *Many* and *fewer* refer to items that can be counted.) Many adults confuse these descriptive words, so it should not be surprising if the children do.

**6. Go Fish!**    This is a popular children's game that provides plenty of opportunity to practice classification. Pictures can be glued onto 3-by-5-inch index cards and chosen according to categories currently under study. One example: classes of animals.

To play the game, each child is dealt five or six cards. In turn, each child asks the next on the left for a class: "Give me a mammal." If the second child has a mammal, she must give the card to the one requesting it. If she does not, she says, "Go fish!" and the child must take a card from the discard pile. Turns move to the left and the first child to lay down sets of four until his hand is empty is the winner.

**7. Fishbowl.**    This activity can be done when the fishbowl is new, then repeated and expanded upon whenever the water needs changing. The teacher decides how much water the fishbowl needs and makes a dark line at that level. Children then use any pitcher to fill the bowl with water and count the number of pitchers required to get to the marked level. If the pitcher is a standard liquid measuring cup, the related vocabulary should be used. When the water needs changing, it can be poured back into the cup for disposal with a recount taking place.

**8. Measuring Tape.**    Any yarn can be used for a measuring tape, but it stretches and occasionally breaks. Bias seam tape provides a sturdy alternative. Try measuring class pets in ways that are appropriate for their type and size. Turtles can be measured from one end of the shell to the other. Small snakes can be held reasonably straight for a (very) quick measure. Rabbits can be measured around the middle. Attach the tape to the wall with the date the measurement was done. If the animal is a fast-growing infant, measure it again in a week or two. Other animals can be measured monthly. Place the second tape near the first and compare lengths. Children can discuss the animal's growth progress or lack of it. From this they learn about the difference between juvenile growth and mature stability, as well as about the difference in growth rates for different animals.

## Social Studies

**9. Community Helpers.**    Using index cards, make a set of pictures of various community workers, preferably those found in the children's own community. Make a matching set of cards with each worker's tools or hats or other articles of identifiable clothing. As children match the appropriate artifact to its worker, they engage in classification.

**10. Birthdays Bar Graph.**    On a large sheet of construction paper, list the months along the bottom. Each child draws a birthday cake on a small piece of construction paper. As children say their date of birth, they glue their cake above the appropriate month. The class then analyzes which month has the most birthdays and which has the fewest. Children can also look for months that have the same number of birthdays and which ones have none at all.

**11. Ordering History.**    As children begin to learn about events that happened in the past, it helps to give them a concrete method of sequencing. Whether it is a news story they have seen on TV or heard about from their parents and older siblings, or the legendary history of the first Thanksgiving, creating a series of pictures provides the needed physical connection. As the children arrange pictures in the order that events occurred, use ordinal numbers informally: "What do you think happened first?" "Yes, that was what happened fourth. . . ."

**12. Follow the Bus.**    Using a blown-up commercial map of your town or section of the city, identify the compass directions and print them on each side of the map. With a small toy school bus, children follow the patterns on the grid to go "north two blocks, then west one block" or "south one block, then east three blocks." If your town's roads are too complex for young children to make sense of, create an easily read grid yourself, and perhaps work with the children to create a town to go on it.

**13. Going Home.**    Using the blown-up commercial map suggested in number 12, have children place small rectangles where their homes are. Or, if you are creating a town on your handmade grid, children can choose where to place their homes. Use a piece of yarn to show how far it is from school to each home "as the crow flies." Each piece of yarn should be cut to size, after which children lay them next to each other along a line to determine who lives farthest from school and who lives closest to it.

Art

**14. Attribute Blocks.**    Children make designs of their choice using a mixture of shapes and colors with commercially made plastic attribute blocks. When they are finished, children can sort the pieces by color into zippered clear plastic bags. If they are able, further sorting can take place according to shape. Bags can then be stored on a section of shelf with a matching symbol (red triangle, green circle, yellow square, etc.).

**15. Art Materials.**    Bring all the art materials—paint jars, fingerpaint containers, crayon boxes, paintbrushes—out for a good cleaning. (Preschool children enjoy the process more than the result. You can do this activity whether the materials actually need cleaning or not.) Put children in smocks and let them participate. When finished, discuss which sets should go in which place and organize according to usage. If children are still interested in working, they can further organize within sets according to color of paint or size of paintbrushes, and so on.

**16. Geometric Collages.**   Have on hand a good supply of geometric construction paper shapes in different colors and sizes. Children can make collages on their own as you informally discuss the names of the shapes and comparative sizes. Or children can be directed to find pieces according to the shape names and colors you suggest. These are then made into collages or other pictures of their choice.

Movement

**17. Move About.**   Children repeat and continue patterns, such as two jumps, one clap, turn around; one step in, one jump, one step out, clap above the head.

**18. Find the Ball.**   In a group effort, the children lay out all the class playground balls in a row according to their size. Then each child identifies "his" or "her" ball as you describe it according to its attributes: "Yours is the largest ball," "Yours is the ball in the middle," "Yours is the second smallest ball." Balls can then be taken to the playground for playtime.

**19. Rhythm Patterns.**   The children sit on the floor in a circle. You clap a rhythm pattern, which the children imitate. Then the sequence is repeated with everyone counting, in rhythm, the number of claps.

**20. Body Numbers.**   Children use any or all of their bodies to make the shape of the number you call out. This can be done with fingers and arms while children sit at their desks. Or it can be done using the entire body in a larger area. Children should not be corrected if their shapes are hard to read.

**21. Stories in Action.**   Children are divided into groups sized according to the "number of the day," for example, 5. As you tell a story problem, the children figure out ways to act it out and discover the answer. Create stories that provide children with opportunities for creative movement.

Example: Five little caterpillars are sitting in their cocoons waiting for the warm spring. Suddenly, two of them push out of their cocoons, wiggle their new butterfly wings, and fly away to the nearest rosebush. How many caterpillars are left in the cocoons? Now, these three caterpillars push out of their cocoons and wiggle their wings and fly to the rosebush to see their friends. How many butterflies are on the rosebush? How many caterpillars are left in their cocoons? How many cocoons did your group leave behind? (If needed, the butterflies can fly back to their cocoons to engage in one-to-one correspondence.)

Table 13.2 summarizes the math activities for curriculum integration.

## Extending Your Learning

1. Observe a preschool class for at least one hour. Make notes of every natural mathematics learning that takes place. Discuss your observations with members of your class.
2. Compare kindergarten and primary mathematics textbooks from several companies. How do they differ in the order and timeliness in which different topics and skills are introduced? Which ones promote the idea of informal, everyday mathematics and which promote structured, teacher-led lessons? Which ones offer ideas for using interesting manipulative materi-

**Table 13.2**
INTEGRATING MATHEMATICS: ACTIVITIES

| ACTIVITY | LEVEL* | CURRICULUM | ADAPTED FROM |
|---|---|---|---|
| Alphabet Blocks | P | Language | Maffei |
| Art Materials | T, P | Art | |
| Attribute Blocks | T, P | Art | Maffei |
| Birthdays Bar Graphs | P, Py | Soc. Studies | |
| Body Numbers | P, PY | Movement | |
| Child-made Books | Py | Language | |
| Community Helpers | P, Py | Soc. Studies | |
| Find the Ball | P | Movement | |
| Fishbowl | P | Science | |
| Follow the Bus | Py | Soc. Studies | Maffei |
| Geometric Collages | P, Py | Art | |
| Go Fish! | P, Py | Science | |
| Going Home | Py | Soc. Studies | |
| Measuring Tape | P, Py | Science | |
| More or Less | P, Py | Science | |
| Move About | P | Movement | Maffei |
| Ordering History | Py | Soc. Studies | |
| Rhythm Patterns | P, Py | Movement | |
| Shelving Books | T, P | Language | |
| Stories in Action | P, Py | Language | |
| Story Sequencing | P, Py | Language | |

*T = Toddler, P = Preschool, Py = Primary.

als and which provide accompanying worksheets? Which books would you choose and why?

3. Invent a board game either for kindergarten/first grade or for second/third grade. Include in it at least two of the concepts discussed in this chapter. Try it out with other members of your class before you try it with children.

4. Give one or two of the Piagetian conservation tasks to a three-year-old, a five-year-old, and a seven-year-old. Two to try: (1) Create two rows of eight or nine pennies each and ask the child which row has more. Then spread out one row to fill more space and ask the same question again. (2) Make two equal balls of clay. Roll one of them into a long cylinder and ask the child which is bigger now.

   Compare the answers the children give and discuss the experience with others in your class who have also tried the tasks.

5. Try any two of the activities in this chapter's final section. Practice them first with other students in your class, then with children of the appropriate developmental level. To make this activity especially useful, create lesson plans for each activity before you try it out. Use the format provided in Chapter 11.

## References

Associated Press (1992). Researcher shows infants can do (very) simple math. *The Bellingham Herald,* 27 Aug., 3.

Baroody, A. (1987). *Children's mathematical thinking.* New York: Teachers College Press.

Bredecamp, S. (ed.) (1987). *Developmentally appropriate practice in early childhood programs serving children from birth through age 8.* Washington, DC: NAEYC.

Colvin, S. (1987). *Introducing addition and subtraction symbols to first graders.* Unpublished doctoral dissertation.

Jensen, R., and O'Neil, D. (1982). Informal geometry through geometric blocks. *Arithmetic Teacher* May 29(9):4–8.

Kamii, C., and DeClark, G. (1985). *Young children reinvent arithmetic.* New York: Teachers College Press.

Kamii, C., and Joseph L. (1989). *Young children continue to reinvent arithmetic—2nd grade: Implications of Piaget's theory.* New York: Teachers College Press.

Maffei, A., and Buckley, P. (1980). *Teaching preschool math.* New York: Human Sciences Press.

National Council of Teachers of Mathematics, Commission on Standards for School Mathematics (1989). *Curriculum and evaluation standards for school mathematics.* Reston, VA: The Council.

Piaget, J. (1975, first published 1948). *To understand is to invent.* New York: Viking.

Read, K., and Patterson, J. (1980). *The nursery school and kindergarten.* New York: Holt, Rinehart and Winston.

Teppo, A. (1991). Van Hiele levels of geometric thought revisited. *Mathematics Teacher* 84(3):210–221.

# 14

# Social Studies

## OBJECTIVE

When you finish reading this chapter, you should be able to

- Plan social studies activities in relation to children's physical, social/moral, and cognitive development.
- Plan social studies activities taking into account the needs of individual children.
- Plan a social studies theme unit that integrates other curriculum areas.

As you think about this chapter on your own, you should be able to

- Observe and analyze your own behavior and attitudes toward children to encourage a more democratic experience.
- Consider and practice conflict resolution approaches that will work well with children and with your teaching peers.

The social studies include a wide array of disciplines: history, geography, economics, anthropology, social psychology, political science, current events, and civics. The thread that ties them all together is their social aspect, the focus on human beings relating to each other. World history is full of evidence that humans frequently do a very bad job of relating to one another. Indeed, history textbooks have frequently been organized according to the buildup and resolution of wars. Current world history is no exception; as peace breaks out in one section of the world, conflict emerges in another.

Perhaps it is too idealistic to hope that helping young children relate well to one another can change the world. On the other hand, it is known that there is a clear connection between children's social successes and failures and their behaviors as adults. Children in the infant room, preschool, and primary grades are learning social behaviors and attitudes that will carry them through many years to come. It may be argued, then, that the most critical social studies learning for young children pertains to human relationships. This is not simply a matter of imposing discipline or managing your classroom effectively so that children get along well with each other. It is making the social studies real and vital to the life of the classroom. Avoidance of war can be taught from a very early age, first on the local level, then with comparisons to events in the wider world.

The vignette that provides the theme for this chapter is a very personal one. Here, the author shares with you her yearlong struggle to create a kindergarten environment based on democratic values and peaceful conflict resolution.

## HANDS-ON SOCIAL STUDIES IN THE KINDERGARTEN

*The year did not begin well, which was something of a surprise to me. The previous June I had sent twenty-three children off to first grade thinking that, at last, I had discovered the secrets of superlative teaching and managing. Now, September had arrived and twenty-five unmanageable, cranky, impudent, and combative children informed me daily that the coming year would be no picnic and that the previous one had succeeded because the children, not I, had been outstanding.*

*Most of the conflict situations occurred during free play, either in or out of the classroom, although teacher-led group discussions could be treacherous, too. Something had to be done.*

*Just before the winter holidays I pored over the children's records and files and discovered that thirteen of the children were younger siblings. As I thought about the children's behavior, this seemingly trivial detail began to make sense. For half of the class, accustomed as they were to struggles with older brothers and sisters, it seemed necessary to fight their way into every-thing they did. And once successful, they became defensive, whining, and accusatory. They didn't know yet that in their classroom they could be coop-erative and generous and still come out ahead.*

*In deciding how to deal with the problem, I concluded that I would con-tinue my usual role as a facilitating guide but that my facilitation would take a different direction. Over the next few months several ideas were tried with varying degrees of success.*

*Since it was impossible to hold large group discussions, I broke the chil-dren up into two or three smaller groups and then dropped in on them as seemed necessary. The small group meetings were kept to no more than ten minutes, although they had sometimes run thirty to forty-five minutes the pre-vious year. Even with smaller groups and shorter time spans, however, discus-sions often provoked fights. Nevertheless, we gradually learned to discuss the pros and cons of controversial issues, to vote, and to live relatively graciously with the will of the majority. This was a hands-on lesson in civics and political science, one that wasn't entirely successful since, at the end of the year, it was still necessary to meet in small groups in order to keep harmony.*

*Another effort might be termed hands-on sociology. Despite my best ef-forts at mixing and matching, free play always found the girls in the house-keeping corner and the boys with the blocks. This situation provided an ap-propriate opportunity to help the children think through why they made the choices they did. One morning, I gathered up my courage, put everyone in a single large group, and asked each gender why they played in one place and not the other. The boys said they didn't have much interest in the doll corner but didn't know why. The girls declared that they would really like to play with blocks but that the boys wouldn't let them. The boys main-tained total innocence and made a great show of inviting the girls in, but, as it turned out, their playing styles were just too different. The boys wanted to construct intricate buildings, while the girls preferred to slap a few blocks together and bring in the dolls. The class was called together in a large group once again, solutions were discussed, and a vote was taken. For the next few weeks there were "girl days" and "boy days" with the opposite sex not allowed within 10 feet (necessary to avoid verbal squabbles). After awhile, the girls lost interest and went back to the doll corner permanently. While this wasn't what I had hoped for, there had at least been a period of time when the children considered a social situation, discussed it, and made group decisions.*

*During the year, a variety of social studies activities were devised in an effort to make the class more cooperative. When we played store with real money (a study of economics), the children were forced to cooperate because every store was required to have two clerks and two customers buying to-*

*gether. When we mapped the inside of the building (geography), the children learned to cooperate because the project was done in small groups. When we posted pictures of our parents as children (history), the children were paired and each of them had to talk about their partner's family rather than their own.*

*Although that school year was the most difficult one in my memory, progress was certainly made. It was a year when everything we did related in some way to the social studies, where the primary focus was on conflict resolution.*

Each year that you teach will be different because the children you teach will be different. Since their collective and individual needs will vary from year to year, your approach to social studies teaching must be flexible. One year you might choose, as I did, to focus on cooperation in virtually every social studies activity, while this might be unnecessary with another class. Whatever direction your decision making takes, it will be more successful if it reflects a sound understanding of the way children develop and learn. The following sections should help you integrate the perspectives of Chapters 1 through 5 with children's learning in the social studies.

## Making Connections: Perspectives on History and Theory

Comenius, whose writings helped to take education out of the Middle Ages and into the Renaissance, provided the foundation for modern-day social studies, even though that term was not used in his time. However, his contention that children first learn about time and space as these concepts relate to their own lives has as much importance for the study of history and geography now as it did then. Thus, young children learn about their own experience (yesterday, last week, and today) before exploring the rest of the world. Likewise, they begin by mapping their desk, their room, and their school before they create maps of larger spaces.

Basing social studies on students' real-life experiences was again put forward at the beginning of this century by Maria Montessori and John Dewey. Montessori believed that children as young as three should be permitted the freedom to create their own little "societies in embryo." You will recall that the last years of her life were spent in exile in order to avoid the fascist control of her schools by Mussolini. It was her belief that, if children were trusted with self-government from a very early age, and if they were given guidance in the creation of a democratic society, they would be less likely as adults to accept the philosophies and control of a Mussolini or a Hitler.

John Dewey's laboratory school at the University of Chicago was a living experiment in the social studies. If you look back at Chapter 1 and review the selections from his pedagogic creed, you will see that his view of an effective classroom included a real-life understanding of democracy. Like Montessori, he believed that children couldn't be taught *about* democratic processes; they had to experience them firsthand.

As a teacher you will find that it takes both courage and experience to provide children with the right balance of independence and adult guidance needed to create a democratic atmosphere. If Dewey and Montessori were right, however, the long-term results may well be worth the effort.

Dewey's philosophy of education was enormously influential in the early years of this century. Both in social studies and other areas of the curriculum, he emphasized educating to the needs and interests of the child rather than to artificially created "disciplines." In 1916 he recommended integrating the various social sciences into a single field termed "social studies." The purpose was to create, in the elementary school, an activity-oriented curriculum where relevant concepts from all the social sciences could be simultaneously used to explore something of inherent interest to the children.

In the following years, Dewey's philosophy influenced developers of early childhood and elementary social studies programs. In the 1930s, Lucy Sprague Mitchell created the "Here and Now" curriculum as a movement away from dry, rote memorization of academic knowledge and toward learning based on children's firsthand experiences, interests, and needs. "Anything that was given to children that was secondhand, before children had an opportunity to experience it for themselves, was considered dangerous to Lucy Sprague Mitchell" (Seefeldt, 1989, p. 8). She, too, argued for a social studies program that began with the home and extended outward, making specific suggestions for each grade:

| GRADE | TOPICS |
|---|---|
| K | Home and Neighborhood |
| 1 | Community and Its Helpers |
| 2 | United States |
| 3 | People in Other Lands |

A similar expanding-communities approach was proposed by Paul Hanna during the same era. Its underlying philosophy was that "we live in a series of communities, each of which is contained in larger communities . . ." (Schuncke, 1988, p. 28). Hanna's suggested topics were:

| GRADE | TOPICS |
|---|---|
| K | The Child |
| 1 | Family and School Communities |
| 2 | Neighborhood Community |
| 3 | The Child's Communities: City, Metropolis, Country |

Stemming from the influence of educators like Mitchell and Dewey, social studies curriculums have tended to begin with social experiences that were most familiar to children (home and neighborhood) and then gradually broaden out to include more abstract national and world events.

Despite these promising moves away from rote learning, subsequent decades of social studies learning took a negative turn. The Dewey-Mitchell-Hanna approach was often interpreted as nondirective learning where children, left to their own devices, should *only* learn about what was near and dear to them. As might be expected, not much learning took place. The eventual backlash from this misapplication of Dewey's theories threatened to return children again to learning singular social sciences through dull, lifeless memorization of facts. Today, we realize that children need directed learning along with freedom to explore, and that they need information about faraway places as well as those nearby. Much of this new understanding can be attributed to the work of Jean Piaget and Jerome Bruner. Bruner (in Maxim, 1987), taking his cue from Piaget's views of development, said that social studies instruction for children should include

- A match between new knowledge and prior knowledge.
- Activities designed to explore social studies data.
- Activities designed to use information, not just memorize it.

To summarize what we have learned from a long history of teaching social studies: Young children are most attracted to learning that reflects their own lives. Such learning is most meaningful to them and provides a natural starting place that can be used to expand their learning outward. Teaching techniques should be activity-oriented and should avoid rote learning that is meaningless in terms of the child's own experience.

## Making Connections: Perspectives on Development

The developmental perspectives provided in Chapters 3 through 5 offer useful guidelines for making curricular choices. Keep in mind that the choices you make should maintain a balance between what children already know and the new knowledge and attitudes you want them to acquire.

### Cognitive Development and the Social Studies

Space and time concepts are elements of cognitive development that are integral to the social studies. Each should be taken into account when planning the content of your lessons and appropriate teaching methods.

Geography, for example, is a social science that requires mapping skills, which, in turn, are based on well-developed concepts of space. Children do not develop these skills and their underlying concepts until the upper elementary years or beyond. Consequently, adult-style mapmaking is inappropriate in the early childhood years. Children must first be able to orient themselves in space, a process that begins at birth and that teachers can nurture through appropriate activities. For example, a geography curriculum designed to help children orient themselves in space can be based on movement exploration (Seefeldt, 1989). Elements of this program can include

- Body awareness: Its shape in space, how it moves and rests.
- Force and time: "limp, energetic, light, fluid, staccato, slow, or quick."
- Space: Where the body is in relationship to the environment; its path through space; high, middle, low positions.
- Locomotion: Moving through space at different levels.
- Weight: Managing body weight in motion, and in relationship to others.
- Isolations: Managing various movements of individual body parts.
- Repetitions: Getting to know a movement better by repeating it. (Adapted from Seefeldt, 1989, p. 164)

While these elements may not directly relate to the adult definition of geography, they do provide children with a better orientation to space, which is a prerequisite for adult geography. Stages in early mapmaking have been designated at three levels:

Stage 1:   The infant can locate objects.

Stage 2:   The child from ages four to seven can "locate and develop reference points and locate items by left, right, in front of, and behind."

Stage 3:   The child, after age seven or so, can locate or place items on a map without difficulty. (Copeland, quoted in Seefeldt, 1989, p. 172)

In relation to Stage 3, keep in mind the Piagetian task described in Chapter 5 in which children tried to imagine what a certain mountain might look like from various viewpoints. This, too, wasn't possible until about age seven. Not until the primary years is it possible to introduce simple mapmaking and map reading for most children.

Concepts of time are closely related to the study of history. As you learned in Chapter 5, children begin to develop the adult sense of time at about age five and are approximately eight before they can grasp a real sense of the future. Not until they are about seven can they tell time in the conventional sense or be sure what a year is. It is for these reasons that the formal study of history doesn't usually begin until the fourth grade.

The following suggestions provide children with a better understanding of the passage of time and prepare them for the later study of history.

■ Use daily routines to help orient children to the repeated passage of time. For the youngest children, this means understanding that outdoor play comes after naptime and that mothers come back following their nap. For older children, different activities that occur on designated days of the week can be recalled and complex weekly schedules written up for all to remember.

■ For children who cannot yet tell time, position play clocks or old, unused clocks next to the room's real one. These can be set to the times when specific events occur. Children should also be given opportunity to play freely with the clocks; you can informally help them compare times with the real clock or learn what the various configurations are called.

■ Adopt a nearby tree that changes with the seasons. Draw pictures of its different cycles and keep them in an album or attach them to the appropriate months on the class calendar.

■ Study the children's own histories, collecting pictures of them from infancy up to the present.

## Social and Affective Development and the Social Studies

In Erik Erikson's (1963) psychoanalytic theory of development there are three stages at which you can expect to observe early social studies learning: Stage 2 (autonomy vs. shame and doubt), Stage 3 (initiative vs. guilt), and Stage 4 (industry vs. inferiority). For children at Stage 2, struggling between autonomy and shame and doubt, the time is right to set the stage for social studies learning. You can encourage the kinds of autonomous decision making that will be needed later when studying democracy. Helping children develop a sense of themselves as self-directed actors provides a foundation for later discussions about their social identity. Informal interventions produce seemingly casual questions such as, "Which do you think you'd like to do now? Play with Lego blocks or try a new puzzle?"

The initiative, attack, and conquest that come with Stage 3 suggest that short-term projects begin to be appropriate. Social studies themes now make sense, particularly if they match children's interests. A four and a half-year-old once asked his teacher, "When are we going to do fire engines in here?" an idea that hadn't yet crossed her mind. Since the rest of the class responded to his idea with a hearty, "Yeah, when?!" they soon embarked on a study of firefighters and their equipment.

Elementary age children, well rooted in the worker/producer role of Stage 4, are ready for thematic units that can be as involved and lengthy as their interests permit. One second-grade class began a simple query into the history of their classroom (the building had once been a very large house), and ended up spending six months on an extended project complete with reports to the PTA. Possible feelings of inferiority, the negative aspect of this stage, can be headed off by providing encouragement rather than negative and judgmental attitudes.

The social learning view of child development, which argues against stages, would suggest teacher modeling for social studies learning. If you want children to learn about such concepts as democracy and conflict resolution and justice, then you yourself should behave democratically toward others, resolve conflicts peacefully, and treat others, particularly your own class, in ways that are just. As was discussed in Chapter 7, young children are often unaware of such modeling unless you explicitly discuss it. For example, two teachers who team taught in a class of four- and five-year-olds once staged an argument to show the children how friendly resolutions could come about. At the end, one of them turned to some nearby children and said, "I'm so glad that Ms. Early and I can disagree and still be friends." Ms. Early then said, "The best part is that we didn't have to hurt each other." The children seemed stunned that teachers might actually argue but relieved that it ended so well. The teachers were rewarded in coming days when they heard their actual words repeated in doll corner disagreements.

The constructivist theory promulgated by Piaget was based, to a great extent, on his observation of children's understanding of rules. Rules, of course, are related to laws, an important element in our society and thus an important part of learning of social studies. In the earliest heteronomous stage, children relate to rules as the rules relate to their self interests. Further, children frequently obey simply because the adults are bigger or have more power, not understanding the knowledge and responsibility that go with these attributes. At this stage, you can have children help create some of the classroom rules, focusing on the idea that rules are important for their own benefit, for their safety, and for the good of their very own class.

Children in the first transitional stage are fascinated, even obsessed, by rules. Since they often believe that rules are unchangeable and made only by higher authorities, it is even more important at this stage to have children join in their creation. By second and third grade children can learn that rules may at times be unjust and that they can participate in changing them.

It is usually during the early elementary years that children begin to recognize the needs of others, to take first steps at putting themselves in others' shoes. It is surprising to many adults when a primary child takes the initiative in starting a class- or schoolwide drive to assist an underprivileged group that is currently in the news. Yet this is the stage when children are first discovering such needs and can relate to them. Their new interest can spur them on to action, particularly if teachers and parents are supportive. It is also important to help young children understand, however, that sending one bundle of food or clothing will not cure all the suffering. Many young children become confused and disillusioned when the media continue to focus on a problem that they have worked to cure.

You will recall that, within the constructivist theory, there is an argument concerning its basis in justice (a male focus) or caring (a female focus). This is one argument that teachers of young children can easily deal with. Both justice and caring should be emphasized as young children learn about the so-

By the second or third grade children are capable of understanding that rules and laws are not immutable but are made by people to help promote justice in their social relations. Having children engage in legal role playing is a good way to develop this human perspective regarding rules and laws.

cial studies. In the unit on conflict resolution that concludes this chapter, there is a focus on both.

## Making Connections: Diversity Among Children

The social studies provide a natural opportunity for creating curriculum that takes into account the diversity found in your classroom and community. As you plan for this teaching, another opportunity presents itself to examine your own understanding of social studies issues. For example, learning about other cultures is an important part of social studies curriculum; so is learning about democracy. Combine these two and you may discover discrepancies in your views when compared with others'. The students at one university were working hard at understanding each other's cultures as they interacted in various organizations. At times, however, their taken-for-granted perceptions hindered their understanding of each other. On one occasion, two student organizations working together needed to make a major decision and, to the students in one group, the democratic process was taking longer than it should. The impatient students were from an all-white organization, and they were heard complaining about the others, who were all Native Americans. "Why can't they get their act together?" one student said. "We know we can't make a perfect decision and get everybody to agree, but we have to decide *something.*" This comment was followed by increasingly derogatory remarks about people from the other culture and their "inability" to make decisions or get anything done. Two days later, the Native Americans returned from discussing the issues with each other and announced that they had come to a unified position. While they were now in total agreement with each other, they had found it necessary to modify some of the original expectations of the two-group project. The white students were a bit taken aback; they were surprised not only by the other students' total unity but by the positive nature of the modifications.

The lack of understanding between the two groups arose from their different views of the democratic process. For the students in the all-white organization, the rule of the majority was an underlying value of democracy. The idea that everyone in the group would have to agree was beyond their expectations. The students in the Native American organization superimposed their traditional value of gaining consensus on group issues onto their understanding of the democratic process. While the first group's method was quicker, the second's was more thorough and, ultimately, more satisfying to everyone.

As you think about teaching the values of democracy and about different cultures to your children, it will be important for you to keep in mind your own definitions and perceptions. Then you must take the time to question those definitions and perceptions to be sure they are shared with your children and their families. Otherwise, you may end up in difficult situations such as those the university students faced.

If the children in your class come from diverse backgrounds, studies of their cultures provide the here-and-now immediacy appropriate to early childhood education. Such studies also contribute to the self-esteem of the children whose cultures are being studied and to the broadening cultural respect of the rest of the class. If your children are more monocultural, it is important to expand their horizons by bringing in cultural studies from other children within the school or from people in the larger community.

Combining studies of your children's cultures with your own growth in cultural understanding may take some effort, but the results can be extremely beneficial for everyone. Here are some suggestions for making your efforts positive:

- Talk to family members who represent the various cultures in your class. Discuss with them your plans to learn about other cultures and ask for suggested books, videos, and information on cultural events that would increase your knowledge.
- Invite family members to participate in the learning experiences of the class. Based on your initial discussions, invite those who are most enthusiastic and comfortable first. As the less enthusiastic observe what is happening in the class, they may become more comfortable about participating.
- Remember that the majority culture needs to be studied as well. When customs and beliefs are brought to the conscious level and examined, they are less likely to be taken for granted as the *right* or *real* way of doing things.
- As you collect materials for classroom activities, question their authenticity and their broad applicability against what you are learning about the culture. Do they represent just one class or group of people? Do they apply to the children in your class who come from that culture? Do they portray stereotyped views that may be colorful but have little to do with modern everyday life?
- If your children speak other languages, find ways to celebrate their ability. Make their knowledge a part of your study, giving the children opportunities to teach some of their language to the rest of the class.
- Try taking nothing for granted about your own culture. This is a *very* difficult suggestion to carry out and should be a lifelong effort. As you communicate with the parents of your children, spend as much effort listening as you do in talking. If you sense that they are not interpreting your comments in the way you meant them, ask questions to see if their cultural definitions and perceptions are the same as yours. This will be important as you study other cultures and the majority culture as well. You might start by thinking about your own definition of democracy and of how that fits into the structure of your classroom. Do you come from a culture that

shares the definition of either of the two university groups described above? Or is your own view slightly different? How will this affect what you want to communicate to your children? Do their parents share your views? If not, what have they communicated to their children and how will this affect your teaching?

Taking into account the varying cultures in your classroom community when creating social studies learning is both an opportunity and a challenge. If you see these opportunities as a way to grow and learn, your experiences should, on the whole, be positive.

## Disciplines of the Social Studies

In the broadest sense, human beings are involved in the social studies from birth. Learning to differentiate self from other and understand a caretaker's response to various types of crying provide the infant with a social education. Social studies continue to be learned in a natural way as the child grows older and enters preschool or kindergarten. The vignette from the author's teaching experience contains many examples of social learning that occurred as part of the ordinary flow of classroom life. Yet such informal social lessons were only a part of the social studies agenda.

Recall that, during that difficult year of teaching, I quite consciously developed social studies lessons and units built around the disciplines of political science, economics, sociology, and civics. The children were exposed to small group lessons in how to discuss controversial issues, and they learned how to vote and to live by the will of the majority. They learned how to confront and to resolve (at least temporarily) a gender-based conflict concerning rights to the block corner. They also learned lessons in consumer economics and money matters in their simulated store, and they learned about space and mapping within the confines of their own school and classroom. Finally, they learned lessons in history and culture by studying the lives of their classmates' parents.

A well-rounded social studies curriculum requires such formal, academic experiences to go with the equally important informal experiences in getting along well together. Inattention to the more formal, teacher-planned activities was directly responsible, in decades past, for the demise of classrooms that followed the lead of John Dewey and Lucy Sprague Mitchell. When they argued that children learn best from their real, personal experience, their intent was to overturn a long tradition of irrelevant rote learning. In their enthusiasm to banish meaningless rote learning, however, many teachers ignored the need for children to actually learn something academic. The "back to basics" movement of recent years was, in large part, an attempt to restore to the social studies curriculum a more even balance between academic learning based on the social science disciplines and less formal lessons keyed to classroom social interactions.

The balance between formal and informal social studies lessons depends in part on the age of the children you teach. It is inappropriate and probably impossible to teach formal social studies to infants and toddlers. Gradually, however, more formal learning is possible, as long as it is balanced by sufficient play and by relating teacher-planned learning to children's real lives. Within this more balanced context, young children can learn much from the formal social studies disciplines.

## History

History is an account of the past: the telling, analyzing, and explaining of the human story up until today. Academic concepts related to history include time, continuity, change, conflict, and the past. As you know from our discussion of cognitive development, these concepts are difficult ones for young children to grasp, even for those who are in the early years of elementary school. Nevertheless, it is during these years that children begin to grapple with these concepts and that teachers can assist them with activities such as these.

### Time

When young children begin to engage in daily routines, they begin to understand the passage of time. Knowing that the day always begins with a song and ends with a story helps them understand the length of a school day. Children in the primary grades can be introduced to time lines. These useful teaching devices are often relied upon in the upper elementary grades to teach major events in history. In the primary grades they can be divided by days, weeks, or months and focused on children's own personal histories. Typically, time lines are made in cooperative groups and are drawn on long sheets of butcher, or similar, paper divided appropriately. They can also be made individually using adding machine strips.

### Continuity

Daily routines can be important for teaching continuity as well as time. If some routines are done continually over long periods of time, the continuity that is sometimes part of history is learned intuitively. As children begin to learn about holidays, their understanding of historical continuity becomes more explicit. The traditions associated with these special days are generally the focus of study, and guests from different generations can share the traditions that have been carried forward through time.

## *Teaching in Another Country: A Conversation with Joan Beecham*

*What better way to learn about another culture than to immerse yourself in it?! Some people find that combining their interest in foreign countries with their talent for teaching can lead to an exciting career. However, the experience is not for everyone. The teacher in this interview is particularly suited to the job, and she tells how you might be too.*

Joan Beecham teaches four-year-olds at the Afcent International School in Brunssum, The Netherlands near the Belgian and German borders. The school is sponsored jointly by the United States Department of Defense, the British Service Children's Education Authority, and the Canadian Department of National Defense. There is also a separate German section. With American, British, and Canadian children in the same classrooms, curriculum planning is an unusually complex challenge.

Each nationality has a list of educational goals it wants the school to meet and, as you might imagine, the lists are not identical. "We have to juggle all three sets of expectations sufficiently that the children can be fed back into their own systems when they go home," Joan says. "The parents expect that we'll equip their children with the skills they need so they won't have trouble later." If Joan were just teaching Canadians and Americans, this would not present too much of a challenge and she could devote her energies to creating a developmentally appropriate curriculum for preschoolers. But, the British system has academic expectations for four-year-olds, and Joan must be sensitive to them. Thus, much of the curriculum in her class is determined by the British needs.

One of those needs is to send even the very young to school for a full day. Joan views this as a mixed blessing. "I like a full-day preschool be-

cause it makes for a more relaxed atmosphere. In a half-day program it's much harder to finish projects." On the other hand, there is also pressure to meet academic goals. For example, the British four-year-olds are expected to do some basic addition and subtraction by the end of the school year. However, since the school's program is developmental (maturationist), the expectations are flexible and just about one-third of the children actually reach the goal.

Joan's school is unique in that it is on a NATO base and, therefore, international. Most Department of Defense schools are on American military bases with children coming only from the United States. Other teaching opportunities are available in a wide variety of international schools in countries throughout the world. Because cultural situations are all so different, the teaching expectations vary from place to place. The schools on the military bases, for example, follow an American curriculum generic enough that children can adapt to most situations when they return home.

International schools tend to set their own curricula and generally provide teachers with the most decision-making freedom. Many of these schools are sponsored by American parents or companies and rely on American texts, materials, and teachers. Nevertheless, the children in the classes may come from several countries and speak English as a second, or even third, language.

In the United States, you might expect a few of your children to speak more than one language and a few of them might have traveled widely. In an overseas school, however, the majority of the children may speak more than one language and be on familiar terms with more than one culture or country. Such a variety of experiences at an early age produces children who have an unusually broad understanding of the world, linguistic expertise, and a veneer of sophistication. At the same time, the children may be disoriented and insecure as the result of having no permanent home base or long-term friends. Thus, their school may well provide the stability they need and the children often form strong and close friendships. The teacher's role as a supportive, stable, and reliable adult is important.

What kind of person is most cut out to be a teacher overseas? A description of Joan's life provides a good example. Born in Tokyo of American parents, she spent a brief kindergarten year in California, then left the country again for Thailand where she lived during her elementary school years. When Joan was twelve the family moved back to the United States, and she finished growing up in Washington, DC. Once out of college, and with some teaching experience, Joan decided she was ready for more foreign adventures, and she happily accepted the position in Holland. She believes that her early life experiences prepared her well for making adjustments to a foreign country, but that others can also do so successfully. Joan suggests:

- It helps if you come with some teaching experience. All around you will be other, perhaps foreign, teaching approaches. You can adopt new ideas more skillfully if you're sure of your own standards.
- You need to be willing to learn from others and be open to learning new ways of doing things. This goes for both teaching and your personal life.
- You need to be a flexible person. Nothing will feel quite the way it does back home and you have to be willing to accept that.
- It helps if you're adventurous. If you are, you already know that adventures have both some good and some bad in them. That's what makes them adventures.

*To discuss: What would make teaching in another culture difficult for you? What would be enjoyable about it? Does your list look like the others in your class? In considering your list, can you surmise how children from other cultures and countries might feel when they come into an American class for the first time? How might that affect your teaching?*

### Change

Young children like to know that "now I can do it and before I couldn't." Helping them see change as personal progress gives children a positive outlook on a part of life and history that can be unsettling at times. Primary children can study the history of their school or neighborhood, combining research into written records with oral history interviews.

### The Past

Daily conversations that touch on yesterday, last week, or earlier this year help children to differentiate lengths of past time. During these informal discussions, it is your responsibility to help children focus on these varying time spans and to observe their understanding of them. One very simple version of a time line can be a division between *today, a little while ago,* and *a long time ago.* Pictures of the way people dressed or different kinds of toys are examples of possible features for this time line.

## Geography

Geography deals with the physical surface of the earth; the earth's division into political units; relationships of people to their physical environments; the use people make of the earth's resources; and cross-space comparisons of single interests such as industry, artistic development, and education. Geographical concepts include place, space, direction, location, region, physical and cultural change, population growth and distribution, maps, and environment.

Some of these concepts provide appropriate learning for the early childhood classroom. Often, two or more concepts interact within a more generalized geography learning experience. A good example of this is found in the concept of maps. When children learn about maps, they must have some understanding of place, space, direction, location, and possibly region and environment. As you know from Chapter 5, young children develop these concepts over quite a few years. Thus, creating adult-style maps is developmentally inappropriate for most children through most of the primary years. Mapping can be done appropriately, but it needs to be redefined to fit children's cognitive development.

Seefeldt (1989) suggests three ways of introducing maps to preschool and primary children:

1. *Survey the children.* Show your class a rather simple map of your city or town and ask if they know what it is. As you listen for answers, note which children seem completely baffled and which ones remark on the things they see. This will give you an idea of the extent of their knowledge and suggest ways to extend it.

Basic economic concepts such as money, scarcity of goods, buying and selling, production and distribution, and making choices can all be taught through activities such as playing store.

2. *Use firsthand experiences.* To help make abstract map concepts more concrete, it is important to relate them to children's interests and needs. Using or making a map for a field trip or a walk around the neighborhood relates directly to their lives.
3. *Develop concepts.* Children cannot comprehend maps until they understand some basic concepts. These include representation, symbolization, perspective, and scale.

*Representation* means that children know that one thing represents something else. When they build cities with blocks, children understand that the blocks represent houses, stores, and so on. Three-dimensional objects such as blocks, boxes, dollhouses, and sticks are appropriate mapping materials in the preschool years. Paper shapes glued on larger sheets of paper may be introduced at some point during these years and carried through the primary grades. Lines on paper are generally appropriate from late kindergarten on.

*Symbolization* is the concept that a symbol represents a real thing. At first, pictures of things children want to put on their maps may be best; later, they can use more abstract symbols. The use of colors in maps is important to explain to children. They readily understand that blue means water, but it can be helpful to take them outside to look at an actual road to see that it's not really blue or red.

*Perspective* on a typical map is a bird's-eye view. Children can attain this by standing on their desk chairs, going to the top of a hill, or looking down from a tall building.

*Scale* is a difficult concept for young children and an absolute understanding should not be expected. Photos of the children and various objects can be used to demonstrate that the real things are larger than the representations. During mapping experiences, point out that, as one child said, it is "just like it is, only this is much smaller" (Seefeldt, 1989, p. 175).

## Sociology

Sociology is the study of humans as they interact within groups: how people affect the groups to which they belong; how groups affect the people within them; the relationships between and among groups; and the ways in which groups are created and structured. Concepts related to sociology include groups, institutions, society, norms, individuals' roles, and socialization.

Children belong to groups and institutions. They bring to school the influence from their families and religious organizations. Within the school there are academic groupings, including the grade they are in and the social groups they create more informally.

An informal study of sociology can and should take place throughout the school year, and an awareness of group interactions can be part of other social studies projects. For example, as you involve parents in school activities, send notes home, or have conferences, you are bringing the concept of family informally into the school. More formally, children may study different configurations for family groups and their own places in them.

## Anthropology

Anthropology is the study of cultures as they have developed over time, as they exist now, and in comparison with other cultures. The concept of culture includes so much—language, literature, art, music, law, religion—that anthropology is often viewed as an umbrella social science that covers all the others.

For young children, there are some useful, enjoyable, and appropriate learnings from anthropology. Having older children teach their favorite games to younger children, for example, not only demonstrates culture but shows how enculturation takes place. Songs and folktales from different parts of the United States or from around the world can be compared to those from the children's own culture. Holiday customs and traditions can be studied in the same way.

## Economics

Human beings have needs and wants that must be satisfied by varying amounts of resources. The study of the patterns and systems by which people do this is the field of economics.

Young children have needs and wants, and economics concepts are part of their lives as soon as they are big enough to sit up while being wheeled through the grocery store in a shopping cart. Sunal (1990) suggests the following concepts as being important and understandable for young children: wants and needs, scarcity, identifying resources, planning, ordering goals, goods and services, buyers and sellers, producers and consumers, money, and making choices.

Activities Sunal suggests include such things as having the class list needs and wants for the classroom, and later checking items off as they are obtained; helping children recognize the factors of production by identifying items needed to complete classroom tasks; and visits to both service-oriented shops (repair shops, beauty shops) and places that sell goods (grocery stores, auto dealerships).

## Political Science

The ways in which social units, both large and small, govern or manage themselves is the focus of political science. Concepts include political systems, political institutions, government, patriotism, public policy, power, authority, and social control.

Even very young children have some understanding of politics, particularly if they have heard of the president or other authority figures. They tend to view such people as positive, benevolent, and personal (Seefeldt, 1989), perhaps believing that they can call them on the telephone or talk to them via the television.

As children are given opportunities to create rules, make various classroom decisions, and generally participate in the running of their schooltime lives, they are creating their own systems of governance. In the primary grades, with some teacher guidance, it is appropriate for children to suggest consequences for those who disobey the rules. (Younger children, and even some primary children, have a hard time choosing consequences that appropriately fit the disobedience.)

Patriotism may be a controversial concept for you as a teacher. Parents and other citizens want to instill patriotic values in children from the earliest years, but the symbols usually associated with patriotism are too abstract for children to understand. A prime example is the flag to which children are asked, often daily, to pledge allegiance. Asked to define *pledge* or *allegiance,* young children may give personally creative but nonsensical answers. If you listen to them as they recite the pledge, you will hear a wide variety of inter-

By the primary grades, children have grown out of much of their egocentrism and begin to see others' points of view during conflict resolution situations.

pretations, with familiar words substituted for the actual ones. Some teaching ideas you might find helpful:

- Focus on a few key words to learn and define.
- Say the pledge less often so it remains special.
- Sing flag-related songs, recite poems, read stories.
- Have children create a flag for the classroom with symbols that have meaning to them.

## Values Education

Even more controversial, potentially, than patriotism, values education is still an important part of children's social studies learning. Again, parents and other citizens want children to learn appropriate values in school. However, most of these people want the children to learn *their* values. In a diverse society such as ours, this means that there are numerous views on what is appropriate, including the view that values education is the responsibility of home and church alone.

In recent years, several approaches to values education have been developed for school use. Probably the best known is values clarification, which provides children with a three-step process for developing a value: thoughtfully *choosing* a course of action, showing satisfaction with the choice by *prizing* it, then *acting* on the prized choice (Raths et al., 1966). The teaching methods and materials associated with values clarification are most appropriate for older children, but other approaches can be applied in the early childhood classroom.

Generally, these approaches are based on Piagetian theory and subsequent work by Lawrence Kohlberg. First, they take into account the developmental levels of children as well as the observation that, within one classroom, children may be operating at a variety of levels. Second, they provide opportunities for children to create their own learning with guidance being offered by the teacher, as necessary. Robert Selman, for example (you met him in Chapter 4), has created a series of filmstrips that elementary teachers can use as springboards to discussion.

Another approach you might try is one that a colleague and I (Schuncke and Krogh, 1983) developed for kindergarten through primary grades. It has three steps:

- *Warm-up.* Introduce the topic in a way that piques their interest. ("Have you ever wished you could use a wonderful toy that wasn't yours?" "Have you ever had a wonderful toy you didn't want to share?") Then read or tell a story in which the protagonist must make a value-laden decision. But stop before the decision is made. You can use a book that is designed for this purpose (such as Schuncke and Krogh's *Helping Children Choose,*) or you can use any good story in which such a decision has to be made.
- *Action period.* Ask the children to suggest courses of action for the protagonist. ("She should only share with her best friend." "She should only share with the girls." "She should share with everybody.") Until they have done this a few times, it may be that only one idea will surface. Accept it and don't push for more; as this step proceeds, children may think of more story endings.

  Have children volunteer as story characters to role play each suggested ending, developing the plot so that they can see the consequences of the action that has been suggested. At first, it may be helpful, especially with younger children, for you to take one of the minor roles in order to move the action along.
- *Debriefing.* At the end of each enactment, ask each of the characters how he or she feels about the way the story turned out. ("I'm a boy and I didn't like it that she only shared with the girls. It wasn't fair." "I didn't mind sharing with everybody, but then I didn't get to play with my new toy very much. I should've just left it at home.")

After all the suggestions have been acted out, children may want to discuss the pros and cons of each. It is important, however, that no one feel pressured into accepting the ideas of others. If they do, they may just be following popular opinion and not growing individually. It's usually not a good idea to take a vote on the best answer. You may find that children will talk to you or each other on an individual basis later, thus providing an opportunity for them to construct their own values in a very Piagetian sense.

The various social science disciplines all contain concepts that are appropriate in some way for young children's learning. Much of the time, learning will be informal, as in our opening vignette. Other times it will be more formal, as in the suggestions just given. In either case, it is important not to make the mistake that occurred over so many decades when the focus was so strongly on the here and now that little or no learning took place. It is equally important that social studies teaching not be rigid and dry.

The social studies, because they have their basis in human endeavors, are naturally interesting to most children. For the same reason, and because they are so varied, the social studies can easily be integrated with each other and with all other areas of the curriculum. We conclude this chapter with an example of how this can be done:

## A Social Studies Theme: Conflict Resolution

A study of conflict resolution can incorporate virtually all of the social studies. For example, studying the Civil War involves the *history* of the experience; learning about the battlefields and their effect on the war's progress involves *geography;* learning how each side financed the war involves *economics;* comparing Northern and Southern governments uses *political science;* while studying the ways in which combatants interacted with one another and with civilians involves *anthropology* and *sociology.* Finally, the difficult decisions made by all participants can be studied as a part of *values education.*

Young children are not yet prepared, either cognitively or affectively, for formal study of this sort. With good reason, the expanding curriculum recommended by social studies researchers does not begin such studies until about the fourth grade. Nevertheless, children are exposed to the perplexing realities of major conflict from a very early age. Sometimes this happens as they watch the evening news on television, or hear older people discussing a story from the newspaper or even read it themselves. Perhaps there are relatives in the military who are engaged in conflict. Certainly children's games are often built around warlike situations.

Depending on what is happening in our current history, children will react to major conflict with varying degrees of interest and fear. There are no firm answers about ways in which teachers can help children deal with these concerns. One place we can look for answers is in the recollections of people who lived through major conflict either as children or as the caregivers of children.

For example, Anna Freud and Dorothy Burlingham, in their 1943 book *War and Children,* described their experiences in World War II England, where they directed three wartime nurseries. Some of the difficulties children had in understanding the war around them arose from their stages of development. For example, one child reminisced, "Do you remember the first night here when we all were so noisy that the Germans dropped a bomb on our house?" As the authors concluded, "In Janet's mind the bomb was dropped as punishment because the children were too noisy" (p. 178).

Kati David (1989), a child survivor of World War II, grew up to interview others who had also lived through the experience as children. She discovered that the 100 survivors she interviewed all experienced the same reactions to their hardships despite very different circumstances. Physical hardships such as cold and hunger left them "relatively indifferent" (p. 14). The primary fear was of being separated from their parents; those who had experienced separation suffered far more. Bombings and air raids were not feared by most children, particularly when they were given extra attention and affection during the raids. Those who had been most fearful claimed that their feelings were transmitted to them from fearful adults. Only 3 of the 100 survivors were still bitter about having gone through the war, with most feeling that they were strengthened by the experience and more appreciative of life.

Even when children have no direct contact with war, they develop concepts about it from an early age. Today, in the United States, many or most children are exposed to conflict in some form on a regular basis during their many contacts with television. Carol Seefeldt's (1989) review of research on children's perceptions of conflict provides a number of conclusions that are useful for teachers:

- Children begin forming ideas of political systems about age three.
- By age seven or eight children understand war and peace fairly well.
- Girls are less likely than boys to be interested in war and war games.
- Six-year-olds demonstrate more hostility than children of other ages.
- Third and fourth graders are most likely to rate wars as glamorous.
- Older children condemn war more frequently than younger ones.
- Young children have difficulty separating real war from fantasy.
- Young children may believe they can cause someone to die if they get angry, or cause war by their misbehavior.

## Dealing with Conflict

Children experience conflict both in the world at large (as they observe it on television or through their parents' eyes) and in their own worlds (as they learn to deal with difficult human relationships). Here are some examples of how you can help children relate their own conflicts to larger conflicts in the adult world.

### Conflict Large and Small

Children not only observe adult conflict, they engage in it themselves. The similarities between the two are noteworthy. Here are a few major sources of conflict, with examples of how they have been played out at both levels.

■ *Conflict over territory.*

—A major cause of World War II was Adolf Hitler's belief that Germany had a need to expand into territory belonging to other countries. The other countries, of course, were not entirely in agreement.

—Yolanda and Chet, focused only on their own game, decided on a long-distance race, thus expanding the space they needed. Zooming their trikes across the blacktop, they broke up a game of hopscotch. The hopscotch players were incensed.

■ *Conflict over resources.*

—A reason given by Saddam Hussein for invading Kuwait in 1990 was that Kuwait was extending its oil lines under Iraq's territory.

—Three groups of first graders were working on an art project that required scissors, glue, and tape. Scissors, however, were in short supply, and the children spent much time and energy trying to convince others that their own need was immediate and greater. Sometimes they hid the scissors under their own paper to have them available when needed.

■ *Conflict over values.*

—As abortions have become more common and easily available in the United States, citizens have disagreed with each other about the morality of legalized abortion. For some, a woman's right to determine her physical state and future circumstances is paramount; for others, the embryo's right to life is more important.

—Joelyn and Tish watched Ben take a few coins from Matt's desk. They whispered about what to do. Joelyn argued that they should inform Mrs. Davis right away, because stealing was wrong. Tish argued just as vehemently that tattling was wrong.

Teachers are not usually in a position to alter world conflict, but they can affect the outcome of disagreements over similar issues at a more personal level. If Yolanda and Chet's teacher has taken the time to instill responsibility and respect for others, the two children will not only apologize but will help restore the hopscotch game to its original condition. The first-grade teacher could try two completely different solutions: only embark on activities when supplies are sufficient, or purposely have too few supplies and develop a system for sharing happily. In Mrs. Davis's case, it will be important to discuss tattling with the class, helping them know when it is important to share information with an adult and when children should work out problems on their own. This kind of discussion may need to continue off and on throughout the entire school year.

### De-escalating Conflict

Response to conflict may sometimes be aggressive ("an eye for an eye") or passive ("turn the other cheek"). But, as William Kreidler (1984) says, "The difficulty with these aggressive or passive alternatives is that they are not, after all, particularly effective ways of handling conflicts. They tend to be accompanied by physical or emotional hurt, humiliation, and suppressed anger. They also tend not to solve problems" (p. 13). Whether the combatants are toddlers or third graders or even warring adults, another option—de-escalation techniques—can work more effectively. "De-escalation cools the conflict, keeping it from spreading and becoming more violent. At its best, conflict resolution is a de-escalation of a conflict that channels it along functional rather than dysfunctional lines" (p. 13).

When you want to help children de-escalate conflict, think of the following four points:

- *Who is involved?* How many children are fighting? How mature (capable of reasoning) are they? How angry is everyone?
- *Is the time right?* Is there time enough now to deal with this, or would it be better to do it later? Are the children still too angry to talk?
- *What de-escalation technique would be most appropriate?* What is the real problem here? Have these particular children used this technique before? Do I need to help them learn the technique?
- *Should the resolution be public or private?* Is this situation one that would be embarrassing or humiliating if other children witnessed the de-escalation time? Could the other children in the class help in the resolution? (Adapted from Kreidler, 1984, p. 17)

Helping children learn to de-escalate and resolve conflict in positive ways is a developmental process. When toddlers first discover that their relationships with their peers cannot always go their way, it is too soon to begin teaching the complex interactions involved in the de-escalation process. Instead, consistently applied interventions usually work best. Examples include:

- Divert the attention of each involved child to another activity of interest.
- Offer hugs and attention all around.
- Remove one or more children from the area.
- Remove the controversial toys or materials from the area.
- Sing or play music as a diversion and peacemaker.

As children grow old enough to talk and understand adult language, their ability to reason grows also. It is at this time that conflict resolution techniques can be introduced. The following activities offer techniques that are appropriate for different ages and levels of development. The techniques may be used informally throughout the school year as a way of helping children experience the social studies firsthand, or you may pick and choose activities for a more formal lesson or unit that takes place over a defined period of time. This is particularly appropriate for children in the primary grades, especially if world conflict is much in the news. Table 14.1 on page 482 suggests the levels at which each activity is most appropriate. However, you should feel free to adapt the activities to different ages. This is particularly true if you are teaching kindergarten where activities suggested for preschool may be most appropriate at the beginning of the year and, toward the end of the year, some of the primary activities may be of more interest. Also listed are other curriculum areas into which that activity may be integrated. Some of the activities are adaptations from other sources, and these are given in abbreviated form. Full references are provided at the end of the chapter.

Activities at the beginning of this section are more appropriate for toddlers and very young children; those at the end are appropriate for primary children only. Most of the activities are suitable, with some adaptation, for all ages.

## Conflict Resolution

### Activities for Classroom Use or Unit Construction

**1. Early Etiquette.** A major reason for the practice of good manners is that it shows thoughtfulness toward others. This alone can go far toward preventing potential conflict situations. Learning to say "please" and "thank you" is possible from the first appearance of speech. Respect for each other's property—even if possessed only for a few minutes—can be taught from toddlerhood on. From the very first day of school, children learn that they walk around, not through or over, each other's toys and projects. With young children, this should include role play and/or a game of follow the leader, with you leading. If you play the game, challenge the children to walk behind you without touching a single thing. Then take them on as complicated and difficult a walk as possible for their age.

Any other aspect of etiquette can be taught in the same way: define the desired behavior, take the time to introduce it, then make the point through a role play or game situation. (It should be noted that etiquette is not simply culturally determined polite behavior. At its best, etiquette is an expression of thoughtfulness toward others.)

**2. Peaceful Sounds.** Play snatches of different kinds of music as the children move to each one. Include music that is extremely loud and thunderous and some that is quiet and peaceful. For very young children, just two choices are sufficient, while older children can concentrate on more. After they have danced, ask the children which music made them feel more peaceful. Play this music again as they move in peaceful ways.

With older children, an amusing, but instructive, discussion can ensue if you ask them to imagine and act out what would happen if the peaceful music were played to accompany a battle.

**3. Hello, I Like You!** Children sit in a circle with one child outside. This child pats another on the head and the two run in opposite directions around the circle. When they meet, they stop, shake hands, and say, "Hello, I like you!" The first player runs back and sits down, and the second player pats someone else on the head to continue the game.

Keep the group small and be sure everyone gets a turn. As children mature, the game may be extended so that each child says, "Hello, I like you because . . ." and thinks up the rest of the sentence.

**4. Ocean Friends.**   Children imagine the room is filled with water. They swim around with beanbags held on their head with just one finger. If a bag is dropped, the player freezes. A nearby friend takes a deep breath and dives down to get the bag and replace it on the player's head.

As children become more proficient, they can try moving without touching their beanbags.

**5. Dance It Out.**   Give the children a clearly explained conflict situation. Have them express through movement a peaceful resolution. A few volunteers can share their solutions by showing them to the rest. If there are many volunteers, children can pair up and show their ideas to their partners.

**6. War Play.**   Despite your best efforts, children may still engage in war play even if they must resort to secrecy and index fingers as weapons. Use this opportunity to help children gain control over their impulses, understand others' points of view, distinguish between fantasy and reality, and better understand world news.

- Engage the children in thoughtful dialogue:
  "Can you use the gun so it catches people instead of kills them?"
  "After you catch the bad guys, how can you help them learn to be good?"
- Help children see a positive resolution to the game. "How can we make this war end peacefully/so everyone is happy/so everybody can be a good guy?"
- Teach the uses of a truce. Introduce a white flag to each side. When it is waved, all fighting stops and one side suggests a way the war can come to a close or has an opportunity to discuss the issues that they are fighting about.
- If the war game reflects current world issues, challenge the children to help the real foes resolve their conflicts by playing out different solutions.

**7. Toy Classification.**   Gather a collection of toys, both the school's and those children bring. Mark off two areas on the floor and label one *War Toys* and the other *Peace Toys.* Individual children place single toys in their correct classification. Once this is done, place a single toy in the other area and challenge children to suggest ways it could be used to fit there. Repeat with others. Children should begin to understand better how nonweapons can be used hurtfully if the attitude is wrong and how weapons can be redefined for peaceful interaction.

**8. Peace Collage.**   From magazines, children cut out pictures that remind them of peace and peaceful solutions to conflict. As these are glued on a large sheet of butcher paper, which is then hung for display, brief conversations can be held about the experience as it teaches them to work harmoniously, cooperatively, and peacefully.

**9. Silent Drawing.**   Two children share one paper and one marker or large crayon. They remain silent while cooperatively making a picture. Afterward, discuss the ways in which it was easy or difficult to communicate peacefully.

**10. Cooperative Musical Chairs.**   Play this like musical chairs, except that children are not removed when the chairs are. Instead, children must share the remaining chairs. Since there is no focus on competition, the game may be stopped at any point, particularly if there is concern about safety.

**11. How Do You Feel?**   Choose an emotion (e.g., anger, frustration, happiness, sadness) and an activity (walking, shaking hands, sweeping the floor, throwing a ball). Children act out one of these, then do the same activity with a different emotion. Discuss possible consequences for acting in these ways. (Walking angrily may lead to bumping into a pole; walking happily may lead to awareness that someone needs your help.)

**12. Talking in More Than Words.**   Children role play both mean and peaceful ways to say different things. Suggestions:

I don't want to play with you.
We don't want you to play with us.
That isn't fair.
You just knocked my work over.
That's my crayon you're using.

As a follow-up, discuss whether it is easier to act in a mean or peaceful way, what makes being peaceful difficult, and why it is worth the extra effort.

**13. Is Everybody Happy?**   Present an interpersonal conflict situation to the children. Define the needs of both sides strongly enough that the solution is not one-sided or simple. For example, Brett and Meredith are building an airport in the block corner. They need one more block to finish the last side and are reaching for it just as Elena and Tim do, too. Elena and Tim need the block as a picnic bench in the doll corner. Ask: "Are Brett and Meredith happy?" "Elena and Tim?" "How could they solve their problem?" As suggestions are given, ask, "Would that make everyone happy?" When the answer is yes, explain that they have created a win-win situation because all sides win.

**14. Drawing on Peaceful Ideas.**   Present a conflict situation as in number 13. Children divide their paper in half (younger) or in fourths (older). Have the children draw one solution to the problem in each section. Children then write or dictate labels for each solution and, perhaps, stick a star on the solution they think is the best one. An informal discussion of why they placed the stars as they did will help children think through the reasons that some solutions may work better than others.

**15. Classifying the News.**   Collect a fairly large group of news and magazine pictures that show people in conflict and in cooperative situations. Mix them together and ask children to classify them as they see fit. Permit them to be free in their classifications. When they choose to classify the pictures into conflict and harmony, ask how they can tell which is which. Identify the body language and other aspects of the situations that convey what is happening.

**16. Rewriting the News.**   This activity is appropriate when children bring up adult conflict that is appearing on the news. Or you may bring in a newspaper article to read to them. Have the children identify the combatants and clarify briefly why they are angry. Show on the globe or a map where the conflict is taking place if the issues are territorial. Children then list possible peaceful solutions to the problem. This should include discussion of the pros and cons of each solution from the point of view of each side.

**17. Open-Ended Stories: Role Play or Puppets.**   Choose any story from your school collection or reading program in which there is interpersonal conflict. Read it to the children, stopping at a point at which a decision must be made to resolve the conflict in some way. The children then suggest a short list of possible solutions and act out each one themselves or with puppets. Let each enactment go further in its plot than the original suggestion to see how the decision might play out in real life. At a good stopping point ask each character how he or she feels about the way things have gone. Permitting, even encouraging, negative solutions will provide more understanding as children see and feel the results.

It is very important to establish a rule that prohibits physical contact in the role play or even between puppets.

**18. Open-Ended Stories: Structured Discussion.**   Essentially, this is the same activity as in number 17, but less active. As each suggestion is made, list it on the chalkboard, leaving extra space between each one. Instead of acting out the solutions, ask the children how each character will feel. To the right of the solution, draw a face of each character with an appropriate feeling expressed. This need be no more than the standard "smiley face" with changes in the mouth's direction and a bit of hair on top to differentiate the characters. Volunteer children may draw in the appropriate mouth after you create the rest.

Once each solution has been illustrated, observe the chalkboard to see

Table 14.1
CONFLICT RESOLUTION: ACTIVITIES

| ACTIVITY | LEVEL* | CURRICULUM | ADAPTED FROM |
|---|---|---|---|
| Classifying the News | P, Py | Math | |
| Cooperative Musical Chairs | P, Py | Music | |
| Dance It Out | P, Py | Movement | |
| Drawing on Peaceful Ideas | P, Py | Art | Kreidler |
| Early Etiquette | T, P | Movement | |
| Hello, I Like You | T, P | Movement | |
| How Do You Feel? | P, Py, | Movement Language | Kreidler |
| Is Everybody Happy? | P, Py | | Kreidler |
| Jumping to Conclusions | Py | Movement | Kreidler |
| Ocean Friends | P | Movement | Sambhava and Luymour |
| Open Ended Stories: Role Play and Puppets | Py | Language | Schuncke and Krogh |
| Open Ended Stories: Structured Discussion | Py | Language | Schuncke and Krogh |
| Peace Collage | P, Py | Art | |
| Peaceful Sounds | T, P, Py | Movement Music | |
| Picturing Peace | Py | Art | |
| Rewriting the News | P, Py | Language | |
| Silent Drawing | P, Py | Art | Sambhava and Luvmour |
| Talking in More Than Words | P, Py | Language | Kreidler |
| Toy Classification | P, Py | Math | Sambhava and Luvmour |
| War Play | P, Py | | Carlsson-Paige and Levin |
| What If . . . | Py | Language | |

*T = Toddler, P = Preschool, Py = Primary

which ideas generated the largest number of satisfied characters. Usually, the most peaceful, fair solution will have the most. Other times, a complex issue will yield no clearly "good" solution. This is also important for children to learn.

**19. Jumping to Conclusions.**   First, explain the meaning of "jumping to conclusions." Show a picture or provide a brief description and ask why. Some possibilities:

This child is crying. Why?
The man is angry at the boy. Why?
The lady is laughing at the man in the truck. Why?

The children suggest possible answers. As they do so, they should jump forward. Have two or three possible conclusions for each situation.

Then discuss how jumping to conclusions can cause problems in human relationships and how it might affect conflict. Give children an opportunity to share times when someone drew an incorrect conclusion about themselves.

**20. What If?**   Children write stories and illustrations describing what would happen in various swords-into-plowshares situations. Some suggestions:

What if tanks became tractors . . .
What if grenades became chickens . . .
What if arrows became pencils when they landed . . .
What if bombs became balloons . . . (and what messages would you put inside them?)

**21. Picturing Peace.**   Either individually or cooperatively, children draw a picture or diagram of the most peaceful world they can imagine. Or they can draw a picture from the current news, imagining the most peaceful possible solution.

## Extending Your Learning

1. Create a mini-unit for a single age group, perhaps one that you are working with now or will in the near future. The suggestions that follow can be supplemented with other ideas you find helpful in Chapter 11. Choose a social studies topic of interest to you and/or to the children with whom you are currently working. Identify the social sciences with which it most closely relates.

   - Define the learning goals of the unit.
   - Choose five or six activities that work toward your identified goals. Identify any other areas of the curriculum that integrate with social studies.
   - Try teaching at least one activity to your children or others who are available (even neighbor children will do).
   - Analyze what went well and what didn't. Adjust your activities accordingly.

2. Choose the social science with which you are least familiar. Visit a store or library to obtain any book in the field that is of interest to you in that field. If you don't have time to read the entire book, try the first three and the final chapters. Then choose one interesting thing you learned from the book and create an activity that can teach that idea, concept, or fact to young children.

3. Begin a collection of social studies resources. Old *National Geographics* are often available at book sales for nominal cost and offer much visual information about the world. Easy-to-read maps of all kinds will be useful if you teach in the primary grades. Write to consulates and embassies for any educational materials they have to share. Check through bookstores and libraries for high-quality social studies literature.

4. Choose a culture or country from those that are represented in your region's schools and about which you know little. Do an in-depth study of this culture or country. Read its history and learn its geography. Read literature written by its best authors. See films, if they are available. Talk to people from the culture or country. As you learn more, ask yourself if your attitudes and, possibly, your stereotyped views of the culture or country have changed. Think, too, about the effect your new knowledge will have on your teaching, if any.

## References

Carlsson-Paige, N., and Levin, D. (1987). *The war play dilemma.* New York: Teachers College Press.

David, K. (1989). *A child's war: World War II through childrens eyes.* New York: Four Walls Eight Windows.

Erikson, E. (1963). *Childhood and society.* New York: Norton.

Freud, A., and Burlingham D. (1943). *War and children.* Westport, CT: Greenwood Press.

Kreidler, W. (1984). *Creative conflict resolution.* Glenview, IL: Scott, Foresman.

Maxim, G. (1987). *Social studies and the elementary school child.* Columbus, OH: Merrill Publishing.

Raths, L., Harmin, M., and Simon, S. (1966). *Values and teaching.*

Rogers F., and Sharapan, H. (1991). Notes to adults on children's concerns about war. *Education Week,* 27 Feb., pp. 33, 35.

Sambhava, L., and Luvmour, J. (1990). *Everyone wins! Cooperative games and activities.* Philadelphia: New Society Publishers.

Schuncke, G. (1988). *Elementary social studies: Knowing, doing, caring.* New York: Macmillan.

Schuncke, G., and Krogh, S. (1983). *Helping children choose.* Glenview, IL: Scott, Foresman.

Seefeldt, C. (1989). *Social studies for the preschool-primary child.* Columbus, OH: Merrill Publishing.

Sunal, C. (1990). *Early childhood social studies.* Columbus, OH: Merrill Publishing.

UNESCO (1983). *Education for international co-operation and peace at the primary-school level.* Paris: UNESCO.

# 15

# Science

When you finish reading this chapter, you should be able to

- Plan science experiences in relation to children's physical, social/moral, and cognitive development.
- Develop science curricula that reflect the needs of individual children.
- Begin to plan units of science study that integrate other curricula.

As you think about this chapter on your own, you should be able to

- Find ways to enhance children's science learning by building on their curiosity.
- Model curiosity yourself as a teacher and a learner.

The sciences include physics, chemistry, biology, and their derivatives and branches, such as astronomy, geology, oceanography, ecology, botany, and zoology. Because the content of these sciences is physical, approachable, and interwoven with children's lives, science is an appropriate and intensely interesting subject for the early curriculum. Environmental studies, which incorporate the various sciences, provide a natural interest for young children because the focus is on their own lives. The following classroom description demonstrates how several learnings can take place at one time by using an activity centers approach.

## FIRST GRADERS MEET THEIR ENVIRONMENT

*Kathleen Sand's first graders have spent many weeks studying the environment of the immediate area around their school, the adjacent fields and forests, and the beach areas of their coastal island. (See the interview with Kathleen on page 502.) Now they are learning about the ways in which the Native Americans of earlier times interacted with the same environment. Their studies have included the Indians' closeness to nature as well as the impact of their behavior on the environment. For example, Kathleen's children understand the positive effects of living without modern construction and facilities and the negative impact of burning all vegetation on the island to make deer easier to catch.*

*Today, the children are working indoors at environmentally oriented centers. Although they may move about as they wish, everyone is expected to spend at least some time at each of the centers before the morning is finished. At one center, the children are making native-style dyes from found materials: marigold petals, green leaves, various mosses, hollyhock seeds, berries, a green tomato. One child observes the changing colors as he stirs his mixture and announces, "I'm making rainbow soup!" Another child gets down to the serious business of labeling the dye she has made from black-berries. Kathleen helps her sound out* blackberries *but doesn't correct the spelling imperfections.*

*At a second center, children are making fruit leather from applesauce and blackberries. When the work is done, the sheets of fruit are placed in the classroom dehydrator, which the children choose to call "the sun," understanding that this method is a modern concession to convenience and speed. Previous to this experience, the children have studied evaporation and the need to keep food edible, when there is no refrigeration, by drying it.*

*At a third center, a large salmon is temporarily in use for an art project. A dark dye is spread over one side of the fish and the children then make prints on large sheets of paper. They are aware that there will be a fol-low-up activity to dissect the salmon to learn how its body is constructed and utilized for survival.*

*The fourth, and final, center requires the children to pound bark strips into smaller pieces for weaving. This is done with heavy rocks. Sharper stones are used to bring out softer fibers for other uses such as kindling, pil-low stuffing, and fine weaving. The children have collected the bark them-selves and can identify the types of trees from which the various pieces come.*

*The entire classroom has been redesigned to resemble a longhouse, in-cluding an impressive entryway from the interior hall and a stone-ringed "fire" for large-group meetings. When center time is finished, the children gather together around the fire to hear Kathleen read the story they have written cooperatively about their visit to a local reproduction of an early longhouse. Kathleen has laminated their individual stories and illustrations and bound them into a Big Book, which will now be kept as part of the class library. Several children were sick when the book was made and she reassures them that, since the book is bound with rings, they will be able to add their contributions in the near future. The entire class seems satisfied with their book, listening attentively to what each child has written and try-ing to guess or remember who drew which picture. It is apparent to the ob-server that what the children learned in the museum reproduction about the Indian environment has been reinforced by the activities at school.*

On the surface, the morning activities in Kathleen's classroom seem to be an interesting collection of social studies activities. After all, the children are studying the historic life ways of Native Americans. Yet the center's focus is on the scientific aspects of local inhabitants' lives: learning successful ways to make dyes and from which materials, applying what they have learned about dehydration to make fruit leather, discussing the salmon's characteristics while creating prints and then dissecting it, and becoming intimately familiar with different kinds of bark. All these activities are practical ways to become acquainted with the physical, biological, and chemical properties of the local environment.

Through these activities the children are exposed to writing, reading, art, and social studies. Also, by labeling dyes, making salmon rubbings, weaving bark strips, and listening to the stories they wrote, they learn more about In-dian life. Because much of their learning happens in this integrated way, Kathleen's first graders are largely unaware of which academic subject they are studying. Instead, they see what they're doing as part of the larger study they are making of their island environment.

Because they have an intense interest in the environment and in preserv-ing it, the children are not intimidated by activities that require scientific processes, or that might be labeled chemistry, physics, or biology. In fact, they are inspired by what Kathleen sometimes labels "difficult tasks." These are activities that, by definition, require extra thought from the children. Most important in this attitude toward scientific learning is Kathleen's own interest and confidence in what she is doing. She is aware that children can only be turned on to science if the teacher first sets an example.

Kathleen's view of early childhood science—hands-on exploration integrated into a curricular theme and encouraged by teacher enthusiasm—is, in some ways, a modern one while also reminiscent of much earlier philosophies. In the following section, we will see how science education for young children has altered its character to suit varying attitudes over time.

## Making Connections: History and Theory

From the beginning of schooling in the United States until today, religion and morality have been linked with children's science learning. Near the end of the eighteenth century, nature books were imported from England with the hope that children would learn about and love God's creation. Today, as we have learned more about this planet's beginnings, parents and education groups from different religious and philosophical views have struggled to ensure that those views are represented in school science curricula.

Additionally, there has been a long-standing controversy regarding age-appropriate science content and the best methods for teaching it. To understand the different views, we can return again to Locke and Rousseau. The Lockean view holds that there is a discrete body of knowledge about the world that children should learn efficiently and enjoyably. This view leads to a model of science education that focuses on choosing which science concepts children are ready to learn, then teaching those concepts in meaningful ways. The Rousseau view, on the other hand, is more permissive, suggesting that children should be allowed to roam free among nature's wonders, questioning the meaning of their surroundings as their interests move them. Only as children express interest should the adult intervene, and then in a facilitative rather than an instructive way.

From the turn of this century until the mid-1950s, derivatives of these two views of childhood science were both prevalent and, thus, in conflict with each other. One, structured and knowledge-based, saw the child as an intellectual learner; the other, based on nature study, played to children's interests, emotional development, and imagination. In 1957, when the Soviet Union began the space race by launching earth's first artificial satellite, science educators took a closer look at the American failure to be first in space and decided that the science curriculum needed revision. The next twenty years produced a number of federally funded science programs that included curricula designed to begin in kindergarten. Eventually, however, concern over civil rights and a back-to-basics curriculum, which didn't include science, dried up the federal dollars. Science became devalued at all levels.

In recent years, interest has again arisen as American students' scientific knowledge has been compared unfavorably with the knowledge of students in other countries. Donna Jean Carter (1990), president of the Association for Supervision and Curriculum Development (ASCD), has said,

> Our science-deficient curriculums are effectively disqualifying the United States from contributing to the worldwide search for scientific and technological solutions and further reducing our economic power. In fact, with the increasing quality-of-life issues facing us today, such as environmental pollution and world hunger, to stay the course is to act as a lamb being led to slaughter. (p. v)

Carter suggests that it is time for teachers to join with administrators, school boards, and communities to "ignite a perpetual flame in the minds of youngsters" (p. 6) so that this negative trend will be halted.

Echoing Carter's concern, a group of eight ASCD science writers point out that,

> [a]lthough only 5 percent of the current student population will choose a scientific career, *all* students will live in a world that is increasingly shaped by science and technology. Science capabilities will be required for individual decision making and for the economic and technological advantage of our country. Making science a priority in schools today can equip students to live in the complex world of tomorrow. (Loucks-Horsley et al., 1990, p. 1)

Today we realize that science education should begin in the earliest years. Young children have a natural enthusiasm for the world around them, and teachers can build on this to enhance their learning and to foster even more enthusiasm. This accomplished, children are far less likely to turn off to science in the late elementary years, a phenomenon all too common today.

The current philosophy and theory behind early childhood science learning is not the focus of as much controversy as in decades past. While there are still some remnants of the "traditional" knowledge-based approach, our constantly developing and changing understanding of science has made it difficult to assume a body of knowledge that children should learn. The developmental, Rousseau-like approach is more popular, particularly in the earliest years in which toddlers and preschoolers can learn much just from exploring freely. The most accepted approach, however, is based on Piagetian theory.

## A Theory of Early Science Learning for Today

In Chapter 13 we discussed the Piagetian view of knowledge, as proposed by Constance Kamii and Rita DeVries, that there are three qualitatively different types of knowledge. The Kamii-DeVries framework can be applied to science learning as well. *Social knowledge* is that which is arbitrarily decided upon by society and includes the naming of objects and ideas. When children learn animal classifications or memorize the names of garden flowers they acquire social knowledge. If memorizing names is the extent of children's learning, however, their knowledge is at a very shallow level. *Physical knowledge* is that gained by interacting with objects. As children act on the objects or observe them, they gain a better understanding of their attributes. If this learning doesn't lead to further connections or meaning, however, again their knowledge remains shallow. *Logico-mathematical knowledge* is that which makes connections and relationships between items of social and physical knowledge. For example, a child may observe that a bright, shiny stone rolls easily down the driveway. Seeing that a dingy, gray stone doesn't roll as easily, she may conclude that ease of rolling is connected to color. Playing with yet another stone, however, shows her that some dingy, gray stones are capable of easy rolling. The child begins to understand that it is the shape of the stone that affects the rolling. According to Piagetian theory, the child constructs this knowledge internally. Such construction is in contrast to externally imposed physical and social knowledge.

Social and physical knowledge are not unimportant. Children need the social knowledge that tells them what things are named, and it is from acting on physical objects that they construct a logico-mathematical framework. But it is self-constructed logico-mathematical knowledge that provides truly internal understanding. Science educator Robert Smith (1987) explains:

> As physical knowledge develops, children become better able to establish relationships (comparing, classifying, ordering) between and among the objects they act upon. Such relationships (logicomathematical knowledge according to Piaget) *are essential for the emergence of logical, flexible thought processes* (p. 35).

Teachers of early childhood science sometimes confuse physical knowledge with logico-mathematical learning. They believe that giving children plenty of hands-on experiences will be sufficient, that they will just "learn by doing." According to Piagetian constructivist theory, the critical logico-mathematical element is then lacking. ASCD science writers Loucks-Horsley et al. (1990) argue that simple, hands-on science makes

> no attempt to help [children] derive meaning from their experiences. They are either left on their own, or they are told what they should have observed or learned. Constructivist science is based on the notion that we

learn best when we are able to construct our own knowledge. Helping children do this from real-life experiences is good science teaching. (p. 49)

Science educators Christine Chaillé and Lory Britain (1991) agree:

The hands-on nature of activities is an important part of a constructivist curriculum, but in and of itself this does not make an activity a constructivist one. This is because the constructivist sees the essential activity as what goes on in the child's head, not in his or her hands. (p. 20)

The following section provides some ways in which teachers can help children progress from physical and social to logico-mathematical knowledge.

## Applying Constructivist Theory in the Classroom

Young children construct their own learning only when they are left free to experiment and manipulate on their own, with guidance and encouragement provided by the teacher when appropriate. Thus, formal instruction is a poor choice of method. Instead, children should be permitted to *be* scientists. That is, they should be allowed to observe, classify, hypothesize, predict, experiment, compute, and communicate the results of their findings. This type of early learning is sometimes called *sciencing*. McNairy (1985) defined it as

the process of active inquiry into and subsequent construction of relationships in both the physical and social world . . . the use of scientific process through physical encounters with the environment for the purposes of creative problem solving and the development of intelligence. (p. 385)

When children encounter the environment on their own terms, and thus engage in sciencing, they can be guided toward a number of the processes or thinking skills that adult scientists use. Children, of course, will use these processes at a level appropriate to their age and development.

*Observation* may be the most important process for young children. It has been described as "the fundamental building block for all of the other processes and thus must be stressed in every way possible throughout *all* of the various activities carried out in sciencing" (Neuman, quoted in Smith, 1981, p. 8). Such an important skill is much more than simply a short viewing session. When young children observe, all their senses participate as they touch, smell, listen, taste, and watch. A baking experiment, for example, allows children to feel the dough's texture, smell the dough as it changes from raw to cooked, listen to the sound of the dough as they punch it down or stir it around, taste the final product, and watch each step as it happens.

*Classification* was addressed in the earlier chapter on mathematics, and it is important in science as well. As children group and regroup objects according to their self-created classification schemes, they construct relationships between and among the objects. Some classifications that children might make as part of science experiences could be edible and nonedible plants or parts of plants, sea- and land-based animals, and frozen and liquid forms of water.

*Prediction* can be nonsensical or magical without some teacher direction. With teacher direction, young children can move toward knowledgeable logic. One school ran a contest for all children from kindergarten through twelfth grade. The object was for each class to make a guess as to how many pieces of bubble gum were in a large glass container on the librarian's desk. The class with the closest estimate would win the bubble gum. The first graders, who had been practicing logical prediction in their science experiences, came in second, right behind the eleventh graders. (The eleventh graders generously shared their prize with the younger children.)

Prediction is guided by such questions as "What do you think will happen if we . . .?" At first, children are not concerned about the accuracy of their predictions, particularly in the preschool years. With practice, however, they can reflect back on the logic of their predictions and become more accurate, as the first graders demonstrated.

*Experimentation* provides children with an opportunity to predict, operate on, and observe changes. Chaillé and Britain (1991) suggest three basic questions to generate early childhood experimentation. The first, "How can I make it move?" leads to experiments in physics. The child who rolled stones of different colors and shapes down the driveway was asking this physics question.

"How can I make it change?" leads to chemistry experimentation. Children at an easel who have been given permission to mix paint colors ask this question of themselves each time they try to create a new shade.

"How does it fit or how do I fit?" leads to experiments in biology. It also leads to the questions: "Who am I in relation to the rest of the world?" "How do my actions affect my world?" Chaillé and Britain view these questions as important in helping children toward social perspective taking, in which children view the effects of their actions and subsequently develop sensitivity, empathy, and appreciation for the natural world. A biological experiment of this sort might be to deprive individual plants of water or sunlight or soil and then chart the results.

*Communication* takes place both during and after a science experience. Children talk informally about what they are doing, often to no one in particular. "I'm mixing the water in now," or "This stuff is turning green," or "Why won't it move anymore?" may be internal thoughts that need to be verbalized but aren't meant as conversation starters. You can talk informally, too, but should have a purpose in doing so. "I wonder what will happen if

Constructivists believe that children should be given the freedom to *be* scientists, that is, to observe, classify, hypothesize, predict, experiment, compute, and communicate the results of their findings just as real scientists do. This type of active learning is sometimes called "sciencing".

we put just one more block on top?" or "Is there some way we could make that a lighter pink?" are questions that foster thinking as well as continued communication.

At the end of a science experience, children can communicate what happened by dictating the events and results or by writing reports on their own. If primary children are working independently or in small groups at a center, it may be helpful to provide worksheets with a simple guiding structure. The sentence starters below are examples that can be changed according to the experience provided.

- The question we asked was
- First we
- Then we
- We observed that

Smith (1981) makes a strong case for the importance of the communication process when he says,

Because preoperational children are egocentric, increased opportunities to interact with classmates, share viewpoints, and listen to others will help children realize there are viewpoints other than their own. Such understandings will help children in their transition from egocentrism to operational thought. (p. 10)

One approach to sciencing that is particularly appropriate to children in the primary grades has been recommended by Canadian early childhood specialist Selma Wasserman (1988). She refers to it as "play-debrief-replay." Wasserman suggests that, in addition to the scientific processes just discussed, children need to learn "what all scientists must know in order to be successful: how to fail and keep trying" (p. 230). Her three-step sciencing process is designed to give children the skills and courage for such risk taking.

- In the first *play* stage of the sciencing experience, the teacher prepares the children and the experience in such a way that scientific inquiry may lead to increased scientific understandings. Wasserman equates this stage with scientific investigation in which children "manipulate experimental variables; generate hypotheses; conduct tests; observe, gather, classify and record data; examine assumptions and evaluate findings" (p. 230). In this stage, the teacher avoids telling the children what to do, but does facilitate their inquiries.
- In the *debriefing,* the teacher helps the children reflect on their experience and extract meaning from it. The teacher uses reflective questioning to help children relate their findings to science concepts, extract new scientific principles, reconsider the conclusions they came to, and lay the groundwork for the next stage.
- When children *replay,* they may repeat the first experience to see if they can replicate their results, or they may alter an experiment based on their reevaluation during the debriefing, or even use the first experience as inspiration for a related but new experience.

This three-step sciencing process is much like the activities of real scientists in actual laboratories, and Wasserman argues that this is the most effective way for children to gain their own best scientific understanding.

## Making Connections: Perspectives on Development

Cognitive, social, and physical development are the focus of this section, with references to previous chapters as well as to developmental issues that relate specifically to science.

## Cognitive Development and Science

Scientists employ mathematics in much of what they do. Astronomers, for example, use mathematical calculations to learn about the universe, including those parts they cannot see. Geologists use math to pinpoint the locations of earthquakes, geographers to calculate surface areas, and chemists to predict the rate of chemical reactions. Even in the primary grades the connections between science and math can be made. Children can learn about these connections by sciencing—by being scientists—rather than by simply studying science as a subject.

The primary division in cognitive maturity is between preoperations and concrete operations. While children at both stages require concrete objects for effective learning, it is in the second stage that logico-mathematical learning develops. Previous to this, the world only makes sense to children based on their egocentric view of it. Since some scientific learning does not evolve at the concrete operational level until late elementary school, children need preoperationally oriented learning experiences well into the primary grades.

In Chapter 13 several aspects of development were discussed that relate to science learning. These developmental changes are those observed by Piaget in his studies of children.

*Seriation* requires children to place objects in a logical order (e.g., from largest to smallest). Preoperational children can find the smallest and largest objects but have difficulty grading things by size. Ordering objects found on a nature walk or on the playground can be an instructive activity for young children.

*Classification* has already been discussed, both as a scientific process and as a mathematics skill. Because young children can focus on just one attribute at a time, complex classification is beyond those students in the preoperations stage.

*Conservation* is another mathematics/science skill that only emerges with concrete operations. As children work with clay, mud, or sand, they don't realize that the quantity remains the same although the shape may change. Or, as they pour water from one container to another, they believe that the quantity changes with the shape of the container. Their understanding of science experiences with materials such as water and clay is affected by their ability, or inability, to conserve.

Children's *perception of time* can affect their experiences with science. Young children's understanding of the passage of time is limited. This will make it difficult for them to comprehend the time needed for an experiment, particularly one that takes place over several days or weeks. You can use simple charts and graphs to help them keep track of time as well as any physical changes. Longer periods of time also present a challenge as children try to understand the distances between our times and those of the dinosaurs or other extinct animals.

Other developmental issues center on the fact that science education involves the study of natural phenomena and young children have not yet learned to respond logically to those that they observe. Until children are in late elementary school, for instance, many have trouble determining whether objects are alive or not. For young children, a deciding factor is whether an object moves or not. Thus, a car or train may seem as alive as a tree or a horse.

The concept of organisms changing over time is also difficult to grasp. Plants whose appearance changes over time are confusing to children, particularly if they must try to understand that a seed grows into a full-fledged plant, which then grows more seeds, which then turn into new plants. The caterpillar-to-butterfly sequence is totally beyond young children's comprehension and should not be studied intensely until a later time, despite the attractiveness of this springtime wonder.

Piaget's studies of children's understanding of cause-and-effect relationships led him to identify three basic characteristics that dominate their explanations of causality (Smith, 1981). The first of these is *animism,* or the belief that inanimate objects make decisions about the ways they act. For example, children may believe that the sun and moon take scheduled turns being asleep and awake, or that the sun shines because it wants them to be happy and warm. The second characteristic is *artificialism,* the belief that everything that exists has been built by humans or by God in a human fashion. Referring again to the sun, a child might explain that God created the sun so we would be happy when we play outside. The third characteristic, *magic,* is used to explain cause-and-effect relationships that are too difficult to explain logically.

## Social and Affective Development and Science

The way young children feel about science is determined, to a great extent, by the feelings of their teacher. Social learning theory explains such development of children's attitudes in terms of adult modeling. Unfortunately, many teachers remember their own science learning as confusing, tedious, or difficult. They are often under pressure to accomplish so much other teaching that such a negative subject is easily deleted. Few have had opportunities or training to think scientifically or engage in meaningful experiments, and conversations in the teachers' lounge and elsewhere serve to reinforce the lack of interest or confidence that teachers have in teaching science (Raper and Stringer, 1987). When teachers communicate their negative attitudes and lack of confidence about science, children respond by becoming more negative themselves. This creates an unfortunate cycle in which, generation after generation, science learning is increasingly neglected.

If you feel undereducated in science or lack confidence, you can break the cycle by reading (many children's books are a good place to start), by taking courses and workshops, and by making an effort to demonstrate a more positive attitude. It is not necessary for you to portray yourself as extremely knowledgeable about science. If children raise questions that you are unable to answer, you can express enthusiasm for exploring the answer together. Modeling scientific curiosity is an important step in helping children keep their own natural curiosity as they grow older.

### Moral Development and Science Learning

For children, as for adults, there is much to science that has a moral dimension. As children gain perspective-taking skills, they start to wonder and worry about the feelings of animals and plants. Their worries may well be compounded if they retain such early views as animism and artificialism. For example, children might believe that plants will suffer pain if they are deprived of water or sunlight. Teachers need to help children sort out their understandings as experiments are undertaken.

Teachers can also direct children's developing perspective-taking skills and moral concerns related to science. Some of today's issues can be adapted to children's levels of understanding. For example, concern for the environment can be applied to the environment in the school. Young children can lead drives to expand recycling activities, join in litter patrols, and care for the grounds. Their concern for animal welfare can be translated into responsible care for classroom pets.

Science usually does have a moral dimension to it. As children become aware of issues and are encouraged to act on their concerns, they increase their understanding of the importance of participating in science in a responsible way.

### Physical Development and Science

An awareness of the body and its senses is a vital part of early science study. The child's own body might be considered the ultimate in concrete learning materials, provoking curiosity and questioning. Such activities as brushing teeth, taking naps, and bathing not only promote health but teach children respect for their bodies. Teaching young children the names of body parts should be accompanied by activities that demonstrate what the body parts can do. If there is a line on the floor where the class gathers, it can be used for this purpose. Children can be asked to touch a knee or a finger to the line or perhaps one hand and the nose. Playing The Hokey Pokey is always popular with children and helps them understand body parts even when they aren't yet able to keep up with the instructions.

## Making Connections: Diversity Among Children

Children's understandings about science must be determined by their cognitive maturity. This is particularly true toward the end of kindergarten and in the primary grades when children achieve concrete operational under-standings at varying rates. Additionally, different children achieve different understandings at different times. Two first-grade girls, for example, loved to classify everything they could find outdoors, and had no trouble sorting leaves and bark according to their appropriate tree names. For one girl, this level of sorting was as far as she could go. Meanwhile, her friend would spend considerable time trying new ways to separate the treasures they had found—by color or size or degrees of perceived beauty. The first girl would watch for a while or wander off, eventually returning to insist, "Now, put everything back where it's supposed to be!"

Activities such as this one make it possible to reach children at different levels. When the girls classified their nature objects, they chose the activity freely. Meanwhile, the second girl increased her understanding of classifica-tion because the teacher came by to ask, "Can you find other ways to group the things you found?" The first girl heard the same question but, being un-ready to respond, continued to engage in classification at her own level. Soon, however, she might be ready to understand more. At such time, she could learn from observing her friend and perhaps recall the teacher's encour-agement. If her teacher was alert, a return visit and skillful questioning would provide further encouragement.

Teachers of young children should be careful not to communicate the view that science is primarily a boy's activity. This stereotype has succeeded in discouraging many genera-tions of young girls from pursuing scientific occupations.

In science as in mathematics, girls and boys eventually come to perform differently and have different interests. Here again, it is the boys who succeed and the girls who fall behind. Yet investigators have not found any biological (genetic or anatomical) or intellectual causes for this difference. Something else seems to be at work. As Barbara Taylor (1993) points out, "attitudes that discourage girls from science participation include teachers not expecting girls to excel in science, families encouraging boys and discouraging girls from taking science classes, and differences in teachers' treatment of girls and boys" (p. 8). Even science textbooks tend to show more boys than girls in their illustrations, as if to send the message that boys should pursue scientific interests and girls should not. Early childhood teachers have a special responsibility to encourage girls as well as boys to engage in and enjoy science, before the textbooks and society can convince the girls that they are not capable.

## The Science Curriculum

Science learning is available everywhere. Writers, educators, and scientists themselves have much to say about the pervasive nature of potential science curriculum.

Their commentary can be poetic, as in this statement from Maryann Ziemer (1987):

> In countless ways, science is at work everywhere and at all times in this beautifully ordered, yet full of surprises, world. It's there for the looking . . . try to see the way children do: Our world is a huge hands-on museum, a well-stocked laboratory, a fascinating never-ending field trip. (p. 45)

Sometimes these experts hope to awaken in teachers an awareness that science curriculum can be pulled from everyday school life, as in this statement from British writers George Raper and John Stringer (1987):

> Even though they are not always recognised as such, by teachers or pupils, many primary classroom activities can be called "science" and many of the attributes of science and ways of working in science are common to other areas of the curriculum. Science can evolve from these areas— possibly by altering the emphasis of the work, increasing the breadth of a topic or by looking at particular aspects in greater depth. (p. 1)

At other times, they feel they must convince teachers that science curriculum even belongs in the school day. Bess-Gene Holt (1977) argues:

> Why plan science into the early childhood curriculum? For one thing, it is entirely appropriate. The study of the phenomena of the world is exactly

compatible with the nature of children. That is not so strange. Children are phenomena of the world, and natural ones at that. . . . The attitudes toward the world and one's place within it form in the early years. (p. 6)

Many seek to promote a science curriculum based on their positive experiences working with young children. Barbara Taylor (1993), whose career has included many of these experiences, says:

It is amazing to see how much time and interest can be involved in events that are seemingly common, and even boring, to older children or adults, such as using magnets to attract paper clips, being mesmerized by water, building up and knocking down blocks, or pouring rice between containers while listening to its crisp sound and watching its jumping action. . . . Science is all around us. We cannot escape it. And it is the magnificence of science that urges us to always move forward while we examine and use the opportunities around us. (p. v)

Taking the world-encompassing subject that is science and organizing it into a teachable framework is the first task of creating the curriculum. There are different approaches from which you can choose. One is to organize the curriculum according to the scientific concepts appropriate to each age: how plants get their food, where animals live, where rain comes from (Good, 1977). Another is to cluster lessons according to children's typical interests, such as the properties of things (color, shape, texture, magnetic properties); ecology and environment (walking in the woods, building a terrarium); or the patterns and relationships within properties (tastes, sounds, colors) (Arnold, 1980). A related approach is to choose topics of interest and plan appropriate activities: air, animals, the body, color, ecology, food, machines, plants, water, weather, and so on (Taylor, 1993). It is also possible to organize the curriculum as adults do, grouping science study according to physics, chemistry, and biology experiences (Chaillé and Britain, 1991), or simply between the natural and physical sciences. Finally, an integrated approach (Schiller and Townsend, 1985) surveys the entire early childhood curriculum and environment and plugs in science activities and learning where they fit naturally. While any or all of these approaches can be used effectively, this curriculum section and the following illustrative unit focus on the final two approaches. In this way, the integrity of each of the sciences remains clear while children's natural learning across the curriculum is given its due.

## The Physical Sciences

The physical sciences deal with inanimate matter or energy and include physics, chemistry, geology, meteorology, and astronomy. While many physical science topics are appropriate for young children, it is always necessary to take into account the children's developmental levels. A lesson on air, for example, may be too advanced for younger students since the idea of unseen gases may be too abstract. Most experts agree that the study of electricity is more understandable if saved for the upper elementary grades, although simple experiments remain popular with many early childhood educators. Whatever decisions you make about your physical science curriculum, be sure that you base them on close observation of the children you teach.

*Physics* deals with the properties, processes, changes, and interactions of matter and energy. Chaillé and Britain (1991) have found that moving objects by pushing, sliding, rolling, tilting, and throwing provides a comprehensible way for young children to learn about physical properties. They suggest four criteria that maximize children's experiences:

■ Children must be able to produce the movement by their own actions, allowing them to make the connection between what they do and how objects respond.
■ Children must be able to vary their actions; otherwise, they will be unable to affect the outcome of the activity significantly. For example, if children are rolling balls down an incline, be sure the incline can be adjusted, so that the children can experiment satisfactorily with different slopes.
■ The reaction of the object must be observable, or else children will make no cause-and-effect connection between their actions and the resulting reactions. For example, if children are rolling objects down a long tube, be sure the tube is made of clear plastic so that the objects in motion can be visible.
■ The reactions of the objects must be immediate so that children can make a cognitive connection between their actions and the results. This is especially important for preoperational children.

Many physics experiences are available throughout the day, simply by focusing children's attention on the physical properties of whatever activity they are engaged in. Other experiences require a plan for science learning accompanied by specialized materials. Some physics activities you might consider:

■ Point out that the playground swing is a pendulum and the slide an inclined plane. Have the class observe them in motion, then experiment with other pendulums and planes. Suggest that children vary the steepness of a wooden board while rolling toy cars down it. Have children determine if steepness alters the velocity of the cars. Attach identical heavy weights to strings of several lengths. Have the children experiment to see if the length of the string affects the length of the swing (adapted from Ziemer, 1987).
■ Collect simple musical instruments from many cultures. Place them in a corner where children can experiment with them. Encourage children to use the instruments in different ways to achieve different types of sounds.

### *Learning from the Environment: A Conversation with Kathleen Sand*

Repeated sailing trips to the San Juan Islands, off Washington's coast, convinced Kathleen Sand and her husband that they should move to the area. She now teaches first grade in one of the small, rural schools that dot these beautiful islands. While her school is known for its dedicated teachers and creative approaches to curriculum development, the building space was designed for the smaller class sizes of earlier generations. Thus, much of the teachers' time and creativity must be dedicated to providing a good education with insufficient space.

In 1988, Kathleen observed early education in England, coming back with ideas for expanding the teaching space to include the outdoors and for creating an environmental curriculum for the entire elementary school. She lists with enthusiasm the positive elements she found in the British infant schools where children ranged from four to eight years: "The children had the natural freedom to go in and out all day doing different studies; there would be ponds outside and laboratories inside . . . the children would bring things in to look at under the microscope; there were rabbit hutches that the children cared for; children could work on a project for a month if they wanted; there were chores and responsibilities for taking care of the environment, but these were tied to whatever they were studying. There was just a feeling of *family,* with their unstructured day, integrated curriculum, and multi-age grouping."

Although the other elementary teachers picked up Kathleen's newfound enthusiasm, they soon realized that their local situation would make some adaptations difficult. For example, her school complex includes grades kindergarten through twelve. Because much of the space is

shared, "We're always dependent on what's going on over there in the high school," Kathleen explains. "We can't figure out a way to unstructure and leave things open because something is always going on that requires us to live by schedules." Kathleen and the other elementary teachers would also like to arrange their classrooms according to multi-age groupings, but they are having difficulty convincing the community that it is a good idea. [The citizens recall all too well that the school was once so tiny that several grades were combined in one classroom. It is difficult to persuade people to switch from the concept of varying *grades* struggling to meet academic achievement requirements while sharing one teacher, to a concept of varying *ages* learning much from each other in an ungraded classroom with team teaching.]

Despite these setbacks, Kathleen has found some measure of success in transporting the British ideas by focusing on the school's natural environment. In one corner of the property there was an unused grassy area with room for a pond and a series of gardens. While transforming the space wouldn't require a great deal of money, it would require more than the school had available, and it would also require some adult time and energy. The resulting community effort included the volunteer efforts of a landscape architect and donated materials, funds from the state's wildlife project and from a "Bingo for Pies" event, and a community construction effort in celebration of Earth Day. The completed project includes a collection of over sixty native trees and plants, a cedar-post fence, a gardening area for each grade, compost bins, birdhouses, an arbor with entry gate, and—the component Kathleen most wanted to adopt from England—a pond stocked with fish. Much of the project's design was planned, measured, and executed by the children themselves.

For her first graders, Kathleen designed a year-long curriculum that used the new environmental center in conjunction with the indoor classroom and with field trips to interesting areas around the island. She soon discovered that using the outdoors as a teaching environment required some adjustment in her approach to teaching. For example, either indoors or out, there had to be time set aside for children to explore new materials in their own way. Outdoors, however, Kathleen found that "you have to plan well ahead of time. It probably isn't that different from what you'd do in the classroom, but it feels different because of the magnitude of the space and the time it takes to work through the initial stage. For example, throughout September and October the children don't develop a sense of stewardship or ownership of the center as an outdoor laboratory. It comes naturally over a period of time because, at first,

it's seen by the children as an extension of the playground. They interact with it in an exploratory manner, but after a series of experiences in which they observe, nurture, measure, water, and care for the growing things the children begin to bond with the center. As a teacher, you have to consciously know that the process is going to happen and that it's okay."

Kathleen points out that even in September and October learning takes place in the outdoor center, but that it would take a very close observer to see beyond the overtly play-oriented attitudes. Right from the beginning, the children enjoy touching and smelling and they start to feel involved. Kathleen has found that the results can be an "almost magical" feeling among the children that inspires extended periods of scientific experimentation, drawing, poetry, and story writing. "I don't think you can initiate or capture that magical feeling in the classroom very often. The situation indoors is synthetic, less natural, and that makes it harder," Kathleen says.

While her hopes for freedom of movement in and out of the classroom and for multi-age grouping still belong to her long-range plans, Kathleen has thoroughly incorporated the outdoors as a natural learning site into her teaching style and into the children's expectations.

*To think about and discuss: There are numerous reasons teachers give for not using the outdoors as a teaching and learning environment. These include time taken away from required learning, a climate that is either too hot or too cold, the lack of enthusiasm of some children for spending time outdoors, some teachers' own dislike for being outdoors, and the accompanying dirt and clutter that tend to take over the classroom. What are some other reasons you can give for not making use of the outdoors? What are some ways in which these problems might be surmounted so that the outdoors can be incorporated into your teaching environment?*

Provide materials for homemade instruments, which can be compared for types of sounds: empty oatmeal boxes, other sturdy boxes, rubber bands, beans of various sizes for shaking instruments, and glasses filled with water at varying levels.

■ As children learn about sounds, they can become aware that movement is necessary to make sounds. Have the class close their eyes while one child at a time makes a movement or does something with an object. Children then take turns trying to guess what object was moved to make noise.

■ Have the class make paper airplanes of various sizes and shapes. Send several into the air at once, then try to determine why some fly farther and higher than others. Try to replicate the design of the most successful. Older children can measure distances, chart results, and revise designs to achieve the greatest success.

■ Ask for donations of old appliances that children can pull apart and try to rebuild. Items with gears and levers are particularly prized.

*Chemistry.* Chemistry deals with the composition and properties of substances, and the reactions that take place when substances are produced or changed into other substances. Since chemical changes often seem mysterious, children frequently believe that it is magic that makes them happen. An important goal for early chemistry experiences, then, is to help children grow beyond a magic orientation. Activities that relate to everyday experiences and materials are preferred over those that may be exciting and flashy but simply reinforce children's confusion. Some chemistry experiences and experiments, such as the following, encourage the transition to logical reasoning:

■ Use rolls of toilet paper and basins of water, combining the two in various ways, then observing the results. Introduce the activity and then follow children's instructions as they try predicting what will happen when different combinations are tried. The paper and water can be placed at an activity center for free use. Some possible experiments: submerge clumps of paper made from large sections of the toilet paper; submerge single sheets; put an entire roll in the water, then squeeze; add food coloring to the water, and either observe its movement or stir in the dye and observe what happens to the paper (adapted from Chaillé and Britain, 1991).

■ Have children experiment with various types of liquids and containers, observing that the liquids take the shape of the containers into which they are poured. Freeze some of the liquids, first having the class predict if they will take the shapes of their containers. Place the frozen shapes in containers of liquid, then watch them melt and take on the containers' shapes.

■ Have children mix paints and observe changes that take place. Some paints may be thicker than others; some may have lumps in them; colors will change in different ways; and all take on the shapes of their containers.

■ Make butter from whipping cream, using junior-size baby food jars. During group time, fill several jars about one-third full of cream, handing them to individual children. Begin by asking children to predict what will happen when the cream is shaken. Each child shakes a jar ten times as everyone counts, then the jars are passed to other children until everyone has had at least one turn to shake. As the cream changes form, have the children observe the differences and repredict what will happen. Eat the butter on crackers and compare its flavor to that of the commercial variety.

## The Biological Sciences

Biology, which includes botany and zoology, is concerned with the origin, history, physical characteristics, life processes, and habits of plants and animals. The effective early childhood setting contains both plants and animals that children interact with as a natural part of their day. These interactions are often less experimental than activities in other areas of science. In early childhood biology, the focus should be on observation of and participation with animals and plants. Your role becomes less facilitative of planned experimentation and more encouraging of a sense of wonder and appreciation of the natural world. Appropriate experiences include the following:

- Obtain one or two crickets from their habitat or from a fish bait shop. Place them in a jar with a ventilated cover. Add 1 to 2 inches of sand or soil and a dry leaf of crumpled paper towel. Keep the crickets for a few days only, providing a fresh bit of lettuce, apple, carrot, or celery every day. Children can observe and describe the crickets—body parts, number of legs, and so on. Discuss how a cricket moves and what it sounds like when it chirps. Demonstrate how a cricket acts as a natural thermometer. You can use it to figure out the current temperature by counting the number of chirps per 15 seconds and adding 40 (Fahrenheit), or by dividing the number of chirps in one minute by 7 and adding 4 (Celsius) (Kramer, 1989).
- Keep a gerbil, hamster, white mouse, guinea pig, or rabbit in the classroom. If you keep a rabbit, you may want to take it out of its cage from time to time. (Check first with all parents to be sure that no one is allergic to animal hair.) Have children observe the animal and describe its characteristics and behaviors. Older children can keep a record of behavior over the period of a day, and several days can be compared. Weigh the animal once a week on a balance or scale and record. A graph can be made to show any changes.
- Capture a spider in its habitat and put it in a large jar with a screened lid. On the bottom of the jar place about 2 inches of moist soil and add a stick or two for a perch and for web building. If you keep the spider more than a few days, provide it with a weekly meal such as a fly, cricket, or other spider. The meal should be alive and smaller than the spider. Have the class observe and describe the spider's parts, how it moves, and how it

Although some critics argue that science need not be taught in the early grades, most experts agree that young children's natural curiosity provides the perfect opportunity to motivate a lifetime interest in science.

catches its prey. If the spider makes a web, observe its shape, how it is attached to the sticks, and how the spider interacts with it once it is built.

■ Obtain one wide-mouthed glass jar for each child. For each jar, wet a paper towel and place it around the inside wall of the jar. Direct the children to wet several dried lima beans and place them between the towel and the wall of the jar. Fill in the empty space with soil. Children should keep the interior of the jar continually moist and observe daily changes as soon as the beans begin to sprout. They can keep a journal to record the beans' growth and measurements taken of their increasing height. Beans can later be transplanted to the class garden.

■ Grow parsley or other herbs. (Parsley is usually the most reliable.) Cut clusters for the children to taste raw and to cook in various projects. Hang some clusters in a cool, dry, and relatively dust-free place. Have the children observe the change from green to greenish gray and from tender to crisp. Let them try the dried parsley and compare its taste and texture with fresh. As a class project, cook soup in two pots: one with fresh parsley and one with dried. Compare the two.

## Integrating Science into the Curriculum

Because science is everywhere and at all times, because young children have a natural affinity for it, and because the most effective science program is one that is integrated into the total curriculum, it is important to incorporate it into children's learning throughout the school day. Some of the ideas presented above, such as those that involve painting or cooking, obviously have crossover value. Here are some other suggestions for integrating science into the curriculum.

- *In the block corner.* Children learn about gravity, simple machines, and inclined planes through their natural play. Posing appropriate questions ("I wonder what would happen if . . .") can lead to extended experimentation.
- *In the housekeeping corner.* Kitchen materials can include measuring cups and spoons, along with beans, flour, and rice. Focus your questions on classification (e.g., color, size, shape) and what would happen if the different items were mixed with water.
- *In the library corner.* Collect books that relate to current classroom science experiences, particularly those concerned with the plants and animals found in the classroom and the local geographical region.
- *As a part of social studies.* Expand on "What would happen if we . . ." science questions by asking similar questions concerning environmental change. Such questions can be starters for research or essays or simply topics for class discussion. Some examples: "What would happen if all the cows became extinct?" "What would happen if the rain stopped falling?" "What would happen if all the water became polluted?"
- *As a part of movement.* Use movement experiences to observe and experiment with physics understandings. For example, throw different objects in the air and observe what happens to them. Discuss why they didn't continue flying away. Children can experiment throwing a ball or beanbag in different ways, using their bodies to fight gravity. Help the children notice how using more of their body and more movement creates more force (Gilbert, 1977).

These are just a few suggestions for incorporating science into other areas of the curriculum. There are additional examples on pages 510–516.

## Curiosity: Critical to Science Learning and Beyond

Curiosity—eagerness to learn and know—is natural to young children, but it needs fostering. Enthusiastic and supportive adults who are themselves curious provide the most encouragement. Uninterested adults who squelch curiosity as creating too much mess, noise, or inconvenience contribute to the deadening of children's desire to learn.

Curiosity, while applicable to any area of learning, is most frequently tied to science, perhaps because it is essential to experimentation, observation of change, and the sense of wonder that underlie true science learning. George Raper and John Stringer (1987) have said that early science learning

> is not merely teaching children a mass of scientific knowledge or content for its own sake, but it is concerned with stimulating the development of a curious and questioning attitude so that children can begin to understand more fully their natural and man-made environments; to begin to appreciate a variety of problems; and to develop a framework for their solution. (p. 1)

Maryann Ziemer (1987) argues for wonder, a focus on discovery, and a sense of fun on the part of both child and adult. She maintains that we "do not 'teach' science; *joyfully, we investigate it together*. . . . We don't have to know all the answers. We may not be teaching facts, but we are teaching curiosity" (p. 45).

Barbara Taylor (1993), writing about young children's science learning, believes that

> adults who interact with young children need to be constantly aware of ways to enliven the curiosity of children. It should be done with truth and excitement, based on the present environment, and with a positive attitude. This will help young children in their observation, invention, exploration, and discovery of the world and people around them. (p. 58)

Children who are curious about science tend to ask questions that begin with *why*. When children ask such questions, they are interested in reasons and explanations, and this attitude is one that leads naturally to investigation. "This interest is similar to that demonstrated by any scientist, in that it leads to a cohesive body of knowledge. In other words, children think as scientists do—or scientists' thinking is much like that of young children—since both are interested in 'why' " (Raper and Stringer, 1987, p. 27).

Teachers can encourage "why?" questions and other questions of scientific interest through an appropriate approach. Taylor (1993) reports research suggesting that children ask more questions when they are in smaller groups than when they are in larger groups; one-on-one relationships between adult and child foster even more questions; and children ask more questions when things are interesting and when toys and materials are rotated. Teachers should also be aware that children express their curiosity in different ways. Some children touch, others verbalize, still others explore intensely, and some just examine objects quietly and independently.

While curious children always seem to have questions waiting to be asked, teachers can promote curiosity by asking questions themselves. These questions should be phrased so that they lead to exploratory thinking. The key is to ask *divergent* rather than *convergent* questions. Divergent questions are those that are open-ended and lead to independent thinking; convergent questions look for a single or right answer. There are times, of course, when a convergent question is appropriate, because there really is a right answer and it is important to know right now. For the purposes of fostering curiosity, however, divergent questions should be asked whenever possible. Some examples and comparisons:

*Convergent:* Can you name the colors in these bottles of paint?
*Divergent:* What will happen if you mix some of these colors together?

*Convergent:* Can you divide these leaves into green and brown piles?
*Divergent:* What are some ways you can divide these leaves?

*Convergent:* How many legs does the spider have? How about the fly?
*Divergent:* What do you think might happen if we put the fly in the jar with the spider?

Curiosity is demonstrated by children when they ask questions and follow them up with exploration. Curiosity is fostered by teachers when they ask open-ended questions and encourage children to follow through on their investigations. While curiosity is basic to good science learning, it applies to all areas of the curriculum as well. When children wonder whether a new book will be good and try reading it to find out, when they wonder whether they

To encourage the spirit of scientific inquiry, teachers should ask divergent, open-ended questions that trigger independent thinking on the part of students.

really are taller than their friends and ask to measure to be sure, or when they wonder what will happen if they place just one more block on an already tall tower, they have carried their curiosity across the curriculum.

The integrated science unit that completes this chapter makes use of children's curiosity, in this case about life in the sea. It is based on a unit that was created by a kindergarten teacher and taught over a period of about two months. Figure 15-1 demonstrates how the activities fit together across the curriculum.

## A Science Theme: Getting to Know Marine Life

"We are increasingly recognizing that our general welfare is associated with the ability to understand the world's oceans, to use their resources wisely and to provide for their continued health" (Fortner and Wildman, 1980, p. 717). After reading this and similar statements by others concerned about deteriorating conditions in the oceans, kindergarten teacher Mari Lou Pilon decided to provide her class with a knowledge and appreciation for marine life. She spent weeks collecting books and other materials and creating activities appropriate for her five- and six-year-old children. Although she lives within driving distance of the Pacific Ocean and has had a longtime interest in reading about marine life, Mari Lou found it important to do some extra informational reading so that she would feel comfortable answering children's questions. Committed to an integrated approach to curriculum, Mari Lou planned the unit's activities so that they would include reading, writing, singing, and mathematics. When the unit was complete, it contained more than fifty activities, games, songs and fingerplays, and resource books. With Mari Lou's permission, a number of the activities have been adapted for this text.

Note how the activities relate to earlier suggestions from this chapter. For example, since this unit is essentially devoted to biology, there is a focus on observation and appreciation rather than on experimentation. The knowledge children gain from this unit is social (animal names and body parts), physical (much hands-on exploration), and logico-mathematical (hypothesizing, decision making, and free exploration). Further, children are given opportunities to observe and hypothesize or predict before they are given information. When experiences happen in this order, children's curiosity is fostered and enhanced.

### Activities

#### General Marine Life

**1. The Mystery Box.** A good activity for starting the unit. In a fairly large box hide a sea star (starfish), a whale model, and a small dish of sand.

FIGURE 15.1
Curriculum Web—Marine Life

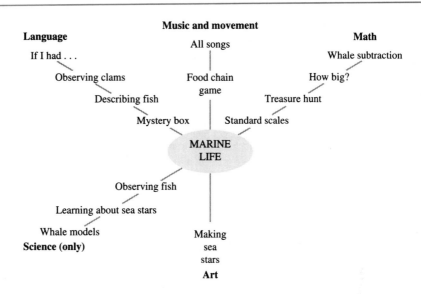

Children take turns asking the teacher questions that will lead them to identify each object. The questions must be phrased so that the teacher can answer yes or no. Once all three items are identified, the children try to determine what they have in common. Their place of origin can then be identified as the topic for upcoming study.

**2. Sand and Scales.**   Children work in pairs or groups of three. Each group has a tub of sand and a simple balance scale as well as an assortment of materials that will fit easily on the scale (scissors, Lincoln Log, Lego block, beanbag, etc.). A tablespoon of sand is placed on one side of the balance. Each of the other items is weighed after the children predict if it will be heavier or lighter than the tablespoon of sand.

Children "record" their findings on a chart with just two words at the top: *heavier* and *lighter.* To do this, they place each item on its correct side. If they choose, children can draw a picture of the item on its proper side so that the chart can be saved.

**3. Treasure Hunt.**   In the sand table, or in small tubs of sand, the teacher hides small, marine-related items (shells, rocks, etc.). The children hunt for the items, then classify them in groups of their choice. The teacher asks informal questions such as, "Which do you have the most of?" "The least?" "Can you group your objects any other way?"

**4. Food Chain Tag.**   For this activity you will need a large bag of popped popcorn, one plastic bag for each child, and approximately thirteen lengths of green yarn, eight lengths of black yarn, and six lengths of red yarn (all long enough to tie around children's waists)

Tie a strand of yarn around each child's waist, identifying the green as plankton, black as clams, and red as crabs. Bags represent the animals' mouths. Children form a large circle and the teacher spreads popcorn inside it.

The teacher gives a *GO* signal, and the plankton start scooping popcorn into their plastic bag mouths. Each clam then tags any plankton that has food in its mouth. Tagged plankton must pour their popcorn into the clams' bags, then sit outside the circle while the clams continue feeding.

Each crab may then tag any clam and take its popcorn. Tagged clams must sit outside the circle while the crabs continue feeding.

The entire game takes just a few minutes, with mostly crabs left in the circle. Discuss the following questions with the children: Why are all the crabs left? What would happen if there were no predators for the crabs? What happens to the clams if the plankton all die? Will this matter for the crabs?

## Activities for Learning about Fish

**5. Observing Fish.**   Use three or four whole fish, preferably of different types. In small groups, children observe the fish by carefully touching and by using magnifying glasses. If a microscope is available, scales can be observed more closely. Children compare the fish with each other and hypothesize what different body parts are for.

Before, during, and after this activity, children should have opportunities to observe the fish in a classroom aquarium. In combination with teacher questioning and children's hypotheses, some teacher explanation will identify the names and uses of the gills, fins, scales, and so on.

One fish can then be dissected for further understanding of its body parts and their functions.

**6. Describing Fish.**   In small groups, or as a whole class, children brainstorm their descriptions of fish. This should be done after there have been plenty of opportunities for observation as in Activity 5. The descriptions can be dictated to the teacher who writes them on a chart, or children can choose their own favorites for their personal journals. Illustrations can follow.

## Activities for Learning about Crustaceans

**7. Crab Observations.**   The children observe two crabs: one live and one cooked. The latter provides an opportunity for close investigation of its eight legs and two pincers as well as the mouth, eyes, and underside. The former provides a demonstration of the use of each.

Observation and activities can be modeled after those in Activities 5 and 6.

Activities for Learning about Sea Stars (Starfish)

**8. Learning about Sea Stars (commonly called starfish).**  This activity works best if you have access to the sea and can collect at least one or two samples of real sea stars, keeping them safe in a pail of seawater. Otherwise, use the books listed in the Resources section on page 516, or others available to you, for pictures of various types as well as descriptions of how they live.

Children observe the slow movements of the sea stars and gently touch them. They can count the legs on the live sea stars (a minimum of five) and those in the pictures. They may be challenged to learn the names of several varieties: crown of thorns, web sea star, sunflower, blood sea star, brittle sea star.

**9. Making Sea Stars.**  Make models of favorite varieties of sea stars using baker's clay. Color can be added during the mixing.

Recipe for baker's clay:

4 cups flour
1 cup salt
1 ½ cups water

Mix well and knead for about five minutes. After molding, bake at 350° for about one hour.

Activities for Learning about Mollusks

**10. Observing Clams.**  For this activity, you will need access to live clams. In a large, plastic dishpan, place about a dozen live clams in seawater. (You should have enough that children can observe in pairs.) Children touch and observe the clams, noting their feet and necks and the way they use them. Use magnifying glasses for a closer look.

Later, give each child a drawing of a cross section of a clam (from the books below or other available sources). Identify the clam's parts and label each one. Children may want to color or paint the clams to match the real ones they have observed.

**11. If I Had.**  Read the class informational material on the octopus, found in the books listed in the Resources section, or from a book such as *Octopus* by Carol Carrick (Clarion Books, 1978).

Children then dictate sentences or stories to finish the starter, "If I had eight tentacles like an octopus, I'd . . ." Children can illustrate their answers.

Activities for Learning about Sea Mammals

**12. How Big?**  Cut several 30-foot pieces of sturdy tape or yarn. Thirty feet is the approximate length of an Orca (killer) whale, and children can use this as a basic measurement for comparison with other whales and familiar objects. Outdoors, lay the tape on the ground and measure how many children, lying down end to end, equal one Orca whale. Place two tapes together, lengthwise, to equal a sperm whale and count children again. Lay three tapes together to equal the largest marine mammal, the blue whale, and, again, count children.

Compare whale sizes with objects around the school, such as buses, classroom wall, and playground equipment.

**13. Whale Models.**  Whale models can be purchased through school equipment catalogs and at educational supply stores. Models can be used to:

- Learn the names and characteristics of the different species.
- Learn how each kind eats and lives.
- Classify according to baleen/toothed.
- Order according to size.
- Refer to for drawing or clay modeling.

**14. Whale Subtraction.**  For this activity you will need a collection of goldfish crackers and a small piece of blue paper for each child. On each paper place a given number of crackers, perhaps five or six. Recite the poem,

> Out in the middle of the deep, blue sea
> Five (or six) little fish swam merrily.
> Along comes a whale as hungry as can be.
> . . . Gulp!

The children eat one fish, then tell how many they have left. The poem is repeated until all fish are gone. This game can be repeated with different numbers of fish, subtracting more than one at a time. Children should also remember which kinds of whales have teeth and eat fish.

Songs

When Mari Lou Pilon taught this unit, she made use of traditional tunes such as "There's a Hole in the Bottom of the Sea." In addition, she created some of her own songs to familiar melodies. One purpose in writing them was to reinforce the children's learning, such as the fact that crabs have *pincers,* not pinchers. Any of these songs can be altered to meet the needs of a particular class. Also, children should be encouraged to create their own songs.

1. *Three Silver Fish*

(sung to "Three Blind Mice")

Three silver fish, three silver fish
See how they swim, see how they swim
Their fins go left, their fins go right
Their gills breathe in, their gills breathe out

Did you ever see such a beautiful sight
As three silver fish?

2. *Crabs Are Walking*

(sung to "Frere Jacques")

Crabs are walking, crabs are walking
On the rocks, on the rocks
Watch out for their pincers
Watch out for their pincers
Pinch, pinch, pinch
Pinch, pinch, pinch

3. *Do You Know?*

(sung to "Do You Know the Muffin Man?")

Do you know the largest mammal
Largest mammal, largest mammal?
Do you know the largest mammal
That swims in the salty sea?

Yes, it is the huge blue whale,
Huge blue whale, huge blue whale
Yes, it is the huge blue whale
That swims in the salty sea.

It's as big as three school buses
Three school buses, three school buses.
It's as big as three school buses
And swims in the salty sea.

4. *Do It!*

(sung to "If You're Happy and You Know It")
(This song is a good choice for extended ideas from the children.)

If you're a clam and you know it
Stick out your neck
If you're a clam and you know it
Stick out your neck.
If you're a clam and you know it,
Then your neck will surely show it.
If you're a clam and you know it
Stick out your neck.

If you're a crab and you know it
Pinch your pincers.
If you're a crab and you know it
Pinch your pincers.
If you're a crab and you know it,
Then your pincers will surely show it.
If you're a crab and you know it,
Pinch your pincers.

If you're a shark and you know it
Show your teeth.
If you're a shark and you know it
Show your teeth.
If you're a shark and you know it
Then your teeth will surely show it.
If you're a shark and you know it
Show your teeth.

## Resources

The following books and kits offer information and ideas for teaching about sea life:

*"Come with Me" Science Series—Sea Animals* by Pat Perea. S/S Publishing Co., Shingle Springs, CA, 1977.
*If You Were a Fish* by S. J. Calder. Silver Press, New York, 1989.
*Investigating Science—Sea Life* by Barbara Laver. Creative Teaching Press, Huntington Beach, CA, 1987.
*Wonders of the Sea* by Louis Sabin. Troll Associates, Mahwah, New Jersey, 1982.
*Sea Creatures Do Amazing Things* by Arthur Myers. Random House, New York, 1981.
*Super Seashells and Other Sea Life.* Kit providing shells and activity and information cards. Educational Insights, Dominguez Hills, CA.

## Extending Your Learning

1. Choose a field of science you would like to know more about. Ask a children's librarian to show you all the books available on the topic. Read them and consider ways you could share them with young children. If there are experiments, try them yourself. Expand your knowledge by checking out books from the adult section. When you feel comfortable with your knowledge and your ability to engage in the experiments, try some of them with children. When done, analyze the experience. Were the experiments too easy? Too hard? Did they encourage independent thinking? Were you able to ask questions that fostered thinking?

2. Choose something in your natural environment about which you are curious. Ask questions about it that will lead you to learn something new. Research the answers to your questions.
3. Try adapting the Marine Life unit to suit your own teaching needs. You can make use of the activities and their principles while changing some specifics. Some suggestions and ideas to think about:

- You'll need to alter reading and writing activities depending on the age and skill level of students.
- You can substitute different animals for study, perhaps comparing animals from different bodies of water.
- Be sure to allow room for firsthand exploration. This is especially important to keep in mind if it is necessary to substitute pictures for some of the real objects.
- Don't hesitate to teach biological terms, including names of body parts, even to very young children.

## References

Arnold, L. (1980). *Preparing young children for science.* New York: Schocken Books.

Carter, D. (1990). Forward. In S. Loucks-Horsley et al. (eds.), *Elementary school science for the '90s,* Alexandria, VA: Association for Supervision and Curriculum Development.

Chaillé, C., and Britain, L. (1991). *The young child as scientist.* New York: HarperCollins.

Fortner, R., and Wildman, T. (1980). Marine education: Progress and promise. *Science Education* 64(5):717–723.

Gilbert, A. (1977). *Teaching the three r's through movement experiences.* Minneapolis: Burgess Publishing.

Good, R. (1977). *How children learn science.* New York: Macmillan.

Holt, B.-G. (1977). *Science with young children.* Washington, DC: NAEYC.

Kramer, D. (1989). *Animals in the classroom.* Menlo Park, CA: Addison-Wesley.

Loucks-Horsley, S., et al. (1990). *Elementary school science for the '90s.* Alexandria, VA: ASCD.

Raper, G., and Stringer, J. (1987). *Encouraging primary science.* London: Cassell.

Schiller, P., and Townsend, J. (1985). Science all day long: An integrated approach. *Science and Children* 23(2):34–36.

Smith R. (1981). Early childhood science education: A Piagetian perspective. *Young Children* 36(2):3–11.

Smith, R (1987). Theoretical framework for preschool science experiences. *Young Children* 42(2):34–40.

Taylor, B. (1993). *Science everywhere: Opportunities for very young children.* Orlando, FL: Harcourt Brace Jovanovich.

Wasserman, S. (1988). Teaching strategies. Play-debrief-play: An instructional method for science. *Childhood Education* 64(4):230–231.

Ziemer, M. (1987). Science and the early childhood curriculum: One thing leads to another. *Young Children* 42(6):44–51.

# 16

# The Expressive Arts

When you finish reading this chapter, you should be able to

- Make decisions for the arts curriculum based on a strong understanding of child development.
- Infuse the arts curriculum into the curriculum as a whole.

As you think about the chapter on your own, you should be able to

- Identify your artistic strengths and plan for carrying them with you into the classroom.
- Identify the artistic areas in which you are lacking and consider ways to expand your knowledge.

In the adult world, the expressive arts include drawing, painting, sculpture, architecture, music, literature, drama, and dance. While not disdaining utility entirely (some artistic products, may after all, be useful), their focus is on the aesthetic, on beauty and creativity. The arts add richness to life, lifting our thoughts and feelings beyond the mundane and commonplace events of our everyday lives. In the world of early childhood, the expressive arts are all this and more. They provide cognitive, social, emotional, and physical development opportunities in the education of the whole child.

Consider, for example, a group of three-year-olds dancing spontaneously to music the teacher has provided as pleasant background during playtime. Perhaps one or two of the children have seen older siblings practicing their ballet steps. They imitate and teach the steps to each other, all the while inventing movements of their own. To this cognitive, social, and physical experience they add the emotion of joy that comes from the freedom, creativity, and beauty of the activity. In this one activity is demonstrated the richness that is added to life through an expressive art and the deeper influence that such an experience brings to the development of young children. Thus, this final chapter has a dual goal: to conclude our discussion of curriculum with those areas that provide a very pleasant "icing" to the "cake" and to argue that those same areas are an important part of the cake itself.

There are three focus topics in this chapter: visual art, music, and movement. Creative writing/literature, too, is often considered an art and, within the whole language philosophy, can often be viewed in this way. Because creative writing and literature were discussed in Chapter 12, the material will not be repeated here. Movement as a general curricular area covers both creative expression and sports activities. The latter were discussed in Chapter 3, while creative movement is the focus of this chapter's discussion. Finally, children's visual art includes drawing, painting of all kinds, various types of sculpture, and work with clay or similar materials.

As in the previous curriculum chapters, we first make connections with the foundational chapters from early in the book. This time, however, you will be asked to help write the text.

## Making Connections

As a professional teacher, you will have many opportunities to make curriculum decisions. This will be true even if your school's philosophy or your district's policy ensures that the overall curriculum is provided for you. Even within guidelines and directives there are opportunities for teachers to make choices. Ideas, materials, games, and so on are easily available in the many trade books available in educational bookstores or departments, in public libraries, and in school collections. Sorting out the good, bad, and indifferent activities takes experience and knowledge. The purpose of this section is to provide you with some of that experience and to demonstrate to you that you have been acquiring much of the needed knowledge.

When choosing arts activities and experiences for children, it is often easy to be swayed by ideas that seem cute or fun or impressive to parents for back-to-school night. The knowledgeable teacher, however, considers the children's developmental levels and needs; the social, emotional, physical, and intellectual diversity within the specific classroom; and the overall goals of the program. This complex consideration requires some extra effort on the part of the beginning teacher. Later on, much of it becomes almost second nature, although periodic attention to detail will help you rejudge the needs and interests of your children. At this point, to help you see how knowledgeable curriculum decisions are made, you will be given an opportunity to do what other chapters have done for you: make connections between curriculum and the issues that should affect it.

For each issue there is a brief discussion with questions for you to think about. At the end of these, there is an empty chart (Table 16.1) for you to copy. It is suggested that you jot down brief summaries of your ideas in each section. When the chart is complete, you will probably have done more than will be necessary when you begin teaching because you will have covered several curriculum areas and ages.

## Development and the Expressive Arts

As you consider the discussion and questions in these sections, it will be helpful for you to refer to the chapters that pertain to each of them. This step will help take you from your academic course work to a professional and knowledgeable real-world application of what you have learned.

### Cognitive Development

Visual art, music, and movement often are not thought of as providing children with intellectual stimulation and cognitive growth. But such growth is an integral part of the experiences associated with each of these. In all of them, cognitive decisions are made about style; harmony of appearance, sound, or movements; mediums of expression; or issues related to time and space. As you review earlier chapters for applicable points related to cognitive development, ask yourself the following questions:

- Which philosophical view of cognitive development seems to provide the best answers to what children need and are capable of doing? What points should be remembered for curriculum development? Or should views be combined? If combined, what is the best that each view has to offer?
- What do children understand about time and space during the preschool years? During the primary years? How might these understandings affect their experiences with visual art? Music? Movement?

■ How is children's cognitive development affected by the people in their environment? How might this affect their understanding of the arts within the school setting?

In Table 16.1, note the answers to those questions that you believe are most important in making curriculum decisions. Put in parentheses those you are unsure about. After you complete the rest of the sections you may have a better feeling for what is important to include.

## Social/Emotional (Affective) Development

Experiences in the arts can be enjoyed alone or in groups, and children may choose one approach one day and the other a day later. Sometimes you will make this choice for the children, although you should consider your choice in terms of development and in relation to the needs of specific children. A review of social/emotional development can help you make such decisions appropriately. Some questions to be asked:

■ Which philosophical view of social development seems to provide the best perspective in relation to the expressive arts? Which points are the most important to remember when planning for interaction among the children? Is there more than one useful philosophy? If so, what are the best attributes of each?
■ What differences are there in social interaction among children of preschool and primary age? How will these differences affect curriculum decisions related to visual art? Music? Movement?
■ In what ways are children affected by the modeled social/emotional ac-

Although not usually thought of in terms of providing opportunities for cognitive development, visual activities such as this involve the child in decisions about sizes, colors, and layout, as well as the content of the picture.

tions of the adults in their environment? How might this affect children's social and emotional experiences in the expressive arts?

■ What are some of the emotional needs that young children might have? What are ways that these might be met by visual art? Music? Movement?

■ Whether the cause seems to be genetic or cultural, there are often differences in social interaction between boys and girls. Are there ways in which any of the expressive arts might affect the developing differences and similarities between them?

Once you have answered these questions, note your comments in Table 16.1. If you are beginning to make observations that are not covered by the questions, don't hesitate to include them.

### Physical Development

All of the expressive arts require at least a minimum of physical involvement, with movement being the most demanding. Yet each of the arts can contribute something to the child's physical development.

■ Review the differences between preschool and primary physical development. Note those that might apply to curriculum decisions in each of the arts.

■ Review the differences between the physical development and growth of boys and girls. Note those that might apply to curriculum decisions in each of the arts.

Once you have jotted down your notes on physical development, pause a bit before going on. Look over your entries in Table 16.1 and see if there are any comments you want to add. At this point, you should feel fairly comfortable in your understanding of children's development so that you can begin to make knowledgeable curriculum decisions.

## Child Diversity and the Expressive Arts

As you know, not every child fits into the standard mold of development, and not every child has the same cultural response to the school environment and curriculum. One of the positive attributes of the arts curriculum is that it naturally provides an appropriate means of expression for the widest possible diversity. Children can move in response to the same music whether they are in a wheelchair or are totally mobile. Or they can use the same art materials to create objects or pictures that portray their own or others' cultures. In your curriculum planning you should take into account the similarities and differences among children. Then you will be able to

**Table 16.1**
CHILD DEVELOPMENT AND THE EXPRESSIVE ARTS

| DEVELOPMENT AREA | | VISUAL ART | MUSIC | MOVEMENT |
|---|---|---|---|---|
| Cognitive | Preprimary | | | |
| | Primary | | | |
| Social/Emotional | Preprimary | | | |
| | Primary | | | |
| Physical | Preprimary | | | |
| | Primary | | | |
| Diversity | Preprimary | | | |
| | Primary | | | |

decide if an expressive art activity provides enough freedom within it to serve various needs or if adjustments should be made so that everyone can participate to the fullest.

- What are the intellectual needs of gifted young children that might affect their participation in visual art? Music? Movement?
- What are the characteristics of intellectually challenged children that might need to be taken into consideration when planning curriculum in each of the arts?
- What are some possible social or emotional difficulties that should be taken into consideration when planning group and individual art activities?
- What are some of the physical challenges that children might have that could influence curriculum plans for each of the arts?
- What are some cultural differences that might influence children's understanding of and participation in each of the arts?
- What are some cultural differences in your own community that might affect children's responses to the arts curriculum?

Child diversity covers many aspects of development and culture. As you write your responses to these questions, be sure to add your own observations.

In the following sections, each of the expressive arts is discussed in turn. Keep Table 16.1 handy, as you will be asked to refer to it from time to time.

## Visual Art and the Young Child

The following story comes from the author's own experience in a Spanish international school. While it took place in a foreign country, the school was American, the children were reasonably fluent in English, and the art curriculum was one that could easily be imported. As you read the account, make a mental list of the elements that you believe made the experience a successful one.

*David, the art teacher, and I had been looking for a way to team teach my second graders, and eventually we more or less stumbled on an idea. The children seemed to love art in all its forms and were as happy to leaf through big art books as they were to experiment with various mediums. One of their favorite books displayed paintings from the Prado Museum in Madrid. As far as they were concerned, the best painting was a huge and complex portrait of the royal family by Diego Velazquez, an eighteenth-century Spanish artist. Called* Las Meninas (The Dwarves), *it depicts the king, queen, royal children, a few dwarves (who at that time were employed as amusing babysitters), and Velazquez himself standing in front of his easel, painting the scene just described. All these elements, plus a mysterious stranger portrayed in a doorway, inspired much imaginative musing by the children.*

*Our school was in Barcelona, many miles east of Madrid, so a field trip to see the painting was out of the question. David and I decided to bring the painting to the children instead, and we began planning ways we might cooperate. Slides of the painting were shown to the children, and the history and artistic detail of the work were discussed. This led to more imaginative musings. The children then acted out the plots they had created. Over several days the plots developed and changed and occasionally appeared in playground dramatic play. To this point, David and I shared responsibility for the children's experiences. Once the children seemed to feel real ownership of the story and the artistry, David took over, discussing with the children ways in which they might reproduce the painting themselves. Using huge sheets of butcher paper taped to each other, the children split up responsibility for different sections of the painting. Here, some friction entered in because each child wanted his or her portion to be the most important, whether it remained true to Velazquez's vision or not. Discussions were held and compromises reached. The final product looked rather like the original painting but with a personalized touch that was most definitely that of a group of strongly individual seven-year-olds.*

*The story doesn't end here, however. Pablo Picasso's cubist version of* Las Meninas *hangs (along with a room full of preparatory studies) in the Picasso Museum in Barcelona. David and I chose not to tell the children about Picasso's version of the painting. Instead, David taught the children about cubism and let them experiment with their own drawings for about three weeks. Art prints of cubist paintings were hung in the classroom, including some from Picasso's* Las Meninas *studies. These, however, were not identified as such to the children. When David felt that the children had a good understanding of cubism, demonstrated in their ability to create their own pictures, we announced a field trip to the Picasso Museum, at last informing them that Picasso had painted a cubist version of* Las Meninas.*

*The museum was expecting us, and we were ushered into the room where Picasso's enormous painting hangs. David, the guards, and I all thought that, when the children first saw the painting, they would be surprised and overwhelmed. At the least we expected an "ooh" or an "aah." Instead, the children stared at it for a minute or two and then quietly went to work with their paper, crayons, markers, and clipboards. A few chose to reproduce the entire* Las Meninas *painting, but most chose their favorite studies, the originals of the slides and prints they had already seen. Most of the children paid no attention to the tourists and other school groups passing through. They were far too busy and focused, both intellectually and emotionally. They worked through morning snack and recess and argued (unsuccessfully) that they didn't need lunch either.*

*After that morning, cubism made irregular appearances in the children's original drawings, although almost everyone developed a preference for the traditional Velazquez painting. For the rest of the year, most of the children's original artwork remained representative. (Adapted from Krogh and Magaña, 1988)*

Have you made a mental list of what made this experience successful? See how much of it matches the one that I made.

- The planning and teaching were done as a team. David is a trained and talented artist, but is accustomed to working with older children. I am trained to work with young children, but any artistic talent has been carefully hidden from me. Our abilities and training complemented each other perfectly.
- The experience grew from the children's own interests. David introduced the art books early in the year, in case the children might enjoy them, and they did, enormously. Soon, they were trying to use some of the artists' techniques, colors, and composition in their own work.

- Role play was used to get the children "into" the painting. Through dramatic play they made the characters their own and learned something of their lives. They didn't simply view the art, they lived it.
- Social give-and-take were necessary for the joint effort. Two of the children were quite stubborn about wanting to take over the lion's share of the available space. It took both teachers, extreme patience, and a great deal of time to make the negotiations successful. The trip to the museum actually had to be postponed a week. The social learning, however, was worth the effort.
- There was a balance between original creativity and skills learning. This project would not have worked with preschool children, but second graders want to make their artwork look like that of the professionals. (Further discussion of this point is found in the Creativity section on page 549.) The children studied and reproduced the Velazquez painting. They also studied cubism and created their own versions of Picasso's work. Then, when the entire project was completed, there was a general return to representational drawing. However, the later work was more skillful and thoughtful than it had been before the project began.
- Not only did the museum officials know we were coming, but they knew about our studies to this point and that the children had only seen the smaller studies of the Picasso painting. Involving them in the plan led to exceptional treatment. We were ushered past countless tourists and other school groups into the main freight elevator and then let out directly in front of the *Las Meninas* room. The two guards who escorted us enjoyed the experience as much as we did, and the children felt welcome in this new and strange place. It is my experience that sharing curriculum goals with others involved in the field trip leads to extraordinarily positive experiences.
- The field trip was focused only on what the children were learning at the time. Often, field trips become simply a day away from school in which as much as possible is crammed into the available time. Children become tired and cranky and remember little of what they experienced. As we left the museum to return to school, David and I took the children slowly through two other rooms that were our personal favorites. The children immediately noticed the difference in style and technique of the paintings there and requested that we return some day to learn how to imitate them. Not many weeks later we did just that.

In upcoming sections, we will discuss ways in which you can foster a close feeling for art in children, both in their production of it and in their enjoyment of the work of others. First, it is important to have a full understanding of the ways in which children develop their art-related skills and abilities.

## Art and Developmental Stages

You have just reviewed developmental stages on your own and may find it helpful to refer again to your chart. In your review, you probably noted the stages in manipulation and scribbling that were discussed in Chapter 3. There, the focus was on children's physical development and its importance to the school setting. Here, we apply these stages and similar ones to art-related skills. The stages given here come from the work of Rhoda Kellogg (1970), Viktor Lowenfeld and Lambert Brittain (1982), and Dennie Wolf and Martha Davis Perry (1988).

### Infants and Toddlers

For the youngest children, process is everything. Simply holding a pencil, crayon, or brush is an interesting challenge, and the tools are treated like any other object or toy. For example, a marker might be wrapped in a piece of paper and called a hot dog just as easily as it might be used to make a mark on the paper. If children do attempt to draw, they watch with extreme interest, fascinated by the marks that appear on the paper. As children watch the marks being made, interesting geometric shapes may appear, but these are made by accident, not by design. Before their second birthday, children are often able to record the correct number and general location of parts on a body. They might, for example, make a slash mark for a head, another below it for the belly, and two at the bottom for feet.

### Preschoolers and Early Kindergartners

During these years, children begin to control their scribbles and eventually give them names, although the labels are generally the result of post-drawing observation, not intention. Once children realize that their scribbles do resemble something, intention becomes a factor and they can engage in beginning attempts at representation. Earlier accidental geometry is replaced by each child's personal system for recording spatial information. Through all these developments, children's feelings may be as important to the drawing as any visualization. Even after attempts are made at representation, feelings may influence the results, as when a smaller but more powerful friend is portrayed as very large. Generally, objects in pictures are found facing forward and floating in space. No understanding of background or dimension is present.

### Late Kindergartners and Primary Children

During the kindergarten year, most children's artwork takes on characteristics that make it more adultlike. Figures in drawings now stand on a baseline and may look at each other instead of at the viewer. A sky is drawn across the top of the page, and for the first time human figures may be given clothing. With experience, children begin to perceive that it is possible to make objects look farther away by making them smaller or by placing them toward the top of the page. They also learn to overlap objects. With this maturation comes a reluctance to experiment with ways to portray everyday objects and people. Each child develops a system of representation and prefers to stick with it once it is comfortable.

## Implications for Teaching

When young children use crayons, markers, paint, and clay, adults often define the processes and results as "art." Yet, employing the adult meaning of the word, this is not the case. Children do not set out to have an aesthetic experience or to be expressive, and they certainly do not conform to any formalized artistic standards. Rather, they use art mediums as one way to interpret their world. As David Baker (1990), a president of the National Art Education Association has said,

> As their mark making becomes picture making, children literally create for themselves a way to mediate reality, to give meaning to the relationships they perceive in the world and the unique encounters they have with them, and to communicate in an abstract manner with what they understand and feel. . . . Picture-making and object-forming activities are in-

Children's initial scribblings are not intentional representations of real life objects, simply the byproduct of manipulating a physical object that to them is like any other.

creasingly understood to be the primary means with which preschool and primary school children prepare themselves to master the conceptual sets, beliefs, values, and behaviors that make them functional within their culture. (p. 22)

Baker argues that what we call art is not produced by children until they mature enough to create their own symbol system and can "manipulate it to communicate abstract ideas about what they see, know, and feel" (p. 23). At that time, their visual work takes on formal properties and expressive qualities that make it deserving of the term "art." Thus, it is inappropriate to call young children "artistic" and to expect adult-style artwork from them. Conversely, it is important to provide young children with developmentally appropriate activities and materials that will meet their current needs as well as lay the groundwork for the real art experiences to come.

Baker cites the recent focus on developmentally appropriate practices as an impetus for rethinking early art education. While theories and curricula are still in the making, some significant trends are observable. Baker (1990) lists five of them:

1. "The tactile/kinetic activity that supports the sense of sight is becoming recognized as an important precondition to image making and the support this, in turn, provides to cognitive development" (p. 23). Early kinetic activities such as reaching, pushing, pulling, and grabbing are important contributors to children's motor control and understanding of space and dimensions. Providing children with three-dimensional activities and resources such as clay, cardboard, and found materials is both appropriate and important. The learnings that come from these experiences become the foundation for later learning in language and mathematics as well as in art.

2. Children have a compulsive need to "explore and master their self-made marks. Drawing thus becomes an essential activity" (p. 24). Because "drawing activities and picture-related behaviors permeate all human modes of comprehension, communication, and expression, they must be central to all that we do with children in schools" (p. 24). Teachers need to offer children plenty of opportunities to draw and let them know that their work is valued. As often as possible, picture making should be incorporated into the general curriculum at every stage of the preschool and primary school experience.

3. "At this level of development, children have a profound need for rich images to contemplate, rich and complex configurations of color, shapes, forms, textures, light, and so on to interact with" (p. 24). Such a need relates to what is called at a more mature level "art appreciation." The teacher's role is to provide these rich images through a well thought out selection of art prints, reproductions of famous paintings, and skilled drawings. These are far more nourishing to children than cute posters and cartoon-

like pictures. Also preferred are blocks, containers, fabrics, yarn, and found objects as opposed to commercially produced games, kits, and cartoon-character dolls.

4. Young children do not yet have the skills to transfer sight to sound, that is, to talk about visual experiences, with ease. Thus, they should be encouraged, but not forced, to share their art experiences "in any manner that seems appropriate to them. . . . While satisfying to adults, formal processes of looking at and talking about art-like things intimidate and constrain young children" (p. 24). If children are unable or unwilling to verbalize their critique of a piece of art or the project they are working on, they should not be forced. Teachers should accept small gestures—a shrug or a pointed finger, perhaps—as an effort to communicate understanding, preference, or feelings.

   When children try to communicate their responses and feelings in words, then teachers should take the cue to encourage. They can be supportive and listen to what children need and want to say; they can discuss children's choice of form, color, or medium; they can discuss solutions to a technical problem; or they can help children analyze what they see.

5. Art should be integrated into the regular curriculum and daily life of the center or classroom. For the most part, it should not be an isolated subject that doesn't connect to children's general experiences. While poor integration is undesirable for any age, it is particularly counterproductive for preschool and primary age children. Instead, there should be art-related activities as a natural part of reading, writing, and other subjects.

   In general, your role as teacher is supportive, providing children with ample opportunity to explore materials, techniques, and the products of others. At the same time, you should not hesitate to provide children with the skills they need to engage in an art-related activity. The important point is to nurture skills that are developmentally appropriate and then to step back (intervening only when desirable) while children construct their own knowledge. For example, young children are often frustrated by scissors, particularly the dull, ineffectual kind frequently found in the classroom. For children who are ready to cut, try to find high-quality scissors. For everyone else, show how to tear paper instead, until they are ready to use the scissors without frustration. For some children, this may be toward the end of kindergarten or even into first grade.

## Materials and Activities

A primary requirement in selecting materials and activities is that they be safe. Young children are fascinated by art-related materials and explore them to the fullest, often placing them in their mouths. For a few children, oral exploration lasts even into the primary grades. Thus, all materials should be checked for toxicity. This includes crayons (which are usually safe), markers, paints, and even the dye in colored papers. Materials used in collage or sculpture are often small, and tasting-stage children should be closely supervised. Additionally, children should not use scissors until they are able to keep them out of their mouths and handle them carefully. Sharp instruments of all kinds should be kept from children who are still awkward in their movements, unless close supervision is provided.

Once safety is established, choose materials for their high quality and aesthetic appeal. High quality does not necessarily mean high expense. Clay and fingerpaint, for instance, can be made from scratch and expensive tempera paint can be extended by adding soap flakes. Novelty and frequent change are not necessary since children enjoy creating new and interesting experiences for themselves using familiar materials. You can bring variety to the familiar by providing paper in different shapes or by setting out crayons from the cool colors one day, warm colors the next.

In considering the materials suggested here, take into account their developmental appropriateness for the children with whom you work.

## Painting

Almost all children love to paint and opportunities should be provided daily, if at all possible, even through the primary grades. Easels provide room to use arms and hands freely, to step back and observe the developing picture, and to be away from the rest of the class for a while. Painting on a table or floor can also be enjoyable, usually allowing for more socialization and, perhaps, less drippy mess. Children can help prepare the paint, an activity that can be expanded to include experimental color mixing.

Probably the easiest way to keep the original color in each container is to provide a brush with each one. The clips holding paper on the easel should be easy enough to handle so that children can learn to remove the paper themselves. Sponges and access to a water source make it easy for children to wipe up all but the most major spills. As you plan your painting area, consider the steps that children will take to paint, clean up, and ready the area for the next painter. Make the steps clear to the children and you will have to intervene only minimally.

For very young children, a joyful "painting" activity is to take buckets of water and broad brushes outdoors on a warm day. Everything in sight can be painted, from the building walls to playground equipment to the concrete sidewalks.

Fingerpaint offers children a sensory experience quite different from tempera paint. Some children are put off by the prospect of touching it and should not be pushed into the experience. One way to encourage these children is to suggest that they try dipping just one finger in the paint to make a few tiny marks on the paper. Over a period of time, most children will become willing to participate with enthusiasm. Traditionally, fingerpainting is done on a flat surface rather than on an easel, as this allows for more upper body control. Despite its name, fingerpainting can make use of palms, fists, elbows, and forearms. Relatively sophisticated pictures are possible with some experimentation.

Fingerpainting is usually done on glazed paper, which protects against leakage. Children could also paint directly on a tabletop, then carefully press paper onto the surface to make a print.

Other types of prints can be made with any interesting (and disposable) object. For instance, children in kindergarten can carve a potato half into an interesting shape for an original design. The potato half can then be dipped into a shallow container of thick paint and pressed onto paper. Notepaper or postcards can be made this way for gift giving. With the addition of laminating paper, placemats can also be made.

## Drawing

Crayons are staples of the early childhood setting. Larger sizes are usually recommended, although, given a choice, children generally reach for the smaller crayons. A combination collection with free choice of size and color is probably the best approach.

Even more popular than crayons are markers. Veteran teacher Sydney Clemens (1991) suggests a homemade marker holder to keep them capped and fresh. Make a mound from clay. Place the caps from a collection of markers in the mound, burying them almost to their edges. When the clay has hardened, place the markers back in their caps. The markers can then be removed and replaced easily during drawing activities.

Chalk is another good drawing tool. It can be used on paper, chalkboard, and sidewalk. It is a good idea to have some chalk handy for spontaneous use outdoors. Children also enjoy having part of the class chalkboard reserved for their own use.

## Construction

Children love working in three dimensions. Construction is an art-related activity that changes depending on the materials at hand. This is the perfect opportunity to make use of found objects and assorted junk. A few of the many items that can be used in construction are

scraps of wood
various styrofoam shapes
shells
buttons
feathers
paper scraps
yarn
fabric scraps

magazine pictures
box lids
leaves and twigs
bits of ribbon

Construction activities can include:

**Collage.** Use sturdy paper, alternating colors for variety. White glue can be squeezed directly onto collage items, or you can put some glue in a small paper cup and have children dip collage pieces into it or smear it on with a popsicle stick. Any lightweight object is appropriate for collage. Vary the collection of objects frequently so that children's interest will remain high. Fabric scraps, bits of colored paper, uncooked macaroni or noodles, and various lengths of yarn are all easily obtained collage items.

**Sculpture.** Objects that are too heavy for collage can be fitted together to make sculptures. Children can use white glue, tape, even string to form free-standing pieces. To make a sculpture transportable, you'll need to provide some sort of base. Scrap plywood is a good choice. More easily obtained, and usually free, are styrofoam meat trays; request them from your market's meat department.

Sculpture can also be done with clay and play dough. Older children will enjoy clay that hardens when dry. Younger children, who primarily enjoy the process of squashing and modeling, will prefer reusable clay that can be worked less formally. To keep interest high for older children, provide plastic knives and other tools for shaping.

**Woodworking.** Kindergarten is a good time to introduce construction with wood. It is important to supply children with real tools, which are generally safer and more successful than toy versions. It is equally important to show children specific techniques for safe and successful construction and to create a list of rules. Scraps of wood may be brought from home or obtained, either free or for a low price, from a lumberyard. Children should sand the wood pieces before using them. (Some children may enjoy the sanding process as much as follow-up construction.) Two bins or boxes can be used to store sanded and unsanded wood. Confining woodworking to the outdoors keeps down noisy confusion in the classroom, but it should only be done there if children can be closely monitored.

## Art Appreciation

Making the classroom beautiful is a first step in helping children appreciate art. Plants and flowers, art prints, sculpture, draped fabric, even carefully arranged objects from science classification activities make the environment more attractive. Carefully display books with good artwork on their covers and discuss the drawings when a story is read. Be sure to hang pictures at children's eye level. Any space above can be filled with broad swaths of color, perhaps from draped fabric.

While most teachers and parents like to see children's artwork posted, younger children often do not share this view. Always ask children first if they would like to have their art products on display. If the experience has been a satisfying one, a child may well prefer to carry the results folded up in a pocket, or hidden safely in a cubby, rather than put on public display.

Museum visits offer an opportunity for children to begin to understand and appreciate the adult concept of art. While you may not live close to a major art museum, most towns have small museums or private galleries. These are actually preferable for young children. Children as young as four can enjoy interacting with a single painting, noting the brush techniques and later imitating them, learning to differentiate the subtle shadings in colors, and talking about the feelings the painting imparts—feelings that might be quite different from those of an adult.

The other two expressive arts discussed in this chapter—music and movement—are often difficult to separate because one so frequently takes place in the company of the other. While this is true for people of any age, it is particularly so for young children, who respond to the sound of music with natural and unself-conscious movement. Just as naturally, they create sounds to accompany their rhythmic movements if no music is readily available. Because each of these arts also makes independent contributions to children's learning and development, we will begin our discussion by treating them individually. Then we will combine them.

## Music and the Young Child

Of the three expressive arts discussed in this chapter, music may be the least influenced by the stages of development that you reviewed earlier. Some thinkers have argued that music deserves special recognition in terms of human development. In his 1983 book *Frames of Mind,* Howard Gardner argued that there are seven separate intelligences that we each possess, and he honored music by making it one of them. (The others are linguistic, logical-mathematical, spatial, bodily-kinesthetic, interpersonal, and intrapersonal.) This concept carries with it the view that children's musical intelligence can be nourished or diminished depending on environmental influences, including those in child care centers and schools. Research that took place in the 1960s and '70s validates this point of view.

In the 1960s, Edwin Gordon (Feierabend, 1990) tested students between the ages of nine and eighteen on their ability to recall the tonality and rhythm patterns presented to them in various musical selections. He found that the musicality of nine-year-olds remained quite stable over the following years,

Music, which has been classified as one of seven forms of intelligence by Howard Gardner, is believed by some to atrophy and die if it is not made a part of children's everyday environment.

whether the children participated in band, choir, or music lessons or had no musical training at all. A decade later, Gordon developed a simplified version of the test to investigate the musicality of younger children. The rather surprising results have important implications for early childhood education.

While scores stayed stable for children over nine, children below that age actually lost their ability to retain tonal and rhythmic patterns when they had no musically stimulating experiences. The greatest loss occurred between the ages of five and six. Gordon did one more study to see what would happen if children in the primary grades were given musical experiences when they had had none before. He discovered that there could be some improvement until age nine, but that children's abilities were never quite as good as if they had had earlier experiences.

Although no studies have been done on children under age five, Gordon's tests, coupled with Gardner's theory of multiple intelligences, have led to the conclusion that children

> are probably born with their own level of music intelligences that begin to atrophy unless supported by a musical environment. . . . In the upper grades, a teacher can teach more music literature or present more infor-

## *The Teacher as Actor: A Conversation with Robert Keiper*

*Early childhood educators rarely think of themselves as actors. Such a view seems to imply a stand-up routine in front of silent rows of immobile high school students. The participant in this conversation, however, has been trained both as an actor and a teacher, and he believes the two are compatible no matter what age the children are. Perhaps this is because his concept of what the actor does is broader than a simple stage performance.*

As an undergraduate Bob Keiper majored in English education, then added a minor in theater as a way to expand his hiring attractiveness. Before long, however, he found that his training as an actor went far in making him a better teacher. As he gained teaching experience, Bob began supervising occasional student teachers and observed that their carefully planned lessons could often have been delivered more successfully if they had been given some training in acting. Later, Bob earned graduate degrees in theater education and curriculum and instruction, while continuing to work with student teachers. It was during this time that he began to develop a unique course called "The Teacher as Actor," which he continues to present in various forms to teachers throughout the United States and in foreign countries. While the majority of his career has been spent working with secondary students and their teachers, Bob believes that much of the teacher-as-actor philosophy is important for early childhood educators as well.

For example, the teacher's use of voice is just as important as the actor's. "I think the most important quality to work on is variance in pitch," Bob says. "As we get older we get more monotonal, especially if we're men. Wo-

men, on the other hand, tend to be more mono-rate. Either of these two things can be a death knell for effective teaching with young children. As I see it, young children's minds are moving at 90 miles a minute as they assimilate and accommodate all they're learning. If you don't have enthusiasm in your voice they'll turn you off. They'll look at you and seem to understand what you say, but if your voice doesn't convey an important message to them, they may choose to assimilate and accommodate something else that's more interesting."

Bob also believes that the teacher should use pitch to indicate different messages. "Children get used to hearing an 'instruction voice,' a 'reprimand voice,' and a 'praise voice.' Those vocal tones can have an effect on the management and control of the classroom if the teacher is consciously aware of using the different voices." Teachers who don't alter their voices, he says, may cause children to tune out if they believe that one type message is being delivered when, in actuality, it is something else.

Body language is important for the teacher as well. For children who are just learning to speak, either because they are very young or because English is a new language to them, body language is critical. "We know that if there's a conflict between the verbal and the nonverbal message, we will hear the nonverbal." For example, "If you praise a child, it's important that they see your face light up and your eyes get big and your body expand itself, so that not only do they hear that they did a wonderful thing, but, even more importantly, they see it from the teacher."

Referring to the importance of getting both voice and body language to work successfully together, Bob turns actor. Putting a dull look on his face, he folds his arms, and, in a monotone, speaks as if to a small group of children, "That was good. This is great. Terrific. Fantastic." Too many teachers, he says, hand out such praise, then wonder why the children don't believe what they say. "How can you fold your arms and say in a monotone, 'Terrific' and expect the child to believe it? The same thing is true of a reprimand. You need to think about the message you want to convey and be sure your voice and body match it."

Bob's philosophy of the teacher as actor includes what he calls "The Three Es." The first

of these is *energy.* "This has to do with your well-being. Energy comes when you think about and take care of yourself first, because it takes a tremendous amount of energy to teach." Next, Bob says, "You need to look at your lesson plans for each day to determine which things will require more energy . . . maybe because it's something the children don't like too much or even that you don't like." Once you identify these areas, you must be ready to follow through with extra effort.

The second E is *enthusiasm,* which Bob says is sometimes tied closely to giving extra effort to an unpopular lesson. "That's probably the area that you should teach with the most enthusiasm. It's really a kind of salesmanship. You're trying to sell the children on the idea that something is important to learn and that it will help them. Enthusiasm, as we know, is contagious and the children will pick it up from you."

The third E is *excitement.* "Students need to believe that the teacher truly finds the job full of excitement and transfers how exciting learning new stuff is to the class. As schmaltzy as this may seem, it is becoming one of the most vital ingredients in good, memorable teaching."

The "Three Es," Bob believes, can go a long way toward dealing with a major problem for today's teachers: making learning attractive for children of the television age who are further distracted by the severe problems that many of them face in their homes.

*To discuss: Share observations you have made of teachers using acting techniques. How did the children respond? What acting skills will be easy for you to adopt and which will you need to work on?*

mation about music, but in kindergarten the teacher can change the children's music intelligence for life. (Feierabend, 1990, p. 15)

The importance of musical experiences for young children is apparent. To make developmentally appropriate curriculum decisions, some understanding of capabilities at each age is important. A general review of cognitive development will be helpful. Add to this the following overview of musical abilities, which is drawn from Bayless and Ramsey (1991) and the Music Educators National Conference (1986).

## Development of Music-Related Abilities

### Birth to Four Months

From earliest infancy, children show their awareness of music by responding in different ways to what they hear. They become more active with lively music and are calmed by lullabies.

### Four to Eight Months

Infants become more actively aware of sounds, turning their heads toward the source of the music.

### Ten to Eighteen Months

Infants begin to have preferences in music and to show them. They might rock and sway or clap their hands to music they like; they may also look with displeasure when music they don't like is played.

### Eighteen Months to Two Years

Toddlers are fascinated by sounds in the environment and may especially enjoy listening to the repeated and familiar tunes from TV shows and commercials, or watching family members play musical instruments.

### Two to Four Years

Children begin to improvise songs during play and are able to learn some folk or composed songs, although they may not stay on pitch. They enjoy creating sounds on instruments and other environmental sources. They learn to recognize the difference between singing and speaking and improvise movements that show their awareness of beat, tempo, and pitch. Closer to age four, children are able to listen attentively to music that they like and maintain a rhythm during movement. For many, music becomes an important way to express and communicate ideas and emotions.

### Four to Five Years

Children's ability to discuss, or show through movement, their musical experiences expands. This capability relates to similarities and differences such as loud-soft, fast-slow, and high-low. Another capability is to match pitches and sing in tune most of the time. Children of this age enjoy singing nonsense and folk songs and participating in musical games. They also like to improvise songs when they are playing and working. Their ability to listen to musical selections expands, making them able to increase the type and number of selections they listen to.

### Primary Years

Increased motor control and ability to synchronize movements make performance in rhythm activities much improved. Children become able to sing in tune, with appropriate musical expression, either alone or in a group. Extended creativity becomes possible and children can sing or play back "answers" to unfinished melodic phrases, create short melodic patterns of their own, create new stanzas to familiar melodies, and dramatize songs. Coupled with their ability to read the written word, children are able to read musical symbols for both pitch and expression.

## Implications for Teaching

The Gordon studies have shown that musical experiences really do make a difference for children at an early age, perhaps even earlier than is now recognized. Some general recommendations for teaching include the following:

- Provide infants with exposure to selected recorded music. Rock, pat, touch, and move with them to the rhythms of music. Sing and chant to them and imitate the sounds they make. As soon as they are old enough to control them, provide infants with safe toys that make musical sounds.
- Give two- and three-year-olds opportunities for improvised singing and teach them some simple songs. Let them explore with basic instruments and objects that make interesting sounds.
- Four- and five-year-olds enjoy singing, participating in song games, and playing classroom instruments in groups. Give them opportunities to experiment with movement, language, and sound.
- Provide primary children with expanded singing experiences by teaching them rounds and by letting them improvise and create new lines to familiar songs or short songs of their own. Continue to give them experiences with musical instruments, showing them simple rhythmic or pitch patterns to accompany singing and dancing activities.
- Make sure that there are musical opportunities every day, even in the primary grades when pressures to ignore music mount.

## Movement and the Young Child

The importance of movement for every facet of young children's learning was discussed in earlier chapters, and your chart no doubt will show the developmental differences in the way children are able to move, depending on their age. In this chapter, our focus is on the aesthetic aspect of children's movement.

*Four-year-old Benjamin ran through the autumn leaves, chasing the rubber ball that his mother had just thrown him. Suddenly, he became aware of the crunchy sound of the leaves and changed his gait to an exaggerated shuffle. "Sluff, sluff, sluff," he said in rhythm with each step. Forgetting the ball entirely, he began to imitate a leaf that had just begun to fall, still saying "Sluff, sluff, sluff," but changing the shuffle to a falling-down dance.*

*Three-year-old Tomiko was on her first visit to an art museum. While her parents asked a guard for directions to the special exhibit they had come to see, Tomiko wandered a short distance away to have a better look at a statue of the Winged Mercury atop the entryway fountain. For a while she just stood, seemingly transfixed. Then, slowly and unself-consciously, she lifted her right arm and left leg in imitation of the statue's stance. She held the position as long as she could, discovered she was about to lose her balance, and recovered by inventing a little dance that permitted her to "fly" back to her parents.*

In both of these illustrations of movement, the children began the episode with basic transportational movement—each one was just going from here to there. And in both cases, the movement became something else. Benjamin lost interest in chasing the ball and was caught up in the beauty of the leaves. Tomiko became so engrossed in the statue that her whole body joined in. As the children engaged in their experiences, in a sense they actually *became* the leaf or the statue. Such becoming, which requires conscious effort and the overcoming of embarrassment for most adults, is natural for young children. Because they are natural to children and because they integrate well with all aspects of the curriculum, aesthetic movement and dance are well suited and important to the early childhood classroom.

What happens in the classroom, of course, should be developmentally appropriate. In addition to the general developmental levels you have included in your chart, and which were discussed at length in Chapter 3, there are characteristics that are specific to an aesthetic movement program. The characteristics and classroom implications in Table 16.2 are adapted from Robert Pangrazi and Victor Dauer's 1981 book *Movement in Early Childhood and Primary Education.*

**Table 16.2**

BEHAVIORAL CHARACTERISTICS AND THEIR IMPLICATIONS—INCORPORATING MOVEMENT IN LEARNING

| CHARACTERISTICS | IMPLICATIONS |
| --- | --- |
| **PRESCHOOL CHILDREN** | |
| Unable to sit still for long periods | Use movement in learning activities |
| Constantly explore environment | Provide opportunities for creativity and exploration |
| Show little differentiation between fantasy and reality | Have movement experiences that use both and help them identify |
| Begin using words to express feelings | Emphasize dramatic play |
| Have fear of heights, falling | Provide successful experiences in jumping off boxes, etc. |
| Like rhythmic activities | Gross motor activities to rhythm; marching |
| Have great desire to imitate | Offer opportunities to imitate animals, machines, significant adults |
| Like to play individually or in groups of two or three | Do movement activities in small groups |
| Show great imagination | Value imagination through creation of make-believe characters that move |
| May walk well but have difficulty with other locomotor skills | Provide wide variety of motor challenges |
| **KINDERGARTEN AND FIRST-GRADE CHILDREN** | |
| Have short attention span | Change activities often; give short explanations |
| Begin to understand teamwork | Have some activities that require group cooperation |
| Are highly creative | Allow children to try new and different ways to move and let them share with friends |
| Seek personal attention | See that everyone has a turn to be the center of attention |
| Are noisy and constantly active | Provide experiences that require much energy |
| May suddenly become tired but soon recover | Use activities of brief duration and include short rest periods |
| Are naturally rhythmical | Provide creative rhythms, folk dances, singing games |
| **SECOND-AND THIRD-GRADE CHILDREN** | |
| Show more interest in group play | Provide group games and simple dances that involve cooperation |
| Are developing more skills and want to excel at them | Suggest movement and dance combinations that provide challenge but are not too difficult |
| Are becoming more socially conscious | Stress social customs and courtesy during dance activities |
| Sex differences still relatively unimportant | Give both boys and girls the same movement opportunities |

Two subgroups of early movement experiences are dance and drama. Note that their definitions are different when applied to young children's experiences.

### Dance and Young Children

Dance specialist Susan Stinson (1989) maintains that,

[w]hile preschoolers can learn some simple steps and routines, they have far more important things to learn and do during these years than train for future careers. They need to explore their world and discover what they can do in it. Through such exploration, they build a rich store of sensory experiences, laying a foundation on which abstract concepts and more complex skills can later be built. Such experiences are the most appropriate steps toward future dance training for those children who might desire it. Even more important, these exploratory experiences contribute to the life of every child, not just those little girls who dream of wearing a tutu. (p. 210)

Dance for young children involves body movement and an inside awareness of that movement, which is sometimes (but not always) an expression of emotion: "To dance is to stay aware of what is ordinarily taken for granted, to discover a new world of sensory awareness provided by the kinesthetic sense" (Stinson, 1990, p. 36). As an art form, dance for young children is based on "natural movement rather than on movement of a particular style of the sort that one might see in tap dance or ballet" (p. 36).

Over a two-year period, researcher Liora Bresler (1992) observed dance education in elementary schools and found little of the natural experience Stinson promotes. Typically, dance experiences were found lacking in any intellectual or aesthetic substance or "tools to explore inner life." Instead, "the infrequent dance sessions were decorative, trivial, and typically associated with the less-important aspects of school life" (p. 20).

Whether in preschool or primary grades, dance experiences for children need to be associated with what is important to children and be developmentally appropriate. Dance is more than fun movement in circle-time sessions (Andress, 1991). It is too important to children's lives for this offhanded treatment. Because young children learn about their world, in great part, through exploratory movement and sensory awareness, seriously taken dance can provide concrete experiences "in which children become more aware of the movement they see in their world, try it on for themselves, and notice how it feels" (Stinson, 1990, p. 36).

Dance, of course, can be fun and joyful. At other times, it can be quite serious. In any case, it should be important and interesting to the children. Dancing about the change in seasons is natural for children, as demonstrated by Benjamin as he "sluffed" through the leaves. Experiences from real life,

Because exploratory movement is a natural learning mode for most children, teachers should take it seriously and look for meaningful ways in which it can be used.

particularly the adult world that children are only permitted to observe, can be meaningful: driving a car, doing the laundry, mowing the lawn. In some ways, such dancing role play has as much in common with drama as it does with dance. As such, it deserves a closer look.

## Drama and Young Children

Just as dance for young children goes a step beyond general movement experiences, drama goes a step beyond dramatic play. Drama for young children is "teacher-initiated dramatic play and can therefore provide a balance between free play and academics." Because it provides experiential learning, children "are more likely to retain information taught through drama because it is multisensory—it gives a visual, physical, and verbal representation of the idea" (Brown, 1990, p. 26).

Drama as a classroom activity can contribute much to children's development. Because it requires interaction, negotiation, and cooperation, and because social themes are often explored, drama promotes social development. Since children are encouraged to express their feelings through drama and because most children find it a positive experience that promotes self-esteem, drama enhances emotional development. Creative movement is often a part of drama, providing physical experience. Cognitive development is fostered when drama is integrated with what is happening in the curriculum. Finally, young children's drama experiences provide opportunities for creativity in problem solving, movement, and use of the imagination.

Drama has proven to be particularly effective in enhancing the language arts curriculum. According to Brown (1990), drama activities

- Promote language acquisition better than many specialized language treatments.
- Enhance speaking skills.
- Foster better reading.
- Encourage verbal flexibility and originality.
- Increase abilities in extemporaneous speaking.

For preschool and kindergarten children, process-oriented drama is a must. Emphasis on product or performance for outsiders defeats the developmental benefits of drama. In the primary grades, process-oriented experiences should continue, but performance-related drama can be added. A few drama experiences that children will enjoy and learn from include acting out

- The falling rain or snow that is keeping them indoors.
- The math story problem that is difficult to understand.
- A story that is currently being read.
- The television news that their parents are talking about but that is difficult to understand.
- The experiences they recall from a field trip.

You should not be afraid of repetition when using drama. Young children learn much from revisiting dramatic experiences. Repetition can reinforce earlier learning and provide a springboard for new understanding.

## Music and Movement Together

As an aesthetic experience for young children, music and movement are more likely to be found together than separated. From the point of view of music education, "Movement experiences are a vital part of the music education program because they represent the sensing-doing stage of learning, which is a means to understanding more abstract musical ideas" (Andress, 1991, p. 22). Conversely, music is vital to movement experiences because it contributes rhythm, mood, and structure.

In their music/movement experiences, children need to be given a balance of freedom (which provides opportunity for creativity) and structure (which provides direction and skills). Music educator Barbara Andress (1991) suggests three ways in which teachers can interact effectively during more structured music/movement experiences: modeling, describing, and suggesting.

*Modeling* does not mean engaging in movements that are to be imitated by the children. Rather, it involves demonstrating free movement to music, expressing your own ideas. This can and should happen at any time of the day, essentially giving the children inspiration and permission to do likewise. For very young children, use tactile modeling to encourage movement to music. Extend your index fingers for a child to grasp, then sway and move gently to the music, guiding the child to explore movement while providing stability and safety.

*Describing* is a way of reinforcing children's behavior, helping them to understand and define what it is they are doing. Describing should take place as the movement is happening, not later when it is forgotten. Some typical statements might be:

- "Julie and Heather are moving quickly when the music sounds quick."
- "Antonio stopped when the music stopped, and he started to move when the music started again."
- "Sandy is stamping her feet hard while the music is loud."

Care should be taken to describe children's actions in a nonjudgmental way and to include everyone.

*Suggesting* is useful when you want the children to feel and demonstrate the music in the way it was intended. For example, "Let's Go Fly a Kite" from *Mary Poppins* matches musical mood to words. You might dance and make such comments as, "My kite is flying very high now . . . the wind is moving it very slowly . . . now my kite is coming back to earth." Overuse of this technique, however, may lead to teacher-imposed learning and imagination killing. One antidote is to let children, once they are comfortable with the idea, take turns being the "teacher."

In the next section, movement, music, and the visual arts are combined together and with the rest of the curriculum to provide you with some specific ideas for classroom experiences.

## Focus for the Expressive Arts: Crossing the Curriculum

The expressive arts lend beauty, sensitivity, and feeling to the curriculum. Without them, life in the center or school is drab and lacking in excitement.

The arts are important in their own right, and children should learn to appreciate them individually. At the same time, the arts enhance and integrate well with other areas of learning. The purpose of this section is to give you some guidance in achieving infusion of the arts across the curriculum. Activities are adaptable to many themes and integrated units.

Activities

Art

**1. Shape Drawing or Collage.**   Provide children with paper that has been cut into geometric shapes. Don't confine these to the usual circle, square, and triangle. Children are equally interested in learning about the rhombus, pentagon, trapezoid, and so on. As they use crayons or markers, or create collages, talk with the children about the shapes of the paper. Tracing the edges with a finger reinforces the learning.

**2. Seed Collage.**   On a sheet of drawing paper, children take a long cord and swirl it into an interesting pattern that should contain several loops (to create enclosed spaces that will be filled in). Glue the cord in place and allow it to dry. Meanwhile, have each child classify a collection of various types and colors of seeds according to the child's own observation and choice. Each grouping should be glued in an enclosed space. Informal discussion during this activity might center on identification of each kind of seed and observations of the differences between them.

**3. Mobiles: Artificial and Natural.**   Use wire coat hangers and string to make mobiles to be hung from ceiling or doorways. Do this as a two-part project: once with all-natural materials, and once with artificial materials. A good source for materials is a nature walk through an area that has litter that can be separated from the natural items. (Be sure any litter that is used in the mobiles is clean and safe.) Discussion of the difference between the two types of materials might lead to an exploration of how some of the materials are made, complete with visits to factories and stores.

**4. Box Town.**   Collect large cardboard boxes from stores that sell appliances. Begin with just one or two, and expand with children's interest. Have the class paint the outside of the boxes with tempera, and either paint or wallpaper the insides. You can lead the children in designing doors and windows and discussing the purpose of each building. Typically, children will begin the project most interested in the painting process and play possibilities. With time, they will become more interested in creating buildings that are functional.

**5. Personalized Clipboards.**   To make clipboards, collect large rectangles of sturdy cardboard. Direct the class in dividing them into smaller rectangles about 10 inches by 13 inches. Primary children can participate in measuring by using nonstandard measuring tools (e.g., a piece of legal-size paper) or with standard rulers if they are learning to read them. A sturdy bread knife is the most effective saw for the board. When the pieces are cut, have children decorate one side with markers or crayons, and write their names on the other. Attach two clothespins to the top to secure paper.

Consider the possibilities for teaching across the curriculum with large boxes that have been arranged into a house: painting windows and doors (that have been measured), cutting out the windows and doors, reinforcing the corners so that they won't crumble, arranging furniture, planning rooms, issuing invitations to a house warming, etc.

## Music

**6. Books About Music.** Choose storybooks that have musical themes or topics. Discuss the musical elements, following through on the children's interests with further explorations of musical instruments, songs to learn, perhaps guest speakers or performers. A few good choices are *Song and Dance Man* (Ackerman, 1988), *Frog Goes to Dinner* (Mayer, 1974), *The Piney Woods Peddler* (Shannon, 1981), and *Busy Monday Morning* (Domanska, 1985).

**7. Predictable Songs.** A predictable song is one with repetitive or predictable language. Choose a song with repetition, such as "Old McDonald" or "Mary Had a Little Lamb," or one with a predictable language pattern, such as the traditional ABC song. Sing it to the children several times and let them join in as they can. Then, write the words on a chart and point to them as they are sung. When the words are familiar, children can take turns doing the pointing. Try chanting the words without the music to focus more on the language. To further develop the reading process, give children strips of words that match a line of the song, or smaller strips with single words on them, and challenge them to find their mates on the chart.

**8. Water Music.** Fill crystal or other fine glass containers with water to different heights. For preschool children, use no more than two or three glasses. For older children, use eight for a full scale. If you have a classroom instrument, tune the glasses to it. Initially, children wet a finger and rub it around the rim of a glass to explore the sound. Later, they can arrange the glasses from lowest to highest tone or try to create a song. They can also try to find the tones on the classroom instrument that match the tones of the glasses. Primary children (and a few kindergartners) will enjoy the challenge of tuning the glasses to the classroom instrument.

**9. Sound Matching.**    Collect empty film canisters from a photography shop. Fill two canisters with each of several items that make different noises when shaken: rice, sand, dried beans in different sizes. On the bottoms of the canisters, paint dots of different colors, indicating the matching sets. At first, children enjoy shaking to explore the sounds. Next, provide them with just two or three sets to match, increasing the challenge to six or seven sets for older children. A further challenge is to arrange the canisters in rows from softest to loudest tones.

## Movement

**10. Dancing the Day.**    At the close of the day, ask children to review the day's activities in the order in which they occurred. Use ordinal numbers to count them. Once the memories have been agreed upon, chant or rap them back to the children as they dance or dramatize the events. Be sure to use the ordinal numbers in the chant or rap.

**11. Becoming Letters and Numbers.**    Children use any part of their bodies they choose to illustrate a letter or number. Once they are accustomed to the activity, you can change it to be a cooperative one with two or three children working together (to form the letter.) Whole words and two- or three-digit numbers can also be created cooperatively.

**12. Where Animals Live.**    As children learn about animals and their homes, ask them to imitate each according to its home. For example: Can you show me an animal that lives in a nest? In a den? In the ocean? In the river? In the jungle?

**13. How Animals Protect Themselves.**    Invite children to share ways that animals protect themselves and add others to extend their learning. As each protection is described, children act it out. For example: Show me what a bull, elk, or rhinoceros uses for protection. Show me how birds protect themselves. How about tigers or crocodiles? Bees or jellyfish?

**14. Dandelion Time.**    When dandelions start to seed, bring in enough for each child to have one (with a few extras for emergencies). Children blow the seeds, then follow one of them to "become" the seed. Narrate to the children the experiences the seed must have to grow into a new plant: being blown by the wind, being rained on, working down into the ground, and so on.

**15. Drawing and Doing.** Provide each child with paper and crayon or marker. Before you suggest a movement, children create it on paper. Examples: Chant, "Dot, dot, dot" as children make dots on their paper. Then, they dance to the chant. Or have children draw a long, straight line accompanied by a prolonged note on an instrument. This is followed by making bodies into long, straight lines. Lively music can be played as children try scribbles. The music is then replayed while the children do a scribble dance.

## Creativity: A Final Word

The topics of this chapter—music, art, and movement—are often thought of as primary vehicles for creativity. Indeed, we have discussed each one of them within that context. Yet the other areas of the curriculum—language, mathematics, science, social studies—should also be considered in terms of creativity. Thus, the final discussion for this chapter on the expressive arts

**Table 16.3**
**THE EXPRESSIVE ARTS: ACTIVITIES**

| ACTIVITY | LEVEL* | CURRICULUM | ADAPTED FROM |
|---|---|---|---|
| Becoming Letters and Numbers | P, Py | Reading, Math | Gilbert |
| Books about Music | P, Py | Literature | Lamme |
| Box Town | P, Py | Social Studies | |
| Dancing the Day | P, Py | Math | |
| Dandelion Time | P, Py | Science | |
| Drawing and Doing | P, Py | Art | Morningstar |
| How Animals Protect Themselves | P, Py | Science | Gilbert |
| Mobiles: Artificial and Natural | P, Py | Science | |
| Personalized Clipboards | Py | Math | |
| Predictable Songs | Py | Reading | Renegar |
| Seed Collage | P, Py | Science | Lewis |
| Shape Drawing and Collage | P, Py | Math | Lewis |
| Sound Matching | P, Py | Classification | |
| Water Music | P, Py | Classification | |
| Where Animals Live | Py | Science | Gilbert |

*P = Preschool, Py = Primary

also pertains to the rest of the curriculum. It also serves as the final summary of the entire text. It is hoped that, as your career in early education is launched, you will regard your teaching tasks with the utmost creativity and that you will provide the children in your care with opportunities to learn creatively.

## Creativity and Development

It has been argued that the innate creativity of younger children is often effectively, rudely, and unnecessarily destroyed by the education system. There is merit in this criticism, particularly when schools focus only on the "basics" and teach them in a basic way. Yet children themselves are also responsible for this change from enormously creative activity to cautious conformity. Within the framework of their developmental stages such change is to be expected.

In their earliest years, children must find ways to make sense of their world. Each day they encounter new learning that they must assimilate and accommodate to their knowledge structure. Unless they are inhibited by physical or mental impairments or by overbearing adults, infants and young children spend much of their time exploring and experimenting with each new bit of knowledge. The result, to the adult eye, is vast creativity. Indeed, young children, being inexperienced and lacking in knowledge, almost have no choice but to create. In doing so, they often draw conclusions or make combinations unlike any that the older people around them have seen.

After about five years, however, the world begins to make more sense. Children start to see patterns and connections as they have repeated contacts and experience with various fragments of knowledge. As they start to move into the stage of concrete operations, the excitement they feel toward learning begins to change character. No longer is it interesting just to mess about fancifully with materials, words, and ideas. Now there is an understanding that there are *right* ways to do and say things, and children want to know what those are and to be able to succeed at them. For many children, it is important to feel comfortable and competent about getting things right before they are ready to think creatively. We might compare this stage to that of the musician who needs to learn theory and the classics before being able to improvise cleverly, or the artist who becomes skilled at draftsmanship before experimenting with new art forms.

One example of the way children change over time is their approach to an art medium such as fingerpaint. Three-year-olds who are introduced to it for the first time are fascinated, attracted to, or repulsed by its texture, coolness, and sloppiness. They are not yet ready to create a product, but need plenty of time to experiment with the material itself, to see what it will do. Even washing their hands is a learning experience as the substance disappears and the hands regain their original color. By the time they are five, most children have overcome any timidity they feel toward fingerpaint and become interested in making designs and pictures. Yet the product may change several times during the creative process and, a short time later, children may not even be able to identify their own pictures. Toward the end of kindergarten and certainly by first grade, most children's interest develops into something quite different. They want to be able to make pictures that really look like something and, unless further instructions are given in the handling of this rather unwieldy substance, children often choose not to use it. Teachers who show them techniques for using the sides of their hands, knuckles, forearms, and fingertips to create specific effects will find that interest in fingerpainting often stays high well into elementary school.

This approach toward fingerpaint demonstrates two stages in creativity development that parallel changes from knowledge gathering to creative expression. In the first stage, the youngest children, faced with a new medium, require time to explore it on its own terms. Process and substance are all-important to them, and little is created. Once they are comfortable with the material and what it does, they begin to create from a limited knowledge base but with enthusiasm. The second stage is similar in that it begins with a need to gain control before creating. Primary children need to learn how to do things "right" or effectively, and then they feel ready to be creative. Developmentally, primary children do not really lose their creativity. Rather, they pause for a reality check. They are then ready to take their creativity to the next level, in which they make use of their extended knowledge.

Teachers who want to support creativity need to be aware of their children's general level of development. When a new material is introduced, much time should be devoted to experimenting with it. Until children become interested in the product, they should not be forced to focus on it rather than on process. Once the product becomes important to them, however, teachers should not become fearful that creativity will be lost if they provide children with the skills to make the products. There are at least two important ways in which primary teachers can kill creativity in their children. One is to focus almost entirely on "serious" academic work while showing little respect for creativity. The other is to try to prolong the early childhood period in which children are left to their own devices during creative experiences. Instead, primary teachers need to build on the children's desire to do things right by showing them techniques that give them the confidence to develop a more mature approach to creating.

The stage development that has just been described is related to Piagetian theory in which preoperations give way to concrete operations. Thus, art is not the only subject area in which this kind of development takes place. Looking across the curriculum we see such development

- *In language:* Children first experiment with sounds, invent their own spellings, create their own versions of stories to accompany their favorite pictures. In the primary grades, they want to read the printed word correctly, spell in a standard way, and speak in a way that makes sense to everyone around them. Their creativity develops as they learn to write their own stories with a beginning, middle, and end; create poetry that they can identify as being different from prose; and, perhaps, give oral reports that entertain their classmates and teacher.

- *In mathematics:* Children first intuit the mathematical attributes of the world around them, count in fanciful ways that may seem creative to adults, and create unusual structures using their limited understanding of spatial relationships. In the primary grades, children need to learn to make change correctly so they can go shopping, measure accurately so they can construct structures that seem accurate to them, and count in a standard way so they can keep score when they play games. When primary children are provided with basic mathematical skills, but are then allowed the freedom to invent their own ways to find the answers, they are given an opportunity to be creative. Now, however, their creativity is based on a structure of knowledge that gives them the courage to take risks.

- *In movement:* Children first move instinctively and with whatever physical skill their current developmental level permits them. As they mature, they enjoy learning specific steps that match various songs and musical compositions, yet they also can invent new steps and movements or make new combinations of the ones they have already learned. Similarly, when children first become aware of sports, they make sense of them by wearing the right clothing and mimicking the movements they have seen. Such early creativity toward the playing of sports is later replaced by an interest in following the rules. Still, some creativity is possible as children develop their own effective ways to be skillful.

- *In music:* As in movement, children first participate instinctively and later become interested in learning real songs and other compositions. Once they have learned them, however, children enjoy creating their own lyrics or melodies.

- *In social studies and science:* Many of the interests and skills from the previous sections can be applied. Choose a topic in social studies or science and consider how children might respond to it creatively, first at the preoperational stage and then at concrete operations.

## Fostering and Supporting Creativity in the Center or School

The importance of creative development cannot be overstated. Children who are encouraged to be creative add a dimension to their lives that has influence far into their adult years. They learn to take risks with less fear of failure. They learn to make decisions based on the ability to consider a variety of outcomes. They learn to participate knowledgeably in a democratic society. They eventually are able to bring creative problem solving to their jobs and careers. And they are more likely to enjoy participating (informally or professionally) in any or all of the expressive arts.

Creativity is so important to some children that they will risk everything for it: the annoyance of their teachers who want them to do things in the proper school way, the anger of their parents who wish they would get tasks done and not make such messes, the ridicule of friends who observe that they are "different." Most children, however, gain courage to be creative only when there is someone—even one person—who encourages them. Historically, it has not been teachers who have felt comfortable about being that one special person. In a 1962 study of the childhoods of 400 eminent people, Goertzel and Goertzel found that the families of these individuals did not place much faith in traditional education. Some of the children were never even sent to school. Those who did attend school found that "it was a place where creativity was stifled, rather than encouraged" (Wasserman, 1992, p. 134) and that the teachers these children liked the best were those who "let them go ahead at their own pace and who gave them permission to work unimpeded in the area of their own special interests" (Goertzel and Goertzel, 1962, p. 267).

All children deserve to have teachers who give them this freedom. Teachers who hope to promote creativity need to keep in mind, no matter what the pressures, that covering required material, turning out high grades on a standardized test, and preparing children for entrance into school or the next grade are not the ultimate goals for the day. Educating the whole child is the goal, and creativity is an important part of that whole.

To promote creativity, children should be given plenty of time to play—with materials and ideas. Selma Wasserman (1992) writes,

> The creation of new ideas does not come from minds trained to follow doggedly what is already known. Creation comes from tinkering and playing around, from which new forms emerge. . . . From all of this play, this messing around, serious and new creative forms are brought to life. (p. 137)

Arguing that play should be taken more seriously by educators, who should recognize its benefits, she says,

> [P]lay allows children to make discoveries that go far beyond the realm of what we adults think is important to know. . . . I believe that with play, we teachers can have it all: the development of knowledge, of a spirit of inquiry, of creativity, of conceptual understanding—all contributing to the true empowerment of children. (p. 137)

A final influence on children's creativity that should be discussed is teacher modeling. As with most behaviors and attitudes, children will respond when they see you expressing creative ideas and behaving in creative ways. In turn, your creative behaviors and attitudes will affect your own growth as a person and a teacher. All the benefits that have been listed for children can be yours as well: greater competence in risk taking, decision making, political participation, artistic creativity, and creative thought in all aspects of your life—including, of course, your career as a teacher.

## Extending Your Learning

1. If you play a portable musical instrument, try using it with young children in a variety of ways. Do a guest presentation in which you explain the physics of how it works. (Be sure to let the children touch the instrument while teaching them to handle it with respect.) Play the instrument for children to create their own movement. Play it quietly as children settle down to a nap. Play a tune and then let the children compose words to go with it.

   If you do not play an instrument, try team teaching the above ideas with someone who does. Consider taking up an instrument now. You may find the experience a restful and enjoyable diversion, and the skills you gain will be a definite plus when you begin teaching.

2. If you feel that your artistic growth stopped many years ago, take some time to rediscover and develop your natural capabilities. Buy some art materials and experiment. Visit an art museum and examine just a few works of art very closely. At home, try to replicate some of the feeling and technique that you observed. Perhaps buy a book that encourages the nonartist to develop. An excellent choice is *Drawing on the Right Side of the Brain* by Betty Edwards (1989). It is written by a college art teacher who has helped nonartists see the world in the ways that artists do, then transfer this capability to drawing skills.

3. Make a collection of songs gleaned from children's music books, from experienced teachers, from children themselves. If you are familiar with musical notation, record the songs on paper. If not, sing them into a tape recorder. Add to your collection, keeping a few favorites in your active memory. When you find yourself with a group of children and a few empty minutes, try introducing one of the tunes to them.

4. You will teach movement activities more easily if you keep yourself agile, strong, and aerobically healthy. Register for a dance or aerobics course. If you currently are working with children, share some of your learning with them.

## References

Ackerman, K. (1988). *Song and dance man.* New York: Alfred Knopf.

Andress, B. (1991). From research to practice: Preschool children and their movement responses to music. *Young Children* vol. 22-27.

Baker, D. (1990). The visual arts in early childhood education. *Arts in Education* 91(6):21-25.

Bayless, K., and Ramsey, M. (1991). *Music: A way of life for the young child.* New York: Macmillan.

Bresler, L. (1992). Dance education in elementary schools. *Arts in Education* 93(5):13-20.

Brown, V. (1990). Drama as an integral part of the early childhood curriculum. *Arts in Education* 91(6):26-33.

Clemens, S. (1991). Art in the classroom: Making every day special. *Young Children* 46(2): 4-11.

Feierabend, J. (1990). Music in early childhood. *Arts in Education* 91(6):15-20.

Gardner, H. (1983). *Frames of mind.* New York: Basic Books.

Gilbert, A. (1977). *Teaching the three r's through movement experience.* Minneapolis: Burgess Publishing.

Goertzel, V., and Goertzel, M. (1962). *Cradles of eminence.* Boston: Little Brown.

Haas, I. (1975). *The Maggie B.* New York: Macmillan.

Kellogg R. (1970). *Analyzing children's art.* Palo Alto, CA: National Press Books.

Krogh, S. and Magaña. (1988). The eyes and hands of second graders: from Velazquez to Picasso. *Newslinks* 8(3):1 and 6.

Lamme, L. (1990). Exploring the world of music through picture books. *The Reading Teacher* 44 (4):294-300.

Lewis, H. (ed.) (1981). *Art for the preprimary child.* Reston, VA: National Art Education Association.

Lowenfeld, V., and Brittain, W. L. (1982). *Creative and mental growth.* New York: Macmillan.

Mayer, M. (1974). *Frog goes to dinner.* New York: Scholastic.

Morningstar, Moira (1986). *Growing with dance.* Heriot Bay, BC, Canada: Windborne Publications.

Music Educators National Conference (1986). *The school music program: Description and standards.* Reston, VA: MENC.

Pangrazi, R., and Dauer, V. (1981). *Movement in early childhood and primary education.* Minneapolis: Burgess Publishing.

Shannon, G. (1981). *The Piney Woods peddler.* New York: Greenwillow.

Stinson, S. (1989). Creative dance for preschool children. *Early Child Development and Care* 47(1):205–209.

Stinson, S. (1990). Dance education in early childhood. *Arts in Education* 34–41.

Wasserman, S. (1992). Serious play in the classroom: How messing around can win you the Nobel Prize. *Childhood Education* 68(3):133–139.

Wolf, D., and Perry, M. D. (1988). *Art, mind and education.* Urbana, IL: University of Illinois Press.

# Glossary

**accommodation**  A cognitive process in which an internal mental structure is changed to incorporate new information.

**achievement tests**  Examinations of the skills and knowledge attained through instruction.

**activity centers**  Classroom areas devoted to a single subject, topic, or theme of interest.

**affective**  Pertaining to attitudes, values, and emotions.

**aide**  A teacher's assistant, usually untrained.

**animism**  The belief that inanimate objects make decisions about the ways in which they will act.

**artificialism**  The belief that everything that exists has been created by humans or by a supreme being in a human fashion.

**assertive discipline**  An approach to behavior management modeled after assertiveness training and using behavior modification techniques.

**assimilation**  A cognitive process in which new information and experiences are incorporated into the existing internal mental structure.

**associative play**  Play in which two or more children are in close proximity, possibly communicating and sharing toys, but not coordinating their efforts.

**attention-deficit disorder**  Hyperactivity or inactive distractibility leading to difficulty in sitting still, paying attention, or behaving in the usually accepted ways.

**autonomy**  Decision making based on self-government.

**back to basics**  Educational emphasis on reading, writing, and arithmetic with little or no emphasis on the arts or other electives. Most recently given this name during the 1980s.

**basal readers**  Book series for reading instruction in which materials are graded and contain controlled vocabulary.

**behavior modification**  A strategy for changing behavior by the use of rewards or other reinforcers.

**big books**  Oversized books with large print, either purchased or handmade.

**child care centers**  Facilities in which children are cared for. Centers may offer educational programs or simply custodial supervision.

**child-centered instruction or curriculum**  Instruction and learning that are planned around children's needs, interests, and capabilities.

**child development associate (CDA)**  A graduate of a program offering the CDA certificate. CDA programs are usually offered in community colleges or vocational institutes and focus specifically on training for effective child care.

**classification**  The systematic grouping of events or objects according to common attributes.

**cognitive**  Pertaining to knowledge, information, and intellectual skills.

**concepts**  A generalized idea of a thing or class of things.

**concrete operations**  A Piagetian stage in which children are able to think about abstract concepts as long as they have concrete objects to manipulate or visualize.

**conflict resolution**  The termination of a disagreement, battle, or war. In education, the focus is on peaceful resolutions.

**conservation**  The understanding that materials or objects remain the same in weight or volume even though their shapes or arrangements in space may change.

**constructivism**  A philosophy of development in which children are seen to construct their own knowledge, intelligence, and morality. Their development takes place in a series of stages by means of assimilation and accommodation.

**cooperative play** Play involving two or more children in which there is cooperation and common agreement as to the play's purpose.

**creativity** The quality of showing imagination and artistic or intellectual inventiveness.

**curiosity** The desire and need to learn and know. Considered natural in young children.

**curriculum web** A diagram drawn in the general shape of a spider's web in which the entire web pertains to a single curricular theme and each radial lists activities pertaining to a subsection or subject area.

**day care** Sites or programs for the care of children while their parents work. May or may not include an educational component.

**decoding** Analysis of written symbols to attain meaning; the reading act.

**developmental-interaction** A philosophy that the best approach to early education is to combine what is known about developmental stages with careful creation of an environment that will produce much learning when children interact with it.

**developmentally appropriate practice** The provision of learning experiences that meet children's developmental needs and interests.

**direct instruction** A method of teaching in which the teacher, as sole leader, passes on knowledge directly to the students.

**disabled** Lagging in cognitive or physical functioning.

**disadvantaged** Lacking the culturally normal advantages of living conditions and opportunities for learning.

**discipline** Teacher control of children for the purposes of enforcing positive behavior.

**dramatic play** Play in which children act out real or imagined experiences by taking on the roles of the characters involved.

**early childhood education** Learning engaged in by children up to about age eight. Typical sites are care centers, preschools, kindergartens, and the primary grades.

**egocentric** In early infancy, being unable to differentiate between what is and is not the self. Later, understanding the world only as it relates to the self.

**empathy** The ability to share in another's emotions, thoughts, or feelings.

**equilibration** The child's continual process of cognitive self-correction; the goal is a better sense of intellectual equilibrium. Assimilation and accommodation are subcategories.

**field trip** A learning excursion outside the classroom, generally for no more than one day.

**Follow Through** Federally funded program for graduates of Head Start to ensure their continued academic success through the primary grades.

**formal operations** The final Piagetian stage, beginning about age eleven and lasting into early adulthood. Abstract thinking is its hallmark.

**fundamental movement phase** A phase of physical development occurring in the preschool years in which children learn movements that are fundamental to later sports activities. Running, jumping, throwing, and catching are examples.

**giftedness** The possession of high ability, usually denoting advanced intellectual capabilities.

**gifts and occupations** Materials developed by Froebel for use with infants and young children.

**hands-on learning** Learning that emphasizes manipulation of objects over more abstract methods.

**Head Start** Federally funded program for disadvantaged preschool children.

**here and now** An approach to social studies curriculum in which children focus on the time and space that is closest to them and therefore best understood and most interesting. Distant geography and history are studied, but in the context of the here and now.

**heteronomous** Decision making based on the rules and influence of others.

**infancy** Birth through the first year of life.

**integrated curriculum** Curriculum content that crosses the traditional subject areas, often organized according to themes of student interest.

**interest centers** See *activity centers.*

**intervention** Method intended to bring special experiences, materials, training, and/or programs to situations of special need, such as to disadvantaged regions, schools, or children.

**intrinsic motivation**   An inner drive to take some action.

**invented spelling**   Nonconventional spelling. Regarded as an early step in learning to spell according to the rules of language.

**kindergarten**   A German word meaning "children's garden," first coined by educator Friedrich Froebel in the mid-nineteenth century. An educational setting for children about five years old.

**kindergartner**   Child of kindergarten age. A kindergarten teacher (obsolete).

**kinetic activity**   Activity involving motion and energy. In early childhood: includes reaching, pushing, pulling, and grabbing.

**learning disability (LD)**   An educationally significant deficit in language or learning capabilities.

**learning stations**   See *activity centers.*

**lesson plan**   A teaching plan, usually written, for a specific activity. Generally includes a statement of goals, objectives, required materials, procedures, and evaluation.

**limited English proficiency (LEP)**   Describes the inadequate English-speaking abilities of a child whose first language is other than English.

**literacy**   The ability to read and write.

**logico-mathematical learning**   Learning that comes from manipulating objects or ideas so that new characteristics of the objects of ideas are introduced to the learner. From this, the learner understands relationships between different characteristics.

**mainstreaming**   Including children with learning disabilities or other special needs in the regular classroom, sometimes on a part-time basis only.

**manipulative play**   Play that provides children with objects for exploration in ways of their choosing.

**maturationism**   A philosophy that views child development as primarily the result of biological programming.

**modeling**   Teaching by example. Also, learning by the examples set by others.

**moral development**   The growth of a child's ability to distinguish between right and wrong and to act upon such growing understanding.

**morphology**   The study of the internal structure and forms of words.

**motor development**   Growth in the ability to use and control the muscles.

**multicultural**   Containing many cultures. In education, the focus is on appreciating the contributions of all cultures.

**multiple intelligences**   The concept, introduced by Howard Gardner, that every person possesses seven separate intelligences: linguistic, logical-mathematical, spatial, bodily-kinesthetic, interpersonal, intrapersonal, and music.

**norms**   The average performance expected of a particular age, grade, or gender.

**nursery school**   A school for young children, typically between the ages of two and five; preschool.

**objectives**   Purposes or expected outcomes, typically of a planned lesson, activity, or program.

**object permanence**   The understanding that an object continues to exist even if it is removed from sight.

**ordering**   Placing two or more objects in some sequence. Also called seriation.

**parallel play**   Play in which two or more children are in the same area, each with an individual agenda or interests. There are few cooperative behaviors and often little awareness of each other.

**peer teaching**   Children teaching other children.

**phonology**   The study of sound systems, or phonetics, of a language.

**physical development**   Growth in body size and weight.

**physical learning**   Learning that is concerned with the physical properties of objects.

**portfolio assessment**   Evaluation of a child's educational performance by means of a collection of artifacts: written work, drawings, tape recordings, journal entries, etc.

**pragmatics**   The application of language to specific and cultural situations.

**predictable stories**   Stories with repetitive language patterns; children are thus able to predict words.

**preoperational**   The second Piagetian stage, from about age two to seven or eight, in which children are able to use mental symbols and imagery; characterized by egocentric thinking linked to perception.

**preschool** A school for young children typically between the ages of two and five; nursery school.

**preschooler** A child of preschool age.

**primary grades** Grades one through three in elementary school.

**punishment** An unpleasant penalty imposed on a child for bad behavior.

**reflexive phase** The physical development phase of early infancy in which involuntary movements are common behavior and a source of learning.

**reinforcement** An event or experience that increases the probability that a behavior will be repeated. Positive reinforcement occurs when a reward is given, negative reinforcement when a painful stimulus ends.

**role play** The intentional mimicking of the behavior of another, or taking on the other's personality in actions.

**rote learning** Learning by memorization alone with little regard to underlying meanings.

**rudimentary movement phase** The period of later infancy in which physical actions tend to be basic and voluntary. Actions include sitting and crawling.

**self-correcting** Pertains to learning materials that have a control of user error built into the material itself.

**semantics** The study of the meaning of words in a language.

**sensorimotor** The first Piagetian stage, from about birth to age two, in which children learn about their environment through sensory input and physical actions.

**significance** In statistics, an observed departure from a hypothesis too large to be reasonably attributed to chance.

**social development** Children's growth in their ability to relate to others effectively and successfully.

**social learning** Learning that relates to culturally determined knowledge, such as the names of objects, places, or people.

**social learning theory** The theory that learning and development take place through contact with the social world.

**solitary play** Play in which one child is alone.

**special needs children** Children with disabilities severe enough to require special education facilities or specific tutoring.

**sport-related movement phase** Movements attained in the fundamental phase are refined and combined and applied to sports situations.

**stereotypies** Infant behaviors that fall between reflex actions and purposive actions. They include kicking, waving, rocking, and bouncing.

**stress** Mental or physical tension or strain.

**symbolic play** Play in which objects or actions represent something else; pretend play.

**syntax** The grammatical structure of a language.

**tabula rasa** A blank slate; a term used by John Locke to represent the inexperienced mind of the child.

**thematic curriculum** A way to integrate curriculum around a focal theme. Specific subject areas are taught as they pertain to the chosen theme.

**transitional kindergarten** A class, midway between kindergarten and first grade, for children who are old enough to be in first grade but not considered ready for school learning.

**whole language** An approach to learning to read and write in which children's natural behaviors and interests are respected; rules and skills are taught within the context of purposeful learning.

**withitness** A characteristic of effective teaching in which the teacher is alert to everything going on in the classroom.

# Photo Credits

# Index